JOHN PLAYER
Cricket Yearbook 1973

EDITED BY TREVOR BAILEY

QUEEN ANNE PRESS LONDON

Compiler: Bill Frindall

Picture Editor: Patrick Eagar
Unless otherwise credited, all pictures were supplied by Patrick Eagar

Executive Editor: Graeme Wright

Designed by Alan Coombes

©Brickfield Publications Ltd 1973
First Published 1973

Published by The Queen Anne Press Ltd,
Paulton House, Shepherdess Walk, London N1

Printed and bound in Great Britain by
Waterlow London and Dunstable

Contents

Foreword by John Player	5
Editorial Preface	7
John Player Limited-Overs Team of 1972	9
A Memorable Year	19

The 1972 Australian Tour
The Fight for the Ashes	24
Dennis Lillee – Man of the Series	41
Statistical Survey of the Series	43
First-Class Matches and Averages	46
The Prudential Trophy	49

County Cricket
The First-Class Counties	54
The County Championship 1972	116
Other First-Class Matches 1972	133
First-Class Averages 1972	137
Where are Our Young Players?	144
John Player League 1972	148
The Gillette Cup 1972	166
Benson and Hedges League Cup 1972	175
Reviving a Cricket Festival: The Fenner Trophy	181
Limited-Overs Averages 1972	183
The Effects of Limited-Overs Cricket	186
Farewell	189

Minor Cricket
The Minor Counties Championship 1972	196
The Second Eleven Championship	200
Under-25 County Cricket Championship	203
The National Club Knock-Out	206
Haig National Village Cricket Championship	208
Club Cricket	210
The Northern Leagues Battle On	213
English Schools' Cricket Association	217
Public School Cricket	221
National Cricket Association	225
Putting Women's Cricket on the Map	227

Overseas Cricket
Cricket in Australia	232
Indian Cricket	238
Two Decades of Pakistan Cricket	242
Is New Zealand's Confidence Justified?	247
South African Cricket is Alive and Well .... and Sponsored	253
West Indies Enters a New Era	258

The Art of Cricket
The Art of Aggressive Batting	264
Bowling Fast	268
Keeping to the Spinners	272
Application and Concentration: Fielding Watchwords	277
Learning from the Stars	280

Register of County Cricketers — 287

Looking Ahead to 1973
Preview	340
England v New Zealand	343
England v West Indies	345
Fixtures 1973	347

Foreword

Many who profess a limited interest in cricket as a sport still recognise its special place in English life. Cricket is a game, a battle, a spectacle, a great skill, the most civilised of contests. Yet the game we love went through a lean patch during most of the sixties. Falling crowds at three-day matches indicated a declining interest among spectators. It was in this climate that the one-day, limited-overs game was introduced.

With several seasons' hindsight, there can be no doubt that the John Player League and other one-day competitions have made a permanent impact on the game. And they've brought back the crowds. In 1972, there were an estimated 2,300,000 paying customers, with millions more following their favourites on television and radio, and in the press.

In publishing this yearbook, John Player and Sons are providing facts, figures and comment for cricket's growing number of adherents. We hope the book fully reflects the John Player policy of bringing the best in sport to the British public.

We've enlisted an editorial panel who really know their cricket, and all are members of the BBC's Test match commentary team.

Our editor, Trevor Bailey, is a former Test match player and cricket correspondent of the *Financial Times*, and he has received enormous support from Bill Frindall, our incomparable statistician, and Patrick Eagar, a first-rate specialist in cricket photography.

Specialist contributors include Alan Knott on wicket-keeping, Fred Trueman on fast bowling, and Colin Cowdrey on fielding. With names like these, I don't think I have to say anything more about the quality of the 1973 *John Player Cricket Yearbook*.

G.A. Iden
Chairman and Managing Director
John Player, Nottingham, England

Preface

The 1972 season will go down in the history of first-class cricket as one of true vintage, with something very close to a renaissance taking place. It produced a nail-biting Test series, a big upsurge in both crowds and interest, and county balance sheets that were unexpectedly healthy. It is appropriate therefore that this, the first *John Player Cricket Yearbook*, should be published to celebrate and record such a memorable summer.

I consider it an honour to have been asked to edit this book, although I must admit that the operation has been rather like setting out on an exciting trip into the unknown without an experienced guide. However, I set myself three main objectives and have tried, as far as possible, to keep to them.

First, I have aimed at producing a book that would be in keeping with the spirit of cricket in the 1970s.

Secondly, it was my intention that this publication would write the game up, rather than knock it. This does not mean that criticism is excluded, because no sport is perfect, not even cricket. In recent years, the administrators have, with the best intentions, tried to cure some of the ills, and the introduction of limited-overs cricket has proved to be an enormous success. Unfortunately some of their other remedies have turned out less successfully.

Thirdly, I have tried to present a book that is interesting and colourful, covers as many aspects as space permits, and will serve as a valuable work of reference – in other words, something that would appeal to many of the game's supporters, old and new.

In trying to accomplish this, I have been fortunate in the many helpers who have rallied round. Some have even provided copy ahead of schedule!

The large and fascinating statistical section has been left entirely in the capable hands of Bill Frindall. He has supplied a wealth of facts and figures, including a most comprehensive piece on limited-overs cricket, and it is no exaggeration to say that, without the wholehearted support of our human computer, the book would never have materialised. In the year of the first women's world cup, it is appropriate that Jacky Frindall and Wendy Wimbush should have helped in the mammoth task of proof-checking this publication.

On this occasion the choosing of the photographs was far from easy, not because it was a question of hunting for pictures to include, but because I had, reluctantly, to exclude so many. Patrick Eagar has such a vast library, and some of his photos are among the finest I have come across. They really bring the game and its personalities to life.

It seemed logical to me that, in a book of this kind, the majority of the articles should be

John Player Cricket Yearbook 1973

written by people with practical experience of Test match cricket; people who know the game at the highest level. Particularly satisfying is the complete absence of 'ghosts'. Unfortunately we have not managed to find space for a piece on those other ghosts of cricket, the umpires – something we hope to remedy in next year's edition. The white-coated brethren do an extremely difficult job so well, and I often feel that they do not receive either the praise or recognition they deserve.

I have been lucky with my Editorial Panel – John Arlott, Ted Dexter, Jim Laker and Denis Compton. All contributed articles and gave very valuable assistance in the preparation of this yearbook. I learned much from this distinguished quartet! John convinced me that my education would not be complete until I had visited the vineyards of France. With Ted's help I now feel confident of breaking a hundred on my next golf outing, at least for the first nine holes. Jim dissuaded me from taking up spin bowling, while Denis surprised us all by turning up for our editorial luncheons on the right day and in reasonable time.

My gratitude is due to all the writers of articles and to the many others who supplied information. I am truly indebted to the secretaries of the first-class counties, the secretary of the Minor Counties Association, and the secretary of the National Cricket Association for their wholehearted co-operation.

The publishers have shown remarkable tolerance and ability in deciphering my writing, and finally I must thank John Player and Sons for making the project possible. T.E.B.

The John Player Cricket Yearbook Editorial Panel, (l-r) Ted Dexter, Jim Laker, Trevor Bailey, John Arlott and Denis Compton, discuss the selection of the limited-overs team of 1972

John Player Limited-Overs Team of 1972

With a high percentage of the side being the automatic choices of the Selection Committee, the John Player Limited-Overs Team of 1972 was chosen in much less time than had been expected. Indeed, the team virtually picked itself, providing few problems for the selectors: Trevor Bailey (Chairman), John Arlott, Denis Compton, Ted Dexter, and Jim Laker.

The aim of the committee was to name a team that was prepared for, and able to cope with, all the eventualities that can occur in the limited-overs game. It should be noted that the John Player team was chosen on form shown last summer, not on potential or performances in other years. For this reason Gary Sobers was not considered, for he was absent injured for the bulk of the 1972 season.

There was complete agreement over the opening pair, Barry Richards and Glenn Turner, and all were unanimous that Rohan Kanhai, who had had such a wonderful season, should go in at No. 3. The selection of Clive Lloyd provoked a certain amount of discussion because he had not been all that successful in the Sunday matches. But, as he so wonderfully illustrated in the Gillette final, he is one of those few players capable of unleashing what is, to all intents and purposes in the one-day game, a match-winning innings. In addition he always goes to the crease with runs in hand because of the large number he saves in the field. So it was Lloyd for No. 4 and the team was provided with the solid basis of four great free-scoring batsmen who had all shown their worth in limited-overs cricket.

The two fast-bowling all-rounders, Mike Procter and Keith Boyce, were perhaps even more self evident. The former is, after Gary Sobers, the finest in the world and in every sense ideally suited to the one-day game. He is such a fine fast bowler and forcing bat that he would probably have commanded a place on either count. Boyce, as the first person to achieve 1,000 runs and 100 wickets in the John Player League, was a must. In 1972 he not only captured 46 wickets at very cheap cost, but the ferocity of his hitting was such that he could transform the entire course of a game in a couple of hectic overs. When it is remembered that in Sunday matches the contest can be decided in only 10 overs, this is a particularly important asset. And on top of his batting and bowling there was the added claim of his tremendous ability anywhere in the field.

It might have been expected that the wicket-keeping spot would have gone to Alan Knott or possibly to Farokh Engineer. But the panel were unable to ignore the remarkable performances by Roger Tolchard with the bat. Last summer he rattled up 650 runs at great pace for Leicestershire, as well as 'keeping in a most lively manner.

The last straightforward position went to John Snow. Though playing for one of the less

John Player Cricket Yearbook 1973

successful one-day teams of the 1970s, he proved himself most economical and also had a high striking rate in terms of wickets per over.

At this stage, the committee decided that they wished to include at least one spinner who would be difficult to get away in all conditions and would run through a team given helpful wickets. The choice was obviously and indisputably Derek Underwood.

The fourth seamer provoked something of an argument, with the relative merits of Graham McKenzie and Tom Cartwright coming under vigorous discussion and John Lever also coming into the reckoning. Cartwright, although lacking the pace of the other two, did have the advantage of being the man to exploit a dusty pitch. But this would be nullified to some extent if it was decided to include two spinners. (Illingworth had already been mentioned as a prospective captain although the actual selection was being left to last.) Strongly in McKenzie's favour were his far superior figures last summer and the fact that when the run-up is limited he is probably the most hostile of all the bowlers. Lever had come on strongly and had enormous potential, though he obviously lacked the experience of the other two. In the end McKenzie got the nod.

Who then was to captain this talented ten? Admittedly it would not need a tactical genius to captain a side of this calibre in a one-day match, but it helps to have an astute captain to ring the bowling changes and keep the pressure on the opposition. Four alternatives were broached. The first was to give the job to Rohan Kanhai and include another out-and-out batsman. The second idea was to choose Tony Lewis, but his record in one-day games had not been especially good. The third alternative was Brian Close, who led England in the one-day internationals. In addition to his ability as a captain, he has the happy knack of hitting the fast bowling

With such glorious attacking strokemakers as Barry Richards (below) and Glenn Turner (bottom) to open the innings, what team needs any more batting?

in an unconventional way. Finally there was Ray Illingworth, who had taken Leicestershire to victory in the Benson and Hedges League Cup and, but for a whole series of injuries, would likely have done the same in the John Player League. He had, therefore, proved himself in this particular form of the game, while his all-round record was also impressive. He is not a natural, flowing stroke-maker, but he can improvise and is the ideal person to have on hand should a collapse occur. After some debate the Committee settled for Illingworth's proven virtues.

The team would bat in the following order:
1. B.A. Richards
2. G.M. Turner
3. R.B. Kanhai
4. C.H. Lloyd
5. M.J. Procter
6. R.W. Tolchard
7. R. Illingworth
8. K.D. Boyce
9. J.A. Snow
10. G.D. McKenzie
11. D.L. Underwood

Barry Wood was named as 12th man.

It might be argued that there is insufficient batting, but it must be remembered that this team has been specifically chosen for single-innings, limited-overs cricket. On good pitches no side ought really to be bowled out in 40 overs unless everything happened to go wrong in a wild slog at the end. There simply is not enough time available to employ an over-long batting line-up. If the match was for 60 or 55 overs, then with Procter at 5, Tolchard 6, Illingworth in preparation for any collapse, and Boyce probably employed as a floater capable of providing a violent assault at the most appropriate time, there should be no shortage of runs. And should the pitch prove really difficult, one would not exactly fancy the opposition's chances of reaching a big score against the John Player side's tight and menacing array of bowlers.

The choice of two spinners may come as some surprise to those accustomed to a fare of seam bowling in limited-overs matches. But both Illingworth and Underwood are highly economical bowlers on good pitches and provide that little extra contrast that is usually of greater benefit in the more protracted encounters than in a 40-over game. Care was taken, in the selection of bowlers, to ensure that another top-class bowler was available should one of the essential five be injured, a measure made possible by the number of exceptional all-rounders.

The most unsatisfactory aspect is that the team is dominated by overseas cricketers, underlining once again the shortage of outstanding home-grown talent at the present time. Had Sobers been fit the position would have been even worse, for presumably he would have replaced Illingworth as captain. This in turn might have reduced the need for one of the bowlers and so provided a place for such an attacking stroke-maker as Majid. English representation could then be reduced to one or two, plus the wicket-keeper.

Because the result of a limited-overs match is more likely to depend on one brilliant individual innings or one distinguished all-round performance than in a first-class game, the top-class import is considered more important than the local prospect. This is not healthy for domestic cricket yet perhaps the truth of the matter is that English cricket is not producing stroke-makers and all-rounders of the highest quality. What, for example, are the chances of an English-born team holding their own in a series of one-day matches against the following: Richards, Turner, Kanhai, Lloyd, Majid, Sobers (capt), Procter, Boyce, Engineer, McKenzie, and Gibbs?

BARRY RICHARDS

Because one is at least entitled to have a look at the bowling before increasing the pressure, it is plainly advantageous to open the innings in limited-overs cricket. But it is doubtful whether any batsman in the world could have capitalised to quite the same extent as Barry Richards. In 1972 he was a mere seven off 1,000 runs with an average of well over 50; a truly remarkable performance, especially as on most occasions all the bowlers were concentrating on keeping him quiet. As a result he was forced to take numerous chances to maintain the run rate.

One of the reasons for Barry's remarkable scoring feats, apart from his class, eye, and exquisite timing, is the brilliance of his footwork; a fundamental of batting that is not always fully appreciated. It not only enables him to be in the best possible position to play the normal strokes, but it allows him to extemporise and so produce the unexpected shot.

Against the faster bowlers he will often advance down the pitch to upset the length and, incidentally, increase the chances of a quick single. When the attack is directed outside the off stump to a packed off-side field, he will move into and across the stumps to facilitate forcing the ball through the less guarded leg side. In the photograph on page ten, his leg stump is being attacked and, to counter, Barry has moved outside the line of his leg stump to give himself sufficient room to force the ball through the covers. To play a stroke of this nature so perfectly is just another indication of his astonishing ability.

GLENN TURNER

It is sometimes difficult to realise that the free-scoring Glenn Turner, with close on 1,000 runs to his credit in one-day matches in 1972, is the same Turner who was such an ultra-defensive member of the last New Zealand team to tour England. His technique has always been exceptional, which means that he is ideally balanced whenever he moves from defence to offence, and even in limited-overs cricket it pays to have the odd batsman who can pace his innings. Provided Glenn is not removed in the opening overs – and his sound defence reduces the chances – the odds are that he will put together a big individual score in which he will gradually, but perceptibly increase his tempo as the overs tick away.

It helps enormously if at least one of the batsmen in at the kill has been at the crease for a considerable period, because he will normally score faster and with greater certainty than anyone who has just arrived. Glenn is also a quick runner between the wickets, and this attribute – highly beneficial in all forms of the game – is especially valuable in limited-overs cricket, in which the eventual result so often depends on the smallest of margins.

ROHAN KANHAI

Rohan Kanhai is a world-class batsman but, now that he is nearing the age of retirement, he is perhaps even better suited to the abbreviated version of the game than to five-day Tests. He is not required to stand for long periods in the field, and his innings of necessity have to be crammed into a comparatively short period of time.

Rohan is naturally a stroke-maker, and his value, when it is necessary to make every over spent at the crease count, is enhanced by his inventiveness. At times this can make a mockery of a bowler's efforts to keep him in check. Cutting a good length ball off the middle stump to the boundary would normally be condemned in a Test, simply because the risk involved is

Limited-Overs Team of 1972

Right: Warwickshire wicket-keeper Deryck Murray and Rohan Kanhai look on as Ray Illingworth scores the winning run for Leicestershire in the Benson and Hedges semi-final. Illingworth's astute handling of Leicestershire, in addition to his value as an all-rounder, made him the ideal choice to lead the John Player side. Kanhai's glorious form in 1972 made him a unanimous selection

Below: Clive Lloyd's bowling would hardly be required by this side

Below right: Mike Procter, now rivalling Gary Sobers as the world's best all-rounder

not proportionate to the reward. But it is highly acceptable when increasing the tempo and the overs are limited. In fact, the ability to play this type of stroke is of great value, because it is more likely to produce runs and upset the bowler than a wild 'heave-ho' across the line.

It would also be true to say that Rohan is likely to score faster by playing comparatively normally than the average batsman attempting to force the pace. He seldom misses putting away the bad ball for four, even though the field is well set and his skill often allows him to score off a really respectable delivery.

CLIVE LLOYD

Apart from being an outstanding stroke-maker, Clive Lloyd has the additional advantage of hitting the ball with so much power that, as long as it is not struck straight to the fielder, a boundary is normally assured. To counter this, captains will sometimes put most of their fieldsmen back near the boundary and present him with a single. But provided the other batsman is also aggressive this move merely assures the pair six runs per over without even trying. When an occasional boundary is added, then the rate of scoring is very high. Because of his pace between the wickets, Clive can run for practically anything. The one danger lies in his partner not having quite the same acceleration.

Even with the field well back Clive, who normally hits with the full face of the bat and avoids the mistake of swinging across the line, can overcome the obstacle by lifting the ball clear over the ropes. He has the confidence and the strength to smite a six straight over deep long-off.

Should Clive fail with the bat, his fielding alone is of immense value to any side, particularly in the one-day game where every run can prove vital.

MIKE PROCTER

This remarkable all-rounder is capable of winning a match with the ball, or the bat, or a combination of both. As an opening fast bowler, who dips the ball in a surprising amount, Mike can destroy the opposing batting line-up in a few hostile overs, while his batting prowess is good enough to savage ruthlessly a good attack. As far as his bowling is concerned he is obviously more effective when the rules of the competition allow him to use his full run-up. In three-day cricket, all-rounders are apt to become tired, but this does not apply to these games, in which the amount of bowling and batting is strictly limited.

Gloucestershire do not have an especially good record in one-day cricket. But when Procter strikes form with bat and ball they are capable of defeating any county, as they have frequently shown in cup games.

ROGER TOLCHARD

Roger is a pugnacious young cricketer who is very alive behind the sticks. He is the type of 'keeper who will personally chase any ball, if there is a chance of the batsman acquiring a couple, and is noticeably quick to get up to the stumps to facilitate possible run-outs.

All this was known before 1972, but what did come as something of a surprise was his consistent scoring. He batted with a swagger and a bravado that was most refreshing to watch and most effective, thus giving the impression that he was almost daring the bowlers to bowl at him. He was helped by his fleetness of foot, a fine eye, a lovely pair of wrists, and his strong cutting.

Up until last season Roger had been regarded mainly as a promising wicket-keeper who could bat, but his performances, especially in one-day cricket, suggested that he is now a wicket-

Below: Roger Tolchard, most capable young 'keeper whose adventurous batting has been a revelation
Bottom: Keith Boyce, limited-overs specialist

Limited-Overs Team of 1972

Ken Kelly

keeper-batsman; a genuine all-rounder. He also showed that he has the makings of a hard, shrewd captain.

RAY ILLINGWORTH

One of the mistakes made about limited-overs cricket is to imagine that this is solely the domain of the hitters, dashing fieldsmen, and an endless procession of short-of-a-length seamers. Fortunately there is also room for the practical cricketer and Ray Illingworth has shown his value both as a player and as a captain.

His position in the Leicestershire batting order normally precludes much chance of a large score, but he has turned in a number of useful, if unspectacular, knocks. Although his 20s and 30s may lack the natural boisterousness of the 'biff bang' expert, they are frequently gathered just as quickly because he uses his intelligence, and will be content to nudge or steer the ball to the boundary, instead of attempting to blast it out of the ground. This is the same approach that little Harry Pilling has employed for Lancashire, though, because he goes in higher up the order he has the opportunity to make a bigger impression on the scorebook.

As a bowler Ray has also proved to be an acquisition in terms of wickets taken and containment. The spinner provides a welcome change from the boredom of a non-stop diet of seam with the 'keeper standing back, but he must be used at the correct time and preferably before the final onslaught. Ray possesses excellent control, avoids the most obvious mistake of bowling too short, and remembers that a flat yorker into the legs is not easy to hit.

Although leading a team in limited-overs cricket is not all that taxing provided the captain can count up to the given number of overs and divide them by the number of bowlers he intends to employ, Ray has nevertheless led Leicester-

15

shire with his customary efficiency. Field placing has become fairly standardised and the England captain can be relied upon to keep things tight, while he has the knack of slipping on his slow men at just the right moment.

KEITH BOYCE

Keith Boyce is a perfect one-day cricketer; a lively bowler who is quick and accurate enough to make the scoring of runs difficult and has the habit of producing an unplayable ball from time to time; a batsman whose inclination is to hit every ball clean out of the ground; and a magnificent fielder anywhere. In three-day cricket Keith's batting has suffered from his being too impetuous, but in the one-day game this can prove a positive advantage when only a few overs remain. He is the type of player who is capable of making 16 or so runs in an over against good bowling with everyone back on the pickets.

Inevitably Keith has become a great favourite with the crowds, because everything he does exudes vitality, and he brings to the county grounds the most exciting features of the game he learnt in Barbados. We do not seem to be able to breed this type of cricketer in England and more is the pity.

JOHN SNOW

As the best fast bowler England has produced for some time, John Snow is an obvious asset to any side. In Test matches he has often caused that early break-through which so frequently decides the whole fate of the match, while his speed is usually too much for the opposing tail. It logically follows that he is a real acquisition in short, one-day skirmishes. He is always liable to pick up wickets at the start of the innings with his pace and lift, while he is sufficiently quick and accurate to make it very difficult indeed for any batsman to maintain a high run rate against him when supported by a heavily defensive field.

It is hard enough for a good player to deal with fast, just short off a length, bowling that is occasionally doing just a little bit and coming up around the ribs, without being expected to take at least four runs an over as well. The best chance of scoring in these circumstances is probably a snick through the non-existent slips.

A bowler of John's pace has another advantage in that he is fast enough to escape punishment when he bowls a loose delivery. It is especially hard to score off any balls, unless they are very short, that miss the leg stump by about a foot.

In first-class cricket the genuine paceman can prove expensive in terms of runs per over. The main reason for this is that he will operate for long spells supported by fields that are ultra attacking. Often the player who patrols the whole of the covers is the only defensive fielder. In these circumstances runs can come quickly without too much effort on the part of the batsman. But it is a very different story in limited-overs cricket. At the start of the innings John Snow may be granted the luxury of a couple of slips. But when he returns for his final spell his field will be entirely defensive, and in certain circumstances he might well have everyone back on the fence.

GRAHAM McKENZIE

Graham McKenzie has a refreshing, and an unusually short, run-up for a fast bowler. Most of his pace and considerable lift come from a high, whippy, powerful body action. The outcome is that in John Player League matches, when the length of a bowler's approach is limited by

Limited-Overs Team of 1972

The John Player team's three specialist bowlers alone would prove a handful for most opponents without the support of the side's all-rounders

Above: Derek Underwood – liable to bowl any side out both quickly and cheaply on a helpful wicket

Left above: John Snow – his speed and hostility make him the perfect spearhead

Left: Graham McKenzie – less inconvenienced by the run-up limitations of the John Player League than most

the rules, he is affected less than most of his quick bowling brethren. As a result he is generally held to be the most hostile bowler under these conditions.

He certainly had a great summer for Leicestershire, picking up a fine haul of 45 wickets at the very low cost of 13 apiece. This is especially economical when it is remembered that he was regularly exposed to the final bombardment.

'Garth', as the big Australian is often called, has never possessed the accuracy and control of a Brian Statham and has always been liable to spray the ball around. His speed, combined with the sharpness of the lift, has ensured that most of the deliveries that were off line have gone unpunished. In any form of cricket it is very disconcerting to receive one ball that rises outside the off stump and swings away towards the slips, the next that necessitates agility from the 'keeper as he moves to leg, and the third a gem that knocks out the middle stump. Garth is not only difficult to score against quickly, but he will suddenly produce a trimmer because everything in his trigger-touch action has fired.

DEREK UNDERWOOD

There are occasions on a perfect pitch in a Test match when Derek Underwood's pace and flatness through the air can be something of a handicap. But in the limited-overs game it is a positive advantage. He is in fact the perfect spinner for it, because, with his accuracy and ability to slip in an in-dipping yorker, he is difficult for the righthander to get after.

His speed, usually closer to medium than slow, means that a batsman has to play him from the crease, unless he starts to go down the pitch before the ball has left Derek's hand, which is an invitation to be set up for a stumping, probably down the leg side. Possibly the most effective way to attack him for a short period is to attempt to swing him to leg, working on the principle that on a really plumb track he will not straighten many.

The 41 wickets that Derek secured at very reasonable cost last season in limited-overs matches, despite missing several games through the Tests, are proof of his effectiveness, and contributed more to Kent's winning the John Player League than was perhaps appreciated.

ONE-DAY MATCHES 1972

M	Runs	Av	Wkts	Av			FIRST-CLASS MATCHES 1972				
							M	Runs	Av	Wkts	Av
22	440	25·88	46	11·91	K.D. Boyce	Essex	22	1,023	30·08	82	20·20
17	249	24·90	20	15·10	*R. Illingworth	Leicestershire	17	538	26·90	39	19·94
27	856	40·76	1	2·00	R.B. Kanhai	Warwickshire	21	1,607	64·28	—	—
25	830	36·08	2	74·00	C.H. Lloyd	Lancashire	18	895	40·68	9	30·66
24	33	5·50	45	13·00	G.D. McKenzie	Leicestershire	23	390	20·52	63	25·04
21	746	39·26	30	17·50	M.J. Procter	Gloucestershire	19	1,219	40·63	58	16·55
21	993	55·16	1	10·00	B.A. Richards	Hampshire	19	1,425	44·53	3	27·33
17	101	12·62	29	13·55	J.A. Snow	Sussex	14	171	10·68	50	21·72
24	650	36·11	36 dis {33 ct / 3 st}		†R.W. Tolchard	Leicestershire	24	979	37·65	58 dis {52 ct / 6 st}	
23	918	43·71	—		G.M. Turner	Worcestershire	21	1,764	51·88	—	—
24	67	9·57	41	16·24	D.L. Underwood	Kent	18	120	10·00	71	20·91
25	579	26·31	30	19·70	B. Wood (12th)	Lancashire	21	1,341	46·24	21	36·38

*captain †wicket-keeper

A Memorable Year

Despite the inauspicious start due to bad weather, 1972 developed into the most memorable first-class cricket season for a long time. The game, which had certainly been on the wane, was on the way up once more. Many of the counties were able to declare a profit, and the wonderful sight of 'Ground Full' notices was seen on several occasions. This was particularly heartening for any lover of the game and marked, one hopes, a genuine renaissance of both Test and County cricket.

The key to the sudden upsurge of interest was the Test series against Australia, which caught the imagination of the public and was followed more intently than any since that of the West Indies, under the late Sir Frank Worrell, back in the early sixties. This in itself was surprising, for whereas the West Indians were at their peak, and contained established stars, the Australian team was comparatively unknown and thought to be far from the strongest to visit this country. In addition the England XI, which just managed to retain the Ashes, was, by international standards, a good but not an especially distinguished combination.

The reason for the success of the series was the competitive way it was fought. In the final Test at Sydney, where England, handicapped by the absence of Boycott and an injury to their key bowler, Snow, regained the Ashes against a substandard Australian side, much of the cricket was quite ordinary, yet the game was a magnificent contest. This was, quite simply, because the two teams were so evenly matched. The advantage kept switching first one way and then the other until, on the final day, Australia required 100 to win with five wickets in hand. The same pattern occurred throughout last summer. The two teams were evenly matched with England, overrated, starting as firm favourites and Australia, slightly underrated, providing perfect opposition.

With practically no interruptions because of bad weather, the two teams fought an honourable and intriguing draw, with two wins apiece and one undecided. To add to the attraction, in each Test the advantage constantly swung from one side to the other. The outcome, after the first Test at Old Trafford, was that the crowds came rolling in to watch the most engrossing series held in England for at least a decade.

Although Ian Chappell's team had several limitations – the absence of one reliable opening bat, the lack of a third top-class seamer, and deficiencies in the spin department – they did possess other big attractions. First, there was Dennis Lillee, the fastest and most exciting pace bowler seen in this country since Wes Hall in his prime. Genuinely quick bowlers are as rare as top-class heavyweights, and they have a similar crowd appeal. In addition, Bob Massie, after his sensational debut at Lord's with one of the most remarkable, and certainly most successful, pieces of seam and swing bowling ever witnessed in a Test on that historic ground, was another newcomer every cricket follower wanted to see in action.

Secondly, Greg Chappell showed he is among the world's outstanding batsmen, and whenever he scored runs the sight of him in action alone was worth the price of admission. Indeed, this Australian team contained several interesting and satisfying batsmen, notably the belligerent Stackpole, Ian Chappell himself, and the rampaging Marsh. Finally, the Australian fielding was a joy to behold.

But the entertainment did not always come from the Australians. Although the early English batting regularly collapsed before the combined threat of Lillie and Massie, time and again the middle-order and the tail staged a series of fighting come-backs to restore the situation. This added greatly to the excitement. Though England's fielding could not match Australia's, their attack was far better balanced.

Adding that little extra spice to the ideal cricket dish – a five-match Anglo-Australian series between two equally balanced teams – was the obvious dislike the teams harboured for each other on the field of battle. Such open hostility meant there was plenty of needle in the matches, which in turn ensured that there was a real fight for the Ashes and that the series was far from being just good clean fun.

The tone of any season is set by the Test matches, and this fine series promoted interest in all forms of the game, just as the 1966 World Cup had aroused enthusiasm for soccer. It would be true to say that in 1972 the counties benefited, directly and indirectly, from the Test matches, and the county sides responded with some of the most interesting cricket they have produced for a considerable time.

The 1972 season marked the introduction of another generously sponsored competition, the Benson and Hedges League Cup, which produced additional revenue for the clubs. The final at Lord's proved the expected success and enabled Leicestershire to win their first major honour. Whether there was a need for yet another tournament, with different rules, other than for purely financial reasons, must be open to some doubt. There is, after all, something vaguely farcical about a mere 17 clubs setting forth in pursuit of the 'quadruple', and each new tournament tends to reduce the importance and the impact of the others. If it was felt that more limited-overs cricket was required, and there was plenty of evidence to substantiate this view, then an extension of the present profitable Sunday League to include Saturdays would have seemed a more logical proposition.

The title for the most improved county in 1972 must assuredly go to Leicestershire. They had a distinguished season – the finest in the club's history – and could justifiably claim to be the most consistent team in the country. If it had not been for the loss of no fewer than five key players during the August run-in, they might well have secured another honour besides the Benson and Hedges Cup.

The County Championship was deservedly won by Warwickshire, who in the process served up some of the most exhilarating batting ever seen at Edgbaston. The Midland club did not lose a single match and finished comfortably ahead of their nearest rivals, Kent. The one sad, and indeed sobering, thought about their triumph was that it attracted comparatively few spectators. When Warwickshire last carried off the title, in 1951, 28,000 and 29,000 paying customers went along to see them in action on separate days. But the total attendance for ten home matches in 1972 was only 17,000. It would be wise not to forget these most disappointing figures in the general euphoria of the summer.

Kent, at full strength probably the most formidable eleven in the country, took the John Player League with the storming finish that was also the feature of their unsuccessful bid for the County Championship. The outcome was eventually decided, amidst scenes of intense excitement, at Canterbury, where they beat Worcestershire before a vast crowd in their final Sunday match.

Lancashire, however, generally failed to play to their full potential, although they did have the satisfaction of winning the Gillette Cup for the third time in a row.

Several other counties can afford to look back with considerable satisfaction on the past summer. Northamptonshire, largely because of three new faces in their attack, made a dramatic climb up the Championship table, while Essex, despite their small playing staff, finished among the leaders in both the Championship and the John Player League. Had they possessed one additional class batsman they would probably have taken the latter. Yorkshire at last appear to have come to terms with the demands of Sunday cricket and showed a welcome all-round improvement, while Gloucestershire, if they can cure their habit of falling away at the end of the season when the pressure is really on, must have high hopes for 1973.

Possibly the most disturbing and unsatisfactory feature of a truly wonderful summer, from an English point of view, is revealed in the best individual performances. The majority of these were achieved either by overseas imports, or by players who have been around for a long time and, in many cases, are in the twilight of their careers.

The two outstanding all-rounders of 1972 were unquestionably Boyce and Mushtaq, who both bowled and batted with tremendous effect. The next places would go to Procter, and Greig (who performed with so much distinction in the Tests) and it is a sad statement on English cricket that all four learned the game abroad.

Batsmen, in general, enjoyed a prosperous summer, with Majid Khan the only player to reach a majestic 2,000 runs and Kanhai conjuring up a whole series of magical performances. Close, who did so well in his first season for his new county, was even more prolific in his second, while Marshall in his final year demonstrated what a loss he will be to Hampshire. The two most successful, comparatively young, English-born middle-order batsmen were probably Keith Fletcher, and David Steele of Northamptonshire.

With bonus points operating in the County Championship and the increase in limited-overs games, the opening batsmen have a considerable advantage, for rarely do those further down the order have the same opportunity to study the bowling before attacking it. Glenn Turner carried on where he had left off for New Zealand in the West Indies, and Barry Richards, although striking a bad patch, still produced several innings of genius. Boycott missed much of the season through injury, yet still finished among the leaders, while Amiss, in what for him was a new role, scored so many runs that he forced his way back into international reckoning. Barry Wood also impressed many critics with his obvious dedication and technique.

For bowlers, however, the season was not one of rich rewards, and for the first time since 1866 no bowler claimed 100 wickets in first-class cricket. One reason for this, of course, was the cutting down of the Championship.

Two bowlers, Tom Cartwright and Barry Stead, took 98 first-class wickets, and with John Dye made up a somewhat unlikely trio to take pride of place in the seam section. The performance of the evergreen Cartwright for Somerset was perhaps no great surprise, even if the size of his haul and his economy continue to be a source of wonder. But few, if any, would have predicted the success of Stead for Notts and of the Kent discard Dye for Northants.

It was only to be expected that the most impressive spinners were all experienced performers – Underwood, Gifford, and Mortimore. They are orthodox and, with the exception of Mushtaq, it proved a bad season for the wrist spinners.

One worrying feature, though, was that the over rate continued to fall, not only in the Tests, but in all first-class matches. This is a problem that needs firm handling. Spectators are prepared to see an outstanding fast bowler, like Lillee, employ a run-up of almost marathon proportions. But they are not happy to watch a fast-medium hack running in more than 20 yards, bowling, and then just ambling back, so that one over takes more than four minutes.

In general the fielding throughout the counties reached a very high standard, as did the wicket-keeping.

In retrospect, then, 1972 will be remembered as a vintage year. It marked a genuine revival in cricket, and contained a great battle for the Ashes, an additional one-day Anglo-Australian series, as well as the start of a new competition for the counties. Crowds and interest increased, and the heavy sponsorship provided large sums of much needed cash for the clubs. Once again, after some years in the doldrums, English cricket could look to the next season with confidence.

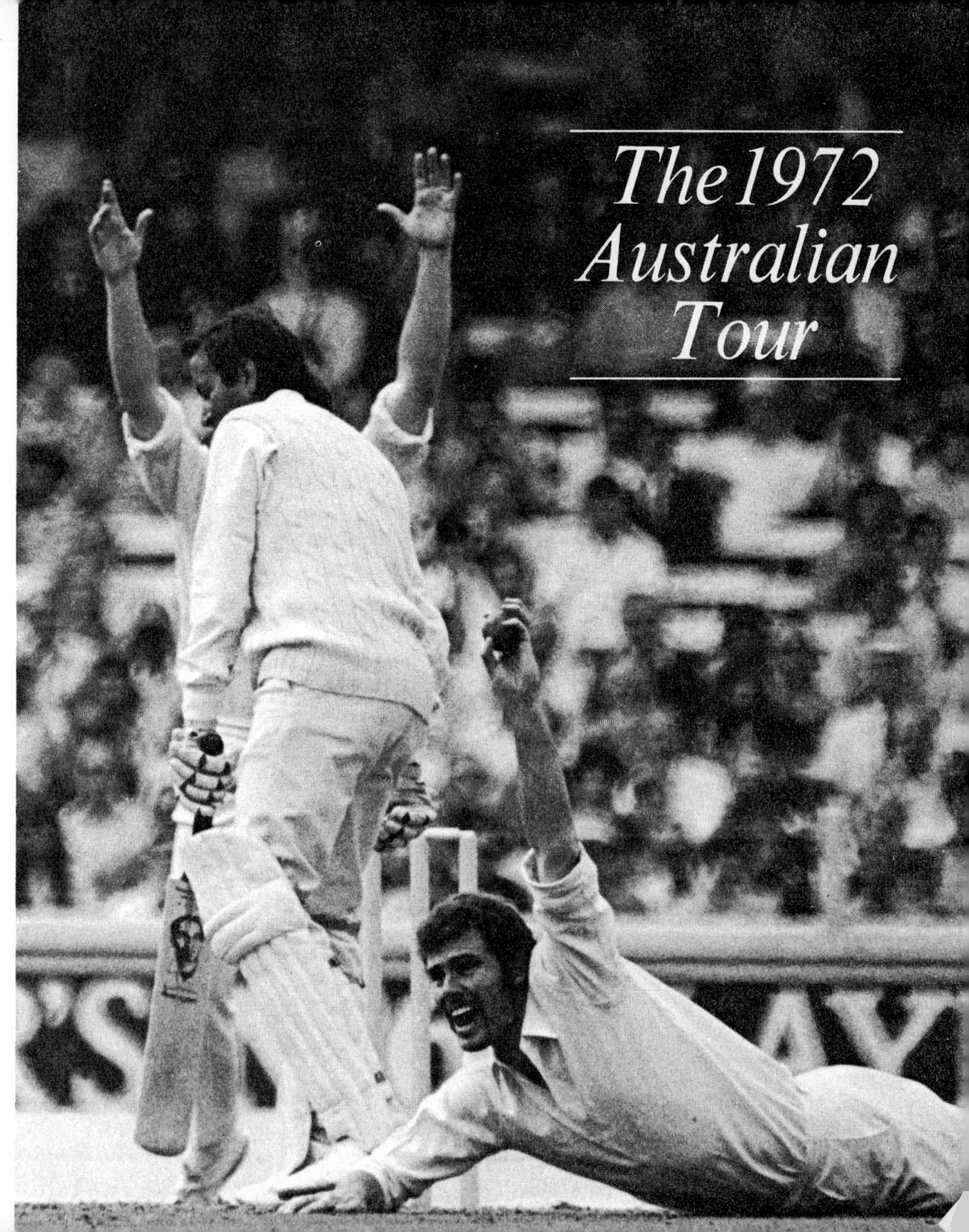
The 1972 Australian Tour

John Player Cricket Yearbook 1973

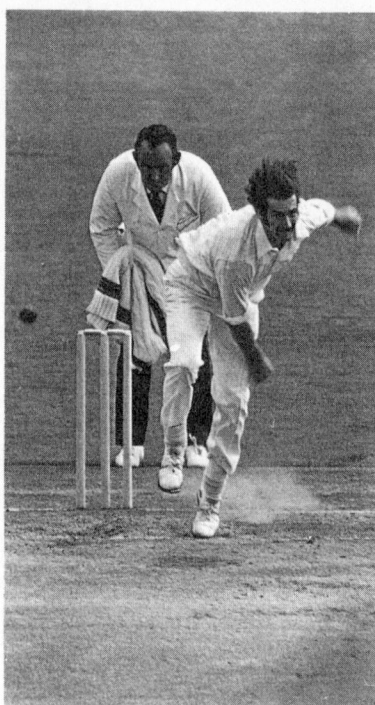

Above: 'Keeper takes 'keeper. Alan Knott catches Rodney Marsh off Underwood and adds support to a vociferous England appeal. Derek Underwood's bowling in this match, the fourth Test at Leeds, produced match figures of 10 for 82 and ensured that the Ashes remained with England

Far left: Ian Chappell in glorious form at The Oval; he top-scored with 118 and shared a partnership of 201 with his brother, Greg, establishing the basis for the victory that squared the series

Left: Dennis Lillee's magnificently fearsome fast bowling kept turnstiles clicking and England wickets tumbling

The Fight for the Ashes 1972

John Arlott

The Tests of 1972 between England and Australia will be remembered by everyone who followed them as a great series. There have been many other rubbers in which more great players took part; but few indeed have ever been so even, fluctuating, exciting, full of character, played in better spirit or with greater enjoyment.

It was clear from the beginning that the essential contest lay between the experience and professionalism of the older English players, accustomed to their own unique conditions, on the one side; and, on the other, the highly talented, younger Australians who would gradually gain all the advantages of understanding and embattled determination which come to a good touring side. Overcoming the depressions and handicaps of appalling weather at the start of the season – they lost a third of their scheduled playing time up to the first Test – they grew up from week to week under the captaincy of Ian Chappell, who learnt quickly, and was unfailingly clear-sighted and resolute. The final drawn series was a fair result; had it been played two years earlier, England would probably have won; two years later it would have gone to Australia.

The figures – justifiably omitting those who played in only one Test – show the Australian top batting far the stronger – four of their batsmen had averages of 45 or over, while no Englishman reached 40. Two Australian bowlers, Lillee and Massie with 54 wickets between them, did better than any three English bowlers in aggregate and all but one – Underwood – in average.

Seen from a different aspect, England won on the two bowlers wickets, Australia on the two fairer ones, and they had the best of the draw on the almost too perfect batting conditions of Trent Bridge.

England were unfortunate in the absence of Boycott – their key batsman, for whom there was no substitute – from three Tests, and the constantly unfortunate Arnold – currently at his finest as a swing bowler – from two. By comparison Australia lost only Massie from one Test – though admittedly that was at Old Trafford where he might have won the game.

This series proved an historic watershed. An England side came to the end of its period of prosperity; and a new generation of Australians entered upon theirs.

England retained the tradition they had established under Illingworth of tenacity in trouble and capacity for recovery from apparent disaster. However, their older batsmen, Luckhurst, Edrich, Smith and Parfitt, were all decisively defeated by Lillee's pace. D'Oliveira plodded gamely but he won no match and saved none. The English successes were Illingworth – at 40 a success in all four departments of his game – Snow, who bowled with fine heart; Arnold, whose due returns were reduced by dropped catches; Underwood, who effectively won the Headingley Test on the kind of wicket where he has no superior in the world; Knott, perkily defiant; Greig, who must have made his place secure for a long time to come; and, on the evidence of The Oval, Wood.

For Australia Walters, despite some spectacular innings in county games, again proved vulnerable at Test level in English conditions. It barely mattered. Stackpole, the most prolific and luckiest batsman of the rubber, gave the side's batting a fine impetus by his gusto and aggressive approach. Greg Chappell, in his early maturity, stepped up to the verge of greatness. His brother Ian batted, and captained the side, with determined concentration. The maturing of Sheahan and the emergence of Edwards and – an immense asset in team balance – Marsh completed a batting strength which should serve Australia long and well. The support bowling was not strong; Gleeson never found a wicket of sufficient pace to suit him; Mallett probably bowled too little; and Colley was a journeyman. That merely emphasises the quality of Lillee and that superb English-style swing-bowler Massie as match-winners. Given two more major bowlers – one of pace and a spinner – they will be extremely hard to beat.

At different times the fielding on both sides wavered. The poor light of Old Trafford afforded some excuse – but too many catches were dropped elsewhere; and England had one sorry day at Trent Bridge. Although he was understandably out of his element at Headingley, Marsh advanced in wicket-keeping as in batting, and Knott, after going through a dim phase, had returned to form.

If there were umpiring errors they probably cancelled out. The feeling between the two sides was friendly enough to survive the grievance of the Headingley wicket; fierce competition on the field was balanced by a convivial spirit off it.

The First Test: Manchester

In conditions which favoured seam bowling, England put out their first choice team for, as it proved, the only time in the series. Australia were without Massie, the likeliest of their bowlers to have exploited the pitch and weather.

After rain which delayed the start by an hour-and-a-half, the first day was largely Australia's and England laboured unsteadily to a meagre 147 for five. Lillee bowled extremely fast; Edrich constantly edged him and Boycott, taking a lifting ball on the arm, retired hurt from lunch until after tea. Gleeson, in contrasting method, turned the ball both ways to batsmen who signally failed to 'read' his hand. His figures, like Lillee's, did his bowling no justice. The English innings was largely a survival exercise in which four catches and a run-out were missed. Edrich hung on for 49 before he was run out: as soon as Boycott returned he was beaten by Gleeson's leg break and caught at slip: while Luckhurst, Smith and D'Oliveira were never secure.

Greig and Knott, together overnight, carried their stand to 63 on Friday; Illingworth and Gifford worked for 41 between them and England's unremarkable 249 was enhanced by their subsequent seam bowling. Arnold made the ball cut alarming curves but, in the indifferent light, four slip catches were missed off him. Nevertheless, he took the wickets of the bold but fortunate Stackpole (dropped twice when he was five) and Edwards, to leave Australia 103 for four that evening.

Next morning Arnold and Snow put out the remaining six Australians for 39 runs and by the end of the day England were 243 in front with seven second innings wickets left. Before a run was scored Walters was dropped in the slips – off the unfortunate Arnold – but Snow, bowling at high speed, soon had the younger Chappell finely taken by Greig at second slip and the rest of the batting was lost against a combination of pace, swing and seam-movement.

Boycott – who studied Lillee with some care, and then played some commanding strokes – and Edrich put on a tactically important 60 for the first wicket. Boycott looked to be in control when he was lbw sweeping uncharacteristically at Gleeson who had now taken his wicket six times in seven Tests.

Almost as soon as Luckhurst came in he edged a catch to Marsh and Edrich, attempting to push the innings along, edged a catch to the 'keeper. While Smith held on against Lillee in the dim evening light, D'Oliveira struck out and they had made 55 together by the close of play.

Another hour-and-a-half was lost to rain on the Monday when Australia achieved individual successes, but England progressed steadily towards winning. Lillee, too fast for all the English batsmen, had D'Oliveira caught in the gully at the start of play and, although Smith defended determinedly and Greig played some fluent strokes, they both often played and missed. Professionally, they put on 40 crucial runs: Greig was top scorer of the innings with an accomplished 62. Then when England seemed to be prospering, Lillee, with the new ball, took three wickets in four balls and was left with a hat trick in perpetual suspension when, in the next over, Greg Chappell yorked Greig. Lillee's six for 66 with little support – Colley was inaccurate – was a fine piece of sustained fast bowling; but Australia needed a distant 342 – the highest innings of the match – to win.

Francis playing back was soon beaten by Snow who, after a stoppage for rain, renewed his old Australian contest with Ian Chappell, who was again caught mis-hooking a bouncer. Australia now were 31 for two; but Stackpole – dropped yet again – and Greg Chappell saw the day out with calm competence.

For the first time in the match a clear, dry day left the seam bowlers without advantage yet, until almost the end of their innings, the Australians, failing to recognize their opportunity, batted irresolutely. In the first half hour two important wickets went down; Stackpole was dropped once more but Greg Chappell in an odd lapse, pulled Arnold to mid-on, and Watson grotesquely mistimed Snow. Stackpole again played gamely; Walters survived with almost comical luck against Arnold, only for Greig to bowl him as soon as he took Arnold's end. Inverarity was taken at slip; Greig's savage breakback bowled Stackpole and when Colley edged Snow to slip, Australia, 147 for eight, had lost six wickets for 90 runs and were 195 short of their aim; and only Stackpole had put a brave face on the day. As if accepting certain defeat, Gleeson swung his bat carelessly and was twice missed. Then, after lunch, Marsh the wicket-keeper, a powerfully built left-hand bat, began to hit with well-judged power; glancing or cutting the short ball, driving anything pitched up. All at once the atmosphere changed.

Gleeson settled to responsible defence and when Gifford – the first English spinner to bowl in the match – came on, Marsh stepped up and hit him for four fine, long, leg-side sixes. He made 91 – with four sixes and nine fours – in a little over two hours. His ninth wicket partnership with Gleeson had put on 104 and offered a threat – remote but real – to England's success when, trying to force Greig through the covers, he was caught at the wicket. England won with three hours to spare; but Australia on the last afternoon had regained much self esteem.

A poor attendance – only 22,816 people paid on the five days – was only partly explained by the cheerless weather.

John Player Cricket Yearbook 1973

ENGLAND v AUSTRALIA 1972 – 1st Test
Played at Old Trafford, Manchester, June 8, 9, 10, 12, 13
Toss: England   Result: England won by 89 runs

ENGLAND
G. Boycott	c Stackpole b Gleeson	8	lbw b Gleeson	47
J.H. Edrich	run out	49	c Marsh b Watson	26
B.W. Luckhurst	b Colley	14	c Marsh b Colley	0
M.J.K. Smith	lbw b Lillee	10	c Marsh b Lillee	34
B.L. D'Oliveira	b G.S. Chappell	23	c Watson b Lillee	37
A.W. Greig	lbw b Colley	57	b G.S. Chappell	62
A.P.E. Knott†	c Marsh b Lillee	18	c Marsh b Lillee	1
R. Illingworth*	not out	26	c I.M. Chappell b Lillee	14
J.A. Snow	b Colley	3	lbw b Lillee	0
N. Gifford	run out	15	c Marsh b Lillee	0
G.G. Arnold	c Francis b Gleeson	1	not out	0
Extras	(b 10, lb 9, nb 4, w 2)	25	(b 4 lb 8, nb 1)	13
TOTAL		**249**	TOTAL	**234**

AUSTRALIA
K.R. Stackpole	lbw b Arnold	53	b Greig	67
B.C. Francis	lbw b D'Oliveira	27	lbw b Snow	6
I.M. Chappell*	c Smith b Greig	0	c Knott b Snow	7
G.S. Chappell	c Greig b Snow	24	c D'Oliveira b Arnold	23
G.D. Watson	c Knott b Arnold	2	c and b Snow	0
K.D. Walters	c Illingworth b Snow	17	b Greig	20
R.J. Inverarity	c Knott b Arnold	4	c Luckhurst b D'Oliveira	3
R.W. Marsh†	c Edrich b Arnold	8	c Knott b Greig	91
D.J. Colley	b Snow	1	c Greig b Snow	4
J.W. Gleeson	b Snow	0	b Greig	30
D.K. Lillee	not out	1	not out	0
Extras	(b 1, lb 4)	5	(w 1)	1
TOTAL		**142**	TOTAL	**252**

AUSTRALIA	O	M	R	W	O	M	R	W
Lillee	29	14	40	2	30	8	66	6
Colley	33	3	83	3	23	3	68	1
G.S. Chappell	16	6	28	1	21.2	6	42	1
Walters	5	1	7	0				
Watson	4	2	8	0	5	0	29	1
Gleeson	24.4	10	45	2	7	3	16	1
Inverarity	9	3	13	0				
ENGLAND								
Snow	20	7	41	4	27	2	87	4
Arnold	25	4	62	4	20	2	59	1
Greig	7	1	21	1	19.2	7	53	4
D'Oliveira	6	1	13	1	16	4	23	1
Gifford					3	0	29	0

FALL OF WICKETS
	England		Australia	
Wkt	1st	2nd	1st	2nd
1st	50	60	68	9
2nd	86	65	69	31
3rd	99	81	91	77
4th	118	140	99	78
5th	127	182	119	115
6th	190	192	124	120
7th	200	234	134	136
8th	209	234	137	147
9th	243	234	137	251
10th	249	234	142	252

Umpires C.S. Elliott and T.W. Spencer

*Captain   †Wicket-keeper

Paying attendance: 22,816   Receipts: £20,337

The Fight for the Ashes

Above left: Boycott hooks Lillee for four in the second round of their confrontation at Manchester

Above right: John Snow sends Gleeson's off stump flying and Australia are all out for 142 in the first innings of the first Test

Left: Bob Massie, the destroyer of England in the second Test at Lord's with 16 wickets on his Test debut

Below: That man Marsh again – on his way to a belligerent 50 at Lord's

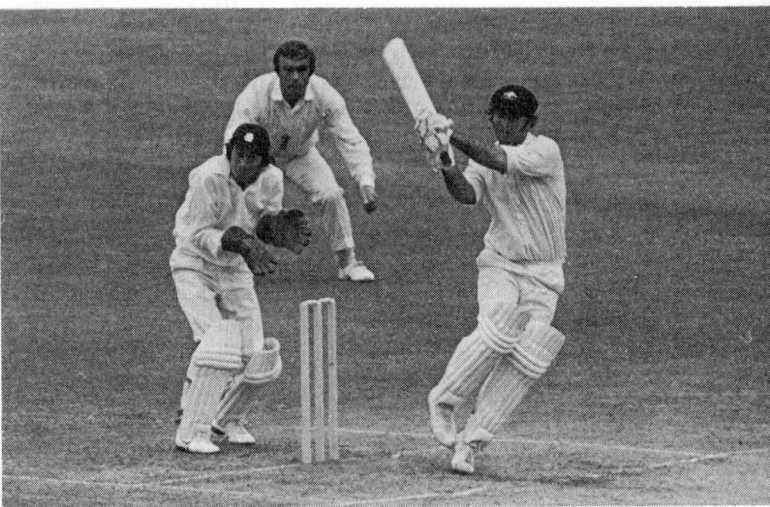

The Second Test: Lord's

The Old Trafford situation was reversed at Lord's; in circumstances ideal for swing-bowling Massie, in his first Test, twice bowled out England while Arnold, who might have been as effective, was not fit to play.

By comparison with Manchester, Australia left out Watson and Inverarity for Massie and Edwards; Price of Middlesex replaced Arnold in the English team.

In the now familiar pattern of recent years, the later English batsmen redeemed the failures of their predecessors. Illingworth won the toss and, in heavy conditions, their first three wickets went down for 28 runs. Boycott and Edrich seemed to have survived the opening bowling when Massie took an illustrious first Test wicket; Boycott took his eye off the ball and was yorked by an inswinger. Statistically Lillee's share of the day was two wickets to Massie's five; but his unsettling effect was of immense tactical value.

While Lillee threatened and hustled the batsmen, Massie's late and well concealed swing, variations – of pace, and between over and round the wicket – confounded them in a different fashion. Yet all the next six men contrived some profit out of their difficulties. Greig further established himself with his third consecutive 50 of the series; and 249 for seven was a higher score than the shape of the play promised.

A second-day crowd of 29,000 promised that the series had caught the public imagination after all: and there was much to interest them as Australia made their way to a position of command. England's three remaining wickets went down for 23 runs, to give Massie an analysis – unequalled by any bowler in his first Test innings – of eight for 84.

Within two overs, however, Australia were seven for two: Francis, again going back instead of forward to Snow, and Stackpole, hooking Price, were out, and the Chappell brothers were left together. They proceeded to bat with shrewd aggression. At first Ian Chappell – hooking the short ball as he had declared he would do, and taking five fours and a six to long leg off Snow – made the going while Greg kept an end secure. Their partnership of 75, which steadied the innings, was broken by Snow – Ian Chappell hooked once too often at his bouncer, and Smith took a tumbling catch on the Mound Stand boundary. Walters was out almost immediately, but Greg Chappell succeeded to seniority with Edwards as his partner. Reading and timing the ball perfectly, he drove with controlled power.

On Saturday the gates were closed on a crowd of 30,000 who watched Australia make a confident way to the verge of winning. Greg Chappell, coolly authoritative – his 131 was the most technically accomplished innings of the series – Marsh with another punitive piece of batting and Colley, took them to a lead of 36 despite the skilfully hostile fast bowling of Snow. Then, in little more than an hour of the afternoon, Lillee and Massie, with two wickets apiece, reduced the English second innings to 25 for four. Boycott was unlucky; he allowed a ball from Lillee to hit him on the thigh and could then only stand helplessly, watching it roll slowly on to his stumps. Edrich, Luckhurst and D'Oliveira were all roundly beaten; and England were still five behind when Greig, failing for the first time in the series, was caught at slip.

Australia duly and comfortably won the match on Monday. Gifford and Price conducted a delaying operation but when Price was caught at slip off Massie – whose match figures of 16 for 137 have only twice been bettered in a Test – Australia needed no more than 81 to win. Stackpole made a breezy 57 of them; they won by eight wickets and the rubber was absorbingly open.

The Fight for the Ashes

ENGLAND v AUSTRALIA 1972 – 2nd Test
Played at Lord's, London, June 22, 23, 24, 26
Toss: England   Result: Australia won by 8 wickets

ENGLAND
G. Boycott	*b* Massie	11	*b* Lillee	6
J.H. Edrich	lbw *b* Lillee	10	*c* Marsh *b* Massie	6
B.W. Luckhurst	*b* Lillee	1	*c* Marsh *b* Lillee	4
M.J.K. Smith	*b* Massie	34	*c* Edwards *b* Massie	30
B.L. D'Oliveira	lbw *b* Massie	32	*c* G.S. Chappell *b* Massie	3
A.W. Greig	*c* Marsh *b* Massie	54	*c* I.M. Chappell *b* Massie	3
A.P.E. Knott†	*c* Colley *b* Massie	43	*c* G.S. Chappell *b* Massie	12
R. Illingworth*	lbw *b* Massie	30	*c* Stackpole *b* Massie	12
J.A. Snow	*b* Massie	37	*c* Marsh *b* Massie	0
N. Gifford	*c* Marsh *b* Massie	3	not out	16
J.S.E. Price	not out	4	*c* G.S. Chappell *b* Massie	19
Extras	(lb 6, nb 6, w 1)	13	(nb 4, w 1)	5
TOTAL		**272**	TOTAL	**116**

AUSTRALIA
K.R. Stackpole	*c* Gifford *b* Price	5	not out	57
B.C. Francis	*b* Snow	0	*c* Knott *b* Price	9
I.M. Chappell*	*c* Smith *b* Snow	56	*c* Luckhurst *b* D'Oliveira	6
G.S. Chappell	*b* D'Oliveira	131	not out	7
K.D. Walters	*c* Illingworth *b* Snow	1		
R. Edwards	*c* Smith *b* Illingworth	28		
J.W. Gleeson	*c* Knott *b* Greig	1		
R.W. Marsh†	*c* Greig *b* Snow	50		
D.J. Colley	*c* Greig *b* Price	25		
R.A.L. Massie	*c* Knott *b* Snow	0		
D.K. Lillee	not out	2		
Extras	(lb 7, nb 2)	9	(lb 2)	2
TOTAL		**308**	TOTAL (2 wkts)	**81**

AUSTRALIA	O	M	R	W	O	M	R	W
Lillee	28	3	90	2	21	6	50	2
Massie	32.5	7	84	8	27.2	9	53	8
Colley	16	2	42	0	7	1	8	0
G.S. Chappell	6	1	18	0				
Gleeson	9	1	25	0				
ENGLAND								
Snow	32	13	57	5	8	2	15	0
Price	26.1	5	87	2	7	0	28	1
Greig	29	6	74	1	3	0	17	0
D'Oliveira	17	5	48	1	8	3	14	1
Gifford	11	4	20	0				
Illingworth	7	2	13	1				
Luckhurst					0.5	0	5	0

FALL OF WICKETS
	England		Australia	
Wkt	1st	2nd	1st	2nd
1st	22	12	1	20
2nd	23	16	7	51
3rd	28	18	82	
4th	84	25	84	
5th	97	31	190	
6th	193	52	212	
7th	200	74	250	
8th	260	74	290	
9th	265	81	290	
10th	272	116	308	

Umpires D.J. Constant and A.E. Fagg

*Captain   †Wicket-keeper   Paying attendance: 82,538   Receipts: £82,914 (world record)

The Third Test: Nottingham

Australia gained a considerable first innings advantage, but on so good a wicket a draw was always on, and England were content with that.

A severe injury to his left hand ruled Boycott out of this and the two following Tests; his place was taken by Parfitt, and Lever of Lancashire was preferred to Price. Australia kept the side that won at Lord's.

When Illingworth won the toss he created some surprise by asking Australia to bat. If he expected to give his bowlers a green first morning wicket to bowl on, he was disappointed; perhaps he simply wanted to ensure that Lillee and Massie had no such chance. In the event the pitch played easily, Australia largely created their own troubles, and England dropped the catches that could have put them in a strong situation. Lever looked weary; Greig suffered from dropped catches and only Snow, rising above tiredness and a steamy afternoon with four good wickets for 65, prevented the game slipping away from England. Stackpole, with support from the Chappells, Edwards, Marsh and Colley, made a typically cavalier and lucky century – remarkably enough the first of the season at Trent Bridge. Australia had not fully accepted their opportunity: their 249 for six left the match open.

On a sunny Friday they made another 66 runs through Marsh and Colley – and then harried the defensively minded English batting down to 107 for four. When England went in, Edrich generally took Massie and Luckhurst Lillee; but if this was a tactical move, neither batsman looked comfortable. Nevertheless they plodded to 55 in two and a half hours before Lillee's pace was yet again too great for Luckhurst's reflexes. Edrich was out relaxing against Colley; the left-handed Parfitt was bowled by a big round-the-wicket inswinger from Massie; and Lillee ended Smith's dogged innings with an explosive breakback.

On Saturday Australia – through Lillee and Massie, with a last wicket from Colley – finished off the English innings for 189 and extended their lead from 126 to 283 with eight wickets left. So England had no more to play for than a draw. Edwards, opening the innings instead of Francis who was ill, scored a distinguished 90 not out. After cutting the first two balls for four, Stackpole went unusually early – caught at slip off Snow – but Edwards, unhurried by pace and intelligent against spin, and Ian Chappell with firm commonsense, took the score from 15 to 139 before Chappell, risking the sweep stroke against Illingworth, was lbw.

Next morning Edwards – in his second Test – and Greg Chappell took command of the game. Only Snow, who never flagged, and Illingworth bothered them; otherwise the English bowling was blunt, and much of their fielding untidy. Chappell had made 72 when he played on to Snow and Walters, in a hurry, was caught square cutting: but Edwards went on his cool way to 170 out of 324 for four, before the declaration left England with 451 to win in a possible nine and a half hours.

This time they batted responsibly and soundly. In three and a half hours they lost only Edrich – bowled middle stump by a late inswinger from Massie – while they scored 111 runs. Luckhurst, at last batting like his usual self, made 60 and remained with Parfitt to begin the last day. They lasted another two hours before Luckhurst, looking for the four to complete his century, tried to sweep Ian Chappell and skied a catch to slip. In Australia's last – new ball – burst, Lillee fired out Smith and Parfitt with two superb balls. Once the shine was gone, though, even he was shackled by the pitch and D'Oliveira and Greig saw England safely to the draw.

The Fight for the Ashes

ENGLAND v AUSTRALIA 1972 – 3rd Test
Played at Trent Bridge, Nottingham, July 13, 14, 15, 17, 18
Toss: England   Result: Match drawn

AUSTRALIA
K.R. Stackpole	c Parfitt b Greig	114	c Luckhurst b Snow	12
B.C. Francis	c Smith b Lever	10		
I.M. Chappell*	c Knott b Snow	34	lbw b Illingworth	50
G.S. Chappell	c Parfitt b Snow	26	b Snow	72
K.D. Walters	c Parfitt b Snow	2	c Gifford b Snow	7
R. Edwards	c Knott b Snow	13	(2) not out	170
R.W. Marsh†	c D'Oliveira b Gifford	41	(6) not out	7
D.J. Colley	c Greig b D'Oliveira	54		
R.A.L. Massie	c Parfitt b Snow	0		
J.W. Gleeson	not out	6		
D.K. Lillee	c Knott b Greig	0		
Extras	(b 4, lb 6, nb 5)	15	(lb 4, nb 1, w 1)	6
TOTAL		**315**	TOTAL (4 wkts dec)	**324**

ENGLAND
B.W. Luckhurst	lbw b Lillee	23	c G.S. Chappell b I.M. Chappell	96
J.H. Edrich	c Marsh b Colley	37	b Massie	15
P.H. Parfitt	b Massie	0	b Lillee	46
M.J.K. Smith	b Lillee	17	lbw b Lillee	15
B.L. D'Oliveira	lbw b Lillee	29	not out	50
N. Gifford	c Marsh b Massie	16		
A.W. Greig	c Marsh b Massie	7	(6) not out	36
A.P.E. Knott†	c Marsh b Massie	0		
R. Illingworth*	not out	24		
J.A. Snow	c Marsh b Lillee	6		
P. Lever	c Walters b Colley	9		
Extras	(b 5, lb 2, nb 13, w 1)	21	(b 17, lb 9, nb 2, w 4)	32
TOTAL		**189**	TOTAL (4 wkts)	**290**

ENGLAND	O	M	R	W	O	M	R	W
Snow	31	8	92	5	24	1	94	3
Lever	26	8	61	1	19	3	76	0
Greig	38.4	9	88	2	12	1	46	0
D'Oliveira	18	5	41	1	7	0	12	0
Gifford	5	1	18	1	15	1	49	0
Illingworth					15	4	41	1

AUSTRALIA	O	M	R	W	O	M	R	W
Lillee	29	15	35	4	25	10	40	2
Massie	30	10	43	4	36	13	49	1
Colley	23.3	5	68	2	19	6	43	0
Gleeson	6	1	22	0	30	13	49	0
I.M. Chappell					12	5	26	1
G.S. Chappell					9	4	16	0
Stackpole					17	7	35	0

FALL OF WICKETS
	Australia		England	
Wkt	1st	2nd	1st	2nd
1st	16	15	55	50
2nd	98	139	60	167
3rd	157	285	74	200
4th	165	295	111	201
5th	189		133	
6th	227		145	
7th	289		145	
8th	298		155	
9th	315		166	
10th	315		189	

Umpires A.E.G. Rhodes and T.W. Spencer

*Captain   †Wicket-keeper

Paying attendance: 52,018   Receipts: £41,748

John Player Cricket Yearbook 1973

Top: Exit the night-watchman with grace. Gifford 'walks' before the umpire confirms his snick off Massie to Marsh in the first innings at Trent Bridge

Above: Mallett's dive beats Knott's run-out attempt in Australia's first innings at Headingley

Far left: Blimey, that was close! Parfitt wonders how Inverarity survived an Underwood delivery

Left: Illingworth's innings of 57 at Headingley proved decisive in England's fight to retain the Ashes

The Fourth Test: Leeds

England retained the Ashes on a freakish, all but grassless, slow, turning wicket caused, according to a subsequent report, by a disease called *fuserium* attacking the grass. The game was over on the third day.

Australia brought in Mallett and Inverarity – their two finger-spinners – and Sheahan for Gleeson, Colley and Francis. On the English side, Arnold returned for Lever, and Gifford and Smith were dropped for Underwood – whom many critics thought should never have been left out – and Fletcher of Essex.

Australia won the toss and batted. After Edwards was out for 0, Stackpole, who again played their biggest and brightest innings, and Ian Chappell handled both pace, and the more threatening spin of Illingworth and Underwood, capably until lunch at 79 for one. In the first over of the afternoon Stackpole snicked Underwood to Knott, and, after the Chappell brothers had made another 14 wary runs, the two English spinners wrecked the innings. Five wickets fell for five runs – three of them to Underwood for one run in 30 balls. Marsh was soon out trying to treat Underwood as he had done Gifford at Old Trafford, but Inverarity and Mallett mustered 47 for the eighth wicket before Snow and Arnold with the new ball finished off the innings at 146.

Although Luckhurst and Edrich made a careful start with 43 overnight, England, too, laboured against the spin of Mallett and Inverarity on Friday. Edrich in a typical unprepossessing, grafting innings made 45 before he lifted Mallett to mid-off; and when the seventh wicket – Greig's – fell, England, at 128, were still 18 behind. Mallett had bowled relatively little on the tour and he had been on, unchanged, since six the previous evening; perhaps decisively, as the afternoon wore on, he tired. At this point Illingworth and Snow embarked on the stand that won the match, growing slowly out of defence until they drove Mallett off with 19 runs off three overs. They had put on a workmanlike 104 in three hours when Snow, swinging at a leg side full toss from Inverarity, was stumped by Marsh. In the final minutes of the day Illingworth went from 48 to 54 – the highest score of the match – by on-driving Mallett for six.

The condition of the pitch and Marsh's difficulties were illustrated by the 46 extras in the English innings which, at 263, gave them a lead of 117. Australia, with reason for anxiety about the spinners, now lost a wicket in each of Arnold's first two overs. Edwards – who thus scored a 'pair' immediately after his 170 not out at Trent Bridge – and Ian Chappell were both caught by Knott. Stackpole hit defiantly; Sheahan played a poised and accomplished innings of 41 not out; and Massie's swings at the end ensured that England batted a second time. On such a pitch Underwood – six for 45 – was too much for them. England, wanting only 20 to win and harried by Lillee and Massie, came carefully in for the loss of Edrich.

So the Ashes were retained. Australia, quite reasonably disturbed about the pitch on which the decision was reached, had the chance to draw the series at The Oval.

John Player Cricket Yearbook 1973

ENGLAND v AUSTRALIA 1972 – 4th Test

Played at Headingley, Leeds, July 27, 28, 29
Toss: Australia   Result: England won by 9 wicket

AUSTRALIA

K.R. Stackpole	c Knott b Underwood	52	lbw b Underwood	28
R. Edwards	c Knott b Snow	0	c Knott b Arnold	0
I.M. Chappell*	c and b Illingworth	26	c Knott b Arnold	0
G.S. Chappell	lbw b Underwood	12	c D'Oliveira b Underwood	13
A.P. Sheahan	c Illingworth b Underwood	0	not out	41
K.D. Walters	b Illingworth	4	c Parfitt b Underwood	3
R.W. Marsh†	c Illingworth b Underwood	1	c Knott b Underwood	1
R.J. Inverarity	not out	26	c Illingworth b Underwood	0
A.A. Mallett	lbw b Snow	20	b Illingworth	9
R.A.L. Massie	b Arnold	0	(11) b Illingworth	18
D.K. Lillee	c Greig b Arnold	0	(10) b Underwood	7
Extras	(lb 2, nb 3)	5	(lb 12, nb 4)	16
TOTAL		**146**	TOTAL	**136**

ENGLAND

B.W. Luckhurst	c G.S. Chappell b Mallett	18	not out	12
J.H. Edrich	c I.M. Chappell b Mallett	45	lbw b Lillee	4
P.H. Parfitt	c Marsh b Lillee	2	not out	0
K.W.R. Fletcher	lbw b Mallett	5		
B.L. D'Oliveira	b Mallett	12		
A.W. Greig	c G.S. Chappell b Inverarity	24		
A.P.E. Knott†	st Marsh b Mallett	0		
R. Illingworth*	lbw b Lillee	57		
J.A. Snow	st Marsh b Inverarity	48		
D.L. Underwood	c I.M. Chappell b Inverarity	5		
G.G. Arnold	not out	1		
Extras	(b 19, lb 15, nb 8, w 4)	46	(lb 3, nb 2)	5
TOTAL		**263**	TOTAL (1 wkt)	**21**

ENGLAND	O	M	R	W	O	M	R	W
Arnold	9.5	2	28	2	6	1	17	2
Snow	13	5	11	2	10	2	26	0
Greig	10	1	25	0				
Illingworth	21	11	32	2	19.1	5	32	2
Underwood	31	16	37	4	21	6	45	6
D'Oliveira	2	1	8	0				
AUSTRALIA								
Lillee	26.1	10	39	2	5	2	7	1
Massie	14	4	34	0				
Mallett	52	20	114	5	5	1	9	0
Inverarity	33	19	26	3				
I.M. Chappell	3	2	1	0				
G.S. Chappell	2	0	3	0				

FALL OF WICKETS

	Australia		England	
Wkt	1st	2nd	1st	2nd
1st	10	5	43	7
2nd	79	7	52	
3rd	93	31	66	
4th	93	51	76	
5th	97	63	108	
6th	98	69	108	
7th	98	69	128	
8th	145	93	232	
9th	146	111	246	
10th	146	136	263	

Umpires D.J. Constant and C.S. Elliott

*Captain   †Wicket-keeper

Paying attendance: 50,016   Receipts: £41,091

The Fifth Test: The Oval

In a match of shifting emphasis, high skill and endeavour, which even on the last morning could have gone either way, Australia deservedly levelled the series. For only the second time in England a Test lasted six days (the previous occasion was in 1930) and the well-made pitch wore evenly and remained honest to the end.

Australia played Watson for Walters; and England left out Luckhurst and Fletcher for Wood, of Lancashire, and Hampshire, of Yorkshire.

True to the pattern of the series, the first day was one of alternating dominance. Australia were well in control until tea; afterwards a slackening of their outcricket allowed yet another English recovery.

When Illingworth won the toss for the fourth time in the series Wood and Edrich opened the batting. Once Lillee had worked up to his full pace Edrich, predictably too slow in reaction, was lbw. Wood made an impressive start against Lillee, Massie and Mallett and, with Parfitt, had brought the score to 50 when, in the last over before lunch, apparently surprised by the bounce of a ball from Watson – a journeyman third seam bowler – he touched a catch to Marsh.

Parfitt and Hampshire went steadily to 133 in the afternoon before Hampshire, chopping Mallett against the spin, was caught at gully, and four wickets fell – three of them to Mallett – for 12 runs in less than half an hour. As England struggled for a foothold, Chappell twice called back Lillee; the first time he bowled Parfitt through a half stroke and, with the next ball, had Illingworth caught at slip: the second, Snow was taken at the wicket and the English innings had fallen from 133 for two to 181 for eight. That was the cue for Knott – dropped in the gully off Massie – to play an impishly quick-footed innings. While Arnold held his end steady, the partnership galloped along for 81 at more than a run a minute. Arnold, in fact, was looking for runs in the last over before the second new ball was due when he was bowled, sweeping at Inverarity. Underwood stayed to the end of the day at 287 for nine which was better than England had expected two hours before.

The second day was dominated by a partnership between the Chappell brothers who, watched by their father, mother and younger brother, became – more humanly than in most records – the first brothers to score centuries in the same innings of a Test.

First of all, England made another 17 runs before Knott edged Lillee and was caught by Marsh, who thus beat Grout's record of 21 dismissals in a five-Test England-Australia series.

Watson and Stackpole were out to Arnold and Snow respectively to bring the Chappells together at 34 for two. In six years of first-class cricket they had only once before shared a century partnership. Now in their different styles they applied themselves to the business of winning a Test match; Ian the strong-armed, quick-eyed practical striker: Greg, a slim, mature stylist. They had accomplished their purpose with a stand of 201 before Greg, beaten in flight by Illingworth, mistimed a gentle catch to midwicket.

In a third day which rain shortened by two and a half hours, England tenaciously confined Australia to 394 – a lead of 110 – for eight wickets. Ian Chappell was out early to Arnold; and Underwood took two quick wickets, but Edwards batted soundly and Inverarity stayed with him in a stand of 73 until, in the last half hour, Underwood took both their wickets. Meanwhile Boycott was scoring 204 not out for Yorkshire against Leicestershire.

On Monday Australia continued their winning progress. Without achieving spectacular figures, Lillee – at an heroic peak of technique and purpose – and Massie effectively destroyed England's last hopes of creating an attacking position. In the now anticipated fashion, Lillee's speed was too great for Edrich and Parfitt. On the other hand Wood, for the second time, batted with confident – even jaunty – skill. Dropped at five he promised to make a first Test hundred when, at 90, Massie beat him through the air and he was lbw. Australia had time on their side but they dared not relax: and they did not. They fretted away, unspectacularly but decisively. Ian Chappell made two important slip catches – when Hampshire slashed at Watson and D'Oliveira, handicapped by a back injury, edged Massie. By the end of the day, England, with Greig and Illingworth together at 227 for five, were only 112 ahead.

On Tuesday the English tail-end batsmen carried out yet another salvage operation. Altogether the last five wickets added 151. Greig, Illingworth – who had spent Sunday in bed with tonsilitis – and Snow all batted determinedly and, above all, Knott, in another defiant innings, made 63 before Lillee, having torn off his cap with a bouncer, heaved out his middle stump with a yorker. By then he had lifted England to 356 and set Australia 242 to win on a pitch where the ball was likely to turn.

England had made themselves another chance. At 16 Watson was lbw to Arnold who, almost immediately afterwards, had Stackpole dropped at slip. It was the tenth time he had been missed in the series.

The tactical reckoning, however, was that the issue would be decided between the Australian batsmen and the English spinners, Underwood and Illingworth. For an appreciable period of the fifth afternoon, those two held the game almost static. Illingworth was bowling with considerable restrictive, and mounting attacking, skill, when, in the delivery stride to Stackpole, he fell over. He had damaged his right ankle and was helped off, leaving Edrich as acting captain. Stackpole and Ian Chappell batted calculatedly and at 116 for one by evening, they had put Australia in a winning position.

So it proved on Wednesday. The two Chappells and Edwards went early to Underwood and Greig: but on an evenly paced turning wicket England had not quite enough fire-power. Illingworth's ankle injury did not allow him to appear – he did not play for the rest of the season – D'Oliveira, whose off-cutters might have helped out, could not take the field because of a back injury; and Snow was suffering from a bruised wrist – sustained while batting – and influenza. Underwood, perhaps trying too hard, bowled too much on or outside the leg stump.

Stackpole was dropped at slip by Hampshire off his first ball of the morning – it was bowled by Arnold, and there we were, back at Old Trafford – but soon he nicked Greig to Knott. Ian Chappell was caught sweeping Underwood, and Edwards was lbw to Greig. With the match again in the balance, Greg Chappell and Sheahan steadied the innings. Their stand was brief but psychologically decisive. Chappell was obviously unhappy at being given out lbw to Underwood but Sheahan's new discovered maturity and Marsh's defiance carried the day and Australia were home with five wickets left.

The Fight for the Ashes

Above: Lillee strikes again and Marsh has his 23rd victim of the series. Tony Greig is the unfortunate batsman

Left: John Hampshire hooks Watson for four in his first innings at The Oval. He fell to Mallett while still eight short of his half-century

Right: An admiring Marsh follows the flight of a Knott boundary in the final Test. The aggression the wicket-keepers displayed with the bat was a highlight of the series

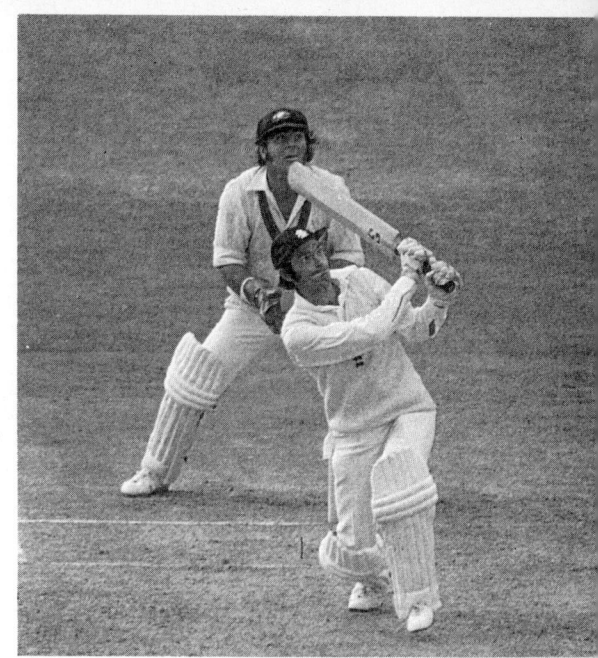

John Player Cricket Yearbook 1973

ENGLAND v AUSTRALIA 1972 – 5th Test

Played at Kennington Oval, London, August 10, 11, 12, 14, 15, 16
Toss: England   Result: Australia won by 5 wickets

ENGLAND

B. Wood	c Marsh b Watson	26	lbw b Massie	90
J.H. Edrich	lbw b Lillee	8	b Lillee	18
P.H. Parfitt	b Lillee	51	b Lillee	18
J.H. Hampshire	c Inverarity b Mallett	42	c I.M. Chappell b Watson	20
B.L. D'Oliveira	c G.S. Chappell b Mallett	4	c I.M. Chappell b Massie	43
A.W. Greig	c Stackpole b Mallett	16	c Marsh b Lillee	29
R. Illingworth*	c G.S. Chappell b Lillee	0	lbw b Lillee	31
A.P.E. Knott†	c Marsh b Lillee	92	b Lillee	63
J.A. Snow	c Marsh b Lillee	3	c Stackpole b Mallett	14
G.G. Arnold	b Inverarity	22	lbw b Mallett	4
D.L. Underwood	not out	3	not out	0
Extras	(lb 8, nb 8, w 1)	17	(b 11, lb 8, nb 7)	26
TOTAL		284	TOTAL	356

AUSTRALIA

G.D. Watson	c Knott b Arnold	13	lbw b Arnold	6
K.R. Stackpole	b Snow	18	c Knott b Greig	79
I.M. Chappell*	c Snow b Arnold	118	c sub (Willis) b Underwood	37
G.S. Chappell	c Greig b Illingworth	113	lbw b Underwood	16
R. Edwards	b Underwood	79	lbw b Greig	1
A.P. Sheahan	c Hampshire b Underwood	5	not out	44
R.W. Marsh†	b Underwood	0	not out	43
R.J. Inverarity	c Greig b Underwood	28		
A.A. Mallett	run out	5		
R.A.L. Massie	b Arnold	4		
D.K. Lillee	not out	0		
Extras	(lb 8, nb 7, w 1)	16	(lb 6, nb 10)	16
TOTAL		399	TOTAL (5 wkts)	242

AUSTRALIA	O	M	R	W	O	M	R	W
Lillee	24.2	7	58	5	32.2	8	123	5
Massie	27	5	69	0	32	10	77	2
Watson	12	4	23	1	19	8	32	1
Mallett	23	4	80	3	23	7	66	2
G.S. Chappell	2	0	18	0				
Inverarity	4	0	19	1	15	4	32	0
ENGLAND								
Arnold	35	11	87	3	15	5	26	1
Snow	34.5	5	111	1	6	1	21	0
Greig	18	9	25	0	25.3	10	49	2
D'Oliveira	9	4	17	0				
Underwood	38	16	90	4	35	11	94	2
Illingworth	17	4	53	1	8.5	2	26	0
					2	0	10	0

FALL OF WICKETS

	England		Australia	
Wkt	1st	2nd	1st	2nd
1st	25	56	24	16
2nd	50	81	34	132
3rd	133	114	235	136
4th	142	194	296	137
5th	145	205	310	171
6th	145	270	310	
7th	159	271	383	
8th	181	333	387	
9th	262	356	399	
10th	284	356	399	

Umpires A.E. Fagg and A.E.G. Rhodes

*Captain   †Wicket-keeper

Paying attendance: 87,473   Receipts: £75,193

Above: Hill-style support for Australia at Trent Bridge

Left: Tony Greig's savage breakback ends Keith Stackpole's innings of 67 at Old Trafford

Below: Great jubilation as Knott edges Lillee to give Rodney Marsh his first catch of the series

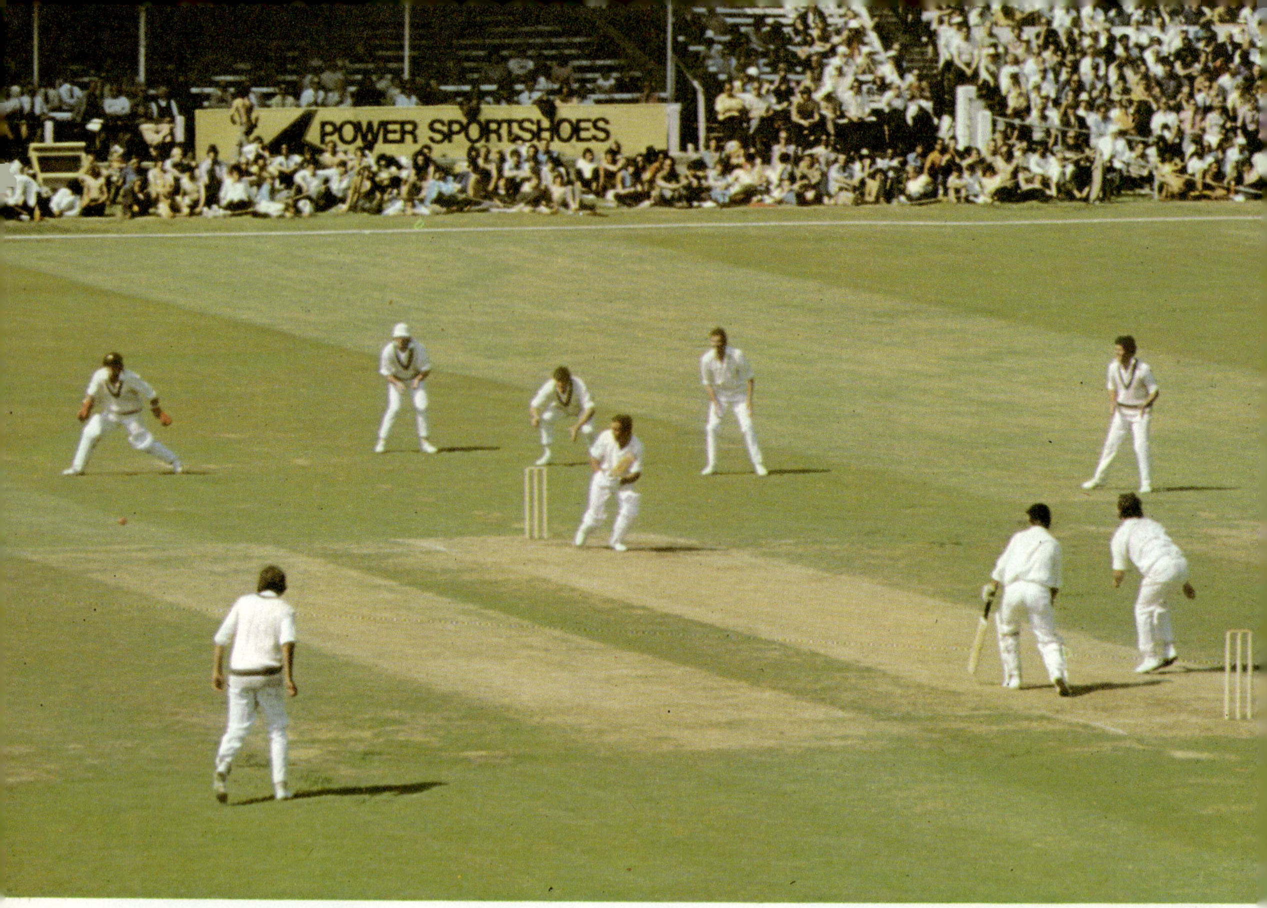
POWER SPORTSHOES

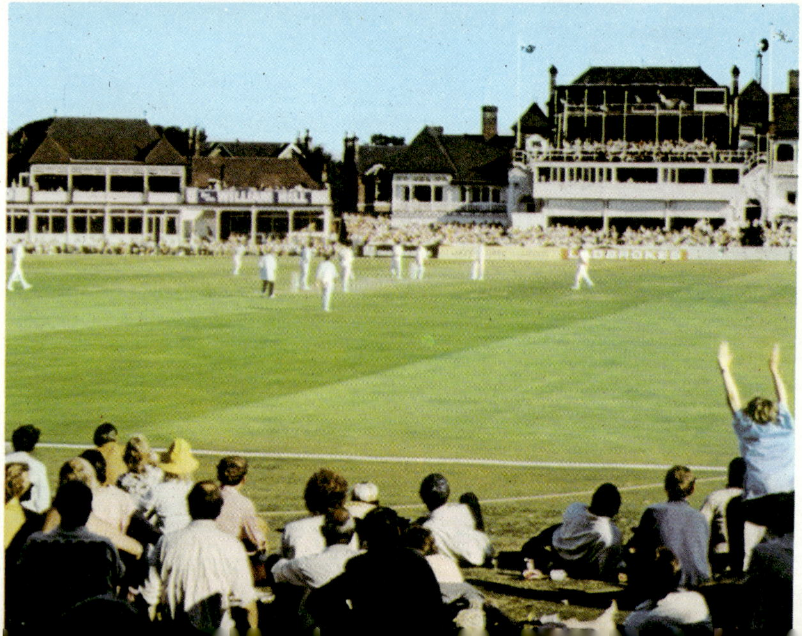

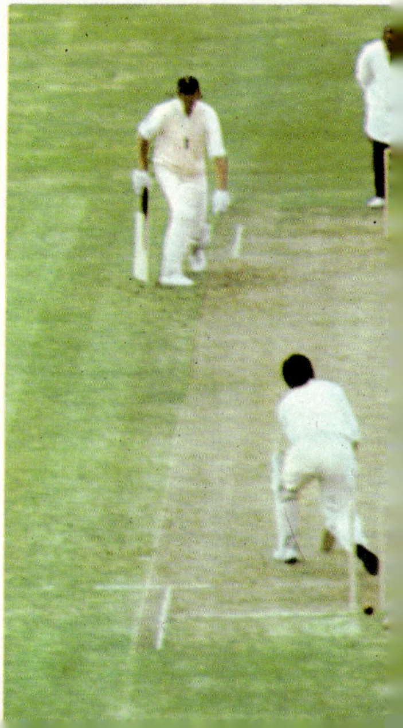

Above: The Underwood rout continues. Inverarity is out for a duck, caught at point by Ray Illingworth, in the second innings of the fourth Test. Derek Underwood, recalled to the England side, fully exploited a freakish, turning Headingley wicket to finish with 10 wickets. Illingworth also had a fine match, scoring a match-winning 57, taking 4 wickets, and holding 4 catches in England's 9-wickets victory

Left above: John Edrich tucks Bob Massie away to leg before a large crowd at Trent Bridge

Far left: Cloudless skies enhance nigh-perfect conditions at Trent Bridge, where the third Test ended in a draw

Left: Lillee sends Parfitt's middle stump flying in the fifth Test. The Middlesex lefthander, recalled to the England side for the third Test, scored 51 and 18 at The Oval before losing his wicket to Lillee each time

Right: Spectators inspect The Oval wicket where Australia won the fifth Test to square a memorable series

The man who brought thousands back to cricket and helped make the Test series such a success – Dennis Lillee, flying into his delivery stride before firing his thunderbolts at the English batsmen. Lillee's 31 Test wickets were a record for an Australian in England, and no batsman played him with confidence

Dennis Lillee — Man of the Series

John Arlott

The outstanding success of the 1972 Australian tour – indeed of that entire English summer – was Dennis Lillee, the fast bowler from Western Australia. Lillee arrived in England 22 years old, with a reputation for high pace but uncertain control and suspect fitness. He left, five months later, unquestionably the fastest bowler in the world, a match-winner of fire, control, strength and stamina. He had taken 31 wickets in the Test series – a record for any Australian in England – and effectively caused the break-up of an ageing English batting side. By that performance alone Dennis Lillee earned himself a place in cricket history; and simultaneously he gave evidence of his capacity to go on winning matches on the highest level.

Lillee's career in first-class cricket has been short, his development rapid: even when he went home at the end of the 1972 season, he had played in only 47 first-class matches – 14 of them on that tour of England when he made his final advance to unquestionable eminence.

The young Australian had his opportunity to play Sheffield Shield cricket when he was 20. In the 1969–70 Australian season, McKenzie and Mayne, Western Australia's regular opening bowlers, were away on the tour of India and South Africa. Tony Lock, then captain of the state, had been impressed by Lillee's pace and potential in net practice and at once he gave him his chance. In the absence of his seniors, Lillee established his team place, took 32 wickets in eight matches, and was chosen for the Australian 'B' team to New Zealand. There, though he played in only one representative match and that with little success, he was top of the bowling averages for the entire tour – 18 wickets at 16·44.

In the following season he played in the last two Tests against Illingworth's visiting England side and took five for 84 in the first of them. For the summer of 1971 he came to England as professional to Haslingden in the Lancashire League where his figures were not so good – in either number of wickets or average – as those of Ken Higgs, Harold Rhodes or Dik Abed.

Lillee returned to Australia to be chosen for the first four international matches with the Rest of the World: he took 24 wickets and had one remarkable spell of eight for 29 in 7·1 overs, on his fast home wicket at Perth. A back injury which kept him out of the fifth game recurred subsequently when he turned out for his state; and, although he was successful when he could play, he had similar trouble in the grim weather at the start of the English season. The entire touring party was clearly concerned about his fitness. As late as mid-May – only about three weeks before the start of the first Test – he had to be rested and undergo intensive treatment. Even after that he was to be seen trying out his bowling action in extremely gingerly fashion.

Ultimately the decision was his – to play for the full stakes and bowl at full bore. Within a month he was the greatest crowd attraction English cricket grounds had known since the heyday of Frank Tyson. He, like Tyson, had the immense elemental appeal of beating batsmen by pure pace. There are fast bowlers and fastest bowlers: Lillee belongs in the second category.

Six feet tall, long-legged, lean, wide-shouldered and hard-trained, with waving dark hair and Mexican-style moustache, he was a striking figure. He walked back 44 strides to his bowling mark, and his run-in was spectacularly furious. Purists said it was too long – and by other men's standards, it was: that he ran too fast too soon – and by coaching manual standards, he did: that he would burn himself out before the end of the tour – but he did not: that he was moving too fast at the point of delivery to profile as a bowler should – but his action seemed to flow through from an adequately side-on position. Lillee's conclusive answer to all his critics lies in his performance – and in the fact that he has an undeniable urge to bowl as fast as he possibly can; he is an instinctive fast bowler.

When he bowled his first ball in front of a crowd that had not seen him before, there was a corporate gasp which told more than many words. In 1972 he bowled at such pace that one experienced Test batsman after another – with his eye in and accustomed to the pace of the wicket – aimed a stroke at him after the ball was past. He commanded an alarming bouncer, the more valuable for the fact that often it was pitched only a little short of good length yet rose steeply; and he often beat the bat around yorker length. One of his speed can hardly be expected to 'move' the ball very much; but when it was new he made it run away towards the slips, and he bowled a savage body-action breakback.

Even when he took few wickets, as in the Lord's Test, his disturbing effect on the English batsmen was of marked tactical value. Massie, of course, took 16 of his 23 wickets for the rubber in that match, Lillee's were spread evenly over the series – eight at Old Trafford, four at Lord's, six at Trent Bridge, three on the spinners' pitch at Headingley where only 11 fell, and ten at The Oval.

Ian Chappell was short of at least one – often two – bowlers for his main purpose of winning the Test series. He recognised the need to keep Lillee fresh; and the figures show that while he bowled him, on average, for 50 overs in each Test, the figure was only 23 in county matches. This meant that, at need against England, he could call him back after an unusually short rest. He did so in the Old Trafford, Lord's, Trent Bridge and Oval Tests – and always the response was of maximum effort. At times, in order to retain a narrow advantage for Australia, in fact, Lillee had almost to be used as a stock bowler. Yet he could still rise to splendid peaks and twice in the series – in the second innings at Manchester and the first at The Oval – he took three wickets in four balls. Both Lillee and his captain paced his effort well. His immense – and decisive – effort at the Oval – 56.4 overs for ten wickets – squeezed almost the last drops of energy out of him.

A faithful but not a great fieldsman, and barely in contention even with his Western Australian team-mate, Massie, for the privilege of not going in last, Lillee is a zestful enthusiast for cricket. He pours all of himself into his bowling, as hostile on the field as he is relaxed and humorous off it. When Dennis Lillee left England, no English batsman of 1972 had been his master; and, on a wicket with the remotest degree of life in it, that would be true for those of any other country in the world today.

Statistical Survey of the Series

BATTING – ENGLAND

*Denotes not out

	Tests	I	NO	HS	Runs	Av	Mins	Balls	Runs/100 balls	4s	6s
B. Wood	1	2	0	90	116	58.00	388	297	39	18	–
A.W. Greig	5	9	1	62	288	36.00	866	719	40	32	1
R. Illingworth	5	8	2	57	194	32.33	738	601	32	17	2
J.H. Hampshire	1	2	0	42	62	31.00	145	118	53	10	–
B.L. D'Oliveira	5	9	1	50*	233	29.12	686	557	42	36	–
A.P.E. Knott	5	8	0	92	229	28.62	523	441	52	33	–
B.W. Luckhurst	4	8	1	96	168	24.00	645	518	32	17	–
P.H. Parfitt	3	6	1	51	117	23.40	534	403	29	9	–
M.J.K. Smith	3	6	0	34	140	23.33	594	452	31	11	1
J.S.E. Price	1	2	1	19	23	23.00	54	38	61	3	–
J.H. Edrich	5	10	0	49	218	21.80	1,005	713	31	25	–
G. Boycott	2	4	0	47	72	18.00	221	166	43	8	–
J.A. Snow	5	8	0	48	111	13.87	372	295	38	12	–
N. Gifford	3	5	1	16*	50	12.50	235	174	29	7	–
G.G. Arnold	3	5	2	22	28	9.33	154	131	21	5	–
P. Lever	1	1	0	9	9	9.00	47	45	20	–	–
D.L. Underwood	2	3	2	5	8	8.00	63	43	19	1	–
K.W.R. Fletcher	1	1	0	5	5	5.00	26	21	24	1	–
TOTALS	55	97	12	(96)	2,071	24.36	7,296	5,732	36.13	245	4

BATTING – AUSTRALIA

†Plus one 'five'

	Tests	I	NO	HS	Runs	Av	Mins	Balls	Runs/100 balls	4s	6s
K.R. Stackpole	5	10	1	114	485	53.88	1,213	949	51	53	–
G.S. Chappell	5	10	1	131	437	48.55	1,163	999	44	51	–
R. Edwards	4	7	1	170*	291	48.50	740	648	45	25†	–
A.P. Sheahan	2	4	2	44*	90	45.00	354	307	29	9	–
R.W. Marsh	5	9	2	91	242	34.57	489	382	63	27	6
I.M. Chappell	5	10	0	118	334	33.40	1,176	938	36	45	1
D.J. Colley	3	4	0	54	84	21.00	216	160	53	9	–
R.J. Inverarity	3	5	1	28	61	15.25	242	234	26	5	–
J.W. Gleeson	3	4	1	30	37	12.33	152	129	29	3	–
A.A. Mallett	2	3	0	20	34	11.33	163	146	23	5	–
B.C. Francis	3	5	0	27	52	10.40	157	137	38	4	–
K.D. Walters	4	7	0	20	54	7.71	193	181	30	4	–
G.D. Watson	2	4	0	13	21	5.25	57	43	49	3	–
R.A.L. Massie	4	5	0	18	22	4.40	68	63	35	2	1
D.K. Lillee	5	7	4	7	10	3.33	80	62	16	1	–
TOTALS	55	94	13	(170*)	2,254	27.82	6,463	5,378	41.91	246	8

HUNDRED PARTNERSHIPS

ENGLAND (2)	Wkt	Runs	Mins	Partners	Venue
	2nd	117	221	B.W. Luckhurst (96) P.H. Parfitt (46)	Nottingham
	8th	104	177	R. Illingworth (57) J.A. Snow (48)	Leeds

AUSTRALIA (6)	Wkt	Runs	Mins	Partners	Venue
	3rd	201†	241	I.M. Chappell (118) G.S. Chappell (113)	The Oval
	3rd	146	128	R. Edwards (170*) G.S. Chappell (72)	Nottingham
	2nd	124	158	R. Edwards (170*) I.M. Chappell (50)	Nottingham
	2nd	116	180	K.R. Stackpole (79) I.M. Chappell (37)	The Oval
	5th	106	148	G.S. Chappell (131) R. Edwards (28)	Lord's
	9th	104‡	82	R.W. Marsh (91) J.W. Gleeson (30)	Manchester

*Denotes not out
†Record partnership by a pair of brothers in Test matches
‡Record Australia ninth wicket partnership in all Tests played overseas

BOWLING – ENGLAND

	O	M	R	W	Av	BB	Balls per wkt	Runs per 100 balls
D.L. Underwood	125	49	266	16	16.62	6–45	47	35
G.G. Arnold	110.5	25	279	13	21.46	4–62	51	42
J.A. Snow	205.5	46	555	24	23.12	5–57	51	45
R. Illingworth	88	28	197	7	28.14	2–32	75	37
B.L. D'Oliveira	83	23	176	5	35.20	1–13	100	35
J.S.E. Price	33.1	5	115	3	38.33	2–87	66	58
A.W. Greig	162.3	44	398	10	39.80	4–53	98	41
N. Gifford	34	6	116	1	116.00	1–18	204	57
P. Lever	45	11	137	1	137.00	1–61	270	51
P.H. Parfitt	2	0	10	0	–	–	–	83
B.W. Luckhurst	0.5	0	5	0	–	–	–	100
TOTALS	890.1	237	2,254	80	28.17	(6–45)	67	42

BOWLING – AUSTRALIA

	O	M	R	W	Av	BB	Balls per wkt	Runs per 100 balls
D.K. Lillee	249.5	83	548	31	17.67	6–66	48	37
R.A.L. Massie	199.1	58	409	23	17.78	8–53	52	34
R.J. Inverarity	61	26	90	4	22.50	3–26	92	25
A.A. Mallett	103	32	269	10	26.90	5–114	62	44
I.M. Chappell	15	7	27	1	27.00	1–26	90	30
G.D. Watson	40	14	92	3	30.66	1–23	80	38
D.J. Colley	121.3	20	312	6	52.00	3–83	122	43
J.W. Gleeson	76.4	28	157	3	52.33	2–45	153	34
G.S. Chappell	56.2	17	125	2	62.50	1–28	169	37
K.R. Stackpole	17	7	35	0	–	–	–	34
K.D. Walters	5	1	7	0	–	–	–	23
TOTALS	942.3	293	2,071	83	24.95	(8–53)	68	37

Lillee's aggregate of 31 wickets is a series record for Australia in England

Statistical Survey of the Series

THREE WICKETS IN FOUR BALLS
D.K. Lillee (Australia) (2)   2nd Inns   Manchester   (W–WW)
                               1st Inns   The Oval   (WW–W)

RECORD BOWLING ON TEST DEBUT
R.A.L. Massie's match analysis of 16–137 at Lord's is a record for a bowler making his first appearance in Test cricket. Only J.C. Laker (19) and S.F. Barnes (17) have taken more wickets in one Test.

FIELDING
England (53 *ct*, nil *st*)
17 – Knott
8 – Greig
6 – Illingworth
5 – Parfitt
4 – Smith
3 – D'Oliveira, Luckhurst
2 – Gifford, Snow
1 – Edrich, Hampshire, substitute

Australia (45 *ct*, 2 *st*)
23* – Marsh (21 *ct*, 2 *st*)
8 – Chappell, G.S.
6 – Chappell, I.M.
4 – Stackpole
1 – Colley, Edwards, Francis, Inverarity, Walters, Watson

*Record for Australia against England. Equals A.T.W. Grout's record in any Test series for Australia

FIVE DISMISSALS IN AN INNINGS
R.W. Marsh (Australia) (2)   2nd Inns   Manchester   (all *ct*)
                              1st Inns   Nottingham   (all *ct*)

EXTRAS
Australia conceded 203 extras in the series (66 byes, 68 leg byes, 55 no balls and 14 wides) – the most they have conceded in any five-match series against England. On only two occasions have more extras been conceded by one team in the history of England v Australia matches: 208 by Australia in 1970–71 (6 Tests) and 204 by England in 1934.
England conceded 91 extras (5 byes, 51 leg byes, 32 no balls and 3 wides)
A.P.E. Knott conceded only 5 byes during the series (one off the bowling of J.A. Snow in the 1st Test and four off a ball from B.L. D'Oliveira in the 3rd Test). He did not concede a bye after the 26th over of the first Australia innings at Nottingham after which Australia scored 1,483 runs.

COMPARATIVE SCORING RATES
AUSTRALIA   43.60 runs per 100 balls (2,345 runs off 5,378 balls)
ENGLAND   39.67 runs per 100 balls (2,274 runs off 5,732 balls)

COMPARATIVE BOWLING RATES
ENGLAND   16 overs per hour   (890.2 overs in 3,327 minutes)
AUSTRALIA   15.1 overs per hour (944.3 overs in 3,744 minutes)

TIME LOST DURING THE SERIES (Because of unfit playing conditions): 7 hours 7 minutes

ATTENDANCE FOR SERIES: 368,361; receipts £261,283

First-Class Matches and Averages

RESULTS
Played 26   Won 11   Lost 5   Drawn 10   (Abandoned 1)

v WORCESTERSHIRE at Worcester, April 29, 30, May 1. Australians won by 6 wickets. Worcestershire 98-2d and 99 (R.A.L. Massie 6-31). Australians 68-2d and 133-4

v LANCASHIRE at Manchester, May 3, 4, 5. Match drawn. Australians 161-6d and 157. Lancashire 97-3d and 92-2

v YORKSHIRE at Bradford, May 7, 8 9. Match abandoned without a ball being bowled.

v NOTTINGHAMSHIRE at Nottingham, May 10, 11, 12. Match drawn. Nottinghamshire 176 (J.R. Hammond 5-46). Australians 270-5

v SURREY at The Oval, May 13, 15, 16. Match drawn. Australians 180 and 281-6 (I.M. Chappell 101). Surrey 300 (J.H. Edrich 110, D.J. Colley 5-72).

v HAMPSHIRE at Southampton, May 17, 18, 19. Australians won by 9 wickets. Hampshire 311 (D.R. Turner 131, R.J. Inverarity 5-67) and 184-5d. Australians 191 and 306-1 (K.R. Stackpole 119 n.o., G.D. Watson 176). *Stackpole and Watson scored 301 for the first wicket to set a new record for Australian opening partnerships in Britain.*

v MCC at Lord's, May 20, 22, 23. Australians won by 4 wickets. MCC 208 (A.A. Mallett 5-61) and 178-4d. Australians 195-6d and 195-6

v GLOUCESTERSHIRE at Bristol, May 24, 25, 26. Match drawn. Gloucestershire 121-8d (D.J. Colley 5-27). Australians 44-1

v GLAMORGAN at Swansea, May 27, 28, 29. Match drawn. Australians 191 (D.L. Williams 5-31) and 158-3d. Glamorgan 93-5d and 6-0

v DERBYSHIRE at Chesterfield, May 31, June 1, 2. Match drawn. Australians 384-9d (B.C. Francis 117, K.D. Walters 109). Derbyshire 257-4 (C.P. Wilkins 100 n.o.)

v WARWICKSHIRE at Birmingham, June 3, 5, 6. Match drawn. Australians 330 (K.D. Walters 154) and 212-5d. Warwickshire 207-9d and 228-5

v ENGLAND (1st Test) at Manchester, June 8, 9, 10, 12, 13. England won by 89 runs. (See p. 28 for full scorecard)

v COMBINED UNIVERSITIES at Oxford, June 14, 15, 16. Australians won by 10 wickets. Combined Universities 277 and 202. Australians 478-8d (B.C. Francis 210) and 2-0

v ESSEX at Ilford, June 17, 19, 20. Match drawn. Essex 238 and 193-6. Australians 435-9d (G.S. Chappell 181)

Below: Another one down in the slips off the unlucky Arnold at Manchester
Bottom: Massie's 6–31 at Worcester gave fair warning

First-Class Matches and Averages

V ENGLAND (2nd Test) at Lord's, June 22, 23, 24, 26. Australia won by 8 wickets. (See p. 31 for full scoreboard)

V SOMERSET at Bath, July 1, 2, 3. Match drawn. Somerset 169 (A.A. Mallett 5–59) and 160–7d. Australians 171–4d and 130–4

V LEICESTERSHIRE at Leicester, July 5, 6, 7. Australians won by an innings and 46 runs. Australians 324–7d (A.P. Sheahan 135 n.o.). Leicestershire 58 (R.A.L. Massie 6–30) and 220 (J.W. Gleeson 5–75)

V MIDDLESEX at Lord's, July 8, 10, 11. Australians won by 5 wickets. Middlesex 192–2d and 207–7d. Australians 167–3d and 233–5

V ENGLAND (3rd Test) at Nottingham, July 13, 14, 15, 17, 18. Match drawn. (See p. 33 for full scorecard)

V MINOR COUNTIES at Longton, Stoke-on-Trent, July 19, 20. Australians won by an innings and 26 runs. Australians 325–5d (R.J. Inverarity 100 n.o.). Minor Counties 161 (J.R. Hammond 6–15) and 138

V SUSSEX at Hove, July 22, 24, 25. Sussex won by 5 wickets. Australians 294 (M.A. Buss 5–69) and 262–2d (K.R. Stackpole 154 n.o., inc. 100 before lunch on third day). Sussex 296–5d (G.A. Greenidge 99) and 261–5 (G.A. Greenidge 125 n.o.)

V ENGLAND (4th Test) at Leeds, July 27, 28, 29. England won by 9 wickets. (See p. 36 for full scorecard)

V NORTHAMPTONSHIRE at Northampton, August 5, 7, 8. Northamptonshire won by 7 wickets. Australians 191 (B.S. Bedi 5–57) and 143. Northamptonshire 210 (G.D. Watson 5–36) and 125–3

V ENGLAND (5th Test at The Oval, August 10, 11, 12, 14, 15, 16. Australia won by 5 wickets. (See p. 40 for full scorecard)

v KENT at Canterbury, August 19, 21, 22. Australians won by 9 wickets. Australians 330–4d (K.D. Walters 150, G.S. Chappell 141 n.o.) and 90–1. Kent 139 (J.W. Gleeson 6–21) and 278

v LANCASHIRE at Manchester, August 30, 31. Lancashire won by 9 wickets. Australians 208 and 154. Lancashire 200–5d and 165–1

v T.N. PEARCE'S XI at Scarborough, September 2, 4. Australians won by 6 wickets. T.N. Pearce's XI 254 and 148 (G.S. Chappell 7–58).

Australians 265–4d (G.D. Watson 157) and 139–4

Note: The Australian Tour also included 11 non-first-class matches, of which all but the two-day fixture against Scotland were played under limited-overs rules. Wins (3): Scotland, England (2nd Prudential Trophy match), T.N. Pearce's XI. Losses (5): Duke of Norfolk's XI, Cricketers' Association, England (1st and 3rd Prudential Trophy matches), T.N. Pearce's XI.

No decision (3): Yorkshire (2), Sussex.

BATTING AND FIELDING

*Not out

	M	I	NO	HS	Runs	Av	100	50	Ct	St
G.S. Chappell	18	28	10	181	1,260	70.00	4	3	26	–
K.R. Stackpole	21	35	5	154*	1,309	43.63	3	7	15	–
A.P. Sheahan	17	26	7	135*	788	41.47	1	4	6	–
K.D. Walters	19	29	5	154	935	38.95	3	–	7	–
G.D. Watson	18	27	2	176	915	36.60	2	4	7	–
R.W. Marsh	17	24	5	91	664	34.94	–	5	38	7
R. Edwards	18	26	3	170*	747	32.47	1	3	9	–
I.M. Chappell	20	34	2	118	1,017	31.78	2	6	19	–
B.C. Francis	18	27	1	210	772	29.69	2	4	5	–
R.J. Inverarity	21	30	9	100*	553	26.33	1	1	13	–
J.R. Hammond	13	6	3	36*	78	26.00	–	–	4	–
H.B. Taber	12	11	3	54	180	22.50	–	1	22	5
D.J. Colley	16	16	3	58*	268	20.61	–	2	5	–
A.A. Mallett	15	13	3	29	146	14.60	–	–	5	–
J.W. Gleeson	17	12	4	30	88	11.00	–	–	3	–
R.A.L. Massie	12	10	1	18	45	5.00	–	–	–	–
D.K. Lillee	14	13	7	11*	30	5.00	–	–	3	–

BOWLING

	O	M	R	W	Av	BB	5 wI	10 wM
I.M. Chappell	43.5	14	106	10	10.60	3–1	–	–
R.A.L. Massie	381.4	115	851	50	17.02	8–53	4	2
D.K. Lillee	456.5	119	1,197	53	22.58	6–66	3	1
J.W. Gleeson	354.5	106	1,014	44	23.04	6–21	2	–
G.D. Watson	244	64	621	25	24.84	5–36	1	–
G.S. Chappell	206.2	51	488	19	25.68	7–58	1	–
R.J. Inverarity	353.5	101	983	37	26.56	5–67	1	–
A.A. Mallett	427	124	1,165	41	28.41	5–59	3	–
D.J. Colley	346.4	73	946	33	28.66	5–27	2	–
J.R. Hammond	278	59	809	26	31.11	6–15	2	–

Also bowled: R. Edwards 1.2–0–15–0; B.C. Francis 2.5–0–15–1; A.P. Sheahan 4–0–19–1; K.R. Stackpole 63–20–164–2; K.D. Walters 35.3–6–117–2.

The Prudential Trophy

A special feature of the Australian visit in 1972 was the first ever series of one-day internationals. It had been intended that a sixth Test be played, but the TCCB, impressed by the public reaction to the one-day international replacing the abandoned third Test in Melbourne in 1970–71, decided to experiment with three one-day matches on different grounds. From a number of interested firms the Prudential Assurance Company emerged as sponsors.

The matches were played under Gillette Cup rules, with one exception: each side was limited to 55 overs instead of 60 to accommodate the painfully slow over-rate of the Test series. It may be argued that the timing of the series was wrong; that it should have come before the final Test, because everything afterwards is inevitably an anticlimax for the visitors – as was seen in the first international. Nevertheless, the outcome was such a success, in terms of both money and interest, that it seems probable for matches of this nature to become an accepted part of future tours. What must not happen, though, is to allow one-day internationals to have an adverse effect on the Test series itself – as has been the case with limited-overs cricket and the County Championship. For all the lively entertainment they provide, they can never hope to produce money on the same scale as one five-day Test.

In terms of publicity, the series got off to an excellent start with the selection of Brian Close as captain in place of the injured Ray Illingworth. Close, relieved of the England captaincy after a time-wasting row in 1967, had left Yorkshire in 1970, and one of the reasons for the termination of his contract was his attitude to one-day cricket and his captaincy in this type of game. His selection, however ironic, was a popular one, and he was given a side well versed in the ways of the limited-overs game. The England selectors chose a party of 15, of whom three – Old, Roope, and Underwood – did not play.

England won the Prudential Trophy by two matches to one, with Dennis Amiss and Keith Stackpole each receiving £200 as the respective Man of the Series. Each match brought the winners £1,000, and the Man of the Match won £200.

First International

England illustrated all their experience and expertise at this type of game with a confidence-boosting six-wicket win with 35 balls to spare in the first international. Admittedly the Australians, drained of enthusiasm after a long tour and a demanding Test rubber, were below their true potential, but even so England, efficiently manoeuvred by Brian Close, fully deserved their victory – one made memorable by batting of high merit from those two most rejected of recent selections, Dennis Amiss and Keith Fletcher.

Old Trafford provided Ian Chappell with conditions most different from those that saw his team's downfall in the first Test ten weeks earlier and, finding an easy-paced wicket and clear skies, he can have had few qualms about batting when he won only his second toss of the season against England. Australia, through the dependable Stackpole and the Chappell brothers, took lunch at 133-3 from 32 of their allotted 55 overs, a sound basis for lusty assault that should have produced a total of nearly 300. But, contained by astute field placing and some accurate seam bowling by Woolmer, who was allowed only ten overs because the official scorers failed to note that D'Oliveira had relieved him for the final pre-lunch over, and Arnold, the Australian innings foundered and England were set the modest scoring rate of four runs an over.

The long-awaited duel between Boycott and Lillee hushed the crowd of 12,000, but remained unresolved. Lillee experimented with an approach reduced by one third, and his pace, though still distinctly sharp, posed fewer problems than feared. England had 48 runs from 11 overs when Boycott edged to where first slip should be and Marsh made a fine diving catch. Amiss, a daring selection that excluded the popular Wood on his home ground, and Fletcher then produced the best English partnership of the season. On the ground where he had nervously bagged a 'pair' in 1968, Amiss scored the first England hundred of the year off 130 balls with nine boundaries. His nomination as Man of the Match was a formality. Fletcher, discarded after a single failure on that bald pitch at Leeds, played an equally majestic innings full of those confident, clean strokes too often reserved only for Essex followers. His 60 took only 76 balls and included eight fours. Their partnership of 125 in only 27 overs ensured a comfortable win.

ENGLAND v AUSTRALIA – 1st Match
Played at Old Trafford, Manchester, August 24
Toss: Australia   Result: England won by 6 wickets

AUSTRALIA
K.R. Stackpole	c D'Oliveira b Greig	37
G.D. Watson	b Arnold	0
I.M. Chappell*	b Woolmer	53
G.S. Chappell	b Woolmer	40
R. Edwards	run out	57
A.P. Sheahan	b Arnold	6
K.D. Walters	lbw b Woolmer	2
R.W. Marsh†	c Close b Snow	11
A.A. Mallett	not out	6
R.A.L. Massie	did not bat	
D.K. Lillee	did not bat	
Extras	(b 2, lb 3, nb 5)	10
TOTAL	(8 wkts – 55 overs)	222

ENGLAND
G. Boycott	c Marsh b Watson	25
D.L. Amiss	b Watson	103
K.W.R. Fletcher	b Massie	60
D.B. Close*	run out	1
J.H. Hampshire	not out	25
B.L. D'Oliveira	not out	5
A.W. Greig	did not bat	
A.P.E. Knott†	did not bat	
R.A. Woolmer	did not bat	
J.A. Snow	did not bat	
G.G. Arnold	did not bat	
Extras	(b 1, lb 6)	7
TOTAL	(4 wkts – 49.1 overs)	226

ENGLAND
	O	M	R	W
Snow	11	1	33	1
Arnold	11	0	38	2
Greig	11	0	50	1
Woolmer	10	1	33	3
D'Oliveira	9	1	37	0
Close	3	0	21	0

AUSTRALIA
	O	M	R	W
Lillee	11	2	49	0
Massie	11	1	49	1
Watson	8	1	28	2
Mallett	11	1	43	0
G.S. Chappell	3	0	20	0
Walters	3	1	16	0
Stackpole	2.1	0	14	0

FALL OF WICKETS
Wkt	Aus	Eng
1st	4	48
2nd	66	173
3rd	125	174
4th	156	215
5th	167	
6th	170	
7th	205	
8th	222	
9th		
10th		

*Captain †Wicket-keeper
Umpires C.S. Elliott and A.E.G. Rhodes
Attendance: 12,000   Receipts: £9,660

Second International

Australia, noticeably more zealous than at Manchester, seized upon English errors in all departments to draw level in this mini-series, their margin of five wickets with 21 balls to spare being as fine as England's at Manchester.

Chappell's decision to ask England to bat seemed vindicated in the third over when Lillee, abandoning his short run of Old Trafford, plucked out Boycott's middle stump with a yorker of howling pace. However, Close took command in conditions that favoured the bowlers. Jaw jutting defiantly and getting courageously in line, he had scored 43 out of 54 in 12 overs, with seven fours and a six, when he sacrificed his wicket after a calling dispute.

Becalmed by a fine spell from off-spinner Mallett, England at lunch were 110 for 3 after 30 overs, but this useful launching pad for a large total was squandered when Fletcher, Hampshire, and D'Oliveira perished to a variety of suicides, leaving Greig and Knott to set a reasonable target. Knott struck 50 off 47 balls as 71 runs came from eight overs. Arnold and Snow extracted nine runs from Lillee's final over and Australia were set 4.3 runs an over to win.

They were speeded on their way by some of the most wayward new ball bowling ever seen at Lord's. (Later a 'rogue' ball was blamed.) In the first three overs 14 extras were conceded, and there was a steady sequence of wides, long-hops, near-wides, and no balls. Before England's astounded captain could banish his opening bowlers, 59 runs had come from only nine overs, 21 of them extras, and it was beyond England's bowlers to prevent the inevitable. Greg Chappell followed up his tidy bowling by dominating a fourth wicket partnership of 103 in 22 overs with Paul Sheahan and was given the Man of the Match award.

The Prudential Trophy

ENGLAND v AUSTRALIA – 2nd Match
Played at Lord's, London, August 26
Toss: Australia   Result: Australia won by 5 wickets

ENGLAND
G. Boycott	b Lillee	8
D.L. Amiss	b Mallett	25
D.B. Close*	run out	43
K.W.R. Fletcher	c Stackpole b G.S. Chappell	20
J.H. Hampshire	st Marsh b Mallett	13
B.L. D'Oliveira	c I.M. Chappell b Lillee	6
A.W. Greig	b Massie	31
A.P.E. Knott†	c Mallett b Massie	50
R.A. Woolmer	run out	9
J.A. Snow	not out	5
G.G. Arnold	not out	11
Extras	(b 1, lb 10, nb 3, w 1)	15
TOTAL	(9 wkts – 55 overs)	**236**

AUSTRALIA
K.R. Stackpole	lbw b D'Oliveira	52
R. Edwards	c Knott b Snow	6
I.M. Chappell*	c Knott b Woolmer	31
G.S. Chappell	lbw b Snow	48
A.P. Sheahan	c Knott b Snow	50
G.D. Watson	not out	11
R.W. Marsh†	not out	6
D.J. Colley	} did not bat	
A.A. Mallett		
D.K. Lillee		
R.A.L. Massie		
Extras	(b 6, lb 14, nb 4, w 12)	36
TOTAL	(5 wkts – 51.3 overs)	**240**

AUSTRALIA	O	M	R	W	FALL OF WICKETS		
Lillee	11	0	56	2			
Massie	11	1	35	2	Wkt	Eng	Aus
Colley	11	1	72	0	1st	11	44
Mallett	11	2	24	2	2nd	65	112
G.S. Chappell	11	0	34	1	3rd	87	116
					4th	114	219
ENGLAND					5th	121	224
Snow	11	2	35	3	6th	121	
Arnold	11	0	47	0	7th	198	
D'Oliveira	11	0	46	1	8th	217	
Greig	9	1	29	0	9th	218	
Woolmer	9.3	0	47	1	10th		

*Captain   †Wicket-keeper

Umpires A.E. Fagg and T.W. Spencer

Attendance: 22,000   Receipts: £23,195

Third International

Inspired by Barry Wood, England won the third and decisive match for the Prudential Trophy by two wickets with 21 balls to spare. This contest was easily the most exciting of the three with England, having held control for most of the day, struggling desperately at the end.

After Close had won the toss and put Australia in, Wood dominated the pre-lunch play. He removed the Chappells with superb demonstrations of throwing and catching. No doubt realising that this was Wood's day (as did the Man of the Match adjudicator), Close gave him a bowl. A slower ball had Sheahan caught at mid-wicket, and lunch saw Australia struggling at 101 for 4. Stackpole (46 not out) had held the innings together, but his partner, Walters, was the last specialist batsman and in desperate form. Just as their partnership was beginning to look threatening, Close again produced his trump card. Success was immediate: Wood's third ball enticed Walters to hit across the line and bowled him. Stackpole was yorked off-stump driving after batting 42 overs.

Boycott and Amiss gave England the best start by either side during the series, 14 runs coming off one Massie over, and at tea England were 65 without loss after 18 overs. But four overs and 11 runs later Amiss edged a square cut; Lillee induced an off-side edge from Close, and then tempted Boycott to hook a bouncer to long-leg. When D'Oliveira was out England needed 76 off 22 overs with six wickets left.

Wood completed a memorable day by helping Fletcher add 39 runs in ten overs, but both fell to rash strokes. Then Walters removed Knott and Woolmer with three balls as the pressure mounted, but Greig, joined by Snow in fading light at 6.52 p.m., took two fours off Massie to steer England home.

ENGLAND v AUSTRALIA – 3rd Match
Played at Edgbaston, Birmingham, August 28
Toss: England   Result: England won by 2 wickets

AUSTRALIA

K.R. Stackpole	b Woolmer	61
R. Edwards	b Arnold	6
I.M. Chappell*	run out	3
G.S. Chappell	c Wood b D'Oliveira	13
A.P. Sheahan	c Woolmer b Wood	19
K.D. Walters	b Wood	15
R.W. Marsh†	lbw b Arnold	0
A.A. Mallett	b Arnold	8
J.R. Hammond	not out	15
D.K. Lillee	c Wood b Arnold	13
R.A.L. Massie	not out	16
Extras	(lb 6, nb 4)	10
TOTAL	(9 wkts – 55 overs)	179

ENGLAND

G. Boycott	c Massie b Lillee	41
D.L. Amiss	c Marsh b G.S. Chappell	40
D.B. Close*	c Marsh b Lillee	5
K.W.R. Fletcher	c Marsh b Hammond	34
B.L. D'Oliveira	run out	2
B. Wood	lbw b Lillee	19
A.W. Greig	not out	24
A.P.E. Knott†	c Mallett b Walters	6
R.A. Woolmer	c Marsh b Walters	0
J.A. Snow	not out	0
G.G. Arnold	did not bat	
Extras	(lb 5, nb 3, w 1)	9
TOTAL	(8 wkts – 51.3 overs)	180

ENGLAND	O	M	R	W
Snow	11	0	29	0
Arnold	11	3	27	4
Greig	10	3	24	0
D'Oliveira	6	1	19	1
Woolmer	11	1	50	1
Wood	6	0	20	2
AUSTRALIA				
Lillee	11	2	25	3
Massie	8.3	3	45	0
Mallett	4	0	16	0
Hammond	9	1	41	1
G.S. Chappell	11	3	20	1
Walters	8	1	24	2

FALL OF WICKETS

Wkt	Aus	Eng
1st	8	76
2nd	15	89
3rd	40	94
4th	87	104
5th	111	143
6th	112	154
7th	127	172
8th	136	172
9th	158	
10th		

*Captain   †Wicket-keeper
Umpires D.J. Constant and A.S.M. Oakman
Attendance: 15,000   Receipts: £11,512

County Cricket

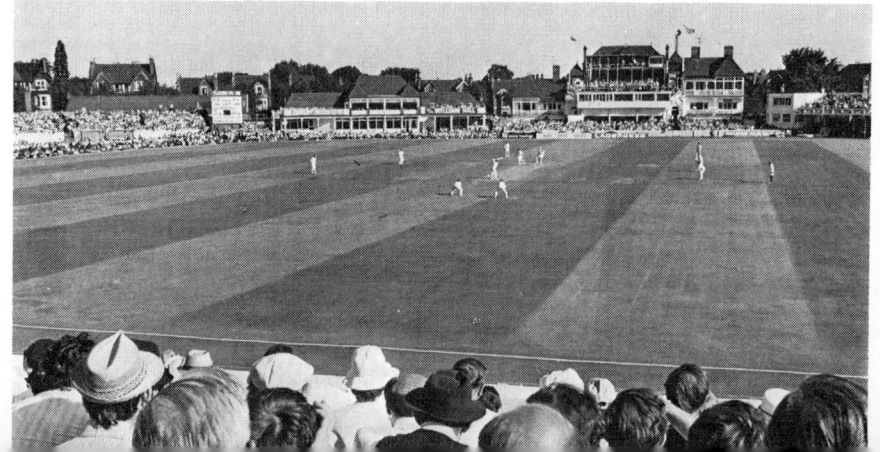

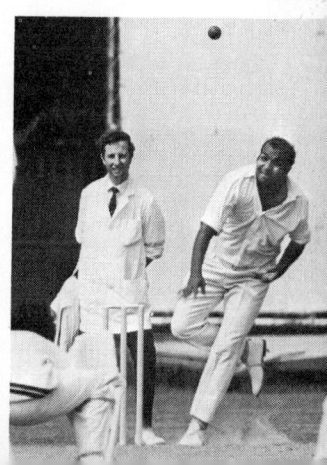

John Player Cricket Yearbook 1973

Above: *Indian off-spinner Venkataraghavan. His special registration should boost the Derbyshire attack in 1973. With his fairly flat flight, 'Venkat' should find English conditions much to his taste*

Above left: *Bob Taylor will be hoping that Derbyshire's import will provide him with plenty of chances behind the stumps. This extremely efficient wicket-keeper can be relied on not to waste them*

Left: *Chris Wilkins, whose retirement has robbed Derbyshire cricket of a most entertaining batsman*

The First-Class Counties

DERBYSHIRE

President: The Duke of Devonshire
Chairman: F.W. Barnett
Secretary: Major D.J. Carr
Captain: 1972 I.R. Buxton
1973 J.B. Bolus
Colours: Chocolate, amber and pale blue
Headquarters: County Cricket Ground, Nottingham Road, Derby DE2 6DA

Honours: County Champions (1) 1936
Gillette Cup Finalists (1) 1969

1st XI Home Grounds 1973:
Derby; Burton upon Trent (Ind Coope Sports Ground); Buxton (The Park); Chesterfield (Queen's Park); Ilkeston (The Rutland Ground)

1972 was another unhappy year for Derbyshire. They finished bottom of the Championship table for the second successive season, making little headway in either of the knock-out cups, and having to settle for a middle of the table position in the John Player League. All this was fairly predictable, because their playing resources were clearly limited and there was a distinct 'relegation' look about them before the season had even begun.

It would be both wrong and unfair to blame Buxton, their captain, for the lack of success. He was given a mediocre outfit and, not surprisingly, was unable to turn them into anything else. It is most unlikely that any other skipper of comparable playing ability would have been able to achieve much more. On occasions the team might have been accused of being negative in their approach, but it is not easy to sparkle positively when there is an acute shortage of runs, wickets, and victories. Understandably Derby became depressed and this was reflected in their cricket.

To make matters worse the County lost the services of their best and most penetrative bowler, Alan Ward, for the majority of the season, while the good start, so essential if the team was to realise its basic potential, was denied them by the terrible weather throughout May and June. By the time the sun had begun to shine they were plainly struggling and doomed.

A quick glance at the Derbyshire batting averages immediately shows an important reason for their lack of success. Not one player achieved the comparative respectability of the thirties, and some accredited batsmen were under twenty. At the head came the South African, Wilkins, who was not only much the best player, but also an entertainer. His decision to retire represents a considerable loss both to his club and to county cricket. Gibbs was the only person to reach a thousand runs in Championship matches and one was left wondering why Page, who has such an admirable technique, did not score more.

A team with such a frail batting line-up, they needed either a very potent attack, or an inordinate amount of luck, to win matches in three-day cricket. Lacking both requirements, Derbyshire had to settle for a solitary victory in 1972.

Their bowling, without the pace of Ward, depended largely upon a battery of seamers, who were normally tight and tidy. However, the similarity of their pace and style made them rather monotonous to watch, except in limited-overs games.

The most encouraging feature of the season for Derbyshire was the form shown by their fast-medium bowler, Hendrick, who captured a fine crop of wickets at a very reasonable cost. He certainly gives every indication of living up to the high traditions of Derbyshire pace bowling in the years that lie ahead. And when fit, Ward did bowl extremely well and formed a most hostile and formidable partnership with Hendrick.

What are Derbyshire's prospects for 1973? Brian Bolus has been specially registered from Notts and will captain the side. He is a sound, rather than a brilliant leader, and, though he himself will bring additional solidity to the batting, he will need several new players if there is to be any substantial improvement.

To make them a middle-of-the-table-team, Derbyshire really require three things. They need to find a couple of batsmen with the ability and the flair of Wilkins; require Alan Ward to remain fit throughout the summer; and Venkataraghavan must prove a match-winning bowler. The scope of the problem facing them is obvious when one realises that the addition of four such players to their team would give at least 75 per cent of the counties in the Championship high expectations of winning at least two of the titles!

County Championship: Played 19 Won 1 Lost 5 Drawn 13 Abandoned 1
Final Position 17th

BATTING

*Denotes not out

	M	I	NO	HS	Runs	Av	100s	50s
C.P. Wilkins	18	34	2	111	933	29.15	3	4
P.J.K. Gibbs	19	36	0	122	1,019	28.30	1	4
M.H. Page	16	30	3	125	739	27.37	1	3
I.W. Hall	9	18	0	105	492	27.33	1	2
I.R. Buxton	19	36	10	46*	591	22.73	–	–
A. Hill	3	6	0	82	120	20.00	–	1
A.J. Borrington	7	13	0	63	251	19.30	–	2
A.J. Harvey-Walker	14	26	0	82	487	18.73	–	4
R.S. Swindell	10	14	6	38	147	18.37	–	–
R.W. Taylor	18	34	10	58*	402	16.75	–	1
J.F. Harvey	12	23	1	98	332	15.09	–	1
F.W. Swarbrook	13	21	2	46*	262	13.78	–	–
P.E. Russell	15	23	4	39	180	9.47	–	–
T.J.P. Eyre	4	3	1	11*	15	7.50	–	–
A. Ward	5	6	2	9*	30	7.50	–	–
M. Hendrick	18	21	6	18	89	5.93	–	–
D. Wilde	9	11	4	12	30	4.28	–	–

BOWLING

	O	M	R	W	Av	BB	5wI	10wM
A. Ward	98.2	13	340	16	21.25	4–77	–	–
M. Hendrick	473.1	115	1,219	51	23.90	8–50	3	1
C.P. Wilkins	228.5	53	566	21	26.95	4–50	–	–
I.R. Buxton	375.4	135	873	32	27.28	5–51	1	–
P.E. Russell	411.3	122	1,109	36	30.80	4–58	–	–
R.S. Swindell	237.2	54	808	26	31.07	5–69	1	–
T.J.P. Eyre	115.2	23	335	10	33.50	3–46	–	–
D. Wilde	211	61	570	15	38.00	3–27	–	–
F.W. Swarbrook	282.1	70	806	17	47.41	3–24	–	–

Also bowled: A.J. Borrington 2–0–8–0; M.H. Page 8–1–46–0.

FIELDING

40 – Taylor (33 ct, 7 st); 16 – Buxton; 13 – Swarbrook; 12 – Page, Wilkins; 11 – Gibbs; 10 – Harvey; 9 – Russell; 7 – Hendrick; 6 – Hall; 5 – Borrington, Swindell; 4 – Harvey-Walker; 2 – Ward; 1 – Eyre, Wilde.

ESSEX

President: T.N. Pearce
Chairman: A.B. Quick
Secretary: S.R. Cox
Captain: B. Taylor
Colours: Blue, gold and red
Headquarters: The County Ground, New Writtle Street, Chelmsford CM2 0RW

Honours: Third in County Championship (1) 1897
John Player League Runners-up (1) 1971

1st XI Home Grounds 1973: Chelmsford; Harlow; Ilford (Valentines Park); Leyton; Westcliff-on-Sea (Chalkwell Park)

Although they failed to win any of the four competitions that are now open to them, Essex nonetheless have every reason to be satisfied with their performances in 1972, because they did far better than they expected. Having lost the services of Francis, their number two batsman of the previous season, who was touring with the Australians, and Barker, their most experienced player, who had retired, their batting line-up, on paper, was extremely fragile.

Because no replacements, other than the inexperienced Keith Pont, were engaged to plug the gap, it seemed probable that runs would be in such short supply, especially in three-day cricket, so that a drop down the County Championship table looked inevitable. But, instead, Essex improved their position from tenth to fifth.

There were four main reasons why they were able to overcome what, at the start of the season, looked likely to prove an unavoidable shortage of runs. First, they were frequently able to camouflage the absence of class in their main batting by some belligerent and effective efforts from an exceptionally confident 'tail'. East, Hobbs, and Lever all produced valuable innings at critical times.

Keith Fletcher, who topped the Essex batting averages, adds to his match-winning 139 not out against Yorkshire in the County Championship

Secondly, Keith Boyce, realising the lack of depth, resisted his natural inclination to try to strike every other ball out of the ground. This self-imposed restraint not only meant that his aggregate increased, but that he was able to score the runs which his ability warranted. Thirdly, Fletcher showed why he is considered to be just about the best middle-order player in the country, and his match-winning century against Yorkshire was unquestionably one of the finest of the entire competition. Fourthly, Brian Edmeades provided that all important solidarity at the start of the innings.

In general it is bowlers who win matches, and the power and the variety of the Essex attack played a major part in the success of the side. Although they lacked a bowler of true international calibre, they were better balanced than any other club. In fact the number of bowlers at his disposal must at times have been something of a headache for Brian Taylor, their very enthusiastic captain.

The new ball was shared by Keith Boyce and the left-handed John Lever. The former was often distinctly hostile and his control has greatly improved. The latter has acquired the ability to move the ball in the air and this, combined with his different line, worried many opening batsmen. With his physique and splendid body action he must rate as one of the best young prospects.

Supporting the seam openers was Turner, who has the advantage of being a shade quicker and better than he looks.

With seamers dominating all versions of the game rather more than is desirable, Essex provided a welcome contrast, as they frequently included three genuine spinners, Hobbs, East, and Acfield, all different in technique and style.

Although Hobbs did not capture as many wickets as in the previous year, he was always liable to win matches. East probably spins the ball as much, if not more, than any other orthodox left-armer. On a helpful pitch he is capable of running through any team, but his overall figures were a shade disappointing. However, he has not yet reached his peak and he has the basic attributes to develop into an outstanding bowler. Acfield was invariably accurate and he was one of the off-spinners who was employed to good effect in limited-overs matches.

Although they have never quite managed to win the trophy, Essex have the most consistent record in the John Player League since its inception, finishing third, fourth, second, and third.

It is easy to understand why they have done so well. In matches where the maximum number of overs is only 40, their lack of batting depth is not such a handicap, while the fact that they

Keith Boyce, whose dynamic all-round ability played a large role in Essex's climb up the Championship table in 1972, punches the ball sweetly to leg. Should, however, he be required by the West Indies tourists in 1973 his absence could hinder his County's title aspirations

possess a number of unconventional strikers is a positive advantage. Boyce, for example, is quite capable of altering the whole course of a game by smiting 20 runs in a single over, and Taylor has the happy knack of being able to pick up accurate seamers and depositing them all round the ground.

In addition to their uninhibited batting, the Essex attack is sharp and, even more important, is supported by just about the best all-round fielding side in the competition. It is undoubtedly this that has been the biggest single contributory factor to their success in Sunday cricket.

Essex have managed to get by with a skeleton staff, but they would have been in serious trouble if either a number of injuries had occurred or they had lost players to Test matches. To guard against these eventualities they do need at least two more batsmen this summer, whom they have already acquired.

County Championship:	Played 20	Won 6	Lost 4	Drawn 10	Final Position 5th

BATTING

*Denotes not out

	M	I	NO	HS	Runs	Av	100s	50s
K.W.R. Fletcher	18	30	6	181*	1,644	68.50	5	9
B.E.A. Edmeades	20	34	2	163	1,207	37.71	2	9
K.D. Boyce	20	30	0	86	925	30.83	–	7
R.E. East	19	20	4	89*	471	29.43	–	4
G.J. Saville	20	33	3	126*	801	26.70	1	5
K.R. Pont	11	16	5	75*	279	25.36	–	2
D.L. Acfield	10	10	8	33*	48	24.00	–	–
B. Ward	20	31	3	72	646	23.07	–	5
S. Turner	20	27	7	66	442	22.10	–	3
K.W. Wallace	2	4	0	46	71	17.75	–	–
B. Taylor	19	29	2	83	448	16.59	–	1
J.K. Lever	20	18	7	38*	130	11.81	–	–
R.N.S. Hobbs	20	22	4	37	210	11.66	–	–

Also batted: R.K. Baker 14*.

BOWLING

	O	M	R	W	Av	BB	5wI	10wM
K.D. Boyce	582.1	126	1,542	80	19.27	7–36	6	–
J.K. Lever	507.2	100	1,337	60	22.28	5–42	4	–
D.L. Acfield	191	55	408	17	24.00	5–42	1	–
S. Turner	495.3	126	1,161	43	27.00	5–39	2	–
R.N.S. Hobbs	409.2	101	1,258	31	40.58	7–118	2	–
R.E. East	463.5	131	1,179	29	40.65	4–25	–	–

Also bowled: B.E.A. Edmeades 16–2–48–0; K.W.R. Fletcher 14–2–49–0; K.R. Pont 13–0–52–1; B. Ward 4–2–5–0.

FIELDING

45 – Taylor (40 ct, 5 st); 21 – Boyce; 18 – Saville; 16 – Fletcher, Turner; 10 – East, Lever; 9 – Pont, Ward; 6 – Edmeades, Hobbs; 2 – Baker; 1 – Wallace.

GLAMORGAN

President: J.C. Clay
Chairman: Judge Rowe Harding
Secretary: W. Wooller
Captain: 1972 A.R. Lewis
　　　　　1973 Majid J. Khan
Colours: Blue and gold
Headquarters:
6 High Street, Cardiff CF1 1YU

Honours: County Champions (2) 1948, 1969

1st XI Home Grounds 1973:
Cardiff (Sophia Gardens); Swansea (St. Helen's); Colwyn Bay (Rhos-on-Sea); Ebbw Vale (Welfare Ground); Neath (The Knoll)

1972 turned out to be a fairly barren year for Glamorgan, who failed to make a genuine impression in any of the competitions. They had the ill luck to lose the services of their captain, Lewis, for much of the summer and, even when he was able to return to his side, he never achieved his best form. Although most counties suffered from the bad weather early in the season, it lasted far longer in Wales.

However, the main causes for Glamorgan's lack of success in the Championship were twofold. First, their attack was thin. There was a complete absence of genuine pace and the spinners did not bowl out the opposition, even on helpful pitches.

Secondly, their batting did not come up to expectations until towards the end of the season. Fredericks experienced a horrid patch early on, Walker was out of touch, and Lewis injured. This meant that, until the arrival of Majid after the University Match, too much depended upon the consistency of Alan Jones.

The combination of Majid and good batting wickets in August produced an absolute flood of runs. The profusion and the pace with which they were gathered came as something of a revelation to everyone who had witnessed the earlier matches.

Majid, who had already done so much for Cambridge cricket, batted quite superbly and inspired the rest of the team, and Fredericks rediscovered his international form, so that the batting sparkled and quite often dazzled. In this purple period Glamorgan should have capitalised on their prowess by winning some matches, but the bowling did not have sufficient penetration to push home the advantage.

Glamorgan's record in limited-overs cricket is undistinguished and last summer merely served to emphasise this point, as they not only finished bottom of the John Player League, but managed to win only two matches in the whole series.

The Welsh county's failure in this form of the game would seem to stem largely from a basic approach which is not technical enough. Until this defect is rectified, they are unlikely to make much impact. Certainly the ability to score fast, which they demonstrated to such good effect in County games at the end of the season is an advantage, but, unless it is supported by tight bowling and fielding, it is not enough to bring success in the short battles of the Sunday afternoon matches. At the moment their seam attack lacks venom, while their fielding did not come up to the high standard set by the great Welsh teams of the past.

The most effective member of the Glamorgan attack was the medium paced, left-armer Nash, who did swing the ball disconcertingly in the air. In addition to securing the largest haul of

Roy Fredericks, Glamorgan's West Indian opening batsman, in aggressive mood

victims at a very reasonable cost, his happy hitting with the bat brought both runs to his side and entertainment to spectators. His main support with the ball came from Williams, who proved himself to be a steady stock bowler.

Their spin attack revolved round Shepherd, Davis, and Walker. Shepherd, who has taken so many wickets for his county, was no longer the menace of previous years and he retired at the end of the season. The county are hoping that Davis will eventually become his successor, but he has a very long way to go, while Walker should be an occasional slow left-arm spinner, rather than a front line bowler.

Although, in terms of performance and results, last summer was largely disappointing for Glamorgan, they can look forward to the future with more confidence than the majority of clubs. They have a very active coaching scheme under the able direction of Phil Clift, with indoor schools at Cardiff and Neath. Apart from overseas stars the County rely largely on home bred talent, a policy which is important not only to Welsh cricket, but also to British cricket.

Their under-25 team, which included no capped members, did very well in the new competition. They appear to have found a crop of promising batsman, including Llewellyn, who scored a century against Cambridge, Hopkins, and Ellis, while Dudley-Jones and Harrison could develop into good seamers.

It will probably be two or three years before a real revival occurs. Although Majid's availability will make a big difference next summer, unless they can unearth a genuinely fast bowler and a match winning spinner the odds must be against Glamorgan carrying off any of the major honours. On the other hand Lewis, who was given the captaincy of the MCC tour of India and Pakistan, should come back a better player, and might establish himself as a regular member

First-Class Counties: Glamorgan

of the England team. This is something he has been promising to do ever since he was up at Cambridge.

Although the whole of Wales would be delighted to see Lewis captain a series of Test matches at home, his selection would automatically lessen Glamorgan's hopes of achieving domestic glory.

County Championship: Played 20 Won 1 Lost 7 Drawn 12 Final Position 13th

BATTING

*Denotes not out

	M	I	NO	HS	Runs	Av	100s	50s
Majid J. Khan	12	22	2	204	1,332	66.60	6	4
R.C. Fredericks	19	31	4	228*	1,159	42.92	4	3
A. Jones	20	33	3	152*	1,089	36.30	3	5
A.R. Lewis	12	19	3	124	529	33.06	1	4
M.A. Nash	20	26	2	82	532	22.16	–	3
J.A. Hopkins	4	6	0	42	123	20.50	–	–
E.W. Jones	20	24	10	33	282	20.14	–	–
R.C. Davis	20	28	2	114	514	19.76	1	1
G.P. Ellis	5	10	1	54	171	19.00	–	1
M.J. Llewellyn	5	7	1	30	108	18.00	–	–
P.M. Walker	17	23	7	60	281	17.56	–	1
J.W. Solanky	10	14	3	45*	172	15.63	–	–
A.E. Cordle	12	11	2	25*	103	11.44	–	–
D.J. Shepherd	12	11	3	16*	47	5.87	–	–
G. Richards	3	4	0	12	21	5.25	–	–
D.L. Williams	19	16	9	15*	25	3.57	–	–
R.D.L. Dudley-Jones	4	4	1	4	6	2.00	–	–
K.J. Lyons	4	4	0	5	7	1.75	–	–

Also batted: S.C. Harrison 5, 6; B.J. Lloyd 0; D.W. White 8.

BOWLING

	O	M	R	W	Av	BB	5wI	10wM
M.A. Nash	519.4	124	1,562	60	26.03	6–64	2	–
D.L. Williams	460.2	116	1,232	41	30.04	5–54	1	–
A.E. Cordle	211.5	36	621	20	31.05	3–47	–	–
D.J. Shepherd	231	83	504	16	31.50	5–47	1	–
R.C. Davis	436.3	81	1,371	38	36.07	5–55	1	–
P.M. Walker	313.3	85	906	21	43.14	3–27	–	–

Also bowled: R.D.L. Dudley-Jones 57.5–6–226–9; R.C. Fredericks 10–1–28–0; S.C. Harrison 10–0–38–1; M.J. Llewellyn 4–0–17–0; B.J. Lloyd 25–5–73–1; K.J. Lyons 19–3–56–1; Majid J. Khan 181–51–466–7; J.W. Solanky 61.1–12–212–6; D.W. White 17.4–2–32–1.

FIELDING

37 – E.W. Jones (33 ct, 4 st); 26 – Walker; 12 – R.C. Davis, Majid Khan; 10 – Nash, Williams; 7 – A. Jones; 6 – Fredericks, Lewis; 4 – Cordle, Ellis, Shepherd; 2 – Solanky; 1 – Dudley-Jones, Hopkins, Llewellyn, Lyons, Richards.

GLOUCESTERSHIRE

Patron: The Duke of Beaufort
President: J.E.C. Clarke
Chairman: M. Jarrett
Secretary: G.W. Parker
Captain: A.S. Brown
Colours: Blue, gold, brown, sky-blue, green and red
Headquarters: County Ground, Nevil Road, Bristol BS7 9EJ

Honours: County Champions (3) 1874, 1876, 1877
Joint Champions (1) 1873

1st XI Home Grounds 1973:
Bristol; Cheltenham (College Ground); Gloucester (Winget Sports Ground); Lydney; Moreton-in-Marsh; Tewkesbury

Gloucestershire remained one of the most unpredictable teams in the country. At one time they looked like winning the County Championship, leading the table from June 20th until July 28th. Their challenge then melted away, and they also finished next to bottom in the John Player League. Nevertheless, on their day they were plainly capable of defeating any side in limited-overs matches, or, to be more accurate, on Procter's day.

Inevitably the success or failure of the county depended to a large degree on Procter, who, with Sobers injured, could justifiably claim to be the finest all-rounder in the world. Indeed he has done rather more for his adopted Club than the West Indian has achieved for Notts. Predictably he once again headed both the batting and the bowling averages, quite simply because he was easily their finest bowler and most productive batsman.

To put his ability into true prospective it is sufficient to say that he was good enough, purely as a fast bowler, to be automatically selected for any Test XI, while his prowess with the bat was such that he could have commanded a place on his batting alone. He is a magnificent cricketer with enormous stamina and it was his injury towards the end of the season which dashed Gloucester's hopes of sustaining the pressure required to carry off the title.

In addition, the Cheltenham Week proved something of a catastrophe and was not helped by internal selection problems.

Gloucester's strength stemmed from their attack rather than their batting, which proved disappointing and was frequently insipid. This was reflected in their inability to pick up batting bonus points and the fact that they were among the slowest scorers in the John Player League. In sharp contrast they regularly dismissed the opposition cheaply and, together with Northants, secured more bowling bonus points than anybody.

Procter was the chief destroyer with a very impressive striking rate of wickets per over. He received some excellent support in the pace section from Davey, with whom he shared the new ball. Rather more surprising was the success of his captain, Brown, who picked up more victims with his medium pace than might have normally been expected, while Knight, although he was still liable to be rather wayward in line, proved to be a useful fourth seamer.

The spin attack was left mainly to the experienced off-break bowler, Mortimore, who was the leading wicket-taker. He was ably assisted by Sadiq and their find of the season, the slow left-armer Graveney. He is only 20 and, as slow bowlers tend to develop late, it would be wrong to become too excited about his potential

Surrey's loss was Gloucestershire's gain when Roger Knight changed counties in 1971. This promising lefthander topped 1,000 runs in his first two seasons with his adopted county during which time Gloucestershire climbed from the foot of the table, where they began the 1971 season, to third place

John Player Cricket Yearbook 1973

Gloucestershire owe much to all-rounder Mike Procter, even if his unusual and open-chested action might make the purists shudder

until he has had at least a couple of seasons in first-class cricket. However, he definitely impressed several good judges among opposing batsmen – despite a rather cramped action – with his control.

The most successful batsman after Procter was the tall left-hander Knight, who showed a marked preference for the front foot in reaching his thousand runs. He was followed in the averages by Shepherd. Unfortunately for Gloucester, Zaheer was unable to play for the complete season and failed to find his touch. Sadiq, their other Pakistan Test player, did not show his true skill. A further disappointment was that the usually dependable Nicholls struggled for runs throughout the season, so Milton was recalled and provided some much needed stability.

It was this comparative failure of the Gloucester batsmen which was a major contributory factor to their disastrous August run-in and to their lowly position in the John Player League.

The outlook for 1973, however, is bright – provided they can translate their batting ability into runs. This should not present too many problems, because Zaheer certainly has the class to enable him to score heavily in county cricket, and Sadiq is much too talented a player not to succeed with the bat next summer. Both these Pakistan cricketers have proven ability as well as youth on their side, whilst Knight is another player who should improve steadily and could well be a challenger for an England place.

Gloucestershire's fielding throughout the season was good. However, they appear to be a team who have the potential to be more of a force in the Championship than in the John Player League and, should Procter find his form at the right moment, they could do well in the Gillette.

First-Class Counties: Gloucestershire

County Championship: Played 20 Won 7 Lost 4 Drawn 9 Final Position 3rd

BATTING

*Denotes not out

	M	I	NO	HS	Runs	Av	100s	50s
M.J. Procter	18	32	3	118	1,215	41.89	3	7
R.D.V. Knight	20	36	1	103	1,085	31.00	1	6
D.R. Shepherd	20	35	4	106	885	28.54	1	6
C.A. Milton	14	24	1	117	637	27.69	1	1
Zaheer Abbas	7	13	0	75	341	26.23	–	4
R.B. Nicholls	19	34	0	90	801	23.55	–	5
J.B. Mortimore	20	27	11	53*	351	21.93	–	1
Sadiq Mohammad	20	35	2	54	665	20.15	–	1
A.S. Brown	19	29	4	63*	408	16.32	–	1
M. Bissex	7	12	1	23	126	11.45	–	–
J.C. Foat	6	12	2	20	87	8.70	–	–
R. Swetman	20	30	6	25*	207	8.62	–	–
D.A. Allen	7	10	5	23*	40	8.00	–	–
D.A. Graveney	5	9	4	11	29	5.80	–	–
J. Davey	18	19	8	12	43	3.90	–	–

BOWLING

	O	M	R	W	Av	BB	5wI	10wM
M.J. Procter	424.1	107	954	58	16.44	6–56	4	1
A.S. Brown	380.2	105	947	48	19.72	4–27	–	–
Sadiq Mohammad	197.4	31	673	33	20.39	4–40	–	–
J.B. Mortimore	635	188	1,396	68	20.52	7–62	2	–
D.A. Graveney	155.2	66	362	14	25.85	5–63	1	–
J. Davey	409.2	81	1,121	43	26.06	5–24	1	–
R.D.V. Knight	152	34	443	15	29.53	3–45	–	–

Also bowled: D.A. Allen 85–19–244–6; M. Bissex 44–3–162–0.

FIELDING

48 – Swetman (42 ct, 6 st); 26 – Knight; 17 – Brown, Milton; 14 – Sadiq; 13 – Procter; 11 – Mortimore; 10 –Shepherd; 8 – Nicholls; 4 – Bissex; 3 – Allen, Davey, Foat; 2 – Zaheer.

John Player Cricket Yearbook 1973

68

Above: *The pride of Hampshire—Barry Richards in full cry. By his own high standards, the South African did not enjoy the best of seasons in 1972, but few county bowlers would welcome a return to prolific form in 1973*

Left: *Bob Herman strikes again as Ken Shuttleworth's off stump goes a-flying*

HAMPSHIRE

President: R. Aird
Chairman: G. Ford
Secretary: E.D.R. Eagar
Captain: R.M.C. Gilliat
Colours: Blue, gold and white
Headquarters:
County Ground, Northlands Road, Southampton SO9 2TY

Honours: County Champions (1) 1961
John Player League Runners-up (1) 1969

1st XI Home Grounds 1973:
Southampton; Bournemouth (Dean Park); Portsmouth (United Services Ground); Basingstoke (May's Bounty)

Hampshire can quite rightly claim to have done rather better in all of the four competitions than their potential warranted. In the last two seasons they have lost the services of their three most experienced and effective seam bowlers, Shackleton, White, and Cottam. The departure of this formidable trio has naturally left an enormous gap, so that in the circumstances ninth in the County table represented a very satisfactory position.

Under the captaincy of Gilliat, they were a happy and contented side, who were able to cover up certain deficiencies by the players' ability to pull out a little extra when the going was hard.

The biggest setback was the serious eye injury to Turner just when he was in the middle of a fine run. Many consider this attractive left-hander to be the best young batting prospect in the country, a view which his impressive century against the Australians tended to support. He was certainly on the short list for India and Pakistan and would probably have made the trip, but for this setback.

The award for the outstanding success of the summer must unquestionably go to Herman, whose haul of victims surprised and delighted everybody. It must also have rather embarrassed Middlesex, who had dispensed with his services at the end of the previous season and must have been astonished to find him finishing with more wickets than any of their own bowlers. The sensational advance made by Herman's seam bowling upon joining his father's old county was one of the most romantic and pleasing highlights of 1972. Two other young players who improved considerably were opening batsman Greenidge and all-rounder Jesty.

Marshall, in his final season with the club for whom he has made so many runs and given so much pleasure, showed that he was still an outstanding batsman with only Richards finishing ahead of him in the averages. The South African was in fact rather out of touch in the early matches, but gradually and inevitably his undeniable genius shone through. His century against Lancashire in the Gillette Cup was not only a great *tour de force*, but one of the most exhilarating innings ever seen in the county. He is a supreme artist with such a perfect technique that he is the ideal model for all aspiring players.

Although Hampshire were not one of the most powerful batting sides in the competition, they were certainly among the most attractive to watch. Gilliat, who can be such an effective striker of the ball, had a disappointing summer and too much depended upon their opening pair and Marshall. Fortunately Sainsbury, who was in form in all three departments, was able to

Roy Marshall's retirement leaves Hampshire with a replacement problem somewhat eased by the improvement of Gordon Greenidge and David Turner

come to the rescue on a number of occasions.

Despite the tremendous advance made by Herman, their attack was a shade short of both penetration and variety for the needs of three-day cricket. The extra pace of White was missed, especially as Holder proved ineffective. Sainsbury bowled more overs than anybody, other than Herman, and though he is not a big spinner, his flight and control brought him a reasonable bag of wickets.

Hampshire were rather better attuned to limited-overs cricket than the three-day game. In the shorter game the brilliance of their outfielding, in which Greenidge and Turner were a source of constant pleasure, proved an even bigger asset and helped to hide a shortage of devilry in their bowling.

Financially the County can look back with considerable satisfaction on 1972 and were very pleased to have enrolled 820 new members.

The retirement of Marshall will be felt, but if both Greenidge and Turner continue to improve, the loss could be partially covered. They are hoping that their new signing, Taylor from Notts, will strengthen both their middle-order and their seam bowling, but they do need another class wicket taker. Although Murtagh, Cowley, and Barrett have promise, Hampshire, at the moment, look a middle-of-the-table outfit, rather than potential champions.

County Championship: Played 20 Won 4 Lost 6 Drawn 10 Final Position 9th

BATTING *Denotes not out

	M	I	NO	HS	Runs	Av	100s	50s
B.A. Richards	17	30	1	118	1,242	42.82	4	6
R.E. Marshall	16	28	5	203	979	42.56	2	5
C.G. Greenidge	20	35	1	142	1,132	33.29	2	4
R.V. Lewis	14	27	5	71*	624	28.36	–	4
P.J. Sainsbury	19	28	7	72	574	27.33	–	3
T.E. Jesty	16	23	2	80	566	26.21	–	6
D.R. Turner	15	24	2	73	573	26.04	–	2
R.M.C. Gilliat	18	29	5	72	555	23.12	–	5
G.R. Stephenson	20	27	4	50*	448	19.47	–	1
D.R. O'Sullivan	11	15	7	33	102	12.75	–	–
D.A. Livingstone	3	6	0	26	71	11.83	–	–
J.M. Rice	8	8	0	26	80	10.00	–	–
R.S. Herman	20	19	6	56	117	9.00	–	1
L.R. Worrell	8	11	3	22*	63	7.87	–	–
J.W. Holder	12	14	4	20	54	5.40	–	–
T.J. Mottram	3	3	2	3	4	4.00	–	–

BOWLING

	O	M	R	W	Av	BB	5wI	10wM
T.J. Mottram	93.2	22	300	17	17.64	5–45	2	–
R.S. Herman	657.1	167	1,614	75	21.52	8–42	3	–
J.W. Holder	301	51	933	37	25.21	7–79	2	1
T.E. Jesty	368.4	98	847	32	26.46	5–37	1	–
P.J. Sainsbury	537.1	188	1,215	45	27.00	5–61	1	–
L.R. Worrell	136.2	27	358	12	29.83	4–33	–	–
D.R. O'Sullivan	394.5	164	866	29	29.86	4–53	–	–
J.M. Rice	208.3	50	581	18	32.27	4–64	–	–

Also bowled: R.M.C. Gilliat 8.3–1–55–0; C.G. Greenidge 41–8–119–2; R.V. Lewis 15–1–68–1; B.A. Richards 45–23–82–3; D.R. Turner 3–1–3–0.

FIELDING

50 – Stephenson (41 ct, 9 st); 27 – Richards; 18 – Sainsbury; 14 – Herman; 12 – Gilliat; 10 – Turner; 8 – Greenidge, Jesty, O'Sullivan; 6 – Rice; 5 – Lewis, Worrell; 1 – Holder, Marshall, Mottram.

KENT

Patron: H.R.H. The Duke of Kent
President: O.J. Grace
Chairman: D.G. Clark
Secretary: L.E.G. Ames
Captain: M.H. Denness
Colours: Red and white
Headquarters:
St. Lawrence Ground, Old Dover Road, Canterbury

Honours: County Champions (5) 1906, 1909, 1910, 1913, 1970
Gillette Cup Winners (1) 1967
John Player League Champions (1) 1972
1st XI Home Grounds 1973:
Canterbury (St. Lawrence Ground); Dartford (Hesketh Park); Dover (Crabble Athletic Ground); Folkestone; Maidstone (The Mote); Tunbridge Wells (Nevill Ground)

At full strength Kent were probably the strongest side in the competition, but were seriously handicapped by the continued absence of three key players for representative matches. With a total staff of only 15 and some injuries it was often impossible to field a truly balanced eleven.

Kent began indifferently in the County Championship. They were not helped by a number of gaps in the fixture list and it was not until late in the season that they began to show their true potential. In July they were lying in the bottom half of the table but, thanks to a wonderful run in August, they climbed to second position. They were never really in with a chance of capturing the Championship, however.

In the Gillette Cup Kent again did well, reaching the semi-final, only to lose by a mere seven runs to the eventual winners, Lancashire. There was nothing to choose between these two fine sides and it was a memorable contest.

Just as in the County Championship, Kent had to rely on a late burst in the John Player League. Fortunately for them Leicester began to slip at the very time that they began their surge, so that by winning their last six matches Kent were able to pip the Midlanders by one point, literally on the post, and carry off the title.

When all their stars were available the Kent batting was most impressive. Their four most successful players all finished with averages of over 40. Luckhurst was once again the most dependable member and Asif conjured up a whole series of exciting innings, after he had recovered from an attack of malaria in the early part of the season. Cowdrey remained an outstanding craftsman, but he now needs a little longer to find his true touch. Denness, the captain, like his team, began indifferently and finished in a blaze of glory.

Although not so successful in Championship matches, Johnson gave his side a number of very good starts in the John Player League, but the main feature of the County's batting was its remarkable depth. On many occasions Shepherd came in at number nine with the dashing

At present primarily a fast-medium left-arm bowler, Bernard Julien has shown his potential to become a dashing stroke-maker

Julien at number ten. Both are highly competent players and can claim to be genuine all-rounders, quite capable of making big scores. Julien did in fact win one match with a dramatic 90 in only 60 minutes.

The Kent attack was not as penetrative as had been expected. It was tidy, but had difficulty in removing the opposition quickly on good pitches. Graham, the left-handed Julien, Shepherd and Woolmer comprised the seam department. This constituted a competent and effective quartet for limited-overs cricket. In Championship matches they could be very dangerous in certain conditions, but there was too much similarity in pace for them to be ideal for a plumb track. What they really needed was a genuinely fast bowler.

Obviously, Underwood, who is the most lethal exponent of a helpful pitch in the whole world, was yet again the pick of the Kent attack. Kent are hoping that Johnson will develop into a sufficiently effective off-spinner to provide him with a contrasting partner at the other end.

The Kent fielding, with Knott setting the tone from behind the stumps, was of an extremely high standard. Their captain proved an inspiration and he was splendidly supported in this department by Luckhurst, Asif, Johnson, and Ealham, in particular.

The most exciting game of the entire season was the final match in the John Player League, when Kent had to beat Worcestershire for the title. The crowd was enormous, while many more sat glued to their television sets. Confronted by the prospect of having to make 191 to win, the odds appeared to favour the visitors but, thanks to a brilliant start from Luckhurst and Johnson, Kent managed to reach their target with two overs to spare, amid scenes of enormous excitement.

Kent's future looks bright. In Denness they

A hefty smite by David Nicholls, unappreciated by the Worcestershire wicket-keeper, takes Kent closer to the John Player League title in the vital match on the last Sunday of the season. Kent won by five wickets amidst scenes of enormous excitement on a Canterbury ground festooned with hops

John Player Cricket Yearbook 1973

have an enthusiastic and capable leader who was well rewarded with the vice-captaincy of the MCC party that toured India and Pakistan. If no Test matches were to be played in 1973, Kent would stand a fine chance of winning at least two of the competitions and, as things stand, they should manage to capture one. The biggest danger would be if the West Indies decided that they require both Shepherd and Julien. This loss combined with other representative calls from the England side would naturally have a serious effect on Kentish prospects.

County Championship: Played 20 Won 7 Lost 4 Drawn 9 Final Position 2nd

BATTING

*Denotes not out

	M	I	NO	HS	Runs	Av	100s	50s
B.W. Luckhurst	13	23	4	184*	1,345	70.78	3	8
A.P.E. Knott	9	13	4	127*	478	53.11	2	2
M.C. Cowdrey	18	31	8	107	999	43.43	2	7
Asif Iqbal	15	25	5	106	868	43.40	1	7
M.H. Denness	19	31	1	162	1,110	37.00	3	7
R.A. Woolmer	18	21	7	75	440	31.42	–	2
A.G.E. Ealham	14	24	5	105	521	27.42	1	2
G.W. Johnson	19	34	2	87	826	25.81	–	4
B.D. Julien	17	22	4	90	406	22.55	–	2
D. Nicholls	19	36	1	60	760	21.71	–	5
J.N. Shepherd	19	25	6	51	320	16.84	–	1
D.L. Underwood	14	13	5	23*	100	12.50	–	–
D.A. Laycock	2	4	0	13	34	8.50	–	–
P.A. Topley	6	5	1	15*	32	8.00	–	–
J.N. Graham	15	14	3	10	23	2.09	–	–

Also batted: R.B. Elms 10*, 11*.

BOWLING

	O	M	R	W	Av	BB	5wI	10wM
R.A. Woolmer	347	85	853	43	19.83	7–65	3	1
D.L. Underwood	472.4	161	1,053	52	20.25	8–70	2	1
J.N. Shepherd	574.2	159	1,423	48	29.64	7–38	2	–
B.D. Julien	446.2	81	1,450	47	30.85	5–57	2	–
J.N. Graham	482.5	102	1,356	42	32.28	5–87	1	–
G.W. Johnson	364.5	117	970	29	33.44	3–28	–	–

Also bowled: Asif Iqbal 37–4–138–2; M.C. Cowdrey 3–0–18–0; R.B. Elms 82.5–16–225–7; B.W. Luckhurst 11.1–6–28–1; D. Nicholls 1–0–5–0; P.A. Topley 54–10–199–3.

FIELDING

28 – Nicholls (27 ct, 1 st); 19 – Denness, Julien; 18 – Luckhurst; 17 – Knott (15 ct, 2 st); 13 – Woolmer; 12 – Cowdrey, Johnson; 10 – Asif Iqbal; 9 – Shepherd; 7 – Ealham; 6 – Underwood; 5 – Topley; 3 – Graham.

LANCASHIRE

Patron: Her Majesty The Queen
President: Sir Neville Cardus
Chairman: C.S. Rhoades
Secretary: J.B. Wood
Captain: 1972 J.D. Bond
1973 D. Lloyd
Colours: Red, green and blue
Headquarters:
Old Trafford Cricket Ground,
Manchester MI6 0PX

Honours: County Champions (8) 1881, 1897, 1904, 1926, 1927, 1928, 1930, 1934
Joint Champions (4) 1879, 1882, 1889, 1950
Gillette Cup Winners (3) 1970, 1971, 1972
John Player League Champions (2) 1969, 1970

1st XI Home Grounds 1973:
Manchester (Old Trafford); Blackpool (Stanley Park); Liverpool (Aigburth); Southport

The 1972 cricket season finished on a triumphant note for Lancashire. The undisputed kings of limited-overs cricket carried off the Gillette Cup for the third successive year. This represents a remarkable hat-trick and it may well be a very long time before it is repeated. The occasion was all the more memorable, because it also marked the retirement of the Lancashire captain, Bond, who has done such a splendid job for his County and has led them to victory at Lord's each time they have appeared there.

This was a wonderful and fully deserved climax, but it could hardly disguise the fact that in most other respects it was a distinctly disappointing season.

At the beginning of the year Lancashire appeared to be the one team who could claim to have serious aspirations in all four competitions, but only in the Gillette Cup did they play to their potential.

Bond's men finished third in the County Championship the previous year and, though this possibly flattered them, they obviously had to be considered as contenders for the title. Instead they ended up an unhappy fifteenth.

The chief reason for their decline, which stemmed from the inability to remove the opposition, was the failure of their opening pair of bowlers, Lever and Shuttleworth, to reproduce their true form. In 1971 they were among the best spearheads in the country and were match winners who headed the bowling averages; but this summer they were less impressive and far more expensive.

The two main Lancashire spinners, Simmons and Hughes, with some support from D. Lloyd, returned figures similar to those of the previous season, which must represent an improvement, because they were not assisted by their seamers achieving an early breakthrough. Simmons and Hughes are both tidy, slow bowlers, who are also effective in limited-overs cricket when containment is so essential. It may well be that their ability in this direction has hampered their advance in the three-day game where one can sometimes afford to buy wickets, and where a high striking rate is preferable to a high maiden rate.

The Lancashire batting remained powerful, with four players, Pilling, who had a fine year, D. Lloyd, the captain elect, C. Lloyd, and Wood all averaging over 40, but they did not score as quickly as in 1971. This is reflected in the big drop in the number of their bonus points. The main reason was that Clive Lloyd, their one stroke-maker of world-class, encountered one of

David Lloyd, Lancashire's new captain for 1973. Though he may find it difficult to emulate the success of Jack Bond, Lloyd is fortunate in having a mature, attractive side well acquainted with the demands of modern cricket

What words of wisdom as the long and the short of Lancashire cricket — Clive Lloyd and Harry Pilling — confer?

those unaccountable bad patches.

The strength and the depth of the Lancashire batting made certain that they seldom lost matches and that, combined with a rather insipid attack, ensured a large number of draws.

With fast scoring batsmen, like Engineer and Hughes, lurking about in the lower part of the order one feels that the purpose that Lancashire showed in the Gillette matches was sometimes missing from County games.

Lancashire had also been third the previous year in the John Player League and, with an outstanding record in limited-overs matches, were firm favourites for the title. But they also lapsed in this competition, ending up in the middle of the table. In some respects this was more disappointing than their form in the Championship, because this was their *forte*, and the players fell well below their potential. They had the batsmen, the know-how, and, even if their bowling was a shade thin, it was largely covered by the high quality of the fielding.

D. Lloyd takes over the captaincy for 1973 and has at his disposal the nucleus of players to win at least one of the honours in limited-overs cricket. It is to be hoped that Lancashire's main attacking bowler, Lever, will be fully fit, and the most obvious requirement is to find an additional paceman.

Although the absence of C. Lloyd, who presumably will be touring with the West Indies, will be felt, D. Lloyd has plenty of batting at his disposal. Wood, who played so impressively for England, when he was eventually chosen, will be striving to establish himself as the regular opener after touring India and Pakistan. If he is successful he will have to miss several games, but this will provide an opportunity for the young talent, and in particular for Hayes, who seems unable to translate his undoubted ability into the all important matter of runs.

John Player Cricket Yearbook 1973

County Championship: Played 19   Won 2   Lost 3   Drawn 14   Abandoned 1
Final Position 15th

BATTING   *Denotes not out

	M	I	NO	HS	Runs	Av	100s	50s
H. Pilling	14	24	4	118	1,031	51.55	2	7
D. Lloyd	19	31	3	177	1,342	47.92	6	3
C.H. Lloyd	16	23	3	181	839	41.95	3	2
B. Wood	16	24	2	186	883	40.13	2	2
J. Sullivan	3	6	1	81*	154	30.80	–	2
F.C. Hayes	16	23	7	71*	472	29.50	–	3
K.L. Snellgrove	9	12	0	83	351	29.25	–	3
K. Shuttleworth	14	10	6	28*	113	28.25	–	–
F.M. Engineer	14	17	5	69	295	24.58	–	1
D.P. Hughes	17	17	4	77	275	21.15	–	2
J.D. Bond	18	18	3	103*	301	20.06	1	–
J. Simmons	18	15	4	26	146	13.27	–	–
P. Lee	16	10	3	18	56	8.00	–	–
K. Goodwin	5	6	1	7	21	4.20	–	–
P. Lever	12	6	0	10	19	3.16	–	–

Also batted: R.M. Ratcliffe 2.

BOWLING

	O	M	R	W	Av	BB	5wI	10wM
J. Simmons	507.1	164	1,379	56	24.62	7–65	2	2
P. Lever	227.3	54	585	20	29.25	7–70	2	–
P. Lee	370.1	80	1,101	37	29.75	5–32	1	–
D. Lloyd	123	49	316	10	31.60	4–70	–	–
D.P. Hughes	527	170	1,454	43	33.81	6–100	2	–
K. Shuttleworth	332.5	60	1,022	30	34.06	4–62	–	–
B. Wood	193.3	56	556	11	50.54	3–62	–	–

Also bowled: C.H. Lloyd 83.2–15–204–5; H. Pilling 11–3–28–0; R.M. Ratcliffe 29–6–76–0; J. Sullivan 52.3–12–166–6.

FIELDING

33 – Engineer (29 ct, 4 st); 25 – D. Lloyd; 16 – Hayes; 13 – Wood; 12 – Simmons; 11 – Bond; 10 – Hughes, Shuttleworth; 8 – Goodwin (3 ct, 5 st); 7 – C.H. Lloyd; 3 – Pilling; 2 – Lee, Lever; 1 – Snellgrove, Sullivan.

LEICESTERSHIRE

President: W. Bentley
Chairman: C.H. Palmer
Secretary: F.M. Turner
Captain: R. Illingworth
Colours: Scarlet and dark green
Headquarters:
County Ground, Grace Road,
Leicester LE2 8AD

Honours: Third in County Championship (2) 1953, 1967
Benson and Hedges Cup Winners (1) 1972
John Player League Runners-up (1) 1972

1st XI Home Grounds 1973:
Leicester (Grace Road)

Not only can Leicestershire claim to have enjoyed the most successful year in the entire history of the club, but they proved themselves to be the best all-round team in the country.

Up until August they were serious contenders for the County Championship. It was then they suffered a whole succession of injuries to key players. They lost two-thirds of their three-pronged spearhead, Higgs and Spencer, two dependable and experienced batsmen, Booth and Norman, and all-rounder and captain, Illingworth. Not surprisingly this proved too large a handicap and they had to settle for sixth place. In addition, of course, Illingworth missed many matches because of his Test match commitments.

The same sad story applied to their campaign in the John Player League. They were front runners until black August ruined their hopes and they finished runners-up. This constituted an admirable performance, when one takes into consideration the loss of three main bowlers at the most critical stage of the competition in limited-overs cricket when five have to be used.

Although Leicestershire were eliminated from the Gillette Cup by Warwickshire, it was by the narrowest of margins, a mere three runs. However, the County did have the satisfaction of gaining one tangible reward for all the good cricket they played and nobody could begrudge them this success.

They had the satisfaction of becoming the first winners of the Benson and Hedges Cup final at Lord's. Their comfortable victory in the final was a just reward for a real team effort and it was also the first major honour ever won by the Club, and, judging from their form last summer, it certainly will not be their last.

Why did the County have such a distinguished season? It largely stemmed from a balanced six-man attack: McKenzie, Higgs, Spencer, Illingworth, Birkenshaw, and Steele. Higgs proved to be a very welcome acquisition, Spencer

Roger Tolchard's pugnacious batting put him into the all-rounder class as a wicket-keeper-batsman

True Yorkshire determination on the face of the Leicestershire captain. With a little more luck and not so many injuries, Ray Illingworth's men might have added the John Player Trophy to the Benson and Hedges Cup they won in 1972

acquired a new lease of life, and McKenzie regularly underlined his claim to a place in the Australian team. Birkenshaw has never bowled better and fully justified his selection to tour India and Pakistan last winter. Steele continued to improve and his left-arm slow bowling provided an excellent foil to the off-spin of Illingworth and Birkenshaw.

The bowlers were finely supported in the field and astutely handled. Roger Tolchard, the most improved player in the side, kept wicket exceptionally well, secured more victims than any other 'keeper, and was a late replacement in the MCC touring side, a just reward indeed. The standard of the fielding was extremely high, and Davison and Steele were both outstanding.

The batting lacked performers of genuine star quality, but proved effective due to their ability to bat down the order. It could be said that no match was ever won until every Leicester player was back in the pavilion, once again emphasising the important part teamwork played in their success.

Their most spectacular player was Davison, whose innings against Warwickshire in the Benson and Hedges League Cup was the highlight of the season, but he was far from consistent. On the other hand, all-rounder Steele proved very reliable with the bat, and Leicestershire-born Haywood in his first full season with the club displayed considerable promise. Tolchard's batting, in addition to his keeping, made a noticeable advance and in the one-day matches he was their most effective performer.

In addition to their performances on the field the County had the satisfaction of showing a profit for the third consecutive year. Next summer their prospects are bright and they must be a good bet to win at least one of the competitions. The obvious danger is that their seam attack is clearly the oldest in the business, and they really do need to find a young fast bowler.

County Championship: Played 20   Won 6   Lost 2   Drawn 12   Final Position 6th

BATTING   *Denotes not out

	M	I	NO	HS	Runs	Av	100s	50s
J.C. Balderstone	3	5	2	81*	161	53.66	–	2
B. Dudleston	19	35	6	132	1,206	41.58	3	6
M.E.J.C. Norman	7	12	0	122	427	35.58	1	2
R.W. Tolchard	20	30	8	111*	777	35.31	1	4
R. Illingworth	8	12	3	57	272	30.22	–	1
J.F. Steele	20	37	1	93	1,065	29.58	–	9
B.J. Booth	14	23	5	44	477	26.50	–	–
B.F. Davison	20	33	2	83	815	26.29	–	5
P.R. Haywood	20	27	4	100*	593	25.78	1	3
G.D. McKenzie	20	23	7	55	366	22.87	–	2
J.G. Tolchard	10	17	1	66	338	21.12	–	2
J. Birkenshaw	20	24	0	77	460	19.16	–	2
R.B. Matthews	6	5	2	16*	37	12.33	–	–
C.T. Spencer	10	9	2	23	69	9.85	–	–
K. Higgs	19	20	11	15*	65	7.22	–	–

Also batted: T.K. Stretton 1; P.M. Stringer 0, 19.

BOWLING

	O	M	R	W	Av	BB	5wI	10wM
C.T. Spencer	120	34	241	16	15.06	3–14	–	–
R. Illingworth	185	44	394	24	16.41	4–29	–	–
J. Birkenshaw	684.1	185	1,587	74	21.44	8–94	5	1
B.F. Davison	136.3	35	344	15	22.93	3–57	–	–
G.D. McKenzie	535.3	122	1,411	57	24.75	5–30	2	–
R.B. Matthews	140.2	25	505	19	26.57	7–51	1	–
K. Higgs	491.5	138	1,183	42	28.16	3–24	–	–
J.F. Steele	276.2	86	692	17	40.70	3–34	–	–

Also bowled: J.C. Balderstone 18–1–50–2; B.J. Booth 16–8–39–1; B. Dudleston 20.4–3–91–4; P.R. Haywood 59–11–155–5; T.K. Stretton 18–3–57–0; P.M. Stringer 34–6–108–1; R.W. Tolchard 2–0–4–1.

FIELDING

48 – R.W. Tolchard (42 ct, 6 st); 30 – Steele; 21 – Higgs; 18 – Dudleston; 15 – Davison; 13 – Birkenshaw; 7 – Booth, McKenzie, Spencer; 4 – Haywood, J.G. Tolchard; 3 – Norman, Stringer; 2 – Illingworth, Matthews; 1 – Balderstone.

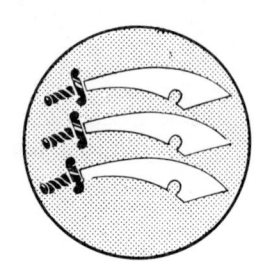

MIDDLESEX

President: G.C. Newman
Secretary: A.W. Flower
Captain: J.M. Brearley
Colours: Blue
Headquarters:
Lord's Cricket Ground, St. John's Wood Road, London NW8 8QN

Honours: County Champions (5) 1866, 1903, 1920, 1921, 1947
Joint Champions (1) 1949

1st XI Home Grounds 1973:
Lord's

1972 will go down at Middlesex as one of those respectable years when the results and the play were reasonable, but a sneaking suspicion lingered that with the material available they could, and perhaps should, have been so much better. After all the team had both ability and experience, and was splendidly led by Brearley – but something was lacking. Possibly they were a shade too complacent and too set in their ways, so that they found it difficult to pull out that little extra something when it might have made all the difference. The impression was that their enthusiasm simmered, but seldom boiled over.

The outcome was that they turned in a middle-of-the-table performance with what, on paper, should have been a rather better than a middle-of-the-table side.

Their batting had class and considerable depth. Smith, who began brilliantly, was talked about as possessing the qualities required of an England opener, while Radley must surely have been on the selectors' short list. In addition their long serving left-hander, Parfitt,

Below: John Murray has given Middlesex valuable service behind the stumps for two decades
Bottom: Middlesex captain Mike Brearley

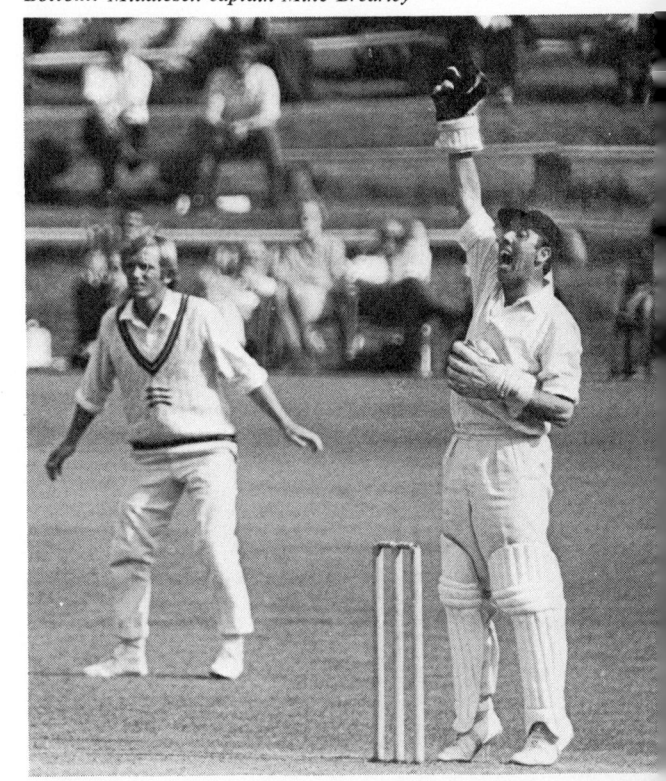

was in such fine form that he was, somewhat surprisingly, recalled to the Test scene.

Brearley contributed several fine innings, but it is strange that a batsman of his ability, who has even been thought of as a future captain of England, has never made a century in Championship cricket.

Although Russell had a lean season and Featherstone, an exciting stroke-maker, was often out of touch, there was still no shortage of runs because of the presence of performers of the calibre of Murray, Jones, and Titmus in the lower regions of the order. On the other hand genuine batsmen in the 'tail' are not always the expected advantage. They have been known, as Middlesex have found to their cost in the past, to induce a relaxed attitude, with the players not worrying as much as they should about losing a wicket, because someone else is bound to make runs.

The Middlesex attack was splendidly spearheaded by the speed of Price. He may have an ungainly approach, as he shifts from gear to gear in his long curving run, but he has pace, control, and heart. These attributes ensured that he was easily their most hostile, economical, and successful bowler. His main seam support came from Jones, who is a good county all-rounder – a third seamer and a useful middle-of-the-order batsman – and Selvey. Another class bowler to share the new ball could have made an enormous difference.

That old campaigner, Titmus, was once again the chief slow bowler. He was always tidy, as he frequently showed in limited-overs games, but his striking rate, in terms of wickets per over, in Championship games dropped. It might have been another story had he had a contrasting spinner at the other end, but unfortunately Latchman experienced a lean time and lost confidence – the kiss of death for any wrist

The long, rather ugly, round-the-corner run-up completed, John Price puts everything into the delivery stride.

Unavailable on a full-time basis in 1973, Price and his stout hearted endeavour will be missed by Middlesex

spinner. In these circumstances it might have paid to have made more use of Parfitt, who is a better off-break bowler than is sometimes realised.

There was a noticeable improvement by Middlesex in the John Player League in which they finished fifth. This was mainly due to a more calculated approach which enabled them to increase their own run rate and reduce that of their opponents. Their attack was accurate and usually brilliantly supported in the field, where Featherstone and Radley were outstanding.

Sunday matches also provided the two most exciting games of the summer, both at Lord's. In the first Middlesex defeated Somerset by five wickets with only two balls remaining, and in the second they lost to Warwickshire by one run off the last ball. Even though there is an element of artificiality about these finishes, nobody can deny their appeal to the general public.

With the departure of Parfitt and Russell, and Price's availability limited, Middlesex will be forced to rely more upon younger players and, in this respect, the winning of the under-25 competition augurs well. It will obviously not be easy to replace batsmen of the calibre of Russell and Parfitt, but in terms of winning matches Price is likely to prove an even bigger loss.

One name to look for next summer will be Gomes, who is a highly talented young strokemaker – but it would be so much more exciting for England supporters if he had learned his cricket in this country, instead of Trinidad.

Given a little luck Middlesex, if they can find a couple of reasonable pace bowlers, should do well in the one-day games. This is especially true of the half-day ones, where the extra mobility and keenness of the youngsters in the field can make all the difference.

County Championship:	Played 20	Won 5	Lost 5	Drawn 10	Final Position 8th		
BATTING	*Denotes not out						
	M	I	NO	HS	Runs	Av	100s	50s
P.H. Parfitt	15	26	3	129*	947	41.17	3	5
C.T. Radley	20	35	1	112	1,287	37.85	3	10
M.J. Smith	20	36	1	147	1,204	34.40	3	4
J.M. Brearley	20	35	7	75	863	30.82	–	4
N.G. Featherstone	11	19	3	76	492	30.75	–	4
W.E. Russell	15	27	1	99	733	28.19	–	5
J.T. Murray	18	28	1	84	654	24.22	–	3
K.V. Jones	18	28	4	57*	466	19.41	–	1
P.H. Edmonds	4	4	2	16*	37	18.50	–	–
F.J. Titmus	20	27	8	49	324	17.05	–	–
H.C. Latchman	15	23	5	96	282	15.66	–	1
J.S.E. Price	20	21	4	34	228	13.41	–	–
M.W.W. Selvey	19	16	10	22	54	9.00	–	–
T. Selwood	2	4	1	7	20	6.66	–	–

Also batted: J.D. Hopkins 0, 4; D.A. Marriott 10*, 0*; H. Pearman 61.

BOWLING

	O	M	R	W	Av	BB	5wI	10wM
J.S.E. Price	479.4	107	1,293	65	19.89	8–85	3	1
K.V. Jones	415.3	102	1,162	41	28.34	6–26	1	–
P.H. Edmonds	184.2	70	402	14	28.71	4–64	–	–
F.J. Titmus	680.5	185	1,661	52	31.94	6–54	3	–
M.W.W. Selvey	562.5	132	1,463	45	32.51	6–43	1	–
H.C. Latchman	270.2	47	1,037	27	38.40	4–57	–	–

Also bowled: N.G. Featherstone 23–1–116–3; D.A. Marriott 34–9–101–3; J.T. Murray 2–0–17–0; P.H. Parfitt 21–2–73–0; H. Pearman 2–0–11–0; C.T. Radley 1–0–6–0; M.J. Smith 0.2–0–4–0.

FIELDING

40 – Murray (38 ct, 2 st); 20 – Brearley; 16 – Parfitt, Radley; 9 – Smith; 8 – Jones, Russell; 6 – Price; 5 – Featherstone, Latchman; 4 – Selvey, Titmus; 3 – Edmonds; 1 – Pearman, Selwood.

NORTHAMPTONSHIRE

President: N.D. Barratt
Secretary: K.C. Turner
Captain: P.J. Watts
Colours: Maroon
Headquarters:
County Ground, Wantage Road, Northampton NN1 4TJ

Honours: County Championship Runners-up (3) 1912, 1957, 1965

1st XI Home Grounds 1973:
Northampton; Wellingborough School; Brackley; Kettering; Luton, Bedfordshire

It was hardly surprising that Northamptonshire should do so much better in the County Championship matches than in the previous year, because they had signed on two class cricketers, Bedi and Cottam, and had also engaged the strong and willing Dye. As all three were very successful with the ball, it meant that from having one of the weakest attacks in the Championship, Northants suddenly found themselves with one of the strongest and most varied. This enabled them to bowl sides out twice.

Cottam and Bedi were expected to do well, but Dye's bowling exceeded all expectations and, compared with his performance for Kent the previous year, he must be regarded as the most improved player in the team. He headed the bowling averages and his 75 wickets for 18 apiece represent fine fast bowling.

When Cottam became available he was quickly among the wickets, and, once he had settled down, Bedi was soon troubling opposing batsmen with his subtle variations of spin and flight. The presence of another brilliant spinner helped to make Mushtaq far more dangerous.

With Bailey and Willey, who also played several valuable innings, providing more than adequate support for the four main wicket-takers, Northampton moved up from 14th to fourth in

First-Class Counties: Northamptonshire

Above: Left-arm spinner Bishen Bedi – a true weaver of spells

Left: Mushtaq Mohammad's importance in the Northamptonshire revival of 1972 is well illustrated by his contribution in the Championship – 1,743 runs and 52 wickets

the table, despite the handicap of a rather fragile batting line-up which largely revolved round two men, Mushtaq and Steele, and had the further disadvantage of a decidedly long 'tail'.

Mushtaq is, of course, a batsman of established international stature and he had his finest season for his adopted county, hitting six centuries and scoring very nearly 2,000 runs. When one remembers that in addition he took over 50 wickets with his leg-breaks and googlies at a very modest cost, one can appreciate his enormous value.

Although Mushtaq's runs, even in that quantity, hardly constituted a surprise, Steele's form came as something of a revelation. Until last summer he has been regarded as a reliable county player, but a first-class average of over 50, together with five centuries and an aggregate of more than 1,600 runs, suggests that this was either a vintage year, or that he has blossomed into something more.

The captain, Watts, who suddenly found himself with a team that was bowling out their opponents, revelled in this new experience and showed his appreciation by batting better than ever.

With so few young batsmen of English origin in the first-class game at the present time, it was pleasant to see two, Cook and Tait, in the side. Although neither scored very many runs, they did enough to suggest that they have important parts to play in the future of Northamptonshire, and possibly even English, cricket.

As a result of the presence of two genuine slow bowlers, as well as seamers able to make that important initial breakthrough, Northants, unlike the majority of the counties, were better equipped for the three-day than the one-day game. There were three main reasons for their lowly 14th place in the John Player League. The batting depended too much on two players –

fatal in this form of the game. There were insufficient natural strikers, and they do not appear to have worked out the best tactical approach to the job of chasing or setting a target. Secondly, although their seamers were more than adequate with Bailey proving very effective in one-day matches, their fielding was too erratic and not nearly efficient enough. Thirdly, and this is a serious condemnation, neither of their two world-class Test match slow bowlers, Mushtaq and Bedi, were effective in these types of matches! Despite the problems of definition, one cannot help feeling that if, in at least one of these one-day competitions, each team had to include and bowl two genuine spinners – not off-breakers who fire in flat, non-turning, yorkers – it would make for a better and more attractive game.

Northants's prospects for 1973 look healthy

David Steele's consistent run-getting in the last two seasons has been remarkable

in the Championship, where the registration of Virgin should provide extra stability to the batting, while both Cook and Tait will be a year older, and, if they are to make that hoped-for progress, this should lead to an increased aggregate.

Provided their attack continues to prove as effective, and they score more runs, they should stay up among the leaders. If their performances in one-day cricket are to improve, it will be necessary to capitalise on the power of their attack by tightening up in the field, while their batsmen will need to be more positive and confident.

County Championship: Played 20 Won 7 Lost 3 Drawn 10 Final Position 4th

BATTING

*Denotes not out

	M	I	NO	HS	Runs	Av	100s	50s
Mushtaq Mohammad	20	35	6	137*	1,743	60.10	6	7
D.S. Steele	20	36	7	131	1,417	48.86	4	6
B.S. Crump	17	25	7	113*	604	33.55	1	3
P.J. Watts	19	32	5	75*	887	32.85	–	8
G. Cook	18	33	2	78	766	24.70	–	5
P. Willey	19	29	3	71	627	24.11	–	3
A. Tait	14	25	0	67	557	22.28	–	4
N. Maltby	3	6	2	36	79	19.75	–	–
G. Sharp	19	25	5	76*	327	16.35	–	1
D. Breakwell	5	8	0	35	83	10.37	–	–
B.S. Bedi	20	20	3	40	145	8.52	–	–
R.M.H. Cottam	13	14	2	16	100	8.33	–	–
J.C.J. Dye	20	17	10	29*	45	6.42	–	–
R.R. Bailey	7	8	2	12	34	5.66	–	–
W. Larkins	5	8	1	20	35	5.00	–	–

Also batted: L.A. Johnson 7.

BOWLING

	O	M	R	W	Av	BB	5wI	10wM
J.C.J. Dye	503.1	123	1,360	75	18.13	6–41	4	–
Mushtaq Mohammad	374.4	120	1,040	52	20.00	6–38	2	–
R.M.H. Cottam	317.1	90	834	41	20.34	6–35	5	1
B.S. Bedi	604	238	1,392	62	22.45	7–34	3	–
R.R. Bailey	197.1	46	559	21	26.61	4–32	–	–
P. Willey	348.5	86	923	26	35.50	5–49	1	–

Also bowled: D. Breakwell 7–1–17–0; G. Cook 1–1–0–0; B.S. Crump 45–17–112–4; N. Maltby 17–3–55–2; D.S. Steele 38.1–10–93–5; P.J. Watts 7–2–15–0.

FIELDING

42 – Sharp (37 ct, 5 st); 25 – Steele; 20 – Watts; 16 – Cottam; 14 – Cook, Mushtaq; 7 – Willey; 6 – Bedi; 4 – Bailey, Crump, Tait; 3 – Dye; 2 – Johnson; 1 – Larkins.

NOTTINGHAMSHIRE

President: F.E. Gregory
Chairman: J.W. Baddiley
Secretary: Group Captain R.G. Wilson
Captain: 1972 J.B. Bolus
1973 G.St.A. Sobers
Colours: Green and gold
Headquarters:
Trent Bridge Cricket Ground,
Nottingham NG2 6AG

Honours: County Champions (12) 1865, 1868, 1871, 1872, 1875, 1880, 1883, 1884, 1885, 1886, 1907, 1929
Joint Champions (5) 1869, 1873, 1879, 1882, 1889
1st XI Home Grounds 1973:
Nottingham (Trent Bridge); Newark (Ransome's Sports Ground); Worksop; Nottingham (John Player Ground)

As Nottinghamshire dropped to 14th in the County Championship and 13th in the John Player League, an immediate reaction would be to write off 1972 as an indifferent year. This may be true, but the team did, in general, play to its potential and in certain respects did rather better than could be reasonably expected.

In the previous season they had looked very much a bottom half of the table side, except on those occasions when the genius of Sobers had lifted them, something he was able to do from time to time, even though suffering from the effects of too much cricket. Last summer injury struck down the greatest all-rounder the game has ever known in his Benefit Year and his appearances were limited to a mere handful. His loss to any team would be enormous and to one with as many limitations as Notts it could have been a catastrophe. The fact that their overall performance was not all that much worse than when he had played a full summer showed clearly that there were good features for the County to savour.

The outstanding success was unquestionably Stead. He is a chunky, fast-medium left-arm bowler who has been around a long time and is middle-aged as far as seamers are concerned. But he turned in a whole series of outstanding performances, finishing with 93 wickets at 20 apiece. It was a remarkable effort and, had it been achieved for a stronger county, could well have won them the title. And had Sobers been available to back him up with both ball and bat there seems little doubt that Notts would have finished in the top half of the table. His sudden development from just another seamer into a lethal destroyer was reminiscent of Sydenham's transformation achieved for Surrey several years ago. In both cases the secret of the great improvement stemmed from the ability to move the ball late in flight, combined with the left-hander's line.

Stead received excellent support from W. Taylor, who made a considerable advance as a bowler, but the attack suffered from the lack of good spinners, although White, who originally went to Notts as a batsman and an occasional off-spinner, now comes into the genuine all-rounder category.

Unfortunately the increased effectiveness and penetration of the Notts bowling, which ought to have brought them more victories than it did, coincided with a decline in the batting. The biggest disappointment was Harris, who had been so prolific in 1971 that he was considered unlucky to have been ignored by the English selectors. On that occasion he amassed over two thousand runs, while last summer he failed to reach a thousand in Championship matches.

Below: Gary Sobers—'His enforced rest may have done him good, both physically and mentally'
Bottom: Barry Stead—the success story of 1972

First-Class Counties: Nottinghamshire

Smedley was another player who was unable to reproduce the touch of the previous summer, but this setback was largely countered by the belligerent and unorthodox Hassan who headed the averages and had the highest aggregate. Bolus, who took over the captaincy, brought his experience and stability to an untrustworthy line up, in which run-getting was often a laboured and painful process.

The absence of Sobers was especially felt in limited-overs matches, where his natural ability has often enabled him to win several matches mainly through his own efforts. In the John Player League the Notts bowling was up to the required standard, but the batsmen failed. They could be faulted on two accounts; insufficient runs and a striking rate which was too low. Unless they managed to start well, the middle order seemed uncertain as how best to approach their task. Although Hassan was a notable exception, too many found it difficult to improvise.

The outlook for 1973 is, perhaps, best described as imponderable. Bolus has joined Derby, while their seam bowler, all-rounder and brilliant field, M. N. S. Taylor, has gone to Hampshire. The latter may never have quite lived up to expectations with either bat or ball, but the County could encounter some difficulty in finding a replacement of comparable ability. The big question mark concerns the future of Sobers. His enforced rest may have done him good, both physically and mentally; but it will be necessary to wait until this winter, when the West Indies meet the Australians, to find if he has completely recovered from his operation. Every cricket lover hopes this will be the case, but if he is fit he will obviously be required by the West Indies touring party next summer, which must automatically reduce his contribution to his own county.

It's that shot again! Derek Randall is bowled round his legs trying to sweep David Steele to square-leg. However, Nottinghamshire have high hopes for this exciting young stroke-player who hit five sixes on his first-class debut

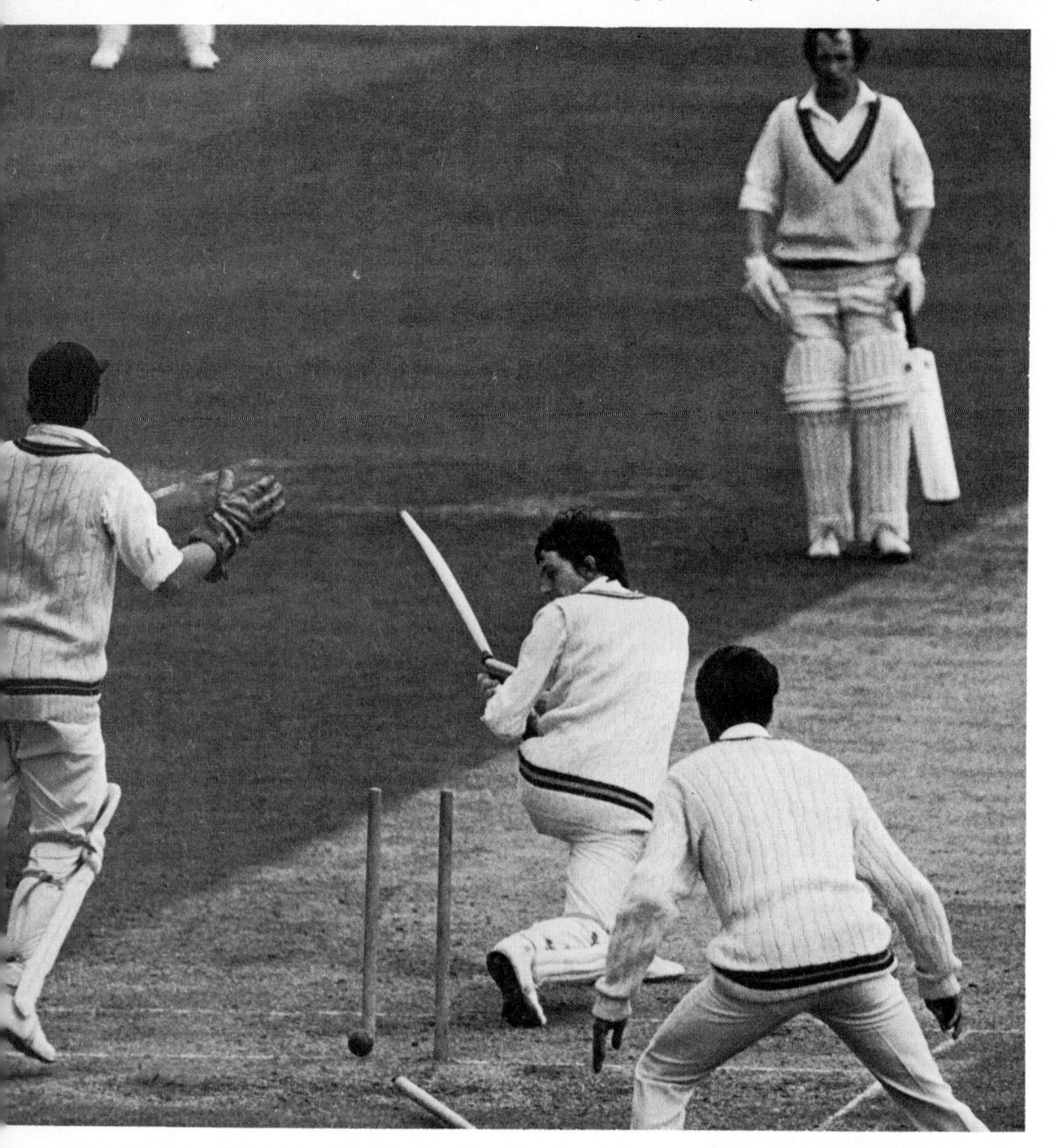

First-Class Counties: Nottinghamshire

It would be fair to predict that Notts are unlikely to be among the honours, unless they are able to find either some exceptional new talent, or to sign on several established cricketers. They need at least one middle-order batsman capable of scoring around 1,500 runs, another incisive seamer – preferably genuinely fast – and a spinner capable of winning two or three matches when the conditions are in his favour.

County Championship:	Played 20	Won 1	Lost 6	Drawn 13	Final Position 14th
BATTING	*Denotes not out				

	M	I	NO	HS	Runs	Av	100s	50s
B. Hassan	19	35	1	111	1,231	36.20	1	9
J.B. Bolus	20	37	4	140*	1,098	33.27	1	8
M.J. Harris	16	28	1	174*	867	32.11	2	6
M.J. Smedley	19	33	3	131	945	31.50	2	5
R.A. White	20	34	6	114*	788	28.14	1	3
G.St.A. Sobers	6	9	1	71	222	27.75	–	1
D.W. Randall	15	26	2	78	550	22.91	–	3
M.N.S. Taylor	20	32	7	71	505	20.20	–	2
N. Nanan	7	12	3	44	153	17.00	–	–
B. Stead	20	29	6	58	361	15.69	–	2
P.J. Plummer	8	11	2	37	107	11.88	–	–
G. Frost	7	13	0	37	109	8.38	–	–
D.A. Pullan	19	24	6	34	125	6.94	–	–
W. Taylor	17	20	9	26*	62	5.63	–	–
P.A. Wilkinson	6	8	3	14	24	4.80	–	–

Also batted: P.A. Todd 66*.

BOWLING

	O	M	R	W	Av	BB	5wI	10wM
B. Stead	700	160	1,891	93	20.33	8–44	5	1
W. Taylor	453.4	71	1,431	64	22.35	6–42	4	1
G.St.A. Sobers	157	45	351	15	23.40	3–37	–	–
R.A. White	488.3	147	1,295	43	30.11	5–56	1	–
M.N.S. Taylor	493	133	1,371	43	31.88	4–74	–	–
P.J. Plummer	132	31	469	10	46.90	3–44	–	–

Also bowled: G. Frost 15–3–42–1; M.J. Harris 94–23–316–3; N. Nanan 10–0–52–0; P.A. Wilkinson 85–14–294–4.

FIELDING

46 – Pullan (45 ct, 1 st); 18 – Hassan; 15 – Harris; 13 – Smedley; 10 – M.N.S. Taylor; 8 – Randall, White; 7 – Stead; 6 – Bolus, Wilkinson; 5 – W. Taylor; 4 – Plummer, Sobers; 2 – Frost, Nanan.

SOMERSET

President: R.V. Showering
Secretary: A.K. James
Captain: D.B. Close
Colours: Black, white and maroon

Headquarters:
County Cricket Ground, St. James's Street, Taunton

Honours: Third in County Championship (4) 1892, 1958, 1963, 1966
Gillette Cup Finalists (1) 1967
1st XI Home Grounds 1973:
Taunton; Bath (Recreation Ground); Bristol (Imperial Ground); Glastonbury (Morlands Athletic Ground); Torquay, Devon (Recreation Ground); Weston-super-Mare (Clarence Park); Yeovil (Johnson Park)

With Close as captain, a well-balanced side under his command, and representative calls unlikely, everything suggested that the promise of the previous season would come to fruition in 1972. Although Somerset were never favourites for any of the major honours, they were an attractive outside bet and clearly had every reason to expect to move up the table in both the County Championship and the John Player League. However, the reverse occurred and they dropped from seventh to eleventh in the Championship and fifth to seventh in the League.

The reasons for this lapse in the three-day matches were easy to pin-point. First, Somerset's two slow bowlers, the Australian wrist-spinner, O'Keeffe, and the long serving off-spinner, Langford, were both considerably less effective and more expensive than in 1971. The outcome was that the County lost some matches which they were expected to win. Secondly, Virgin, who had been the most consistent and productive batsman in the team for many years, was woefully out of touch, because he was not happy with the situation and he has since left to join Northants.

Once again Cartwright was Somerset's leading wicket-taker, easily heading the averages, and enjoying another wonderful season in which he secured 93 victims at 18 apiece. He remained what he has been for several years, the finest medium-paced bowler in the country, and probably in the world. His control, allied to his ability to move the ball either way, was a joy to behold and served as a perfect answer to those critics who claim that seam bowling is not an art, but merely consists of running up and banging the ball down on the seam.

His chief support was supplied by Jones, the former Sussex bowler who was the most improved player in the eleven. The lively West Indian, Moseley, also turned in several good performances and, with all-rounder Burgess bowling effectively and Close himself always available, the County were well equipped with seam. If their spinners had been as penetrating then Somerset must surely have finished near the head of the table.

However, the batsmen must also share some of the blame because they were inclined to score so slowly that there was insufficient time left to enable the bowlers to remove the opposition twice. This was also one of the reasons for the high number of drawn matches, 14 out of 20 with four victories and only two defeats. It was significant that they acquired fewer batting bonus points than most teams in the Championship, but more bowling bonus points, thanks very

First-Class Counties: Somerset

Above: After a season in which he was woefully out of touch, Roy Virgin has moved to Northants for 1973. Somerset, trying to re-establish themselves after a poor season in 1972, can ill afford to lose this most accomplished opener

Left: Tom Cartwright was yet again accuracy and economy personified as he proved himself without peer as a medium-pace bowler. His 98 first-class wickets in 1972—joint leading aggregate of the season—cost just 18 runs each

*Since his arrival in 1971, Brian Close has made a vital contribution to Somerset cricket, both with the bat and, last season, as an **astute** captain*

largely to Cartwright, than Warwickshire or Kent! Although many of the draws were unavoidable, there were occasions when a slightly more adventurous approach might have produced more definite results. If in fact they had won three more and lost three more matches as well as picking up a few extra bonus points for batting they would almost certainly have ended in the first five!

In his second season with his adopted county, Close had an even better summer than last with the bat and made more runs than anyone else in his team. The only other player to top a thousand was Kitchen, and the rest of the batting is best described as sketchy and unreliable. Nevertheless, there was a considerable resilience in the side, because all the lower order did produce useful innings from time to time. This is reflected by the fact that of the 14 in their batting averages, 13 achieved scores of 40 or more.

It is obviously an advantage to possess a 'tail' that is capable of towing the team out of trouble, but this happened far too frequently in the case of Somerset and was yet another reason for their slow rate of scoring.

In some respects the most encouraging feature of the summer, other than the marked advance of Jones, was the form shown by their young left-hander, Rose. In only five innings he scored 252 runs and topped the averages, thus transforming into figures the promise he had shown as a schoolboy several years before.

What are Somerset's prospects for 1973? They have lost the services of Virgin, and possibly Langford. They will be hoping that Breakwell, the left-arm spinner who has left Northants because of the arrival of Bedi, will strengthen their slow bowling department.

It is extremely difficult to make predictions about Somerset. The immediate reaction is to

Above: Harry Pilling, trying to reach his century with one mighty blow, is bowled by Peter Sainsbury for 94. Just 5 ft 3 in tall, Pilling found his lack of height no handicap as he accumulated more than 1,000 runs in an entertaining way to top the Lancashire averages for 1972

Right: A full house at Lord's for the second Test between England and Australia. In 1972, the Mecca of cricketers was host to all from Test players to villagers competing for the Haig Trophy

Above: West Indies fast bowler Vanburn Holder, one of four overseas players in the Worcestershire side who might be required for tour duty in 1972

Above right: Peter Parfitt ended a 17-year association with Middlesex in 1972 and gave an indication that his first-class playing days might be over – the latter in spite of the impressive form that earned him a Test recall against Australia

Right: The Oval and its famous gasometer, both an integral part of cricket lore

put them into the 'middle-of-the-road' category, but if their batting finds the necessary solidarity then theirs could be an entirely different tale. On the other hand how much longer can one expect the bowling of Cartwright to be so devastating? Close is both a fine and an experienced captain, but one wonders if there is sufficient character in the team as a whole to maintain the pressure needed to win any of the competitions, other than, aided by luck in draw and toss, the Gillette Cup.

County Championship: Played 20   Won 4   Lost 2   Drawn 14   Final Position 11th

BATTING
*Denotes not out

	M	I	NO	HS	Runs	Av	100s	50s
B.C. Rose	3	5	0	125	252	50.40	1	–
D.B. Close	18	29	5	135	1,192	49.66	3	5
M.J. Kitchen	20	33	0	156	1,078	32.66	2	4
S.G. Wilkinson	8	12	2	69	264	26.40	–	2
K.J. O'Keeffe	20	26	9	43*	397	23.35	–	–
R.T. Virgin	19	32	1	121	668	21.54	2	2
B.A. Langford	17	21	8	68*	268	20.61	–	1
P.W. Denning	19	29	3	54*	524	20.15	–	2
P.J. Robinson	3	3	0	55	57	19.00	–	1
T.W. Cartwright	20	29	3	93	492	18.92	–	3
G.I. Burgess	17	28	1	63	484	17.92	–	1
H.R. Moseley	16	18	4	67	234	16.71	–	1
D.J.S. Taylor	20	23	7	43	250	15.62	–	–
A.A. Jones	18	15	7	22*	67	8.37	–	–

Also batted: R.C. Cooper 4, 0. R.J. Clapp played in one match but did not bat.

BOWLING

	O	M	R	W	Av	BB	5wI	10wM
T.W. Cartwright	822	358	1,735	93	18.65	8–94	6	1
A.A. Jones	409	83	1,192	50	23.84	9–51	2	1
G.I. Burgess	228.3	52	578	21	27.52	4–80	–	–
H.R. Moseley	357	73	915	33	27.72	4–26	–	–
B.A. Langford	249.4	60	831	16	51.93	3–60	–	–
K.J. O'Keeffe	361.3	98	1,077	18	59.83	3–31	–	–

Also bowled: R.J. Clapp 29–3–118–3; D.B. Close 35–10–128–3; P.W. Denning 8–1–25–0; M.J. Kitchen 9–3–19–1; B.C. Rose 2–0–5–1; R.T. Virgin 1–0–5–0; S.G. Wilkinson 2–0–9–0.

FIELDING

31 – Taylor (28 ct, 3 st); 16 – Close; 15 – Virgin; 11 – Moseley, O'Keeffe; 10 – Cartwright; 9 – Denning; 7 – Jones, Kitchen; 5 – Burgess; 4 – Rose, Wilkinson; 3 – Langford.

John Player Cricket Yearbook 1973

Above: Intikhab Alam, Surrey's leg-break bowler and hard-hitting batsman. Though The Oval wicket is not always sympathetic to his wrist-spinners, 'Inty' is always prepared to bowl and bowl, tempting the batsmen with his teasing flight

Right: Dudley Owen-Thomas, for whom Surrey have high hopes now that he is available for the whole season. While at Cambridge, he produced many fine innings that suggested he could go on to win higher honours

SURREY

Patron: Her Majesty The Queen
President: M.J.C. Allom
Secretary: C.G. Howard
Cricket Manager: A.J.W. McIntyre
Captain: 1972 M.J. Stewart
1973 J.H. Edrich
Club colours: Chocolate
Headquarters:
Kennington Oval, London SE11 5SS

Honours: County Champions (18) 1864, 1887, 1888, 1890, 1891, 1892, 1894, 1895, 1899, 1914, 1952, 1953, 1954, 1955, 1956, 1957, 1958, 1971
Joint Champions (2) 1889, 1950
1st XI Home Grounds 1973:
The Oval; Guildford (Woodbridge Road); Byfleet (BAC Ground); Sunbury; Tolworth (Decca Ground)

Nothing seemed to go right for the County Champions in 1972. Hopes that Surrey would retain their title soon disappeared and they finished 12th in the table. Although this represented a considerable slump, the difference in playing ability between the counties is so small these days that it would be wrong to regard it as especially significant.

The two main causes for their decline were the injury to Arnold which restricted his appearances in County Championship matches to seven and the departure of Willis, for whom no adequate replacement was found. This effectively reduced what had been one of the strongest spearheads in the County game to the solitary Jackman. Although he responded splendidly to the additional burden, and was probably the most improved player in the side, the County were unable to achieve those early breakthroughs of the previous year and in fact won only three games.

This lack of penetrative pace bowling also meant that their two fine attacking spinners, Pocock and Intikhab, frequently had to be introduced too early and in unsuitable conditions, while in 1971 they had often been able to exploit and press home the advantage initially won for their team by the quickies. Pocock had a good season and he and Intikhab formed a very dangerous pair, particularly on a dusty track.

Surrey's lack of success in three-day matches also applied to the restricted-overs competitions, where the loss of two above-average seamers proved an even bigger handicap. However, although the County did have its problems, there was no disguising the fact that they simply did not play to their potential. Their batting remained strong, but the impression remained that it should have been even more productive, and several players failed to return the figures expected from them. It was the same story in the field, where Roope confirmed that he is one of the finest fieldsmen in the country, both close to the bat and in the deep, but the overall standard was not up to that of the previous year.

Yet again the reliable Edrich, who will take over the captaincy from Stewart this summer, headed the batting averages. He missed several matches because of his selection for Test duty against the Australians and, although he had a disappointing time in the Tests, runs continued to flow regularly from his bat for his county.

Roope had another impressive season and is clearly one of that rare breed, a young English born, middle-order batsman with serious aspirations to making the Test side.

The highly talented Younis amassed the

highest batting aggregate in Championship matches, despite a bad patch in which he was well below his true form.

After the University Match Owen-Thomas played several good innings and will be available throughout this summer, when he hopes to prove that he has the ability to become something more than a competent county bat.

But too many of the Surrey players did not do themselves justice. How does such a dangerous striker of the ball as Intikhab finish with an average of 12? It must have been particularly disappointing for Stewart, who was in his last season with the Club for whom he has given such fine service, both as captain and as player.

It is difficult to predict what 1973 holds for Surrey. The committee have decided to adopt a policy of blooding young cricketers for the next year or so. Whether this produces the results must inevitably depend upon the calibre of these new recruits. As far as the limited-overs games, and especially the John Player League, are concerned, the newcomers will, or at least should, bring fresh verve to the fielding, while there ought to be sufficient batting talent around to make the runs.

Probably the key to success lies in whether Surrey can find a pace bowler, who is at least as good as Willis, and also adequate cover for Arnold, in case of injury or representative calls. At the moment Surrey appear to have rather too many batsmen who can turn an arm over but lack the bite needed to produce the type of figures that win matches, especially three-day games on a good pitch.

County Championship: Played 20   Won 3   Lost 5   Drawn 12   Final position 12th

BATTING   *Denotes not out

	M	I	NO	HS	Runs	Av	100s	50s
J.H. Edrich	11	20	3	168	848	49.88	2	4
G.R.J. Roope	18	31	7	122	1,009	42.04	1	5
Younis Ahmed	18	33	2	143	1,156	37.29	2	6
R.M. Lewis	13	22	1	78	769	36.61	–	6
D.R. Owen-Thomas	10	18	2	112	531	33.18	2	–
S.J. Storey	18	31	9	92*	596	27.09	–	4
M.J. Edwards	15	29	0	121	654	22.55	1	2
R.D. Jackman	20	21	11	43	203	20.30	–	–
M.J. Stewart	13	23	3	79	395	19.75	–	2
G.P. Howarth	4	6	0	55	114	19.00	–	1
A. Long	20	26	5	55	397	18.90	–	2
L.E. Skinner	2	4	0	30	75	18.75	–	–
P.I. Pocock	20	24	4	52*	305	15.25	–	2
Intikhab Alam	16	22	3	42	234	12.31	–	–
G.G. Arnold	7	8	3	22	47	9.40	–	–
A.R. Butcher	7	5	2	20	28	9.33	–	–
C.E. Waller	8	7	2	3*	8	1.60	–	–

BOWLING

	O	M	R	W	Av	BB	5wI	10wM
P.I. Pocock	585.4	145	1,729	69	25.05	7–67	4	–
A.R. Butcher	106	22	281	11	25.54	6–48	1	–
Intikhab Alam	392	105	1,112	43	25.86	6–22	3	1
R.D. Jackman	602	121	1,809	69	26.21	5–49	4	–
C.E. Waller	150	33	433	16	27.06	4–36	–	–
G.G. Arnold	211.1	44	548	15	36.53	3–32	–	–
S.J. Storey	254.5	70	659	14	47.07	3–25	–	–
G.R.J. Roope	230.3	36	684	14	48.85	3–46	–	–

Also bowled: G.P. Howarth 3.2–0–14–0; R.M. Lewis 1–0–5–0; Younis Ahmed 2–2–0–0.

FIELDING

44 – Long (36 ct, 8 st); 26 – Roope; 23 – Storey; 10 – Jackman; 9 – Edwards, Stewart; 6 – Edrich, Intikhab, Lewis; 5 – Waller, Younis; 4 – Howarth, Pocock; 3 – Butcher; 2 – Arnold, Owen-Thomas.

SUSSEX

President: The Duke of Norfolk
Chairman: D.W. Wilshin
Secretary: A.A. Dumbrell
Captain: 1972 M.G. Griffith
1973 A.W. Greig
Colours: Dark blue, light blue and gold
Headquarters: County Ground, Eaton Road, Hove BN3 3AN

Honours: County Championship Runners-up (6) 1902, 1903, 1932, 1933, 1934, 1953
Gillette Cup Winners (2) 1963, 1964

1st XI Home Grounds 1973:
Hove; Eastbourne (The Saffrons); Hastings (Central Ground)

The Sussex side, at least on paper, looked capable of more than holding their own against the majority of the other counties, but once again they failed to do themselves justice.

Certainly there were extenuating circumstances for their finishing 16th in the Championship table. First, Snow, their international fast bowler, and Greig, their international all-rounder, both missed half the matches owing to Test calls. Secondly, Tony Buss, a thoroughly experienced opening bowler, was out of action for most of the summer. The absence of this trio for so many games made an enormous difference. To make matters worse, their two above-average second string seamers, Spencer and Phillipson, were not available until late in the season. The outcome was that the attack was at times distinctly anaemic, and made the more so because Joshi, their only recognised spinner, met with little success.

However, despite these handicaps, one feels that Sussex should have managed to win a few more matches and have ended up somewhere near the middle of the table. Their batting on occasions appeared to lack determination, or was it, perhaps, dedication?

In the other competitions, with the exception of zonal matches in the Benson and Hedges League Cup, Sussex can hardly be said to have played to their true potential. They were eliminated in the first round of the Gillette Cup, largely due to some indifferent batting, while their 15th place in the John Player League was extremely disappointing.

Sussex, who have a distinguished record in Gillette matches – admittedly of longer duration than the Sunday League – like some other sides still do not appear to have worked out their best tactics for these short encounters. In particular the early batsmen seemed unable to pace their innings. This point is illustrated by the fact that only two counties had a slower run rate, rather a ridiculous state of affairs when one examines the calibre and the ability of the Sussex batsmen.

Another reason for their lowly position was that collectively their fielding was not as consistently good as it might have been.

Three of the batsmen had averages of over 40, Greig, Prideaux, predictably with the highest aggregate, and the evergreen Parks. After these three it was down to the less satisfactory twenties. Geoff Greenidge did enough to suggest that he will become a good batsman, possibly even a great one. Griffith produced several rescue innings for his team, and might have warranted an extended trial higher up the order, but Mike Buss failed to make as many runs as expected.

The most improved batsman was Graves, who when he opened the innings showed the form that he has promised for so long.

The outstanding Sussex discovery was their right-arm fast-medium bowler, Phillipson. Had he been either a batsman or a spinner, his name would have already come up as a future Test cricketer, but it is a name to note for the future nonetheless.

Although Snow is currently the finest English fast bowler, his record with the ball for his county is not exceptional. He leads the bowling averages, but he does not win the matches for his county which one might expect.

Greig had a splendid all-round season and the one danger next year, when he captains the side, is that he will burn himself out trying to do too much. There never has been any doubt as to the quality of his batting, but, until his tour of Australia with the World XI, there had been a chameleon-like quality about his bowling. Now he has acquired the control essential for anyone who wishes to establish himself as the third seamer in an International XI.

The great moment in Sussex cricket last summer was their splendid victory against the Australian tourists. The Australians made 294 in their first innings, to which the County's reply was 296 for 5. The visitors sportingly closed their second innings at 262 for 2. This left Sussex to make 261 for victory against the clock. Thanks to some splendid batting, especially from Greenidge, Graves, and Prideaux, this target was reached, much to the delight of some of the keenest and enthusiastic members in the land.

With seam bowlers of the quality of Snow, Greig, Phillipson, Spencer, and the Buss brothers, Sussex could, under the direction of Greig, prove to be a force in any of the limited-overs competitions next summer. They should have more than adequate support in the field and sufficient strokemakers to provide the runs. Until they find at least one class spinner, they are, however, unlikely to make much impression in the County Championship.

First-Class Counties: Sussex

Sussex captains old and new:

Above: *Mike Griffith, whose batting may well benefit now that he is no longer burdened with the worries of the captaincy*

Right: *Tony Greig—success with Sussex would make him a prime candidate for the captaincy of England*

John Player Cricket Yearbook 1973

County Championship:	Played 20	Won 2	Lost 8	Drawn 10	Final Position 16th

BATTING

*Denotes not out

	M	I	NO	HS	Runs	Av	100s	50s
A.W. Greig	9	14	3	112	640	58.18	1	5
R.M. Prideaux	20	35	5	169	1,438	47.93	4	6
J.M. Parks	20	33	9	87	968	40.33	–	7
M.G. Griffith	20	31	8	78	673	29.26	–	5
G.A. Greenidge	20	36	2	142*	940	27.64	1	6
P.J. Graves	20	33	1	77	780	24.37	–	4
M.A. Buss	20	35	1	94	822	24.17	–	5
J.D. Morley	11	14	3	76	236	21.45	–	1
J. Denman	14	15	1	24	154	11.00	–	–
A. Buss	5	6	0	19	56	9.33	–	–
U.C. Joshi	19	20	8	14*	111	9.25	–	–
J.R.T. Barclay	5	6	1	25	39	7.80	–	–
J.A. Snow	8	9	1	16	60	7.50	–	–
J. Spencer	13	14	3	21*	73	6.63	–	–
C.P. Phillipson	13	11	4	10	28	4.00	–	–

Also batted: A.A. Henderson 2, 9; N.I. Thomson 1*, 1.

BOWLING

	O	M	R	W	Av	BB	5wI	10wM
J.A. Snow	192	55	453	26	17.42	6–82	1	–
A.W. Greig	255.4	75	560	26	21.53	6–20	2	1
A. Buss	121	18	403	11	36.63	3–51	–	–
M.A. Buss	389.3	111	1,201	32	37.53	6–68	1	–
C.P. Phillipson	270	61	756	20	37.80	6–56	1	–
U.C. Joshi	474.5	124	1,341	33	40.63	4–56	–	–
J. Spencer	345.2	69	1,038	24	43.25	3–40	–	–
J. Denman	276.1	51	932	21	44.38	3–22	–	–

Also bowled: J.R.T. Barclay 41–13–95–1; P.J. Graves 7–2–32–1; A.A. Henderson 40.1–4–132–5; R.M. Prideaux 10.2–5–27–0; N.I. Thomson 32–9–81–1.

FIELDING

26 – Parks (22 ct, 4 st); 17 – Graves; 16 – Griffith; 14 – Prideaux; 13 – Joshi; 10 – Denman; 9 – Greenidge; 7 – M.A. Buss; 6 – Greig; 5 – Spencer; 4 – Morley; 3 – Snow; 2 – A. Buss, Phillipson.

WARWICKSHIRE

President: Lt.-Gen. Sir Oliver Leese, Bt.
Chairman: C.C. Goodway
Secretary: L.T. Deakins
Captain: A.C. Smith
Colours: Blue, yellow and white
Headquarters: County Ground, Edgbaston, Birmingham B5 7QU

Honours: County Champions (3) 1911, 1951, 1972
Gillette Cup Winners (2) 1966, 1968

1st XI Home Grounds 1973:
Birmingham (Edgbaston); Coventry (Courtaulds)

Warwickshire not only carried off the County Championship, but accomplished it in the grand manner. They proved themselves to be the best team in the competition and produced some outstanding cricket in the process. The only regret is that they did not draw the crowds which their efforts deserved.

The Championship normally goes to a team with an exceptional attack, but in the case of Warwickshire, it was their batting line-up, rather than their bowling, which proved the deciding factor. Their batsmen had a wonderful summer in which Kanhai, Amiss, Kallicharran, and Mike Smith were outstanding. This quartet demonstrated that there is no substitute for class, but more important than the runs they made was the manner in which they were acquired. Their rate of scoring was extremely high and this was very valuable on plumb pitches, because it gave a good, rather than an outstanding, attack, a big total to bowl against, plus *the time to bowl out the opposition twice.*

For Kanhai it was truly an Indian summer and the sheer beauty of his stroke production will be treasured by all who were lucky enough to have seen him in action. He showed that he is still a world-class performer. From the purely domestic angle the re-emergence of Amiss was the most exciting feature. Amiss started indifferently and even lost his place, but he came storming back in such a way that it was hard to understand why he has never established himself as a permanent member of the England team.

Although Kallicharran was a newcomer to the county scene, he was, of course, already an established player of international repute, but he turned out to be an even better and more exciting batsman than had been anticipated. Mike Smith, who was recalled to the England team, displayed yet again his accustomed ability and flair.

Main support for this exhilarating foursome came from Murray, Whitehouse, and Jameson. Whitehouse, who had been so impressive in the previous season, was a little disappointing, while Jameson, who many considered the correct partner for Boycott in the England XI, had a surprisingly lean season.

The Warwickshire attack really revolved around six men. The fact that five of these fall into the seam category meant a lack of balance and emphasised the important part played by the fast run-rate.

McVicker was the leading wicket-taker and he was admirably assisted by the wholehearted Brown, newcomer Willis, the promising left-armer, Rouse, and, somewhat surprisingly, Alan Smith, who actually headed the averages. This meant that the only spinner of consequence was the veteran Gibbs. But Tidy and Lewington

John Player Cricket Yearbook 1973

Left above: Mike Smith's consistent performances for Warwickshire saw his recall to the England side in 1972. He disappointed in the Tests, but was in excellent form for his County as they won the Championship and reached the finals and semi-finals of the Gillette Cup and Benson and Hedges League Cup respectively

Left: Warwickshire owe much to the dynamic batting of Rohan Kanhai for their attractively-won success of 1972

Above: Bob Willis will be looking for a Test place in 1973

should eventually provide the support that is at present lacking.

Warwickshire enjoyed a certain amount of success in limited-overs cricket and indeed were the losing finalists at Lord's in the Gillette Cup. It could be argued that they contributed to their own downfall on that occasion, but on the other hand they were a trifle fortunate in two earlier rounds, especially against Leicestershire.

As a result there is a feeling that with the talent available plus the exceptional reserve strength, the County ought to do better in this form of the game. Why should a team with such a fast scoring record finish 12th in the John Player League? The answer probably lies in the fact that in afternoon games the ability to gather runs quickly is possibly not quite as vital as the ability to restrict the run-rate of the opposition.

Although the Warwickshire seamers, admirably complemented by the accuracy of Gibbs, were as efficient as those of several teams that finished higher in the order, the mobility of their fieldsmen was not. This was understandable because their side can hardly be said to be in the first flush of youth. In County Championship matches Warwickshire's fielding was generally good and Kanhai at slip was brilliant, but when the main purpose was the denial of runs they had their limitations.

Whether Warwickshire are able to retain their title must depend to a large degree on the West Indian selectors. It is possible that they will include as many as four of the County's team in their party to tour England. In addition England could well require Amiss and Willis.

Even though they have a strong second XI, which contains considerable talent, the possible loss of that number of class cricketers would obviously make a considerable difference to their chances.

County Championship: Played 20 Won 9 Lost 0 Drawn 11 Final Position 1st

BATTING   *Denotes not out

	M	I	NO	HS	Runs	Av	100s	50s
D.L. Amiss	15	24	7	192	1,129	66.41	5	1
R.B. Kanhai	20	28	4	199	1,437	59.87	7	3
A.I. Kallicharran	20	29	5	164	994	41.41	2	3
M.J.K. Smith	16	23	5	102	743	41.27	1	6
D.L. Murray	14	21	6	54	412	27.46	–	1
J. Whitehouse	15	24	1	55	528	22.95	–	3
J.A. Jameson	15	24	2	78	469	21.31	–	3
A.C. Smith	14	13	4	26*	161	17.88	–	–
N.M. McVicker	20	23	5	65*	297	16.50	–	2
D.J. Brown	15	15	4	79	174	15.81	–	1
R.G.D. Willis	9	6	2	12	39	9.75	–	–
L.R. Gibbs	19	12	6	24	54	9.00	–	–
R.N. Abberley	3	4	1	25	26	8.66	–	–
P.J. Lewington	5	3	2	8*	8	8.00	–	–
K. Ibadulla	5	5	0	12	22	4.40	–	–
S.J. Rouse	12	7	1	9	26	4.33	–	–

Also batted: W.N. Tidy 0. W. Blenkiron played in two matches but did not bat.

BOWLING

	O	M	R	W	Av	BB	5wI	10wM
A.C. Smith	202.3	66	449	20	22.45	5–47	1	–
N.M. McVicker	527.1	137	1,496	63	23.74	6–72	3	–
L.R. Gibbs	551.1	148	1,324	50	26.48	6–77	2	–
D.J. Brown	332.2	70	902	34	26.52	5–49	1	–
S.J. Rouse	288.2	52	894	32	27.93	5–47	1	–
P.J. Lewington	106.1	26	322	11	29.27	4–62	–	–
R.G.D. Willis	246.1	57	732	25	29.28	8–44	1	–

Also bowled: R.N. Abberley 6–1–12–0; W. Blenkiron 56–10–199–7; K. Ibadulla 92–26–251–5; J.A. Jameson 80–14–216–3; A.I. Kallicharran 54.4–5–232–6; R.B. Kanhai 8–1–23–0; M.J.K. Smith 2–1–4–0; W.N. Tidy 17–0–119–3; J. Whitehouse 46–9–123–2.

FIELDING

44 – Murray (40 ct, 4 st); 26 – Kanhai; 16 – Gibbs; 13 – Amiss, A.C. Smith (12 ct, 1 st); 11 – Kallicharran; 8 – Rouse; 6 – Brown, Whitehouse; 5 – Jameson (4 ct, 1 st); 4 – M.J.K. Smith, Willis; 3 – Abberley; 2 – Blenkiron, McVicker; 1 – Ibadulla, Lewington.

WORCESTERSHIRE

President: C.G.D. Smith
Chairman: G.J. Dorrell
Secretary: M.D. Vockins
Captain: N. Gifford
Colours: Dark green and black
Headquarters:
County Ground, New Road,
Worcester WR2 4QQ

Honours: County Champions (2) 1964, 1965
John Player League Champions (1) 1971
Gillette Cup Finalists (2) 1963, 1966

1st XI Home Grounds 1973:
Worcester; Kidderminster (Chester Road); Dudley

Although Worcestershire did not win any of the four competitions, they can afford to look back with satisfaction on the summer. It is true that their eventual position in the County Championship was slightly disappointing, but they were handicapped by the following factors. D'Oliveira was able to take part in only eight matches, Carter was unable to play after July 14th, and both Hemsley and Cumbes had to return to their footballing commitments in mid-July. If they had been in a position to field their full side throughout, they would certainly have finished higher.

Turner is now a world-class opening batsman. He enjoyed another fine season for his adopted county and was easily their most prolific scorer. He is defensively sound and straight, but he can also, when in the mood, take an attack apart. In all games for the County he scored over 1,800 runs and, when it is remembered that he made over 2,000 runs for New Zealand in the West Indies, he can be said to have had a remarkable

First-Class Counties: Worcestershire

Above: *The New Zealander Turner and the West Indian Headley go out to open Worcestershire's innings in the Gillette Cup semi-final against Warwickshire. Worcestershire's world-class opening partnership will be affected by the tours of England by New Zealand and the West Indies in 1973*

Left: *Worcestershire's other New Zealander, John Parker (here batting against the Australians), made his Test debut against Pakistan at Wellington in 1972–73*

year in which he showed an appetite for batting which rivals that of Boycott.

The most improved player was probably Hemsley, who, in a very limited period, batted with an authority and style that further underlined what his absence meant to the Club. His method and approach suggested that he is one of the best uncapped middle-order players in the country, while he also possesses the additional advantage of being a natural competitor.

Parker, another New Zealander, clearly possesses the attributes needed to become, at the very least, a good county player. The all-round skill of D'Oliveira was yet again of enormous value and his batting was generally powerful. Although Headley missed several matches through injury, he played a number of fine innings, while the experienced and stylish Ormrod almost reached a thousand runs in Championship matches.

However, the bowling was not so impressive, despite the presence of Holder, who captured 76 wickets at a very economical cost. This was all the more praiseworthy, because he frequently had to make do without front-line support. The other seamers, D'Oliveira excepted, were all inclined to be too expensive.

Gifford led his side shrewdly and did well to win a place in the England XI with his left-arm spin bowling. He topped the bowling averages and deservedly gained a place in the MCC touring party.

Worcester's hopes of reaching the Gillette final died in the semi-final against Warwickshire, when they were never really in the hunt after the first few overs. Their biggest disappointment, however, occurred in the John Player League, which they won the previous year and in which they dropped to 11th place.

The three major causes for this decline were as follows. First, rain seriously interfered with the first five matches. Secondly, their bowling was not sufficiently tight, which caused them to lose several games, after their batsmen had put together what would normally be regarded as match-winning totals. Thirdly, there was a general rise in the standard of opposition.

Behind the stumps Wilcock did well, but eventually lost his place to Cass, who literally fought his way back into the side by his efforts with both bat and gloves in the Second XI.

Their most exciting match was against Warwickshire in the John Player League. Headley and Turner began with a full-blooded assault which amassed 182 runs for the first wicket, with 150 coming in only 88 minutes. Their innings eventually closed with 247 runs on the board, which seemed to guarantee a comfortable victory. In the process Turner registered a century which, as he made another two hundreds against the same opponents that weekend, suggested a distinct partiality for the Warwickshire attack.

After a brisk start there was a collapse and the game appeared to be over, but this failed to take into account the opposing 'tail' who smashed 118 runs off 18 overs to win a remarkable contest which produced no fewer than 496 runs.

It is difficult to assess the County's prospects for 1973, because so much will depend upon the whims of three different groups of selectors. New Zealand and the West Indies both have short tours and the former will obviously want the services of Turner, and possibly Parker, while the latter are likely to call upon Holder and could include the experienced Headley. England used D'Oliveira and Gifford last summer and may need them again. If all the selectors show a liking for Worcester players, then the chances of acquiring any domestic honours must be remote. On the other hand it is difficult to sympathise too much with a county with so many overseas players in their team.

First-Class Counties: Worcestershire

| County Championship: | Played 20 | Won 4 | Lost 4 | Drawn 12 | Final Position 7th |

BATTING
*Denotes not out

	M	I	NO	HS	Runs	Av	100s	50s
G.M. Turner	20	36	4	170	1,649	51.53	6	6
E.J.O. Hemsley	8	13	3	92	485	48.50	–	4
B.L. D'Oliveira	8	14	3	107	508	46.18	2	3
J.M. Parker	12	20	2	118	701	38.94	1	3
R.G.A. Headley	17	28	1	131	881	32.62	1	5
J.A. Ormrod	20	35	5	157*	963	32.10	1	4
P.J. Stimpson	11	18	2	88	426	26.62	–	4
D.E.R. Stewart	5	10	1	40	196	21.77	–	–
K.W. Wilkinson	9	12	4	49*	170	21.25	–	–
T.J. Yardley	20	31	6	59	501	20.04	–	2
N. Gifford	16	17	5	46*	228	19.00	–	–
H.G. Wilcock	17	20	6	39	238	17.00	–	–
I.N. Johnson	4	6	1	27	67	13.40	–	–
V.A. Holder	20	17	6	23*	139	12.63	–	–
K. Griffith	3	4	0	24	38	9.50	–	–
J. Cumbes	7	3	0	17	24	8.00	–	–
R.G.M. Carter	11	6	3	19*	19	6.33	–	–
G.R. Cass	3	5	1	7	21	5.25	–	–
A.P. Pridgeon	7	7	3	4*	9	2.25	–	–

A. Shutt played in two matches but did not bat.

BOWLING

	O	M	R	W	Av	BB	5wI	10wM
N. Gifford	489.5	134	1,175	59	19.91	7–66	4	1
V.A. Holder	621.2	129	1,596	76	21.00	6–60	4	–
B.L. D'Oliveira	161.5	37	387	17	22.76	5–24	2	–
J. Cumbes	151.1	24	452	17	26.58	5–36	1	–
K.W. Wilkinson	220.2	37	719	21	34.23	3–57	–	–
R.G.M. Carter	240.4	40	866	25	34.64	4–63	–	–
J.A. Ormrod	166	25	626	17	36.82	5–27	1	–

Also bowled: K. Griffith 22–1–105–1; E.J.O. Hemsley 47–12–150–2; I.N. Johnson 81–9–272–5; J.M. Parker 2–0–14–1; A.P. Pridgeon 133–17–513–7; A. Shutt 50–8–181–2; D.E.R. Stewart 13–0–58–0; P.J. Stimpson 5–2–19–0; T.J. Yardley 1–0–6–0.

FIELDING

38 – Wilcock (35 ct, 3 st); 19 – Ormrod; 13 – Turner; 12 – Gifford; 11 – Wilkinson, Yardley; 6 – Cass; 4 – Carter, Headley, Holder, Pridgeon; 3 – Cumbes, Griffith, Hemsley, Johnson, Parker, Stimpson; 1 – Stewart.

YORKSHIRE

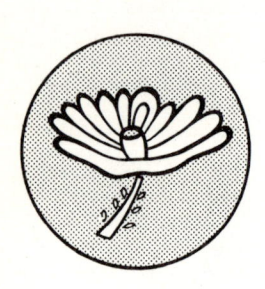

Patron: H.R.H. The Duchess of Kent
President: Sir William Worsley, Bt.
Chairman: A.H. Connell
Secretary: J. Lister
Captain: G. Boycott
Colours: Oxford blue, Cambridge blue and gold

Headquarters:
Headingley Cricket Ground, Leeds LS6 3BU

Honours: County Champions (31) 1867, 1870, 1893, 1896, 1898, 1900, 1901, 1902, 1905, 1908, 1912, 1919, 1922, 1923, 1924, 1925, 1931, 1932, 1933, 1935, 1937, 1938, 1939, 1946, 1959, 1960, 1962, 1963, 1966, 1967, 1968
Joint Champions (2) 1869, 1949
Gillette Cup Winners (2) 1965, 1969
Benson and Hedges Cup Finalists (1) 1972
1st XI Home Grounds 1973:
Leeds (Headingley); Bradford (Park Avenue); Harrogate; Hull; Middlesbrough; Scarborough; Sheffield (Bramall Lane)

After the disappointments of the previous season Yorkshire displayed far better all-round form in 1972. They could, by no stretch of the imagination, compare with any of their great teams of the past, but there were several indications that things are getting better. This is good news, because a powerful Yorkshire and a powerful England are usually synonymous.

In the County Championship matches they were rather let down by their batting. Perhaps they unconsciously relied too much on Boycott, who was out of the side for long spells with injury, and later representative calls. His absence gave a great opportunity to both the newcomers and the old brigade, but neither took full advantage. Hampshire remained an enigma. In the course of a season he will produce about four innings of a brilliance that makes one wonder why he is not a regular member of the England side, and in the other games the reason becomes all too clear.

Lumb was probably the pick of the hopefuls and looked capable of becoming a reliable opener, Leadbeater sparkled in the one-day games, and Squires was an interesting prospect. One of the peculiarities of Yorkshire cricket in recent years has been the number of young batsmen who have promised so much initially and have then faded from the scene. Unfortunately neither Hutton nor Sharpe were really in touch with the bat.

The attack was impressive, Nicholson and Old, at least on a helpful pitch, were just about the best opening pair in the country; the former takes a well deserved benefit in 1973 and the latter could well take over from Snow in a year or so. They received excellent support from both Hutton and the rapidly improving Cooper. This seam quartet was sufficient in the limited-overs games, but the lack of penetrating spinners proved a serious handicap in the three-day matches. The loss of Cope, because of action trouble, was one cause, but it was difficult to understand why such an experienced campaigner as Wilson should finish at the bottom of the averages, although it is true he did miss some games through injury.

Yorkshire have a reasonably good record in the Gillette Cup, but this was the first season that they seemed to come to terms with the requirements of the John Player League. The side realised that there were many occasions

Despite missing much of the season with a broken finger, Geoffrey Boycott topped the 1,000-runs mark once more, finishing with a Championship average just short of 100.

As a captain he has improved greatly, and under his leadership Yorkshire have shown they are capable of making a strong claim for the major trophies

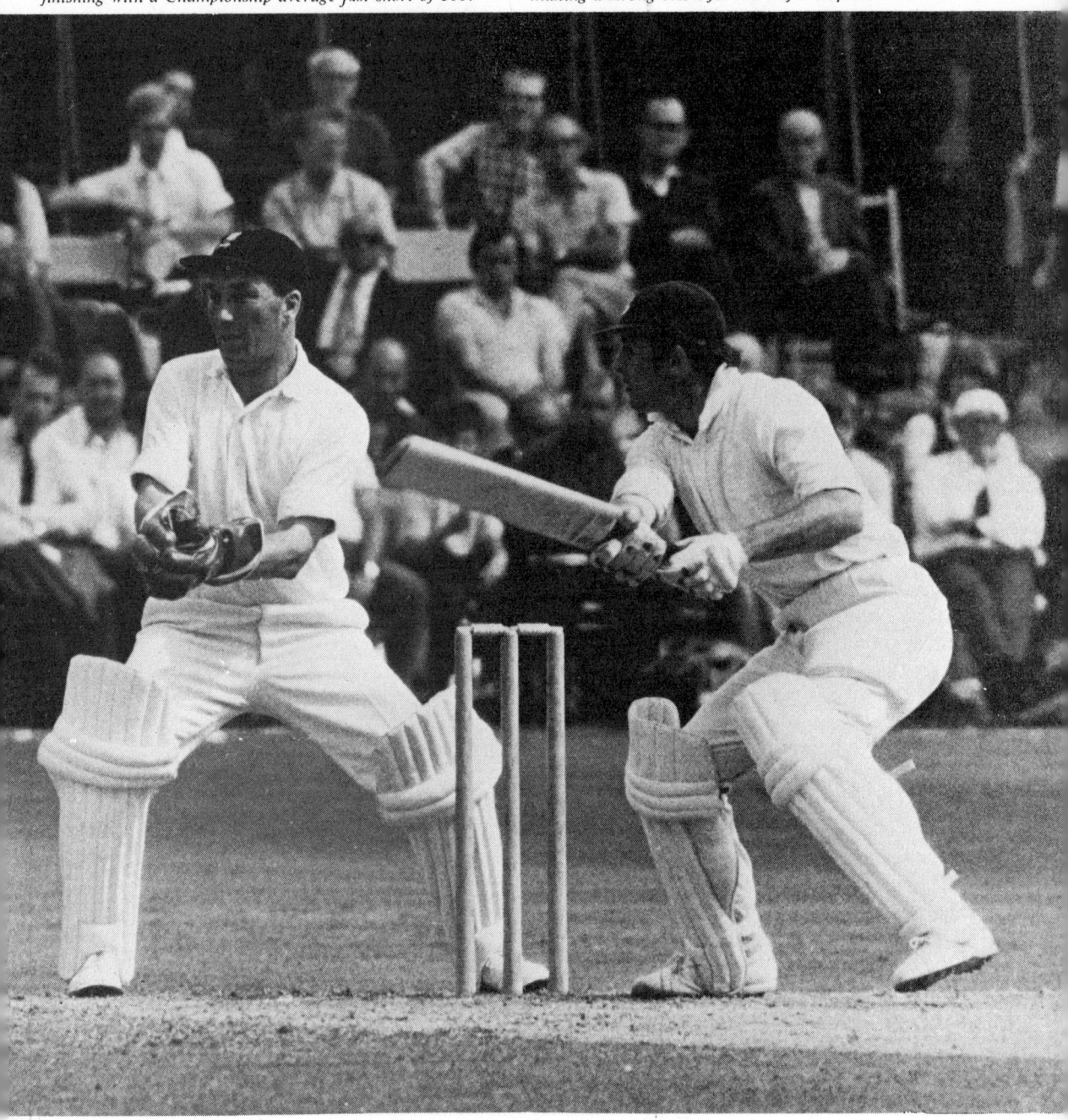

David Bairstow adds the wicket of Nottinghamshire's Taylor to an already impressive tally of dismissals

when they could not afford the steady build-up which is possible in whole-day, as distinct from afternoon, matches, and also the need to improvise with strokes which are not to be found in a coaching manual. Aided by a strong and naturally mean seam attack, which was supported by tight field placing, the Northerners began their campaign impressively and looked as if they might win the title, until they lost one or two games they should have won, including a somewhat farcical defeat by Essex at Scarborough, which was eventually to cost them third place in the League. However, moving up from 15th to fourth and finishing with three successive wins hinted at greater things for 1973.

Although eliminated in the first round of the Gillette Cup, in a close match, by Warwickshire, Yorkshire were far from disgraced and, but for Boycott's broken finger, would probably have gone further.

In the first ever League Cup, Yorkshire were well satisfied to have reached the final where Leicester beat them well. Whether the Midlanders would have triumphed if Boycott had been able to play remains a matter for conjecture.

The outlook for 1973 is encouraging. Boycott, in his second year as captain, made a noticeable advance and, with more experience and increasing tact, should become even better. He is such a magnificent batsman himself that he is perhaps inclined to expect too much from less talented performers.

Although capable of climbing the Championship table, much clearly depends on whether Cope has been able to make his action legitimate and also effective, or, alternatively, whether Yorkshire can unearth another spinner. In Yorkshire a class bowler of this type in three-day cricket is absolutely essential. The supporters will also be expecting Sharpe to recover the form which deserted him in 1972 and led to his being dropped from the team. His omission certainly underlined his enormous value as the finest slip fieldsman in the country.

Yorkshire also need one or two of their young batsmen to establish themselves in a very definite fashion. They need to make runs regularly and to include two or three centuries in their aggregate.

County Championship: Played 20   Won 4   Lost 5   Drawn 11   Final Position 10th

BATTING

*Denotes not out

	M	I	NO	HS	Runs	Av	100s	50s
G. Boycott	10	17	5	204*	1,156	96.33	6	4
A.J. Dalton	3	4	0	128	178	44.50	1	–
J.H. Hampshire	17	26	2	111	734	30.58	2	3
R.G. Lumb	14	22	0	79	611	27.77	–	4
B. Leadbeater	18	29	3	53	670	25.76	–	1
R.A. Hutton	20	28	4	57*	535	22.29	–	1
P.J. Sharpe	10	15	0	53	313	20.86	–	1
C. Johnson	19	26	4	53	391	17.77	–	1
C.M. Old	15	21	3	64	302	16.77	–	1
H.P. Cooper	7	10	4	47	97	16.16	–	–
P.J. Squires	8	14	0	64	210	15.00	–	1
D.L. Bairstow	20	25	3	52*	267	12.13	–	1
A.G. Nicholson	17	18	8	31	113	11.30	–	–
M.K. Bore	9	6	1	15	49	9.80	–	–
D. Wilson	13	17	1	25	148	9.25	–	–
J.D. Woodford	2	4	0	18	36	9.00	–	–
G.A. Cope	8	5	2	7*	19	6.33	–	–
C.C. Clifford	10	12	4	12*	39	4.87	–	–

BOWLING

	O	M	R	W	Av	BB	5wI	10wM
C.M. Old	378.5	101	931	54	17.24	6–69	3	–
A.G. Nicholson	522.5	144	1,149	60	19.15	7–49	4	–
H.P. Cooper	200.1	45	495	24	20.62	4–37	–	–
R.A. Hutton	405.3	84	1,093	51	21.43	5–27	2	–
G.A. Cope	171.5	70	348	15	23.20	4–31	–	–
C.C. Clifford	238.5	89	614	24	25.58	5–70	1	–
M.K. Bore	239	106	531	15	35.40	3–56	–	–
D. Wilson	244	72	665	18	36.94	4–83	–	–

Also bowled: J.H. Hampshire 24–10–34–3; C. Johnson 12–4–31–0; J.D. Woodford 7–2–42–0.

FIELDING

44 – Bairstow (40 ct, 4 st); 18 – Hampshire; 14 – Hutton, Lumb; 10 – Sharpe; 9 – Johnson; 6 – Old; 5 – Boycott, Leadbeater; 4 – Clifford, Cooper, Wilson; 3 – Nicholson, Squires; 2 – Cope.

John Player Cricket Yearbook 1973

Above: *Warwickshire, winners of the County Championship in 1972. Standing (l–r): Deryck Murray, John Whitehouse, Norman McVicker, Bill Blenkiron, Bob Willis, Steve Rouse, Warwick Tidy, Alvin Kallicharran. Sitting (l–r): Dennis Amiss, Rohan Kanhai, Mike Smith, Alan Smith (captain), David Brown, Lance Gibbs, John Jameson*

Below: *Norman McVicker, spearhead of the Warwickshire attack*

The County Championship 1972

COUNTY CHAMPIONSHIP 1972 FINAL TABLE

		P	W	L	D	Bat.	Bowl.	Total Points
1	WARWICKSHIRE (2)	20	9	0	11	68	69	227
2	Kent (4)	20	7	4	9	69	52	191
3	Gloucestershire (8)	20	7	4	9	38	77	185
4	Northamptonshire (14)	20	7	3	10	34	77	181
5	Essex (10)	20	6	4	10	50	63	173
6	Leicestershire (5)	20	6	2	12	43	68	171
7	Worcestershire (15)	20	4	4	12	59	68	167
8	Middlesex (6)	20	5	5	10	48	61	159
9	Hampshire (9)	20	4	6	10	50	64	154
10	Yorkshire (13)	20	4	5	11	39	73	152
11	Somerset (7)	20	4	2	14	34	71	145
12	Surrey (1)	20	3	5	12	49	61	140
13	Glamorgan (16)	20	1	7	12	55	61	126
14	Nottinghamshire (12)	20	1	6	13	38	73	121
15	Lancashire (3)	19	2	3	14	42	56	118
16	Sussex (11)	20	2	8	10	46	49	115
17	Derbyshire (17)	19	1	5	13	27	60	97

Figures in brackets show 1971 positions.
The match between Derbyshire and Lancashire at Buxton (June 24, 26, 27) was abandoned without a ball being bowled.

(Figures in brackets after each county in the match result line show the total number of points gained from that match, followed by a breakdown of bonus points, e.g. Essex (9:5/4) shows that Essex took 9 points from the match with 5 batting bonus points plus 4 bowling bonus points.)

May 3rd, 4th, 5th
MIDDLESEX (4:2/2) drew with LEICESTERSHIRE (6:4/2) at Lord's. Middlesex 332–9d (C.T. Radley 112, P.H. Parfitt 53). Leicestershire 365–5 (P.R. Haywood 100 not out, J.F. Steele 93, B.F. Davison 62)

SUSSEX (5:3/2) drew with ESSEX (9:5/4) at Hove. Sussex 248 (M.G. Griffith 59, K.D. Boyce 5–41) and 31–2. Essex 355–7d (K.W.R. Fletcher 114, K.D. Boyce 71)

WORCESTERSHIRE (7:2/5) drew with SOMERSET (4:0/4) at Worcester. Somerset 109 (B.L. D'Oliveira 5–24) and 108–3 (M.J. Kitchen 55). Worcestershire 202 (G.M. Turner 88 not out – carried bat through innings, R.G.A. Headley 64)

May 10th, 11th, 12th
GLAMORGAN (4:0/4) drew with HAMPSHIRE (0) at Neath. Hampshire 141–8 (M.A. Nash 5–56). Rain.

LANCASHIRE (7:4/3) drew with SURREY (7:4/3) at Manchester. Lancashire 290–8d (D. Lloyd 90, C.H. Lloyd 87) and 32–2. Surrey 297 (M.J. Edwards 121, D.P. Hughes 6–100)

LEICESTERSHIRE (4:0/4) drew with KENT (4:1/3) at Leicester. Kent 223 (Asif Iqbal 59, G.D. McKenzie 5–30) and 184 (J.N. Shepherd 51, G.W. Johnson 50). Leicestershire 252 (J. Birkenshaw 59, P.R. Haywood 55, D.L. Underwood 6–67) and 84–4

NORTHAMPTONSHIRE (14:0/4) beat ESSEX (5:0/5) by 5 wickets at Northampton. Essex 147–9d (B.E.A. Edmeades 65 not out) and 153–1d (G.J. Saville 67 not out, K.W.R. Fletcher 63 not out). Northamptonshire 129 (K.D. Boyce 7–36) and 172–5 (P.J. Watts 55)

SOMERSET (2:0/2) drew with MIDDLESEX (3:3/0) at Taunton. Middlesex 283–6d (M.J. Smith 147, N.G. Featherstone 54 not out). Rain.

WARWICKSHIRE (3:0/3) drew with SUSSEX (6:5/1) at Birmingham. Sussex 278–6d (A.W. Greig 72 not out, J.M. Parks 71). Warwickshire 92–3

YORKSHIRE (16:1/5) beat GLOUCESTERSHIRE (5:0/5) by 126 runs at Middlesbrough. Yorkshire 185 (R.A. Hutton 57 not out) and 173 (G. Boycott 68, M.J. Procter 6–56). Gloucestershire 135 (A.G. Nicholson 5–55) and 97

May 17th, 18th, 19th
DERBYSHIRE (8:4/4) drew with LEICESTERSHIRE (5:3/2) at Derby. Derbyshire 323–6d (P.J.K. Gibbs 122, I.W. Hall 81) and 185–6d. Leicestershire 254 (J.F. Steele 69) and 144–3 (B.F. Davison 65, B. Dudleston 53 not out)

WARWICKSHIRE (19:4/5) beat LANCASHIRE (3:1/2) by an innings and 41 runs at Manchester. Lancashire 181 (S.J. Rouse 5–47) and 149 (D.J. Brown 5–49). Warwickshire 371–7d (R.B. Kanhai 199, N.M. McVicker 65 not out, A.I. Kallicharran 53)

GLOUCESTERSHIRE (17:2/5) beat NORTHAMPTONSHIRE (5:1/4) by 6 wickets at Northampton. Northamptonshire 179 (M.J. Procter 5–16) and 250 (B.S. Crump 58, A. Tait 50). Gloucestershire 226 (M.J. Procter 74) and 206–4 (R.D.V. Knight 74, R.B. Nicholls 56)

NOTTINGHAMSHIRE (4:1/3) drew with SOMERSET (8:3/5) at Nottingham. Somerset 302–8d (M.J. Kitchen 74, P.W. Denning 51) and 107 (B.Stead 8–44 including hat-trick). Nottinghamshire 175 (R.A. White 61, M.J. Harris 51) and 135–6

SURREY (7:5/2) drew with WORCESTERSHIRE (6:4/2) at The Oval. Worcestershire 307–7d (B.L. D'Oliveira 107, J.A. Ormrod 56, P.J. Stimpson 52) and 201 (T.J. Yardley 59, R.D. Jackman 5–81). Surrey 310–7d (Younis Ahmed 112, G.R.J. Roope 89) and 171–4 (M.J. Stewart 79)

May 24th, 25th, 26th
ESSEX (5:3/2) drew with HAMPSHIRE (8:7/1) at Chelmsford. Hampshire 367 (C.G. Greenidge 124, R.E. Marshall 63, D.R. Turner 57, J.K. Lever 5–73) and 185–0d (B.A. Richards 104 not out, R.V. Lewis 71 not out). Essex 297–5d (B.E.A. Edmeades 73, G.J. Saville 70, K.W.R. Fletcher 62) and 198–5 (B.E.A. Edmeades 102)

GLAMORGAN (1:0/1) drew with WORCESTERSHIRE (0) at Cardiff. Worcestershire 85–2d and 93–3d. Glamorgan 0–0d and 81–4

MIDDLESEX (8:6/2) drew with NOTTINGHAMSHIRE (4:2/2) at Lord's. Nottinghamshire 289–7d (G.St.A. Sobers 71, J.B. Bolus 53, M.J. Smedley 51) and 209–4 (R.A. White 114 not out, M.J. Harris 51). Middlesex 394 (C.T. Radley 100, W.E. Russell 99, M.J. Smith 77, W. Taylor 5–87)

NORTHAMPTONSHIRE (5:0/5) drew with WARWICKSHIRE (7:5/2) at Northampton. Northamptonshire 238–8d (B.S. Crump 75 not out, G. Cook 71) and 264–4d (G. Cook 78, Mushtaq Mohammad 72 not out). Warwickshire 297 (R.B. Kanhai 121, J.A. Jameson 66, J.C.J. Dye 6–66) and 45–2

SOMERSET (5:3/2) drew with YORKSHIRE (8:3/5) at Taunton. Somerset 242 (T.W. Cartwright 93, R.A. Hutton 5–72) and 109–2 (D.B. Close 55 not out). Yorkshire 226–4 G. Boycott 122 not out)

May 27th, 29th, 30th
ESSEX (5:3/2) drew with WARWICKSHIRE (10:6/4) at Chelmsford. Warwickshire 303–5d (M.J.K. Smith 102, R.B. Kanhai 98) and 28–1. Essex 289–9d (B.E.A. Edmeades 78, K.W.R. Fletcher 70)

GLOUCESTERSHIRE (10:5/5) drew with SOMERSET (3:0/3) at Bristol. Gloucestershire 298–7d (M.J. Procter 118, D.R. Shepherd 71). Somerset 87 (J. Davey 5–24) and 146–4 (R.T. Virgin 59)

KENT (7:5/2) drew with SURREY (8:4/4) at Maidstone. Kent 302 (A.P.E. Knott 127 not out, R.A. Woolmer 57) and 216–5d (A.P.E. Knott 118 not out, B.W. Luckhurst 68). Surrey 297–7d (J.H. Edrich 168) and 128–5

Below: Keith Fletcher's consistent Championship performances for Essex resulted in his selection for the 1972-73 MCC tour
Bottom: Basil D'Oliveira – reliable as ever for Worcestershire

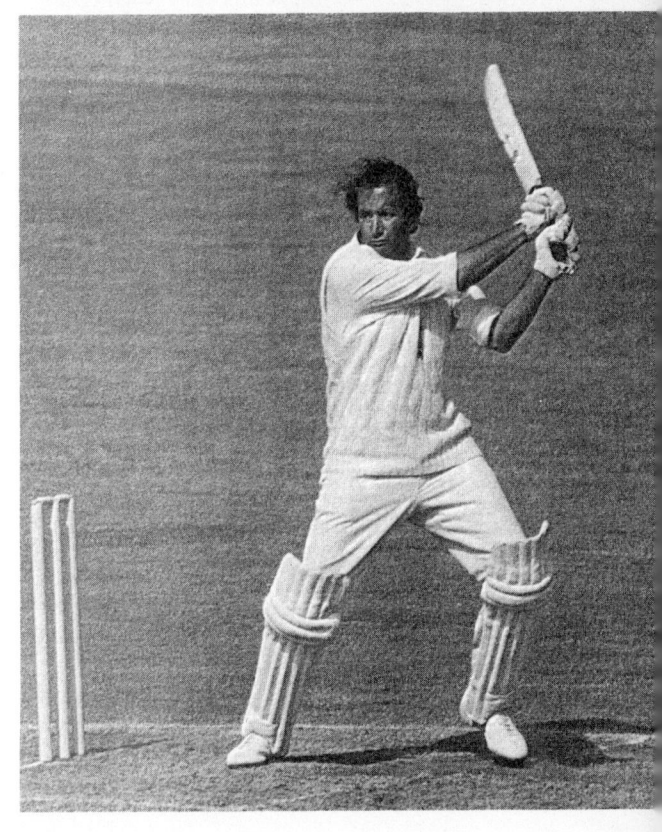

MIDDLESEX (19:4/5) beat SUSSEX (1:0/1) by 9 wickets at Lord's. Sussex 173 (P.J. Graves 68, R.M. Prideaux 58, M.W.W. Selvey 6–43) and 180 (A.W. Greig 62, J.S.E. Price 8–85). Middlesex 279–6d (M.J. Smith 136, P.H. Parfitt 52) and 76–1

HAMPSHIRE (16:3/3) beat NORTHAMPTONSHIRE (8:3/5) by 5 wickets at Northampton. Northamptonshire 247–7d (D.S. Steele 81, Mushtaq Mohammad 54) and 218–9d (G. Cook 65). Hampshire 238 (B.A. Richards 77, R.M.C. Gilliat 54) and 228–5 (B.A. Richards 69, R.E. Marshall 58, R.M.C. Gilliat 52)

LEICESTERSHIRE (18:3/5) beat NOTTINGHAMSHIRE (5:0/5) by 105 runs at Nottingham. Leicestershire 248 and 137–4d (B. Dudleston 70). Nottinghamshire 143 and 137

WORCESTERSHIRE (15:0/5) beat DERBYSHIRE (3:0/3) by 87 runs at Worcester. Worcestershire 247 and 143–6d (J.M. Parker 79). Derbyshire 109 (J. Cumbes 5–36) and 194 (C.P. Wilkins 51)

YORKSHIRE (8:3/5) drew with LANCASHIRE (4:1/3) at Leeds. Yorkshire 253–8d (G. Boycott 105) and 95–9d (P. Lever 5–27). Lancashire 190 (F.M. Engineer 69, A.G. Nicholson 7–49) and 36–2

May 31st, June 1st, 2nd
LANCASHIRE (12:0/2) beat KENT (0) by 5 wickets at Manchester. Kent 63–4d and 164–5d. Lancashire 20–0d and 208–5 (K.L. Snellgrove 71)

LEICESTERSHIRE (15:2/3) beat GLOUCESTERSHIRE (5:2/3) by 123 runs at Leicester. Leicestershire 303–7d (R.W. Tolchard 111 not out, G.D. McKenzie 51 not out) and 114–4d. Gloucestershire 201–7d (R.B. Nicholls 74) and 93 (J. Birkenshaw 7–30)

NOTTINGHAMSHIRE (7:2/5) drew with ESSEX (3:0/3) at Newark. Essex 119 and 236–7 (B.E.A. Edmeades 89, K.W.R. Fletcher 68, B. Stead 5–43). Nottinghamshire 277 (J.B. Bolus 78, D.W. Randall 78, K.D. Boyce 5–65)

SOMERSET (17:2/5) beat SURREY (1:0/1) by an innings and 8 runs at The Oval. Somerset 300–3d (R.T. Virgin 111, S.G. Wilkinson 69, P.W. Denning 54 not out). Surrey 124 (T.W. Cartwright 5–45) and 168 (Younis Ahmed 89)

WARWICKSHIRE (3:0/3) drew with NORTHAMPTONSHIRE (8:3/5) at Birmingham. Warwickshire 133 (J.C.J. Dye 6–41) and 209–8 (J.A. Jameson 78). Northamptonshire 246–7d (D.S. Steele 107 not out)

WORCESTERSHIRE (6:1/5) drew with MIDDLESEX (3:1/2) at Kidderminster. Worcestershire 252 (B.L. D'Oliveira 104 not out, F.J. Titmus 6–54) and 216–4d (E.J.O. Hemsley 92, J.A. Ormrod 67). Middlesex 192 (H.C. Latchman 96) and 253–9 (P.H. Parfitt 118)

YORKSHIRE (19:4/5) beat GLAMORGAN (3:0/3) by an innings and 124 runs at Scarborough. Yorkshire 345–8d (J.H. Hampshire 111, C.M. Old 64, D.L. Bairstow 52 not out). Glamorgan 86 (R.A. Hutton 5–27) and 135 (A.G. Nicholson 5–32)

June 7th, 8th, 9th
ESSEX (16:4/2) beat SOMERSET (5:1/4) by 9 wickets at Colchester. Somerset 239–9d (D.B. Close 88, S.G. Wilkinson 50, J.K. Lever 5–42) and 116 (S. Turner 5–39). Essex 250 (K.D. Boyce 74, B.E.A. Edmeades 54) and 106–1 (K.W.R. Fletcher 70 not out)

GLAMORGAN (5:0/5) drew with LEICESTERSHIRE (6:3/3) at Cardiff. Leicestershire 245 (B. Dudleston 79, M.A. Nash 6–64). Glamorgan 89–6d

HAMPSHIRE (7:2/5) drew with GLOUCESTERSHIRE (6:2/4) at Basingstoke. Gloucestershire 215 (M.J. Procter 87) and 88–4. Hampshire 223 (R.V. Lewis 51)

KENT (6:3/3) drew with DERBYSHIRE (5:2/3) at Tunbridge Wells. Kent 335–9d (M.H. Denness 113, G.W. Johnson 81, I.R. Buxton 5–51) and 154–5d (M.C. Cowdrey 52). Derbyshire 253 (A.J. Harvey-Walker 82) and 101–7

MIDDLESEX (7:2/5) drew with YORKSHIRE (6:2/4) at Lord's. Middlesex 227 (W.E. Russell 68, C.T. Radley 56) and 109–3. Yorkshire 212 (J.H. Hampshire 103)

NORTHAMPTONSHIRE (12:1/1) beat SUSSEX (6:3/3) by 9 wickets at Hove. Sussex 317–5d (G.A. Greenidge 83, J.M. Parks 81 not out, M.A. Buss 80) and 118. Northamptonshire 287–7d (Mushtaq Mohammad 118, G. Sharp 76 not out) and 149–1 (Mushtaq Mohammad 60 not out)

June 10th, 12th, 13th
SOMERSET (15:0/5) beat GLAMORGAN (1:0/1) by an innings and 25 runs at Swansea. Somerset 314–7d (D.B. Close 108). Glamorgan 145 (T.W. Cartwright 5–50) and 144

GLOUCESTERSHIRE (15:0/5) beat KENT (5:0/5) by 2 wickets at Tunbridge Wells. Kent 162 (M.H. Denness 50) and 153. Gloucestershire 132 (J.N. Shepherd 7–38) and 185–8 (Sadiq Mohammad 54, R.D.V. Knight 53)

LEICESTERSHIRE (15:0/5) beat SURREY (4:0/4) by 6 wickets at Leicester. Surrey 159 and 120. Leicestershire 140–8d (R.D. Jackman 5–49) and 142–4 (J.F. Steele 64)

HAMPSHIRE (13:1/2) beat MIDDLESEX (6:1/5) by 5 wickets at Lord's. Middlesex 296 (J.T. Murray 52) and 86 (R.S. Herman 5–47). Hampshire 190 (R.M.C. Gilliat 72, K.V. Jones 6–26) and 193–5 (R.M.C. Gilliat 50 not out)

WORCESTERSHIRE (14:9/5) drew with WARWICKSHIRE (1:0/1) at Worcester. Warwickshire 165 and 90–0 (J. Whitehouse 51 not out). Worcestershire 375–3d (G.M. Turner 156, R.G.A. Headley 94, E.J.O. Hemsley 79 not out)

YORKSHIRE (0) drew with DERBYSHIRE (0) at Sheffield. (Rain prevented play on first two days.) Derbyshire 121 (M.H. Page 55, C.M. Old 5–26). Yorkshire 116–8

June 17th, 19th, 20th
DERBYSHIRE (4:0/4) drew with YORKSHIRE (9:4/5) at Chesterfield. Yorkshire 276 (J.H. Hampshire 56, P.J. Sharpe 53) and 110–1d (G. Boycott 54 not out). Derbyshire 136 (A.J. Harvey-Walker 55, A.G. Nicholson 5–49) and 150–8

GLOUCESTERSHIRE (15:0/5) beat HAMPSHIRE (6:1/5) by 2 wickets at Gloucester. Hampshire 190 (B.A. Richards 64) and 218–8d (T.E. Jesty 50). Gloucestershire 164 (J.W. Holder 6–49) and 245–8 (M.J. Procter 100, R.B. Nicholls 80, J.W. Holder 7–79)

LANCASHIRE (3:0/3) drew with GLAMORGAN (6:2/4) at Manchester. Glamorgan 263 (R.C. Davis 114, A. Jones 56, P. Lever 7–70). Lancashire 143–9 (D.J. Shepherd 5–47)

NORTHAMPTONSHIRE (15:0/5) beat NOTTINGHAMSHIRE (5:0/5) by 9 wickets at Northampton. Nottinghamshire 136 and 119. Northamptonshire 148 (P.J. Watts 62) and 109–1 (G. Cook 63 not out)

John Player Cricket Yearbook 1973

Bob Herman left Middlesex for Hampshire, and in 1972 emerged as one of the outstanding young players of the season with fine Championship performances

SURREY (4:2/2) drew with KENT (5:3/2) at The Oval. Kent 354–6d (B.W. Luckhurst 184 not out, A.P.E. Knott 55) and 143–2d (B.W. Luckhurst 63 not out, D. Nicholls 52). Surrey 271–9d (S.J. Storey 78, G.P. Howarth 55) and 85–4

SUSSEX (8:5/3) drew with WORCESTERSHIRE (6:2/4) at Hove. Sussex 277 (A.W. Greig 112) and 165–3d (G.A. Greenidge 60). Worcestershire 202–6d (R.G.A. Headley 77) and 76–2

WARWICKSHIRE (18:3/5) beat MIDDLESEX (1:0/1) by 10 wickets at Birmingham. Middlesex 158 (C.T. Radley 63, N.M. McVicker 5–52) and 176 (L.R. Gibbs 6–77). Warwickshire 334–4d (D.L. Amiss 151 not out, M.J.K. Smith 74, A.I. Kallicharran 54) and 4–0

June 21st, 22nd, 23rd
DERBYSHIRE (5:3/2) drew with GLAMORGAN (5:4/1) at Derby. Derbyshire 302–5d (I.W. Hall 105, M.H. Page 82, C.P. Wilkins 55 not out) and 152–5d (P.J.K. Gibbs 55). Glamorgan 259–4d (R.C. Fredericks 70, A. Jones 64) and 110–6

ESSEX (16:1/5) beat SURREY (3:0/3) by 8 wickets at Ilford. Surrey 118 (K.D. Boyce 5–50) and 201 (R.M. Lewis 59). Essex 234 (S. Turner 53, R.D. Jackman 5–87) and 87–2

GLOUCESTERSHIRE (18:3/5) beat SUSSEX (3:1/2) by 230 runs at Gloucester. Gloucestershire 327–9d (R.D.V. Knight 103, D.R. Shepherd 59) and 170–2d (M.J. Procter 64 not out, R.D.V. Knight 54 not out). Sussex 184 (M.G. Griffith 66, M.J. Procter 5–20) and 83

WARWICKSHIRE (16:1/5) beat HAMPSHIRE (5:0/5) by 5 wickets at Portsmouth. Hampshire 79 and 284 (B.A. Richards 105, C.G. Greenidge 61, T.E. Jesty 56 not out). Warwickshire 177 (R.S. Herman 8–42) and 189–5 (R.B. Kanhai 121 not out)

The County Championship 1972

LEICESTERSHIRE (3:3/0) drew with LANCASHIRE (7:2/5) at Leicester. Leicestershire 249 (B.F. Davison 83, R.W. Tolchard 51 not out, J.F. Steele 50) and 131–1 (J.F. Steele 73 not out, B. Dudleston 50). Lancashire 383–5d (B. Wood 186, D. Lloyd 146)

NOTTINGHAMSHIRE (5:2/3) drew with KENT (7:3/4) at Nottingham. Kent 263 (M.C. Cowdrey 91, R.A. Woolmer 75) and 162–7d (R.A. White 5–56). Nottinghamshire 214–8d (M.J. Harris 67) and 165–7 (B. Hassan 95)

SOMERSET (5:0/5) drew with NORTHAMPTONSHIRE (6:1/5) at Bath. Northamptonshire 176 (P. Willey 71) and 194–7d. Somerset 109 (R.M.H. Cottam 6–35) and 185–8 (P.J. Robinson 55, R.M.H. Cottam 5–54)

June 24th, 26th, 27th

DERBYSHIRE (0) v LANCASHIRE (0) at Buxton Match abandoned without a ball being bowled.

GLAMORGAN (5:0/5) drew with SUSSEX (2:2/0) at Cardiff. Sussex 224 (J.M. Parks, 87 R.M. Prideaux 74). Glamorgan 13–0

LEICESTERSHIRE (5:0/5) drew with NOTTINGHAMSHIRE (6:1/5) at Leicester. Nottinghamshire 176 and 110 (J.B. Bolus 58, J. Birkenshaw 5–34). Leicestershire 143 (W. Taylor 6–75) and 120–7 (B. Stead 5–43).

NORTHAMPTONSHIRE (2:0/2) drew with SURREY (8:3/5) at Northampton. Northamptonshire 134 (Mushtaq Mohammad 60, R.D. Jackman 5–61) and 403–5d (D.S. Steele 131, Mushtaq Mohammad 120, A. Tait 67). Surrey 312 (G.R.J. Roope 122, R. M. Lewis 64) and 66–3

SOMERSET (4:2/2) drew with ESSEX (2:0/2) at Bath. Somerset 311–7d (R.T. Virgin 81, G.I. Burgess 63, M.J. Kitchen 50, S. Turner 5–65). Essex 139–5 (B.E.A. Edmeades 52, K.W.R. Fletcher 50 not out)

WORCESTERSHIRE (6:3/3) drew with GLOUCESTERSHIRE (8:6/2) at Worcester. Worcestershire 302–7d (E.J.O. Hemsley 79, P.J. Stimpson 63, G.M. Turner 51) and 9–0. Gloucestershire 300–7d (C.A. Milton 117, R.D.V. Knight 77, M.J. Procter 51)

YORKSHIRE (5:1/4) drew with WARWICKSHIRE (1:0/1) at Sheffield. Yorkshire 266 (R.G. Lumb 70). Warwickshire 60 and 114–4.

July 1st, 3rd, 4th

ESSEX (17:2/5) beat DERBYSHIRE (5:1/4) by 41 runs at Burton upon Trent. Essex 222 (B. Ward 53) and 171–5d (K.W.R. Fletcher 80). Derbyshire 193 (P.J.K. Gibbs 50, J.K. Lever 5–54) and 159

GLAMORGAN (6:2/4) drew with GLOUCESTERSHIRE (7:2/5) at Swansea. Gloucestershire 217 (J.B. Mortimore 53 not out). Glamorgan 201 (A.R. Lewis 78, J.B. Mortimore 7–62)

LEICESTERSHIRE (17:2/5) beat HAMPSHIRE (4:0/4) by 9 wickets in 2 days at Bournemouth. Hampshire 168 and 96 (J. Birkenshaw 5–28). Leicestershire 207 (R. Illingworth 57) and 61–1

LANCASHIRE (1:0/1) drew with NORTHAMPTONSHIRE (7:6/1) at Liverpool. Northamptonshire 333–3d (Mushtaq Mohammad 137 not out, D.S. Steele 76, P.J. Watts 72 not out). Lancashire 81–3

NOTTINGHAMSHIRE (7:2/5) drew with YORKSHIRE (5:3/2) at Worksop. Yorkshire 228 (G. Boycott 100, B. Stead 6–58) and 155–2 (G. Boycott 75 not out). Nottinghamshire 270 (M.J. Harris 101)

SURREY (6:5/1) drew with MIDDLESEX (4:3/1) at The Oval. Surrey 327–4d (Younis Ahmed 143, J.H. Edrich 96) and 229–1d (J.H. Edrich 127 not out including 101 before lunch on 3rd day, Younis Ahmed 53 not out). Middlesex 307–3d (P.H. Parfitt 129 not out, C.T. Radley 52) and 215–9 (J.M. Brearley 75, K.V. Jones 57 not out, P.I. Pocock 5–79).

SUSSEX (17:2/5) beat KENT (3:0/3) by 10 wickets at Hastings. Sussex 244 (A.W. Greig 94) and 13–0. Kent 54 (A.W. Greig 6–20) and 199 (M.C. Cowdrey 59 not out, A.W. Greig 5–26).

WARWICKSHIRE (11:8/3) drew with WORCESTERSHIRE (9:7/2) at Birmingham. Worcestershire 380–7d (G.M. Turner 122, E.J.O. Hemsley 61, T.J. Yardley 57 not out, B.L. D'Oliveira 52) and 201–4d (G.M. Turner 128 not out). Warwickshire 350–5d (D.L. Amiss 156 not out, A.I. Kallicharran 72) and 72–1.

July 5th, 6th, 7th

KENT (17:6/1) beat MIDDLESEX (7:4/3) by 7 wickets at Maidstone. Middlesex 312–7d (M.J. Smith 88, C.T. Radley 72, J.M. Brearley 54) and 253–7d (C.T. Radley 82, W.E. Russell 50). Kent 310–8d (B.W. Luckhurst 77, D. Nicholls 51) and 258–3 (B.W. Luckhurst 98 not out, A.G.E. Ealham 89).

LANCASHIRE (3:0/3) drew with ESSEX (4:3/1) at Southport. Essex 351–7d (K.W.R. Fletcher 85, S. Turner 61 not out, B.E.A. Edmeades 58, K.D. Boyce 57, R.E. East 53 not out). Lancashire 97–3.

July 8th, 10th, 11th

GLOUCESTERSHIRE (3:0/3) drew with SURREY (7:3/4) at Bristol. Surrey 228–6d (S.J. Storey 65 not out, A. Long 55) and 126–6d. Gloucestershire 134–8d (D.R. Shepherd 54 not out) and 121–5

HAMPSHIRE (2:0/2) drew with SOMERSET (3:1/2) at Bournemouth. Somerset 223 (D.B. Close 77, P.J. Sainsbury 5–61) and 105–6d. Hampshire 124–5d and 95–2.

KENT (7:5/2) drew with ESSEX (7:4/3) at Maidstone. Kent 275–6d (B.W. Luckhurst 77, A.P.E. Knott 62, M.H. Denness 50). Essex 352–8 (K.W.R. Fletcher 115, B. Ward 60, G.J. Saville 56)

LANCASHIRE (5:2/3) drew with SUSSEX (5:2/3) at Manchester. Lancashire 219–7d (K.L. Snellgrove 83, B. Wood 53) and 147–5d. Sussex 217–6d (G.A. Greenidge 81, J.M. Parks 58 not out) and 147–7

LEICESTERSHIRE (2:1/1) drew with NORTHAMPTONSHIRE (9:4/5) at Leicester. Northamptonshire 252–3d (Mushtaq Mohammad 122, D.S. Steele 109 not out) and 137–9d (D.S. Steele 59 not out). Leicestershire 194 (J.F. Steele 91, Mushtaq Mohammad 6–58) and 34–1.

NOTTINGHAMSHIRE (5:0/5) drew with DERBYSHIRE (5:0/5) at Nottingham. Nottinghamshire 149 (M. Hendrick 6–43) and 168–3d (M.J. Harris 67, B. Hassan 58). Derbyshire 131 (B. Stead 5–54) and 52–6

WARWICKSHIRE (15:1/4) beat GLAMORGAN (8:3/5) by 8 wickets at Birmingham. Glamorgan 226–9d (R.C. Davis 77 not out, A.C. Smith 5–47) and 220–3d (M.J. Khan 113, A.R. Lewis 51). Warwickshire 198 (J. Whitehouse 55, D.L. Williams 5–54) and 250–2 (R.B. Kanhai 123 not out, M.J.K. Smith 66 not out)

YORKSHIRE (5:2/3) drew with WORCESTERSHIRE (8:3/5) at Sheffield. Worcestershire 228–6d (G.M. Turner 76) and 133 (B.L. D'Oliveira 58, C.M. Old 5–39). Yorkshire 222 (R.G. Lumb 79) and 36–2.

July 12th, 13th, 14th

DERBYSHIRE (15:4/1) beat SUSSEX (7:3/4) by 3 wickets at Derby. Sussex 282–4d (R.M. Prideaux 169 not out, P.J. Graves 65) and 229–6d (P.J. Graves 77). Derbyshire 252 (I.W. Hall 72, C.P. Wilkins 52) and 261–7 (C.P. Wilkins 105, A.J. Harvey-Walker 57)

ESSEX (8:5/3) drew with MIDDLESEX (6:4/2) at Westcliff-on-Sea. Essex 306–8d (K.W.R. Fletcher 121, K.D. Boyce 63) and 201 (R.E. East 59, K.D. Boyce 55). Middlesex 292–9d (M.J. Smith 112, N.G. Featherstone 76, J.K. Lever 5–63) and 189–8 (W.E. Russell 54)

GLOUCESTERSHIRE (16:3/3) beat WORCESTERSHIRE (8:3/5) by 9 runs at Bristol. Gloucestershire 228 and 179 (R.D.V. Knight 97, J.A. Ormrod 5–27). Worcestershire 294–7d (G.M. Turner 170) and 104

KENT (18:4/4) beat NORTHAMPTONSHIRE (4:1/3) by 5 wickets at Dover. Northamptonshire 185 and 304–4d (D.S. Steele 106 not out, P.J. Watts 68 not out). Kent 295 (M.C. Cowdrey 107, B.D. Julien 59, R.M.H. Cottam 5–66) and 195–5 (B.D. Julien 90, Asif Iqbal 55 not out).

SURREY (17:2/5) beat HAMPSHIRE (3:0/3) by 126 runs at Guildford. Surrey 264 (G.R.J. Roope 69, Younis Ahmed 51) and 206–2d (Younis Ahmed 83 not out). Hampshire 171 (A.R. Butcher 6–48) and 173

WARWICKSHIRE (21:9/2) beat LANCASHIRE (2:2/0) by 35 runs at Birmingham. Warwickshire 423–3d (D.L. Amiss 192, R.B. Kanhai 165, J. Whitehouse 54) and 181–6d (R.B. Kanhai 54 J.A. Jameson 52). Lancashire 343–7d (D. Lloyd 99, J. Sullivan 64, H. Pilling 52, K.L. Snellgrove 51) and 226 (B. Wood 77)

July 15th, 17th, 18th

GLOUCESTERSHIRE (16:1/5) beat ESSEX (6:1/5) by 107 runs at Westcliff-on-Sea. Gloucestershire 184 (D.R. Shepherd 59, M.J. Procter 51) and 238 (M.J. Procter 102). Essex 178 (B.E.A. Edmeades 72) and 137 (M.J. Procter 5–30 including the hat-trick; all lbw bowling round the wicket).

Procter is the first player to score a century and take a hat-trick in the same first-class match in Britain since 1937, when E. Davies did so for Glamorgan v. Leicestershire at Leicester. It is only the tenth recorded instance in the history of first-class cricket. Only two other bowlers, H. Fisher for Yorkshire in 1932 and J.A. Flavell for Worcestershire in 1963, have taken an all-lbw hat-trick in a first-class match.

GLAMORGAN (7:5/2) drew with NOTTINGHAMSHIRE (7:4/3) at Cardiff. Nottinghamshire 291 (M.J. Smedley 108, J.W. Solanky 5–37) and 263–5d (M.J. Smedley 76, J.B. Bolus 66, D.W. Randall 61). Glamorgan 316–9d (A.R. Lewis 124, A. Jones 66) and 189–7 (M.J. Khan 116 not out)

HAMPSHIRE (5:2/3) drew with KENT (5:2/3) at Southampton. Kent 291 (M.C. Cowdrey 75, D. Nicholls 55, J.W. Holder did the hat-trick) and 174 (T.E. Jesty 5–37). Hampshire 267–7d (P.J. Sainsbury 72, R.E. Marshall 52, G.R. Stephenson 50 not out) and 106–4

MIDDLESEX (19:4/5) beat LANCASHIRE (4:2/2) by 7 wickets at Lord's. Lancashire 215 (J.D. Bond 103 not out, J.S.E. Price 5–33) and 180. Middlesex 348–6d (W.E. Russell 81, C.T. Radley 69, J.M. Brearley 50 not out) and 48–3

NORTHAMPTONSHIRE (16:1/5) beat YORKSHIRE (6:3/3) by 151 runs at Northampton. Northamptonshire 229 (Mushtaq Mohammad 90) and 254–9d (Mushtaq Mohammad 119, A. Tait 59). Yorkshire 227 (J.H. Hampshire 72) and 105

SURREY (4:1/3) drew with DERBYSHIRE (4:2/2) at The Oval. Surrey 267–7d (G.R.J. Roope 92 not out, R.M. Lewis 56) and 222–5d (D.R. Owen-Thomas 100 not out, R.M. Lewis 64). Derbyshire 282–8d (A.J. Harvey-Walker 63, R.W. Taylor 58 not out) and 104–5

SOMERSET (18:3/5) beat SUSSEX (2:0/2) by 110 runs at Hove. Somerset 301–6d (M.J. Kitchen 156) and 178–5d. Sussex 157 (M.A. Buss 67, A.A. Jones 9–51 – the best first-class analysis of the 1972 season) and 212 (R.M. Prideaux 50, M.A. Buss 50, T.W. Cartwright 6–91)

WORCESTERSHIRE (14:3/1) beat LEICESTERSHIRE (7:5/2) by 44 runs at Worcester. Worcestershire 337–8d (J.A. Ormrod 157 not out) and 240–6d (R.G.A. Headley 52, G.M. Turner 50). Leicestershire 323–4d (B. Dudleston 132, J.F. Steele 76, J.C. Balderstone 51) and 210 (J.C. Balderstone 81 not out, V.A. Holder 5–44)

July 22nd, 24th, 25th

ESSEX (15:1/4) beat WORCESTERSHIRE (3:1/2) by 90 runs at Worcester. Essex 316 (B. Ward 72, B.E.A. Edmeades 70, S. Turner 66, N. Gifford 7–66) and 87–9d (N. Gifford 5–20). Worcestershire 176 (J.A. Ormrod 57) and 137 (D.L. Acfield 5–42)

July 26th, 27th, 28th

DERBYSHIRE (6:1/5) drew with NORTHAMPTONSHIRE (5:0/5) at Chesterfield. Derbyshire 177 (B.S. Bedi 5–72) and 191 (M.H. Page 50, J.C.J. Dye 5–42, R.M.H. Cottam 5–60), Northamptonshire 97 (M. Hendrick 8–50) and 202–8 (B.S. Crump 113 not out)

WARWICKSHIRE (20:6/4) beat KENT (4:3/1) by 4 wickets at Dartford. Kent 311 (Asif Iqbal 64, D. Nicholls 50) and 272 (A.G.E. Ealham 67, M.H. Denness 52, L.R. Gibbs 5–80). Warwickshire 372–5d (R.B. Kanhai 115, M.J.K. Smith 87, D.L. Amiss 63) and 214–6 (D.L. Amiss 121 not out)

LEICESTERSHIRE (19:5/4) beat SOMERSET (4:2/2) by 83 runs at Taunton. Leicestershire 334 (M.E.J.C. Norman 122, R.W. Tolchard 71) and 177–2d (B. Dudleston 102 not out). Somerset 213 (D.B. Close 93) and 215 (H.R. Moseley 67, J. Birkenshaw 8–94)

SURREY (16:1/5) beat YORKSHIRE (4:0/4) by an innings and 12 runs in 2 days at The Oval. Yorkshire 96 (Intikhab Alam 6–22 including the hat-trick) and 133 (Intikhab Alam 6–56). Surrey 241 (M.J. Stewart 69, P.I. Pocock 52 not out, C.C. Clifford 5–70).

SUSSEX (10:7/3) drew with NOTTINGHAMSHIRE (4:2/2) at Hove. Sussex 346–4d (R.M. Prideaux 160, G.A. Greenidge 60, M.A. Buss 59) and 200–6d (J.D. Morley 76, M.G. Griffith 54 not out). Nottinghamshire 290 (J.B. Bolus 88, R.A. White 55 not out, M.A. Buss 6–68) and 240–9 (M.J. Harris 99, B. Hassan 52, C.P. Phillipson 6–56)

WORCESTERSHIRE (2:1/1) drew with LANCASHIRE (8:3/5) at Worcester. Worcestershire 190 and 212–7. Lancashire 399 (D. Lloyd 177, H. Pilling 82, N. Gifford 6–111)

July 29th, 31st, August 1st

LANCASHIRE (22:7/5) beat YORKSHIRE (2:0/2) by an innings and 34 runs at Manchester. Lancashire 358–4d (C.H. Lloyd 181, F.C. Hayes 71 not out, H. Pilling 65). Yorkshire 132 (D.P. Hughes 5–59) and 192 (R.G. Lumb 56, J.H. Hampshire 54, J. Simmons 6–50)

LEICESTERSHIRE (6:3/3) drew with DERBYSHIRE (7:2/5) at Leicester. Leicestershire 230 (M.E.J.C. Norman 55, G.D. McKenzie 55). Derbyshire 216–6 (C.P. Wilkins 104, A.J. Borrington 52)

The County Championship 1972

Above left: *Allan Jones of Somerset, whose 9-51 in the Sussex first innings at Hove was the best first-class analysis of the 1972 season*

Above: *Sussex were hampered in their Championship season by injuries to opening bowler Tony Buss*

Left: *Bob Cottam was another seam bowler who found success with his adopted county – in this case Northamptonshire – in 1972*

MIDDLESEX (7:3/4) drew with KENT (8:6/2) at Lord's. Middlesex 294 (C.T. Radley 96, M.J. Smith 53, J.N. Graham 5–87) and 166–7 (C.T. Radley 51, B.D. Julien 5–57). Kent 310–8d (G.W. Johnson 87, D. Nicholls 60, M.C. Cowdrey 51 not out)

NORTHAMPTONSHIRE (4:2/2) drew with WORCESTERSHIRE (4:0/4) at Northampton. Northamptonshire 288 (P.J. Watts 58, A. Tait 54). Worcestershire 143–4 (R.G.A. Headley 92)

NOTTINGHAMSHIRE (2:0/2) drew with HAMPSHIRE (10:6/4) at Nottingham. Hampshire 392–6d (B.A. Richards 118, R.E. Marshall 114 not out, D.R. Turner 73). Nottinghamshire 116–8

SOMERSET (5:2/3) drew with GLAMORGAN (11:8/3) at Taunton. Glamorgan 382–8d (M.J. Khan 191, A.R. Lewis 86, A.A. Jones 5–56) and 88–3d. Somerset 267 (T.W. Cartwright 55) and 165–6 (B.A. Langford 68 not out)

SURREY (3:3/0) drew with SUSSEX (1:0/1) at The Oval. Surrey 328–4d (D.R. Owen-Thomas 112, G.R.J. Roope 93 not out). Sussex 127–1 (P.J. Graves 69 not out)

WARWICKSHIRE (3:0/3) drew with GLOUCESTERSHIRE (5:3/2) at Birmingham. Gloucestershire 312–7d (D.R. Shepherd 106). Warwickshire 149–5 (M.J.K. Smith 55 not out)

August 5th, 7th, 8th
DERBYSHIRE (7:2/5) drew with NOTTINGHAMSHIRE (3:1/2) at Ilkeston. Derbyshire 257 (A.J. Borrington 63, C.P. Wilkins 50) and 86. Nottinghamshire 177 (R.S. Swindell 5–69) and 146–8

ESSEX (6:1/5) drew with LEICESTERSHIRE (4:1/3) at Leyton. Leicestershire 177 (R.W. Tolchard 61, J.F. Steele 51, K.D. Boyce 5–51) and 222–9. Essex 325 (B.E.A. Edmeades 163, R.E. East 53 not out)

GLOUCESTERSHIRE (3:2/1) drew with LANCASHIRE (8:3/5) at Cheltenham. Gloucestershire 218 (C.A. Milton 63) and 174–9 (P. Lee 5–32). Lancashire 354–7d (D. Lloyd 104, H. Pilling 94, C. H. Lloyd 72)

HAMPSHIRE (15:2/3) beat WORCESTERSHIRE (5:1/4) by 9 wickets at Portsmouth. Worcestershire 225 (B.L. D'Oliveira 69, G.M. Turner 56) and 90 (T.J. Mottram 5–45). Hampshire 253 (R.S. Herman 56, B.L. D'Oliveira 5–84) and 63–1.

KENT (15:4/1) beat GLAMORGAN (4:2/2) by 7 wickets at Canterbury. Glamorgan 318–4d (A. Jones 152 not out, M.A. Nash 59, M.J. Khan 56) and 164 (M.J. Khan 96 not out, R.A. Woolmer 6–42). Kent 302–7d (M.H. Denness 162, M.C. Cowdrey 63) and 181–3 (B.W. Luckhurst 79)

MIDDLESEX (4:0/4) drew with SURREY (8:4/4) at Lord's. Surrey 276–9d (G.R.J. Roope 55) and 171–5d (J.H. Edrich 79 not out). Middlesex 206 (J.T. Murray 84) and 154–7 (P.H. Parfitt 74)

SOMERSET (6:1/5) drew with WARWICKSHIRE (3:0/3) at Weston-super-Mare. Somerset 217 (D.B. Close 108, N.M.McVicker 5–46) and 81–3. Warwickshire 151

YORKSHIRE (2:0/2) drew with SUSSEX (3:1/2) at Bradford. Sussex 283–5d (R.M. Prideaux 69, J.M. Parks 51 not out). Yorkshire 128–5

August 9th, 10th, 11th
ESSEX (2:2/0) drew with WORCESTERSHIRE (8:4/4) at Leyton. Essex 275 (G.J. Saville 92, R.E. East 89 not out, V.A. Holder 5–93) and 234–6d (K.R.Pont 75 not out, G.J. Saville 50). Worcestershire 303–9d (G.M. Turner 154, J.M. Parker 91, K.D. Boyce 5–52) and 93–3

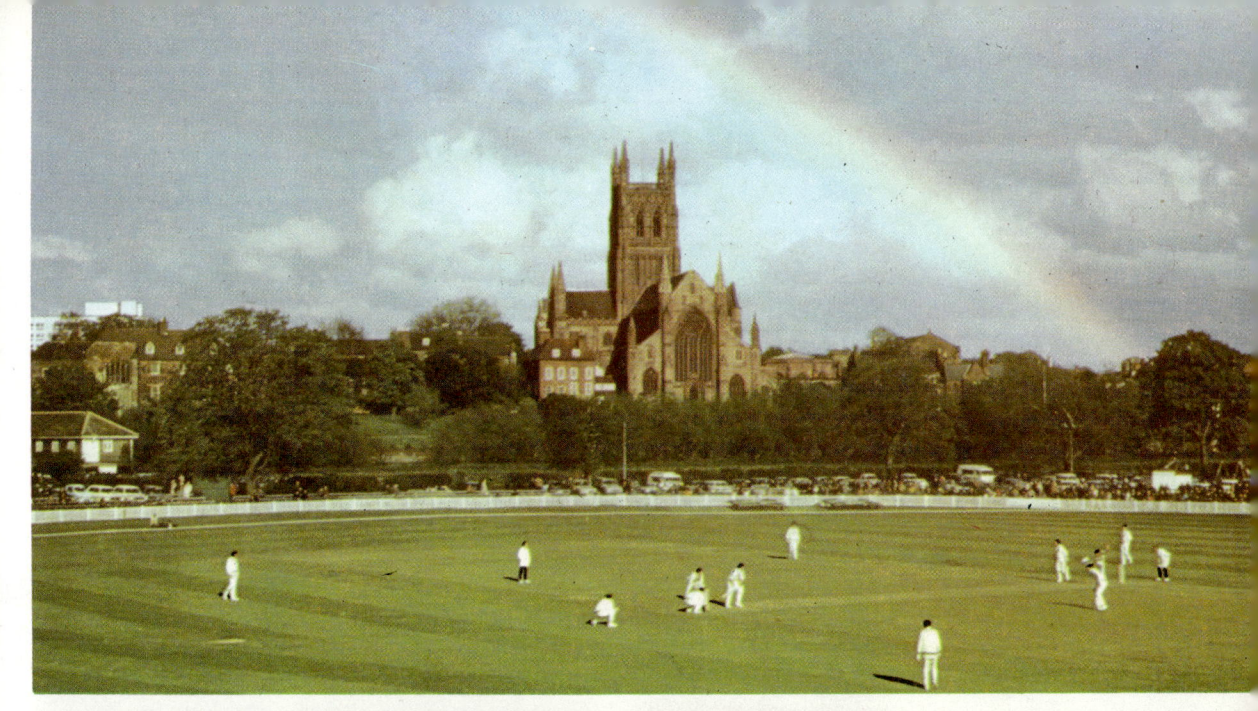

Top: *A rainbow adds further charm to the County Ground, Worcester, where cricket is played under the protective majesty of a most famous cathedral*

Above: *Leicestershire's Jack Birkenshaw, capped by England on the 1972–73 tour of India and Pakistan*

Left: *The majestic Majid Khan, the only batsman to score 2,000 runs in first-class cricket in 1972*

Left: Leicestershire's ultra-aggressive Brian Davison hammers the Sussex bowling to the square-leg boundary. His batting was a major factor in his county's success in one-day matches in 1972, but his first-class record, by comparison with that of 1971, was disappointing

Below: The St Lawrence Ground at Canterbury, headquarters of Kent CCC and home of the Canterbury Festival. This ground, with its famous lime tree standing inside the boundary, has witnessed the feats of such great Kent players as Woolley Chapman, Ames, Evans and Cowdrey

GLOUCESTERSHIRE (18:3/5) beat DERBYSHIRE (4:1/3) by 5 wickets at Cheltenham. Derbyshire 176 and 232 (C.P. Wilkins 111, D.A. Graveney 5–63). Gloucestershire 303 (M.J. Procter 95, R.B. Nicholls 82) and 106–5

GLAMORGAN (16:3/3) beat HAMPSHIRE (4:1/3) by 4 wickets at Portsmouth. Hampshire 216 (P.J. Sainsbury 56) and 210 (C.G. Greenidge 71). Glamorgan 258–9d (A. Jones 137) and 169–6 (G.P. Ellis 54)

KENT (16:3/3) beat SUSSEX (4:3/1) by 9 wickets at Canterbury. Sussex 243 (R.A. Woolmer 6–70) and 193 (R.A. Woolmer 7–65). Kent 372–5d (B.W. Luckhurst 92, M.H. Denness 76, G.W. Johnson 75, Asif Iqbal 61 not out) and 65–1

NORTHAMPTONSHIRE (18:3/5) beat MIDDLESEX (3:0/3) by an innings and 65 runs in 2 days at Lord's. Northamptonshire 250 (Mushtaq Mohammad 110 not out). Middlesex 96 (J.C.J. Dye 6–47) and 89

SOMERSET (10:5/5) drew with LANCASHIRE (4:1/3) at Weston-super-Mare. Somerset 350–9d (M.J. Kitchen 139, D.B. Close 65). Lancashire 196 (H. Pilling 118) and 351–3 (D. Lloyd 155 not out, C.H. Lloyd 100)

WARWICKSHIRE (24*:9/5) beat NOTTINGHAMSHIRE (9:4/5) by 9 wickets at Coventry. Nottinghamshire 263 (D.W. Randall 72, J.B. Bolus 65) and 144 (M.J. Smedley 59 not out). Warwickshire 388 (A.I. Kallicharran 164, D.L. Amiss 120, D.L. Murray 54) and 20–1
*Record number of points obtained from one match since present scoring system began in 1968.

YORKSHIRE (15:1/4) beat SURREY (3:1/2) by 9 wickets at Scarborough. Surrey 206 (Younis Ahmed 93) and 130. Yorkshire 296 (P.J. Squires 64, B. Leadbeater 53, C. Johnson 53, P.I. Pocock 5–71) and 41–1

August 12th, 14th, 15th
DERBYSHIRE (2:0/2) drew with HAMPSHIRE (7:4/3) at Derby. Hampshire 354–8d (R.E. Marshall 203, B.A. Richards 52, P.J. Sainsbury 51). Derbyshire 195 and 179–7 (P.J.K. Gibbs 62)

ESSEX (22:8/4) beat GLAMORGAN (7:7/0) by 2 wickets at Swansea. Glamorgan 338–9d (R.C. Fredericks 119, M.J. Khan 108, M.A. Nash 52) and 299 (A. Jones 87, M.J. Khan 79, R.N.S. Hobbs 7–118). Essex 350–1d (K.W.R. Fletcher 181 not out, G.J. Saville 126 not out) and 290–8 (K.D. Boyce 78, K.W.R. Fletcher 65, B. Ward 61)

MIDDLESEX (16:2/4) beat GLOUCESTERSHIRE (6:3/3) by 6 wickets at Cheltenham. Gloucestershire 260 (Zaheer Abbas 75, J.S.E. Price 7–40) and 177 (Zaheer Abbas 58, F.J. Titmus 5–56). Middlesex 288 (C.T. Radley 72, H. Pearman 61, J.T. Murray 50) and 150–4

LANCASHIRE (7:5/2) drew with NOTTINGHAMSHIRE (2:2/0) at Manchester. Nottinghamshire 315–6d (J.B. Bolus 140 not out, M.N.S. Taylor 58) and 230–5d (B. Hassan 78 not out, J.B. Bolus 50). Lancashire 275–1d (D. Lloyd 126 not out, H. Pilling 117 not out) and 149–5 (F.C. Hayes 60, D.P. Hughes 51 not out)

LEICESTERSHIRE (2:0/2) drew with YORKSHIRE (4:1/3) at Leicester. Yorkshire 310–7d (G. Boycott 204 not out, J. Birkenshaw 5–81) and 146–6d. Leicestershire 231 (M.E.J.C. Norman 68) and 141–4

NORTHAMPTONSHIRE (5:0/5) drew with SOMERSET (3:0/3) at Wellingborough. Northamptonshire 226 (T.W. Cartwright 5–104) and 210–5d (B.S. Crump 69 not out). Somerset 173 (B.S. Bedi 6–24) and 154–8 (T.W. Cartwright 59 not out)

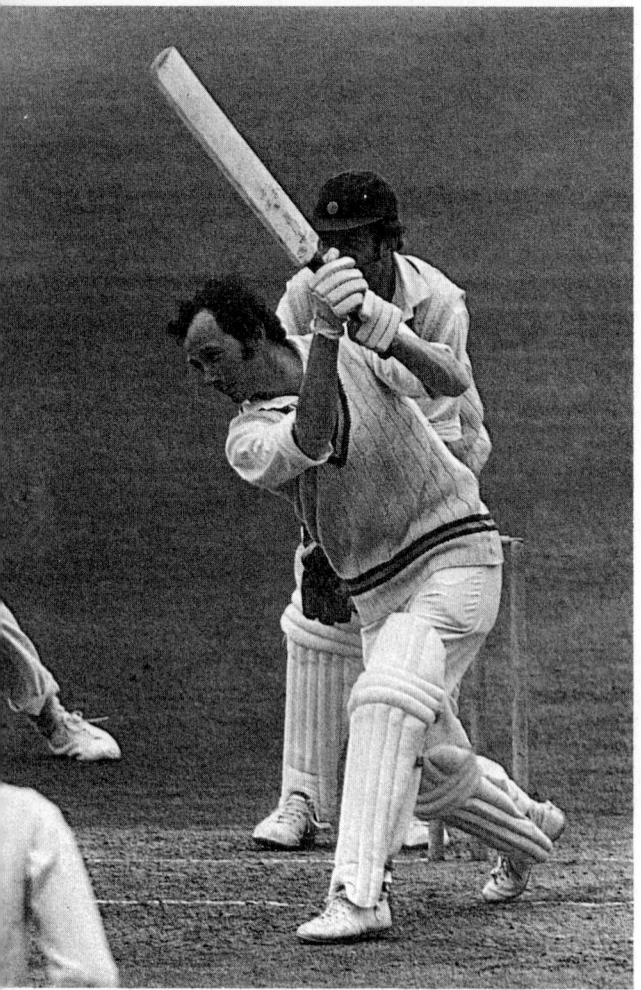

Mike Smedley, although making some good scores for Nottinghamshire in 1972, failed to reproduce his form of the previous summer

SUSSEX (5:3/2) drew with SURREY (8:6/2) at Eastbourne. Surrey 300–4d (M.J. Edwards 81, R.M. Lewis 72) and 130–5d. Sussex 226–5d (R.M. Prideaux 106 not out) and 202–9 (R.M. Prideaux 97, G.A. Greenidge 68, P.I. Pocock 7–67 – including the hat-trick, 4 wickets in 4 balls, 5 in 6 balls, 6 in 9 balls and 7 in 11 balls)

KENT (18:6/2) beat WORCESTERSHIRE (6:4/2) by 3 wickets at Worcester. Worcestershire 347–8d (P.J. Stimpson 88, J.M. Parker 59) and 141 (J.N. Shepherd 5–24). Kent 346–5d (Asif Iqbal 106, B.W. Luckhurst 80, M.C. Cowdrey 57 not out, M.H. Denness 57) and 146–7

August 19th, 21st, 22nd
ESSEX (17:5/2) beat YORKSHIRE (7:4/3) by 6 wickets at Chelmsford. Yorkshire 285–6d (G. Boycott 121) and 239–5d (G. Boycott 86). Essex 282–7d (K.D. Boyce 86, K.R. Pont 52) and 246–4 (K.W.R. Fletcher 139 not out)

MIDDLESEX (19:4/5) beat DERBYSHIRE (2:1/1) by an innings and 61 runs at Lord's. Derbyshire 198 and 166 (F.J. Titmus 5–72). Middlesex 425–6d (P.H. Parfitt 129, C.T. Radley 109, N.G. Featherstone 58 not out, J.M. Brearley 56)

NORTHAMPTONSHIRE (6:1/5) drew with LEICESTERSHIRE (5:1/4) at Northampton. Leicestershire 187 (P. Willey 5–49) and 266–8d (R.W. Tolchard 65, P.R. Haywood 60). Northamptonshire 204 (D.S. Steele 78) and 128–6

NOTTINGHAMSHIRE (9:4/5) drew with LANCASHIRE (4:2/2) at Nottingham. Nottinghamshire 365–9d (M.J. Smedley 131, B. Hassan 89, B. Stead 53 not out) and 176–2d (B. Hassan 75, J.B. Bolus 52 not out). Lancashire 218 (C.H. Lloyd 111, H. Pilling 72, W. Taylor 5–37) and 262–8 (D.P. Hughes 77, H. Pilling 62)

SOMERSET (9:4/5) drew with GLOUCESTERSHIRE (3:0/3) at Taunton. Gloucestershire 94 and 484–7 (R.B. Nicholls 90, M.J. Procter 74, D.R. Shepherd 74, A.S. Brown 63 not out, Zaheer Abbas 59). Somerset 331 (D.B. Close 135)

HAMPSHIRE (19:4/5) beat SUSSEX (5:2/3) by 156 runs at Hove. Hampshire 289 (C.G. Greenidge 142, J.A. Snow 6–82) and 224–2d (C.G. Greenidge 68, R.M.C. Gilliat 63 not out, R.V. Lewis 61 not out). Sussex 200 (R.M. Prideaux 80, M.G. Griffith 56) and 157 (A.W. Greig 88 n.o.)

WARWICKSHIRE (22:7/5) beat SURREY (5:0/5) by 9 wickets at Birmingham. Surrey 143 and 237 (R.M. Lewis 78, J.H. Edrich 75). Warwickshire 344 (A.I. Kallicharran 149 – incl 124 before lunch on 2nd day, M.J.K. Smith 71) and 37–1

WORCESTERSHIRE (20:5/5) beat GLAMORGAN (4:1/3) by an innings and 23 runs in 2 days at Worcester. Worcestershire 399–8d (R.G.A. Headley 131, J.A. Ormrod 80). Glamorgan 176 (V.A. Holder 5–47) and 200 (R.C. Fredericks 68, A. Jones 59, N. Gifford 6–78).

August 23rd, 24th, 25th
NORTHAMPTONSHIRE (18:3/5) beat ESSEX (2:0/2) by 164 runs at Chelmsford. Northamptonshire 258 (P.J. Watts 69, P. Willey 68, D.S. Steele 68, R.N.S. Hobbs 5–85) and 184–5d (Mushtaq Mohammad 68 not out). Essex 140 (Mushtaq Mohammad 6–38) and 138 (B.S. Bedi 7–34)

KENT (15:1/4) beat HAMPSHIRE (11:6/5) by 5 wickets at Folkestone. Hampshire 317 (B.A. Richards 101, T.E. Jesty 80, B.D. Julien 5–104) and 198–8d (T.E. Jesty 52). Kent 179 (M.H. Denness 52, R.S. Herman 5–55, T.J. Mottram 5–80) and 338–5 (M.H. Denness 146, Asif Iqbal 97 not out)

WORCESTERSHIRE (20:6/4) beat NOTTINGHAMSHIRE (6:4/2) by 4 wickets at Nottingham. Nottinghamshire 282 (R.A. White 59, M.J. Harris 54, V.A. Holder 6–60) and 308–2d (M.J. Harris 174 not out, B. Hassan 75). Worcestershire 320–5d (J.M. Parker 118, P.J. Stimpson 66, G.M. Turner 53) and 271–6 (G.M. Turner 107)

SURREY (4:3/1) drew with GLAMORGAN (9:5/4) at The Oval. Glamorgan 374–8d (M.J. Khan 204, P.M. Walker 60, R.C. Fredericks 50) and 183–4d (R.C. Fredericks 107). Surrey 261 (S.J. Storey 92 n.o. P.I. Pocock 50) and 252–8 (S.J. Storey 65)

SUSSEX (14:1/3) beat LEICESTERSHIRE (6:1/5) by 7 wickets at Hove. Leicestershire 263 (J. Birkenshaw 77, B. Dudleston 66) and 224–5d (B.F. Davison 78 not out, B. Dudleston 52). Sussex 187 (R.B. Matthews 7–51) and 301–3 (G.A. Greenidge 142 not out, R.M. Prideaux 100)

YORKSHIRE (17:3/4) beat MIDDLESEX (4:1/3) by 98 runs at Leeds. Yorkshire 266 (A.J. Dalton 128) and 173. Middlesex 206 and 135

August 26th, 28th, 29th
NORTHAMPTONSHIRE (14:4/0) beat GLAMORGAN (9:6/3) by 29 runs at Swansea. Northamptonshire 300 (P.J. Watts 75 not out, Mushtaq Mohammad 59, P. Willey 51, R.C. Davis 5–55) and 293–4d (D.S. Steele 73 not out, G. Cook 63, P.J. Watts 51 not out). Glamorgan 346–2d (R.C. Fredericks 228 not out, A. Jones 105) and 218 (M.J. Khan 66, A.R. Lewis 60, R.M.H. Cottam 5–52)

HAMPSHIRE (8:6/2) drew with LANCASHIRE (5:2/3) at Bournemouth. Lancashire 301 (D. Lloyd 116, F.C. Hayes 51) and 247–5d (H. Pilling 94, J. Sullivan 81 not out). Hampshire 309 (C.G. Greenidge 85, T.E. Jesty 77) and 183–8 (B.A. Richards 83, R.E. Marshall 63)

LEICESTERSHIRE (18:3/5) beat ESSEX (6:2/4) by 7 wickets at Leicester. Essex 222 (B. Ward 52, G.D. McKenzie 5–45) and 273 (B. Taylor 83). Leicestershire 248 and 248–3 (B. Dudleston 116 not out, J.G. Tolchard 53)

SOMERSET (3:2/1) drew with KENT (8:6/2) at Glastonbury. Kent 351–5d (B.W. Luckhurst 142, Asif Iqbal 77, M.H. Denness 69) and 234–5d (A.G.E. Ealham 105, M.C. Cowdrey 101 not out). Somerset 345–6d (B.C. Rose 125, M.J. Kitchen 69) and 154–7

SURREY (17:2/5) beat NOTTINGHAMSHIRE (5:0/5) by 21 runs at The Oval. Surrey 214 (A. Long 51) and 229–8d (J.H. Edrich 64, Younis Ahmed 64, M.J. Edwards 56). Nottinghamshire 148 (B. Hassan 52, Intikhab Alam 5–25) and 274 (B. Hassan 111, M.J. Smedley 55, P.I. Pocock 5–107)

MIDDLESEX (13:1/2) beat SUSSEX (7:3/4) by 3 wickets at Hove. Sussex 345 (M.G. Griffith 78, J.M. Parks 56) and 144–8d. Middlesex 236 and 257–7 (C.T. Radley 55, N.G. Featherstone 55)

August 30th, 31st, September 1st
SOMERSET (16:3/3) beat DERBYSHIRE (6:2/4) by 2 wickets at Chesterfield. Derbyshire 292–9d (J.F. Harvey 98, P.J.K. Gibbs 70, T.W. Cartwright 8–94) and 91 (T.W. Cartwright 5–14). Somerset 257 (R.T. Virgin 121, M. Hendrick 7–65) and 127–8

GLAMORGAN (6:3/3) drew with MIDDLESEX (6:3/3) at Cardiff. Middlesex 306 (P.H. Parfitt 72) and 243–4d (M.J. Smith 64, P.H. Parfitt 58). Glamorgan 319 (R.C. Fredericks 126, M.A. Nash 82) and 137–6

NOTTINGHAMSHIRE (16:2/4) beat GLOUCESTERSHIRE (6:1/5) by 42 runs at Bristol. Nottinghamshire 217 (B. Hassan 85, B. Stead 58) and 178 (M.J. Smedley 69 not out). Gloucestershire 201 and 152

HAMPSHIRE (10:5/5) drew with SUSSEX (4:0/5) at Bournemouth. Sussex 146 and 359–5d (M.A. Buss 94, G.A. Greenidge 89, J.M. Parks 70 not out, A.W. Greig 62). Hampshire 292 (R.V. Lewis 61, T.E. Jesty 53) and 110–4 (C.G. Greenidge 56)

LEICESTERSHIRE (8:3/5) drew with WARWICKSHIRE (3:1/2) at Leicester. Leicestershire 331–9d (J.G. Tolchard 66, P.R. Haywood 64, B.F. Davison 63, N.M. McVicker 6–72) and 165–8d (J.F. Steele 51). Warwickshire 197 (R.B. Kanhai 53) and 171–8 (M.J.K. Smith 58)

KENT (23:8/5) beat YORKSHIRE (5:0/5) by an innings and 81 runs in 2 days at Bradford. Yorkshire 98 and 183 (D.L. Underwood 8–70). Kent 362 (B.W. Luckhurst 109, Asif Iqbal 67, C.M. Old 6–69)

September 6th, 7th, 8th
WARWICKSHIRE (13:8/5) drew with DERBYSHIRE (6:1/5) at Birmingham. Derbyshire 188 (M.H. Page 125, R.G.D. Willis 8–44 including the hat-trick) and 97–5. Warwickshire 351 (R.B. Kanhai 124, D.J. Brown 79)

September 9th, 11th, 12th
GLOUCESTERSHIRE (3:0/3) drew with GLAMORGAN (9:4/5) at Bristol. Gloucestershire 168 (Zaheer Abbas 62) and 289–9d (D.R. Shepherd 78 not out, R.D.V. Knight 62). Glamorgan 273 (M.J. Khan 116) and 105–7 (J.B. Mortimore 5–25)

HAMPSHIRE (1:0/1) drew with YORKSHIRE (9:4/5) at Southampton. Yorkshire 255–3d (G. Boycott 105, R.G. Lumb 70). Hampshire 147 and 224–3 (B.A. Richards 82, R.E. Marshall 69 not out)

LANCASHIRE (9:5/4) drew with DERBYSHIRE (3:1/2) at Blackpool. Lancashire 282–5d (B. Wood 150, D. Lloyd 57) and 77–3d. Derbyshire 177–9d (A. Hill 82, J. Simmons 7–65) and 81–5

WARWICKSHIRE (14:0/4) beat NOTTINGHAMSHIRE (10:5/5) by 4 wickets at Nottingham. Nottinghamshire 294 (M.N.S. Taylor 71, P.A. Todd 66 r.h.) and 26–0d. Warwickshire 169 (N.M. McVicker 53, W. Taylor 6–42) and 154–6

Other First-Class Matches 1972

Cambridge University
Played 8   Won 1   Lost 3   Drawn 4

April 26th, 27th, 28th LEICESTERSHIRE beat CAMBRIDGE U. by 8 wickets at Cambridge
Cambridge U. 260–7 declared (R.P. Hodson 84, M.J. Khan 54, P.D. Johnson 54 not out) and 148 (P.D. Johnson 56). Leicestershire 249–7 declared (B.F. Davison 82, J. Spencer 5–28) and 162–2 (J.F. Steele 65, R.W. Tolchard 59 not out)

May 3rd, 4th, 5th CAMBRIDGE U. drew with WARWICKSHIRE at Cambridge
Warwickshire 277–9 declared (M.J.K. Smith 119) and 101–1 (A.I. Kallicharran 53 not out). Cambridge U. 198 (W. Snowden 104)

May 10th, 11th, 12th CAMBRIDGE U. drew with WORCESTERSHIRE at Cambridge
Cambridge U. 243 (H.K. Steele 68, M.J. Khan 67, N. Gifford 7–49) and 140 (M.J. Khan 70 not out, N. Gifford 7–27). Worcestershire 241–5 declared (G.M. Turner 111, J.M. Parker 61) and 91–5

May 17th 18th, 19th CAMBRIDGE U. drew with GLAMORGAN at Cambridge
Glamorgan 265–8 declared (K.J. Lyons 92) and 265–5 declared (P.M. Walker 61 not out, R.C. Davis 55 not out, A. Jones 55). Cambridge U. 257–4 declared (M.J. Khan 109 not out, D.R. Owen-Thomas 61 not out) and 178–9 (W. Snowden 57)

June 7th, 8th, 9th SURREY beat CAMBRIDGE U. by 8 wickets at Cambridge
Cambridge 216 (M.J. Khan 139) and 120. Surrey 274–9 declared (G.R.J. Roope 83) and 64–2

June 10th, 12th, 13th CAMBRIDGE U. drew with SUSSEX at Cambridge
Cambridge U. 248 (H.K. Steele 103 not out, D.R. Owen-Thomas 57, J. Denman 5–45) and 195–7 declared (R.P. Hodson 66). Sussex 153 (M.G. Griffith 57, R.J. Hadley 5–31) and 183–5 (M.A. Buss 57, R.M. Prideaux 53 not out)

June 28th, 29th, 30th GLAMORGAN beat CAMBRIDGE U. by 6 wickets at Swansea
Cambridge U. 177 (D.R. Owen-Thomas 81, H.K. Steele 56, D.L. Williams 5–18) and 207 (J. Spencer 55). Glamorgan 274–7 declared (M.J. Llewellyn 112 not out, A.E. Cordle 81) and 111–4

July 1st, 3rd, 4th CAMBRIDGE U. beat OXFORD U. by an innings and 25 runs at Lord's
Cambridge U. 280–6 declared (D.R. Owen-Thomas 114 not out, W. Snowden 51)
Oxford U. 121 (J. Spencer 5–21) and 134 (M.P. Kendall 6–43)
This was the first win by either university in this match since 1966 and the first by Cambridge since 1958.

Oxford University
Played 13 Won 1 Lost 7 Drawn 5

April 22nd, 24th, 25th LEICESTERSHIRE beat OXFORD U. by 8 wickets at Oxford
Oxford U. 133 and 207. Leicestershire 239–9 declared and 104–2

April 26th, 27th, 28th OXFORD U. beat WARWICKSHIRE by 2 wickets at Oxford
Warwickshire 237 and 266–4 declared (R.B. Kanhai 167 not out, M.J.K. Smith 80). Oxford U. 286–6 declared (M.G. Heal 124 not out, M.J.J. Faber 57) and 218–8 (A.K.C. Jones 62, D. Williams 52)

April 29th, May 1st, 2nd OXFORD U. drew with HAMPSHIRE at Oxford
Oxford U. 150–9 declared and 39–2. Hampshire 233–4 declared (B.A. Richards 77, C.G. Greenidge 67)

May 3rd, 4th DERBYSHIRE beat OXFORD U. by 9 wickets at Oxford
Oxford U. 153 and 98. Derbyshire 234–2 declared (I.W. Hall 136 not out, P.J.K. Gibbs 76) and 19–1

May 6th, 8th, 9th OXFORD U. drew with MIDDLESEX at Oxford
Oxford U. 188 (R.J. Lee 68, F.J. Titmus 5–33). Middlesex 31–2

May 13th, 15th, 16th OXFORD U. drew with NOTTINGHAMSHIRE at Oxford
Nottinghamshire 216–4 declared (M.J. Harris 82, M.J. Smedley 70) and 65–2 declared. Oxford U. 117–8 declared (M.N.S. Taylor 6–46) and 143–8 (P.J. Plummer 7–71)

May 17th, 18th ESSEX beat OXFORD U. by an innings and 90 runs at Oxford
Oxford U. 89 and 116 (R.N.S. Hobbs 6–57). Essex 295–6 declared

May 20th, 22nd NORTHAMPTONSHIRE beat OXFORD U. by an innings and 105 runs at Oxford. Oxford U. 55 (R.M.H. Cottam 8–14) and 89 (Mushtaq Mohammad 5–36). Northamptonshire 249–5 declared (D.S. Steele 122)

May 24th, 25th, 26th LEICESTERSHIRE beat OXFORD U. by 44 runs at Oxford
Leicestershire 289–9 declared (J.F. Steele 126, P.R. Haywood 63) and 149–5 declared. Oxford U. 125 (J. Birkenshaw 5–33) and 269 (C.B. Hamblin 123 not out)

June 3rd, 5th, 6th LANCASHIRE beat OXFORD U. by 5 wickets at Oxford
Oxford U. 255 and 161. Lancashire 271–8 declared (F.C. Hayes 74, B. Wood 53, M.J.D. Stallibrass 5–80) and 146–5 (B. Wood 52)

June 7th, 8th, 9th OXFORD U. drew with WORCESTERSHIRE at Oxford
Worcestershire 248–5 declared (E.J.O. Hemsley 74) and 102–5. Oxford U. 187 (C.B. Hamblin 65)

June 21st, 22nd, 23rd YORKSHIRE drew with OXFORD U. at Harrogate
Oxford U. 173 (G.A. Cope 6–40) and 133. Yorkshire 190–6 declared (B. Leadbeater 71, J.H. Hampshire 56) and 115–8

July 1st, 3rd, 4th CAMBRIDGE U. beat OXFORD U. by an innings and 25 runs at Lord's (*see Cambridge U. section for scores*)

Combined Universities

June 14th, 15th, 16th AUSTRALIANS beat COMBINED UNIVERSITIES by 10 wickets at Oxford (*see Australian Tour section for scores*)

MCC v Surrey

April 26th, 27th, 28th MCC drew with SURREY at Lord's
MCC 285–6 declared (M. H. Denness 82, A.W. Greig 62, B.W. Luckhurst 50) and 181–7 declared (M.H. Denness 68, B.W. Luckhurst 54 not out). Surrey 266–8 declared (J.H. Edrich 124) and 133–4 (M.J. Edwards 59 not out)

Scotland v Ireland

June 24th, 25th, 26th SCOTLAND drew with IRELAND at Greenock
Scotland 219–4 declared (T.B. Racionzer 58 not out, D.S. Mackintosh 57) and 74–6 declared. Ireland 106 (G.F. Goddard 8–34) and 163–9

CAMBRIDGE UNIVERSITY AVERAGES 1972

BATTING and FIELDING

	M	I	NO	HS	Runs	Av	100	50	Ct	St
M.J. Khan†	9	16	2	139	742	53.00	2	5	9	–
D.R. Owen-Thomas†	7	13	2	114*	431	39.18	1	4	1	–
W. Snowden†	7	12	0	104	347	28.91	1	2	1	–
H.K. Steele†	9	15	1	103*	400	28.57	1	2	3	–
R.P. Hodson†	8	14	0	84	345	24.64	–	2	4	–
P.D. Johnson†	9	15	2	58*	276	21.23	–	3	4	–
J. Spencer†	9	15	3	55	179	14.91	–	1	1	–
P.H. Edmonds†	9	15	1	42	166	11.85	–	–	13	–
C.R.V. Taylor†	9	15	1	25	97	6.92	–	–	18	3
M.P. Kendall†	7	9	3	13	39	6.50	–	–	–	–
R.J. Hadley †	8	11	5	8*	13	2.16	–	–	2	–

Also batted: I. Coomaraswamy 0, 0; N.G.H. Draffan 3, 0, 1, 0 (1 ct); A.M. Hutson 0*; S.A. Woolfries 3.

BOWLING

	O	M	R	W	Av	5 wI	BB
J. Spencer†	234.3	83	490	31	15.80	2	5–21
R.J. Hadley	155	52	425	14	30.35	1	5–31
M.P. Kendall†	168	43	451	14	32.21	1	6–43
M.J. Khan†	273	81	625	16	39.06	–	3–33
P.H. Edmonds†	341.4	107	812	20	40.60	–	4–93

Also bowled: R.P. Hodson† 17–4–34–2; A.M. Hutson 18–1–54–0; P.D. Johnson† 12–0–58–0; D.R. Owen-Thomas† 5–1–21–1; W. Snowden† 0.3–0–4–0; H.K. Steele† 115–35–288–3.

*Not out   †Blue 1972
Note: these figures include the Combined Oxford & Cambridge Universities XI v Australians match at Oxford

OXFORD UNIVERSITY AVERAGES 1972

BATTING and FIELDING

	M	I	NO	HS	Runs	Av	100	50	Ct	St
C.B. Hamblin†	13	22	4	123*	526	29.22	1	1	6	–
M.J.J. Faber†	12	23	2	57	477	22.71	–	1	7	–
A.K.C. Jones†	11	20	1	62	403	21.21	–	1	1	–
M.G. Heal†	13	24	1	124*	440	19.13	1	–	5	–
J.M. Ward†	4	7	0	56	121	17.28	–	1	2	–
R.J. Lee†	11	20	0	68	344	17.20	–	1	6	–
M.C. Wagstaffe†	13	23	7	42	233	14.56	–	–	5	–
D. Williams	11	20	0	52	291	14.55	–	1	5	–
R.G.L. Paver	5	9	1	30	116	14.50	–	–	6	3
R.C. Kinkead-Weekes†	4	8	1	25*	72	10.28	–	–	6	1
C.J. Sutton Mattocks	4	8	0	37	78	9.75	–	–	1	–
P.C.H. Jones†	13	23	3	24*	191	9.55	–	–	7	–
M.J.D. Stallibrass	8	13	1	13	68	5.66	–	–	3	–
S.C. Corlett†	4	7	1	11*	29	4.83	–	–	3	–
R.E.D. Storer	4	6	3	9	13	4.33	–	–	2	–
B. May†	3	5	0	14	18	3.60	–	–	1	–
A.D. Leech	9	11	4	8*	24	3.42	–	–	3	–

Also batted: W.J. Maidlow 45, 1, 0, 7 (2 ct); A.R. Wingfield Digby 7, 35, 4.

BOWLING

	O	M	R	W	Av	5 wI	BB
D. Williams	34	8	110	5	22.00	–	3–16
M.J.D. Stallibrass	96.4	25	305	13	23.46	1	5–80
S.C. Corlett†	112	36	274	11	24.90	–	4–34
M.C. Wagstaffe†	373.1	135	870	28	31.07	–	4–96
R.J. Lee†	230	46	660	17	38.82	–	4–56
A.D. Leech	158.5	24	521	12	43.41	–	3–40
A.R. Wingfield Digby	91	25	246	5	49.20	–	3–98
C.B. Hamblin†	245	37	787	14	56.21	–	3–33

Also bowled: M.J.J. Faber† 1–1–0–0; M.G. Heal† 1–0–3–0; A.K.C. Jones† 1.3–0–7–0; P.C.H. Jones† 9.2–0–58–1.

*Not out   †Blue 1972
Note: these figures include the Combined Oxford & Cambridge Universities XI v Australians match at Oxford

First-Class Averages 1972

BATTING (Qualification: 8 innings, average 10)   *Not out

	M	I	NO	HS	Runs	Av	100s	50s
G. Boycott	13	22	5	204*	1,230	72.35	6	4
R.B. Kanhai	21	30	5	199	1,607	64.28	8	3
Majid J. Khan	21	38	4	204	2,074	61.00	8	9
Mushtaq Mohammad	23	40	7	137*	1,949	59.06	6	8
K.W.R. Fletcher	22	36	6	181*	1,763	58.76	5	10
D.L. Amiss	18	29	7	192	1,219	55.40	5	1
B.W. Luckhurst	20	37	6	184*	1,706	55.03	3	12
D.S. Steele	22	39	8	131	1,618	52.19	5	7
G.M. Turner	21	38	4	170	1,764	51.88	7	6
D.B. Close	20	33	6	135	1,396	51.70	3	7
R.M. Prideaux	22	39	6	169*	1,596	48.36	4	8
D. Lloyd	22	37	5	177	1,510	47.18	6	3
E.J.O. Hemsley	9	15	3	92	565	47.08	–	5
B. Wood	21	34	5	186	1,341	46.24	2	8
H. Pilling	17	30	5	118	1,137	45.48	2	8
A.W. Greig	16	27	4	112	1,031	44.82	1	9
B.A. Richards	19	33	1	118	1,425	44.53	4	8
M.J.K. Smith	22	34	6	119	1,247	44.53	2	8
J.H. Edrich	18	33	3	168	1,305	43.50	4	4
Asif Iqbal	15	25	5	106	868	43.40	1	7
M.C. Cowdrey	19	33	8	107	1,080	43.20	2	8
A.I. Kallicharran	22	33	6	164	1,153	42.70	2	5
A.P.E. Knott	15	23	5	127*	765	42.50	2	4
R.E. Marshall	18	31	6	203	1,039	41.56	2	5
C.T. Radley	22	37	3	112	1,413	41.55	3	11
C.H. Lloyd	18	26	4	181	895	40.68	3	2
M.J. Procter	19	33	3	118	1,219	40.63	3	7
R.C. Fredericks	21	35	5	228*	1,199	39.96	4	3
J.M. Parker	15	26	4	118	869	39.50	1	4
M.H. Denness	21	35	1	162	1,339	39.38	3	10
G.R.J. Roope	22	38	7	122	1,202	38.77	1	7
P.H. Parfitt	20	35	5	129*	1,154	38.46	3	7
R.W. Tolchard	24	37	11	111*	979	37.65	1	5
J.M. Parks	22	37	10	87	1,014	37.55	–	7
B. Dudleston	22	41	6	132	1,303	37.22	3	6
B.E.A. Edmeades	22	37	2	163	1,257	35.91	2	9
B.L. D'Oliveira	15	26	4	107	784	35.63	2	4
D.R. Owen-Thomas	17	31	4	114*	962	35.62	3	4

M.E.J.C. Norman	7	12	0	122	427	35.58	1	2
A. Jones	22	37	4	152*	1,169	35.42	3	6
Younis Ahmed	21	38	3	143	1,232	35.20	2	6
R.M. Lewis	14	24	1	78	807	35.08	–	6
I.W. Hall	11	21	2	136*	665	35.00	2	2
B. Hassan	21	38	2	111	1,253	34.80	1	9
M.J. Smith	21	38	1	147	1,271	34.35	3	5
M.J. Harris	18	31	1	174*	1,020	34.00	2	8
J. Sullivan	5	9	2	81*	236	33.71	–	2
J.A. Ormrod	23	41	8	157*	1,105	33.48	1	4
J.B. Bolus	22	39	5	140*	1,135	33.38	1	8
C.G. Greenidge	22	38	1	142	1,230	33.24	2	6
G.A. Greenidge	22	40	3	142*	1,213	32.78	2	7
C.P. Wilkins	20	35	3	111	1,033	32.28	4	4
M.J. Smedley	22	38	4	131	1,082	31.82	2	6
P.J. Watts	21	34	6	75*	890	31.78	–	8
R.E. East	21	22	5	89*	538	31.64	–	4
M.J. Llewellyn	6	9	2	112*	221	31.57	1	–
M.J. Kitchen	21	35	0	156	1,098	31.37	2	4
J.F. Steele	24	44	1	126	1,347	31.32	1	10
R.G.A. Headley	19	32	1	131	961	31.00	1	5
J.H. Hampshire	19	30	2	111	867	30.96	2	4
D.R. Turner	17	27	2	131	766	30.64	1	2
R.D.V. Knight	21	37	1	103	1,100	30.55	1	6
B.S. Crump	18	27	7	113*	608	30.40	1	3
M.G. Griffith	22	35	10	78	757	30.28	–	6
J.M. Brearley	22	37	8	75	877	30.24	–	4
A.R. Lewis	14	22	3	124	574	30.21	1	4
K.D. Boyce	22	34	0	86	1,023	30.08	–	8
F.C. Hayes	19	27	8	74	563	29.63	–	4
C.B. Hamblin	13	22	4	123*	526	29.22	1	1
N.G. Featherstone	13	22	4	76	523	29.05	–	4
B.F. Davison	24	41	4	83	1,074	29.02	–	7
D.R. Shepherd	21	36	4	106	927	28.96	1	6
W. Snowden	7	12	0	104	347	28.91	1	2
A.G.E. Ealham	15	26	5	105	604	28.76	1	3
P.J.K. Gibbs	21	39	0	122	1,119	28.69	1	5
H.K. Steele	9	15	1	103*	400	28.57	1	2
P.J. Sainsbury	21	31	9	72	628	28.54	–	3
B.J. Booth	16	26	6	44	568	28.40	–	–
R.V. Lewis	14	27	5	71*	624	28.36	–	4
K. Shuttleworth	15	10	6	28*	113	28.25	–	–
R.A. Woolmer	19	23	7	75	449	28.06	–	2
R.G. Lumb	14	22	0	79	611	27.77	–	4
G.St.A. Sobers	6	9	1	71	222	27.75	–	1
W.E. Russell	16	28	1	99	749	27.74	–	5
C.A. Milton	14	24	1	117	637	27.69	1	1
R.A. White	22	36	7	114*	801	27.62	1	3
P.R. Haywood	23	32	5	100*	745	27.59	1	4
F.M. Engineer	16	18	6	69	331	27.58	–	1
D.L. Murray	14	21	6	54	412	27.46	–	1
S.J. Storey	21	35	10	92*	682	27.28	–	4
B. Leadbeater	19	31	3	71	761	27.17	–	2
M.H. Page	18	33	4	125	787	27.13	1	3

First-Class Averages 1972

T.E. Jesty	17	23	2	80	566	26.95	–	6
R. Illingworth	17	26	6	57	538	26.90	–	3
K.L. Snellgrove	10	14	0	83	375	26.78	–	3
D.L. Acfield	12	11	9	33*	52	26.00	–	–
G. Cook	20	36	2	78	880	25.88	–	6
G.J. Saville	22	36	3	126*	853	25.84	1	5
J.T. Murray	19	29	1	84	722	25.78	–	4
G.W. Johnson	20	36	2	87	858	25.23	–	4
Zaheer Abbas	8	14	0	75	353	25.21	–	4
K.R. Pont	12	17	5	75*	300	25.00	–	2
S.G. Wilkinson	9	14	2	69	299	24.91	–	2
R.P. Hodson	8	14	0	84	345	24.64	–	2
P.J. Stimpson	14	24	2	88	540	24.54	–	4
B. Ward	22	34	3	72	757	24.41	–	6
M.A. Buss	22	39	1	94	925	24.34	–	6
P.J. Graves	22	37	1	77	874	24.27	–	4
P. Willey	21	31	4	71	652	24.14	–	3
J. Whitehouse	18	30	2	55	674	24.07	–	3
D.E.R. Stewart	6	12	2	40	238	23.80	–	–
K.J. Lyons	7	8	2	92	142	23.66	–	1
K.J. O'Keeffe	21	28	10	43*	419	23.27	–	–
M.J. Edwards	19	36	2	121	791	23.26	1	3
R.B. Nicholls	20	35	0	90	807	23.05	–	5
D.W. Randall	15	26	2	78	550	22.91	–	3
R.C. Davis	22	31	4	114	617	22.85	1	2
B.A. Langford	19	24	10	68*	320	22.85	–	1
M.A. Nash	23	28	3	82	569	22.76	–	3
K.W. Wilkinson	10	14	6	49*	182	22.75	–	–
I.R. Buxton	20	36	10	46*	591	22.73	–	–
D. Nicholls	20	38	1	60	841	22.72	–	6
M.J.J. Faber	12	23	2	57	477	22.71	–	1
J.B. Mortimore	21	28	12	53*	355	22.18	–	1
D.P. Hughes	21	20	5	77	330	22.00	–	2
A. Tait	16	27	0	67	589	21.81	–	4
P.J. Sharpe	11	17	0	53	370	21.76	–	1
P.M. Walker	19	26	9	61*	370	21.76	–	2
R.M.C. Gilliat	20	32	5	72	575	21.29	–	5
J.D. Morley	12	16	4	76	255	21.25	–	1
R.T. Virgin	22	38	1	121	786	21.24	2	2
P.D. Johnson	9	15	2	58*	276	21.23	–	3
A.K.C. Jones	11	20	1	62	403	21.21	–	1
S. Turner	22	30	7	66	483	21.00	–	3
R.A. Hutton	21	30	4	57*	544	20.92	–	1
B.D. Julien	18	24	4	90	414	20.70	–	2
B. Taylor	22	33	3	83	616	20.53	–	3
G.D. McKenzie	23	26	7	55	390	20.52	–	2
A. Long	23	29	6	55	469	20.39	–	2
J.G. Tolchard	13	21	1	66	406	20.30	–	2
G.P. Ellis	6	12	1	54	223	20.27	–	1
J.D. Bond	20	18	3	103*	301	20.06	1	–
G.R. Stephenson	22	29	5	50*	481	20.04	–	1
Sadiq Mohammad	21	36	2	54	679	19.97	–	1
A.J. Harvey-Walker	15	27	1	82	514	19.76	–	4
J.A. Jameson	19	32	2	78	592	19.73	–	3

P.W. Denning	20	31	3	54*	550	19.64	–	2
M.N.S. Taylor	22	33	7	71	508	19.53	–	2
A.J. Borrington	7	13	0	63	251	19.30	–	2
M.J. Stewart	16	27	3	79	463	19.29	–	2
M.G. Heal	13	24	1	124*	440	19.13	1	–
A.C. Smith	17	17	5	28	227	18.91	–	–
J. Birkenshaw	24	31	1	77	566	18.86	–	2
K.V. Jones	20	29	4	57*	466	18.64	–	1
E.W. Jones	22	26	10	33	298	18.62	–	–
J.A. Hopkins	6	9	0	42	166	18.44	–	–
R.S. Swindell	10	14	6	38	147	18.37	–	–
R.D. Jackman	23	24	12	43	216	18.00	–	–
T.J. Yardley	22	34	6	59	504	18.00	–	2
J.W. Solanky	11	15	3	45*	215	17.91	–	–
T.W. Cartwright	21	31	3	93	497	17.75	–	3
A.E. Cordle	14	14	2	81	212	17.66	–	1
G.I. Burgess	18	30	1	63	501	17.27	–	1
R.J. Lee	11	20	0	68	344	17.20	–	1
N. Gifford	21	23	6	46*	291	17.11	–	–
F.J. Titmus	22	27	8	49	324	17.05	–	–
C. Johnson	20	28	4	53	409	17.04	–	1
N. Nanan	7	12	3	44	153	17.00	–	–
C.M. Old	15	21	3	64	302	16.77	–	1
N.M. McVicker	22	25	6	65*	318	16.73	–	2
H.R. Moseley	16	18	4	67	234	16.71	–	1
J.N. Shepherd	20	27	7	51	333	16.65	–	1
G. Sharp	20	25	5	76*	327	16.35	–	1
A.S. Brown	20	30	4	63*	420	16.15	–	1
R.W. Taylor	22	35	10	58*	402	16.08	–	1
H.G. Wilcock	19	21	6	39	238	15.86	–	–
J.F. Harvey	14	24	1	98	364	15.82	–	1
P.I. Pocock	23	27	5	52*	342	15.54	–	2
B. Stead	22	30	6	58	367	15.29	–	2
D.J.S. Taylor	21	25	8	43	260	15.29	–	–
D.J. Brown	17	17	4	79	195	15.00	–	1
I.N. Johnson	5	8	3	27	75	15.00	–	–
P.J. Squires	8	14	0	64	210	15.00	–	1
J. Simmons	21	16	5	26	164	14.90	–	–
H.C. Latchman	17	24	5	96	283	14.89	–	1
M.C. Wagstaffe	13	23	7	42	233	14.56	–	–
D. Williams	11	20	0	52	291	14.55	–	1
R.G.L. Paver	5	9	1	30	116	14.50	–	–
Intikhab Alam	18	24	3	59	304	14.47	–	1
J.S.E. Price	23	23	5	34	251	13.94	–	–
F.W. Swarbrook	15	21	2	46*	262	13.78	–	–
R.N.S. Hobbs	23	27	6	37	279	13.28	–	–
D.R. O'Sullivan	11	15	7	33	102	12.75	–	–
P.H. Edmonds	13	19	3	42	203	12.68	–	–
D.L. Bairstow	21	27	4	52*	284	12.34	–	1
H.P. Cooper	8	12	4	47	98	12.25	–	–
J.K. Lever	22	19	7	38*	143	11.91	–	–
J. Denman	15	16	1	24	177	11.80	–	–
V.A. Holder	21	28	6	23*	139	11.58	–	–
M. Bissex	7	12	1	23	126	11.45	–	–

J.M. Rice	9	9	0	26	102	11.33	–	–
J. Spencer	23	29	6	55	252	10.95	–	1
G. Frost	9	16	0	37	175	10.93	–	–
P.J. Plummer	10	12	2	37	107	10.70	–	–
J.A. Snow	14	17	1	48	171	10.68	–	–
D. Breakwell	5	8	0	35	83	10.37	–	–
A.G. Nicholson	18	19	8	31	114	10.36	–	–
R.C. Kinkead-Weekes	4	8	1	25*	72	10.28	–	–
D.L. Underwood	18	19	7	23*	120	10.00	–	–

BOWLING (Qualification: 10 wickets in 10 innings)

	O	M	R	W	Av	BB	5wI	10wM
A. Ward	164.5	35	506	31	16.32	4–45	–	–
M.J. Procter	426.1	107	960	58	16.55	6–56	4	1
C.M. Old	378.5	101	931	54	17.24	6–69	3	–
C.T. Spencer	164	46	333	19	17.52	3–14	–	–
G.A. Cope	221.5	97	407	23	17.69	6–40	1	–
J.C.J. Dye	530.1	132	1,427	79	18.06	6–41	4	–
R.M.H. Cottam	364.3	109	918	50	18.36	8–14	6	1
T.W. Cartwright	863	373	1,827	98	18.64	8–94	6	1
N. Gifford	580	157	1,395	74	18.85	7–27	6	2
A.G. Nicholson	547.3	152	1,203	62	19.40	7–49	4	–
A.S. Brown	387.2	109	955	49	19.48	4–27	–	–
Mushtaq Mohammad	408.2	135	1,130	57	19.82	6–38	3	–
R. Illingworth	376.3	105	778	39	19.94	4–29	–	–
K.D. Boyce	616.1	131	1,657	82	20.20	7–36	6	–
B. Stead	747	173	1,998	98	20.38	8–44	5	1
Sadiq Mohammad	197.4	31	673	33	20.39	4–40	–	–
B.S. Bedi	661	258	1,533	75	20.44	7–34	4	–
R.A. Hutton	413.3	87	1,109	54	20.53	5–27	2	–
J.B. Mortimore	635.3	188	1,398	68	20.55	7–62	2	–
R.A. Woolmer	363	90	906	44	20.59	7–65	3	1
V.A. Holder	636.2	131	1,647	79	20.84	6–60	4	–
D.L. Underwood	652.4	227	1,485	71	20.91	8–70	3	2
H.P. Cooper	226.2	51	549	26	21.11	4–37	–	–
R.S. Herman	730.1	190	1,755	81	21.66	8–42	3	–
J.A. Snow	418.5	103	1,086	50	21.72	6–82	3	–
J.S.E. Price	555.5	116	1,566	72	21.75	8–85	3	1
J. Birkenshaw	830.3	224	1,976	90	21.95	8–94	6	1
J.K. Lever	535.2	110	1,399	61	22.93	5–42	4	–
M. Hendrick	527.1	130	1,334	58	23.00	8–50	3	1
J. Simmons	605	209	1,565	68	23.01	7–65	2	2
W. Taylor	483.4	75	1,527	65	23.49	6–42	4	1
J. Cumbes	174.3	32	498	21	23.71	5–36	1	–
N.M. McVicker	580.1	159	1,571	66	23.80	6–72	3	–
P.I. Pocock	696.2	178	2,010	83	24.21	7–67	4	–
J.W. Holder	323	59	971	40	24.27	7–79	2	1
A.C. Smith	233.2	73	540	22	24.54	5–47	1	–
R.D. Jackman	699.1	141	2,076	84	24.71	5–49	4	–
D.L. Williams	534.1	144	1,375	55	25.00	5–18	3	–
G.D. McKenzie	609.3	143	1,578	63	25.04	5–30	2	–
A.A. Jones	437	84	1,281	51	25.11	9–51	2	1
B.L. D'Oliveira	270.5	69	607	24	25.29	5–24	2	–

Intikhab Alam	433	110	1,294	51	25.37	6–22	3	1
A.R. Butcher	106	22	281	11	25.54	6–48	1	–
C.C. Clifford	266.5	103	666	26	25.61	5–70	1	–
T.E. Jesty	385.4	105	865	33	26.21	5–37	1	–
D.J. Brown	369.2	78	973	37	26.29	5–49	1	–
B.F. Davison	158.3	41	396	15	26.40	3–57	–	–
K. Higgs	565.2	158	1,328	50	26.56	4–31	–	–
J. Davey	416.2	83	1,144	43	26.60	5–24	1	–
R.R. Bailey	197.1	46	559	21	26.61	4–32	–	–
A.W. Greig	468.2	130	1,102	41	26.87	6–20	2	1
P.J. Sainsbury	597.1	220	1,317	49	26.87	5–61	1	–
I.R. Buxton	399.4	143	916	34	26.94	5–51	1	–
P. Lee	434.1	94	1,267	47	26.95	5–32	1	–
R.B. Matthews	166.2	37	543	20	27.15	7–51	1	–
C.E. Waller	154	35	439	16	27.43	4–36	–	–
L.R. Gibbs	596.1	162	1,428	52	27.46	6–77	2	–
S.J. Rouse	321.3	58	989	36	27.47	5–47	1	–
M.A. Nash	589.4	137	1,761	64	27.51	6–64	2	–
D.L. Acfield	243	74	525	19	27.63	5–42	1	–
H.R. Moseley	357	73	915	33	27.72	4–26	–	–
S. Turner	530.3	131	1,256	45	27.91	5–39	2	–
J. Spencer	599.5	157	1,577	56	28.16	5–21	2	–
D. Lloyd	134	53	339	12	28.25	4–70	–	–
A.E. Cordle	241.5	49	681	24	28.37	3–24	–	–
M.N.S. Taylor	546.5	152	1,474	51	28.90	6–46	1	–
G.I. Burgess	235.3	52	610	21	29.04	4–80	–	–
K.V. Jones	443.3	110	1,236	42	29.42	6–26	1	–
R.D.V. Knight	152	34	443	15	29.53	3–45	–	–
D.R. O'Sullivan	394.5	164	866	29	29.86	4–53	–	–
R.J. Hadley	155	52	425	14	30.35	5–31	1	–
F.J. Titmus	721.5	202	1,732	57	30.38	6–54	4	–
C.P. Wilkins	245.5	57	639	21	30.42	4–50	–	–
P.E. Russell	472.3	149	1,219	40	30.47	4–58	–	–
J.N. Shepherd	591.2	165	1,469	48	30.60	7–38	2	–
G.G. Arnold	401	89	1,016	33	30.78	4–62	–	–
B.D. Julien	461.2	84	1,517	49	30.95	5–57	2	–
R.G.D. Willis	297.1	66	901	29	31.06	8–44	1	–
R.S. Swindell	237.2	54	808	26	31.07	5–69	1	–
M.C. Wagstaffe	373.1	135	870	28	31.07	4–96	–	–
D.J. Shepherd	281	102	593	19	31.21	5–47	1	–
K. Shuttleworth	367	69	1,106	35	31.60	4–38	–	–
M.P. Kendall	168	43	451	14	32.21	6–43	1	–
R.A. White	527.3	157	1,392	43	32.37	5–56	1	–
R.G.M. Carter	317.4	62	1,053	32	32.90	4–63	–	–
D.P. Hughes	636	209	1,745	53	32.92	6–100	2	–
M.W.W. Selvey	597.1	146	1,549	47	32.95	6–43	1	–
J.N. Graham	501.5	103	1,421	43	33.04	5–87	1	–
L.R. Worrell	175.2	40	435	13	33.46	4–33	–	–
P. Willey	385.2	94	1,005	30	33.50	5–49	1	–
P.J. Plummer	153	32	570	17	33.52	7–71	1	–
J.M. Rice	236.2	53	688	20	34.40	4–64	–	–
M.A. Buss	468.3	138	1,417	41	34.56	6–68	2	–
D. Wilson	271	84	731	21	34.80	4–83	–	–
R.N.S. Hobbs	483.5	114	1,534	44	34.86	7–118	3	1

First-Class Averages 1972

G.W. Johnson	379.5	118	1,051	30	35.03	3–28	–	–
P. Lever	297.3	72	772	22	35.09	7–70	2	–
M.K. Bore	239	106	531	15	35.40	3–56	–	–
P.H. Edmonds	526	177	1,214	34	35.70	4–64	–	–
T.J.P. Eyre	140.2	29	397	11	36.09	3–46	–	–
J.F. Steele	397.4	145	903	25	36.12	4–88	–	–
R.E. East	523.5	151	1,304	36	36.22	4–25	–	–
B. Wood	273.3	77	764	21	36.38	3–62	–	–
K.W. Wilkinson	252.2	42	801	22	36.40	3–57	–	–
P.M. Walker	392.3	107	1,081	29	37.27	4–49	–	–
R.C. Davis	486.3	88	1,543	41	37.63	5–55	1	–
D. Wilde	211	61	570	15	38.00	3–27	–	–
J. Denman	323.1	67	1,027	27	38.03	5–45	1	–
J.A. Ormrod	174	27	647	17	38.05	5–27	1	–
R.J. Lee	230	46	660	17	38.82	4–56	–	–
C.P. Phillipson	295	62	838	21	39.90	6–56	1	–
F.W. Swarbrook	338	89	946	23	41.13	3–24	–	–
H.C. Latchman	298.2	54	1,180	28	42.14	4–57	–	–
U.C. Joshi	531.5	142	1,520	36	42.22	4–56	–	–
A.D. Leech	158.5	24	521	12	43.41	3–40	–	–
Majid J. Khan	454	132	1,091	23	47.43	4–48	–	–
G.R.J. Roope	268.3	40	801	16	50.06	3–46	–	–
B.A. Langford	275.2	64	959	19	50.47	3–60	–	–
S.J. Storey	316.3	80	829	16	51.81	3–25	–	–
C.B. Hamblin	245	37	787	14	56.21	3–33	–	–
K.J. O'Keeffe	376.3	103	1,129	19	59.42	3–31	–	–

The following bowlers took ten wickets but bowled in less than ten innings:

G.F. Goddard	35	17	77	11	7.00	8–34	1	1
T.J. Mottram	129.2	30	405	20	20.25	5–45	2	–
G.St.A. Sobers	157	45	351	15	23.40	3–37	–	–
M.J.D. Stallibrass	96.4	25	305	13	23.46	5–80	1	–
J. Sullivan	91.4	22	248	10	24.80	3–42	–	–
S.C. Corlett	112	36	274	11	24.90	4–34	–	–
D.A. Graveney	155.2	66	362	14	25.85	5–63	1	–
W.N. Tidy	64	10	288	10	28.80	3–43	–	–
P.J. Lewington	139.1	31	471	16	29.43	4–62	–	–
A. Buss	121	18	403	11	36.63	3–51	–	–

FIELDING STATISTICS

58	R.W. Tolchard (52 ct, 6 st)	40	E.W. Jones (36 ct, 4 st)	25	D.S. Steele
54	G.R. Stephenson (45 ct, 9 st)	37	J.F. Steele	24	J.A. Ormrod
52	B. Taylor (44 ct, 8 st)	35	A.P.E. Knott (33 ct, 2 st)	23	K. Higgs
51	A. Long (42 ct, 9 st)	32	J.M. Parks (27ct, 5 st)	22	J.M. Brearly
51	D.A. Pullan (49 ct, 2 st)	32	G.R.J. Roope	22	B.W. Luckhurst
50	R.W. Taylor (39 ct, 11 st)	32	D.J.S. Taylor (29 ct, 3 st)	22	P.H. Parfitt
48	R. Swetman (42 ct, 6 st)	30	S.J. Storey	21	K.D. Boyce
47	D.L. Bairstow (42 ct, 5 st)	28	R.B. Kanhai	21	B. Dudleston
46	G. Sharp (40 ct, 6 st)	28	D. Nicholls (27 ct, 1 st)	21	Majid J. Khan
44	F.M. Engineer (38 ct, 6 st)	28	B.A. Richards	21	C.R.V. Taylor (18 ct, 3 st)
44	D.L. Murray (40 ct, 4 st)	27	R.D.V. Knight	20	R.M.H. Cottam
42	H.G. Wilcock (37 ct, 5 st)	27	D. Lloyd	20	J.H. Hampshire
41	J.T. Murray (39 ct, 2 st)	27	P.M. Walker	20	P.J. Watts

Where are Our Young Players?

Denis Compton

When Australia announced their side to tour England in 1972 and it was seen they had left out players of the calibre and experience of Graham McKenzie, Bill Lawry and Ian Redpath, the reaction in informed circles in English cricket was a mixture of astonishment and jubilation. England, having regained the Ashes after 12 years, in a series in which Australia failed to win a home Test against their oldest rivals for over 80 years, seemed odds-on favourites to win again and by an even more handsome margin. In the event England managed to retain the Ashes, but it was a desperately close thing and for once they had luck on their side.

Australia's policy of taking a chance on youth was entirely justified and when MCC next go 'Down Under' in the winter of 1974-75 they face a formidable job indeed.

Of course there will be new names in the English touring party. There have to be. The march of time has finally overtaken players like Basil D'Oliveira, Ray Illingworth, Peter Parfitt; and possibly men like John Edrich and Norman Gifford will feel a little too long in the tooth to undertake the most rigorous of all tours. The point is that the newcomers will be exposed to the responsibility and demands of Test cricket in the areas of Sydney, Melbourne, Adelaide and Brisbane with no previous experience of international cricket with the Australians as opponents.

The 1972 season, despite the appalling weather of May and much of June, saw the game overall continue along its path back to health and vigour, but the current panel of selectors showed a marked lack of faith in the rising generation of first-class cricketers. Before the series started the selectors admitted to being worried about England's middle batting. In 1971 the batting averages reflected the changes imposed upon the art of run-making by the growth of limited-overs cricket, and the chase for bonus points in the first innings of three-day Championship fixtures.

Of the overseas stars playing regularly in English cricket the names of Rohan Kanhai, Gary Sobers, Asif Iqbal, Mike Procter and Majid Khan were high on the list of middle-order batsmen but practically all the leaders of English birth are openers – Geoff Boycott, Mike Harris, Brian Luckhurst, John Edrich. The selectors seemed to have two solutions, and when they named no fewer than seven men, who at one time or another had opened the innings, for the MCC side to meet the Australians at Lord's in May, in the match which has come to be regarded as an unofficial Test trial, it seemed they had taken what they regarded as the logical step in the circumstances. The cold and wet of what was the worst May in memory did not permit a fair or searching test of this plan, and when the party for the first Test at Old Trafford was named, it was seen the selectors were either bankrupt of ideas or moral courage. They recalled M.J.K. Smith of Warwickshire, after an absence from Test cricket of six years, to fill the problem number four position. Mike had finished fourth in the national averages in 1971, with an aggregate less than 50 short of 2,000 in 48 innings – but he was almost 39.

Suspect against real pace at the highest level and never the outstanding success in Test cricket that he is in the County game, the Warwickshire skipper was clearly going to be a major risk against the likes of Lillee. 'M.J.K.', one of the most respected and popular players of the post-war period, gave all he had in terms of bravery and expertise, but his eyes and reflexes could not cope with Australia's new ball attack and he was out six times in the three Tests in which he played for 140 runs, Lillee getting his wicket four times and Massie twice.

I charge our selectors with placing an impossible burden on a man not far short of 40. It would have made far more sense to have said to Graham Roope of Surrey, 13 years Smith's junior, 'You are in at number four for the first three Tests, see what you can do'. Roope had more than his youth to recommend him. He finished the last six weeks of the 1971 season with five centuries, which brought his aggregate for the season to nearly 1,650 runs from two innings less than Smith. He had also held 59 catches, the highest total by a fielder as opposed to a wicket-keeper since 1962. To be sure he had no form behind him prior to the first Test – but who had?

It must never be forgotten that the players in that remarkable game at Manchester came to it quite ridiculously short of match practice and all depressed by a nearly total absence of sun, warmth and decent light. John Snow, for example, had bowled just 36 first-class overs and taken four wickets before a game in which he was to make the major contribution with a match analysis of eight for 128.

Roope might well have bagged a pair as Amiss did in an earlier Test at Old Trafford against Australia, when Test match nerves petrified him and gave his undoubted talent no chance to assert itself. But even if this had happened, Roope's 25-year-old athleticism and eagle eye must have justified his choice in the slips where he has held so many of his catches. The selectors obstinacy in refusing to give youth a chance, in

Surrey's Graham Roope, punching the ball wide of mid-on, might have added zest to the England side in 1972 but was never given the chance

Roger Tolchard, Leicestershire's promising young wicket-keeper-batsman, appeals eloquently for an lbw decision against M.J.K. Smith

the shape of Roope, sent England into battle without a slip specialist, and the number of catches spilled in this area reached near record proportions. As it happened Australia's inability to put together more than 142 against the moving ball in their first innings really decided the issue, but this was no thanks to a board of selectors who seemed obsessed by the idea that the emerging cricketer was not half the man his counterpart of 20 years before had been.

This policy persisted even when the top half of England's batting failed four times in the opening two Tests, and at Nottingham the selectors not only retained Mike Smith but dug out another Test discard, Peter Parfitt. Parfitt certainly performed a stout job in the record innings at Trent Bridge, where his occupation of the crease for nearly four and three-quarter hours was a major contribution in denying Australia victory and keeping us in the series. But his recall, like that of Smith, was in the long term purely negative.

At Leeds we were provided with another baffling piece of the selectional thought processes. They called up the other Mike Smith, Middlesex's 30-year-old opening bat. He did not make the side at Headingley but it was said he would benefit by the Test match atmosphere. Before the second day's play was over he was on his way back to Lord's to appear for Middlesex in their match against Kent starting on the Saturday. He was ignored for the final Test at The Oval, although England by winning at Leeds on a controversial pitch had made sure of keeping the Ashes, and then, even more staggering, was not picked to tour India and Pakistan under Tony Lewis even after Boycott had withdrawn. It made his summons to Leeds entirely without any point that I can think of. If Michael Smith was one of the most hurt and disappointed professional cricketers in England last winter he must try to derive some small measure of consolation from the fact that he is by no means the first to suffer in this inexplicable and inexcusable way.

And while we are on the subject of the tour to India and Pakistan, how could the non-selection of Bob Willis be justified, in view of his quite considerable success when pitchforked into a tour of Australia when he was the rawest of novices? He came back to a period of his career when he was dissatisfied and unsettled at The Oval, and switched to Warwickshire. When he was over this and into the first team at Edgbaston there were many days when he showed he was still in the process of mastering his craft. But that he is unquestionably made of the right stuff he showed when he clinched the Championship for the Midland county by taking 8 for 44 against Derbyshire in their penultimate match, a performance which brought him his county cap.

Willis will be only 25 when we next go to Australia to defend the Ashes and, with John Snow by that time nearing the end of his maximum effectiveness, certainly at Test level, the big, happy-dispositioned lad from Sunderland will surely be our spearhead, especially with the future of Derbyshire's Alan Ward so open to grave doubt. Not to have kept Willis busy in the winter of 1972-73 is another sin of omission on the part of the selectors which I cannot find it in my heart to forgive. Chris Old is a good cricketer, but I do not see him as a possible match winner in Australia next time. Yet he was the man the selectors saw fit to give Lewis rather than Willis.

It seems the selectors are incapable of learning by their mistakes. Barry Wood, Lancashire's 29-year-old opening bat from Ossett in Yorkshire, who looks like a compact edition of Boycott at the crease, was around at Old Trafford for the first Test last summer. As was to be expected he was not picked and he then disappeared from the reckoning until the final Test when the selectors took their one 'daring' gamble of the entire series and played him at The Oval. Wood made 90, looked every inch the class player so many of us had been saying he was all season, and made sure he would spend four months of the next English winter in the sun.

Yet it did not seem to occur to the selectors that if Wood could prove such an instant success a lot of other untried players of the younger school might be able to do an equally good job for England.

The selectors should dedicate themselves to the task of filling the England eleven with as many young players as possible in the summer of 1973, and with mini-series against New Zealand and West Indies they will never have a better opportunity. If some of the young swans turn out to be geese what will it matter? The great thing is to find three or four good young 'uns who have both the talent and the temperament for the job that matters in Australia in 1974-75.

John Player Cricket Yearbook 1973

Above: The thrilling climax to the John Player League season: Kent, needing victory for the title, meet Worcestershire at Canterbury

Left: An anxious Kent supporter. But she need not have worried. Kent won by 5 wickets

Below: Mike Denness shows the John Player Trophy to the crowd

John Player League 1972

FINAL TABLE		P	W	L	T	NR	Pts	Run rate	6s	4w
1	Kent (8)	16	11	4	–	1	45	4.361	23	5
2	Leicestershire (4)	16	11	5	–	–	44	4.214	11	4
3	Essex (2)	16	10	5	–	1	41	4.059	22	4
4	Yorkshire (15)	16	10	5	–	1	41	3.983	23	4
5	Middlesex (13)	16	8	6	–	2	34	4.456	29	3
6	Hampshire (6)	16	7	5	1	3	33	4.689	30	2
7	Somerset (5)	16	8	7	–	1	33	4.580	22	4
8	Lancashire (3)	16	8	7	–	1	33	4.180	23	6
9	Derbyshire (11)	16	7	7	–	2	30	4.282	25	3
10	Surrey (9)	16	7	7	–	2	30	4.191	28	2
11	Worcestershire (1)	16	7	8	–	1	29	4.882	21	6
12	Warwickshire (17)	16	7	8	–	1	29	4.322	29	2
13	Nottinghamshire (12)	16	6	10	–	–	24	3.898	19	4
14	Northamptonshire (14)	16	5	8	1	2	24	3.720	8	4
15	Sussex (7)	16	5	8	–	3	23	3.861	13	8
16	Gloucestershire (16)	16	3	10	2	1	17	3.984	28	1
17	Glamorgan (10)	16	2	12	–	2	10	3.804	30	–

Positions for teams finishing with an equal number of points are decided by the highest run rate per over. Figures in brackets show the 1971 position.

PREVIOUS CHAMPIONS   1969   Lancashire   1970   Lancashire   1971   Worcestershire

RESULTS
Win=4 points; Tie=2 points each; No result= 1 point each

April 30th
MIDDLESEX beat GLOUCESTERSHIRE by 8 wickets at Lord's
Gloucestershire 185–8 in 40 overs (M.J. Procter 58). Middlesex 187–2 in 35.1 overs (M.J. Smith 92, C.T. Radley 56)

May 7th
SURREY beat DERBYSHIRE by 16 runs at Derby (18 overs match)
Surrey 170–3 in 35.5 overs (J.H. Edrich 108 not out) set Derbyshire a target of 86 in 18 overs. Derbyshire 70 in 16.5 overs (R.D. Jackman 6–34)

GLOUCESTERSHIRE beat ESSEX by 6 wickets at Moreton-in-Marsh (33 overs match)
Essex 131–9 in 33 overs (B. Taylor 59). Gloucestershire 132–4 in 28.5 overs (D.R. Shepherd 56 not out, M.J. Procter 52)

MIDDLESEX beat NORTHAMPTONSHIRE by 35 runs at Northampton
Middlesex 76 in 29.2 overs. Northamptonshire 41 in 32 overs *(record lowest total in John Player League)*

LANCASHIRE beat NOTTINGHAMSHIRE by 74 runs at Nottingham (20 overs match)
Lancashire 251–3 in 37 overs (C.H. Lloyd 89 not out, K.L. Snellgrove 62) set Notts a target of 136 in 20 overs. Nottinghamshire 62–9 in 20 overs (K. Shuttleworth 5–13).

KENT beat SUSSEX by 12 runs at Hove (39 overs match)
Kent 174–9 in 39 overs (B.W. Luckhurst 69, J. Denman 4–28). Sussex 162–7 in 39 overs

HAMPSHIRE beat WARWICKSHIRE by 10 wickets at Birmingham (10 overs match)
Warwickshire 58–7 in 10 overs (R.S. Herman 4–22). Hampshire 59–0 in 8.1 overs

WORCESTERSHIRE beat SOMERSET by 12 runs at Worcester (10 overs match)
Worcestershire 84–7 in 10 overs. Somerset 72–8 in 10 overs

May 14th

ESSEX beat NORTHAMPTONSHIRE by 41 runs at Chelmsford (35 overs match)
Essex 159–6 in 35 overs (K.D. Boyce 93 not out). Northamptonshire 118–9 in 35 overs

YORKSHIRE beat GLAMORGAN by 6 wickets at Swansea
Glamorgan 113 in 39.2 overs. Yorkshire 116–4 in 36.5 overs

HAMPSHIRE beat NOTTINGHAMSHIRE by 7 runs at Bournemouth (27 overs match)
Hampshire 155–9 in 40 overs set Notts a target of 105 in 27 overs. Nottinghamshire 98 in 26.3 overs (T.J. Mottram 4–35).

KENT beat WARWICKSHIRE by 5 wickets at Canterbury
Warwickshire 134 in 38.3 overs (D.L. Underwood 4–28). Kent 136–5 in 32.3 overs (B.W. Luckhurst 60 not out)

LANCASHIRE beat GLOUCESTERSHIRE by 67 runs at Manchester (39 overs match)
Lancashire 182–5 in 39 overs (J. Sullivan 71 not out). Gloucestershire 115–8 in 39 overs

DERBYSHIRE beat LEICESTERSHIRE by 4 wickets at Leicester
Leicestershire 117 in 40 overs (I.R. Buxton 5–19). Derbyshire 118–6 in 39.3 overs

SOMERSET beat SUSSEX by 4 wickets at Taunton (37 overs match)
Sussex 94 in 39 overs set Somerset a target of 87 in 37 overs. Somerset 92–6 in 33.1 overs

SURREY beat WORCESTERSHIRE by 6 wickets at Leatherhead (19 overs match)
Worcestershire 83–5 in 19 overs. Surrey 84–4 in 18 overs

May 21st

DERBYSHIRE beat GLAMORGAN by 6 wickets at Ilkeston (19 overs match)
Glamorgan 105–8 in 32 overs set Derbys a target of 63 in 19 overs. Derbyshire 66–4 in 15.5 overs

GLOUCESTERSHIRE tied with HAMPSHIRE at Bristol (39 overs match)
Hampshire 198–6 in 39 overs (D.R. Turner 99 not out, B.A. Richards 51). Gloucestershire 198–5 in 39 overs (Sadiq Mohammad 93, R.D.V. Knight 58)

MIDDLESEX beat ESSEX by 68 runs at Lord's
Middlesex 161–8 in 40 overs (J.M. Brearley 55, K.D. Boyce 4–34). Essex 93 in 30.5 overs

John Player League 1972

NORTHAMPTONSHIRE beat LANCASHIRE by 4 runs at Peterborough (34 overs match)
Northamptonshire 133–8 in 37 overs (J. Simmons 5–28) set Lancs a target of 123 in 34 overs. Lancashire 118–9 in 34 overs

NOTTINGHAMSHIRE beat KENT by 9 wickets at Nottingham
Kent 151–9 in 40 overs (W. Taylor 4–26). Nottinghamshire 154–1 in 38 overs (M.J. Harris 67 not out, B. Hassan 59)

SUSSEX beat SURREY by 5 wickets at Hove
Surrey 150 in 38.5 overs (J.H. Edrich 56, J.A. Snow 5–15). Sussex 152–5 in 39.1 overs

WARWICKSHIRE beat SOMERSET by 6 wickets at Birmingham (26 overs match)
Somerset 128–7 in 32 overs (K. Ibadulla 4–20) set Warwicks a target of 105 in 26 overs. Warwickshire 108–4 in 24.1 overs

LEICESTERSHIRE beat WORCESTERSHIRE by 10 wickets at Dudley (28 overs match)
Worcestershire 84–9 in 28 overs (R. Illingworth 4–5). Leicestershire 85–0 in 25.4 overs

May 28th
ESSEX beat NOTTINGHAMSHIRE by 4 runs at Chelmsford (23 overs match)
Essex 150–8 in 40 overs (K.D. Boyce 52) set Notts a target of 87 in 23 overs. Nottinghamshire 82–8 in 23 overs

KENT beat GLOUCESTERSHIRE by 9 wickets at Maidstone
Gloucestershire 104 in 35.4 overs (D.L. Underwood 5–19). Kent 108–1 in 23.5 overs (D. Nicholls 56)

SOMERSET beat LANCASHIRE by 84 runs at Manchester (33 overs match)
Somerset 160 in 33 overs. Lancashire 76 in 32.3 overs (G.I. Burgess 5–16)

LEICESTERSHIRE beat SUSSEX by 1 wicket at Leicester
Sussex 144 in 37.5 overs. Leicestershire 146–9 in 39.5 overs

WARWICKSHIRE (3.74) beat SURREY (3.33) by a faster run-rate when rain stopped play at Charterhouse School, Godalming
Surrey 133–8 in 40 overs. Warwickshire 88–4 in 23.3 overs

YORKSHIRE beat DERBYSHIRE by 7 wickets at Bradford (28 overs match)
Derbyshire 109 in 26.3 overs. Yorkshire 110–3 in 26.2 overs

June 4th
ESSEX V LANCASHIRE at Colchester – no result. Lancashire 98–4 in 24.5 overs (C.H. Lloyd 50 not out). Rain.

SOMERSET (4.66) beat GLOUCESTERSHIRE (3.00) by a faster run-rate when rain stopped play at Bristol
Somerset 177–8 in 38 overs. Gloucestershire 60–4 in 20 overs

MIDDLESEX V HAMPSHIRE at Lord's – no result. Hampshire 42–4 in 16 overs. Rain.

KENT beat NORTHAMPTONSHIRE by 4 wickets at Northampton
Northamptonshire 147–9 in 40 overs (W.J. Stewart 55, B.D. Julien 4–28). Kent 149–6 in 33.3 overs (Asif Iqbal 67 not out)

SURREY beat NOTTINGHAMSHIRE by 5 wickets at Nottingham
Nottinghamshire 157–6 in 40 overs (G.St.A. Sobers 96 not out). Surrey 160–5 in 38.5 overs (Younis Ahmed 60)

SUSSEX V GLAMORGAN at Hove – no result. Match abandoned without a ball being bowled

LEICESTERSHIRE (5.91) beat WARWICKSHIRE (5.73) by a faster run-rate when rain stopped play at Birmingham
Warwickshire 229–6 in 40 overs (R.B. Kanhai 120). Leicestershire 201–6 in 34 overs (B.F. Davison 80, R.W. Tolchard 68 not out)

WORCESTERSHIRE beat YORKSHIRE by 4 wickets at Worcester
Yorkshire 135 in 39.2 overs (N. Gifford 4–44). Worcestershire 136–6 in 36.2 overs

---

June 11th
DERBYSHIRE V WORCESTERSHIRE at Chesterfield – no result
Match abandoned without a ball being bowled

GLAMORGAN beat WARWICKSHIRE by 7 wickets at Swansea
Warwickshire 85 in 38 overs. Glamorgan 86–3 in 33.4 overs

ESSEX beat HAMPSHIRE by 129 runs at Basingstoke
Essex 172 in 40 overs (K.W.R. Fletcher 69). Hampshire 43 in 24.1 overs (K.D. Boyce 4–6).

MIDDLESEX beat KENT by 1 run at Folkestone.
Middlesex 127 in 39.2 overs. Kent 126 in 39.3 overs (D. Nicholls 54)

LEICESTERSHIRE beat NOTTINGHAMSHIRE by 3 wickets at Leicester (26 overs match)
Nottinghamshire 100–7 in 26 overs. Leicestershire 103–7 in 25.1 overs

NORTHAMPTONSHIRE beat SOMERSET by 6 wickets at Taunton (33 overs match)
Somerset 136–9 in 40 overs set Northants a target of 113 in 33 overs. Northamptonshire 113–4 in 24.3 overs

SURREY beat GLOUCESTERSHIRE by 9 wickets at Sunbury (38 overs match)
Gloucestershire 133–8 in 40 overs set Surrey a target of 127 in 38 overs. Surrey 130–1 in 25.5 overs (Younis Ahmed 64 not out)

YORKSHIRE V SUSSEX at Leeds – no result.
Match abandoned without a ball being bowled

June 18th
DERBYSHIRE V MIDDLESEX at Buxton – no result.
Match abandoned without a ball being bowled.

KENT beat ESSEX by 6 wickets at Ilford (10 overs match)
Essex 81–6 in 10 overs. Kent 84–4 in 8.5 overs

LEICESTERSHIRE beat GLOUCESTERSHIRE by 7 wickets at Gloucester (38 overs match)
Gloucestershire 142–8 in 38 overs (C.A. Milton 53). Leicestershire 146–3 in 29 overs (B.F. Davison 68)

HAMPSHIRE beat LANCASHIRE by 20 runs at Manchester (10 overs match)
Hampshire 77–2 in 10 overs. Lancashire 57–3 in 10 overs

NORTHAMPTONSHIRE V SURREY at Northampton – no result
Match abandoned without a ball being bowled.

NOTTINGHAMSHIRE beat GLAMORGAN by 65 runs at Nottingham (31 overs match)
Nottinghamshire 176–2 in 35 overs (M.J. Harris 82 not out, B. Hassan 80 not out) set Glamorgan a target of 156 in 31 overs. Glamorgan 91–6 in 31 overs

YORKSHIRE beat SOMERSET by 8 wickets at Sheffield (21 overs match)
Somerset 103–8 in 21 overs (D.B. Close 55 not out, A.G. Nicholson 6–36). Yorkshire 106–2 in 20.1 overs (G. Boycott 52 not out)

A fine hook by Barrie Leadbeater, who headed the John Player averages and shared second place in the batsmen's pool with 11 sixes, each worth £2.60

June 25th
DERBYSHIRE beat WARWICKSHIRE by 40 runs at Chesterfield
Derbyshire 234–7 in 40 overs (C.P. Wilkins 94, A.J. Borrington 56). Warwickshire 194–4 in 40 overs (A.I. Kallicharran 101 not out, D.L. Amiss 57)

GLAMORGAN beat GLOUCESTERSHIRE by 7 runs at Cardiff
Glamorgan 140–8 in 40 overs. Gloucestershire 133 in 39.5 overs

LANCASHIRE beat KENT by 33 runs at Maidstone (39 overs match)
Lancashire 178–7 in 39 overs (D.L. Underwood 4–30). Kent 145 in 36 overs

LEICESTERSHIRE beat NORTHAMPTONSHIRE by 7 wickets at Leicester (31 overs match)
Northamptonshire 141 in 39.5 overs set Leics a target of 110 in 31 overs. Leicestershire 110–3 in 23 overs (B.F. Davison 63)

SOMERSET beat ESSEX by 55 runs at Bath
Somerset 175–9 in 40 overs. Essex 120 in 37.3 overs

SURREY beat MIDDLESEX by 3 runs at Byfleet
Surrey 144–8 in 40 overs (G.R.J. Roope 50 not out, D.A. Marriott 4–12). Middlesex 141–8 in 40 overs (Intikhab Alam 4–17)

WORCESTERSHIRE beat SUSSEX by 170 runs at Dudley (*Record margin of victory in John Player League matches*)
Worcestershire 258–4 in 40 overs (G.M. Turner 121, R.G.A. Headley 77). Sussex 88 in 32.1 overs (R.G.M. Carter 4–16)

YORKSHIRE beat NOTTINGHAMSHIRE by 8 runs at Hull
Yorkshire 150–6 in 40 overs (B. Leadbeater 69, C. Johnson 51 not out). Nottinghamshire 142 in 39.2 overs (J.B. Bolus 52, A.G. Nicholson 5–17)

July 2nd
ESSEX beat SURREY by 1 wicket at Harlow
Surrey 165–8 in 40 overs (Younis Ahmed 54). Essex 168–9 in 40 overs

HAMPSHIRE V KENT at Portsmouth – no result
Hampshire 142–9 in 39 overs (J.N. Shepherd 4–18). Rain.

YORKSHIRE beat LANCASHIRE by 8 wickets at Manchester
Lancashire 177–7 in 40 overs (K.L. Snellgrove 55, D. Lloyd 53). Yorkshire 178–2 in 38.1 overs (J.H. Hampshire 106 not out)

LEICESTERSHIRE beat MIDDLESEX by 19 runs at Lord's
Leicestershire 206–5 in 40 overs (R.W. Tolchard 103 – out 'obstructing the field'). Middlesex 187 in 39 overs (C.T. Radley 88, B.F. Davison 4–33, C.T. Spencer 4–39)

NORTHAMPTONSHIRE (4.63) beat GLAMORGAN (4.28) by a faster run-rate when rain stopped play at Northampton
Glamorgan 171–8 in 40 overs (A.R. Lewis 60). Northamptonshire 74–2 in 16 overs

DERBYSHIRE beat NOTTINGHAMSHIRE by 66 runs at Nottingham (39 overs match)
Derbyshire 147–6 in 39 overs (J.F. Harvey 52 not out). Nottinghamshire 81 in 38.4 overs (M. Hendrick 6–7).

WARWICKSHIRE beat WORCESTERSHIRE by 4 wickets at Birmingham
Worcestershire 247–4 in 40 overs (G.M. Turner 108, R.G.A. Headley 82). Warwickshire 249–6 in 39.3 overs (D.L. Amiss 59)

July 9th
ESSEX beat GLAMORGAN by 60 runs at Purfleet (38 overs match)
Essex 196–9 in 38 overs (K.D. Boyce 92). Glamorgan 136 in 35.4 overs (M.A. Nash 68, J.K. Lever 4–21)

HAMPSHIRE beat SURREY by 5 wickets at Southampton
Surrey 164–8 in 40 overs (J.H. Edrich 75). Hampshire 167–5 in 38.2 overs (C.G. Greenidge 57, R.E. Marshall 51)

SOMERSET beat KENT by 6 wickets at Canterbury (22 overs match)
Kent 90–9 in 22 overs (H.R. Moseley 4–33). Somerset 92–4 in 21.2 overs

LANCASHIRE beat LEICESTERSHIRE by 1 wicket at Manchester
Leicestershire 90 in 39.4 overs. Lancashire 91–9 in 39.3 overs

YORKSHIRE beat MIDDLESEX by 13 runs at Lord's (21 overs match)
Yorkshire 122–6 in 21 overs. Middlesex 109–7 in 21 overs

DERBYSHIRE beat NORTHAMPTONSHIRE by 1 wicket at Northampton
Northamptonshire 154–8 in 40 overs. Derbyshire 156–9 in 40 overs (P.J.K. Gibbs 55, P.J. Watts 4–14)

NOTTINGHAMSHIRE beat SUSSEX by 4 wickets at John Player & Sons Ground, Nottingham
Sussex 102 in 39.5 overs (W. Taylor 4–11). Nottinghamshire 105–6 in 38.1 overs (M.J. Harris 58, J.A. Snow 4–15)

July 16th
DERBYSHIRE beat GLOUCESTERSHIRE by 51 runs at Derby (39 overs match)
Derbyshire 260–6 in 39 overs (A.J. Borrington 84). Gloucestershire 209 in 37.5 overs (D.R. Shepherd 70)

MIDDLESEX beat GLAMORGAN by 7 runs at Cardiff
Middlesex 212–4 in 40 overs (M.J. Smith 84). Glamorgan 205 in 40 overs (A.R. Lewis 64)

LEICESTERSHIRE beat ESSEX by 6 wickets at Leicester
Essex 141–8 in 40 overs (K.W.R. Fletcher 50, G.D. McKenzie 5–15 including hat-trick). Leicestershire 142–4 in 36.2 overs (M.E.J.C. Norman 63 not out)

SOMERSET beat HAMPSHIRE by 3 wickets at Bristol
Hampshire 222–5 in 40 overs (C.G. Greenidge 84, B.A. Richards 52). Somerset 227–7 in 39.4 overs (R.T. Virgin 74)

SURREY beat LANCASHIRE by 6 wickets at The Oval
Lancashire 140–7 in 40 overs (D.P. Hughes 50 not out). Surrey 141–7 in 38.3 overs (J. Sullivan 5–29)

WARWICKSHIRE beat SUSSEX by 7 runs at Hove
Warwickshire 156–7 in 40 overs (R.B. Kanhai 58, J. Denman 4–37). Sussex 149 in 40 overs

WORCESTERSHIRE beat NOTTINGHAMSHIRE by 38 runs at Worcester
Worcestershire 227–4 in 40 overs (G.M. Turner 88). Nottinghamshire 189–6 in 40 overs (M.J. Harris 92)

YORKSHIRE beat NORTHAMPTONSHIRE by 10 runs at Sheffield
Yorkshire 211–4 in 40 overs (B. Leadbeater 86 not out, R.G. Lumb 56). Northamptonshire 201–8 in 40 overs (Mushtaq Mohammad 71, D.S. Steele 56, C.M. Old 5–38)

July 23rd
WORCESTERSHIRE beat GLOUCESTERSHIRE by 22 runs at Lydney
Worcestershire 160–8 in 40 overs (G.M. Turner 83). Gloucestershire 138 in 36.4 overs (B.L. D'Oliveira 5–26)

NORTHAMPTONSHIRE beat HAMPSHIRE by 24 runs at Portsmouth (19 overs match)
Northamptonshire 110–6 in 19 overs. Hampshire 86–8 in 19 overs (R.R. Bailey 6–22)

MIDDLESEX beat LANCASHIRE by 9 wickets at Manchester (22 overs match)
Lancashire 82 in 21.3 overs (M.W.W. Selvey 4–21). Middlesex 85–1 in 14.1 overs

LEICESTERSHIRE beat GLAMORGAN by 10 wickets at Leicester
Glamorgan 133–6 in 40 overs. Leicestershire 137–0 in 34.4 overs (M.E.J.C. Norman 71 not out, B. Dudleston 56 not out)

NOTTINGHAMSHIRE beat SOMERSET by 4 wickets at Torquay
Somerset 213 in 39.2 overs (G.I. Burgess 55, B. Stead 4–24). Nottinghamshire 214–6 in 39.2 overs (N. Nanan 58)

KENT beat SURREY by 16 runs at The Oval (27 overs match)
Kent 200–8 in 39 overs. Surrey 122 in 26.5 overs

WARWICKSHIRE beat YORKSHIRE by 109 runs at Birmingham
Warwickshire 183–5 in 40 overs (D.L. Amiss 73). Yorkshire 74 in 35 overs

Barry Richards in full cry. His 14 sixes put him at the top of the batsmen's pool and gave immense delight to thousands of Sunday supporters

July 30th
LANCASHIRE beat GLAMORGAN by 2 runs at Ebbw Vale
Lancashire 206-7 in 40 overs (B. Wood 67, H. Pilling 53). Glamorgan 204-7 in 40 overs (M.J. Khan 83, A. Jones 57)

HAMPSHIRE beat LEICESTERSHIRE by 120 runs at Leicester
Hampshire 248-5 in 40 overs (B.A. Richards 105, C.G. Greenidge 83 not out). Leicestershire 128 in 22.2 overs

MIDDLESEX beat SOMERSET by 5 wickets at Lord's (38 overs match)
Somerset 176-8 in 38 overs (T.W. Cartwright 61). Middlesex 177-5 in 37.4 overs (J.M. Brearley 67 not out)

GLOUCESTERSHIRE beat SUSSEX by 2 wickets at Arundel
Sussex 178-9 in 40 overs (J.M. Parks 64, M.J. Procter 5-10). Gloucestershire 179-8 in 39.4 overs (D.R. Shepherd 68 not out, J. Spencer 4-27)

NOTTINGHAMSHIRE beat WARWICKSHIRE by 7 wickets at Birmingham (32 overs match)
Warwickshire 152-3 in 32 overs (R.B. Kanhai 65 not out). Nottinghamshire 155-3 in 29 overs (B. Hassan 86 not out)

WORCESTERSHIRE beat NORTHAMPTONSHIRE by 9 wickets at Worcester
Northamptonshire 134 in 39.5 overs. Worcestershire 137-1 in 18.2 overs (G.M. Turner 57 not out)

ESSEX (4.40) beat YORKSHIRE (3.45) by a faster run-rate when rain stopped play at Scarborough. Yorkshire 92-5 in 26.4 overs. Essex 44-1 in 10 overs

August 6th

ESSEX beat DERBYSHIRE by 10 runs at Leyton (32 overs match)
Essex 135–6 in 32 overs. Derbyshire 125 in 31.5 overs

GLOUCESTERSHIRE V WARWICKSHIRE at Cheltenham – no result
Gloucestershire 135–3 in 23 overs (M.J. Procter 109 not out). Rain.

HAMPSHIRE V GLAMORGAN at Southampton – no result
Match abandoned without a ball being bowled

KENT beat LEICESTERSHIRE by 5 runs at Gillingham
Kent 172–7 in 40 overs. Leicestershire 167–9 in 40 overs (R.W. Tolchard 50)

MIDDLESEX (5.62) beat WORCESTERSHIRE (4.31) by a faster run-rate when rain stopped play at Lord's
Middlesex 146–9 in 26 overs (J.M. Brearley 66, V.A. Holder 6–33). Worcestershire 107–9 in 24.5 overs (D.A. Marriott 4–32)

NORTHAMPTONSHIRE V SUSSEX at Brackley – no result
Match abandoned without a ball being bowled

SOMERSET V SURREY at Weston-super-Mare – no result
Match abandoned without a ball being bowled

August 13th

LANCASHIRE beat DERBYSHIRE by 14 runs at Chesterfield
Lancashire 152–9 in 40 overs (F.C. Hayes 50). Derbyshire 138–9 in 40 overs (P.J.K. Gibbs 68, P. Lee 4–17).

KENT beat GLAMORGAN by 7 wickets at Cardiff
Glamorgan 136–8 in 40 overs. Kent 139–3 in 35 overs (G.W. Johnson 65)

LEICESTERSHIRE beat SOMERSET by 18 runs at Leicester
Leicestershire 180–6 in 40 overs. Somerset 162–8 in 40 overs (P.W. Denning 71 not out)

GLOUCESTERSHIRE beat NOTTINGHAMSHIRE by 67 runs at Nottingham
Gloucestershire 191–6 in 40 overs (Zaheer Abbas 92, W. Taylor 4–43). Nottinghamshire 124 in 34.1 overs (B. Hassan 67)

SUSSEX beat MIDDLESEX by 29 runs at Eastbourne
Sussex 210–7 in 40 overs (P.J. Graves 101 not out). Middlesex 181 in 39.2 overs (N.G. Featherstone 53, C.P. Phillipson 4–25)

WARWICKSHIRE beat NORTHAMPTONSHIRE by 60 runs at Birmingham
Warwickshire 179 in 39.2 overs (A.I. Kallicharran 63). Northamptonshire 119 in 36.4 overs (A.C. Smith 5–19)

ESSEX beat WORCESTERSHIRE by 7 wickets at Worcester (39 overs match)
Worcestershire 195–6 in 39 overs (P.J. Stimpson 52, T.J. Yardley 52 not out). Essex 197–3 in 36.1 overs (B. Ward 99, K.W.R. Fletcher 50)

HAMPSHIRE beat YORKSHIRE by 3 wickets at Bradford
Yorkshire 161–9 in 40 overs. Hampshire 165–7 in 39.1 overs (C.G. Greenidge 69)

August 20th

ESSEX beat SUSSEX by 6 wickets at Chelmsford
Sussex 102–7 in 40 overs. Essex 103–4 in 36.1 overs

DERBYSHIRE (5.43) beat HAMPSHIRE (5.38) by a faster run-rate when play closed at 6.30 p.m. under rule 2(A) at Portsmouth
Derbyshire 217–5 in 40 overs (C.P. Wilkins 84, P.J.K. Gibbs 57). Hampshire 183–9 in 34 overs (B.A. Richards 95)

KENT beat YORKSHIRE by 9 wickets at Folkestone (39 overs match)
Yorkshire 159–9 in 39 overs. Kent 163–1 in 34.5 overs (B.W. Luckhurst 74 not out)

LANCASHIRE beat WORCESTERSHIRE by 76 runs at Manchester
Lancashire 197–7 in 40 overs (B.M. Brain 4–35). Worcestershire 121 in 34 overs (J. Sullivan 4–20)

WARWICKSHIRE beat MIDDLESEX by 1 run at Lord's
Warwickshire 182–6 in 40 overs (R.B. Kanhai 60). Middlesex 181–5 in 40 overs

NORTHAMPTONSHIRE beat NOTTINGHAMSHIRE by 40 runs at Kettering
Northamptonshire 146–9 in 40 overs. Nottinghamshire 80 in 30.4 overs (R.M.H. Cottam 4–17)

SOMERSET beat GLAMORGAN by 120 runs at Glastonbury
Somerset 234–5 in 40 overs (B.C. Rose 61 not out, P.W. Denning 54). Glamorgan 114 in 37.4 overs (G.I. Burgess 6–25)

LEICESTERSHIRE beat SURREY by 4 wickets at Guildford
Surrey 183–5 in 40 overs (J.H. Edrich 53). Leicestershire 185–6 in 39.5 overs (R.W. Tolchard 83)

August 27th
KENT beat DERBYSHIRE by 4 wickets at Derby.
Derbyshire 151–7 in 40 overs. Kent 152–4 in 37.5 overs

SURREY beat GLAMORGAN by 3 wickets at Swansea
Glamorgan 205–7 in 40 overs (R.C. Fredericks 67). Surrey 206–7 in 39.2 overs (Younis Ahmed 62)

GLOUCESTERSHIRE tied with NORTHAMPTONSHIRE at Bristol
Gloucestershire 154 in 40 overs (J.C.J. Dye 4–41). Northamptonshire 154–9 in 40 overs

SUSSEX beat LANCASHIRE by 80 runs at Hove.
Sussex 214–5 in 40 overs (E.R. Dexter 70 not out). Lancashire 134 in 35.5 overs (C.P. Phillipson 4–26)

HAMPSHIRE beat WORCESTERSHIRE by 44 runs at Worcester
Hampshire 215–8 in 40 overs (B.A. Richards 101, B.M. Brain 4–29). Worcestershire 171 in 37.2 overs

YORKSHIRE beat LEICESTERSHIRE by 3 runs at Leeds
Yorkshire 176–9 in 40 overs (R.G. Lumb 55). Leicestershire 173–8 in 40 overs (B. Dudleston 61)

ESSEX beat WARWICKSHIRE by 4 wickets at Birmingham
Warwickshire 120 in 36 overs (M.J.K. Smith 50, J.K. Lever 5–18). Essex 122–6 in 37 overs

September 3rd
WORCESTERSHIRE beat GLAMORGAN by 2 runs at Colwyn Bay
Worcestershire 177–7 in 40 overs (D.E.R. Stewart 62). Glamorgan 175–8 in 40 overs (M.J. Khan 58)

YORKSHIRE beat GLOUCESTERSHIRE by 8 wickets at Tewkesbury
Gloucestershire 90 in 39.1 overs. Yorkshire 91–2 in 29.2 overs

NOTTINGHAMSHIRE beat MIDDLESEX by 5 runs at Nottingham (39 overs match)
Nottinghamshire 174–7 in 39 overs (J.B. Bolus 62). Middlesex 169–8 in 39 overs

SUSSEX beat DERBYSHIRE by 8 wickets at Hove.
Derbyshire 154–7 in 40 overs (P.J.K. Gibbs 50).
Sussex 155–2 in 36.1 overs (E.R. Dexter 70 not out, G.A. Greenidge 67 not out)

September 10th
SUSSEX beat HAMPSHIRE by 18 runs at Bournemouth
Sussex 193–7 in 40 overs (P.J. Graves 63). Hampshire 185 in 39.3 overs (B.A. Richards 59, J.A. Snow 4–37).

KENT beat WORCESTERSHIRE by 5 wickets at Canterbury to become 1972 John Player League Champions
Worcestershire 190–5 in 40 overs (J.A. Ormrod 69, R.G.A. Headley 66). Kent 191–5 in 38 overs (B.W. Luckhurst 67)

LANCASHIRE beat WARWICKSHIRE by 4 wickets at Manchester
Warwickshire 135–8 in 40 overs (J. Sullivan 4–23). Lancashire 138–6 in 31.3 overs (C.H. Lloyd 51)

SOMERSET beat DERBYSHIRE by 35 runs at Taunton (39 overs match)
Somerset 164 in 30 overs (P.E. Russell 4–36). Derbyshire 129 in 35.5 overs (H.R. Moseley 4–19)

YORKSHIRE beat SURREY by 4 wickets at The Oval (39 overs match)
Surrey 148–9 in 39 overs (R.A. Hutton 4–18). Yorkshire 152–6 in 38.3 overs

Review of the Season

In ideal conditions before a capacity crowd on a sunny, early autumn day at Canterbury, that most delightful of settings, Kent won their first John Player League title when they beat Worcestershire by five wickets in the final week of the season. Thousands of happy Kent supporters and just about everything else on the ground were so covered in hops that one had serious qualms about the future of the beer industry. It was a perfect climax to a competition in which Leicestershire, who led the table for more than half the season, appeared to have established an unassailable lead as early as mid-July.

After Lancashire's domination of the first two years of this 40-over Sunday league, the past two seasons have seen breathtaking finishes. No one, least of all an Essex supporter, needs reminding that Worcestershire won the 1971 title by 0.0037 of a run per over and the presence of an electronic calculator when the two counties finished level on points. This time a single point separated Kent from Leicestershire.

Such a grand finale was scarcely predictable after a torrential June in which only 13 of the scheduled 30 matches were not reduced by rain. Seven games had to be abandoned, and BBC2 viewers were particularly unlucky, being entertained to six consecutive Sundays of almost continuous rain. This sequence was followed by the only match to be abandoned in July, and with the cameras becoming renowned as rain-making devices, a visit from the BBC team was something to be dreaded.

Kent had to win their last six matches to pip Leicestershire at the post. After winning four of their first five games, they had won only one of the next five and had dropped to seventh place – 11 points behind the leaders – by mid-July. Yet the counties above them all faltered just as they had done in the County Championship of 1970. Moreover Kent beat each of the three sides immediately below them in the final table, frequently often sacrificed Knott, Luckhurst, Underwood and Woolmer to England's cause and even lost Asif through malaria for three matches. The batting of Luckhurst (445 runs, average 44.50) and the bowling of Underwood (28 wickets, average 12.42, plus three shares in the bowling jackpot) played a leading part in Kent's success, as did their magnificently athletic fielding. They fully deserved their £2,000 prize money, which had been doubled by the sponsors since 1971, and the honour of introducing 40-over cricket to the West Indies.

Leicestershire began in tremendous form, winning seven consecutive matches and nine out of ten. At this stage they had already won the new Benson and Hedges Cup by a street and were challenging in third place for the Championship. Then the loss of key players through injury proved too much and they won only two of their last five matches. Kent beat them by five runs and, when they went down by three runs to Yorkshire in their final fixture, they were kept in suspense for a fortnight waiting for Kent to play Worcestershire. Roger Tolchard had a most remarkable John Player League season. Besides equalling the wicket-keeping record of 24 dismissals, he hit 480 runs, including his county's first John Player century (an innings ended by the first 'obstructing the field' in limited-overs cricket) and, in Illingworth's absence, led the team to victory six times out of seven.

Essex finished level on points with Yorkshire and should, under the new ruling, have had a play-off to decide third place. When neither a date nor venue could be agreed upon, Essex took the higher place on average run-rate by 0.076. This was some compensation for their 1971 experience. Essex is the only county to finish in the top four every season of the John Player League, and no one has contributed more to this amazingly consistent record, nor indeed to the success of the League itself, than Keith Boyce. He has regularly entertained with his aggressive fast bowling, splendidly uninhibited batting, and superb fielding. No other player approaches his all-round contribution of 1,131 runs and 117 wickets, and the sponsors acknowledged this 'double' with a special £100 award at their end of season dinner.

Yorkshire, whose previous final positions had been 8th, 14th, and 15th, seem to be mastering the art of one-day cricket. Although twice winners of the Gillette Cup, they had seldom shown much enthusiasm for the shorter versions, but 1972 saw them win the Fenner Trophy, reach the final of the Benson and Hedges Cup, and play a vital part in deciding the John Player title when, with a team including seven uncapped players, they beat Leicestershire.

Other highlights of 1972 included Gloucestershire's two tied games at Bristol, Barry Richards' 73-minute hundred at Leicester, Glenn Turner's record run of 122, 108, 88, 83, and 57 not out for a disappointing Worcestershire, Bob Woolmer's delightfully illegal ninth over at Portsmouth, and the return of Fred Trueman who, in six matches for Derbyshire, bowled perfect late-outswingers and enacted his own slow-motion playback after each dismissal!

John Player League 1972

Above: A plainly jubilant Asif Iqbal dashes for the safety of the pavilion as young Kent supporters swarm on to the ground to congratulate their heroes

Left: Keith Boyce, the Essex all-rounder whose hostile fast bowling and dynamic batting enabled him to complete the first double in the John Player League

Below: Derek Underwood, with 28 wickets at 12 apiece, played a vital role in Kent's John Player League triumph

John Player Cricket Yearbook 1973

JOHN PLAYER LEAGUE AVERAGES – DISTRIBUTION OF PRIZE MONEY

AWARDS
Presented by John Player & Sons (total prize-money £12,950)
  £2,000 to League Champions: KENT
  £1,000 to runners-up: LEICESTERSHIRE
  £500 to third placing: ESSEX
  £50 each match to winners (shared in event of a 'no result')

£1,000 batsmen's pool – one share for every six hit. 384 sixes (38 fewer than in 1971) were hit by 124 players – each six being worth £2.60. Six-hitters:
  14 – B.A. Richards (wins special £150 award for most sixes).
  11 – B. Leadbeater, Younis Ahmed.
  10 – D.R. Shepherd, C.P. Wilkins.
   9 – M.J. Procter.
   8 – C.G. Greenidge, G.W. Johnson, R.B. Kanhai, M.J. Khan.
   7 – K.D. Boyce, D.B. Close, J.H. Hampshire, A.I. Kallicharran, M.J. Smith.
   6 – J.M. Brearley, B.F. Davison, Intikhab Alam, G.M. Turner.
   5 – T.W. Cartwright, N.G. Featherstone, R.C. Fredericks, G.St.A. Sobers, J. Sullivan.
   4 – A.S. Brown, G.I. Burgess, B.L. D'Oliveira, M.J. Harris, A.J. Harvey-Walker, R.G.A. Headley, B.D. Julien, C.H. Lloyd, B.W. Luckhurst, N.M. McVicker, M.A. Nash, G.R.J. Roope, M.J.K. Smith, K.L. Snellgrove, B. Taylor, R.W. Tolchard, S. Turner.
   3 – I.R. Buxton, P.W. Denning, M.J. Edwards, P.J. Graves, G.A. Greenidge, F.C. Hayes, R.N.S. Hobbs, D.P. Hughes, J.A. Jameson, A. Jones, K.V. Jones, M.J. Llewellyn, R.E. Marshall, J.T Murray, J.W. Solanky, B. Stead, D.S. Steele.
   2 – C.J.R. Black, H. Cartwright, A.E. Cordle, E.R. Dexter, J.H. Edrich, K.W.R. Fletcher, B. Hassan, M. Hendrick, T.E. Jesty, R.D.V. Knight, R.G. Lumb, Mushtaq Mohammad, N. Nanan, D. Nicholls, G.R. Stephenson, D.E.R. Stewart, F.S. Trueman, R.A. Woolmer.
   1 – Asif Iqbal, W. Blenkiron, J.D. Bond, G. Boycott, G.R. Cass, R.C. Cooper, J. Denman, M.H. Denness, R.E. East, P.H. Edmonds, G. Frost, A.W. Greig, K. Griffith, M.G. Griffith, W.H. Hare, E.J.O. Hemsley, J.M.M. Hooper, M.J. Kitchen, W. Larkins, J.K. Lever, D. Lloyd, N. Maltby, J.B. Mortimore, H.R. Moseley, D.L. Murray, R.B. Nicholls, C.M. Old, J.A. Ormrod, P.H. Parfitt, J.M. Parks, R.M. Prideaux, C.T. Radley, D.W. Randall, P.E. Russell, Sadiq Mohammad, D.J. Shepherd, J.N. Shepherd, J. Simmons, R.W. Taylor, D.R. Turner, C.T. Spencer, P.J. Stimpson, S.J. Storey, P.J. Squires, P.M. Walker, P.J. Watts, J. Whitehouse, B. Wood.

£1,000 bowlers' pool – one share for taking four or more wickets in a match.
62 instances (3 fewer than in 1971) by 45 bowlers – each share being worth £16.13.
Shareholders:
  3 – J.A. Snow, J. Sullivan, W. Taylor, D.L. Underwood (share special £150 award for most shares).
  2 – K.D. Boyce, B.M. Brain, G.I. Burgess, J. Denman, J.K. Lever, D.A. Marriott, H.R. Moseley, A.G. Nicholson, C.P. Phillipson.
  1 – R.R. Bailey, I.R. Buxton, R.G.M. Carter, R.M.H. Cottam, B.F. Davison, B.L. D'Oliveira, J.C.J. Dye, N. Gifford, M. Hendrick, R.S. Herman, V.A. Holder, R.A. Hutton, K. Ibadulla, R. Illingworth, Intikhab Alam, R.D. Jackman, B.D. Julien, P. Lee, G.D. McKenzie, T.J. Mottram, C.M. Old, M.J. Procter, P.E. Russell, M.W.W. Selvey, J.N. Shepherd, K. Shuttleworth, J. Simmons, A.C. Smith, C.T. Spencer, J. Spencer, B. Stead, P.J. Watts.

£250 for the fastest fifty scored in a match televised on BBC 2:
G.M. Turner (Worcestershire) who hit 50 off 32 balls against Northamptonshire at Worcester on July 30th

£100 special award to K.D. Boyce (Essex) for completing the John Player League 'double' of 1,000 runs and 100 wickets

John Player League 1972

BATTING (Qualification: 8 Innings, Average 23.00)   *Not out

	M	I	NO	Runs	HS	Av	100	50	6s
B. Leadbeater	13	12	4	440	86*	55.00	–	2	11
B.A. Richards	14	14	2	643	105	53.58	2	4	14
J.H. Edrich	10	10	1	413	108*	45.88	1	3	2
G.M. Turner	15	15	1	642	121	45.85	2	3	6
B.W. Luckhurst	14	13	3	445	74*	44.50	–	4	4
R.W. Tolchard	16	14	2	480	103	40.00	1	3	4
M.E.J.C. Norman	15	15	4	421	71*	38.27	–	2	–
Younis Ahmed	13	13	1	446	64*	37.16	–	4	11
M.J. Harris	14	13	3	360	92	36.00	–	4	4
B. Hassan	16	16	3	463	86*	35.61	–	4	2
R.G.A. Headley	12	12	0	408	82	34.00	–	3	4
J.M. Brearley	15	13	3	333	67*	33.30	–	3	6
C.G. Greenidge	15	15	2	428	84	32.92	–	4	8
K.W.R. Fletcher	15	14	2	395	69	32.91	–	3	2
C.T. Radley	15	14	2	385	88	32.08	–	2	1
M.J. Procter	14	14	1	417	109*	32.07	1	2	9
G. Boycott	9	9	1	256	52*	32.00	–	1	1
C.H. Lloyd	13	13	2	350	89*	31.81	–	3	4
E.R. Dexter	11	11	2	286	70*	31.77	–	2	2
R.B. Kanhai	16	15	1	444	120	31.71	1	3	8
C.P. Wilkins	13	13	0	409	94	31.46	–	2	10
A.I. Kallicharran	16	15	4	340	101*	30.90	1	1	7
M.J. Khan	8	8	0	240	83	30.00	–	2	8
M.J. Smith	15	14	0	407	92	29.07	–	2	7
K.D. Boyce	16	14	2	345	93*	28.75	–	3	7
P.J.K. Gibbs	14	14	0	402	68	28.71	–	4	–
D.L. Amiss	12	11	2	256	73	28.44	–	3	–
G.R.J. Roope	14	13	3	280	50*	28.00	–	1	4
C. Johnson	14	8	2	166	51*	27.66	–	1	–
Asif Iqbal	13	11	4	190	67*	27.14	–	1	1
P.J. Graves	12	12	1	293	101*	26.63	1	1	3
J.A. Ormrod	15	13	2	280	69	25.45	–	1	1
D.L. Murray	15	11	4	177	46*	25.28	–	–	1
B. Wood	14	13	2	276	67	25.09	–	1	1
D.B. Close	15	15	1	347	55*	24.78	–	1	7
D.R. Turner	11	10	1	221	99*	24.55	–	1	1
P.R. Haywood	14	13	3	243	38*	24.30	–	–	–
D. Nicholls	13	12	0	287	56	23.91	–	2	2
M.H. Denness	15	13	2	258	49*	23.45	–	–	1
J.T. Murray	13	10	1	211	40	23.44	–	–	3
A. Jones	13	13	1	280	57	23.33	–	1	3
P.W. Denning	15	15	3	277	71*	23.08	–	2	3
B.F. Davison	16	14	0	323	80	23.07	–	3	6
J.M. Parks	13	12	1	253	64	23.00	–	1	1

John Player Cricket Yearbook 1973

BOWLING (Qualification: 15 wickets, Average 23·00)

	O	M	R	W	Av	4w	BB
J.A. Snow	63.5	7	183	18	10.16	3	5–15
J. Sullivan	63	11	214	20	10.70	3	5–29
J.K. Lever	103	14	342	29	11.79	2	5–18
R.G.D. Willis	46.4	5	179	15	11.93	–	–321
K.D. Boyce	108.2	17	370	31	11.93	2	4–6
A.G. Nicholson	80.4	13	284	23	12.34	2	6–36
D.L. Underwood	95.5	16	348	28	12.42	3	5–19
R.R. Bailey	98	13	310	23	13.47	1	6–22
G.I. Burgess	88	9	354	26	13.61	2	6–25
T.E. Jesty	49.3	3	227	16	14.18	–	3–30
J.S.E. Price	86.5	10	277	19	14.57	–	3–17
J.C.J. Dye	107	18	371	25	14.84	1	4–41
D.A. Marriott	67	8	240	16	15.00	2	4–12
G.D. McKenzie	120	15	407	27	15.07	1	5–15
V.A. Holder	105.1	11	388	25	15.52	1	6–33
R.D. Jackman	104.1	18	378	24	15.75	1	6–34
C.T. Spencer	84.5	7	343	21	16.33	1	4–39
W. Taylor	121.3	22	468	28	16.71	3	4–11
M. Hendrick	91.4	15	353	21	16.80	1	6–7
R.S. Herman	92	5	400	23	17.39	1	4–22
B. Stead	124.4	17	419	24	17.45	1	4–24
B.M. Brain	75	6	338	19	17.78	2	4–29
C.P. Phillipson	82.1	6	290	16	18.12	2	4–25
B.D. Julien	100	8	430	23	18.69	1	4–28
M.W.W. Selvey	109	14	494	26	19.00	1	4–21
P.I. Pocock	94.3	10	306	16	19.12	–	2–13
T.W. Cartwright	108	23	327	17	19.23	–	3–19
K. Shuttleworth	91	13	347	18	19.27	1	5–13
J.N. Shepherd	115	10	406	21	19.33	1	4–18
J. Denham	84	4	385	19	20.26	2	4–28
S. Turner	105.5	17	329	16	20.56	–	2–19
A.A. Jones	104.3	10	399	19	21.00	–	3–45
H.R. Moseley	83.4	8	362	17	21.29	2	4–19
J.N. Graham	112.4	10	385	18	21.38	–	3–24
B.F. Davison	88	5	417	19	21.94	1	4–33
J. Simmons	96	18	376	17	22.11	1	5–28
M.J. Procter	92.1	18	336	15	22.40	1	5–10
K. Higgs	113.5	16	409	18	22.72	–	2–27

MOST ECONOMICAL BOWLING (Qualification: 60 overs)

	O	M	R	W	Runs/over
J.A. Snow	63.5	7	183	18	2.87
T.W. Cartwright	108	23	327	17	3.03
G.G. Arnold	71.3	12	217	11	3.03
S. Turner	105.5	17	329	16	3.11

John Player League 1972

	O	M	R	W	Runs/Over
R.R. Bailey	98	13	310	23	3.16
J.S.E. Price	86.5	10	277	19	3.19
P.I. Pocock	94.3	10	306	16	3.24

WICKET-KEEPING

Dismissals: 24 (equalling record) – R.W. Tolchard (21ct, 3st). 20 – A.P.E. Knott (17c, 3st). 19 – B. Taylor (16ct, 3st). 18 – D.L. Murray (18ct), G. Sharp (18ct). 17 – D.L. Bairstow (16ct, 1st), J.T. Murray (16ct, 1st), R.W. Taylor (13ct, 4st).

FIELDING

Catches: 11 – K.W.R. Fletcher, C.T. Radley. 10 – M.H. Page, C.P. Wilkins. 9 – J.M. Brearley, A.S. Brown, C.H. Lloyd, M.J. Smith.

PLAYING RECORD OF THE COUNTIES 1969–1972

*Not out

	P	W	L	T	NR	Run Rate	6s	4w	Highest Total	Lowest Total	HS	BB
Derbyshire	64	30	30	–	4	4.17	66	12	260	70	94	6–7
Essex	64	40	19	–	5	4.36	108	17	265	93	107	8–26
Glamorgan	64	21	37	–	6	3.89	117	10	215	65	87	6–36
Gloucestershire	64	23	34	2	5	4.01	85	13	229	90	127*	5–10
Hampshire	64	34	26	1	3	4.47	111	11	248	43	155*	5–31
Kent	64	40	22	1	1	4.38	133	21	261	84	142	5–19
Lancashire	64	43	18	–	3	4.53	106	18	255	76	134*	5–13
Leicestershire	64	34	25	–	5	4.31	82	12	262	90	103	5–13
Middlesex	64	27	31	–	6	4.45	87	18	241	56	133*	6–6
Northamptonshire	64	22	37	1	4	4.02	86	15	239	41	115*	6–22
Nottinghamshire	64	24	37	1	2	4.11	88	19	252	66	116*	5–23
Somerset	64	27	31	–	6	4.18	87	10	234	92	128*	6–25
Surrey	64	31	28	–	5	4.04	79	6	215	82	108*	6–34
Sussex	64	19	37	–	8	4.27	89	15	288	63	121	6–28
Warwickshire	64	26	31	–	7	4.37	92	10	249	85	120	5–13
Worcestershire	64	32	27	–	5	4.36	78	17	258	86	121	6–33
Yorkshire	64	27	30	–	7	4.13	105	17	235	74	119	7–15

The Gillette Cup 1972

FIRST ROUND – Wednesday July 5th

CAMBRIDGESHIRE V BUCKINGHAMSHIRE at Fenner's, Cambridge
Buckinghamshire won by 183 runs
Buckinghamshire 224–7 in 60 overs (D.A. Janes 95, D.C. Wing 4–40). Cambridgeshire 41 in 20 overs* (R.E. Bond 5–17, F.W. Harris 4–21).

Record lowest total in Gillette Cup matches

HAMPSHIRE V WILTSHIRE at Bournemouth
Hampshire won by 8 wickets
Wiltshire 115 in 59.5 overs. Hampshire 116–2 in 22.4 overs (B.A. Richards 64 not out).

NORTHAMPTONSHIRE V GLAMORGAN at Northampton
Glamorgan won by 43 runs
Glamorgan 241–8 in 60 overs (R.C. Fredericks 82, A. Jones 63)
Northamptonshire 198 in 56.3 overs (M.J. Khan 4–38).

OXFORDSHIRE V DURHAM at Morris Motors Ground, Oxford
Durham won by 4 wickets
Oxfordshire 140 in 60 overs (R.D. Montgomerie 64). Durham 141–6 in 30.2 overs (A.J. Burridge 95, S.A. Hattea 4–32).

SUSSEX V WORCESTERSHIRE at Hove
Worcestershire won by 3 wickets
Sussex 185–8 in 60 overs (G.A. Greenidge 72). Worcestershire 187–7 in 58.5 overs (E.J.O. Hemsley 73, B.L. D'Oliveira 50).

YORKSHIRE V WARWICKSHIRE at Headingley, Leeds
Warwickshire won by 4 wickets
Yorkshire 173 in 60 overs (R.A. Hutton 61, R.G.D. Willis 4–21). Warwickshire 176–6 in 58 overs (D.L. Amiss 52, R.B. Kanhai 62).

SECOND ROUND – Wednesday July 19th

KENT V GLOUCESTERSHIRE at Canterbury
Kent won by 33 runs
Kent 240–9 in 60 overs (G.W. Johnson 65). Gloucestershire 207 in 56.2 overs (Sadiq Mohammad 53).

WARWICKSHIRE V LEICESTERSHIRE at Edgbaston, Birmingham
Warwickshire won by 3 runs
Warwickshire 218–7 in 60 overs (M.J.K. Smith 66 not out, C.T. Spencer 4–28). Leicestershire 215 in 59.4 overs

The Gillette Cup 1972

Above: Barry Richards lofts Hughes out of the ground during his brilliant innings of 129 in the third round of the Gillette Cup

Right: Essex fast bowler John Lever devastated Middlesex in the second round, taking 5–8 in their disastrous 41

Below: Glenn Turner is bowled by David Brown in the semi-finals, and with him go Worcestershire's hopes

DERBYSHIRE V WORCESTERSHIRE at Derby
Worcestershire won by 9 wickets
Derbyshire 214–6 in 60 overs (I.R. Buxton 81, J.F. Harvey 54 not out). Worcestershire 215–1 in 51.4 overs (G.M. Turner 101 not out, R.G.A. Headley 68).

DURHAM V SURREY at Chester-le-Street
Surrey won by 75 runs
Surrey 217–9 in 60 overs (M.J. Stewart 101). Durham 142 in 52.3 overs (J.G. March 78).

NOTTINGHAMSHIRE V HAMPSHIRE at Trent Bridge, Nottingham
Hampshire won by 79 runs
Hampshire 283–9 in 60 overs (T.E. Jesty 62 not out, B.A. Richards 55). Nottinghamshire 204 in 55.3 overs (M.N.S. Taylor 58, T.E. Jesty 4–32).

BUCKINGHAMSHIRE V GLAMORGAN at Amersham
Glamorgan won by 4 runs
Glamorgan 174 in 58 overs (F.W. Harris 4–33). Buckinghamshire 170–9 in 60 overs (J.B. Turner 65).

LANCASHIRE V SOMERSET at Old Trafford, Manchester
Lancashire won by 9 runs
Lancashire 243–9 in 60 overs (C.H. Lloyd 86, H.R. Moseley 4–36). Somerset 234 in 58.4 overs (M.J. Kitchen 116, D.P. Hughes 4–61).

ESSEX V MIDDLESEX at Westcliff-on-Sea
Essex won by 8 wickets
Middlesex 41 in 19.4 overs* (J.K. Lever 5–8, K.D. Boyce 5–22). Essex 43–2 in 18 overs

*Equalled record lowest total in Gillette Cup matches. This match equalled the earliest finish (2.20 p.m.) in the competition's history and was completed in fewer overs (37.4) than any Gillette Cup match not reduced by rain.

THIRD ROUND – Wednesday August 2nd*
HAMPSHIRE V LANCASHIRE at Bournemouth
Lancashire won by 4 wickets
Hampshire 223 in 58.2 overs (B.A. Richards 129). Lancashire 227–6 in 58.3 overs (B. Wood 66).

WORCESTERSHIRE V SURREY at Worcester
Worcestershire won by 6 wickets
Surrey 106 in 55.3 overs (N. Gifford 4–7). Worcestershire 109–4 in 44.4 overs

WARWICKSHIRE V GLAMORGAN at Edgbaston, Birmingham
Warwickshire won by 10 runs
Warwickshire 214–9 in 60 overs (A.I. Kallicharran 88). Glamorgan 204–9 in 60 overs (A. Jones 58, P.M. Walker 51).

ESSEX V KENT at Leyton
Kent won by 10 runs
Kent 137 in 52 overs (Asif Iqbal 52). Essex 127 in 57.3 overs (J.N. Shepherd 4–23).

*The Birmingham match continued on Thursday, August 3rd, while that at Leyton was postponed until August 3rd.

Semi-Final:
Warwickshire v Worcestershire

Winners of the Gillette Cup in 1966 and 1968, Warwickshire reached the final of the competition for the fourth time when they overwhelmed Worcestershire by eight wickets, with 12.5 overs in hand, at Edgbaston. This abnormally large margin of victory for a limited-overs match was well deserved, for Worcestershire could not match their neighbour's depth of batting, or the penetration and economy of their bowling. Only a substantial innings from their key player, Turner, could transfer the pressure from their

The Gillette Cup 1972

suspect attack to Warwickshire's batsmen, and with his dismissal went most hope of winning.

Overcast skies prevented neither 10,500 spectators from enjoying the splendid amenities of the best equipped cricket ground in Britain nor Gifford from deciding to bat first. Worcestershire began well enough, scoring 16 off 4 overs before Headley top-edged a hook at a slower ball and was caught at short square-leg. Yet his rash hit almost escaped penalty when Murray challenged Jameson for the catch. Stimpson soon edged to first slip's right, but Turner, undeterred, continued with a series of handsome drives and cuts. His crucial dismissal occurred in the 15th over when he was completely baffled by a good length ball that broke back to hit the off-stump.

Certainly Worcestershire were unable again to strike at a rate of 4 runs an over. At lunch they were 70 for 3 off 27 overs, Ormrod having scored 7 in 15 overs with a 20-minute break for rain. Five overs afterwards they lost D'Oliveira – a spectacular dismissal this, with the ball cutting back to beat a majestic cover-drive and take the middle stump. When the score showed 111 for 7 in the 48th over at 2.54 p.m., it looked as if the match would be over soon after tea. Yardley (52 in 103 minutes off 80 balls) and the bowlers had other ideas, and Warwickshire were set 175 at almost 3 runs an over.

If tea encouraged Holder to dream of an early breakthrough, Jameson ensured that he was not disappointed by dragging a widish off-side ball into his stumps. That was Worcestershire's last hope. Without taking undue risks, Amiss and Kanhai scored 143 together in 40 overs. The operation was expertly paced with a queue of reserve batsmen not even tested. Amiss hit eight fours before being caught, but Kanhai, Man of the Match for the third time in Gillette Cup games, was still there at the finish.

WARWICKSHIRE v WORCESTERSHIRE at Edgbaston, Birmingham on August 17th
Warwickshire won by 8 wickets
Toss: Worcestershire
Man of the Match: R.B. Kanhai

WORCESTERSHIRE
R.G.A. Headley	c Jameson b Willis	4
G.M. Turner	b Brown	31
P.J. Stimpson	c Kanhai b Rouse	8
J.A. Ormrod	run out	17
B.L. D'Oliveira	b Willis	21
T.J. Yardley	c Kallicharran b Willis	52
G.R. Cass†	lbw b Brown	4
N. Gifford*	lbw b McVicker	0
V.A. Holder	c Jameson b Rouse	7
B.M. Brain	not out	16
A. Shutt	not out	0
Extras	(b 5, lb 7, nb 2)	14
TOTAL	(9 wkts – 60 overs)	174

WARWICKSHIRE
J.A. Jameson	b Holder	1
D.L. Amiss	c Cass b Holder	67
R.B. Kanhai	not out	85
M.J.K. Smith*	not out	6
A.I. Kallicharran		
D.L. Murray†		
N.M. McVicker		
S.J. Rouse	did not bat	
D.J. Brown		
R.G.D. Willis		
L.R. Gibbs		
Extras	(b 2, lb 7, nb 6, w 1)	16
TOTAL	(2 wkts – 47.1 overs)	175

WARWICKSHIRE
	O	M	R	W
Willis	12	1	53	3
McVicker	12	1	34	1
Brown	12	2	27	2
Rouse	12	0	31	2
Gibbs	12	5	15	0

WORCESTERSHIRE
	O	M	R	W
Holder	12	4	25	2
Brain	11	1	48	0
Shutt	11.1	1	48	0
Gifford	9	1	23	0
D'Oliveira	4	0	15	0

FALL OF WICKETS
Wkt	Wo	Wa
1st	16	4
2nd	43	147
3rd	47	
4th	81	
5th	96	
6th	109	
7th	111	
8th	132	
9th	168	
10th		

Umpires: W.E. Alley and D.G.L. Evans
Attendance: 10,500

Semi-Final:
Lancashire v Kent

In a repeat of the 1971 final, Lancashire, the holders, earned an attempt at a Gillette Cup hat-trick when they beat Kent by seven runs at Old Trafford, their experience and expertise carrying them through the pressures of a nail-biting finish.

Kent's disadvantage in losing the toss was doubled when morning rain delayed the start beyond an early lunch and took the match into a second day. They had to endure an unbroken session of 185 minutes (52 overs) in the field, whereas Lancashire's bowlers were refreshed by a night's rest after 34.4 overs of the Kent innings.

Lancashire followed their one-day match policy of a steady start by scoring only 15 runs from ten accurate overs by Graham (4 maidens) and Julien. With the damp outfield reducing several normal boundaries to threes, the opening stand of 59 took 23 overs, but a typically lively partnership of 46 in 14 overs between Pilling and Clive Lloyd began the acceleration phase. However, this progress was impeded by much brilliant ground fielding and two memorable catches. First, Johnson ran in from deep square-leg to hold a sweep from Clive Lloyd, then Asif held a most improbable skier from Hayes, covering 30 yards and holding the catch knee-high while running at full tilt as the batsmen were completing their second run.

Tea was taken after 52 overs with Lancashire 160 for 4. Pilling – chiefly through cuts – and Hughes – with swinging drives – plundered 63 runs from the remaining eight overs. Even Kent's magnificently athletic fielding could not prevent 76 coming from the last ten. Curiously Lancashire's 224 equalled their total in the 1971 final.

Lee, whose umpteenth shout for lbw gained Luckhurst's wicket, frequently beat the bat in a splendid six-over spell that cost only four runs. Johnson fell in the 13th over, but Cowdrey, in vintage form, and Denness stemmed any fears of collapse. Their stand, which added 76 elegant runs in 22 overs, continued through ever-darkening murk when the batsmen charitably declined the umpires' invitation to call it a day to avoid disappointing the 20,500 spectators who had paid £18,182. But the return of Lee saw the immediate departure of Cowdrey and the end of play, with Kent, 110 for 3 off 34.4 overs, needing 4.5 runs per over.

The 2,500 who watched under two hour's play the next day saw a splendid finish. Denness and Asif made 45 in the first half-hour to put Kent in a strong position before off-spinner Simmons dismissed them both in three balls. Four overs later he induced a reckless sweep from Knott, and even Julien, with a 4-ball onslaught worth 4, 2, 6, 6, could not shake Lancashire's grip on the match. Relentlessly the holders, who did not concede a boundary after the 48th over, drove Kent below the required rate. Twelve were needed from the final over and Underwood's attempt to score 8 off the last ball ended in a stumping by the gore-stained Engineer, who had had his brow split and eye closed by a ball ricocheting off Shepherd's pads.

John Shepherd's four wickets against Essex in the third round helped Kent win a place in the semi-finals where they met, and lost to, Lancashire

LANCASHIRE V KENT at Old Trafford, Manchester on August 17th and 18th
Lancashire won by 7 runs
Toss: Lancashire
Man of the Match: H. Pilling

LANCASHIRE
D. Lloyd	c and b Underwood	33
B. Wood	b Woolmer	29
H. Pilling	c Knott b Julien	70
C.H. Lloyd	c Johnson b Underwood	32
F.C. Hayes	c Asif b Underwood	13
D.P. Hughes	not out	35
J. Simmons	c Denness b Julien	0
F.M. Engineer†	not out	0
J.D. Bond*		
K. Shuttleworth	did not bat	
P. Lee		
Extras	(b 1, lb 10, w 1)	12
TOTAL	(6 wkts – 60 overs)	224

KENT
B.W. Luckhurst	lbw b Lee	10
G.W. Johnson	c Engineer b Wood	12
M.H. Denness*	lbw b Simmons	65
M.C. Cowdrey	lbw b Lee	44
Asif Iqbal	c Engineer b Simmons	23
A.P.E. Knott†	lbw b Simmons	3
B.D. Julien	lbw b Shuttleworth	35
R.A. Woolmer	c Bond b Hughes	3
J.N. Shepherd	c Simmons b Hughes	9
D.L. Underwood	st Engineer b Hughes	5
J.N. Graham	not out	1
Extras	(lb 4, nb 1, w 2)	7
TOTAL	(60 overs)	217

KENT	O	M	R	W	FALL OF WICKETS		
Graham	12	4	40	0			
Julien	12	2	35	2	Wkt	La	K
Shepherd	12	0	38	0	1st	59	17
Woolmer	12	1	51	1	2nd	67	34
Underwood	12	2	48	3	3rd	113	110
					4th	160	155
LANCASHIRE					5th	223	155
Lee	12	4	16	2	6th	223	163
Shuttleworth	12	3	47	1	7th		188
Wood	12	4	42	1	8th		192
Simmons	12	1	48	3	9th		213
C.H. Lloyd	3	0	18	0	10th		217
Hughes	9	0	39	3			

Umpires: H.D. Bird and G.H. Pope
Attendance: 20,500 (1st day) and 2,500 (2nd)

Final: Lancashire v Warwickshire

For the tenth year running the Gillette Cup final, the climax to the season, was blessed with fine weather and completed in the day. The 26,586 who paid £47,571 saw an ideal match played on a good, reasonably fast Lord's pitch, despite the fact that neither side was at full strength. Lancashire were without opening bowlers Lever and Shuttleworth, while Warwickshire, minus the ubiquitous Alan Smith, had a dangerously long tail. In the event, Warwickshire, over-concerned about their batting, failed to take advantage of their opponent's makeshift attack, and Lancashire, owing much to a truly great innings by Clive Lloyd, won the Gillette Cup for the third successive year.

Jack Bond, under whose captaincy Lancashire won the Gillette Cup in three successive years

Mike Smith's decision to bat first in sunny, dew-free conditions on a dry, hard wicket looked a sound one when Whitehouse and Amiss gave Warwickshire a sound start, scoring 50 in 20 overs. But when Amiss played across the line and Kanhai holed-out on the square-leg boundary, fears of the long tail reduced the captain to 15 runs off 14 overs. Only 21 overs remained when lunch was taken at 114 for 2.

Two overs later, Hughes deceived Whitehouse, so bringing Kallicharran to the wicket to begin the delayed acceleration phase that produced 85 runs in 15 overs. The Guyanese left-hander reached his half-century off 56 balls with a six and 6 fours before he edged a skier to Engineer. Murray helped Smith take 15 off the next two overs, but then five wickets fell for six runs in the space of eight balls. Three were grotesque run-outs involving Brown.

Lancashire, faced with a target of 235 at 3.9 runs an over – 20 more than the previous best second innings score in a final – were soon in trouble at 26 for 2 in the tenth over. Pilling and Clive Lloyd developed slowly, pressed by attacking fields, and the early part of Lloyd's innings gave scant indication of the onslaught to follow. He confined himself to just six singles in eight overs before launching himself with a four and a six off Brown. At tea the match was still evenly poised with Lancashire, 73 for 2 after 23 overs, needing another 162 at 4.4 runs per over. After tea, Lloyd's form made nonsense of all predictions. In sharing stands of 97 in 24 overs with Pilling and 86 in 17 overs with Hayes, he hammered every bowler, the violence of his hitting, allied to a fast outfield, bringing him 14 fours in addition to three sixes. His 50 took 68 balls, his century 110, and his nomination as Man of the Match after Lancashire's four-wicket victory with 20 balls to spare was merely a formality.

Clive Lloyd, hero of Lancashire and Man of the Match following his magnificent 126 that took the Gillette Cup back to Old Trafford

The Gillette Cup 1972

LANCASHIRE V WARWICKSHIRE at Lord's, London on September 2nd
Lancashire won by 4 wickets
Toss: Warwickshire
Man of the Match: C.H. Lloyd

WARWICKSHIRE

J. Whitehouse	st Engineer b Hughes	68
D.L. Amiss	lbw b Wood	16
R.B. Kanhai	c D. Lloyd b Hughes	14
M.J.K. Smith*	lbw b Simmons	48
A.I. Kallicharran	c Engineer b Sullivan	54
D.L. Murray†	lbw b Sullivan	10
N.M. McVicker	run out	1
D.J. Brown	run out	5
S.J. Rouse	run out	0
R.G.D. Willis	not out	2
L.R. Gibbs	not out	4
Extras	(b 5, lb 7)	12
TOTAL	(9 wkts – 60 overs)	**234**

173

LANCASHIRE

D. Lloyd	lbw b Brown	10
B. Wood	c and b McVicker	15
H. Pilling	run out	30
C.H. Lloyd	lbw b Willis	126
F.C. Hayes	c Murray b Brown	35
J. Sullivan	not out	9
F.M. Engineer†	b Willis	0
D.P. Hughes	not out	4
J.D. Bond*		
J. Simmons	did not bat	
P. Lee		
Extras	(lb 6)	6
TOTAL	(6 wkts – 56.4 overs)	**235**

LANCASHIRE

	O	M	R	W
C.H. Lloyd	12	2	31	0
Lee	10	1	48	0
Wood	12	2	27	1
Hughes	12	0	50	2
Sullivan	5	1	27	2
Simmons	9	0	39	1

WARWICKSHIRE

	O	M	R	W
McVicker	12	1	44	1
Willis	12	1	29	2
Brown	12	1	67	2
Rouse	10.4	0	45	0
Gibbs	10	0	44	0

FALL OF WICKETS

Wkt	Wa	La
1st	50	26
2nd	69	26
3rd	122	123
4th	207	209
5th	222	219
6th	222	223
7th	224	
8th	227	
9th	228	
10th		

Umpires: C.S. Elliott and A.E.G. Rhodes
Attendance: 26,586   Receipts: £47,571

Rohan Kanhai tickles one away down the leg side during his attractive innings of 85 in the Warwickshire-Worcestershire semi-final. Kanhai's superb form last summer belied his increasing years and contributed much to Warwickshire's successful season

GILLETTE CUP FINALS

1963 SUSSEX beat Worcestershire by 14 runs
1964 SUSSEX beat Warwickshire by 8 wickets
1965 YORKSHIRE beat Surrey by 175 runs
1966 WARWICKSHIRE beat Worcestershire by 5 wickets
1967 KENT beat Somerset by 32 runs
1968 WARWICKSHIRE beat Sussex by 4 wickets
1969 YORKSHIRE beat Derbyshire by 69 runs
1970 LANCASHIRE beat Sussex by 6 wickets
1971 LANCASHIRE beat Kent by 24 runs
1972 LANCASHIRE beat Warwickshire by 4 wickets

Benson and Hedges League Cup 1972

Zonal Results

MIDLANDS	P	W	L	Bwlg Pts	Pts
LEICESTERSHIRE	4	4	0	4	16
WARWICKSHIRE	4	3	1	1	10
Worcestershire	4	2	2	1	7
Northamptonshire	4	1	3	0	3
Cambridge U.	4	0	4	0	0

Matches begun on Saturday April 29th

LEICESTERSHIRE (4 points) beat NORTHAMPTONSHIRE by 7 wickets at Leicester
Northamptonshire 120 in 51.4 overs (G.D. McKenzie 4–19). Leicestershire 121–3 in 40.4 overs (R.W. Tolchard 63 not out).

WARWICKSHIRE (3 points) beat CAMBRIDGE U. by 7 wickets at Edgbaston, Birmingham
Cambridge U. 179–9 in 55 overs. Warwickshire 180–3 in 47.1 overs (R.B. Kanhai 81 not out).

Matches begun on Saturday May 6th

WORCESTERSHIRE (4 points) beat CAMBRIDGE U. by 87 runs at Cambridge
Worcestershire 196–7 in 55 overs (G.M. Turner 89, J. Spencer 4–29). Cambridge U. 109 in 49.5 overs

WARWICKSHIRE (4 points) beat NORTHAMPTONSHIRE by 5 wickets at Northampton
Northamptonshire 132 in 53.5 overs. Warwickshire 133–5 in 51.2 overs

Matches begun on Saturday May 13th

WORCESTERSHIRE (3 points) beat NORTHAMPTONSHIRE by 8 wickets at Northampton
Northamptonshire 162–8 in 55 overs (A. Tait 51). Worcestershire 163–2 in 51.5 overs (R.G.A. Headley 71, J.A. Ormrod 63 not out)

LEICESTERSHIRE (4 points) beat WARWICKSHIRE by 184 runs at Coventry
Leicestershire 327–4 in 55 overs (B.F. Davison 158 not out, M.E.J.C. Norman 86). Warwickshire 143 in 48 overs (K. Higgs 4–31)

Matches begun on Saturday May 20th

LEICESTERSHIRE (4 points) beat CAMBRIDGE U. by 8 wickets at Leicester
Cambridge U. 135 in 54.1 overs. Leicestershire 136–2 in 35.1 overs (M.E.J.C. Norman 63 not out)

WARWICKSHIRE (3 points) beat WORCESTERSHIRE by 8 wickets at Worcester
Worcestershire 178–6 in 55 overs (T.J. Yardley 75 not out). Warwickshire 179–2 in 50.3 overs (D.L. Murray 82)

John Player Cricket Yearbook 1973

Barry Wood, here off driving with power and conviction, gave a fine all-round performance for Lancashire against Derbyshire

Matches begun on Saturday June 3rd

NORTHAMPTONSHIRE (3 points) beat CAMBRIDGE U. by 8 wickets at Cambridge
Cambridge U. 141–8 in 55 overs. Northamptonshire 142–2 in 44.1 overs (G. Cook 54, D.S. Steele 51 not out)

LEICESTERSHIRE (4 points) beat WORCESTERSHIRE by 56 runs at Worcester
Leicestershire 202–8 in 55 overs. Worcestershire 146 in 47 overs (B.L. D'Oliveira 52, G.D. McKenzie 4–12)

NORTH	P	W	L	Bwlg Pts	Pts
YORKSHIRE	4	3	1	2	11
LANCASHIRE	4	3	1	2	11
Nottinghamshire	4	3	1	1	10
Derbyshire	4	1	3	0	3
Minor Counties (N)	4	0	4	0	0

Matches begun on Saturday April 29th

NOTTINGHAMSHIRE (3 points) beat DERBYSHIRE by 5 wickets at Trent Bridge, Nottingham.
Derbyshire 162–6 in 55 overs (A.J. Harvey-Walker 79). Nottinghamshire 163-5 in 52.3 overs (M.J. Harris 92 not out)

YORKSHIRE (4 points) beat LANCASHIRE by 9 wickets at Bradford
Lancashire 82 in 47.2 overs (D. Wilson 5–26). Yorkshire 84–1 in 41.1 overs

Matches begun on Saturday May 6th

LANCASHIRE (3 points) beat DERBYSHIRE by 29 runs at Old Trafford, Manchester
Lancashire 174 in 54.2 overs (B. Wood 56). Derbyshire 145–8 in 55 overs (B. Wood 4–34).

Above: Worcestershire's Glenn Turner in attacking mood. Though he has always possessed an excellent defensive technique – and would use it for hours on end if necessary – Turner in recent years has developed as a stroke-player of high quality. His aggression has been especially marked in limited-overs matches, in which he amassed 918 runs during the 1972 season. 121 of these came in Worcestershire's 170 runs victory over Sussex in the John Player League – a record margin of victory for that competition

Right: John Shepherd, Kent's medium-pace seamer, in action against Worcestershire in the John Player League match that brought Kent the 1972 title

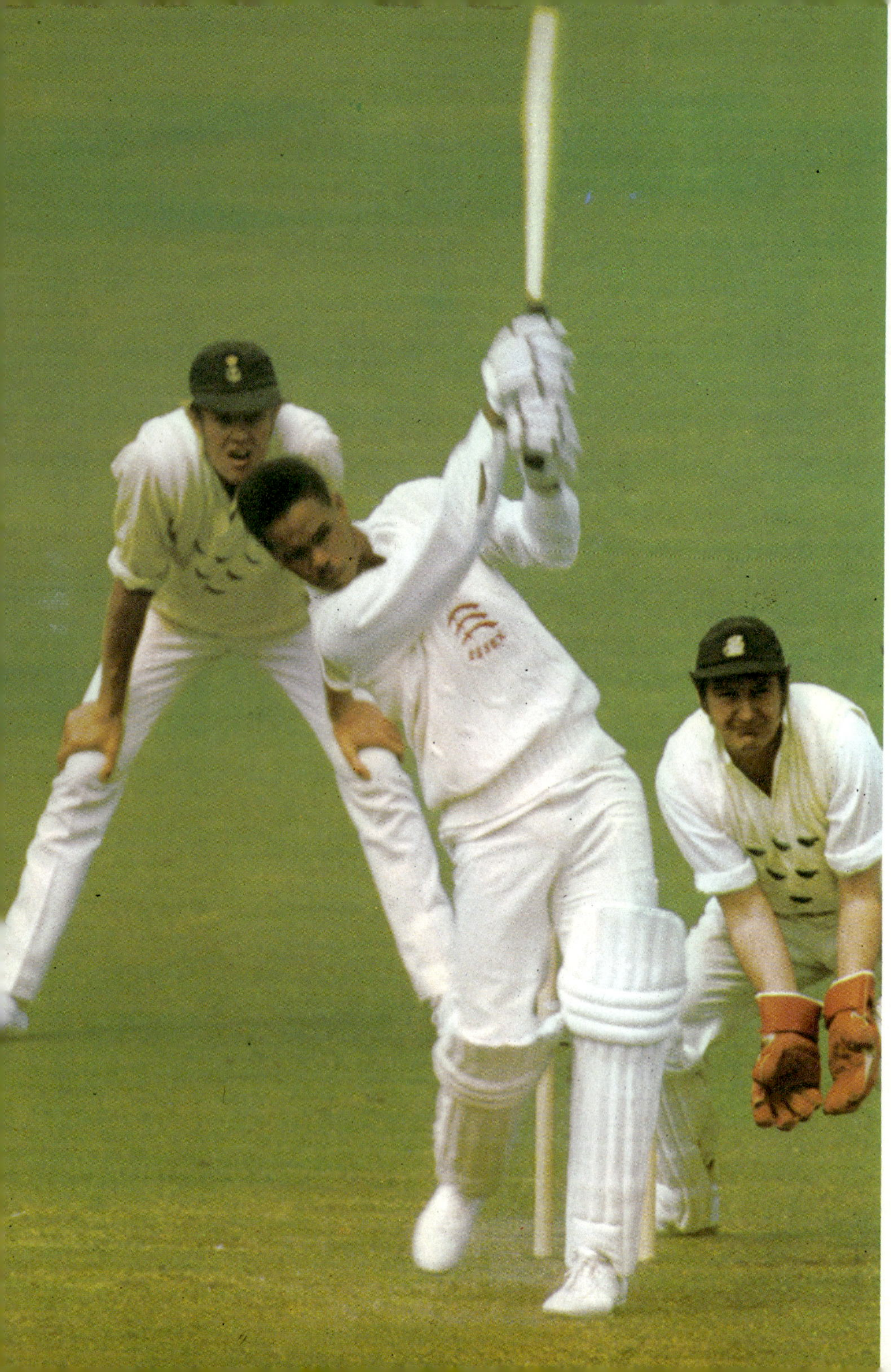

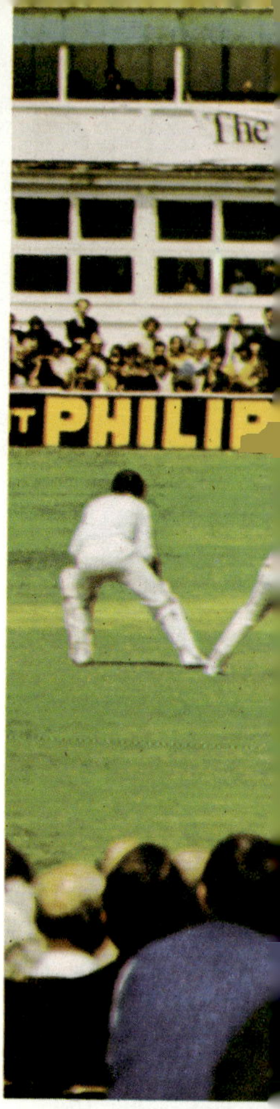
The
PHILIP

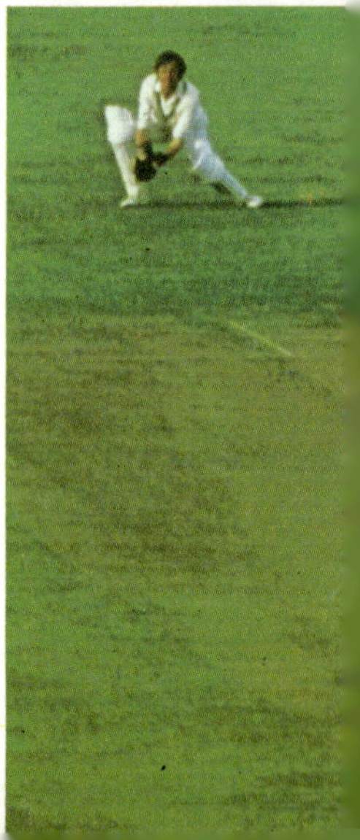

Above: Ken Higgs yorks David Brown, and Warwickshire are all out for 96 in the Benson and Hedges League Cup semi-final at Leicester. Leicestershire reached 98 for the loss of only three wickets and went on to beat Yorkshire in the first final

Far left: Keith Boyce, Essex's Barbadian all-rounder, batting against Sussex. His John Player League double was recognised with a special award

Left: Rohan Kanhai unleashes a majestic square drive during his innings of 85 not out in Warwickshire's 1972 Gillette Cup semi-final against Worcestershire

Above: Barry Richards, whose 993 runs for Hampshire in one-day games put him at the top of the limited-overs averages for 1972. His average of 55.16 was the only one to top the 50 mark. Statistics alone, however, give no indication of the immense pleasure Richards gave spectators with the grace and power of his stroke-play

Right above: Kent supporters with little doubt as to who was going to win the John Player Trophy for 1972

Right: Oh, Dolly! Basil D'Oliveira's middle stump is knocked back by Bob Willis, and Worcestershire are in real trouble in the 1972 Gillette Cup semi-final against Warwickshire

NOTTINGHAMSHIRE (4 points) beat MINOR COUNTIES (N) by 55 runs at Cleethorpes
Nottinghamshire 206 in 53.5 overs (G.St.A. Sobers 97 not out). Minor Counties (N) 151 in 54 overs

Matches begun on Saturday May 13th
YORKSHIRE (4 points) beat DERBYSHIRE by 6 wickets at Chesterfield
Derbyshire 127 in 53.5 overs (A.G. Nicholson 4–26). Yorkshire 128–4 in 47.1 overs (G. Boycott 58 not out).

LANCASHIRE (4 points) beat MINOR COUNTIES (N) by 88 runs at Boughton Hall, Chester
Lancashire 216–4 in 55 overs (H. Pilling 53, C.H. Lloyd 57). Minor Counties (N) 128 in 48.3 overs (R.M.O. Cooke 53, P. Lever 5–21).

Matches begun on Saturday May 20th
LANCASHIRE (4 points) beat NOTTINGHAMSHIRE by 156 runs at Old Trafford, Manchester
Lancashire 251–5 in 55 overs (K.L. Snellgrove 66, H. Pilling 62). Nottinghamshire 95 in 44.3 overs

YORKSHIRE (3 points) beat MINOR COUNTIES (N) by 9 wickets at Middlesbrough
Minor Counties (N) 170–9 in 55 overs (R.M.O. Cooke 63, A.G. Nicholson 6–27). Yorkshire 173–1 in 47.5 overs (P.J. Sharpe 89 not out, B. Leadbeater 64)

Matches begun on Saturday June 3rd
DERBYSHIRE (3 points) beat MINOR COUNTIES (N) by 24 runs at Derby
Derbyshire 179–8 in 55 overs. Minor Counties (N) 155–9 in 55 overs (A.J. Burridge 76)

NOTTINGHAMSHIRE (3 points) beat YORKSHIRE by 3 wickets at Trent Bridge, Nottingham.
Yorkshire 122–8 in 55 overs. Nottinghamshire 123–7 in 52.2 overs

SOUTH	P	W	L	Bwlg Pts	Pts
MIDDLESEX	4	3	1	1	10
SUSSEX	4	3	1	1	10
Kent	4	2	2	2	8
Surrey	4	2	2	1	7
Essex	4	0	4	0	0

Matches begun on Saturday April 29th
MIDDLESEX (3 points) beat KENT by 3 wickets at Lord's, London
Kent 234–5 in 55 overs (M.C. Cowdrey 107 not out). Middlesex 235–7 in 53.4 overs (M.J. Smith 73)

SUSSEX (4 points) beat SURREY by 57 runs at Hove
Sussex 182–8 in 55 overs (R.M. Prideaux 63 not out). Surrey 125 in 48.4 overs

Matches begun on Saturday May 6th
KENT (4 points) beat SUSSEX by 49 runs at Tunbridge Wells
Kent 173 in 50.5 overs (B.W. Luckhurst 55). Sussex 124 in 48.4 overs (R.A. Woolmer 4–14)

SURREY (3 points) beat ESSEX by 19 runs at The Oval, London
Surrey 176–9 in 55 overs (J.H. Edrich 75, J.K. Lever 4–33). Essex 157–8 in 55 overs

Matches begun on Saturday May 13th
KENT (4 points) beat ESSEX by 3 wickets at Chelmsford
Essex 166 in 53.4 overs. Kent 167–7 in 54.1 overs (D. Nicholls 51)

SUSSEX (3 points) beat MIDDLESEX by 47 runs at Hove
Sussex 224–6 in 55 overs (M.A. Buss 78). Middlesex 177–8 in 55 overs (C.T. Radley 55)

John Player Cricket Yearbook 1973

Below: M.J. Smith, who enjoyed a fine season for Middlesex in 1972
Bottom: Gordon Greenidge of Hampshire

Matches begun on Saturday May 20th

SUSSEX (3 points) beat ESSEX by 28 runs at Chelmsford
Sussex 172–8 in 55 overs. Essex 144–8 in 55 overs

MIDDLESEX (4 points) beat SURREY by 13 runs at The Oval, London
Middlesex 199–9 in 55 overs (J.M. Brearley 68 not out). Surrey 186 in 54.2 overs (C.J.R. Black 4–39)

Matches begun on Saturday June 3rd

SURREY (4 points) beat KENT with scores level, having lost fewer wickets, at Blackheath
Kent 172 in 53.2 overs (M.H. Denness 53). Surrey 172–7 in 55 overs

MIDDLESEX (3 points) beat ESSEX by 51 runs at Lord's, London
Middlesex 232–6 in 55 overs (P.H. Parfitt 110). Essex 181–7 in 55 overs (G.J. Saville 85 not out)

WEST	P	W	L	Bwlg Pts	Pts
GLAMORGAN	4	3	1	2	11
GLOUCESTERSHIRE	4	3	1	1	10
Somerset	4	2	2	2	8
Hampshire	4	2	2	1	7
Minor Counties (S)	4	0	4	0	0

Matches begun on Saturday April 29th

GLOUCESTERSHIRE (3 points) beat GLAMORGAN by 6 wickets at Swansea
Glamorgan 194–9 in 55 overs (M.J. Procter 5–37). Gloucestershire 195–4 in 50.4 overs (Sadiq Mohammad 108)

SOMERSET (4 points) beat MINOR COUNTIES (S) by 65 runs at Plymouth
Somerset 169 in 54 overs (R.C. Cooper 95). Minor Counties (S) 104 in 52.5 overs

Matches begun on Saturday May 6th
HAMPSHIRE (4 points) beat GLOUCESTERSHIRE by 99 runs at Moreton-in-Marsh
Hampshire 169 in 47.3 overs. Gloucestershire 70 in 32.4 overs (P.J. Sainsbury 4–17, R.S. Herman 4–20)

GLAMORGAN (3 points) beat MINOR COUNTIES (S) by 37 runs at Chippenham
Glamorgan 180–5 in 55 overs M.A. Nash 92 not out). Minor Counties (S) 143–6 in 55 overs (T.I. Barwell 64 not out)

Matches begun on Saturday May 13th
GLAMORGAN (4 points) beat SOMERSET by 15 runs at Pontypridd
Glamorgan 136 in 54.2 overs (G.I. Burgess 4–12). Somerset 121 in 47.4 overs

HAMPSHIRE (3 points) beat MINOR COUNTIES (S) by 104 runs at Southampton
Hampshire 215 in 54.2 overs (C.G. Greenidge 81). Minor Counties (S) 111–8 in 55 overs

Matches begun on Saturday May 20th
GLOUCESTERSHIRE (3 points) beat MINOR COUNTIES (S) by 7 wickets at Bristol
Minor Counties (S) 161–8 in 55 overs (H.B. Hollington 78). Gloucestershire 162–3 in 38.5. overs (R.D.V. Knight 82 not out)

SOMERSET (4 points) beat HAMPSHIRE by 51 runs at Yeovil
Somerset 264–7 in 55 overs (D.B. Close 88, G.I. Burgess 58). Hampshire 213 in 49.1 overs (R.M.C. Gilliat 62, C.G. Greenidge 51)

Matches begun on Saturday June 3rd
GLAMORGAN (4 points) beat HAMPSHIRE by 33 runs at Bournemouth
Glamorgan 208–9 in 55 overs (R.C. Fredericks 87). Hampshire 175 in 50.4 overs (D.L. Williams 5–30)

GLOUCESTERSHIRE (4 points) beat SOMERSET by 38 runs at Taunton
Gloucestershire 252–7 in 55 overs (M.J. Procter 154 not out). Somerset 214 in 50.2 overs (R.C. Cooper 53, M.J. Procter 5–26)

QUARTER-FINALS

Matches begun on Wednesday June 14th
WARWICKSHIRE beat GLAMORGAN by 5 wickets at Cardiff
Glamorgan 104–9 in 55 overs. Warwickshire 108–5 in 45.5 overs

LEICESTERSHIRE beat LANCASHIRE by 7 wickets at Leicester
Lancashire 135 in 55 overs. Leicestershire 138–3 in 49.4 overs (B. Dudleston 65 not out)

GLOUCESTERSHIRE beat MIDDLESEX by 62 runs at Lord's, London
Gloucestershire 238–9 in 55 overs (R.D.V. Knight 92, M.J. Procter 56, M.W.W. Selvey 5–39). Middlesex 176 in 49.5 overs (C.T. Radley 63, A.S. Brown 4–43)

YORKSHIRE beat SUSSEX by 5 wickets at Bradford
Sussex 85 in 51.1 overs. Yorkshire 89–5 in 51 overs

SEMI-FINALS

Played on Wednesday June 28th
LEICESTERSHIRE beat WARWICKSHIRE by 7 wickets at Leicester
Warwickshire 96 in 39.5 overs. Leicestershire 98–3 in 37.2 overs

YORKSHIRE beat GLOUCESTERSHIRE by 7 wickets at Headingley, Leeds
Gloucestershire 131 in 55 overs. Yorkshire 134–3 in 48.4 overs (G. Boycott 75 not out)

Final

For England and Leicestershire captain Ray Illingworth, the result of the first Benson and Hedges Cup final was doubly satisfying. Not only did he have the honour of leading Leicestershire, his adopted county, to their first title in 93 years as a club; he also had the personal satisfaction of beating his former county, Yorkshire, before a near-capacity crowd at Lord's. Furthermore, his team's victory by five wickets with 49 balls to spare brought them the £2,500 prize, cricket's richest reward of the summer.

Leicestershire's improvement was one of the season's main features. They dominated the early rounds of this new competition, being the only side to win every match and gain maximum points by bowling out the opposition each time. Moreover, they were never bowled out themselves and, thanks to an incredible innings of 158 not out by Davison, scored a record 327–4 in 55 overs against Warwickshire at Coventry.

Yorkshire, desperately unlucky to be without Boycott, who had damaged a finger, eventually made the winners struggle, but they never recovered from some woeful batting. Sharpe chose to bat on a pitch with plenty of life for the faster bowlers, and he must have regretted his decision when both he and Lumb were back in the dressing room after ten overs with just 21 runs on the board. At lunch, with 18 overs left, they were 72 for 4 with Leadbeater retired hurt.

Leicestershire's start was no better than Yorkshire's: 24 for 2 after 14 overs. Even the ebullient Davison found the pitch difficult, while Norman's 38 in 35 overs allowed Yorkshire thoughts of victory. When Illingworth was caught off a leg-glance, his side were 97 for 5 and needing 40 to win off 15 overs. This was the cue for another Yorkshire exile, Balderstone. His 41 off 53 balls decided the contest and won him the Man of the Match award.

LEICESTERSHIRE V. YORKSHIRE at Lord's, London on July 22nd
Leicestershire won by 5 wickets
Toss: Yorkshire
Man of the Match: J.C. Balderstone

YORKSHIRE

P.J. Sharpe*	c Tolchard b Higgs	14
R.G. Lumb	b McKenzie	7
B. Leadbeater	run out	32
J.H. Hampshire	lbw b McKenzie	14
R.A. Hutton	c Spencer b Steele	8
J.D. Woodford	c Spencer b Illingworth	1
C. Johnson	b Higgs	20
C.M. Old	lbw b Illingworth	6
D.L. Bairstow†	c Tolchard b McKenzie	13
H.P. Cooper	not out	7
A.G. Nicholson	not out	4
Extras	(lb 9, nb 1)	10
TOTAL	(9 wkts – 55 overs)	136

LEICESTERSHIRE

B. Dudleston	c Bairstow b Nicholson	6
M.E.J.C. Norman	c Sharpe b Woodford	38
R.W. Tolchard†	c Bairstow b Cooper	3
B.F. Davison	b Cooper	17
J.C. Balderstone	not out	41
R. Illingworth*	c Bairstow b Hutton	5
P.R. Haywood	not out	21
J.F. Steele	} did not bat	
G.D. McKenzie		
K. Higgs		
C.T. Spencer		
Extras	(b 1, lb 3, nb 1, w 4)	9
TOTAL	(5 wkts – 46.5 overs)	140

LEICESTERSHIRE

	O	M	R	W
McKenzie	11	2	22	3
Higgs	11	1	33	2
Spencer	7	2	11	0
Davison	11	2	22	0
Illingworth	10	3	21	2
Steele	5	1	17	1

YORKSHIRE

	O	M	R	W
Old	9.5	1	35	0
Nicholson	9	2	17	1
Hutton	11	1	24	1
Cooper	9	0	27	2
Woodford	8	1	28	1

FALL OF WICKETS

Wkt	Y	Le
1st	17	16
2nd	21	24
3rd	60	58
4th	65	84
5th	77	97
6th	83	
7th	113	
8th	122	
9th	124	
10th		

Umpires: D.J. Constant and T.W. Spencer
Attendance: 19,725   Receipts: £20,446

Reviving a Cricket Festival

The Fenner Trophy

There was a time when cricket was the supreme summer sport. Not any more. Television, motoring and continental holidays are taking their toll, and the soccer season has extended into August and May. Often, the new generation of county cricketers play their matches before empty enclosures. Or rather they did, until the advent of knock-out cricket – those one-day, sudden-death struggles that have aroused as much partisanship as football matches.

Such was the case at Scarborough, where attendances for the traditional Yorkshire v MCC fixture were dwindling steadily. The North Marine Road ground had once been packed with spectators eager to see giants like Hobbs, Sutcliffe, Rhodes, Hirst, Woolley and Bradman in festival mood. Now, the last and greatest of these cricketing showcases was dying on its feet.

And then in September, 1971, in the 85th year of the Festival, the Hull power transmission company of J.H. Fenner brought new life to the event. A three-day, knock-out tournament was sponsored. Three of the best cricketing sides in the country were invited to compete against the host county, Yorkshire, for the Fenner Trophy and £1,000 in prize money.

Yorkshire, Lancashire, Kent and Nottinghamshire played a series of one-day matches which culminated in a Lancashire v. Kent final. This was a needle encounter very much to the taste of the Yorkshire spectators, because Kent had been beaten by the Red Rose county in the Gillette Cup final only a week earlier. This time Kent were the victors by 66 runs, and became the first holders of the new trophy. The combined gate for three exciting days of 50-over cricket exceeded 30,000 – almost tripling the attendance for the previous season's Yorkshire v MCC fixture. The crowds had returned to Scarborough.

Fenner has supported Yorkshire cricket for many years. Benefit matches held on the Company's Marfleet ground at Hull have helped to swell many a testimonial fund for a long-serving county player. Sponsorship was a logical progression, and Scarborough the ideal venue. This was to be proved beyond doubt a year later when the holders, Kent, went into the hat with Yorkshire, Surrey, and Gillette Cup winners, Lancashire.

The standard of cricket was even better, with Lancashire putting out Kent by 90 runs, and Yorkshire disposing of Surrey, 1971 County champions, by five wickets. From a northern point of view this resulted in a dream final – the first time that a Roses match had been held at Scarborough. Naturally, the one-day specialists, Lancashire, were red-hot favourites to add the Fenner Trophy to the Gillette Cup.

But this was a War of the Roses remember, and urged on by a near-capacity crowd, Yorkshire pulled themselves from 76 for 5 to a more respectable 234 for 9 – mainly due to a

Below: Boycott and Lumb walk out to open for Yorkshire
Bottom: Jack Bond receives the last of many awards as Lancashire's captain

staggering 106 in 75 minutes from Man of the Match, Chris Old. In reply, Lancashire never really got into their stride and ended up 60 runs short, having to settle once again for the £300 runners-up award, and leaving their rivals with the cup and the £600 first prize. This time the total attendance over the three days topped the 34,000 mark.

Already, this tournament has become known as the 'Championship of the Champions'. The entries for the 1973 competition prove this conclusively. Yorkshire are no longer hosts by courtesy, but Fenner Trophy holders in their own right. Warwickshire headed the County Championship table, and Kent the John Player League. Lancashire have a hat-trick of Gillette Cup wins to their credit. The scene is set for a battle of the giants, and the gloomy prophets who predict that cricket is a dying game should take themselves off to Scarborough next September. The sea air will bring some colour to their cheeks, and the high quality of the cricket will do much to restore their appetite for what is still our finest summer sport.

The Fenner Knock-Out Trophy 1972

Played at Scarborough September 6th, 7th, 8th

LANCASHIRE beat KENT by 90 runs
Lancashire 225–9 in 50 overs (F.C. Hayes 64, D. Lloyd 58, D.L. Underwood 5–36). Kent 135 in 29.2 overs

YORKSHIRE beat SURREY by 5 wickets
Surrey 131 in 46.2 overs. Yorkshire 135–5 in 43.2 overs

FINAL
YORKSHIRE beat LANCASHIRE by 60 runs
Yorkshire 234–9 in 50 overs (C.M. Old 106, G. Boycott 75). Lancashire 174 in 50 overs

PREVIOUS WINNERS   1971 Kent

Limited-Overs Match Averages 1972

The combined one-day cricket averages include performances in the Prudential Trophy Internationals, Gillette Cup, John Player League, Fenner Trophy, Benson and Hedges Cup, and the Challenge Match between the JPL champions and the winners of the Gillette Cup.

BATTING (Qualification: 10 innings, average 23)   *Not out

	M	I	NO	HS	Runs	Av	100s	50s
B.A. Richards	21	21	3	129	993	55.16	3	6
G.M. Turner	23	23	2	121	918	43.71	3	4
G.St.A. Sobers	10	10	3	97*	299	42.71	–	2
G. Boycott	20	20	5	75*	638	42.53	–	4
M.E.J.C. Norman	21	21	5	86	671	41.93	–	4
R.B. Kanhai	27	26	5	120	856	40.76	1	6
M.J. Procter	21	21	2	154*	746	39.26	2	3
M.J. Harris	19	18	4	92*	528	37.71	–	5
D.L. Amiss	24	22	4	103	654	36.33	1	5
R.W. Tolchard	24	22	4	103	650	36.11	1	4
C.H. Lloyd	25	25	2	126	830	36.08	1	5
J.H. Edrich	16	16	1	108*	540	36.00	1	4
T.J. Yardley	20	17	6	75*	392	35.63	–	3
B.W. Luckhurst	23	22	3	74*	664	34.94	–	5
B. Leadbeater	23	22	5	86*	589	34.64	–	3
F.C. Hayes	14	13	2	64	371	33.72	–	2
C.G. Greenidge	22	22	2	84	645	32.25	–	6
K.W.R. Fletcher	23	22	3	69	610	32.10	–	4
R.G.A. Headley	18	18	0	82	576	32.00	–	5
J.M. Brearly	21	19	4	68*	475	31.66	–	4
C.T. Radley	21	20	2	88	552	30.66	–	4
B. Hassan	21	21	3	86*	547	30.38	–	4
Younis Ahmed	20	20	1	64*	560	29.47	–	4
B.F. Davison	24	22	2	158*	581	29.05	1	3
E.R. Dexter	12	12	2	70*	290	29.00	–	2
R.C. Cooper	13	13	1	95	343	28.58	–	2
A.I. Kallicharran	26	23	4	101*	537	28.26	1	3
R.D.V. Knight	23	23	4	92	537	28.26	–	3
P.R. Haywood	20	16	4	43	331	27.58	–	–
P.J.K. Gibbs	19	19	0	68	521	27.42	–	4
J.A. Ormrod	23	20	3	69	464	27.29	–	2
E.J.O. Hemsley	12	12	3	73	245	27.22	–	1
M.J. Smith	21	20	0	92	540	27.00	–	3

H. Pilling	18	18	1	70	449	26.41	–	4
J.T. Murray	19	16	3	40	343	26.38	–	–
Sadiq Mohammad	21	21	1	108	527	26.35	1	2
B. Wood	25	24	2	67	579	26.31	–	3
D.S. Steele	19	19	2	56	442	26.00	–	2
C.M. Old	24	13	4	106	234	26.00	1	–
J.F. Harvey	19	19	4	54*	389	25.93	–	2
K.D. Boyce	22	19	2	93*	440	25.88	–	3
Asif Iqbal	21	19	4	67*	385	25.66	–	2
D.L. Murray	26	20	6	82	357	25.50	–	1
M.H. Denness	24	22	2	65	506	25.30	–	2
M.J.K. Smith	24	23	3	66*	505	25.25	–	2
D.R. Owen-Thomas	12	12	3	46	227	25.22	–	–
Majid J. Khan	14	14	0	83	351	25.07	–	2
C.P. Wilkins	18	18	0	94	450	25.00	–	2
R. Illingworth	17	14	4	39	249	24.90	–	–
D.R. Turner	17	16	1	99*	368	24.53	–	1
D.B. Close	23	23	1	88	533	24.22	–	2
R.E. Marshall	15	14	2	51	288	24.00	–	1
B.L. D'Oliveira	19	17	3	52	333	23.78	–	2
R.M. Prideaux	19	19	1	63*	427	23.72	–	1
R.C. Fredericks	22	22	0	87	521	23.68	–	3
Mushtaq Mohammad	19	19	1	71	422	23.44	–	1
M.G. Griffith	18	16	5	39	257	23.36	–	–
A. Jones	21	21	1	63	461	23.05	–	3

BOWLING (Qualification: 20 wickets)

	O	*M*	*R*	*W*	*Av*	*5w*	*BB*
J.K. Lever	250	28	510	43	11.86	2	5–8
K.D. Boyce	170.2	31	548	46	11.91	1	5–22
A.G. Nicholson	161.5	33	458	38	12.05	3	6–27
R.G.D. Willis	106.4	13	357	29	12.31	–	4–21
G.D. McKenzie	191.1	32	585	45	13.00	1	5–15
J.A. Snow	159.4	28	393	29	13.55	1	5–15
J. Sullivan	98.3	19	353	26	13.57	1	5–29
T.E. Jesty	94.3	15	335	23	14.56	–	4–32
R. Illingworth	84	25	302	20	15.10	–	4–5
R.R. Bailey	140	26	379	25	15.16	1	6–22
P. Lee	123.1	23	406	26	15.61	–	4–17
C.J.R. Black	73	5	328	21	15.61	–	4–39
J.C.J. Dye	157	29	501	32	15.65	–	4–41
C.T. Spencer	138.5	21	466	29	16.06	–	4–28
D.L. Underwood	189.3	35	666	41	16.24	2	5–19
G.I. Burgess	136.2	18	561	34	16.50	2	6–25
J.S.E. Price	141.5	20	417	25	16.68	–	3–17
B.D. Julien	182.3	21	681	40	17.02	–	4–28
V.A. Holder	192.4	31	615	36	17.08	1	6–33
D. Wilson	129	27	427	25	17.08	–	3–22
R.D. Jackman	173.4	35	586	34	17.23	1	6–34
B.L. D'Oliveira	141.5	19	448	26	17.23	1	5–26
T.J. Mottram	100	11	399	23	17.34	–	4–35
M.W.W. Selvey	172.2	23	700	40	17.50	1	5–39
M.J. Procter	162	32	525	30	17.50	3	5–10

Limited-Overs Match Averages 1972

B. Stead	180.4	29	578	33	17.51	–	4–24
H.R. Moseley	125.5	18	465	26	17.88	–	4–19
K. Shuttleworth	163.4	33	549	30	18.30	1	5–13
R.S. Herman	164.2	26	623	34	18.32	–	4–20
P. Lever	136.2	20	434	23	18.80	1	5–21
T.W. Cartwright	163	45	437	23	19.00	–	3–12
M. Hendrik	121.4	20	437	23	19.00	1	6–7
A.A. Jones	157.3	25	538	28	19.21	–	3–19
J.D. Woodford	163.1	27	559	29	19.27	–	3–14
K. Higgs	192.2	33	617	32	19.28	–	4–31
W. Taylor	175.3	28	679	35	19.40	–	4–11
B. Wood	170.1	32	591	30	19.70	–	4–34
J.N. Shepherd	214	21	730	37	19.75	–	4–18
P.I. Pocock	163.5	30	478	24	19.91	–	3–38
J. Denman	149.4	12	595	29	20.51	–	4–28
C.M. Old	204.3	37	608	29	20.96	1	5–38
S. Turner	161.5	27	462	22	21.00	–	3–26
J. Spencer	129	22	446	21	21.23	–	4–27
D.J. Shepherd	151	26	505	23	21.95	–	3–27
J. Davey	151.1	31	468	21	22.28	–	3–13
J.N. Graham	195.4	28	604	27	22.37	–	3–24
B.F. Davison	126	9	540	24	22.50	–	4–33
J.F. Steele	145	25	450	20	22.50	–	3–17
R.A. Hutton	202.1	28	616	27	22.81	–	4–18
G.G. Arnold	176.3	35	653	28	23.32	–	4–27
J. Simmons	206	36	758	32	23.68	1	5–28
N.M. McVicker	230	26	763	32	23.84	–	3–19
D.L. Williams	134.4	16	530	22	24.09	1	5–30
A.W. Greig	160.4	30	525	21	25.00	–	3–15
R.A. Woolmer	185.2	20	662	26	25.46	–	4–14
A.S. Brown	167	22	655	25	26.20	–	4–43
N. Gifford	159	27	528	20	26.40	–	4–7
M.N.S. Taylor	166	18	665	22	30.22	–	3–18
D.J. Brown	180	21	666	22	30.27	–	3–25
I.R. Buxton	151	22	816	25	32.64	1	5–19
S.J. Rouse	226.4	22	839	20	41.95	–	3–32

FIELDING

MOST WICKET-KEEPING DISMISSALS

		Ct	St
36	R.W. Tolchard	33	3
34	A.P.E. Knott	29	5
30	D.L. Bairstow	29	1
28	D.L. Murray	28	0
28	B. Taylor	24	4
26	J.T. Murray	24	2
25	A. Long	19	6
23	D.J.S. Taylor	19	4
23	R.W. Taylor	17	6
22	F.M. Engineer	18	4

MOST CATCHES (excluding wicket-keepers)

Ct		Ct	
15	A.S. Brown	11	N. Gifford
15	B.A. Richards	11	R.M.C. Gilliat
14	C.H. Lloyd	11	M.J. Smith
13	C.T. Radley	11	J. Simmons
13	B. Wood	10	P.J. Graves
13	R.B. Kanhai	10	P.M. Walker
12	R.C. Fredericks	10	M.J. Harris
12	K.W.R. Fletcher	10	C.T. Spencer
11	M.H. Page	10	T.W. Cartwright
11	C.P. Wilkins	10	G.W. Johnson
11	G. Boycott	10	J.M. Brearley
11	R.E. East	10	D.L. Underwood

The Effects of Limited-Overs Cricket

Jim Laker

Some 25 years ago the average programme for a county cricket club would consist of 28 three-day county fixtures, plus matches against the Universities and the touring side. It was not uncommon for 25,000 people to watch Surrey play Middlesex on the Saturday alone, or for the gates to be closed at Old Trafford for the Roses matches. The Bank Holiday fixtures at Trent Bridge and Swansea drew similar crowds. There were of course many less popular fixtures which attracted very meagre gates but despite this the overall picture was a healthy one.

Gradually over the years the scene began to change dramatically and no one in all honesty could pinpoint one particular reason. It was due to a combination of circumstances. The pace of life had begun to increase. No longer were people content to sit in the sun and while away an entire Saturday. They looked for new avenues to explore and many thousands found a new way of spending leisure time. Possibly the biggest single factor was the motor car, a luxury even in early post-war years, but a necessity as life and time moved on. Of all the major sports, cricket, which demanded so much time, was the principle sufferer. Crowds dwindled to a hard core of real enthusiasts; officials and players became desperate and this appeared to reflect in performances. Cricketers went on the defensive, and the game as a whole reached its lowest ebb.

Something had to be done to give the game a shot in the arm; to fill the grounds again; to increase the tempo of cricket in line with the modern way of living. The demand was for all-action entertainment, even at the risk of losing the supreme skills and arts of what has always been a complicated game. Cricket does not change overnight and the traditionalists were slow to appreciate that a new and more positive approach was needed. The Gillette Company, sponsoring a cup for knock-out cricket, was the first in the field to introduce a new format for first-class cricketers.

However, probably the greatest single factor in rousing the old establishment was the phenomenal success achieved by the International Cavaliers, linked with the name of Rothmans, who began to draw enormous Sunday crowds all over the country. These games, televised on BBC 2, included top names from every cricketing country and provided a new cricketing public with instant and dynamic performances. One became patently aware that some day limited-overs cricket must become a permanent feature of the summer calendar.

The break-through initiated by the Cavaliers was subsequently taken over by MCC, and under the sponsorship of John Player the Sunday League was born. Almost instantly this competition prospered and, with the Gillette Cup proving an unqualified success, room was found for yet another competition, initiated in 1972, the Benson & Hedges Cup. To accommodate all the additional games and the travelling they involved, it was necessary to cut down on the three-day match programme, a decision which met with strong opposition.

I agree with the majority of first-class cricketers, senior officials and a large proportion of county members that the County programme of 25 years ago was ideal for playing and watching cricket, but one must appreciate that a continuance of the game under the old structure would have led only to bankruptcy and the end of the first-class game. I, for one, welcome and enjoy cricket in its instant form and feel greatly indebted to Gillette, to John Player and to Benson & Hedges for the great steps they have taken to re-establish our game.

The last of these limited-overs competitions, the Benson & Hedges Cup, has yet really to get off the ground. Introduced only last season, it had the great misfortune to be dogged by bad weather but the whole concept of the competition is first class, with the initial rounds played on a regional basis, and it may well develop into a most popular form of limited-overs cricket.

This then leaves us with the Gillette Cup competition and the John Player League. The first named has caught the imagination of the public, growing in popularity year by year, and indeed has finally been accepted by the die-hards who could see no further than three-day county cricket. The chief reason for this is that 60 overs per side does not automatically result in a slogging contest from the word go. There is no limitation on bowlers' run-ups, though each bowler is allowed to bowl only 12 overs.

Initially I believed this to be a good rule as it meant that at least five bowlers had to be used, and this would presumably mean the inclusion of a fair proportion of the slower variety. Instead, of course, teams picked their attack with quick and medium paced bowlers and have paid the penalty. Three of the most successful sides in recent Gillette years, Lancashire, Warwickshire and Kent have been indebted to Simmons and Hughes, Gibbs, and Underwood for their success. It has always been my opinion that it is unfair to take a bowler off or to make an enforced change when he is bowling well, and for this reason *in a competition of 60 overs per side*, I would like to see the restriction of 12 overs per bowler removed. This amendment apart, it would be foolish to offer criticism of the Gillette, which at Lord's in September produced 25,000 people, gate receipts of £50,000, a superb Clive Lloyd century and 469 runs – a wonderful climax to an enthralling competition.

The John Player League is quite different. Played on Sundays from April to September, this competition begins with the basic disadvantage of time being at a premium. Forty overs per side is the maximum that can possibly be bowled and so the rules must include limited run-ups – quite rightly in this case – with only eight overs allowed to each bowler. Interest in this League has become nationwide and, given good weather, it has proved a first-class competition. Naturally, batsmen must take far more chances than they would in a 60-over match, but even so any team which scores at a rate of $4\frac{1}{2}$-5 runs an over should gain a very high percentage of victories.

The problems arise when bad weather interferes and, to ensure a result, the number of overs is drastically reduced. In common with many other devotees of the game I find it very difficult to assess the merits of a game of cricket which is reduced to less than 25 overs per side. At the moment a match counts for points in the John Player League, if each side is able to complete ten overs, or 30 minutes of batting. So, after a long and hard season one may reach a situation where the championship itself rests on the result of a ten-over slog. But despite this the Sunday League continues to have an enthusiastic following, and rightly so, for not only has it taken County cricketers to lesser known grounds within the county, spreading the gospel still further, but in a summer when rain badly interfered with early games, together with a further soccer encroachment and the magnetic appeal of the Munich Olympics, the amazing figure of approximately 22,000,000 viewers followed the televised games on BBC 2.

What then are the overall general effects, the objectives and the criticisms of the arrival of limited-overs cricket? It is felt very strongly in some quarters that limited-overs cricket does not provide a training ground for Test match cricketers, and with a reduced three-day programme Test match cricket will suffer. Surely this thinking can only bring smiles to the faces of our friends in Australia and the West Indies. Australia still has to pick its Test teams on the evidence of eight first-class matches, whilst the Barbadian has only half that number of first-class games in which to prove his ability to selectors.

Even now our County cricketers play 20 three-day games which surely is an answer in itself. Many cricketers believe that it is detrimental to their own performance to continually switch from the staid, solid cricket of the County match to the hurly-burly requirements of limited-overs cricket. Surely, in the past, a very large number of County games have reached a thrilling climax thanks only to artificial declarations. Teams have jogged along steadily, scoring 250 runs per day for the first two days and then, in an effort to reach a three-day decision, 400 runs are scored on the last day, when teams have been asked repeatedly to score at 90 or even 100 runs an hour to win on a declaration. No need to emphasise that this is a rate of scoring rarely achieved in a limited-overs game.

The shortened game is also attacked because it offers little for the middle-order batsman, and never before has there been such a dearth of these specialist performers. Unquestionably it is a game in which batsmen one to four have an enormous advantage, but my belief is that the present shortage of future Test cricketers at number five and number six can be attributed to two other major factors. I agreed with the policy of immediate registration of a limited number of world-class overseas players, but since the floodgates have been opened to allow an influx of overseas cricketers, who are often no better than our own up and coming players, the newcomers have, in so many counties, monopolised the middle-order positions and retarded the advance of our own colts.

Secondly, the counties who have resisted these temptations and persevered with their own youngsters have been hit unmercifully by the introduction of the system of batting bonus points. For the sake of collecting an extra point these players have found themselves thrown into a conflict with instructions to 'have a go', when instead they should be taking the opportunity of gaining experience and learning how to build an innings.

There can be little argument that the one department of the game which has improved out of all recognition, due to limited-overs cricket, is the outfielding and throwing. It was generally possible, in years gone by, quite effectively to hide a couple of players in the field. This is no longer the case in a game where every run is vital, which demands of all 11 cricketers not only speed and accuracy in the field, but a far higher degree of physical fitness than was ever attained by myself and my own contemporaries. This great improvement has permeated through to all types of cricket and the fielding has been a joy to watch.

Farewell

It is always sad to say goodbye to cricketers, all of whom have contributed something to the game. At the end of 1972, 22 first-class players retired, and in wishing them well in their new careers we thank them for the entertainment and enjoyment they have provided.

In this group there are six who, for various reasons, stand out above their contemporaries and we pay them special tribute.

David Allen

In some respects David Allen was unfortunate in that his career coincided with that of John Mortimore, for both more than upheld Gloucestershire's remarkable tradition for producing top-class off-spinners. It may have been fine for the County to have two international off-break bowlers, but either of these fine operators would have been even more effective if the other had been a left-arm spinner, thus providing contrast.

At his peak, David was a bigger finger spinner than most of his contemporaries. He gave the ball a real tweak, and there were occasions on a sticky wicket when he could be criticised for doing too much with the ball – in spite of going round the wicket!

Along with his ability to impart a large amount of spin, David had a deceptive flight and a much more curving, less flat trajectory than the average English bowler of his type. This brought him considerable success on tour, especially on the good batting pitches in the West Indies, where he obtained an unusual amount of bounce, and his excellent control ensured his wickets were bought economically.

Another great asset was his ability to deceive batsmen in the air, as well as beating them off the track. He was, certainly in this country, essentially an attacking bowler, willing to buy his wickets. This meant he was not as well suited to the needs of limited-overs cricket as a less able off-break bowler who fired the ball in flat. On the other hand it made him infinitely superior in three-day and Test matches.

As a batsman, David Allen was an effective tailender with an ugly, rather crab-like style. He had plenty of determination, with a preference for the back foot, a liking for the cut, and a temperament that responded to the challenge of a crisis.

Jack Bond

When Jackie Bond took over the captaincy of Lancashire, they were one of those counties that seemed unable to play to their potential. Yet, under his leadership, Lancashire carried off the Gillette Cup on three successive occasions (1970–72), won the John Player League in 1969 and 1970 and were third in 1971, and took third place in the County Championship in 1970 and 1971. The record is a considerable tribute to his quiet, efficient handling of the Club.

Jack Bond (right) holds aloft the Gillette Cup that Lancashire won for three successive seasons under his inspiring captaincy

Jack Bond brought a thoroughly professional approach to limited-overs cricket, with the result that Lancashire became the acknowledged experts in the sphere. Where they especially excelled was in the field, where the captain's influence was most felt. Aware of the importance of both preventing runs and holding catches in one-day games, he made sure his side improved considerably in this department. In addition he supported his bowlers to the hilt with most astute field placings, and consequently very few sides found runs easy to come by against Lancashire's accurate attack.

A good, correct county batsman with plenty of determination himself, Jack impressed on his lower-order batsmen what could be achieved if they hit hard and straight.

In addition to the honours that Jack Bond brought to the Club, Lancashire have perhaps greater reason to thank him. He attracted the crowds back to Old Trafford, not only because there was a winning side to support but because it was playing bright, attractive cricket. Jack, himself, led unobtrusively, gaining the confidence of the players and planning meticulously. His successor has been set a high precedent, but Jack Bond has left him with a side full of attacking potential. No captain could ask for more.

Roy Marshall

It may seem difficult to appreciate today, but there was a time when it was neither necessary nor fashionable for overseas countries to call their Test players from the ranks of the first-class counties. Consequently, when the young Roy Marshall chose to qualify for Hampshire in the early 1950s he was effectively ending the Test career that had seen him win four West Indies caps in Australia and New Zealand in 1951-52.

Just how great a loss Roy Marshall was to his country is a matter of guesswork, but there is no doubting that he was a much better player than many who represented West Indies. What is beyond conjecture is that for 18 seasons he was an enormous asset to his adopted county. Hampshire batting revolved largely around Roy, and by far the largest proportion of his 35,725 runs were made on their behalf. However, his real value should not be assessed by mere statistics, no matter how impressive, for they could never illustrate the entertainment his batting provided.

Tall, bespectacled, and rather severe in appearance, Marshall looked more suited to the ranks of the Roundheads, but he batted like a Cavalier. To Hampshire he brought the flashing strokes he had learnt in the Caribbean: the square cut, the slash through the covers, the pull and the hook. Allied to these was the ability to hit the ball on the rise, from the first ball of the innings if necessary.

Although Roy was most effective on true, hard

The end of an innings: Roy Marshall returns to the pavilion for the last time after nearly two decades with Hampshire

pitches, on which his full follow-through was seen at its best, he quickly learnt to cope with the many varieties of wickets found in England. Without losing his shots he tightened his defence, but he never forgot that a half-volley should be dispatched to the boundary whether the wicket was playing true or not. He was probably least impressive on a 'green top', where the ball moved about and his beloved cut and hook were liable to prove fatal.

In his prime Roy was an aggressive opening bat who, on his day, could take an attack apart by the power and variety of his strokes. He made life especially hard for the fast-medium brigade, exasperatingly smiting the good ball to the boundary and seldom failing to punish anything loose. In addition, his ability to collect runs at well above the average rate gave his own team more time to bowl the other side out – an important factor when it is remembered that Hampshire have rarely had the most balanced of attacks.

Roy Marshall succeeded Ingleby-Mackenzie as captain of his Club and did a sound job. Rather surprisingly, his captaincy inclined towards caution and defensive fields; quite the reverse of his approach to batting. In the twilight of his career he dropped down the order to number four, where his experience and ability continued to keep him among the runs.

He will be sorely missed in Hampshire, not only by the Club but by its supporters. County cricket will not seem quite the same without Roy Marshall dominating an innings with a panache that automatically drew spectators from the bars and beer tents.

Eric Russell

Eric Russell was a fine opening batsman who looked the part. Everything about him, from his clothes to his style, was ordered, neat, and elegant.

He clearly came from the same stable that produced his Middlesex predecessor, Jack Robertson, and, like him, he was an excellent model for all budding batsmen. His stance was upright and relaxed, and he always appeared to have time to play his shots. This, combined with a technique that was close to copy book, meant that he at times made the art of batting appear simpler than it is.

Although Eric could play cross-bat shots, the bulk of his runs flowed from straight-bat strokes. He was a most impressive driver off both front and back foot, possessing a high backlift and clean follow-through which enabled him to pierce the field with shots that seemed stroked, rather than hit. With so much inswing and off-spin about, it was inevitable that he should have developed a partiality and expertise for scoring runs on the leg-side, and he was especially adept at putting the ball away off his legs with a straight bat.

Possibly Eric did not assert himself sufficiently, and there were occasions when he allowed himself to be dominated by an attack he might easily have mastered. Nevertheless, he was clearly one of the most efficient and reliable openers in the last decade, and many feel he warranted more opportunities in international cricket. He played in ten Tests, but this was over a considerable period and he was never able to establish himself as a regular.

On the other hand, it might be argued that he lacked the spark that so often divides the outstanding county player from the true international. This is, perhaps, substantiated by his career figures – more than 25,000 runs for the highly respectable average of 34. Averages can be, and often are, misleading, but a true international opening batsman would be expected to finish with an average in the forties.

Don Shepherd

As did so many excellent off-spinners, Don Shepherd began his career as a lively seamer. Indeed, for several years he opened the Glamorgan attack, and his fast-medium bowling was effective enough to bring him 120 wickets in 1952 for 22 apiece, despite the not-inconsiderable handicap of having to bowl so much on Welsh pitches, which have never been famed for their sympathy towards pace.

The summer of 1956 was the turning point of Don's career. Until then he had proved himself a useful county seamer, but that season he gave up quick bowling and turned to off-cutters with immediate success, taking more than 170 wickets for only 15 runs apiece. Until he retired at the end of last season he was the main spinner for his County, and, in many respects, the most effective Wales has every produced.

Although his remarkable career figures of 2,218 wickets at 21 apiece speak for themselves, they do not by any means tell the full story. Don filled two vital roles for Glamorgan. First, he was their chief match-winner on pitches that gave him the slightest encouragement. Secondly, he was their main stock bowler, his accuracy allied to his exceptional stamina always making him a difficult proposition to score off.

When Don first abandoned seam, he was more of a cutter than a spinner, operating from over the wicket with the keeper standing back. But as the years went by, Don, always a thoughtful cricketer, learnt to vary his pace, used the crease intelligently, was able to go round the wicket, and thought batsmen out. He was not a classical off-spinner like Glamorgan's Clay and McConnon who combined spin with flight and high graceful actions. Quick through the air, flat trajectory with a whirling delivery that had little aesthetic appeal, he was essentially a practi-

Don Shepherd, who for so long was Glamorgan's main wicket-taker – accurate, persistent, and a true competitor

cal bowler who must surely rank as the best uncapped spin bowler since the war. Certainly there have been many with less ability and heart who have been honoured. This second attribute, heart, is another reason for Don's success. He was a natural competitor who brought his fast bowler's detestation of opposing batsman into his new style.

In addition to his bowling, Don was a fine athletic outfielder in his younger days, and an old-fashioned slogger, much beloved by crowds everywhere. He was a tailender who deliberately forsook the prosaic defensive push for the delights of the full-blooded 'mow', which sometimes paid off in a most spectacular fashion.

Why did Don Shepherd capture so many wickets? First and foremost, he possessed the cardinal virtues of immaculate line and length. Then, too, his pace through the air was a great asset on his home pitches, which are so frequently slow turners.

He was an outstanding bowler with a passionate love of cricket, and it will be a long time before Glamorgan are lucky enough to find a replacement of his calibre.

Micky Stewart

It was not surprising that the England selectors called on Micky Stewart when Hall and Griffith were causing mayhem in 1963. The neat, courageous little Surrey opener had always been prepared to stand up to the fastest bowling and counter-attack by hooking the bouncer.

Indeed, Micky always looked sounder against pace and seam than against spin, despite the fact that he was prepared to go down the wicket to the slow bowlers. Among his most effective, and spectacular, strokes was a forcing shot off the back foot, played late, that sent the ball crashing past cover. As one would expect of a former footballer, he was exceptionally nippy on his feet and an excellent runner between the wickets. His ability to pinch quick singles meant he was able to keep the score moving along without taking too many chances.

In addition to his batting, Micky must rank as one of the truly great close short-legs, where he picked up many brilliant catches. There were times when he was much too close to the bat for both comfort and safety, but his presence ensured the pressure was always on the batsman.

As captain of Surrey for a considerable period, Micky Stewart had the satisfaction of leading them to the County Championship title in 1971. He wanted to retire then, but the County asked him to stay for 1972, and he did. A sound, rather than brilliant, leader, he was perhaps over-conscientious, which led him to worry too much, but this is hardly a failing in times of changing loyalties.

CAREER STATISTICS OF PLAYERS WHO RETIRED FROM ENGLISH FIRST-CLASS CRICKET IN 1972

\multicolumn{7}{l	}{BATTING AND FIELDING}		\multicolumn{6}{l}{BOWLING}
M	I	NO	HS	Runs	Av	100s	Ct	St		Runs	Wkts	Av	BB	5wI	10wM
456	641	147	121*	9,291	18.80	1	252	–	D.A. Allen (Gs)	28,585	1,209	23.64	8–34	56	8
212	354	35	104*	6,492	20.35	2	133	–	M. Bissex (Gs)	6,783	237	28.62	7–50	11	2
345	524	76	157	11,880	26.51	14	218	–	J.D. Bond (La)	69	0	–	–	–	–
177	163	94	23	317	4.59	–	55	–	R.G.M. Carter (Wo)	13,630	521	26.16	7–61	17	2
321	479	111	133*	8,789	23.88	5	144	–	B.S. Crump (Nh)	20,163	814	24.77	7–29	30	5
197	264	49	102	3,436	15.98	1	83	–	T.J.P. Eyre (D)	10,305	359	28.70	8–65	8	–
270	483	32	136*	11,666	25.86	9	189	–	I.W. Hall (D)	23	0	–	–	–	–
206	344	32	168	7,538	24.16	4	87	–	J.F. Harvey (D)	21	1	21.00	1–0	–	–
47	49	14	33	374	10.68	–	12	–	J.W. Holder (H)	3,415	139	24.56	7–79	5	1
416	702	78	171	17,039	27.30	22	337	–	K. Ibadulla (Wa)	14,264	462	30.87	7–22	6	–
301	519	63	200	12,722	27.89	16	243	2	D.A. Livingstone (H)	93	1	93.00	1–31	–	–
54	89	13	92	1,513	19.90	–	26	–	K.J. Lyons (Gm)	205	1	205.00	1–36	–	–
602	1,053	59	228*	35,725	35.94	68	293	–	R.E. Marshall (H)	5,092	176	28.93	6–36	5	–
406	569	191	63	5,367	14.19	–	707	119	B.J. Meyer (Gs)	–	–	–	–	–	–
33	37	7	46	386	12.86	–	16	–	P.J. Plummer (Nt)	2,016	63	32.00	7–71	2	–
88	106	22	72	1,221	14.53	–	60	–	P.E. Russell (D)	5,765	196	29.41	6–61	3	–
448	796	64	193	25,525	34.87	41	302	–	W.E. Russell (M)	993	22	45.13	3–20	–	–
668	837	248	73	5,696	9.67	–	251	–	D.J. Shepherd (Gm)	47,298	2,218	21.32	9–47	123	28
530	898	93	227*	26,492	32.90	49	634	–	M.J. Stewart (Sy)	99	1	99.00	1–4	–	–
56	63	21	22	333	7.92	–	27	–	P.M. Stringer (Le)	2,772	88	31.50	5–43	1	–
73	94	27	90	1,096	16.35	–	45	–	F.W. Swarbrook (D)	5,157	162	31.83	6–48	4	–
111	200	14	156	6,431	34.57	12	134	6	C.P. Wilkins (D)	2,182	61	35.77	4–21	–	–

*Not out

Minor Cricket

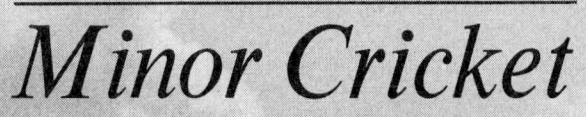

Minor Counties Championship 1972

Despite the fact that the early part of the season saw several matches interfered with by rain, 1972 proved to be a successful year for the Minor Counties. With some counties, particularly those in the South, not commencing their programme until July, when university players and schoolteachers are available, much of the Championship was played in ideal weather. There was enterprising cricket, and the Championship remained in balance until the very last match.

The Championship table was eventually headed by Yorkshire II, who had been at the top in 1971, and remained thereabouts for most of 1972. Bedfordshire, who returned to their 1970 form after a slide in 1971, emerged as runners-up. Staffordshire, who had been lying third, had to wait until the final fixture between Buckinghamshire and Bedfordshire to see whether they or Bedfordshire would be runners-up. And the matter was not decided until the very last ball of the game, which was, appropriately, hit for four by the Bedfordshire captain.

As Bedfordshire and Yorkshire II had not met during the season, the rules of the competition allowed Bedfordshire to challenge Yorkshire II to decide the Championship. This match was held over three days at Barnsley in September, and in a ding-dong struggle Bedfordshire eventually won by three wickets, so becoming champion county for 1972. As far as the records show, this is the first time that a challenging minor county has defeated the 2nd XI of a major county, and congratulations are due to Jack Smith and his players for their notable success.

During last season the Minor Counties took part in the new Benson and Hedges League Cup, fielding two representative teams, Minor Counties (North) and Minor Counties (South). Although none of the games were won, the one between Minor Counties (N) and Derbyshire went very close, there being a difference of only 24 runs in it. It is felt that, with the experience gained in 1972, a considerable improvement should be shown this season. Once again the Minor Counties were represented in the Gillette Cup, by Cambridgeshire, Buckinghamshire, Wiltshire, Durham, and Oxfordshire, and the 1973 qualifiers are Bedfordshire, Staffordshire, Durham, Dorset, and Wiltshire. Now only two counties have not figured in this competition since the Minor Counties joined in 1964.

From time to time, suggestions have been made regarding alterations in the method of awarding points in Minor Counties Championship matches, and at last December's Annual Meeting a new system was agreed on. It is hoped that this will lead to a more interesting game with the emphasis on winning cricket. However no matter how much the rules are altered, in the end everything depends on the captains to give a positive attitude to Minor Counties Championship matches in 1973.

Review of the Counties

Bedfordshire finished second in the table and then beat Yorkshire II in the Challenge Match to win the Championship for the second time in three years. The inspiring captaincy of J. Smith was a potent factor and the side responded enthusiastically to his lead. In the Challenge Match, Trevor Rosier inspired the county to victory with a magnificent all-round performance, taking 8-35 as Yorkshire were skittled out for 108 and then scoring 118 in Bedfordshire's first innings.

Berkshire completed the season undefeated for the first time in 40 years, winning two games and drawing eight. The preponderance of drawn games was a disappointment, but this was not due to defensive cricket so much as to the inability of the bowlers to achieve a breakthrough at crucial moments, and to good batting wickets.

Buckinghamshire somewhat surprisingly annihilated Cambridgeshire at Fenners in the first round of the Gillette Cup, dismissing them for 41 in 20 overs – the lowest score in the competition at the time. At home in the second round they failed by only four runs to defeat Glamorgan. Raymond Bond, Man of the Match at Fenners, failed to connect with the last ball and so win Bucks a place in history.

After these performances, the county failed to do themselves justice in the Championship. All too often winning positions were not exploited, and the bowling, in the main, lacked penetration.

Cambridgeshire, for the first time in many years, were twice bowled out for less than 50. The big disappointment was the crushing defeat by Bucks in the first round of the Gillette Cup. In the Championship the County fared a little better, managing to finish just below half-way. Terry Jenner, the Australian professional, had a good season with the bat.

Cheshire found 1972 a season of missed opportunities in terms of overall performance, although it proved a highly successful one in terms of ripening of younger players.

Cornwall must have had their worst season on record. They failed to win a match and finished at the foot of the Championship table. The batsmen rarely found their true form, two of the leading bowlers in 1971 were not available, and there was a high percentage of dropped catches.

Cumberland had a disappointing season. On paper they had what promised to be a fairly strong side, but once again the availability of players was the great problem. During the season they had to call on 21 players, which did not help the skipper or develop good team work.

Devon once again finished well down the Championship table. The main reasons were inconsistent batting, frequently indifferent fielding, and the unavailability of three key players. Some good individual performances included three centuries, which indicates the side is capable of better things. It is hoped that 1973 will show an all-round improvement.

Dorset had their best season for several years, as regards both weather and results, and on the completion of their programme were assured of participation in the Gillette Cup in 1973. The side's success was largely due to the way their captain, D.M. Daniels, directed operations. He appreciated that the quickest way to score runs was to play proper shots and run like scalded cats between the wickets.

Durham had a most successful season, finishing third among the true Minor Counties, and so qualified for the Gillette Cup for the fifth time.

Maximum points were obtained from four matches, one was lost, first innings points were gained on four occasions, and one match ended without any result. Russell Inglis, the newly appointed captain, was unable to play regularly, but nevertheless the team blended well and a happy spirit was maintained throughout the season.

Hertfordshire finished 12th in the Minor Counties table, with two wins only, though rain interfered with several games when the county were in a strong position. Eighteen players represented Hertfordshire in what proved to be a transitional season, with several members of previous years no longer available.

Lancashire II, captained again by E. Slinger, had an average season in the Minor Counties competition, due partly to bad weather and partly to 1st XI calls. An ability to get runs was spoilt by lack of penetration in the bowling. However the opportunity was used to give trials to many promising cricketers, and of these, B. Reidy, who toured the West Indies with the Young Cricketers side, has been engaged on the professional staff.

Lincolnshire, though not enjoying one of their best seasons, still managed to finish in quite a respectable position in the Championship table. Ian Moore, in his first season as captain, filled this position with much credit, setting a fine example with his batting. Sonny Ramadhin, as usual, headed the Minor Counties bowling averages with 36 wickets at 12.30.

Norfolk, though showing some improvement on their previous dismal season, nonetheless experienced another disappointing summer. The batting was generally adequate, with Ken Taylor (Norfolk's first winner of the Wilfred Rhodes Trophy) and Robin Huggins outstanding. But lack of penetrative support for Tracey Moore in the bowling, considerable fallibility about the close catching, and a high proportion of days completely 'washed out' prevented the side from pressing home a number of advantageous positions.

Northumberland suffered in 1972 from the non-availability of some of their more experienced players – in particular bowlers. As a result the county were always struggling to bowl sides out, this being reflected in the season's results. Only one game was won, and of six games in which first innings points were obtained, five were subsequently lost.

Oxfordshire experienced what can only be described as a very disappointing season. They started by losing to Durham in the first round of the Gillette Cup and never seemed to recover. In the Minor Counties Championship they won only one game, and went from 6th place in 1971 to 19th in 1972, registering only 23 points from 10 games. It is true that in three rain-ruined matches, they were in a more favourable position than their opponents, but it seems that the real reason for their lack of success was inconsistency, which can be attributed to shortcomings in batting, bowling and fielding.

Shropshire have little reason to remember 1972 from the point of view of their performances or the weather, although their only victory was a convincing one, over Somerset II. In September they said farewell to their popular Australian professional, Tony Mann, who was a great inspiration, and for 1973 they have engaged Douglas Slade of Worcestershire. The new season also sees their fixture list increased by home and away games with Devon.

Somerset II did not enjoy such a successful season as in 1971, but there were several good performances, particularly the win at Weston-super-Mare against the strong Cheshire team.

Roy Virgin made several appearances in an attempt to recapture his batting form and Brian Rose's very consistent batting won him promotion to the County XI. The leading wicket-taker was again off-spinner Roy Kerslake, who continued to captain the side in his quiet, efficient way.

Staffordshire enjoyed one of their most successful playing seasons for many years, going through the season undefeated. (They have not lost a match since August 1970.) They rose from 11th to 3rd place in the Minor Counties table and it was not known until the final ball of the last Minor Counties match of the season whether Staffordshire or Bedfordshire would finish in second place. The ability to keep a settled side again proved a great advantage, only 17 players being called on during the season, and Douglas Henson again led his men enthusiastically.

Suffolk, if one were to go by their position in the Championship table, had a season that was little short of disastrous. Yet the picture is not as gloomy as it might first appear. Suffolk experienced perhaps their worst ever crop of injuries and were without their talented all-rounder Dick English for the entire season. They were close to victory on several occasions, and there were some fine individual performances.

Wiltshire, soundly beaten by Hampshire in the 1972 Gillette Cup, have a chance to show they can do better in 1973. The county again finished near the top of the Minor Counties Championship and so qualify to take part in the Gillette Cup for the fifth time.

B.H. White has led the side for the past two years, and much of Wiltshire's success can be attributed to the good team spirit he has engendered and to his personal achievements with the bat. He finished at the top of the averages and made over 500 runs.

Yorkshire II had another successful season in 1972, again heading the Minor Counties Championship table. However, in the Challenge Match against Bedfordshire they were defeated by three wickets, and so ended the season as runners-up. They were captained this year by D.E.V. Padgett, who must take a lot of credit for his team's success, leading the side with great enthusiasm and efficiency.

MINOR COUNTIES CHAMPIONSHIP

BEDFORDSHIRE beat Yorkshire Second Eleven by 3 wickets in the Challenge Match at Barnsley on September 15, 16, 17 and so became Champion Minor County under Rule 16.

Final Table		P	W	L	W 1st Inn	L 1st Inn	NR	Pts	Av
Yorkshire II		10	5	1*	3	—	1	64	6.40
BEDFORDSHIRE	G	10	5	—	3	2	—	61	6.10
Staffordshire	G	10	4	—	4	1	1	55	5.50
Durham	G	10	4	1	4	—	1	54	5.40
Dorset	G	8	3	—	3	1	1	42	5.25
Wiltshire	G	8	3	—	2	3	—	39	4.87
Cheshire		12	4	3‡	1	2	2	58	4.83
Lincolnshire		10	4	2	1	3	—	46	4.60
Somerset II		10	4	3	1	2	—	45	4.50
Buckinghamshire		12	3	2*	4	3	—	48	4.00
Berkshire		10	2	—	4	4	—	36	3.60
Hertfordshire		10	2	2*	2	4	—	33	3.30
Cambridgeshire		8	1	3*	2	1	1	22	2.75
Cumberland		8	1	4*	2	1	—	20	2.50
Devon		10	1	2*	2	4	1	25	2.50
Lancashire II		8	1	1	1	3	2	20	2.50
Northumberland		12	1	6§	—	5	—	30	2.50
Shropshire		8	1	4†	—	2	1	20	2.50
Oxfordshire		10	1	3	3	2	1	23	2.30
Norfolk		10	—	5†	3	1	1	18	1.80
Suffolk		10	—	3*	3	4	—	16	1.60
Cornwall		8	—	5*	1	1	1	9	1.12

G qualified for Gillette Cup 1973.
* 1st Innings lead (3 points) in *One* match lost.
† 1st Innings lead (3 points) in *Two* matches lost.
‡ 1st Innings lead (3 points) in *Three* matches lost.
§ 1st Innings lead (3 points) in *Four* matches lost.

The Second Eleven Championship

A distinct lack of publicity has relegated the Second Eleven Championship to the status of a poor relation in cricket. Few people are aware of how the competition operates and the counties themselves are often uncertain of their progress in the table because up-dated figures are issued only four times a year. It seems strange that such a fertile schooling ground for first-class cricket should receive so little coverage.

The competition is run on similar lines to the County Championship and involves only the second strings of the regular professional counties. It is not intended to be a zonal tournament but, because of the financial problems experienced by most counties, southern teams do tend to play each other twice, as do the Midland sides. The travelling and hotel expenses of a match between Lancashire II and Kent II would obviously be prohibitive.

Games are spread out over the whole season. Unfortunately one or two counties play very infrequently and for them the weather conditions are all important. Surrey 2nd XI now try to play all their cricket in July and August when the weather is generally better and when more players of a better standard are available – these are usually university students, training college students and the more mature schoolboys. Early season games often cause selection headaches to counties with small professional staffs when such players are not available. Surrey are setting a precedent which other counties could do well to follow.

Matches are of three and two days' duration. The three-day match is a recent innovation designed to prepare young cricketers for three-day Championship cricket. The 1972 competition also saw the introduction of bonus points earned in an identical way to the method used in first-class cricket: one point for every 25 runs scored above 150 within 85 overs, and one point for every two wickets taken within 85 overs. Unfortunately not all counties are able to afford three-day 2nd XI cricket, Gloucestershire for instance only play two-day games – others play up to 50 per cent of their fixtures as three-day cricket. The two-day games have a different method of attaining bonus points. Here one point is gained for every 25 runs scored above 100 within 70 overs and one point gained for every two wickets taken within 70 overs.

This ruling, which also came into being for the first time last season, although good in principle, did not work too well in practice because of the time taken to bowl the 70 overs. At a bowling rate of 20 overs per hour three-and-a-half hours would be taken up in bowling the required amount, and in most cases either side are perfectly entitled to use the full quota of time in pursuit of bonus points. Hence seven hours of a two-day game could, theoretically, be used on the first innings, but in practice it was rare to find a side bowling at that rate, and more often a total of eight hours or more were involved. This left a mere four and a half hours for the remainder of the match. An unsatisfactory situation to say the least. A figure of 55 or at the outside 60 overs would be better and it is to be hoped that this will be approved for 1973.

Total points from a game come in the form of bonus points in the first innings, plus an extra ten points for a win. The competition is decided on a points average system – the only possible way when there is such variance in the number of games played by each county.

The teams themselves usually have a nucleus of professionals. The number varies from county to county depending on the size of their professional staffs and the number of first eleven injuries at the time of the game. Occasionally a side may field as few as two professionals or on other occasions a full eleven of professionals and part-time professionals.

The part-timers usually arrive in July and are university or training college students whose studies prevent them from being available earlier. Several enjoy the life and show sufficient ability to try their luck professionally once they have completed their studies.

From time to time players discarded by other counties who wish to stay in the game come as trialists, and they are normally played in the second eleven. Any person can play for more than one county second eleven in any given season without any special registration rules being applied, so anyone seeking a living in the game has the opportunity to impress more than one prospective employer. This is a good aspect of the rules and contrasts strongly with the stringent qualifying rules of first-class cricket, by which a contracted and registered player must abide.

Good club cricketers with plenty of free time are also given the opportunity to play. Occasionally the better and more mature schoolboys make up the side. They are also considered trialists, but very few come straight from school to join the groundstaffs – these days they are more conscious of the need for some form of training on which they can fall back if things go against them in the professional game. It is wise to adopt such an outlook but it often makes it harder for counties looking to bring in youngsters from the age of 17 or 18.

Captains in second-eleven cricket vary considerably in age and experience. In general the county coach will skipper the side and this enables him to see from close quarters how the players react to various situations in the game. However, this is not the method every county employs. Some coaches, as they become older, take on a kind of managerial post, watching from the boundary and meting out due punishment to offending youngsters at lunch and tea intervals. In this case the side may be captained by an ex-first eleven player, not necessarily currently connected with the professional staff. One or two counties appoint an ex-professional whose job it is to skipper the side. Others without a regular captain appoint the most senior player in the side at the time – an example of this in 1972 was David Allen, the England off-spinner in his last season with Gloucestershire, who captained the second eleven when not required for first team duty.

The lack of publicity and advertising for this type of cricket is reflected in the attendances. Hampshire have proved that better advertising and coverage in the local press has had a beneficial effect on attendances. An average crowd in Hampshire in good weather now consists of about 30–35 people! A *good* crowd totals about 50 people and one has the urge to lock the gates to keep them in! General opinion is that Hove draws the biggest gates with sometimes several hundred spectators in the ground, but sadly this is the exception rather than the rule.

A cold, wet start followed by a noticeable lack of sun did little to encourage attendances or enhance playing conditions for the 1972 season. Many early games suffered from interruptions caused by rain, and whole days were washed out. This was particularly true of Glamorgan where they had their wettest spring on record.

The season eventually fell into a pattern, and by September four of last year's top six sides had repeated their successful performances.

The 1971 champions, Hampshire, although undefeated for the second successive year, slipped to sixth position. Notts deservedly won the competition, impressively winning half their matches – a very high proportion.

Kent and Gloucestershire dropped considerably in the table compared to their performances in the previous season; Kent from third to tenth and Gloucestershire from fourth to thirteenth. Such inconsistency in results from one season to another can be attributed to either an increase or decrease in professional staffs or high demands on the side because of first eleven injuries.

The 1972 season will be remembered as a particularly cold, wet and miserable one. If more sides were able to play as many games as Warwickshire in future, the loss of so many days play would not be quite so noticeable.

FINAL TABLE — 1972

1972		P	W	L	D	Bt	Bw	Total	Av
1	NOTTINGHAMSHIRE	14	7	0	7	44	52	166	11.85
2	Surrey	11	4	1	6	29	51	120	10.90
3	Warwickshire	23	5	2	16	69	78	197	8.56
4	Northamptonshire	17	4	3	10	50	55	145	8.52
5	Middlesex	14	1	4	9	48	54	112	8.00
6	Hampshire	12	2	0	10	34	40	94	7.83
7	Leicestershire	13	3	5	5	29	38	97	7.46
8	Worcestershire	15	4	3	8	23	46	109	7.26
9	Essex	8	1	1	6	17	28	55	6.87
10	Derbyshire	12	1	3	8	35	34	79	6.58
11	Kent	10	1	1	8	12	36	58	5.80
12	Lancashire	12	1	3	8	23	36	69	5.75
13	Sussex	12	0	3	9	27	42	69	5.75
14	Gloucestershire	10	0	3	7	28	25	53	5.30
15	Glamorgan	15	1	3	11	35	34	79	5.26

Under-25 County Cricket Competition

An historic event of 1972 was the start of a brand new county cricket competition. Aimed at encouraging the budding young talent in the first-class counties, the County Cricket Competition for players under 25 is sponsored by the Warwickshire County Cricket Supporters' Association, under the chairmanship of C.C. Goodway – whose idea the competition originally was. Alan Oakman, the Warwickshire senior coach, is secretary and treasurer.

The tournament takes place under the rules governing the John Player League. The 17 counties are divided into four zones and play against each other on a league basis within these groups. The winners from each zone then go on to contest the semi-finals and final on a knock-out principle. The eventual winners of the competition receive £500, a trophy, and a special Under-25 tie; the runners-up receive £250, and the two losing semi-finalists each receive £125.

It came as no surprise that Warwickshire should win the Midland zone, because they possess the strongest reserve section among the counties. This meant they were able to field a side containing players of the calibre of Whitehouse, who would surely command a permanent place in most other first teams. In addition, they also played two genuine Test cricketers, the West Indian Kallicharran and England's Bob Willis, who were both qualifying.

Northamptonshire also were able to call upon several players with first-class experience and, but for a rain affected game with Worcestershire, could have been involved in a play-off with Warwickshire. The batting of both Tait and Cook clearly indicated that here are two youngsters with genuine potential.

The Northern zone was, somewhat surprisingly, won by Derbyshire, which, considering their lack of success in Championship matches, was very encouraging for them. Although their batting was fragile in the extreme, they were able to remove their opponents cheaply, due to some hostile bowling from Hendrick, Swarbrook, and Wilde. It was expected that either Yorkshire or Lancashire would be the winners, especially as all their cricketers had had considerable experience of limited-overs cricket in the Leagues, but the Derbyshire attack proved too strong.

The two best teams in the Southern zone were Surrey and Middlesex. The former, largely through the efforts of Skinner, Waller, and Roy Lewis, began exceptionally well and seemed certain to qualify for the semi-final, but were overtaken by a Middlesex side, capably led by Selwood, who batted well and camouflaged a fairly innocuous attack by some fine, aggressive fielding. The pick of the Middlesex batting was the West Indian Gomes, who seems clearly destined for a big scoring future. The weakest team in this zone, and probably in the competition, was, not surprisingly, Essex. They suffered from a minute staff and the fact that, apart from Pont, who joined them last summer, they have taken on no players for several years, apart from two overseas cricketers, neither of whom was with them last season.

Before the start of the competition it was assumed that Gloucester, who could include a Pakistan Test cricketer, as well as Roger Knight, would cruise into the semi-final, but it was the young, keen, and comparatively unknown Glamorgan who proved to be the most efficient side in this division. The form displayed by Hopkins, Llewellyn, and Reynolds in particular bodes well for Glamorgan's future. What must have been especially pleasing for the Welsh county was that the success was obtained by players who had been found and developed by their own coaching system – a very healthy sign.

The first semi-final at Edgbaston was between Derbyshire and Middlesex. On winning the toss for Derbyshire, Peter Eyre elected to bat. Against tight bowling from Edmonds, whose eight overs cost only 11 runs and produced two wickets, and Vernon, whose figures were 3 for 26, Derbyshire managed to reach only 133. The main contributions were 21 apiece from Swindell and Hill and an aggressive 16 from Hendrick. Middlesex realised that on an easy-paced wicket this was a fairly small target in 40 overs, but on the other hand the Derby attack was formidable. They were certainly made to fight for their runs, but an inspired 60 from their captain, Tim Selwood, saw them home, despite a fine piece of very accurate seam bowling from Hendrick.

In the second match, Warwickshire versus Glamorgan, Glamorgan won the toss and, as in previous matches, elected to field. Their captain, Reynolds, is a great believer in batting last. Warwickshire, in spite of four run-outs, reached 173 off 40 overs – the main contributions coming from Kallicharran 54, and Hemmings 51. Against experienced bowlers such as Willis, Rouse, Abberley and Hemmings, Glamorgan realised they had a very difficult task on their hands. A solid start by Reynolds and Ellis, followed by another good stand between Llewellyn and Hopkins, took Glamorgan within easy reach of the Warwickshire total. With the return of Rouse and Willis to bowl the last eight overs Francis and Richards rose to the occasion and saw Glamorgan home to victory by four wickets with an over to spare. It represented a splendid piece of intelligent batting from a young side.

In the final, Glamorgan again won the toss, put Middlesex in to bat and needed 183 off 39 overs. For Middlesex, Barlow 31, Edmonds 30, and Hopkins 34, were the main run-getters against tight bowling and first-class fielding. Selvey, pegging away with accurate bowling, tied Glamorgan down, but at one point 50 runs were scored during four overs which put Glamorgan well back in the hunt. Only 23 runs were needed with seven overs left when Hopkins, who had scored the bulk of the 50 runs during the whirlwind attack, was run out.

Middlesex brought back Selvey who dismissed Gwyn Richards for 24, and from then onwards the Glamorgan batsmen offered little opposition, and Middlesex won by 8 runs in what had been a splendidly contested match.

At the end of the season all agreed that the competition had been a great success with limited teething troubles. This type of competition will be of great benefit to young cricketers up and down the country.

During the competition, three counties selected players who had represented their country in Test cricket, but from 1973 the competition will be limited to uncapped players

– county or country – but allowing Oxford or Cambridge Blues. It will, however, permit players to continue to play in the competition throughout a season in which they are awarded their county or country caps.

There was a strong feeling the captain should also be under 25, but it was ultimately decided he should be a senior, experienced player, to train young cricketers and give experience. The captain of the Under-25 side would be the normal Second XI captain.

Suggestions to increase the number of overs to either 55 or 60 from the existing 40 found little support as problems arose, such as Glamorgan having to travel from Cardiff to possibly Southampton, involving travelling time of $3\frac{1}{2}$ hours. This was coupled with the fact that players found it easier to take half-a-day off instead of a whole day to play a game of cricket and also bearing in mind that this competition was designed specially to prepare young cricketers for the 40 over game.

U-25 COUNTY CRICKET COMPETITION

	P	W	L	NR	Pts
NORTH					
Derbyshire	6	4	0	2	18
Lancashire	6	3	2	1	13
Yorkshire	6	2	2	2	10
Nottinghamshire	6	0	5	1	1
MIDLANDS					
Warwickshire	6	5	1	0	20
Northamptonshire	6	4	1	1	17
Worcestershire	6	1	4	1	5
Leicestershire	6	1	5	0	4
SOUTH					
Middlesex	8	7	1	0	28
Surrey	8	6	2	0	24
Kent	8	4	4	0	16
Sussex	8	3	5	0	12
Essex	8	0	8	0	0
WEST					
Glamorgan	6	4	0	2	18
Gloucestershire	6	3	2	1	13
Hampshire	6	3	2	1	13
Somerset	6	0	6	0	0

SEMI-FINALS   MIDDLESEX beat Derbyshire
              GLAMORGAN beat Warwickshire
FINAL   MIDDLESEX beat Glamorgan

England Test bowler Bob Willis was available for Warwickshire's under-25 side while qualifying for the county

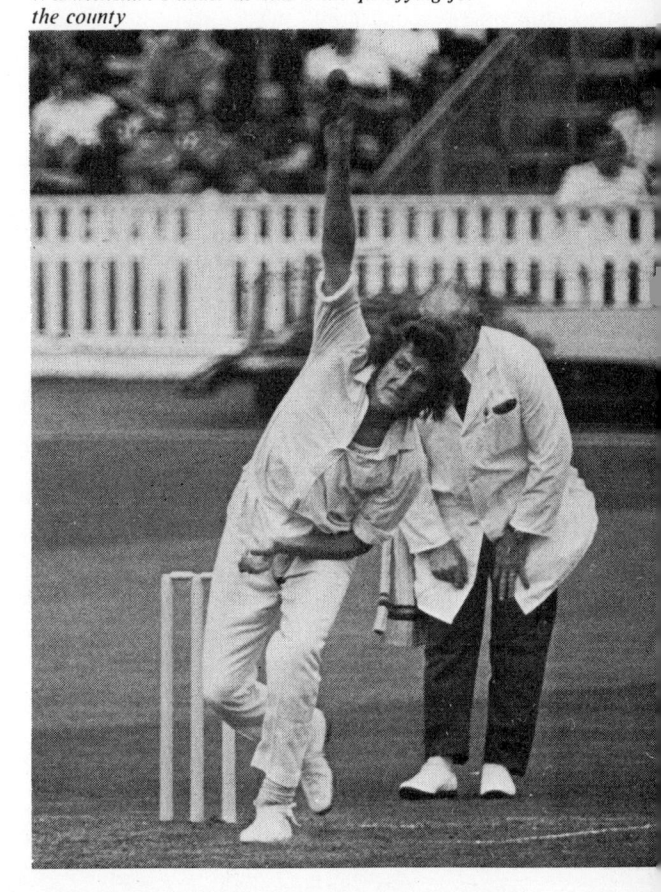

The National Club Knock-Out

It all started by accident. Jim Swanton and the Coventry City Football Club chairman, Derrick Robins, were discussing the popularity and success of The Cricketer Cup, the competition for Public School Old Boys. Derrick, a keen club cricketer of many years standing, whose D.H. Robins XI will be playing against both New Zealand and the West Indians in 1973, decided that it would be a good idea to have a similar tournament for club cricket. He had a magnificent trophy designed and donated prize money of £250 for the winning club, £150 for the losing finalist, and £50 each for the losing semi-finalists.

The competition is regionalised so that in the early stages not too much travelling is involved, but in the later stages Aberdeen may well find themselves playing Penzance. Plaques are presented to all the regional winners.

In the first year, 1969, the final took place at Edgbaston, but since then it has taken place at Lord's, and each year it becomes more and more popular. The club cricketers now come 'Up for the Cup' and it is very much the club cricketers day at Lord's, because every club cricketer in the country naturally wants to play there.

The first final was fought out between Hampstead CC and Pocklington Pixies – the old boys of Pocklington School in Yorkshire. Hampstead had the best of the day. They won the toss and batted in reasonable light while Pocklington had to bowl with a wet ball. There were some splendid innings; C.J.R. (Sam) Black got 49 and captain Nick Alwyn 34 in the all-out total of 191. In dim light and facing the dry ball with which Hampstead bowled, Pocklington made a great and spirited reply, with veteran Guy Willett scoring 40 and C. Johnson, 43, taking them to within 14 runs of the total. But the bowling of M. Willard, 4 for 26, and B. Davison, 2 for 22, was just a little too strong and Hampstead were the worthy winners.

And so to Lord's in 1970. This was a fantastic game of cricket between Stockport CC from the Lancashire League and Cheltenham CC – the surprise team of the year. Captained by David Brown of Gloucestershire they were most certainly the underdogs and Stockport, with the help of Mankad, the Indian Test player, were expected to win. However, the beauty of cricket lies in its uncertainty, and Stockport used up all their 45 overs, achieving a total of only 169. Mankad started from the first and finished with 83 not out, but, with his experience, should have been able to have made more runs in the time. Cheltenham were left with 170 to make at a rate of almost four per over.

They attacked their task in a magnificent way, and by the most exciting running between the wickets and the most hazardous risks they forced themselves to keep up with the run rate despite losing wickets regularly. However, in the last three overs, they got slightly behind the clock and when the last over was called Cheltenham required eight runs. Stockport placed all their fielders on the boundary and the task seemed beyond Cheltenham's grasp. With the help of an overthrow and some frantic running it came to the magnificent situation whereby Cheltenham required four off the last ball of the match, and with every Stockport fielder on the boundary it seemed all over. But no. We saw the last ball, not one of the highest quality, smacked straight over the top of the Tavern virtually into the street for the most glorious of sixes and Lord's erupted. Cheltenham had won the trophy.

The 1971 final was famous for some swing bowling of considerable ability. It was one of those days that happen at Lord's from time to time – as when Ian Thomson was bowling for Sussex against Warwickshire in the Gillette final, and other occasions at Lord's when the ball moves all over the place.

Ealing CC, playing against Blackheath CC, won the toss and elected to bat, and they faced up to the first overs from the Blackheath West Indian bowler, Toppin. His early overs were quite remarkable. They consisted of huge away swingers, and every three or four balls, a big inducker which kept on knocking the stumps down. It was most disconcerting to bat in these circumstances, but to those sitting behind the bowler's arm, who were able to see what was happening with the ball, it really was no surprise to find Ealing, a fairly strong London club, move from 8 for 2, to 17 for 4, to 23 for 6. John Poore with a good 45 stabilized the damage to a certain extent, but the batting was broken and Ealing were all out for 105. Toppin turned in the magnificent figures of 5 for 10.

Blackheath, helped by several players with Kent Second XI experience, had no trouble in getting the runs and won comfortably by seven wickets.

And so to last year's final. Brentham CC, who have a number of Middlesex Second XI players in their side, fought through the London regions of the competition to be a surprise finalist at Lord's. Their opponents were the very famous Scarborough CC, who have shown a tremendous interest in this competition from the beginning. It was therefore fitting that they should reach the final, having lost in the semi-final the previous year.

Brentham won the toss and on a perfect wicket made the mistake of batting first. This Lord's final is a tense and nervous occasion to the club cricketer, and one was left with the impression that Brentham were determined that they were not going to get over excited. They seemed to take this too literally and their batting became quite casual, and their running not particularly urgent. On the other hand Scarborough were right on their toes, fielding like demons and keeping a very tight grip on the situation. Much was expected from Graham Barlow, the Middlesex Second XI player, but unfortunately he failed. Wickets fell regularly, and in the end Brentham were dismissed for the dismal total of 129 in 42 overs, Pincher taking four for ten and Kirby three for 17.

This proved to be no serious obstacle for Scarborough who got the runs very comfortably for four wickets in 33.4 overs. There was, in fact, only one time when they seemed to be ruffled and that was when Swan came on to bowl his leg spinners (who says spinners are out of favour in limited-overs cricket?). He bowled magnificently for an analysis of none for 7 in eight overs. Nevertheless there really was never any doubt and Scarborough became the worthy winners and the first northern team to have won the Derrick Robins trophy.

Haig National Village Cricket Championship

208 The Haig National Village Cricket Championship was born in the winter of 1970. The National Cricket Association and *The Cricketer* magazine had conducted a joint survey of English club cricket and from this decided that village cricket deserved, and indeed would benefit from, some form of encouragement. They therefore decided to seek a sponsor to back a competition at village level.

At the same time, John Haig & Co. Ltd were investigating the question of sports sponsorship. After looking at more than 50 different sporting activities, Mr. Michael Henderson, Managing Director of Haig, decided that he had no need to look further – Haig would sponsor a national village cricket tournament.

From then on the Haig National Village Cricket Championship gathered momentum. Rules were drawn up stating that 'The object of the competition shall be to promote the best in village cricket and give an opportunity to village cricketers to compete in a national event'. It was agreed that *The Cricketer* would organise the Championship and that the Laws of Cricket should apply, with the addendum that each side should bat for 40 overs unless their innings was completed earlier, or unless the captains agreed to a lesser number of overs before the start of the match.

A village was deemed a rural community of not more than 2,500 inhabitants; players had to be paid-up members of their club who had played an aggregate of eight games in less than three years, although players did not have to live in the village. Players were ineligible if they had ever played first-class cricket (unless they were over 60) or if they were competing in the National Club Knock-Out during the same year, or if they received a fee for playing.

Entries poured in from throughout the country, with teams from every county in England, plus entries from Wales and Scotland. In the end 795 village cricket clubs took part. For the purposes of the Haig, the country was divided initially into 32 county groups. Clubs played off within their groups, and then the groups, divided into four regions, the North (including Scotland), the Midlands, the South East and the South West, played off against each other. Therefore one team from each region competed in the semi-final rounds.

The North played the Midlands, producing the Astwood Bank team from Warwickshire as one finalist, and the South East played the South West, with the other finalist coming from Troon in Cornwall.

The highlight of the championship was, of course, the final at Lord's which was held on Saturday, 9th September. In keeping with the dreadful summer weather of last year, the day of the final dawned grey and wet. Play was due to commence at 12 noon, but had to be delayed

Their aim is to play at Lord's for the Haig Challenge Trophy, but for the moment these cricketers content themselves with the idyllic surroundings of Welford Park in Berkshire

to allow the pitch to dry out from the heavy rain of the day before. Play eventually started at 1.30 p.m. Troon won the toss and sent their opponents in to bat first. Astwood Bank made 165 for 8 in their 40 overs. Troon got off to a bad start with opening bat John Spry getting out for only 2 runs. However, a magnificent innings of 79 not out by Terry Carter assured Troon's victory with a score of 170 for 3 in 33.4 overs.

The magnificent £1,000 Haig Challenge Trophy, in the form of a silver Dimple Haig bottle with crossed bats, was presented to Troon's captain Terry Carter by Michael Henderson. Freddie Brown, President of the MCC and former England captain, when congratulating the two teams, spoke of 'this unique tournament which has captured the interest of all in the game'. 'Man of the Match' awards were also made and presented by Ian Redpath, Australian Test batsman, to Terry Carter of Troon and Brian Spittle of Astwood Bank.

The saddest story of the day at Lord's was of the Troon supporters who had chartered a train from British Rail to bring over 600 people to see their club battling for the title. A derailment of a goods train at Dawlish blocked a tunnel and the Troon train had to return to Cornwall, taking with it a crowd of very disappointed and very angry people. But Troon's victory was well and truly celebrated, with a civic reception and a special reception laid on at Troon by Haig.

Apart from the final of the Village Cricket Championship, Haig also organised a cricket ball throwing competition for members of clubs who had entered the Haig. The best 25 'throwers' were invited to Lord's to 'throw off' before the start of the game. Michael Richardson, 17, a schoolboy from Belsay in Northumberland, won with a throw of 106 yd 2 ft 1 in, winning for himself a superb trophy, half a gallon of Haig whisky and a cheque for his club.

Club Cricket

Tony Pawson

Club cricket is now so wide in scope that it defies definition. The term covers not just the traditional club sides such as Free Foresters or Buccaneers with their programmes of friendly matches, but also those who indulge their competitive inclinations in the National Club Knockout or the leagues.

Two things only are certain. The vitality everywhere apparent in the game in 'Australia Year' was reflected in the strength and enthusiasm of club cricket. And the tide of change is flowing strongly towards being more competitive.

Until a few years ago the South looked askance at league cricket. But the drift of the past few seasons has become a flood, with most of the leading clubs joining leagues. In the Club Cricket Conference area stretching from Bedfordshire to the Kent coast there are already 22 leagues, with Hampshire on the verge of launching another with five divisions and eighty clubs interested.

The Middlesex County Cricket League is another that officially starts in the 1973 season, although several of the clubs were keeping a tally of points when they played each other last season. Most of the leading clubs like Hornsey, Hampstead, Richmond, Ealing and Finchley have joined the new League.

Surrey were earlier off the mark, with their League Cricket Championship started in 1969, and won last season by Guildford. Here, too, most of the strong club sides such as Beddington, Malden Wanderers, Old Whitgiftians, Epsom and Honor Oak are in the League.

The Kent League, in only its second season, staged its second taut finish with everything depending on the final match. This time it was a club rich in tradition, Sevenoaks Vine, that came through to steal the championship, just as Ashford had done the year before. Once more, the main sufferer was Tunbridge Wells, who again lost their vital match to a Folkestone team that had struggled to beat anyone all season. The Sevenoaks' success owed much to the new captain, Bob Golds, and to Chris Tavaré, the 17-year-old who had made so many runs for Sevenoaks School and averaged nearly 50 for the Vine.

Underlining the conversion in the South, the Sussex League is also thriving after its second season. Eastbourne were the champions going ahead of Brighton and Hove when they won their last match against Gorsham by 78 runs. The former Cambridge Blue, Chris Pyemont, was their most successful all-rounder.

The Club Cricket Conference representative side was as strong as ever, unbeaten in any match and with two notable wins. The Army was shot out for 70 and beaten by ten wickets though their side was good enough to win the Inter-Service matches. MCC were also beaten in a two-day game with no declarations needed to ensure a finish. The Conference also came close to defeating the United London Banks, the most consistent of the strong sides they play.

D.J. Evans celebrated his third year as captain of the Conference side with a notable success of his own, passing the thousand runs in representative matches. Only one other Conference player, P.J. Whitcombe, has ever achieved this before, not surprising as there are only seven or eight representative games a season.

So far the emphasis has been on competitive club cricket in the South, but the main club prize went to a Northern team. The National Club Knock-out for the Derrick Robins Trophy was won by Scarborough whose solid teamwork was well emphasised in the final at Lord's on September 10th. This was the fourth season of the competition and the first time a Northern team had taken the trophy, the previous winners being Hampstead (1969), Cheltenham (1970) and Blackheath (1971).

It was too much to hope that the excitement could match that first Lord's final when a six by the last man off the last ball gave Cheltenham the victory over Stockport. But Scarborough's comfortable win by 6 wickets with 11.2 of their 45 overs left underlined the strength of Yorkshire Club cricket. (See *The National Club Knock-Out*.)

Another popular competition with a charitable purpose is Kemp's Cup run by Bertie Joel and open to clubs within 40 miles of London. The entrance fee is donated to Sparks and nearly 200 clubs are glad to pay. Vauxhall Motors took the trophy, winning by 44 runs against a Mote team which included five Kent 2nd XI players, but which never scored fast enough to look like matching Vauxhall's 176 in 45 overs.

This happy combination of club cricket and charity was further enhanced by the Mote who staged the match between Old England and Lord's Taverners on their Maidstone ground. Over £1,200 was collected in this game sponsored by Ladbrokes. The fund raising got the better of the weather as in so many of the Lord's Taverners' games, but the only hint of a golden summer was the memory evoked by a fine partnership between Edrich and Compton.

Lord's Taverners did not neglect those other talented cricketers, the England Ladies XI. Their meeting ended in a tie that included three run-outs in the last over and the irrepressible Rachael Flint scoring 99.

While Australia gave such challenge to our first-class game, club cricketers were enjoying the visits of the Argentine and East African teams. The Argentine side lost only two of its twelve matches, one to Frank Sanderson's XI at Torquay and one to MCC at Lord's. Peter Richardson, the former England batsman, with scores of 105 and 153 not out at Torquay and 81 at Lord's was the man to upset their record, but nothing disturbed the sporting spirit in which the games were played. The Argentinians indeed gave lessons in ' walking ' as well as in playing ability.

MCC were also too good for the East Africans who travelled from Hove to Blackburn and from Taunton to Colwyn Bay in their first-ever tour of this country. Harilal Shah with 690 runs and 22 wickets was their most successful all-rounder.

These tours helped to mix club cricketers with first-class players and that is also one of the successful achievements of the Cricketer Cup. For the second year running Old Tonbridgians won this competition for Old Boy teams, with its attractive award of a trip to Epernay organised by Moët and Chandon and *The Cricketer*.

The final was played at Burton Court, that charming tree-lined ground in the heart of London enlivened by a colourful marquee and the band of the Irish Guards. To the obvious enjoyment of the Chelsea Pensioners in the crowd, Colin Cowdrey made batting look disarmingly simple, scoring 49, but it was Colin Smith's murderous assault on the Old Malvernnian bowling that decided the match. Though Moët and Chandon were the sponsors, there was no champagne cricket from the Old Malvernians who made hard work of losing by 114 runs.

Club cricket owes a great debt to individuals for so often much of the work and inspiration comes from one man. Such a person was Henry Grierson who founded the Forty Club and made it such a powerful force. His death was a sad loss for cricket, for in his deep love of the game, his kindly humour and his great enthusiasm, he expressed the best ideals of club cricket.

Two others who embody this spirit and who have served club cricket well over many years are Doug Kesby and Geoff Hunnybun. Doug Kesby was President of the Club Cricket Conference and also celebrated his fiftieth year as a playing member of Old Parkonians. Geoff Hunnybun last season completed 50 years in club cricket, 30 with Mill Hill, the rest with North Mymms. To recognise his service to Hertfordshire cricket their captain, John Appleyard, brought down a strong Hedgehogs XI to play the North Mymms side led by Hunnybun.

There were celebrations for clubs as well as cricketers. Notable was the Grange Cricket Club centenary of its ground at Raeburn Place in Edinburgh. Ian Peebles, who is the only Scottish cricketer, apart from Mike Denness, to play for England and captain a county side, was the principal guest at this most successful of Scottish clubs. Their centenary cricket week included games against MCC, Sussex Martlets, Free Foresters and a Scotland XI. Another centenary was the Roundhay Park Cricket Club in Leeds, which plays in the Barkston, Ash and Yorkshire Central League.

Despite the strength of league cricket in Yorkshire there are many thriving clubs who keep to the old tradition of friendly matches. The Saints, with no little assistance from Fred Trueman, continued to provide challenging opposition in a wide range of fixtures, while the Craven Gentlemen turned nomadic for a Southern tour.

Two club sides used to wide ranging travel are the Arabs and Buccaneers, both of whom had highly successful tours. For the Arabs M.J.J. Faber, the Oxford blue, scored 102 in 101 minutes in the match against Sussex Martlets at Arundel. Cambridge were to the fore for the Buccaneers, Gwyn Hughes taking 17 wickets in their Southern tour. But the honours for an all-rounder went to J.P. Bramall of Downside School who scored over 400 runs for an average of 58 and took 13 wickets.

Cricketers sometimes complain of soccer's encroachment into the summer, though the surfeit of football has probably helped rather than hindered the great upsurge of interest in cricket. But some clubs fight back. The Jack Frost XI which played its first match in October 1961 has been reversing the trend for the past 11 years. Though its fixture list is not in the main as wintry as its name, the Jack Frost XI enjoys its 20-over matches on Boxing Day. These were first played at Teddington, now at Surbiton, and the number of clubs playing cricket on Boxing Day is steadily spreading. The Northern Cricket Society started the Boxing Day craze in Leeds in 1949, with Brian Close often captaining the side, and the weather over the years has been surprisingly good. But the first club side to play regularly was in Sussex, where Noel Bennett's Yule Log XI have been playing on Boxing Day since 1945. Such is the keenness of the club cricketer.

The Northern Leagues Battle On

John Kay

It takes more than a spell of bad weather to daunt the keen and determined league cricketers of the North of England. They have known crisis after crisis and battled on to win through. It was the same in 1972 as in 1932, 1942 and 1952 . . . and possibly in 1962 as well. The weather kept the crowds away in the early part of the season and, when the sun did shine, the holiday season had reduced the ranks of would-be spectators to a mere trickle when only a flood of support at the turnstiles could make amends for the cold, damp and often windy days of April, May and early June.

In the mighty Lancashire League – the field that boasts that only the best players in the world are good enough to become club professionals – secretary Jack Isherwood describes the gate receipts as the 'worst in years', and crowd support as the smallest he can recall. Yet he adds that his clubs will emerge with a smile and a spirit that cannot be faulted, in readiness for a new season this April.

What lies ahead cannot be foreseen. What happened in 1972 is now cricket history but it will be remembered as the year in which batsmen had to fight harder than ever for runs; bowlers had to master lifeless pitches and cold hands to gain success, and the fieldsmen had to shiver in two and sometimes three sweaters to survive the arctic conditions that passed for England's spring and early summer. In the mighty Lancashire League, East Lancashire were the champions and Bacup the Worsley Cup Winners.

The big town teams and the small ones too shared the honours. In the Central Lancashire League two of the smaller clubs collared the glory. Milnrow and Castleton Moor, off-shoots of the larger Rochdale township, were champions and Wood Cup winners respectively, and each had good amateurs and professionals.

East Lancashire owed a great deal to their former Australian Test seamer Neil Hawke, and Bacup had reason to thank Western Australian spinner, Tony Mann. Hawke proved himself a sound all-rounder. He captured 71 wickets at just over 11 runs each and hit 536 runs for an average of 33.50, to keep East Lancashire at the top of the Lancashire League table for most of the season. In the end his side had 12 points to spare and were defeated only five times in 26 limited-overs games. Figures may tend to suggest that Hawke's was a 'one-man' performance yet he is the first to pay tribute to the support accorded him by a bunch of talented and enthusiastic amateurs.

Brian Ratcliffe was a skipper of much consequence. Always willing to take a chance and ever ready to accept a challenge, East Lancashire lacked nothing in what was for them a successful season. Jim Kenyon and Roger Sharp provided the bowling support for Hawke, and chipped in with useful runs as well. Mann's 71 wickets cost

Bacup 13 runs each, and his batting return of 841 runs for an average of 40.04 was the best in the League. Bacup finished in fourth position but gleefully took the Worsley Cup in a magnificent final with East Lancashire.

Dik Abed, possibly the best coloured South African to grace league cricket since Basil D'Oliveira made such an impact with Middleton in the Central Lancashire League, was seldom found wanting with Enfield. His return of 89 wickets and 558 runs kept the side pressing on the heels of the champions most of the season, and it was certainly not Abed's fault that the pace became too hot in the closing weeks. Of the newcomers to the professional ranks in this testing sphere none did better than Sarfraz Nawaz, the Pakistan and former Northamptonshire bowler, who joined Nelson and contributed 716 runs and 79 wickets to keep the Seedhill side in the top half of the table.

Abdul Barnes, coming from the coloured ranks in South Africa, had an unlucky first season at Colne, but looked a promising player once the sun began to shine. His record of 467 runs and 33 wickets may not look or sound impressive, but for a newcomer to league cricket and Lancashire conditions there was much to admire about this likeable cricketer's potential.

In the Central Lancashire League, where professionalism operates on a more modest basis, a young amateur bowler collared the headlines, and took Milnrow to a championship they seldom looked like losing right from the early days of a cold and cheerless May. Peter Wilson became the first unpaid seamer to capture more than 100 wickets for years and his 110 victims for 11.99 each was not bettered.

They were superbly skippered by Ken Grieves. The former Lancashire all-rounder from Australia, now playing out his last few seasons as an amateur, saw to it that Milnrow lacked nothing in leadership. Astute bowling changes and shrewd field placings were matched by thoughtful use of a keen set of young amateurs and the building of a tremendous team spirit in the Milnrow dressing room. And when runs were wanted, Grieves seldom failed. His return of 407 runs for an average of 40 placed him ahead of all other amateur run-scorers.

Heywood, with Colin Lever a consistent all-round professional, came second best to Milnrow, and Middleton, always a team of sound all-round ability, filled the third position without seriously threatening Milnrow's domination of the scene. There was much merit in the Wood Cup success of Castleton Moor who humbled Milnrow in a final that attracted a crowd of 5,000 and receipts topping £400.

It would be unfair not to mention the successful return of the once fiery Roy Gilchrist to the sphere which first launched him on an adventurous league career after successful spells with the West Indies in Test cricket. Always a stormy character and frequently a misjudged one, Gilchrist joined Crompton and picked up 85 wickets at 10.75 runs each. Alas, his team finished at the bottom of the League table, but Gilchrist did more than his fair share for a side lacking real amateur support. Rochdale had a successful and hard-working professional in Cheshire's Alan Barratt, whose 91 wickets and 411 runs represent excellent value.

To refute the point that spinners have no real part to play in over-limited cricket, it must be mentioned that young Derek Parker, a leg-spinning reject by Lancashire, joined Royton to claim 89 wickets – and was often seen making the new ball lift and turn. At Littleborough, Yacoob Omar, one of South Africa's coloured players tilting at the sort of windmills D'Oliveira successfully demolished, hit 702 runs and captured 30 wickets, but found himself replaced by

Neil Hawke, cheerful, articulate swing bowler who has become a great favourite in the Lancashire League. Like so many Australians he is also a useful batsman

Gloucestershire's Mike Bissex for 1973.

There was much good cricket against the odds in several of the minor Lancashire leagues and in the Bolton League Little Lever were the champions, and a likeable West Indian player of much league experience, Syl Oliver, was the most successful batsmen with 630 runs on Egerton's behalf. But the man who meant most was Sonny Ramadhin!

At an age when regular cricket means hard work the gallant West Indies wizard of spin joined Little Lever and picked up 100 wickets for a mere eight runs each. Opposition batsmen were often heard to credit 'Ram' with all his old-time deadliness, but he steered his side to the championship by the simple but effective means of bowling a good line, a perfect length and stationing his fieldsmen astutely.

The Lancashire and Cheshire League championship went to Stalybridge and the Walkden Cup to Denton St. Lawrence, and in this realm officials have taken the plunge with a bold league cricketing gamble. This summer they have recruited ten new clubs who will play for places in two divisions with promotion and relegation issues brought into operation for the 1974 season. 'Crowd support and membership have been dwindling for years – we must do something new to attract the waverer', says secretary Gilbert Burrows. He admits to reservations and accepts criticism, but believes a new look essential for a long-established league that will in future draw clubs from Derbyshire and Yorkshire, as well as Lancashire and Cheshire. He also reports that, in readiness for the experiment, most clubs are recruiting professional aid after several years of mainly amateur cricket.

Over in Yorkshire it is the Bradford League that matters most. Promotion and relegation have long been the pattern in their two divisions and in 1972 Bankfoot were Division I champions, with Bradford runners-up. Great Horton and Farsley were relegated to Division II, with Hartshead Moor and Pudsey St. Lawrence regaining senior status. Prominent among the batsmen in this highly competitive and well supported league was Doug Padgett, now Yorkshire's chief coach and second-team captain. From the bowling point of view Bob Platt, another former Yorkshire player, and Howard Cooper, one of the best of the new White Rose brigade, did well, with Platt taking 42 wickets at 8.89 each, and Cooper picking up 50 victims for Bankfoot at 8.92 each.

All in all 1972 was not a vintage year for league cricket. The weather was the major culprit, but there are still a few snags to be ironed out in over-limited cricket. The Central Lancashire League found accusations of gamesmanship and criticism of their umpires a common complaint, but acted with welcome promptitude when suspending Malcolm Hilton for six matches. The former England and Lancashire spin bowler, now skipper of Werneth, ignored several warnings for conduct detrimental to the game and eventually paid the penalty. The League's action is to be commended. No player, however high his status, is more important than the game – and no club must be allowed to play fast and loose with the rules!

LANCASHIRE LEAGUE

Club	P	W	L	D	Pts	Professional	Runs	Av	Wkts	Av
East Lancashire	26	17	5	4	82	N.J.N. Hawke	536	33.50	71	11.01
Enfield	26	15	5	6	70	Dik Abed	558	26.57	89	11.31
Rawtenstall	26	13	7	6	60	D.L. Orchard	619	34.38	57	15.59
Bacup	26	12	11	3	58	A. Mann	841	40.04	71	13.00
Nelson	26	11	9	6	55	Sarfraz Nawaz	716	37.68	79	10.21
Accrington	26	12	9	5	54	L. Varis	458	24.10	77	10.97
Todmorden	26	12	9	5	54	P.T. Marner	578	36.12	35	20.22
Burnley	26	11	8	7	52	H.J. Rhodes	31	7.75	39	10.84
Church	26	9	10	6*	47	C. Forbes	402	26.80	63	12.34
Ramsbottom	26	9	8	9	44	R.G. Nadkarni	382	19.10	61	12.83
Rishton	26	7	14	5*	35	K. Barker	462	23.10	37	23.70
Colne	26	5	15	6	28	A.L. Barnes	467	20.30	33	15.36
Lowerhouse	26	5	14	7	25	D.G. Carter	312	19.50	61	12.83
Haslingden	26	5	14	7	24	P. Nicholls	678	37.66	35	16.14

*Tied game included. Four points awarded for a win, two points for a tie and, in a completed match, one extra point awarded for dismissing the opposition

CENTRAL LANCASHIRE LEAGUE

Club	P	W	L	D	Pts	Professional	Runs	Av	Wkts	Av
Milnrow	26	20	3	3	89	R. Miller	192	12.00	84	10.15
Heywood	26	17	6	3	70	C. Lever	821	34.20	82	11.51
Middleton	26	12	7	7*	66	J. Burton	356	23.73	72	13.41
Radcliffe	26	12	11	3	61	C. Abrahams	404	17.57	54	12.35
Littleborough	26	13	9	4	61	Y. Omar	702	30.52	30	17.33
Werneth	26	10	12	4	50	R. Kelsall	478	19.91	50	20.84
Rochdale	26	10	12	4	48	A. Barratt	411	27.40	91	10.05
Castleton Moor	26	10	13	3	47	J. Howarth	100	8.33	80	11.38
Royton	26	9	12	5*	47	D. Parker	140	10.00	89	10.87
Walsden	26	10	12	4*	47	C. Wright	179	9.94	90	13.61
Oldham	26	9	13	4	46	I. Elahi	335	15.22	72	13.27
Ashton	26	7	12	7*	43	C. Watson	474	23.70	72	14.00
Stockport	26	8	15	3	41	R. Scarlett	413	18.77	63	15.00
Crompton	26	5	14	7	32	R. Gilchrist	166	8.30	85	10.75

*Tied games included. Four points awarded for outright victories, three points for 'limited' wins, two points for a tie and one point for an unfinished match

English Schools' Cricket Association

For a body that began in 1948 with 12 county associations in membership, the English Schools' Cricket Association (ESCA) has come a long way. On the playing field, its success is registered by the status of players 'capped' by the Association – Dennis Amiss, Geoff Arnold, Jack Birkenshaw, Derek Underwood, Alan Knott, Chris Old, and Pat Pocock of the 1972-73 MCC touring side to India and Pakistan. These and the many others who grace the first-class scene reflect fully the value of the Association's encouragement of schoolboy cricketers.

On an administrative level, the ESCA progressed rapidly, and by 1969 it boasted 43 County associations in membership, and every county in England had a Schools' Association in affiliated membership. Because the individual schools affiliate to their respective counties, or in some cases to the district associations, the exact number of schools affiliated indirectly to the ESCA can never be precisely stated, but it would be fair to say that virtually every school in England is associated with the national body.

Ever since its inauguration, the Association has been responsible for school cricket at all ages: Primary, Junior (under 15 on September 1 of the current school year), and Senior (under 19 on the same date). In the early days the strongest section was undoubtedly the Junior, for the Senior representative teams were certainly not fully representative of the available schools' talent. Gradually, however, more and more County Associations themselves put on Senior county matches, and at the present time few outstanding boys fail to be nominated for the Senior games.

At Junior level an annual festival is arranged in which representative sides from the four regions – Midlands, North, South, and West – participate, each region playing the other. In the earlier days the North were generally the strongest, but more recently the other regions have come more and more into contention. A representative side selected from the four regions plays a two-day match against the Public Schools. Unfortunately, efforts to provide other matches for this side have not yet been successful.

The Senior representative side has a much wider programme. In 1949 it played its first match, against the Welsh Schools, which since then has become an annual fixture on a home and away basis. Too often this match results in a draw, but over the years this has been more the fault of the weather than of the cricket played. In 1968 a series began against the Scottish Cricket Union Colts, matches which have provided some interesting cricket, and each year the team also plays a two-day match against the Public Schools. In addition matches have been played against the South African Schools, whom the ESCA defeated in the only match played here, Dutch sides, and the Canadian Colts.

In 1970-71 the Association sent its first team abroad, a party of 15 boys going to India for a six-week visit. Though England lost the only completed 'test' of the five played, the tour was a successful one and all matches attracted large and enthusiastic crowds. Included in that side were John Barclay, Peter Booth, Graham Clinton, Geoffrey Miller, and Andrew Stovold, all of whom were in the Young England side, captained by John Barclay, that toured the West Indies in 1972. In 1973 the English Schools are welcoming here the Indian Schools for a six-week tour.

From the first, the Association has realised the importance of coaching, and two residential courses have been held each Easter at which some 70 to 80 boys are coached annually. Such is the enthusiasm for these courses that a third is being organised for 1973.

The 1972 season was a milestone in the history of the Association, for it saw the start of the Esso Trophy Competition, an individual-schools event generously sponsored by the Esso Company at the suggestion of *The Cricketer* and organised by the English Schools' Association. This is a two-tier competition. At Under-15 level each county has one school representative in a national competition to find a national winner, while at Under-14 level each county organises a schools competition, the winner of which will be the county representative in the next year's national competition. Well over 400 schools competed in the first season of this competition, and it is interesting to note the number of Public and Independent Schools that took part – Winchester, Millfield, Cheltenham, Christ's Hospital, and Lancing, to name only a few.

At national level 31 schools competed, and there will be more in 1973. Though it was plagued by bad weather in the early season, the competition provided much enjoyable cricket and some extremely close finishes. In the first semi-final, the Grammar School of King Edward VI, Morpeth, defeated Warwick School by ten runs, and in the other Brighton, Hove and Sussex Grammar School defeated Wellsway Comprehensive of Somerset by six wickets. The final between these two schools, about as geographically distant as possible, was played at the Oval. As with all the matches there was a limit of 40 overs each, and the game was a tense and exciting one of fluctuating fortunes. Batting first the Morpeth School lost six wickets for 54, but the next two wickets more than doubled the score and at the close they were 115 for 8. Brighton made a fine start putting 85 on the board for the loss of three wickets, but then good bowling and fine fielding, coupled with over anxiety on the part of the batsmen, brought about a collapse and Brighton were all out for 107, leaving King Edward VI the winners by eight runs.

Mr Campbell, Esso's Marketing Director, supported by Mr Bray, Esso's Advertising Manager, presented the fine new trophy and the winner's pennant to the winning team. But because they failed to win this year's Northumberland Under-14 competition, Morpeth will not have the opportunity to retain the trophy, whereas the Sussex side did win the Sussex Under-14 and thus will have a second chance.

The 1972 Junior Festival was organised by Warwickshire, with all matches being played on the historic grounds of Rugby School. Fortunately rain fell only once – and that during a tea interval – during the five days, and there was much good batting. There was little bowling of a comparable standard, however, with the result that, of the 12 innings played, only three were completed. Declarations were the order of the day, but only once did such a declaration bring a result, and then the declaring side lost. The Mid-

English Schools' Cricket Association

Among those who grace the first-class arena each summer are numerous products of the English Schools' Cricket Association.

John Hampshire (above left), Dennis Amiss (above), Alan Knott (far left), and Chris Old (left) are examples of ESCA caps who have gone on to win England honours

lands drew two matches and lost one, the North won two, but lost to the South, who only drew their other two matches. The West also drew two, but lost one.

In the match against the Public Schools, the ESCA side batted first and declared at 318 for 8. Gatting of Middlesex made 115, the first century in this match since 1961. For the Schools Christopher Cowdrey batted well for 75 and Gower for 85, these two putting on 130 for the first wicket, and their declaration came at 236 for 8. ESCA made a further declaration at 153 for 4, leaving the Public Schools 239 to get in 190 minutes. They needed a good start, but both Cowdrey and Gower were soon out and the task looked formidable. There was a third wicket stand, but the later batsmen failed and the side were all out for 122, so giving ESCA victory after three consecutive defeats.

The Senior side began the season with the problem of selecting a new side. All their 'capped' players, who usually formed the nucleus, were selected for the Young England touring side to the West Indies. In their first two matches 21 players were tried. Against the touring University of California, the Senior side were dismissed for 122, and after much excitement the tourists won by one wicket. The two-day match against Millfield produced some very high scoring and few wickets fell. Neale of Lincoln and Davies of Cheshire both made centuries. Millfield, left to get 251 in 200 minutes, put on 179 for the first wicket but failed to keep up the pace and the match was drawn.

As so often in the past, rain at Beckenham interfered with the match against the Public Schools, and what could have been an interesting finish petered out into a draw. At Colwyn Bay only two hours play was possible in the two-day game against the Welsh Schools.

The final match of the season was against the Scottish Cricket Union at Penrith. ESCA declared at 127 for 9 and in reply the Scots declared at 178 for 8, Larkin's 106 not out being a slow but very useful century. ESCA declared at 160 for 6, which left the Scots to score 110 in 70 minutes and a whirlwind opening partnership of 86 in 49 minutes put them well on the way. But the scoring then slowed, and it was not until the fifth ball of the last over that they scored the winning run to notch up the first Scottish victory over the English Schools.

1973 Indian Schoolboys Tour of Great Britain

(Provisional Programme)

Date	Opponent	Venue
July 20	London Schools	London
July 21	President's XI	Arundel
July 23, 24	South of England	Canterbury
July 26, 27, 28	First test match	Hove
July 30, 31	Public Schools XI	Winchester
August 2, 3	West of England	Bristol
August 6, 7	Welsh SSCA	Cardiff/Swansea
August 8, 9	Midlands	Trent Bridge
August 12, 13, 14	Second test match	Bradford
August 16, 17	North of England	Blackpool
August 19, 20	Scottish Cricket Union	Edinburgh
August 22, 23, 24	Third test match	Edgbaston
August 27, 28, 29	National Association of Young Cricketers	BP Sydenham

Public School Cricket

Tony Pawson

Twenty-six years ago a 13-year-old Tonbridge schoolboy named Colin Cowdrey startled the cricket world by his phenomenal performance at Lord's. His scores of 74 and 44, and his 8 wickets for 117 were mainly responsible for the Tonbridge victory over Clifton. Colin's son, Christopher, hasn't quite matched the unmatchable, but at 15 he scored prolifically for Tonbridge last season and played for the Public Schools XI against the English Schools. In the Eastbourne Festival he had scores of 76 not out, 47 not out 116 not out and 70. This was C.S. Cowdrey's first season in the eleven and he had a happy introduction into a mature and successful team captained by S.R.R. Edlmann. Tonbridge won eight and drew three of their school matches, aided by an effective pair of spinners in C.M. Davies and M.E. Allbrook.

The most exciting batsman of the season, however, was only a few miles distant at Sevenoaks. C.J. Tavaré scored 791 runs in the 13 matches played and averaged 113. With an average of nearly 50 for Sevenoaks Vine he also proved himself equally at home in the highest class of club cricket. Not surprisingly Sevenoaks School responded to his captaincy and his batting. Unbeaten by any school side for the previous two years, they were undefeated by any side last season and won nine of their matches. Tavaré was closely rivalled by C. Aworth of Tiffin with 1,017 runs for an average of 107.

But school cricket is very much a team game, and this is perhaps best expressed in the traditional rivalry between Eton and Harrow. A draw is also traditional for this meeting, and so it was last year. The game was often exciting, but neither side was willing to be adventurous at the critical moments. J.C. Lepp of Harrow was the most successful batsman, with 99 runs in his two innings, and Harrow's W.R. Worthy the best bowler with eight wickets in all. But for Eton P.W.R Leigh took a hat-trick – last achieved in the game by R. Neame in 1955 – and the captain, J. MacDonald, scored a match-saving 36, after Eton had lost five second innings wickets for 35.

It was sad to see so little visible support for a game that once packed Lord's, but at least cricket in the schools is healthy where it really matters – on the field. Perhaps neither Eton nor Harrow were the best examples of its flourishing state.

Harrow, indeed, went through the season without winning a game, all seven matches with other schools being drawn or abandoned. Lepp and Worthy apart they were not a formidable side and on balance Eton were little more successful. They lost to Marlborough and Wellington, though getting the better of Charterhouse and Bradfield.

Another of the great traditional fixtures is Eton and Winchester, and this too was drawn.

Colin Cowdrey, whose son Christopher made a fine impression in Public School cricket in 1972, first captured public notice as a 13-year-old Tonbridge schoolboy

But Winchester, with a splendid pair of opening bowlers in E.J.W. Jackson and R.H. Purser, were an attacking side, always going for a positive result, winning five and losing five out of 17 games. The only defeats by schools were from Tonbridge and Clifton in the Eastbourne Festival. Their spirited play was a heartening send-off for G.H.G. Doggart, President of ESCA, so long in charge of cricket at Winchester and now moving as headmaster to King's Bruton.

Before leaving Winchester Hubert Doggart also had the pleasure of seeing an under-14 Winchester side qualify for the 1973 Esso Colts trophy by winning the Hampshire knock-out competition. It is a healthy sign that a number of Public Schools will be taking part in the Esso Colts National Trophy.

Back with the first elevens there were a number of consistently successful sides unbeaten, like Sevenoaks, for the whole season. Canford had a young team, but still won seven and drew six of their matches, their tally including a win over Sherborne. P.E.B. Frampton took 32 wickets, and the outstanding all-rounder was C.C. Taylor, only 16 but in his third year in the side.

Cheltenham were just as talented, winning seven and drawing seven. They were unable to force a finish in the two-day games against Haileybury and Marlborough but in their seven school matches had five wins and two near misses. K.G.D. Thomas played a captain's part with 857 runs and 37 wickets.

Reed's (Cobham) went one better with eight wins and four draws. P.F. Grainger, the wicket-keeper, celebrated a fifth season in the eleven with a batting average of over 60. Nottingham High School had an even better record with ten wins and 14 draws, the result of all-round excellence rather than individual brilliance.

In Scotland, Edinburgh Academy were masters of the field with nine wins, six of them against schools, and five draws. W.D.G. Loudon and T.F. MacLeod were the bowlers with a strong arm in their results. But perhaps the most successful of all was Loretto's D.J.M. Hutchinson who took 58 wickets at 8.34 apiece, including the destruction of Fettes with 8 for 22. The Loretto batsmen were not in the same class, one sole individual score of over 50 confining them to four wins and three defeats in eight school matches.

Fettes too had their bowling hero with K.R. Gillies taking 10 for 17 in 15 overs against Merchiston Castle. This was a new experience for Merchiston who had not lost a match to another school in the previous four years. In their re-building last season frail batting let them down too often.

Of the Northern schools Pocklington had a particularly well-balanced side, winning ten of their 17 matches and drawing the remainder. A.H. Woodhead, D.N. Allison and D. Stollmeyer all scored over 450 runs and seven different bowlers took more than ten wickets. One team they drew with was St. Peters, York, who were unbeaten all season and won six of their 13 matches. Appropriately the most effective player was the captain, S.P. Coverdale, in fine form as wicket-keeper and batsman.

Ampleforth had rather more talent than success, but at least they beat another good side, Sedbergh. That was despite Sedbergh's powerful attack, with the fast-medium C.D. Weston taking 23 wickets and the left-arm spin of W.T. Rogers always difficult to play.

The Merchant Taylor's (Crosby) captain, R.G. Lewis, held 19 catches at short-leg and also scored 630 runs. With seven wins and only two defeats Merchant Taylor's had no nightmares over the departure of W. Snowden, scorer of 1,018 runs at an average of 127 in 1971 and winner of his Blue as a freshman at Cambridge. St. Bees suffered their first school defeat for three years when Durham beat them by 17 runs. To compensate they had six wins and five draws in the other games.

Elsewhere a number of leading schools fell below their usual high standards. Haileybury lost three and won only one of their school games, with six drawn. But they had the excitement of close finishes, losing to Bedford by four runs and beating Highgate by two.

Westminster won against Lancing early on, but despite the useful batting of J.F.W. Sanderson and the destructive bowling of A.P. Macwhinnie their only other victory was against Ardingly. Bradfield had similar troubles, beating Westminster in their first school match but winning none of the others.

Malvern beat Dean Close and lost to Cheltenham before the frustrating experience of seven draws in the remaining games, six of them after they had declared. Uppingham had a strong batting side, but failed to win a match, only once dismissing their school opponents. And Oundle had no encouragement either, other than a victory over Bedford, who in turn could only beat Haileybury. Rugby too had a moderate season, brightened only by the defeat of Clifton and by J.M. Vivian's batting.

One team's depression is another's opportunity and there was no lack of teams with good results. The experienced Dulwich side had encouraging victories over King's Canterbury, Epsom, Whitgift, and Christ's Hospital. Whitgift too had the sweet taste of success with five consecutive wins to start the season and nine victories in 14 matches.

For Mill Hill P.J. Dean hit three centuries during the term and in the three school games they defeated Merchant Taylor's, St. Paul's and

Felsted. No school side reached 150 against Stowe, with their two baffling spinners R.G.L. Cheattle and G.L. Macleod-Smith, and six out of eight games were won. Only a batting collapse led to defeat by Radley.

Wellington drew with them and the two sides were well matched. For apart from a defeat by Tonbridge, Wellington won against Eton, Radley, Haileybury and The Leys. Radley could beat only Stowe and Abingdon, but T.E. Harris scored 817 runs in ten completed innings.

Felsted were a powerful batting side, beating five schools and losing only to Tonbridge and Mill Hill. Brentwood won five and lost only two games, but Denstone had the perfectly balanced season, seven wins, seven draws and six losses. H.J.W. Wright took 41 wickets in his fifth year in the Repton XI to bring his total for the school to 136. Needless to add Repton had a good season beating Rugby and Uppingham, with only a disastrous day at Cheltenham to mar their results. Shrewsbury were also in trouble against Cheltenham and lost to Wreken as well, but this was off-set by their win against Rossall.

King's Canterbury suffered early defeats by Dulwich and the St. Lawrence club, but thereafter won five and drew five. Sutton Valence also won five matches and lost only once, to Cranbrook by four runs.

Clifton had five victories over other schools, losing only to Rugby and Cheltenham. But their game of the season was a tie with Millfield, the only side to defeat Marlborough. Millfield were again a fine team unbeaten by schools and winning against Bryanston, Taunton, and Bristol Grammar School as well as Marlborough – a happy note on which to end one of the happiest of seasons.

Notable individual performances of the season are recorded in the *Slazenger* monthly awards for the best batting and bowling performance in games involving Public Schools. The list indicates some remarkable achievements:

MAY AWARDS

R.J. Evans 146 for Ipswich v Gentlemen of Suffolk. N. Clewett 8 for 26 for Bristol Grammar School v Queen Elizabeth's Hospital.

Other notable feats included P.M. Roebuck 134 not out for Millfield v XL Club and N.E.G. Wright 7 for 22 for Radley v OU Authentics.

JUNE AWARDS

C. Aworth 200 not out for Tiffin v Kingston Grammar School and K.R. Gillies 10 for 17 for Fettes v Merchiston Castle. Other fine efforts were D.H. Knights 161 not out for Ipswich v Colchester Royal Grammar School, A.N. Ricks 9 for 7 for Reed's (Cobham) and T.S. Smith 8 for 3 for Bishop's Stortford.

JULY AWARDS

D.R. Vincent 200 not out for Woodhouse Grove v Giggleswick and C.J. Tucker 8 for 13 for Price's Fareham v Portsmouth. Other honourable mentions go to C.J. Tavaré 187 not out v Holmesdale CC and J.C. Lepp 157 not out for Harrow v Butterflies.

National Cricket Association

Development of Coaching

Though cricket's administrators can feel well satisfied after the revival of the game in 1972, one disturbing feature of the season must not be lost amidst the euphoria. There were few young English-born cricketers making an impact.

One reason for this is the decline of cricket in the schools. Recent surveys have indicated a diminishing interest in the game in English schools, partly because children today have a greater freedom of choice, and partly because good facilities are not provided. Fortunately, the challenge to compete with other sports and leisure activities has been accepted, and the National Cricket Association (NCA) is vigorously involved in the urgent task of developing young cricketers through its coaching scheme.

Not that coaching in schools is by any means new. In 1952 MCC formed their Youth Cricket Association with the main task of setting up a coaching structure on a national basis. There were awards for those who successfully undertook training at coaching courses and for 18 years the scheme progressed encouragingly. But with the setting up of the National Cricket Association in 1968 and the subsequent phasing out of the Youth Cricket Association, changes in the coaching scheme were inevitable. Now it is to the Colleges of Education, to the teachers in the schools, and to club cricketers that the NCA has turned in order to stimulate a greater interest in the game amongst boys and girls.

The Award Scheme originated by the MCC has now been extended to include three main coaching awards. First, there is the recently introduced Teachers Award for those who are able to teach some of the basic skills of the game and to organise games periods where there is a greater involvement and participation by children. Secondly, there is the Coaching Award for all cricketers who wish to become involved in the coaching of the skills of the game. Finally, for coaches who wish to undertake the organisation of courses, there is the Advanced Award. The Advanced Coach is the key figure in the coaching scheme. He should have a wide knowledge of the game and must be able to coach at all levels, to act as course tutor, and to examine candidates for both the Teachers and the Coaching Awards.

Today there are more than 500 holders of the Advanced Award. The NCA is responsible for the organisation of all Advanced Coaching courses throughout the country, and these are held at centres such as the Lilleshall National Sports Centre, Loughborough Colleges of Education, and Scarborough College of Education. Courses for the Coaching Award certificate, however, are the responsibility of county cricket associations and other bodies throughout the country, although the NCA retains control as regards the choice of examiners and the standard of examination required.

It is hoped to introduce, in the spring of 1973, a Proficiency Awards scheme aimed at encouraging youngsters to learn more about cricket. There are three tests, which will be held at schools and clubs, and for those who are successful there will be badges and a certificate of competence. The co-operation of physical education advisers, teachers, and cricketers will be essential for the conduct and success of this scheme.

Any such project needs financial backing, and this is being obtained from the Wrigley Cricket Foundation. The NCA are indeed greatly indebted to the Wrigley Company, who have made available, over a period of five years, £50,000 to stimulate and encourage interest in the playing of cricket by the young and their achieving greater proficiency and skill in the game. Grants are made primarily towards coaching courses for boys and girls and for the training of coaches. In addition, the sponsorship of representative School and Youth matches, including overseas tours, is a part of the activities of the Foundation. It seems ironic that such a traditionally English game as cricket has to depend on the generosity of an American firm.

Coaching alone, however, will not solve the problem. Our young cricketers need, and deserve, better facilities, particularly in the form of non-turf pitches at schools, and until these are provided cricket will decline still further at youth level. Those who are concerned with the welfare of our summer game must, therefore, look well beyond the problems facing first-class and senior cricket. Our young cricketers need every encouragement if cricket is to flourish.

England Young Cricketers Tour to the West Indies 1972

In the summer of 1972 a team of England Young Cricketers visited the West Indies on a six weeks tour. The team had been selected from the best young cricketers available throughout the country; with two limiting factors. The boys had to be under 19 years of age on September 1, 1971, and no player contracted to a county club was eligible for selection.

The team visited Jamaica, Nevis, Barbados, St Vincent, Trinidad, and Guyana, playing representative matches against schoolboy and youth teams on each island. Unfortunately, the tour took place during the rainy season in the Caribbean and on a number of occasions matches were rained off before a result could be reached. Because of a number of minor injuries, the team was seldom at full strength and though the batting never let the team down, inevitably it was difficult to bowl out the opposition on easy paced pitches. The only match won was against the Leeward Islands, while the Young England Cricketers were beaten by the Guyana Schoolboys in a match of declarations. All the other matches were drawn.

Though the results may appear disappointing on paper, there was plenty of good cricket played by both sides, many friendships were made, and the team returned – in the words of the manager – as England Young Ambassadors.

Ivan Johnson, who had been playing for Worcestershire during the summer, headed the batting averages, having made 497 runs at an average of 62. Geoffrey Miller, who has joined Derbyshire, was the most successful all-rounder, averaging 42 with the bat and taking 29 wickets, including a hat-trick against the Leeward Islands, with his off-spinners.

The touring party was: J.T. Ikin (Manager), A.R. Duff (Assistant Manager), J.R.T. Barclay (Captain), G.S. Clinton (Vice-Captain), A. Backhouse, P. Booth, B. K. Gardom, G.A. Gooch, A.J. Good, T.E. Harris, I.N. Johnson, M.I. McLaren, G. Miller, S.A. Milner, B.W. Reidy, W. Snowden, A. Willis-Stovold.

Putting Women's Cricket on the Map

Rachael Heyhoe

Women's cricket throughout the world is currently passing through a phase of great activity and enterprise. The summer of 1973 should be a memorable one, for the first ever Women's Cricket World Cup is to be staged in this country. Seven teams will be competing for the trophy; Australia, New Zealand, Trinidad and Tobago, Jamaica, an International Invitation XI, England, and Young England.

This ambitious venture, designed to put women's cricket on the map, will run from mid-June until the end of July, with limited-overs games being played all over the country. The final match will be at Edgbaston, between England and Australia on July 28 – so book the date now in your diary!

Each of the visiting sides will have to work frantically to raise the necessary money to cover their travelling expenses because all women cricketers are true amateurs, and when they are selected to go on an overseas tour, they each have the task of paying their own fares.

In the world of women's cricket, the host country bears the loss (or appreciates any profit!) from a tour. In 1973, England has the task of supporting the World Cup, but they are extremely fortunate to have the promised patronage of the Bahamas-based businessman Jack Hayward – of *SS Great Britain* and Lundy Island schemes fame. Jack Hayward sponsored winter tours by the England women cricketers to the West Indies in 1970 and 1971. These two successful tours both revitalised the interest in international women's cricket and provided a stimulus for the inauguration of the World Cup.

The World Cup will be a true test of the relative abilities of women cricketers throughout the world, although the games will not be of the normal three-day Test match duration. On the world scene currently England would seem to lead the field. They have not lost a Test since 1951; they hold the female version of the Ashes, which they successfully defended in Australia in 1968-69; on that same tour, they beat New Zealand in two out of the three Tests, and since then they have returned undefeated again from the tours in the West Indies in 1970 and 1971.

New Zealand are a team who are improving year by year. Only two winters ago they defeated Australia in one Test at the St. Kilda Ground in Melbourne and then continued on an undefeated nine-match, seven-week tour of South Africa during which they won the three-match Test series.

South Africa have been visited by only two touring teams in the last 12 years. Apart from the New Zealanders, Holland played a short visit in 1969 and England played there in 1960-61. However five South Africans will be included in the International Invitation XI, which will help to keep a very keen cricketing country

John Player Cricket Yearbook 1973

Above: Showing the men what cricket is all about. Rachael Heyhoe Flint dispatches the ball to the square-leg boundary, leaving the men of Hampshire to wonder what the world's coming to

Left: Kent's medium-fast bowler Mary Pilling, a member of the England team that will contest the first-ever World Cup of women's cricket in 1973. England, hosts of this ambitious venture, start as favourites but will face strong opposition from six other sides in their bid for the trophy

in touch with other women's cricketing nations.

Because of the 1973 World Cup, with all its attendant publicity, women's cricket should come to the forefront and notice of the general public. There is a vast ignorance about the sport – many seriously believe that the women bowl under arm, use a soft ball and bat with a type of willow more associated with beach cricket!

Few people realise that women's cricket has been on the scene for more than 225 years. The earliest record of a women's cricket match dates back to 1745, when at Gosden Common, Guildford, 'eleven maids of Hambleton dressed all in white' beat 'eleven maids of Bramley' by 127 notches to 119. And although many more mentions of women's cricket are to be found since that first record, it was not until 1926 that the Women's Cricket Association was formed in England. This was at a time when the country was very conscious of the rise of female emancipation.

Other countries were not long in following England's example, and official bodies were set up in Australia in 1931, and the Netherlands and New Zealand in 1934. South Africa and Rhodesia was formed in 1952, Jamaica in 1966 and Trinidad and Tobago in 1967. All these countries are now members of the International Women's Cricket Council (IWCC) which was founded in 1958 and determines tour schedules between member countries.

More hints of the resurgence of women's cricket in the world came with the news in 1972 that Barbados – the birthplace of so many wonderful West Indian stars in the men's cricket world – applied to join the IWCC.

Lack of financial resources in the past has prevented freguent tours between member countries of the IWCC, although the British Government supported England's 1968-69 tour of Australia and New Zealand with a grant of £2,000 – the first of its kind received by the WCA. The first ever tour was made in 1934, when England, captained by Betty Archdale, toured Australia and New Zealand. The first women's Test, played in Brisbane, was won by England by nine wickets. In the second Test at Sydney, Myrtle Maclagan made 119, to become the first century-maker in women's Tests.

In the only Test against New Zealand, at Christchurch, on that first tour, Betty Snowball scored 189 – still the highest individual Test score by a woman. During that innings Betty Snowball also shared in a record Test partnership of 235 with Molly Hide of Surrey. Again, this record still stands. Molly Hide was to become the next England captain and remained so from 1937 until 1954, when she was succeeded by Mary Duggan who led England for the next 12 years.

Both Molly Hide and Mary Duggan were great all-rounders, particularly the latter, whose bowling was apparently praised by first-class cricketers at Worcester, where she practised. It was suggested that her left arm orthodox spin bowling could have earned her a place in a man's first-class county team. By coincidence, another outstanding all-rounder of more recent years, Enid Bakewell who comes from Nottinghamshire, is also a slow left arm orthodox spinner.

Enid Bakewell, in 1968-69 in Australia, achieved the first ever double on a women's tour. Playing in 20 of the 26 matches she scored 1,031 runs at an average of 39.6 and took 118 wickets with the amazing average of 9.7. Many people might scoff at that and say 'Well, it's only women's cricket'. But, it has to be remembered that with the best women cricketers of one country matched against the best of another those averages are commendable in any class of cricket.

In one match against a New South Wales XI at Manly, near Sydney, Enid Bakewell took what is believed to this day to be a unique hat-trick in first-class cricket. All her victims were caught out by the *same* player, June Stephenson of Yorkshire, who was fielding at silly mid-off.

Australia, New Zealand, and South Africa all have inter-state or inter-provincial matches, while in Jamaica and Trinidad and Tobago, club sides know no other cricket than league cricket. In England, however, competitive cricket is practically non-existent. Here the majority of club, inter-college and area matches are played on a friendly basis. Yet the strength of English women's cricket is such that of the 14 Test series played since 1934 England have lost only one. That was in Australia in 1948-49.

Women all over the world play to the MCC Laws with the exception of the ball which they use. The official WCA cricket ball is five ounces compared with the $5\frac{1}{2}$-$5\frac{3}{4}$ ball used by the men.

On the coaching side, several members of the WCA hold the MCC Advanced Coaching Certificate and dozens are holders of the Youth Coaching award.

Many people ask how women's cricket compares with men's cricket. It really is very difficult to make exact comparisons because it's rather like comparing men's tennis with women's tennis. If, for example, Virginia Wade played tennis against Rod Laver, technique-wise their game would look exactly the same, but the strength quality would be very different. It would be just the same if an England women's team were to play against a men's first-class county. The sheer pace of the men fast bowlers would be too much for the women. Perhaps with practice we might be able to develop the reactions to cope with such speed, but the fastest bowlers in the England women's team today – Mary Pilling and Pam Ferdinand – have been classed by the men against whom they have bowled as medium to medium fast.

This brings me back to this year when there is a wonderful chance for our game to be seen. The England and Young England parties of 15 have been named, from which the final teams will be chosen, and these 30 players will be practising hard through the winter months.

The England 15 has only three players who are new to international cricket, Lesley Judd, Jane Gough and Sue Hilliam. All the others have played Test matches in this country and abroad and are a very experienced side.

All the overseas teams arrive in this country from June 6 onwards and a friendly opening tournament with all the seven sides will take place at the Civil Service Sports Grounds, Chiswick, on Saturday June 16. Thereafter, every Wednesday and Saturday until the final match, World Cup games will be taking place all over the country.

ENGLAND

Rachael Heyhoe Flint (West Midlands) Enid Bakewell (North Midlands) Lesley Clifford (Yorkshire) Jill Cruwys (West Midlands) Heather Dewdney (Kent) Jane Gough (West) Kay Green (West) Sue Hilliam (West Midlands) Shirley Hodges (Sussex) Lesley Judd (East Anglia) Pam Mather (East Anglia) Mary Pilling (Kent) June Stephenson (Yorkshire) Lynne Thomas (West) Chris Watmough (Kent)

YOUNG ENGLAND

Sue Goatman (Kent, captain) Caroline Brown (Kent) Kate Brown (Kent) Jackie Court (Middlesex) Gerry Davies (Surrey) Shirley Ellis (Sussex) Lynn Green (North Midlands) Julia Greenwood (Yorks) Lyn Hanson (Kent) Glynis Hullah (Middlesex) Megan Lear (Kent) Julie Lloyd (East Anglia) Lynn Read (East Anglia) Wendy Swinhoe (Lancs and Cheshire) Margaret Wilks (West).

Overseas Cricket

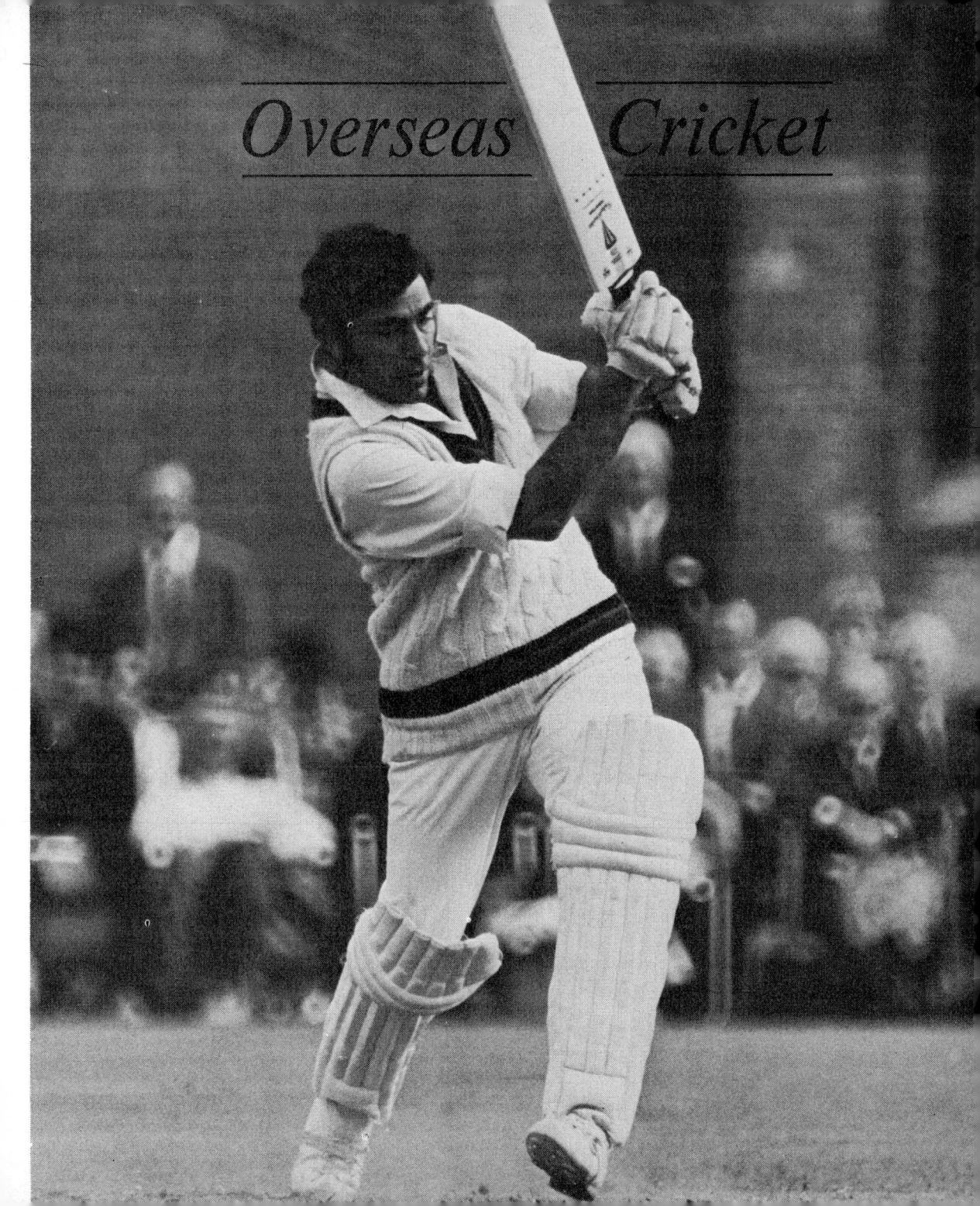

John Player Cricket Yearbook 1973

Australian News and Information Bureau

Above: The Sydney Cricket Ground, one of the most famous of Test cricket venues; home of the notorious 'Hill'

Right: The belligerent Rodney Marsh, one of the many Western Australians to make the Test side in recent years

Below: Ian Chappell, following in the footsteps of his grandfather, Vic Richardson, as Australia's captain

Cricket in Australia

Richie Benaud

The strange thing about cricket in Australia is that, structurally, it bears little relation to cricket as known in England, the home of the game. Test matches are the same in both countries; vast crowds thronging to the biggest arenas in the land, and tremendous interest throughout each country in the deeds of the players and the results of the matches. But at that point the similarity ends, even though players of similar temperament and skills compete in the various spheres of cricket below Test match standard.

England's background is more that of the village green and the village community, where cricketers can, if necessary, cut their own pitch in the local meadow. Mid-week and evening games are commonplace, but this system does not hold in Australia. The game in Australia has never really got past the part-time stage, for all cricketers have full-time jobs, whether they work for themselves or for an employer.

Broadly speaking, the Australian cricket set-up can be divided into sections of junior cricket, senior cricket, first-class cricket, and, as the ultimate offshoot of the latter, Test cricket. That is the situation in the capital cities. Country cricket, however, is something entirely separate. Each country association is affiliated with its state association, and cricket in the country area or group is controlled by country administrators.

Let us take the hypothetical case of a young cricketer born and reared in a country area of New South Wales and wanting eventually to become a Test cricketer; his path would run roughly along the following lines. We will assume he is born in Dubbo – miles from Sydney. He would attend the local primary school and play in the primary school competition on Wednesday afternoons against teams from half a dozen other primary schools in the area. On Saturday afternoons he would be eligible to play for a club in the Dubbo district. Most clubs have two grades, so he would probably start in the B Grade team and make his way eventually to the A Grade side. Then, if good enough, he would be chosen for the Dubbo district side to play against combined teams from other districts, in some cases up to 100 miles away.

Good performances in these matches would bring him under the notice of group selectors, who choose combined sides to play against other groups within the state. In addition, his name would be passed on to the N S W selectors as a promising youngster who may be of interest to them when they choose their Colts teams. And, if really promising, he would be asked to travel to Sydney for special coaching classes during the Christmas holidays, when the N S W Cricket Association looks at young country talent for the future.

His name would now be on the list of country schoolboys who go to Sydney for special trials and are considered for inclusion in the state schoolboys' team. Each state plays against the other five states in a carnival organised by the Australian Schoolboys' Cricket Association.

If he stayed in the country, his performances would then range over the games and spheres mentioned above, and also he would most likely play in combined country teams against Cricket Association sides sent to the country, and overseas touring teams who play country matches as part of their schedule. If he is good enough though, he will have been earmarked by the state selectors for a place in one of the combined country sides to play against Metropolitan at the Sydney Cricket Ground. Or he may have been asked to go to Sydney and join a Grade club, where he would then be on the same footing as the Sydney cricketers. If, in fact, a Sydney club looked favourably on a young player and asked him to join them, he would certainly go straight into First Grade cricket, thus bypassing the other spheres available to players in each capital city. He would join city players who had gone through their own system to arrive at the point where they were likely to be considered for representative honours.

My own playing career spanned most of the possibilities of this city system. First of all, I attended the Burnside Primary School, played in combined school matches, and then attended Parramatta High School, where I represented the Combined High Schools XI against Combined Northern High Schools. That was as far back as 1945. At that point a young cricketer has two alternatives: the first is that he can play junior cricket, in which the game is played, for the most part, on matting over concrete, or he can join a Grade club where there are five Grade teams, and possibly more, playing in different competitions but still connected with the club. Moreover, he would be playing on turf wickets.

Thousands upon thousands of cricketers turn out every Saturday afternoon in the capital cities to take part in the junior cricket competitions, which range from churches competitions to those run by individual metropolitan associations. On Saturday mornings there are age competitions and senior and schools competitions catering, in the main, for the young cricketers.

Again, in junior cricket, there are several representative teams available to the player who wants to move on from merely Saturday afternoon exercise. These representative teams often produce high quality players, and indeed the junior cricket system throughout Australia is one of the main reasons why cricket here is so strong.

For the young cricketer intent on joining a Grade club, there are several avenues open. He can join one of the City and Suburban clubs, which have their own competition, often with players who consider themselves past their best but still feel the need for exercise and want to enjoy cricket on a Saturday afternoon. There is scope for the young player here, particularly if the club has two City and Suburban teams. In that case, it is probable one would comprise the older players and the second the younger players who are eager for advancement to one of the higher grades.

Then there is the Municipal and Shire competition, run under the auspices of the NSW Cricket Association. These days there are three divisions in this competition, the participating clubs playing for the R.B. Clark Cup, the S.J. Mayne Trophy, and the J.B. Hollander Trophy. Forty teams take part in those competitions every Saturday afternoon, and that is the first stepping-stone for the young player on his way up through the Grade ranks. In Sydney Grade cricket there are two age competitions, the

Poidevin-Gray Shield for players under 21 and the A.W. Green Shield for players under 16 years of age. I played in both those competitions once I moved on from high school to the Grade cricket ranks and they are widely regarded as the most important parts of the NSW cricketing set-up.

There are 16 Grade cricket clubs in Sydney, most of them long-established, though there are some that have been amalgamated in recent years with one or two new areas coming in because of the population explosion in the outer suburbs. Each of those Grade cricket clubs has four teams who play, respectively, for the Belvidere Cup, the Albert Cup, the Mitchell Cup, and the Reid Cup. Then, in addition, there is a Fifth Grade competition, in which some clubs have two teams turning out and which is used as a nursery for young players. The youngster who makes a Fifth Grade team faces a natural progression through Fourth, Third, and Second Grade until he arrives in First Grade to play with and against players who, at the same time, are representing their state and Australia.

There are approximately 750 First Grade cricketers taking the field every Saturday in the five main states of Australia. In theory, each one of these has a chance of taking the next step forward in the Australian cricket framework – selection to play for his state in Sheffield Shield cricket. In fact, of the 750, somewhere between 60 and 70 will play first-class cricket in Australia in any one year. In New South Wales the state selectors will nominate 12 players for the initial

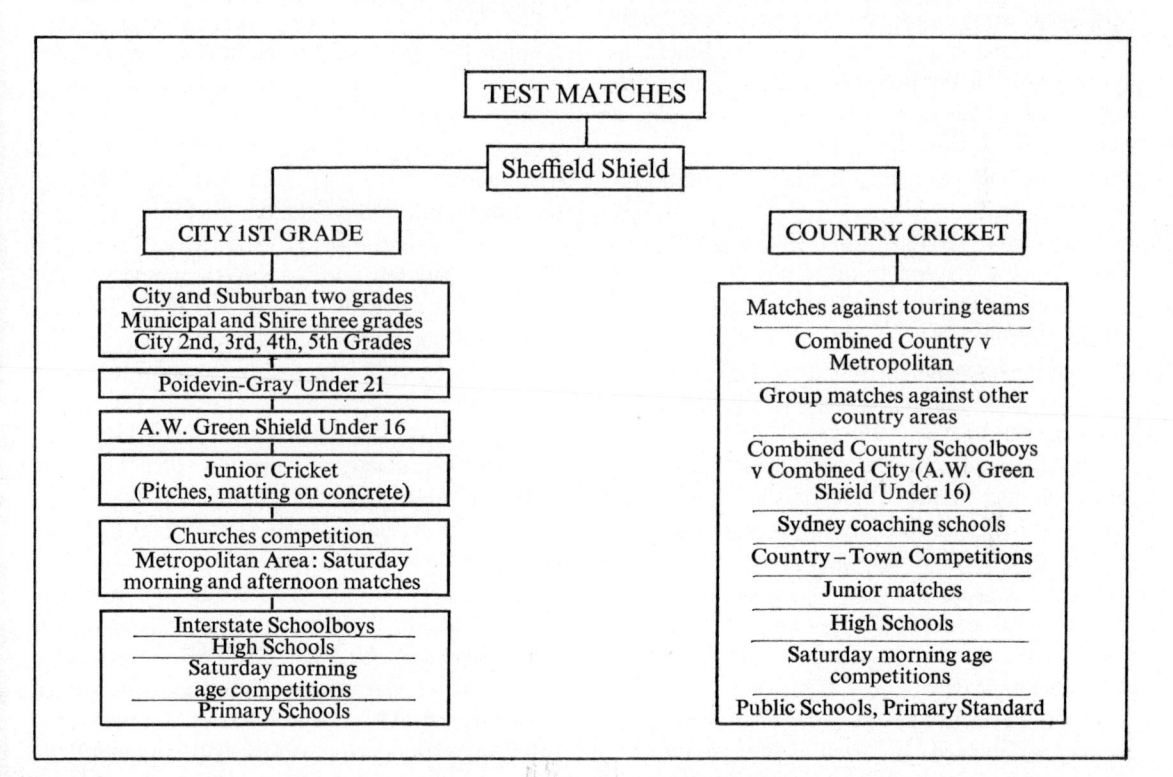

```
                        TEST MATCHES
                        Sheffield Shield

    CITY 1ST GRADE                          COUNTRY CRICKET

City and Suburban two grades          Matches against touring teams
Municipal and Shire three grades      Combined Country v
City 2nd, 3rd, 4th, 5th Grades           Metropolitan
                                      Group matches against other
Poidevin-Gray Under 21                   country areas
A.W. Green Shield Under 16            Combined Country Schoolboys
Junior Cricket                          v Combined City (A.W. Green
(Pitches, matting on concrete)          Shield Under 16)
                                      Sydney coaching schools
Churches competition                  Country – Town Competitions
Metropolitan Area: Saturday           Junior matches
morning and afternoon matches         High Schools
Interstate Schoolboys                 Saturday morning age
High Schools                             competitions
Saturday morning                      Public Schools, Primary Standard
age competitions
Primary Schools
```

first-class match of the season.

It is at this point that it is possible to show the enormous difference between cricket in England and Australia. In Australia those available for selection in Sheffield Shield cricket play only on Saturday afternoons, and it is impossible to play Test cricket for Australia without going through the Sheffield Shield ranks. In some cases, players have only a handful of matches to produce performances that will ensure the three Australian selectors, appointed by the Board of Control, consider them for selection.

Unlike his English counterpart, who can play for his county virtually seven days a week, the Australian Test cricketer plays a limited number of matches in a season. A Sheffield Shield cricketer can play in eight matches, four home and four away, against the other four main States. Tasmania is excluded from the Shield, as is the Northern Territory. With these eight games spread over four and a half to five months, it can be readily seen that first-class cricket is, by English standards, played on a remarkably restricted basis.

If selected in the Australian side to play one or more Tests, a player will quite possibly miss out on a Sheffield Shield match or, in some cases, as many as four. These games will coincide with the Tests because of the relatively crowded weekend programme. Consequently a top-line batsman might play a full quota of ten innings in the Test matches and then have only eight other innings in the whole of the season with which to persuade the Australian selectors he is worthy of a tour overseas.

In recent years in Australia, a one-day competition has been introduced, sponsored by the Coca-Cola Bottlers of Australia, and this includes New Zealand, who send a team over to participate at the semi-final stage. Other knock-out cricket is played in each state, Rothmans supporting a competition in Sydney and various sponsors helping the state associations elsewhere in Australia. One-day cricket, however, is very much secondary to the first-class cricket and is always likely to remain so, although there is definitely a place for the limited-overs game.

That, in broad terms, is the playing structure as far as the thousands of participants are concerned. But there are two other aspects of the game in Australia that bear close examination. The first of these concerns the media – newspapers, radio, and television – and the second concerns coaching.

Whereas in England, a smaller country, almost unlimited television is allowed through the BBC, this is not the case in Australia. When a first-class game is in progress in any of the capital cities, television is permitted by the Board of Control only between the tea interval and stumps on any day. That applies to Sheffield Shield matches, games against a touring side, and Test matches. However, a really worthwhile piece of administration by both the Australian Broadcasting Commission and the Board of Control has ensured that, for Test matches, viewers in all states but the one holding the game can see television for the full six hours of play. This has allowed housewives and others who normally might not be able to get to the ground to take a greater interest in the game, and it has been one of the most important factors in cricket's increased popularity in Australia. The ABC and some commercial stations provide radio broadcasts of the Test matches, and the ABC also cover Sheffield Shield games in each state. The commercial stations will often give summaries and comments for listeners on Sheffield Shield games and Tests and will also run comments by their sports broadcasters. The television broadcasts are not only sent to the capital cities in the other states but are also relayed throughout the country areas by the ABC. Again, this provides a tremendous upsurge in interest in cricket.

There is no question that attendances have fallen at Test and first-class matches over the past 15 years. But I don't find this particularly surprising. Attendances at racecourses, football matches, tennis tournaments, and practically all other sports meetings have decreased at the same time, with most people now owning cars and having much more leisure time than before World War II.

But a realistic look at attendances and at the people who watch cricket on television and listen to it on the radio makes it quite clear that there is more interest in the game in Australia than ever before. A few years ago the ABC had to make a decision on whether or not they would telecast five-day Test matches live into the states other than where the match was being played. When they did, they found the rating of the programme was amongst the highest ever. The ratings showed, in fact, that more Australians watched the Test matches on television than had watched any other single event – excepting perhaps the telecast of the first moon-landing, which had been taken by all channels.

Newspapers generally have a good knowledge of the popularity of various sports and, in Australia, plenty of space is given to cricket. Whereas in England there are two national daily afternoon papers and several national mornings, in Australia the newspapers are on a state basis. One national, *The Australian*, has a cricket writer in each state and all the other papers employ cricket correspondents. This television, radio, and newspaper coverage has played an important role in the continuing upsurge of interest.

The area of coaching is one that was largely neglected for many years, but now all states are showing an awareness of the situation. The Board of Control was fortunate when, in 1971, the Rothmans National Sport Foundation agreed to employ a national coach, as New Zealand have done with Martin Horton. Brian Taber was appointed to the Australian post and he is at present engaged in setting up a completely new structure of coaching in Australia, which will be based broadly on the one in operation in England. Emphasis will be placed on the coaching of coaches.

At the moment Western Australia have former Test player Laurie Mayne as state coach, Queensland had Tom Graveney (and it was a sad day for Queensland cricket when he decided to resign), and Ernie Clifton is the South Australian coach. Tasmania use England Test and county players such as John Hampshire, Peter Lever, Rodney Cass, and Jack Simmons, all of whom have done a fine job. But the surface has been only slightly ruffled, and it will be through Taber and the organisation he sets up that even more interest and skill will be engendered.

Although administrators are constantly looking to improve the standard of the game and to keep it well publicised within the limits of available funds, it can be said that Australian cricket is in an extremely healthy state. Every youngster in Australia has an equal chance. Out here it is not so much a question of how a player looks but what he does, and though it is remotely possible that a youngster of great ability could be missed in the constant search for future first-class players, it is just that – a remote possibility. If he plays in a country area, no matter how far from the 'big smoke', he will come under notice and be recommended for coaching in Sydney and for minor representative honours. If he plays in Sydney or any other capital city, he has every opportunity to develop into a star – or just enjoy his Saturday afternoon cricket.

Whether opening or batting in the middle-order, Farokh Engineer plays his strokes with a panache and total disregard for bowlers' reputations that have established him as a firm favourite from Bombay to Old Trafford

Indian Cricket

Farokh Engineer
(India and Lancashire CCC)

During an interview at the end of last season Frank Bough asked me for my views on limited-overs cricket. As a member of a Lancashire side which has reaped so many glorious victories in this sphere of the game in recent years, it would have been difficult for me to deny that I enjoy this type of cricket. But 'instant' cricket also appeals to me as an individual. My approach to batting remains exactly the same as in the three-day game, so I have no problems of adapting my style. I love the atmosphere in which this type of cricket is played. The enthusiasm of the big crowds is contagious and it reminds me of the big audiences I used to play in front of in India.

In Bombay, where I come from, cricket of any sort attracts vast crowds and the game itself is immensely competitive at all levels. There is a somewhat mistaken notion in this country that Indian Test cricketers are, in the main, weekend cricketers. This was perhaps true of the Indian sides that visited England before the war, but it is certainly not so today.

The structure of Indian cricket now is vast and complex. There are national competitions held at all levels of the game and it is virtually impossible for any cricketer of talent to go unnoticed.

Our domestic first-class season kicks off with the Irani Trophy match, which is between the previous season's Ranji Trophy champions and the Rest of India. This fixture is by no means a gentle 'shoulder-loosener'. It is played in earnest, with the Test selectors watching intently.

Then comes the Ranji Trophy tournament, which is the equivalent of the County Championship. It was instituted purely as a knock-out tournament in 1934-35, with only a dozen teams participating. This number has now doubled and the competition is played under a modified system, introduced in the late 1950s. The revision was introduced because, under the old system, the weaker teams had very little opportunity of progressing in the competition and gaining more experience.

The latest system is almost identical to the one under which the English counties play in the Benson & Hedges Cup. The country is split into five geographical zones. Teams within each zone initially play a one-leg league. The first two teams in each league then go on to play a knock-out. The competition now totals 56 matches in all.

Unfortunately, many of the weaker teams do not measure up to accepted first-class standards. One or two of them have gone through their respective zonal leagues for years without winning a single match. The enormous disparity between the strong sides and the weak also tends to give a distorted view of individual performances. It would benefit both the strong and the weak if the tournament were split up into two divisions.

While the selectors certainly do not ignore Ranji Trophy performances, they attach a lot more weight to the Duleep Trophy Tournament, which is played more or less simultaneously by teams representing the best talent in each zone. This tournament was instituted shortly after the war, but did not become popular and was abandoned. However, its revival in 1961 coincided with the surge of new interest in the game and it now enjoys a tremendous following.

In the Ranji Trophy, the league games and early rounds of the knock-out are played over three days. The semi-finals are extended to four days and the final to five. Of course, there have been experiments with six-day and limitless finals in the distant past, and Denis Compton was involved – and very brilliantly so – in one such marathon during the war.

On the 1971 England tour, the Indian team won more county games than any of its predecessors. But it will be noticed that all these victories were gained by bowling the other side out. Rarely did the tourists chase runs, nor did they set targets in the accepted English fashion.

I am not making this statement to criticise Wadekar. Instead, it is meant to throw light on the system of Indian cricket. In the league part of the Ranji Trophy, an outright win is worth eight points, which is only three more than for a first-innings lead in a drawn match. But, so great is the disparity between various sides that victory either comes in the straightforward manner or, if two strong sides are pitted against against each other, they play primarily for first-innings points. In the knock-out rounds or the Duleep Trophy matches, a first-innings lead is also very vital, because it decides the winner in the event of an unfinished match.

Despite the present enthusiasm and the financial turnover of Indian cricket, there is no professional system like England's. This does not, however, mean that cricketing prowess is not financially rewarded. In the old days, leading cricketers received the patronage of the Maharajas and the Nawabs. The patronage of the ruling princes has now been taken over by the bigger industrial houses and state-owned corporations. Also, the connection between them and the cricketers can no longer be described as 'patronage', for all the cricketers thus employed hold genuine appointments, depending on their academic qualifications.

This is a very desirable system, because while the cricketer gets all the time off and all facilities during his playing days, he has a secure job to devote himself to when he gives up the game.

Most of the big cricketing centres in India have separate tournaments for business houses and easily the most important of these is the 'Times of India Shield' in Bombay, which has been run for over 30 years.

One rung below the first-class level are two national competitions for universities. The older of the two is run on almost the same lines as the Ranji Trophy, except that even at zone level, the tournament is played on a knock-out basis. Teams are mustered for the other tournament on the same basis as the zonal sides for the Duleep Trophy.

Next come the schools. They first play an inter-state tournament among the zones. Then each zone picks the best side from all the teams within their borders and they play a separate tournament. And, of course, we now have schoolboy tours and schoolboy Tests as well.

How is all this furious activity financed? While the Board, unlike the English TCCB, does not allocate shares from Test receipts, all its affiliated associations receive an annual grant to finance their participation in the All-India Schools Tournament.

Sunil Gavaskar began his Test career for India with 774 runs at an average of 154.80 in the series against West Indies in 1970-71

All this gives the impression that cricket in India today has reached the proportion of an industry. Indeed it has. Dividends have already been realised in the form of our victories in the West Indies and in England in 1971, and bonus issues, I am sure, are well on the way.

Enthusiasm for cricket is nationwide, but the heart, the very soul of Indian cricket, lies in Bombay. I am not being carried away because I was born and reared in this proud and mighty city. This was where Indian cricket took its roots.

Right in the heart of the city, within a radius of two miles from our fabulous Brabourne Stadium, are four gigantic open spaces which we call 'maidans'. Several clubs, some of them over one hundred years old, have their little patches on these grounds.

A lot of the wickets are very good, but one club's patch is so near the other's that mid-off in one match stands alongside mid-on in another match – facing the other way, of course. Boundaries fall within the playing area of another club and there is chaos galore, but the sight is quite fascinating.

These little grounds have no pavilions. Marquees are pitched at weekends and when these marquees are taken down at the drawing of stumps, players and supporters squat on the cool green grass and talk cricket till well after dark.

In Bombay, cricket goes on round the year, even through the monsoon, which brings a hundred inches of rain in five months. First-class cricket is played from October to March but the game in some form or other never ceases.

We seem to throw our youngsters in at the deep end of first-class cricket much earlier than in England. For them the three-day game is nothing new, for even schools' cricket at home is played over two or three days. In fact, the final of the Inter-School competition in Bombay was, till I left the country, a limitless affair. These finals would be played on one of the bigger club grounds on the maidan and would be watched by thousands.

I started on the theme of limited-overs cricket, and that's where I am going to end. This form of the game is by no means unknown to India. In fact, Bombay started a 50-overs competition for clubs about the time, or probably just before, the Gillette Cup was first played in England.

Our tournament is known as the Talim Shield. It is a popular event, but treated very much as a diversion from the big competitions. At the moment, at least, there are no signs of instant cricket being played at inter-state level. In England, one-day games came about entirely through the circumstances surrounding English cricket. As things stand, Indian crowds are happy enough with the present state of affairs.

John Player Cricket Yearbook 1973

Above: Over them, not at them, might be Wasim Bari's reaction, despite the run out. In the third Test of the 1971 tour of England, Wasim set a Test record for Pakistan by holding eight catches in the match

Right: Majid Khan, Pakistan's new captain

Below: Intikhab Alam, former captain of Pakistan

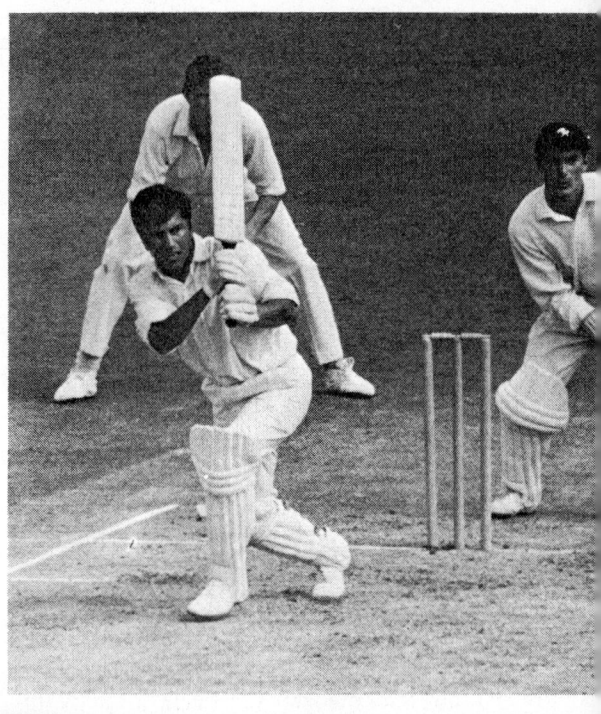

Two Decades of Pakistan Cricket

Intikhab Alam
(Pakistan and Surrey)

Pakistan became a separate political entity 26 years ago, on August 14, 1947, and her national cricket team dates only from 1952. In that year, after proving her strength by defeating the 1951-52 MCC touring team which included Graveney and Statham, she was admitted to the ICC and played her first official series of Tests.

The present Pakistan team is the best we have ever had, and it is worth tracing the development of this strength through the short history of our international cricket. Pakistan has played against every major cricketing country in the world apart from South Africa, and has had the proud privilege of winning Test matches against each of them.

A.H. Kardar played the most crucial part in those difficult, formative years by captaining the side in its first 23 Tests. Now, as President of the BCCP (Board of Control for Cricket in Pakistan), he is playing another vital role as our game's chief administrator. He gained valuable experience of international cricket when, as Abdul Hafeez, he toured Britain with the 1946 Indian team. After playing for Oxford University and Warwickshire, he returned home and led Pakistan on her first official tour – to India in the closing months of 1952.

Pakistan's first official Test was a humiliating baptism that resulted in defeat by an innings and 70 runs. Revenge was swift though and, despite losing the toss again, Pakistan won the second Test at Lucknow by an innings and 43 runs. Nazar Mohammad (no relation to Hanif) and Fazal Mahmood were the heroes of that first victory. Nazar carried his bat through an innings of 331 for Pakistan's first official Test century, 124 not out, while Fazal Mahmood's medium-pace cutters earned the splendid match analysis of 12 for 94 in 51·4 overs on a jute-matting wicket.

Pakistan's wicket-keeper and opening batsman during that series was Hanif Mohammad. He was then only 17 but had already proved himself a player of the highest class. Hanif, 'The Little Master', formed the backbone of Pakistan batting for many years. I have seen him play some truly great innings, and if he had represented a country that played in more Test matches, he would probably have smashed all the batting records. On numerous occasions Hanif was criticised for his slow tactics but nobody ever realised that his approach was dictated, not by his personal liking, but by the requirements of the team. Indeed Hanif possessed every stroke in the book, but time and again the role of sheet-anchor was thrust upon him. It is to his credit that he always adjusted superbly. The team always depended on him and seldom did he disappoint them.

The Mohammad brothers have played a very considerable part in Pakistan's Test history and, with Mushtaq and Sadiq having, we hope, many years of cricket ahead of them, they are continuing to do so. Before our 1972-73 tour of Australia and New Zealand, Wazir, Hanif, Mushtaq, and Sadiq had made a total of 106 Test appearances and scored 17 of Pakistan's 38 centuries. Hanif missed only two of our first 57 Tests and no Pakistan team has taken the field in an official Test match without at least one of the Mohammad brothers. On one memorable occasion, three of them played – Hanif (his last appearance), Mushtaq, and Sadiq (his debut) – thereby equalling the record of the Grace brothers at The Oval in 1880. A fifth brother, Raees, was very unlucky to miss the 1954 tour of Britain. Their mother takes a fanatical interest in their cricket and Wazir told me that she refuses to receive visitors at her home it if means interrupting a radio commentary on a match in which one (or more!) of her sons is playing. He also recalls how on one lamentable occasion Raees, Hanif, and himself were all dismissed without scoring in a domestic first-class match and his mother took this as a personal insult, refusing to receive them for several days.

At the last count, Hanif had one son and six nephews, and it will be most surprising if our cricket records of the future do not include the names of at least one of this new generation. Names to look out for in about ten years' time are Wazir's son, Waqar; Raees' sons, Shakir, Shahid and Asif; Hanif's son, Shoaib; and Mushtaq's sons, Munaf and Suheil.

English crowds must still remember the young and immature Pakistan team of 1954 being thrown into battle against the full might of England. Their initial performances prompted some critics to write them off but, as the tour progressed and the players became used to one of England's wettest summers, our team improved beyond recognition. On Tuesday, August 17, 1954, Pakistan covered themselves with glory by becoming the only side to win a Test match on their first visit to England. Our 24-run victory at Kennington Oval enabled us to draw the rubber.

Our first home series was against India in the early months of 1955 and all five Tests were drawn. New Zealand paid her first visit to our country later in the year and were beaten in the first two Tests of a three-match rubber. In the second match, Imtiaz Ahmed scored Pakistan's first double Test century. One of the most popular of sportsmen, this dashing wicket-keeper-batsman was a tremendous hooker of the fastest bowling. I shall always recall two hooks off consecutive balls from Wes Hall in 1959. Bowling on the lively Bagh-e-Jinnah ground at Lahore, with a 50-mph gale behind him, Wes had just struck down the other opening batsman, Ijaz Butt, with a ferocious bumper. He then tried two at Imtiaz, who hooked with such perfect timing that Butcher at long-leg had no time to move before the ball had rocketed into the fence.

Ian Johnson's 1956 Australians played their first Test against us at Karachi on their way home from a disastrous tour of England. This time it was not Laker's off-spin that caused their downfall but some magnificent fast bowling from Fazal Mahmood and Khan Mohammad on a matting pitch. This pair bowled unchanged through the 53·1 overs of Australia's first innings as the visitors struggled to 80 all out. They went on to share all 20 wickets in the match; Fazal's share being 13 for 114.

Next came a strenuous tour of the West Indies in 1958. Pakistan drew the first Test after following-on 473 runs behind on the first innings. Their recovery was due to a monumental innings of 337 by Hanif that lasted for 16 hours 39 minutes and remains comfortably the longest innings in first-class cricket. It began on the third day and did not end until the sixth and final one. There is that lovely story, probably apocryphal, about the spectator watching the start of Hanif's innings from a tree. He dozed off, fell from his lofty perch, and was carted off to hospital. After spending three days there, he was discharged and, undaunted, climbed back up to his usual position among the branches – only to find Hanif still batting!

The West Indies were then at the height of their power. With Gary Sobers emerging as a new star – he beat Hutton's record by scoring 365 not out in the third Test – they overwhelmed Pakistan in the next three matches. Yet Pakistan gained some revenge by winning the final Test by an innings.

The West Indies were beaten 2-1 when they paid a return visit to Pakistan the following year. These victories produced a wave of optimism amongst our supporters and showed the world that our cricket was of the highest class. That same season saw Hanif add to his list of world records by scoring 499 in 640 minutes for Karachi. Sadly he was run out off the last ball of the day going for his 500.

To prove that pride does come before a fall, Pakistan did not win another Test for six years. In that time we toured India, Australia, New Zealand, and England, and played home series against Australia and England, 22 Tests in all. It was not until New Zealand were beaten by an innings and 64 runs at Rawalpindi in March 1965 that we gained our next victory.

Hanif had now succeeded to the captaincy. Under him we toured England in 1967 and, although we lost the three-match rubber 2-0, we showed a marked improvement on our 1962 form. Thus the stage was set for a very interesting series when the MCC came to Pakistan in 1968-69 under Colin Cowdrey. Pakistan was formed at a time of tremendous political, social, and economic turmoil. This unrest and confusion has seldom been far from the surface and it came to a head again during MCC's visit. After the first two Tests at Lahore and Dacca had been interrupted, the third had finally to be abandoned because of continuous rioting. Pakistan was then in the midst of a major political upheaval and the current was so strong that it swept the MCC tour with it. It all earned Pakistan some very unkind remarks in the foreign Press but I think that these assessments were rather harsh. I sincerely feel that visiting teams have always been accorded the warmest of welcomes and have enjoyed our traditional hospitality. At the time of the MCC's visit the prevailing situation was beyond control.

That brief and sadly interrupted series showed that Pakistan, depleted after the retirement of several key players, would soon have a team to match the best in the world. The 1971 tour of England confirmed these hopes and although we lost the three-match rubber 1-0, I think a draw would have been a fairer result; rain had ended the first Test when we were almost sure to win. The find of this tour was the spectacular Zaheer Abbas, who, after his brilliant 274 in the Edgbaston Test, has gone from strength to strength and has been rated by Gary Sobers as the finest number three batsman in the world.

For Pakistan to produce players of genuine class is miraculous because both our playing facilities and our first-class programme are of an extremely limited nature. Our domestic first-class cricket consists of two competitions: The Quaid-e-Azam Trophy and the BCCP Trophy. 'Quaid-e-Azam' means 'The Great Leader', an epithet given to the late Mr Jinnah who played a major part in the creation of Pakistan. This competition was inaugurated as Pakistan's national championship in the 1953-54 season and, although the number of competing teams and the basis of competition have varied from season to season, it is usually run on a league-cup basis; zonal knock-out or league champions compete in a final knock-out stage. Karachi, with a large number of established players at its disposal, has tended to dominate this trophy. Often the major cities have enough first-class cricketers to enter more than one side: hence, Karachi Blues (1st XI) and Karachi Whites (2nd XI). In 1963-64 both Karachi teams reached the final, the Blues winning by 18 runs.

The BCCP Trophy, formerly the 'Ayub Trophy', dates back to the 1960-61 season. Run on a zonal knock-out basis, it had a rather chequered career with the fifth competition being spread over three seasons! Renamed and enlarged in 1970-71, this competition was won in both seasons of its short life by the Pakistan International Airlines 'A' team, captained by Hanif. It was a remarkable tribute to the strength of interest in cricket in Pakistan that this competition should have been held during the war against India.

In complete contrast to professional cricket in England, our programme is organised so that on occasions a team might play only one three-day first-class fixture in the entire season. On the other hand, club cricket consisting of 50-overs matches is played all the year round. It is this version of the game that now breeds many of our best players and it probably explains why Pakistani batsmen in England are inclined to have a fling regardless of the situation once they are well-set with 30 or 40 runs on the board. Lack of major cricket means that our players are not physically attuned to the rigours of cricket six days per week. Members of Pakistani touring teams to England frequently break down for this very reason.

I wrote at the start that the present Pakistan team is the best we have ever had. We have more players of genuine class than ever before. Majid Khan is a batsman with so much time to spare while playing his strokes that sometimes he just seems to be lazily going through the motions. Zaheer Abbas was selected for the World XI in Australia after his first full Test series and is likely to form the backbone of our batting for many years. Mushtaq is now a very seasoned and mature all-rounder; Asif Iqbal is also a very fine player; and Wasim Bari is a constant source of confidence behind the stumps.

As I write this, we are about to embark on our most strenuous season of international cricket, playing nine Tests in a little over three months and in three different countries: Australia, New Zealand, and Pakistan (against England). If we can produce positive results during these series, cricket in Pakistan will receive a tremendous impetus. Cricket still holds a massive spectator appeal in Pakistan and, once this interest has been regenerated, it will bring extra money into the game and allow the BCCP to concentrate more on perfecting the organisation of cricket throughout the country.

* * *

Intikhab Alam has modestly made no mention of his own considerable part in the development of Pakistani cricket. From the moment that he took the wicket of Colin McDonald with his first ball in Test cricket in 1959, Intikhab made his presence felt at international level. Prior to leading Pakistan in six of their nine Tests in 14 weeks against three countries in 1972-73, 'Inti' had played 29 times for Pakistan, including six as captain, scoring 802 runs at 20·05 and taking 57 wickets at 45·10.

Having toured England with three Pakistani teams – the last as captain – and played for Surrey since 1969, this large, genial man is no stranger to English cricket. He is an immense and thrilling striker of the ball and one of the game's most subtle exponents of that absorbing art, leg-spin and googly bowling.

Is New Zealand's Confidence Justified?

John Reid
(N.Z. captain 1956-65)

For a New Zealander to assert that a Kiwi cricket side could pose a threat to the side that holds the Ashes may well seem the height of optimism. Indeed, to those who remember the less inspiring of our performances in England in 1958 and 1965, such an assertion must appear arrogant. But I believe there are followers in Britain sufficiently aware of recent events in the world of Test cricket who will accept that in 1973 the New Zealanders should cause England more bother than any New Zealand side since 1949.

It does not require the foresight of an oracle to say this; merely recognition of New Zealand's expanding Test programme and our increasing success at international level. And, most significantly, it requires the acceptance of Bruce Taylor, Bevan Congdon, Hedley Howarth, and Glenn Turner as players of world class.

Perhaps, before introducing specific reasons why this 1973 tour will lift New Zealand's image in England, I first should relate New Zealand's Test record in the past three seasons. In 1969, after losing two of the three Tests to England, New Zealand cricket began to show signs of blossoming again. The first two Tests with India saw the series level at one apiece, and the Kiwis had the better of the third match when a mysterious fire in the grandstand stopped the match—and cost New Zealand the series! By way of consolation New Zealand won the only Test against Pakistan. In 1970 an Australian team, including such players as Greg Chappell and Dennis Lillee, did not often hold the upper hand in three drawn matches.

The following season saw Ray Illingworth's men in New Zealand. In the first Test, on a substandard wicket at Lancaster Park, Christchurch, that great exploiter of bad wickets, Derek Underwood, bowled England to an easy win. But in the second Test the English team, admittedly tired after the demanding tour of Australia, would have suffered their first ever Test defeat by New Zealand had it not been for a certain chap by the name of Alan Knott. The England wicket-keeper failed by only four runs in his second dig to notch a century in each innings.

Since then we have met the West Indies on their own pitches, before their own colourful spectators and underneath their baking sun. It was this tour that most vividly illustrated the success of the New Zealand administrators' decision to increase our participation in Test cricket. One of that team, Jack Alabaster, first toured with a New Zealand side in 1955, while Graham Dowling, the captain, had been to South Africa in 1961–62. And among the others Terry Jarvis, Congdon, Graham Vivian, Taylor, and Richard Collinge had toured England in 1965. For a change New Zealand had sent a side overseas full of experienced, but still relatively young, Test cricketers, and consequently New Zealand, though lacking the attack to win a Test, did not buckle under pressure as so often before. Five tests, five draws: nothing, it might be claimed, to restore great heart to any cricketing nation. But it is largely on the basis of New Zealand's performance in the West Indies that I base my confidence in the team to tour Britain. Although, at the time of writing, it is yet to be selected, I feel that unless our administrators reverse their current selection policy – to pick from what is now a core of proven Test cricketers – New Zealand should have its most successful tour of England since Walter Hadlee took us there in 1949.

The four I have already mentioned, Taylor, Congdon, Howarth, and Turner, will no doubt be the men on whom New Zealand will be most dependent. But the great strength of the touring side will be that the onus to score runs, take wickets, and hold catches will not be on just a few men. Too often in the past too much has depended on too few players. But of the players likely to visit England this summer at least six will have made Test centuries. At January this year, Congdon, Mark Burgess, and Turner had scored three each, and two of Turner's were double centuries. Brian Hastings and Taylor have both scored two and Terry Jarvis has one to his credit. Compare this with the team I took to England in 1965. Of the players selected only three had scored Test centuries.

So my confidence in the 1973 team will not be based entirely on optimism.

The player whose name I expect English followers to hear most of is Bruce Taylor, a remarkable cricketer who has developed with giant steps since he made his Test, and almost his first-class, debut in 1965. After only three first-class games Taylor was plucked into the Kiwi team and, in his first Test, against India, made 105 and took 5–86 with his brisk inswingers and cutters. I can't remember a more sensational debut to Test cricket, certainly not by a New Zealander.

Since then Taylor has become New Zealand's most reliable and penetrative bowler. He has that rare ability to produce the unplayable ball, and the heart to nag at all batsmen, even on a plumb track. As a batsman, he is more than just a hitter. In 1968–69 he scored his first 50 against West Indies in just 30 minutes. He must have tired a little after that for it took him another 56 minutes to get to his hundred. Yet it has often been said in New Zealand that Taylor is a lucky cricketer, an opinion that is either a churlish way of downgrading his ability or a way of expressing surprise that such a spectacular player should have achieved consistent results. But Taylor silenced a few of the sceptics with his performance in the West Indies. On wickets tailor-made to make a bowler take up marbles, 'Haystacks', as Taylor is known, took a record-equalling 27 wickets at an average of just over 20 apiece. And he didn't even play in the first Test.

Bevan Congdon, in another way, is also an unorthodox cricketer but one supplied with an equal amount of courage. Gritty, eager to bat for as long and as profitably as he is able, he has been of great service to New Zealand cricket. And when he took over the captaincy in the West Indies after Graham Dowling's back injury had forced his withdrawal from the tour, he managed to lift New Zealand's performance by leading from the front. He scored more runs than any other batsman except Turner, he took crucial Test wickets with his tidy medium-pacers, and he upheld New Zealand's high reputation in the field. In addition, he is a good runner between the wickets.

There is not a great deal I can say of Glenn Turner. County bowlers and cricket spectators in England will know more of him than we in New Zealand do. A prolific scorer in County and

"Is New Zealand's Confidence Justified?"

Above: The Basin Reserve, Wellington. This ground, like many of New Zealand's major cricket grounds, has suffered from being used for winter sport also. The turf does not always have sufficient time to recover, with the result that New Zealand's batsmen sometimes find themselves on sub-standard pitches that do not encourage stroke-making

Left: Glenn Turner, on whom the 1973 New Zealand tourists will depend greatly, slashes gloriously backward of point

Test cricket, Turner brings to the New Zealand side a solidity that makes it extremely difficult for the other side to win the match. He has excellent powers of concentration, he is dedicated, and he is almost impossible to fault technically. In the West Indies he saved one Test with a time-consuming double century, in another Test he set a New Zealand record with an innings of 259. In 1969, at Lord's, he batted through a Test innings against England, a feat he repeated against West Indies in 1972. He has shown, though in the main he has restricted this ability to limited-overs cricket, that he has the shots as well as the concentration to become a truly great cricketer.

The fourth player I singled out earlier, Hedley Howarth, is also well known in England. On his maiden tour in 1969, Howarth emerged as a left-arm spinner of world class, and we in New Zealand thought he was a little unlucky not to be included in the Rest of the World team that played Australia. He has accuracy, control, stamina, and the ability to move the ball away from the right-hand batsman or float it in. He is certain to get his share of bowling on the tour, and I am confident that only the best hitters will collar his spinners.

So, we have four cricketers recognised beyond New Zealand as players of international calibre. In addition to them we have two other batsmen, both exciting players, whom I would commend readers to watch closely. They are Mark Burgess and Graham Vivian. Both players are brilliant shot-makers, both are in the Colin Bland or Martin Donnelly class as fieldsmen, both are potential match-winners. And perhaps equally important, both have already experienced English conditions.

Of the two, Burgess has had the more tangible successes, having scored Test hundreds against Pakistan, England, and West Indies.

The first of these, against Pakistan in 1969, came under most trying circumstances with New Zealand heading for defeat until Burgess, farming the bowling, took over. Against England in our summer of 1971, he scored a superb hundred, and in doing so became the first New Zealand batsman to master Underwood's wizardry – a great psychological victory. Not only did Burgess master Underwood, but he took New Zealand to a position from which victory was the logical conclusion until Knott proved otherwise.

Vivian, though technically inferior to Burgess, is one of those rare athletes with almost superhuman reflexes, an attribute that gives him the chance to play shots few other batsmen could try and take catches other fieldsmen would not get near. Sadly, New Zealand do not seem to realise the full potential of this young man, for since he was first chosen for his country at the age of 18 he has suffered unfairly from the whims of selectors. Only once, in a match against Victoria, has he been able to fulfil his batting potential, which he did with a match-saving but entertaining century. Yet it is not always the big scores that win matches. A quick 30 at the right time is often as valuable as any century, and there are not many New Zealand batsmen better equipped for a quick 30 than Vivian. In addition he bowls leg-spinners, albeit at an inconsistent length and he is one of the first players I would select for the team. Indeed it will be an injustice if he fails to make the side to England.

Another batsman I see as a strong candidate for Britain is Brian Hastings, one of our more successful batsmen in the 1969 series. A fluent stroke-maker, Hastings in full cry is a joy to watch, but he has, not unjustifiably, acquired a reputation as a poor starter. A tour of England, of course, is the best possible way for any batsman to overcome this affliction, for a long string of innings removes the worry New Zealanders often have: that is, if they lose their wicket early they probably have to wait another week before they bat again. Like most of the team Hastings is a fine fieldsman, particularly in the gully.

At the time of writing, as the tour hopefuls participate in the current Plunket Shield competition, there are only two other players I would regard as certainties for the team. They are Jarvis and Wadsworth, both of whom emerged from the West Indies with credit.

Terry Jarvis, in the 1965 side, had ill luck at the start of his international career, catching the 'dreaded lurgy' *en route* to England through India and Pakistan. But since then this personable young man has fought his way back to Test cricket, and with Turner put on 387 in an opening partnership against West Indies. Ken Wadsworth, picked to tour England in 1969 as a batsman who could keep wicket, failed on his first tour, though his wicket-keeping improved immeasurably. However, he fought back and reached a high level of maturity with his batting in the West Indies, twice playing leading roles in back-to-the-wall recoveries.

These, then, are the players who stimulate the confidence of followers here; the players who have done enough to prove their worth at international level. But there is one additional reason for a New Zealander's confidence, an aspect of our cricket I have already mentioned briefly: fielding. The most successful tour I have ever been associated with was the Kiwi tour of South Africa in 1961–62, when we shared the five-Test series two apiece with a South African team that included Adcock, Heine, McGlew, MacLean, Waite, Peter Pollock, and Bland. And one of the reasons for our success was the fielding. In the Tests we held 95 per cent of our catches.

The side New Zealand has now should be every bit as good in the field as the team that went to South Africa. Vivian and Burgess, as I have already said, are of exceptional value in the field, and there are a host of other skilled fieldsmen. Turner is a superb slip fielder, Jarvis excells in any position, Congdon and Hastings miss little close to the wicket. In fact, the side fielded so well in the West Indies that local commentators claimed it was the best fielding side to tour there.

However, having listed the strengths of the side, I suppose I should add the qualifications.

The chief weakness will be the spin bowling. For unless our Plunket Shield competition unveils an off-spinner this department will be ominously thin. The obvious spin partner for Howarth is Jack Alabaster, now something over 40 but still an accurate leg-spinner with rare control. Never will I forget the yeoman services he performed on the tour of South Africa, where he bowled 1,200 overs and was so adaptable that I was able to use him as a stock bowler or, when the occasion allowed, as our main attacking bowler. Unfortunately he suffered a back injury in the West Indies and it is doubtful that he will be available for the tour.

Should this be the case the New Zealand selectors will probably have to think again about Vic Pollard or Bryan Yuile, the only other spinners in New Zealand who have had any success in Test cricket. But here there is a problem. Both these players hold strong religious convictions that prevent them from playing on Sundays. It is not for me to debate this issue, but I will say that as a captain of any touring team I would be far from happy with players in my side who could not guarantee being available.

Another player in this category is Bruce Murray, probably, in terms of his ability to get on top of the bowling, the most successful opening batsman in New Zealand. He, too, has an international century to his name, and when he made his hundred, against Australia, he came close to making 100 runs in a session. There is talk in New Zealand that Murray may be selected for England because he has said he would make himself available for Sunday play should the circumstances demand it.

Were Graham Dowling fit and available he would be an obvious choice, both as an opening batsman and as a captain, but Dowling, who has given invaluable service to New Zealand, is now considering retirement following a run of bad luck. This began when he broke his finger deputising as a wicket-keeper in Australia, and when it failed to mend he had it amputated to allow him to continue with cricket. Then he injured his back in the West Indies and, at last reports, that has made little progress.

A further problem for the selectors will be finding pace bowlers to support Taylor. The first choice will probably be Richard Collinge, a burly young left-armer who came into Test cricket at 18 with immediate success. But in recent seasons Collinge too has had fitness problems, and he has not always been a success in Test matches. Nonetheless, his pace is brisk and he does have experience. Murray Webb, another speedster who has taken a great deal of wickets in Plunket Shield cricket, was unable to hold a Test place in the West Indies and will need plenty of wickets this season to get to Britain.

I do not see Bob Cunis getting to England, though the English batsmen have reason to respect him. He took six wickets in an innings against England during the second Test in 1970-71. But the problems he has had with his knees seem to be catching up on him, and he had a most disappointing tour of West Indies after a fairly unproductive time in Australia with the 1971-72 World XI side. The man I would like to see tour is Bryan Andrews, an experienced bowler who has been unlucky never to rise beyond the fringe of the New Zealand team. He has a striking similarity to Australia's Bob Massie in the way he moves the ball sharply and could well prove an effective force in English conditions.

The only other pace bowlers who, at this time, look to have much chance of getting to England are young Richard Hadlee and the strong-armed Taranaki player Alistair Jordan. Hadlee, a younger brother of Dayle Hadlee, who toured England in 1969, and the son of Walter Hadlee, created such an impression in his three first-class games last year that he made the New Zealand B team that played in the knock-out tournament in Australia. He is still young and a bit raw, and his fitness is suspect, but he does have an outside chance of continuing the family tradition. Jordan is from a different kennel. He is a young man of impressive dimensions, has great stamina, and is learning more with each match.

Lastly, the selectors are going to have a problem finding middle-order batsmen to support Congdon, Burgess, and Hastings. They could solve it by batting Jarvis down in the order, though, personally, I see him as the Test opener with Turner, should Murray be left behind. My probable choice is Rodney Redmond, a left-handed opener from Auckland who gives the ball a decent whack and who fulfils the proper opener's role by getting on with the task of scoring runs once the shine has gone off the ball.

Whoever makes this team, however, will have merited his place. New Zealand cricket is no longer at that level where a couple of Plunket Shield fifties meant a Test chance. We in New Zealand will be bitterly disappointed should the 1973 Kiwis prove to be an unattractive side, or one that will bow meekly when faced with the strength of your Test sides. I hope they fulfil our expectations . . . and I do not think the odds against New Zealand gaining their first Test victory over England are too long to be discounted.

South African Cricket is Alive and Well ...and Sponsored

Peter Pollock

The grave fear that South African cricket, in its current isolation, would lack incentives for young, up-and-coming players has, I feel, been allayed. Despite the tragic lack of international competition, the game is flourishing, albeit only at a provincial level. There are no signs of decline in standard or potential, nor has there been a slackening of competitiveness. In fact, such is the enthusiasm, dedication, and intensity of purpose among the five teams in the glamour 'A' section of the Currie Cup that some pundits are already expressing doubts about the cause of all this apparent rejuvenation – namely sponsorship.

It has long been my contention, both as player and paid scribe, that South African cricketers should be able to reap the rewards of their talents. And I mean this in the monetary sense. After all, cricket must move with the times, and today, whether we care to acknowledge this or not, we are all basically mercenaries. It is naive to suggest that any sport at top level is played for the sheer thrill and fun of the game. Everything has become more specialised and scientific, and cricketers, the same as other sportsmen, find that it is virtually a full-time job keeping themselves in trim for the rigours of life at the top.

More important, though, cricketers are also entertainers, and it is the players alone who draw the crowds, keep those turnstiles clicking, and pour funds into the coffers of the provincial unions. To Barry Richards and Mike Procter goes the credit for the change in attitude. These two, with their county cricket background as a platform, have not only exploited their respective abilities but have shown the way in cajoling sponsors into the act.

But now the sponsors are there, some people are beginning to have second thoughts. The South African Breweries have taken on the overall sponsorship of the Currie Cup competition, but the basis of their financial aid is covering expenses, though part of the money does find its way back to the players, either directly or indirectly. Everyone welcomes this participation. What apparently are not welcomed are the added financial bonuses being offered, either by the unions or outside sponsors, to individual or team performances. In this respect, it is generally felt that the added carrots dangling before the players are introducing a 'needle' atmosphere which in turn breeds gamesmanship rather than sportsmanship. Already there is evidence of this.

I have always maintained that the 'A' section of the Currie Cup represents the highest standard of first-class cricket apart from Test matches. The secret of this high standard is that it is restrictive and highly competitive, and none but the strong survive. The men are sorted out from the boys in extra-quick time and temperament is severely tested. I feel that this is healthy, although to youngsters it is a torrid introduction to the top echelon of world cricket. I say it without reservation – it is this tough school that has made South African cricket what it is today.

But the purists, and those who benignly believe that cricket is only cricket when played socially, on a village green on a Saturday afternoon, are not convinced that sponsorship and the attendant professional, mercenary approach are good for the game. Well, who is to argue?

Umpires are finding their lot considerably more unenviable. They are being tested, and tested severely, and the weak are being exploited. The incompetent are being hounded to the extent where life in the middle is hardly bearable. Not so long ago, there was an apparent misunderstanding between the two umpires and the Eastern Province captain, Lorrie Wilmot. It revolved around a decision on just when the final 20 overs of the match would be started. It turned out to be a real thriller with Rhodesia, captained by Mike Procter and supported by a partisan home crowd at Bulawayo, launching a pulsating bid for victory. But came the final over, with Rhodesia only six runs away from their target and with four wickets in hand, and the game came to an abrupt and controversial finish. Eastern Province skipper Wilmot, refusing to accept the umpire's decision on a change with regard to the final 20 overs, trooped off the field, followed by his team. Wilmot felt that the match was over and steadfastly stuck to his opinion that the umpires had no legal right to make any alterations. He was, of course, right from a purely legal point of view. But had he, by walking off, committed the cardinal sin of bad sportsmanship?

The two umpires awarded the match to Rhodesia, a decision that was subsequently overruled by the South African Cricket Association. And at the time of writing (December), Rhodesia have given warning that they are going to appeal. Irrespective of the final outcome, this major incident, and others where umpires have been abused or even 'shanghaied' into decisions, is being used by the critics of sponsorship. 'They don't worry about the game any more. It's the money they are after', said one former member of the SACA. And this opinion is shared by many. After all, an umpire's decision, right or wrong, must be abided by in the true spirit of sportsmanship.

Personally, I feel that sponsorship might have something to do with this bold new spirit. But, by the same token, I find the advent of this spirit most welcome, even though there are aspects of it that leave a sour taste. South African cricket has at least found an answer to the isolation that faces it. And as long as this dedicated approach remains I can see no reason why future Springbok teams, when, or if, they are accepted back into the international fold, should not carry on from where Ali Bacher's illustrious side left off in 1970, just before the door was closed. I must admit my reservations about some of the things being accepted in the rather wide category of 'legal gamesmanship'. Yet the publicity that these issues are being accorded and the resultant 'needle' atmosphere have certainly helped to fill the void for player and spectator, both of whom mark time till the day when they are once again part of this great game at international level.

But what of the individuals? Who are the stars shining in forgotten South Africa? The names are familiar. Barry Richards, his fair hair distinctively worn like a mane, is still the lion of South African batsmanship. I watched him nonchalantly stroking an undefeated century the other day. He was both unobtrusive and obtrusive as he charmed by his skilful dominance – a mixture of arrogance and shyness. 'Pardon me for being so brilliant', I could almost hear him say as he chalked up the rands – two rands for every run he makes. I thought to myself that he has, believe it or not, improved. 'When he sets his mind on

South African Cricket

Africamera

Left: *The Wanderers Stadium in Johannesburg, the largest Test ground in South Africa. Its pitches and outfield are as fast as anywhere in the world, and it was here, in 1966–67, that South Africa beat Australia for the first time in South Africa*

Below left: *One of the most magnificent sights in cricket: Graeme Pollock hoisting a six over the long-on boundary. In this match, against Hampshire in 1965, Pollock scored 94 in 66 minutes*

Below: *Should South Africa be allowed back into the fold of Test cricket, they have in Barry Richards the finest attacking opening batsman in the world*

making a century, there is nothing we can do about it on these hard wickets', complained one bowler the other evening, his brow covered with sweat and his feet sore and aching. Some laughed, some smiled, but I knew just how he felt. And I complimented myself on retiring from the game, for now it is possible to enjoy a Barry Richards innings. It wasn't when I was battling to dismiss him.

Natal depend heavily on Richards. If he fails the team fails, relatively speaking. Not that there are no other fine players in the team. There are, but they are somewhat overshadowed by the brilliance of this outstanding batsman.

Mike Procter, too, walks like a Greek god. The white man's Gary Sobers is his current tag, and he certainly lives up to it. Procter's batting has now reached a maturity that places him not far behind Richards as both a consistent run-getter and a stroker of the ball. His 'wrong footed' fast bowling is still the most feared in the country, especially when the spirit moves him into full throttle. And then, just for good measure, Mike Procter's off-spinners – yes, off-spinners – have also turned a match. At the start of this season, Procter, on the final afternoon of the vital match against Transvaal, decided to bowl spinners. Later that afternoon he was being chaired from the field, having scalped nine wickets – eight with his spinners – in spearheading Rhodesia to a superb outright triumph. Indeed nothing appears beyond Procter's capabilities. Rhodesians have come to expect miracles from Procter, and he rarely lets them down.

Transvaal, too, have their main star, the left-handed Lee Irvine. Such is Irvine's improvement over the past two seasons that he is talked about much in the same breath as Graeme Pollock – and that, in this country, is a compliment of the highest order. Quick-footed with lightning reflexes, Irvine has the ability to pierce the field either side of the wicket. Aggression is his watch-word, but he is not reckless in choosing the ball to strike to the boundary, or over it. His defence is also very solid. In fact he is almost as complete a player as Barry Richards, save that he is more prone to committing the odd indiscretion. There was once a question-mark against his tempera-ment, but over the past two seasons he has saved Transvaal from so many delicate situations that bowlers no longer entertain false hopes of a nervous error.

In the Eastern Province there is Graeme Pollock, still a force to be reckoned with, though this season cruel luck has kept him out of the firing line. In a Gillette Cup match against Griqualand West, he notched up the fastest century ever in this competition – in a mere 72 minutes – only to break his finger later in the day taking a catch in the slips. Unfortunately the injury did not mend properly and required a further operation. As I write, he is still likely to be out for another six weeks, and so Eastern Province, fighting grimly to avoid the wooden spoon in the 'A' section, will, at their luckiest, have Pollock available for only the final two matches of the season.

Finally, we have Western Province, the team that depends so heavily on Eddie Barlow for both material and psychological contributions. Barlow is still as irrepressible as ever, and even though he has not quite recaptured some of his old form, his presence on the field is enough to spur his team-mates on.

As I have made a brief run through the five sides making up the 'A' section, it would not be a misguided observation for any reader to remark: 'But there are only five players in South Africa.' Perhaps I might be permitted to quote Geoff Dakin, a former provincial captain who is convenor of the Eastern Province selection com-mittee. 'Take Procter from Rhodesia, Richards from Natal, Irvine from Transvaal, Barlow from Western Province, and Graeme Pollock from Eastern Province and the rest of the mortals will have a very evenly contested Currie Cup competition.' There is a lot of sense in this remark, but let me hasten to add that, though South Africa boasts these five stars, cricket here does not lack depth. Those five are all match-winners on their own. They are in world class, and I wouldn't hesitate suggesting any of them for a current world side.

But the fact that they are geniuses, and I use that word somewhat liberally, does not mean that the supporting cast pales into insignificance. Andre Bruyns, formerly of Western Province and now of Natal, is a fine No. 3 batsman. Natal also have Arthur Short, an opener who has twice been picked for South Africa and has twice had his tour cancelled. Then there is Vintcent van der Bijl, a giant of a man who stands at 6 ft 8 in. He uses his height to devastating effect to gain bounce, and this, together with his ability to swing and seam the ball, makes him a highly promising bowler. He too has been picked for South Africa on one of its aborted tours.

And in Natal a spinner has been unearthed! He is Pelham Henwood, a left-armer who is not afraid to vary his flight and give the ball air. Rhodesia also have an orthodox left-armer, Richie Kaschula, who relies heavily on accuracy and a devastating arm ball and has proved himself over the past two seasons. The fact that Kaschula is successful in Gillette Cup cricket bears testimony to his accuracy, control, and ability to fill an Underwood-type role. Unfortunately South African pitches rarely sympathise with spin bowlers, but I have no doubt, were he to play overseas, he would be a veritable match-winner.

The outstanding newcomer as far as Eastern Province is concerned is Simon Bezuidenhout, an opening batsman who looks a little awkward but is nevertheless highly efficient. Gifted with a tremendous eye, he is able to chance the odd shot across the line of flight, though basically he is orthodox in defence. I remember back in 1965, when Peter van der Merwe's Springboks arrived in England, some critic looked at Ali Bacher, saw how he tended to play across the line, and promptly suggested that he had no chance on English wickets. I hope that gentleman's face was red when he glanced at the tour statistics, for Bacher was second only to Graeme Pollock as a run-maker on that tour. I would say that Bezuidenhout is something of a Zaheer Abbas in that he looks vulnerable from the pavilion but is remarkably effective. Both Abbas and Bezuidenhout get away with technical transgressions thanks to their good eyes and quick reflexes.

Ali Bacher, incidentally, is still an astute captain, even if his Transvaal side are finding it increasingly hard to maintain their grip on the Currie Cup. He appears to have lost a little form but nevertheless remains a highly respected competitor.

There is only one real problem at the moment – finding an opening bowler to partner Mike Procter. Were a Springbok team to be selected right now, Procter would have to play the spearhead role alone, with someone like Vintcent van der Bijl at the other end. However, I have no doubt that in the not-too-distant future a partner for Procter will present himself, even if the cupboard does seem a little bare at the moment.

In summing up, might I say again that South African cricket, despite its isolation, is keeping up the standard that saw it reach such glorious heights until 1970. And I am optimistic that it will survive, especially if the current highly competitive spirit prevails. I see no reason why it should not.

John Player Cricket Yearbook 1973

Above: Cricket-loving Barbadians make use of the best vantage points to watch Barbados bat against the 1971–72 New Zealanders

Right: Clive Lloyd's powerful hitting has produced thousands of runs for Lancashire, but his recent record in Tests for West Indies has disappointed. However, his brilliant fielding compensates for any batting lapses, and his ability to change the course of a match in a matter of overs can never be ignored

Far right: Gary Sobers relinquished the West Indies captaincy after 39 Tests

West Indies Enter a New Era

Gerry Gomez
(Former West Indies Test captain and selector)

With the Australians about to visit our islands, the West Indies tour of England in the latter half of 1973 can be justifiably regarded as part of the distant future. At the moment everyone's attention is riveted on the Australian Sheffield Shield season and the performances of likely tourists. Lillee, with his early successes against the visiting Pakistanis and his flattening of Paul Sheahan, has already established such an imposing and frightening image that he looms like a colossus ready to hurl thunderbolts. Indeed, there are so many exciting new players coming here that interest in the Australians has tended to overshadow our problems of team building. Consideration of our England visit comes well down the list. Nevertheless, in spite of this momentary lack of interest I will consider the prospects of the West Indies' 1973 visit to England and the likely contenders for the team.

My first thought is that now is the time to make a policy decision that will have a profound bearing on the West Indies team of the near future. With Gary Sobers's withdrawal from the captaincy, there is an urgent need to establish his successor securely, and also to restore the importance and intrinsic value of the captaincy to West Indian cricket. Such action would afford the new captain the satisfaction of being recognised first and foremost as a leader, irrespective of any consideration of his finding a place in the team. It will give him a psychological boost, and a sense of authority from which he will derive much courage and enthusiasm.

Captaincy of a West Indies team during a Test series at home is fraught with pressures and influences that are peculiar products of our small communities. It requires a man with experience and toughness of character to overcome them. Another factor is that the home captain functions in a tight five-Test schedule without the benefit of handling teams day by day which he obtains on tour. The man for this job must, therefore, take a group of players and fashion them into an efficient unit in the least possible time. The present situation calls for a man of stature in the eyes of both the opposition and his own team.

The contenders for the job are Kanhai, Holford, Carew, and Murray. The immediate circumstances lessen the claims of Holford and Murray, but I would choose Murray as vice-captain to prepare him for the captaincy of the side going to England in July. It is a pity that Holford, with his undoubted cricket acumen, was not recognised as captaincy material earlier in his career by both Barbados and West Indies. This leaves us with Kanhai and Carew.

Kanhai, the distinguished batsman much respected by his adversaries, is admired by his contemporaries but is short on experience as a practising captain; Carew, after his successful trip to Australia in 1969, is also highly regarded, and he has been an outstanding captain of

Trinidad – purposeful, searching, aggressive, and unsettling. But Carew might not get the nod because his forthright and aggressive approach has given rise to some emotional and unreasonable thinking among officials. This is unfortunate, because he is definitely the man to bring to flower much of the talent that lies untapped, unused, and in need of purposeful direction in the West Indian team; a team that must fight tooth and nail with a young, confident Australian team in the next few months.

Carew's appointment, however, is strictly a case of horses for courses. In the comparative serenity of English tour conditions, to which he is no stranger, Murray can take over. At 30, Murray has already enjoyed a distinguished Test career against England, captained Cambridge and played for World elevens.

It is the hope and prayer of every cricket lover that Gary Sobers, the world's greatest all-rounder, will be available for yet another tour. As less bowling demands will be made on him he will carry, with Kanhai, the responsibility of the batting. Both possess perfect knowledge of English conditions, and possibly on this tour there will be the long, exciting partnerships which in the past have remained the dream of most West Indian followers. The certainties for the opening places are Roy Fredericks and Geoff Greenidge, who also have English playing experience. Fredericks is a busy opener difficult to contain, and Greenidge, more orthodox, has the memory of coming within one run of separate hundreds for Sussex against Chappell's team last year still fresh in his mind. Both are useful change bowlers, Fredericks bowling chinamen and wrong 'uns and Greenidge leg-breaks.

Lloyd and Kallicharran, already established as part of the English summer scene, will delight with their dashing approach to batting. Lloyd is under a cloud as a Test certainty at the moment (his omission from the invitation list for the Australian series must have raised many Lancashire eyebrows, but he has not achieved anywhere near his run-making potential in Tests). Kallicharran, off to a good start with a hundred on his Test debut, plays with a panache reminiscent of the great Neil Harvey. And if Lloyd's fielding alone is worth the price of admission Kallicharran's is not far behind.

Another strong candidate is Charlie Davis. He has tours of England and Australia behind him and was a great success at home against India and New Zealand. Like Lloyd, he is a useful seam and swing bowler – a type so much used and so necessary in England.

With his meteoric entry onto the Test scene against New Zealand, Rowe of Jamaica is a class player gifted with a good temperament, a well organised batsman both correct and thoughtful. His countryman, Foster, also comes into the reckoning as a batsman of much ability who favours the on-side and as a bowler of off-spin at a pace that makes him hard to get at.

Now I come to a gifted West Indian who, surprisingly, has won only one Test cap – Keith Boyce. In English conditions he should be a great asset, as a hard-hitting batsman, fast-medium seam bowler, and a brilliant fieldsman – just as he has been for Essex in recent seasons. Only once in the West Indies has he favoured us with a glimpse of his great power and too often has brought about his own demise by playing across the line on our faster surfaces. Like Lloyd he is a joy to watch in the field, and his rocket-like throw places him in the same bracket as the Australians O'Neill and Sheahan.

This brings me to the end of the accredited batsmen, but there are several youngsters who might come good in the next few months and so force their claims on the selectors. I refer to openers Baichan of Guyana, Ashby of Barbados, and Morgan of Jamaica. Baichan's painstaking methods have earned him useful scores on our true wickets, while the other two contenders have a wider stroke range and consequently are more prone to error.

With Murray holding the number one wicket-keeping position, there is little to choose between Findlay of Windwards and Lewis of Jamaica. The former, with tours to England and Australia and a full series against New Zealand, has the edge on experience, is unobstusive in his methods, and a valuable team man. Lewis gained his Test cap against India and blossomed forth as a correct, watchful batsman, getting two 80s. The following year, against New Zealand, he lost his place to Findlay, basically the better wicket-keeper, and there, perhaps, lies the deciding factor.

With the retirement of Hall and Griffith, the West Indies bowling attack lost its real penetration and replacements have been long in coming to the fore. Holder is an intelligent quick bowler, bowls well within himself, but lacks that extra yard of pace to be truly fearsome and devastating. There is, however, in young Dowe of Jamaica a bowler of genuine pace and aggression. If handled properly he could be a great striking force. He has played in Tests against India and New Zealand, and recently he spent three months in Barbados undergoing thorough coaching and training from the terrible duo – Hall and Griffith. Apprenticeship to these two great exponents should round him off as a bowler of real fire, zest for the job, and guile. Boyce, very much at home in English conditions, will enjoy fast and 'green topped' wickets if and when they are provided, and he should prove a very useful third prong to the fast attack. Of the other claimants for a place among the quickies, only Shillingford has had previous tour and Test experience. His fellow Windward and Leeward Islanders, Phillip and Roberts, have had their inspired spells but so far have not impressed sufficiently to merit Test selection.

To give the attack more variety and penetration, there must be a place for Inshan Ali with his chinamen and googlies. This little man has developed physically while his confidence and control have been improving by leaps and bounds. It will be interesting to see how he handles the Australians, who do not play this type of bowling from the crease, but in England

Vanburn Holder, for whom the West Indies have yet to find a regular opening partner

he will be encouraged by the fact that few, if any, England batsmen will go down the track to him. For orthodox left-hand spin, Ali's team-mate Jumadeen should find a place ahead of Willett. He uses the air better and imparts more spin with little loss of control.

The off-spin department presents an interesting situation. The best man in these parts is still Lance Gibbs, but considerations of grooming a young man might open the door for Persaud of Guyana and Howard of Barbados. Gibbs, at 38, is a seasoned player and a Test cricketer in the truest sense of the word. He has been a great stiffening influence on West Indian teams in the past and would be a great source of knowledge and encouragement to the new captain.

With the development of youth cricket in the West Indies there are a number of fine young players on the fringe of representative cricket. Although the present strength of the batting in the Test team does not leave much room for young middle-order batsmen, there is no reason to worry about the future with players like Johnson and Clarke of Barbados, Bacchus of Guyana, and L. Gomes of Trinidad. Along with the young openers mentioned earlier they are undoubtedly the best of the present crop.

In the bowling department, there is an outstanding prospect in Imtiaz Ali, with his leg-breaks and wrong 'uns. Playing for Trinidad against the Young England tourists he was the leading wicket-taker and impressed Jack Ikin, the England manager. For one so young (only 17) he approaches his job with skill and confidence, and his control improves with every game. Indeed I am prepared to say at this early juncture that there is a place and a need for this rising young leg-spinner in the team that goes to England in July.

England are always a difficult proposition at home, where their players possess the technique to adapt to their weather, light, and pitches. Nevertheless, I fancy West Indies' chances given their blend of experience and youth as represented in the players I have mentioned. There is one aspect of the tour to which I must draw attention and that is the approach of the tourists to county fixtures. On recent tours we have tended to regard only Test matches as important. I urge the 1973 West Indian team, in the interests of our own cricket and that of the host counties, to play positive match-winning cricket in each fixture. This attitude serves the double purpose of creating an attractive public image and of instilling in the team a match-winning attitude. It is really the obligation of all touring sides to spread the gospel of entertaining cricket instead of going through the motions in provincial games and leaving everyone bored until the Tests.

Cricket, at the best of times, is possibly the worst game in which to attempt prophecy, and West Indies cricket is at present in a state of flux. But change of captain, older players receding from Test level, and, happily, promise of talented young replacements all give rise to optimism. The imminent encounter against the vibrant Australians should sharpen the West Indian team and so there is every reason to expect an English tour full of good cricket, tension, exhilaration, and excitement. Two top appointments for this tour have already been made by the West Indian Cricket Board of Control: Esmond Kentish, a former Test player, knowledgeable, charming, and efficient, will be manager, and Glendon Gibbs, another former Test player, will be assistant manager. Both these men bring to their jobs a knowledge and understanding, not merely of cricket at the highest level but of players and their welfare. It is an important factor that augurs well for the success of the trip.

The Art of Cricket

Ted Dexter goes for the big one and the ball is on its way to the mid-on boundary for six. Note the full follow-through, which is why he has opened his chest. The shot is a fine example of power, grace, and confidence, the latter being an essential part in the make-up of the aggressive batsman

The Art of Aggressive Batting

Ted Dexter

Experienced mechanics will no doubt remember the first piece of advice given to them as apprentices: 'If all else fails, it is sometimes worth taking a look at the instruction manual.'

Of course the said manuals continue to gather dust in this age as in every other – that's what happens to the work of people who write to instruct rather than amuse, and I suspect that it was for this reason, rather than a professed unfamiliarity with the subject, that our editor, Trevor Bailey, shifted the burden of this batting homily on to me.

'I rather wanted to do this one myself', he said, 'but for some extraordinary reason, everyone seemed to think that you were better suited'. Now I come to think back, he might just have been fishing. Perhaps my reply should have encouraged him to think otherwise – after all I distinctly remember Trevor hitting a six somewhere along the line – a Tuesday in July some years back, downhill and wind-assisted admittedly – but a six nevertheless!

Only the thought that he might reciprocate and encourage me to think I knew something about medium-pace swing bowling persuaded me to short-circuit the whole situation and do as I was bid.

One consolation at least tends to ease my mind. That is my conviction that there has never been a batsman in the history of the game who did not dream of hitting the bowler out of sight. What actually happens to that aggressive desire when, in cold daylight, generations of batsmen have trudged out to the middle to face their first ball, is another matter altogether. Some lose their heads completely. Others change character second by second, step by step, as they walk in, all their good intentions suddenly forgotten. As often as not they are replaced by a fierce competitive desire not to get out under any circumstances: a cricketing virtue in itself, let it be said, but not always the best approach, if the ambition to be a Milburn or a Clive Lloyd burns strongly enough.

For the purposes of this discussion I must, therefore, try to define the term 'aggressive batting' more closely, before the stonewallers' union writes and tells me that their defensive attitude is simply *their* way of being aggressive towards the opposition. I take the point. However, in this context I am being asked to give pointers on quick scoring rather than slow.

Statistically it is also perfectly possible to prove how quick scoring can lose a match when a steadier rate might have produced a different result. It could be said, for instance, of an innings of mine against Australia at Old Trafford in 1961. I was promoted to number three by Peter May on the basis that I might as well have a biff early, before my somewhat suspect temperament could be subjected to too much pressure later on. The psychology was spot-on.

The runs came thick and fast, and when I was out some 76 runs and as many minutes later England were in a winning position. Unfortunately they were also committed to winning with barely a chance of a draw if the victory chase failed. Fail it did and the match was lost. See what I mean about statistics!

I am therefore forced to make a further assumption, which is that we are interested for the time being in quick scoring, which is in fact advantageous to the team, as in all limited-overs cricket, and in most other games as well. The big difference between the two, of course, is that for most of the time in limited-overs cricket, the bowler is using extreme defensive tactics as his best method of restricting the scoring rate and, incidentally, as his best chance of getting the batsman out, while in more open and extended forms of the game the bowler may be conducting an aggressive policy himself.

The latter case is surely infinitely easier to deal with and it was certainly this kind of situation which appealed most to my fairly simple philosophy in Test and County matches. The more fielders the bowler used in supposedly aggressive positions, slips, short-legs and in the 'silly' positions, the better the odds, it seemed to me, in favour of scoring runs easily and quickly. The open spaces always seemed so inviting, just as the prospect of surrendering lamely, popping a catch to someone under my nose, seemed particularly dismal.

Batsmen with absolute confidence in a defensive technique can perhaps take a different view, but in my experience they are a rare breed, and for 99 out of 100 batsmen attack is surely the best form of defence whenever the bowler gets over-adventurous with his field placings.

Quite honestly, I'm not sure there is a great deal more to be said about that kind of quick scoring. It demands no more expertise than good batting in general, all of which can be gleaned from the instruction manual supreme, the MCC coaching book, or from great authorities on the subject such as Sir Donald Bradman; an ability to position yourself quickly and easily to play a wide variety of strokes, the nerve to wait until the ball is in the air before committing yourself, and so on. Without those special talents quick scoring is not feasible in any case. But many people possess these abilities. If only they would give them rein by taking that first bold decision.

Limited-overs cricket is a different kettle of fish altogether. The agony of actually making that decision is largely removed, as the rules of the game insist that you get on with it – or else.

But unfortunately there are 11 men out there in the field dedicated to the task of stopping you doing so. They can't afford the luxury of giving you enough rope to hang yourself as in other forms of the game. They want to keep you on tight rein from the word go and it's the devil's own job to beat the system.

Some people take the view that there is only one way out, to take a smack at every ball and hope it falls in the vacant spots. In fact it is mighty tempting to opt out of your responsibilities in this way.

The trouble is that you succeed only very occasionally and there is precious little satisfaction when you do, so – back to the drawing board. The trouble is that the traditional methods do not necessarily apply.

The editor asked me 'particularly to emphasise the importance of hitting straight rather than across the line'. This is fool-proof advice most of the time, but it can hardly be correct when the whole aim of the fielding side may well be to induce the batsman to do precisely that. Sussex won the first two Gillette Cups in 1963 and 1964 by sticking exclusively to a pattern of bowling and field placings which made the batsman play in a narrow arc in front of the wicket. As a matter of policy we all bowled well up to the bat and straight at the wicket, and the harder and straighter the batsman replied, the better we were pleased.

The awkward batsmen were the clever deflectors on either side of the stumps, people like Harry Pilling and Ray Illingworth, not everyone's idea of match-winners in limited-over cricket – until you look at their records.

Of course, there are exceptions. Who will ever forget Clive Lloyd's magnificent century in last year's Gillette Cup final, particularly those scorching straight drives which beat the fielders, even when they were posted right on the fence? Remember, though, we are talking about an exceptionally powerful hitter who hit peak form on that special occasion. In fact, prior to that innings, Clive Lloyd's capacity for big hitting had shown modest returns in 1972 – as opposed to a fine 1971 season – largely, I think, because the pattern of bowling and field placing was developing constantly to put a choke on his kind of tearaway tactics.

The more I play John Player League cricket, the more I am convinced that quick scoring must start with really electric running between the wickets. Run first – biff bang later, if you survive. A scoring rate of one run per ball, or 240 off 40 overs, wins a League match 19 times out of 20, and it needs this startling kind of running more than anything to achieve that kind of total.

Short singles are a must, but even more damaging to the morale of the fielding side is the longish single which good runners can turn into two.

Placing the ball accurately becomes more important than hitting it hard. In fact, it is sometimes a better proposition to hit the ball steadily to a boundary fielder and run two, than to lash it in his direction for a hopeful boundary which turns out to be worth only a single.

More than anything there is a lesson here for the over-30s. Fitness can be more important in the four-hour Sunday afternoon game than it is in some first-class county matches.

I could go on about the new demands of the game as played in the John Player League and similar length matches – the increased awareness of 'team' as opposed to the individual, for instance, is a subject on its own.

But I will stick to my brief. As the game constantly develops and changes, batting techniques must also change rapidly to accommodate each new discovery of the bowlers. How do you best treat Tom Cartwright's eight overs on a Sunday? That is a problem that nobody has yet satisfactorily solved.

On the other hand it is nice to know that there is always a place in cricket, and in batting particularly, for boldness and adventure. The art of aggressive batting lies as much in the hands of future great players as it does in the dusty files belonging to big-hitters of the past, and I am sure that in the final reckoning there will never be much to choose between them.

Fred in full cry – one of the most exhilarating sights seen on the cricket grounds of the world. His run-up began slowly and gradually worked up into a crescendo of fury. With his black mane flowing, Fred Trueman epitomised the hostility and the dislike of batsmen that is the trademark of the true fast bowler

Bowling Fast

Fred Trueman

If you think that all I have to do to bowl fast is take my coat off, roll up my sleeves, flex my muscles, and swing my arms, you could not be further than the truth. There's a lot more to it than that. Forget all about that old saying that fast bowlers are strong in the back and weak in the head. Nothing could be more ridiculous. True, fast bowlers have to be strong, but unless they think as well their chances of success will be severely limited.

Strength and fitness do play their part in a fast bowler's make-up. For, to be a top-class fast bowler, you must be prepared for the hardest of work; for heartache, blood, sweat, tears, and utter frustration. You must be prepared to accept the goadings of captains or team-mates, who will try anything that will spur you on . . .anything to make you extract that little extra effort and pace from your aching body that can mean victory or defeat in any match.

Top-flight fast bowlers who are lucky enough to be gifted with genuine pace are, in the eyes of their captain, potential match-winners long before the start of any game. But unless they give a lot of thought to the job in hand, they will rarely get the full benefit of their talent. A bowler must at all times be able to pick out the weaknesses of the batsmen, left or right-handed.

I found the best way to do this was to watch every player closely, concentrate on his first movements, and to make a mental photograph of whether he favoured playing off his back or front foot. At times I would also try to remember if he shuffled across his wicket to bring him into the line of flight. You see, I believe that a batsman can do one of four things; he can play back or forward, off side or on side. It is up to you then to decide what line of attack is most likely to succeed.

It is quite easy, if you use all your powers of concentration. If, for instance, a batsman is basically a front-foot player, you should by the law of averages be bowling a little shorter than usual. If he is a back-foot player, you will be able to pitch the ball further up to him, which gives you more chance of swinging the ball – the theory being the further you are allowed to pitch the ball up, disregarding a full toss, the more you should be able to move it. If his strength is the on side, you want to be on the line of the off stump, and if he favours the off side you should be using a line of attack, say leg, or leg and middle. It is very rare to run across a player who is able to play off back foot and front foot equally well.

When the batsmen are getting on top is the time to have a word with your skipper to tell him your ideas about removing them. It is an odds-on bet that 90 times out of 100 his ideas will be different from yours, but he will probably let you try yours first. If you do not succeed, he will then say, 'Well, shall we try mine?'

By pooling your knowledge it is possible to achieve the aim that you are both striving for – another wicket.

It was this simple, but basic, philosophy that I worked on. I know a lot of people who think they could bowl fast before my time will say I am talking a lot of codswallop, but, believe me, I am fortunate enough to have a stock answer. 'Look in the record book, it is all there.'

You can never put into words the thrill that runs through your whole body when, for the first time, you pitch the ball on leg and middle and see it move away to hit the top of the off stump, sending it cartwheeling through the air and leaving the batsman completely mystified, only able to look back sadly at his shattered wicket. When this happens it is usually followed up by the inevitable question. How did you bowl that one? This is where you come into your own. Puffing your chest out and pulling yourself to your full height you say, 'Ah well, if I told you how I did it, next time I bowl at you, you will see the way I hold the ball and be able to get yourself into position to play it'.

What you must not say is, 'If I knew, I would tell you'. Because if every bowler who uses the new ball told the truth, he would admit that a lot of deliveries do things he knows nothing about. Mind you, if he does not know himself what is happening, the batsman facing him will be even more baffled and it will be impossible for him to detect any significant change in the action. Many bowlers I have heard say, 'I grip the ball this way for an outswinger', or 'I grip the ball that way to bowl an inswinger'. In theory this sometimes works, but believe me, once you put it into practice things do not always work out that way. I defy anyone to say to me, 'I will make this delivery do exactly what I want at real pace'. It is different for a medium-pace seamer. Some balls will swing in and some will swing out, and with an ordinary bowler it is a fair comment to say that nothing will happen at all.

The great Len Hutton, the finest batsman I have ever had the pleasure of playing with, always reckoned a batsman did not like playing forward all the time. It meant he had to work harder for his runs, particularly against bowlers of lesser pace. He always said that a batsman on his back foot was being allowed to rest, which gave him that precious second longer to play his shot and place the ball where he wanted. I learnt a lot from 'The Master' about the art of fast bowling, in which he was a great believer. It was his predecessor in the Yorkshire and England side, Herbert Sutcliffe, who said the following about fast bowling: 'Some people can play it and some cannot, but if we all tell the truth there is nobody who likes to face it.'

In my opinion a genuine fast bowler should be used in short spells, thus keeping him fresh at all times to be flung into the attack whenever the situation arises. If a fast bowler is used in one-and-a-half and two-hour spells as I was, under some inexperienced skippers he will find that trying to come back, after tea, say, to bowl really fast with a second new ball will be like running a 100-yards sprint wearing a pair of wellingtons. I don't want to sound like an 'ear bashing' old-timer, but I sit and laugh when I read of bowlers, who try to bowl fast, saying they are tired after 20 overs in a day, or 600 overs in a season. I thought nothing of 25 or 30 in a day, or 1,000 or more in a year. I got tired, you bet I did, but I enjoyed bowling so much that I didn't have time to complain.

Before you reach maturity as a fast bowler, you will have to learn to take harsh criticism and listen to grossly exaggerated stories about yourself. These usually come from people who don't know you, who have little or no knowledge at all about the finer points of bowling, or who are able to see your potential – and are loath to admit to it. They will argue fiercely that you cannot bowl straight, that you bowl too short, that you can't swing the ball, that your action is all wrong. Someone in a high position will probably malign you, because at some time or another you have dared to argue with him. All such criticisms will be hurled at you, because you have become a dangerous bowler and could be playing against the club they happen to support.

This is where the frustration and the sweating comes in. You won't be able to understand why you are not in the first eleven when you are sure you are worth your place. But you will have to grin and bear it, and go on striving to turn in the performances that must eventually convince the people who matter.

Fast bowlers come in different shapes and sizes, and I have met bowlers whose build would contradict the theory that height is of great importance. The ideal height, throughout history, has been between 5 ft $9\frac{1}{2}$ in and 6 ft. Over the years the men in this bracket, usually barrel chested, with strong legs and, believe it or not, thin arms, seem to have been the strongest and most consistent. It is also noticeable that most fast bowlers usually carry a broad beam, but whether this has anything to do with their speed I honestly don't know. I was built on these lines and found it a great advantage, because in my first-class career I never pulled a muscle and seldom missed a match.

Fast bowlers usually hunt in pairs, Larwood and Voce, McDonald and Gregory, Lindwall and Miller, to name a few of the famous ones... and, of course, Statham and Trueman. It often applies that their outlook on life is entirely opposite; even their outward appearances are at times noticeably different. On the field their bowling is of the same nature, but of contrasting styles. Brian Statham favoured moving the ball into the batsman, whereas I favoured moving it away. This is where averages rarely tell the full story. The ball leaving the bat will get batsmen out quicker, but in the process it will give more runs away.

Brian moved the ball into the batsman, mainly off the seam. This was because of his high and whippy action and his tendency to bowl wide of the crease, looking down the wicket from the inside of the left elbow, which brought him slightly chest on to the batsman. He was a model of accuracy and personified the 'you miss and I hit' bowler.

In contrast, I favoured bowling close to the stumps, left arm pointing towards fine leg, eyes looking over my left shoulder on the outside of my left elbow, which brought me perfectly sideways on to the batsman. I then had to bring my right arm over and across my body, with my right hand finishing on the outside of my left leg. Being sideways on made me drag my right toe in order to get round, and this enabled me to make the ball move away.

In my own humble opinion there is no finer sight on a field of sport than that of a great fast bowler moving to the wicket in a rhythmic build-up. The greatest of them all was Ray Lindwall. He reminded me of a ballet dancer with his grace and balance as he reached his crescendo before releasing the ball on its 90 mph journey.

Not everyone will reach such perfection, but it is something for which to strive. It will take hours of practice and years of toil to master this exacting art. And it is an art. The truly fast bowler is an artist, and like all great artists he is born, not made.

Alan Knott neatly whips the bails off, but Ian Chappell had his foot back just in time. This stumping attempt by Knott was, however, a remarkable effort. The ball from Derek Underwood went between bat and pad, which meant that Knott did not see it clearly all the time. And to make life more difficult it kept low

Keeping to the Spinners

Alan Knott

This winter I will be returning to the East to play cricket on wickets which have character all of their own. The ball does not rise very high from the lifeless flat wickets and there never seems to be a great deal of pace. This, coupled with the fact that the shine of the ball rapidly disappears on the dry, dusty outfields, makes fast bowling a thankless occupation. The spinners, therefore, are soon in the action, where they stay for most of the day at one end, if not both.

Pakistan have Mushtaq, Pervez and Intikhab, and India have that brilliant threesome, Bedi, Chandra and Venkat to get everything that is possible out of the slow, turning wickets. Our spin attack will be in the capable hands of Pat Pocock, Derek Underwood, Jack Birkenshaw and Norman Gifford.

I have kept wicket to all of them, except Jackie Birkenshaw, which means one of my first jobs will be to get early practice with him in the nets to study his variations and deceptions in flight and spin.

No two bowlers ever seem the same. For example, when Norman Gifford regained his England place, although most people regarded him as a similar bowler to Derek Underwood, I found considerable differences in their styles. He generally bowls slightly slower, from wider of the crease and his lower arm action really angles his left-arm deliveries into the right-hander's body. Balls pitching on the stumps from him, just short of a length, can finish up well down the leg side if they go on with the arm, or alternatively may turn and beat the outside edge – problems for the wicket-keeper!

From what I have said already, you will appreciate how vitally important it is for a wicket-keeper to study the many variations of all his bowlers. This is one of the major reasons I spend many hours in a vacant net with them, bowling exactly as they would in a match, that is with the same run up and at their normal pace.

Sometimes I put a stump in the ground to represent the bat. This can give the bowler a better idea of what length to bowl and also you can have deflections off the stump. A colleague batting can also be a great help, especially if he plays with a stump or an old cut down bat.

I encourage the bowlers to pitch quite a few balls well up to me, even with the occasional half-volley, so that I am accustomed to taking these rare and difficult deliveries. They are difficult because the ball, pitching much closer to you, gives you less time to 'sight' it off the pitch. A full half-volley, however, is a simpler proposition than a ball pitching two to four feet in front of you. The half-volley can be taken just after it has hit the ground, there is no time for any unusual bounce or change of direction, but the ball pitching shorter, especially if it hits in the rough, has enough space to become unpredictable. The time left for you to detect any unusual movement is so brief that these deliveries are the hardest to take, particularly from a spin bowler who is making the ball bite.

If this well-pitched up ball is bowled outside the leg stump, there is a good chance of it coming through to the wicket-keeper, because the batsman, attempting a 'straight bat' shot, is forced to play uncomfortably across his body. Even if he goes for 'the sweep', as most top class players do against the spinner, there is still a good chance of him missing it, because he will invariably be surprised at such an inaccurate delivery and consequently will be late with his shot. The batsman being late often leads to the ball striking his gloves, so possible chances to an alert wicket-keeper may occur.

People often judge a wicket-keeper by the way he takes the ball on the leg-side, but in fact with these deliveries he generally has a sense of anticipation of the ball coming through to him. On the off-side, however, where most half-volleys or full tosses are hit comfortably by the batsman, the wicket-keeper will have to use his full powers of concentration in assuming every ball is coming to him.

On the rare occasion that a top class batsman does play and miss at these deliveries, the ball normally comes under the bat, or between bat and pad, which means at some time the ball is hidden from the wicket-keeper's view. For these reasons, therefore, the off-side work of a wicket-keeper can be as hard if not harder than that on the leg-side, contrary to what most people think.

The shorter pitched ball from a spinner, while giving the wicket-keeper more time to sight it off the pitch, can present the problem of higher bounce. One bowler who seems able to produce this bounce on any kind of wicket is Pat Pocock of Surrey and England, and the wicket-keeper must always be alert to the likelihood of a top-edged catch when a batsman attempts to cut him. His bounce comes from his high action, the tremendous spin that he imparts on the ball and the exceptional 'loop' in his flight.

This 'loop' of Pat's is very deceptive. He often draws the unsuspecting batsman down the wicket to drive. Deceived by the flight the player may well turn the delivery into a yorker and plays over the top of it, or is beaten 'through the gate' by the off spin.

This gives the wicket-keeper the kind of stumping chance which looks easy to the spectator because the batsman is well out of his ground. It must be remembered, though, that he has actually played at the ball only just out of his crease and the momentum of his 'charge' has taken him on, well down the wicket. The wicket-keeper has had the problem of re-sighting the ball as it reappears under the bat, or between bat and pad, making this type of stumping much more difficult than it might look.

On the other hand, when a batsman pushes forward defensively, just dragging his back foot, and is out by half an inch, the stumping is often acclaimed as brilliant. In fact, although the wicket-keeper did well to whip the bails off quickly, he would have seen the good length delivery all the way, with the ball being pitched that much shorter and beating the outside edge of the bat.

So do not judge the difficulty of a stumping chance by the distance a batsman is out of his ground. Rather judge it on where the ball passed the bat and the batsman's body, whether the wicket-keeper was unsighted at some stage, and on what length the ball pitched in relation to the wicket-keeper.

When an off-spinner of Pat Pocock's class is getting the ball to turn, quite a lot of a wicket-

A jubilant Farokh Engineer claims the wicket of Roy Marshall. Standing close to the wicket calls for the sharpest reactions, especially when chances come from batsmen who favour the cut

keeper's work can be taking the ball down the leg-side. Before making your move to the leg-side to take these deliveries, you must try to see the ball off the pitch, and so judge the bounce and deviation. Otherwise you must be just guessing where the ball is coming to you, which on turning wickets can only result in failure.

With the ball pitched right up outside the batsman's legs, or even further than that, you cannot, of course, sight it off the pitch, but you will have logged in your mind the right line from its flight, and moved your gloves behind it. You will then have to judge what height to hold your hands, but with a ball of such full length the amount of lift should be only very small before reaching your gloves. Such deliveries can be extremely difficult to gather when they land in the rough or the bowlers' foot marks.

When I am standing up and see the ball heading for the leg-side, I begin to move my hands to where I feel the ball will end up and also start to lean and move my body towards the line of the ball. However, I leave my head where it is as long as possible so that my eyes peer round the batsman's body to see the ball pitch. My movement to the leg-side is always parallel or forwards, never backwards, and I always try to keep my body weight slightly directed towards the stumps ready for a stumping.

Derek Underwood is another world class spinner to whom I have had the pleasure of wicket-keeping regularly over the last eight years, both for Kent and England. Through the seasons an almost telepathic link has developed between us, so that I feel that I know which of his many varied deliveries he is about to bowl as he starts his run up.

Thinking that some batsmen could also 'work him out', two or three seasons ago Derek changed his approach. He adopted the idea of running in behind the umpire, thus obscuring himself from view, until the last few strides.

While this definitely made life more difficult for the batsman, it also presented me with the problem of not reading him until those last few strides. However, having 'kept' to him for so long my reaction has become almost automatic.

On any type of wicket, Derek is a wonderful bowler, but on a wicket which is giving him any assistance, he can be a real headache to the batsman, and at times also to the wicket-keeper.

On these helpful wickets he bowls at a lively pace and often makes the ball rear awkwardly from a good length. This means that the wicket-keeper must be prepared to take the ball at chest, or even neck, height. In these difficult circumstances, I find that I must keep my body inside the line of the ball, so that if the ball does 'kick' then I can move my hands freely to take the ball with my fingers pointing to the side. With the body kept in line you will find that you are forced to catch these high deliveries with your fingers pointing towards the ball, which if done consistently can lead to bruised or dislocated joints, or even a breakage.

While one is obviously looking for the chances from the outside-edge off the 'spin-ball' and off the glove from the 'lifter', with a bowler of Derek Underwood's class I have always to be on the look-out for his straight-on seamer. He often bowls this as a quick yorker, which with it generally pitching in the rough can be extremely difficult to take, especially as the batsman often plays over the top of it. It was from this type of delivery that I feel I made my best ever stumping. Roger Prideaux attempted a drive but 'dragged' enough to give me the chance to whip off the bails.

There have been days, however, when even Derek has failed to worry the batsman unduly. On one occasion at Lahore, he bowled for two hours without one ball coming through to me. When one did eventually come through and finished up safely in my gloves, he was given a round of ironical applause by his Young England team-mates. This light-hearted incident, however, does illustrate a vital aspect of a wicket-keeper's job: that of believing every ball is coming through to him and into his gloves, so that, even after long spells of the ball not passing the bat, he is always ready for the occasion when it does.

One of the regrettable things about today's County game is the lack of the wrist-spinner, caused by the recent slower English wickets. They can give great pleasure to the spectators and really bring the wicket-keeper into the game by luring the batsman down the wicket. Like the batsman facing this type of bowler, a wicket-keeper has the problem of picking the googly. After hours of practice with the bowler, if he still finds difficulty, then a well disguised pre-arranged signal must be decided upon. There can be nothing more discouraging to a bowler of this type than to deceive the batsman only to see that the ball has also deceived the wicket-keeper, with the batsman out of his ground.

With the wickets gradually improving and gaining in pace, let us hope that the wrist-spinner will again soon become an important feature of our game. Wicket-keepers will certainly welcome them back, because not only are they fun to keep to, but they will also produce more stumpings.

Application and Concentration: Fielding Watchwords

Colin Cowdrey

When I think of the way Clive Lloyd, Colin Bland, or Paul Sheahan can thrill the crowds with their glorious fielding, their superb gifts of athleticism and fitness, it makes me all too aware that the truly great outfielders are born, not made. Close fielding, on the other hand, is different. I know several top-class cricketers – David Sheppard in particular comes to mind – who started off with a weakness but by sheer application and determination reached the highest standard as a short-leg or gully.

Nevertheless, just because we are not born gifted does not mean we can't improve our outfielding with practice and by adhering to the basic principles with a little discipline. You might not be able to bound gracefully around the outfield like a Lloyd or Sheahan, to swoop on the ball and return it with glorious power and freedom, but you could improve your own standard, and in doing so gain a lot more enjoyment from fielding. For example, you can make certain that you watch the ball more carefully as you pick it up before throwing. Don't snatch at it. If the ball is in the air, position yourself more skilfully, especially for the high catch, and try to keep your eyes on the ball all the time. Throwing, both in length and accuracy, you can improve with practice. But don't be too ambitious. Set your sights at a reasonable level so as not to become disheartened too soon. In time you will improve, and your team, especially the bowlers, will benefit from that improvement.

But, whether you practice or not, never think of fielding as a bore. I love fielding, and I always have done. If someone suggests a fielding practice I am the first to volunteer, and I could not have survived in the game for more than 20 years – and am still thirsting to play a little longer – without such enthusiasm. Several of my batsmen colleagues have fallen by the wayside because, as much as they loved their batting, their faces became a study in dejection when the captain came into the dressing room on the first day of a match to say we had lost the toss and were destined for a day in the field.

Mind you, there are days of fielding one does not like to be reminded about. If you had asked my opinion on the game of cricket at lunch on the third day of my first Test match, by which time Australia had batted for seven consecutive sessions in gruelling, humid heat, I would not have been very proud of my reply. But I learnt a lesson; one has to take the rough with the smooth and be determined to maintain a positive, level-headed approach, come what may.

For though fielding demands a good eye, a safe pair of hands, and a few technical tricks, more than anything else it is the mental approach that is so vital for success. Concentration, concentration... and more concentration. It has become a rather over-worn word with regard to sport and sportsmen, and I wish I could think of a new one. But the simple fact is that the cricketer who can learn the art of sensible concentration is the one who is most successful – and this probably applies to fielding more than any other branch of cricket. There is a right way and a wrong way to concentrate.

Sadly, the wrong way is usually born out of an excess of zeal. I see it so often, and I picture it in my mind's eye: the cricketer who arrives very early at the ground, full of pent-up enthusiasm, bursting at the seams with energy and excitement. During the first half hour of play he has spent himself in over-exuberance; after an hour his attention is beginning to wander, and unless the game happens to be exceptional he has to fight with himself to keep concentrating. I know it all so well for I have done precisely this myself.

First, I would like to give you, as an example, Godfrey Evans, who looked as lively in the last over of the day as he did in the first. This he set out to do quite deliberately. That he was able to do it was due to his capacity to switch off his concentration and then switch it on again at the vital moments. As he viewed the whole day in the field ahead, he would not regard it as a six-hour day. Rather, he would think of it as so many vital seconds of concentration to be spent on each ball, and when one comes to think about it in that way it makes a tremendous difference. In any six-hour day you might expect 700 balls to be bowled, and if the wicket-keeper is giving his full attention for something less than ten seconds a ball, he has to give rather less than two hours total absorption to the game.

How does this work out in practice? Those of you who idolised Godfrey Evans, as I did, will recall that as the bowler turned at the end of his run Godfrey would knock his gloves together before assuming the crouched position. This was a conscious action to switch on his concentration, and from that moment until the stroke was completed and he was no longer required in the action, nothing short of an earthquake would divert his eye from watching the ball. Then, just as quickly as he had switched on his concentration he would switch it off, only for a few seconds – the vital seconds needed to recharge the battery in readiness for the next spurt.

Godfrey Evans's method taught me that the key to it all was to be able to rivet one's attention at the vital moment to the vital spot – and that is all that mattered. To keep up a state of anxious suspense throughout was a needless sapping of nervous energy and was quite ineffective when it came to holding catches.

I have elaborated this at some length purposely. The art of sensible concentration is not inborn; it has to be learnt and adapted to our game by trial and error. In the same way as Godfrey Evans touched his gloves together, I try to say something to myself just before the bowler bowls. I rivet my attention on the outside edge of the bat, and just before the batsman strikes the ball I try to say to myself, under my breath, 'Catch it'. In this way I can stay relaxed until the last possible moment and perhaps concentrate fully for only two or three seconds on each delivery. In terms of effectiveness, I am achieving much more than if I were to stay crouched in a tense state throughout the bowler's run-up.

At both Test and County level, I have taken a lot of catches, and I have dropped my share as well. But one thing I am certain; I have never dropped a catch if my hands were properly warm and my eye had a clear view of the ball from the edge of the bat. Without warm hands, catching can be a nightmare. Fielding on overseas tours under a hot sun is such a delight. But what agonies our visiting teams have to undergo in April or May!

What can one do on a cold day? I make a point of filling a basin with hot water, as hot as my hands will stand, and soaking my hands for three or four minutes just before the umpires are due to go out. Even on a reasonable day, should there be a chilly wind, it is worth running the hot tap over the palms for a few minutes. For, by immersing the hands in hot water, one is artificially creating that same feeling of warmth and puffiness that comes into the fingers after a sharp ten-minute practice session of short catches.

If this sounds trivial, I challenge you, next April on a cold, grey day, to submit yourself to this experiment. Go straight out, without any preparation, and ask someone to hit you 20 catches, fairly firmly, from a distance of six to eight yards. The first dozen will really sting, and only the last two or three will start to go into the hands properly, if they are not already bruised. Next time, on a cold or grey day, warm your hands first and you will find those 20 catches will be so much easier.

The problem of background is not nearly as easy to control. Few people realise the significance of a good background for catching. Luck really does play a part. I still feel the heart beat when I remember a day at second slip in a Lord's Test when Freddie Trueman, bowling from the pavilion end, found the outside edge of Conrad Hunte's bat. I saw the ball leave the edge of the bat very clearly, but almost at once it seemed to disappear against the bright red-coloured brickwork of the pavilion and I was conscious only of a haze. I simply could not focus the position or the speed it was travelling – and I panicked. Suddenly the ball moved out of the edge of the brickwork and was mirrored against the white lunch marquee. I got a picture again, shot my left hand up, not to catch it but just in time to knock it into the air and then catch it as it came down. It was flukey, of course. But as I had a clear picture to start with and my hands were warm, I am sure I would have caught it – until I lost sight of it. Once that happened I was in real trouble.

You can help yourself in this matter of background. When you take up a new position in the field, assess the line along which a likely catch is going to come and then see if moving a yard or two to the left or the right can help your vision. Often you will find a move of one yard will alter the background from the red tiles of a house, some red cars, or a tree to something better. Bobby Simpson once told me that in Australia, where the bright coloured shirts of a crowd can make life difficult, he rarely bends down low. By standing up, unorthodox as that may sound, he is able to create a background for catching out of the white-painted fences around the ground and so has a better chance of pulling off a catch. Awareness of background is much more important than is generally realised.

Fitness, practice, concentration, warm hands, and a good background – all these, then, contribute to the fun and success of fielding. A high standard of fielding, close to the wicket or in the outfield, is something well worth striving for, because fielding has always been the key to winning matches. Look how Kent's performances in the field helped them win the John Player League last season. And remember how Barry Wood dramatically swung the last one-day international against Australia England's way with his inspired fielding. Indeed, the advent of limited-overs cricket, with its extra pressures, has heightened the significance of fielding, and for this we should be grateful. Cricket must be entertaining, and good fielding, at any level, is one of the great enjoyments of the game.

Learning from the Stars

The Forward Defensive

The forward defensive stroke is not only the most used stroke in cricket, but without it no batsman can hope to remain at the crease for any length of time. For those who shudder at the word defensive, I must point out that this shot is merely an extension of the drive and, although the main aim of every player is, normally, to score runs, good bowlers make sure that this is not possible off every delivery.

The forward defensive stroke provides the perfect counter to the good length, straight, ball, especially the one that breaks, or moves after pitching. It is particularly valuable against both the spinner and the medium-paced seamer, but it can be physically dangerous against a genuine fast bowler, unless the wicket is extremely passive.

Here we see Tony Lewis employing the forward defensive with locked wrists and no follow-through. The picture has been taken immediately after contact, and the stroke has effectively killed the ball.

Points to note:—

The straight bat which is angled to make absolutely sure the ball is kept on the ground.

The head right over the ball and the bent left leg.

The bat and pad close together so that there is no chance of being bowled 'through the gate'.

The weight on the left foot, but the right remaining behind the crease to eliminate all chances of being stumped should the ball turn sufficiently to beat the bat.

Learning from the Stars

The Off Drive

The off drive is normally used to a half volley pitching just outside the off stump. A class player, like Boycott, can also play the stroke on the up, yet still keep the ball on the carpet. Lesser mortals, however, would be wise to employ it against overpitched deliveries.

The bat is brought down in a pendulum and should meet the ball with the full face. At the top of the backswing for the off drive the bat should be pointing towards fine leg.

In this picture Geoff Boycott has sent the ball between cover and extra and has opened his shoulders in the follow-through. At the moment of contact his left shoulder was pointing at the ball and on this occasion he has deliberately timed the shot a shade late to avoid the fieldsmen.

Points to note:—

The weight firmly on the bent left leg with the left foot pointing towards mid-off. A common fault is for the left foot to point up the wicket which, when playing the off drive, means that the batsman is inclined to swing across the line and in consequence is in danger of being caught out in the slips, or at the wicket.

The weight is on the left foot, but Boycott has not made the very common error of walking, or dragging his right foot.

The obvious control, concentration, and timing which have combined to produce an exquisite boundary.

Driving Off the Back Foot

The ability to drive off the back foot is the sure sign of the class batsman. It is played to the short ball with an absolutely straight bat and a full follow-through. The foot moves back, but not quite as far across as in the back defensive, in order to give sufficient room for the swing of the bat.

It supplies the perfect answer to the medium pacer who can contain the scoring by bowling straight and just short of a length.

In this picture Mike Denness is driving through the covers off the back foot. At the moment of contact he was sideways on, but has opened up in the follow-through.

Points to note:—

The position of the right foot.

Denness has risen on to his toes, because of the bounce of the ball and because he wants to get right over it to keep it along the ground.

One of the main reasons why batsmen have difficulty in playing this shot is that they are unable to achieve a perpendicular swing of the bat, and become too square on at the moment of contact. One way to ensure that this does not occur is to have the right foot parallel to the batting crease.

Learning from the Stars

The Square Cut

The square cut is a cross-bat stroke played to a short ball outside the off stump which has not risen too high. There are two golden rules to remember about this lucrative shot. First, cut down and roll the right wrist at moment of contact to keep the ball on the ground. Secondly, cut as hard as possible. This will not only increase the chances of beating the field, but it will also decrease the likelihood of giving a chance, should the stroke be edged. A mistimed, full-blooded cut tends to fly over the heads of the slips rather than provide a catch.

This picture shows Keith Fletcher on his way to one of the most spectacular centuries of the season against Yorkshire. He has already sent the ball scudding to the boundary and has reached his follow-through.

Points to note:—

Fletcher has moved his right foot back and across the wicket.

He has leaned into the stroke to provide extra power and control. A common fault is to lean back.

Because the ball has lifted a little, Keith has risen on his right foot to give himself additional leverage.

All the weight is clearly on his right foot.

The wrists have been rolled.

In general it can be said that cutting off-spinners invites trouble, and to do it on a turning wicket is suicidal.

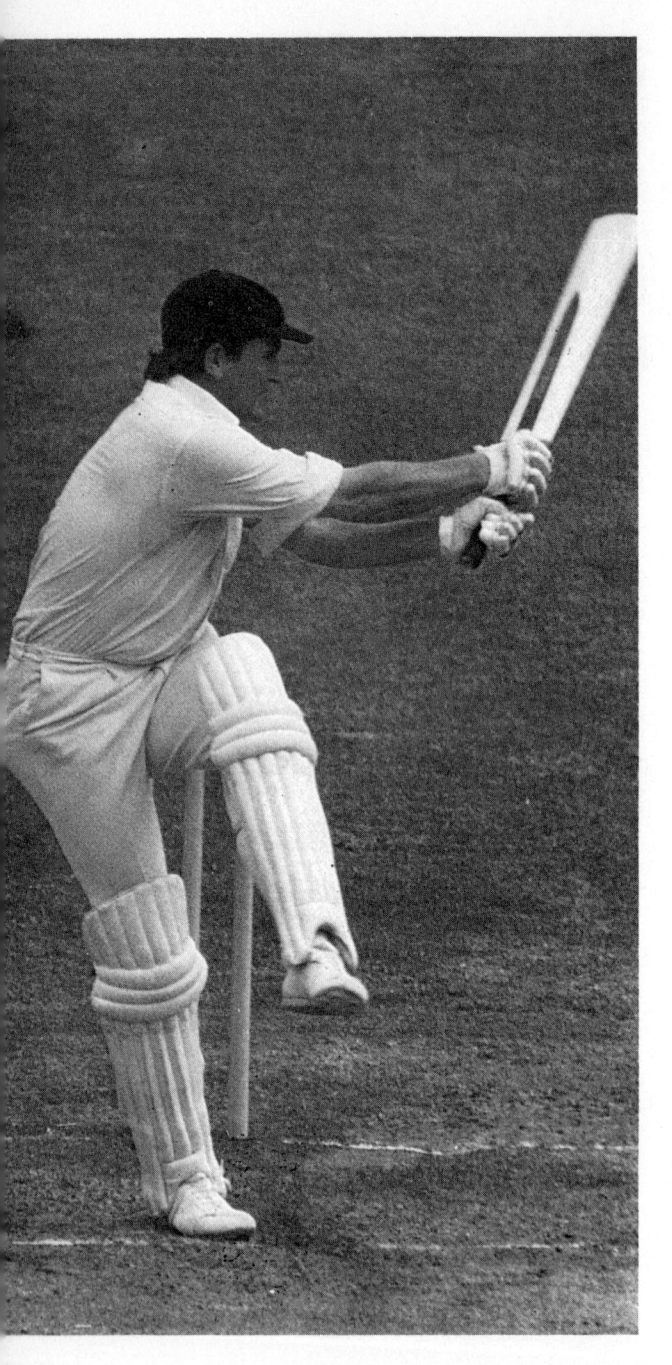

The Hook

The hook is played to a short, fast, rising ball and is the one effective and productive method of dealing with the bouncer. The batsman moves back and across his stumps to give himself time and to get inside the line of the ball. If he fails to make contact it will merely pass over his left shoulder. Some of the finest hookers are prepared to play the stroke immediately in front of their face, but this method is advisable only for the expert.

The stroke is made with a cross bat and, because the ball will often be travelling fast somewhere between the batsman's chest and throat it is not an easy shot to perfect. Obviously the quicker the bowler the more difficult and dangerous in both respects it becomes. A common error is to try to play the stroke to a ball that has risen too high. The outcome is that the bat cannot be horizontal at impact, which increases the chance of giving a catch.

In this picture Keith Stackpole has hooked a short ball to the boundary in the Lord's Test. It is a stroke in which he revels.

Points to note:—

Stackpole has moved back and across his wicket.

He has rolled his wrists to keep the ball down. It is easier to hook up, and if the ball has bounced above a certain height, impossible to do anything else. But there is a chance of being caught out on the boundary, as Ian Chappell found to his cost. On this occasion Stackpole sent the ball along the ground to the square-leg boundary.

The power of the stroke has been such that he has swivelled right round on his right foot and has lifted his left leg after contact, as his shoulders have moved into the follow-through.

Learning from the Stars

The Off-break

This picture was taken of Ray Illingworth in the fourth Test at Headingley. He is bowling his off-breaks from over the wicket. The ball is just about to be released with the break itself obtained by a combination of the fingers, especially the first, and a sharply turned wrist. He has landed on a braced left leg with his toe pointing towards fine-leg and has already started to swivel round and rise on the toes because his left shoulder has moved into the body action.

What is especially interesting is that the left foot has come down in *front of the leg stump* and this means that he lets go of the ball just about in line between wickets.

The advantages of an off-spinner bowling so close to the stumps are considerable.

He can obtain an lbw that would be denied to him if he had bowled exactly the same ball from wide of the crease.

From this position it is far easier to make the odd ball run away, or leave the righthanded batsman. This is a most important delivery for an off-spinner to have in his armoury, particularly on good pitches. Ray bowls and conceals this ball very cunningly, and it has brought him many victims over the years, either caught by the 'keeper or at first slip.

An off-spinner should cultivate the one which goes with his arm, but he must learn to do this without changing his grip to that of a seamer, since any good batsman will spot this immediately.

A Glorious Action

One of the main reasons why Dennis Lillee is the fastest bowler since Wes Hall, and is able to maintain his pace for so long, is his perfect body action. It could be argued that his run-up is too long, although he is perfectly entitled to answer by simply pointing to the number of wickets he has taken.

The purpose of a run-up is to provide the bowler with added impetus for the actual body action which begins during the last but one stride of the run-up. In order to gain maximum speed it is necessary to spring the last pace from the left foot (on to the right foot) at the same time twisting the body so that the left shoulder is pointing down the wicket. This is exactly what Lillee is doing in pictures (a) and (b). Note how, from running normally, he has swung his left shoulder right round and how, in picture (b), his body is leaning back to produce a catapult effect when he grounds his right foot.

When the right foot comes down it should land behind and parallel to the bowling crease. The weight should be on the right leg and the body should be leaning slightly away from the batsman. The left arm should be high, with the bowler looking round the left-hand, not the right-hand, side. All these points can be seen in picture (c).

From the ideal position arrived at in picture (c) Lillee is perfectly placed to uncoil. He will come down hard on the braced left leg. His left arm will be thrown out towards the batsman and his right arm will be flung back to a position behind his right buttock before being brought over to chase his left arm across his body.

The ball which is held between fingers and thumb is released from a high right arm immediately the left foot has hit the deck.

Notice the loose wrist in picture (a) which helps to give just a little extra zip. The height of a bowler's leap will depend on his pace. In the case of Lillee, who runs up very fast, it is considerable.

Register of County Cricketers

Register of County Cricketers

All first-class career and Test match statistics are complete to the end of the 1972 season, but where a player has improved his highest score or best bowling analysis in the 1972–73 overseas season, before this Yearbook went to press, these have been amended.

The forename by which a player is known is in bold type, and the county in which a player was born is given only when this differs from the one he now represents.

Test match records include the 1970 England v Rest of the World series and all Tests involving South Africa and Pakistan since those countries left the Commonwealth. As the Australian Board of Control stated that the 1970–71 Australia v Rest of the World matches were not Tests these are excluded.

Abbreviations

*	Not out
†	Played first-class cricket in 1972–73 season
av	Average
b	Born
BB	Best innings bowling analysis
cap	Awarded county 1st XI cap
ct	Catches
F-c	First-class
HS	Highest score
LB	Bowls leg-breaks
LF	Bowls left-arm fast
LFM	Bowls left-arm fast-medium
LHB	Bats left-handed
LM	Bowls left-arm medium
OB	Bowls off-breaks
occ	Occasional
RF	Bowls right-arm fast
RFM	Bowls right-arm fast-medium
RHB	Bats right-handed
RM	Bowls right-arm medium
SLA	Bowls orthodox slow left-arm
SLC	Bowls slow left-arm 'chinamen'
st	Stumpings
WK	Wicket-keeper

ABBERLEY, Robert Neal, b Birmingham 22 Apr 44. RHB, occ OB. WARWICKSHIRE cap 1966. F-c career: 6,191 runs (av 24.56) 2 hundreds; 2 wkts (av 74.50) HS 117* v Essex (Birmingham) 1966. BB 2–19 v Oxford U. (Oxford) 1972.

Neat, rather on-side conscious, opening bat whose opportunities for f-c cricket have been limited lately.

ACFIELD, David Laurence, b Chelmsford 24 Jul 47. RHB, OB. ESSEX cap 1970. F-c career: 767 runs (av 8.24); 313 wkts (av 28.69). HS 42 Cambridge U. v Leics (Leicester) 1967. BB 6–28 Cambridge U. v Sussex (Cambridge) 1967.

Extremely accurate off-break bowler who is also effective in limited-overs cricket. He is not a big finger spinner, but is capable of winning a match on a pitch giving assistance.

†AMISS, Dennis Leslie, b Birmingham 7 Apr 43. RHB, occ SLA/LM. WARWICKSHIRE cap 1965. 10 England caps 1966-71, scoring 317 runs (av 21.13), HS 56. F-c career: 14,173 runs (av 36.34), 23 hundreds; 14 wkts (av 37.07). HS 192 v Lancs (Birmingham) 1972 BB 3-21 v Middx (Lord's) 1970.

A talented batsman who has consistently failed to do himself justice at Test match level. Originally a middle-order strokemaker, he gained a new lease of life when he began to open for Warwickshire and went in that role to India and Pakistan with the MCC. He is still young enough to make the grade in international cricket. His grip is rather low for an attacking batsman and he does occasionally become becalmed. A fine fieldsman, especially close to the wicket.

†ARNOLD, Geoffrey Graham, b Earlsfield 3 Sep 44. RHB, RFM. SURREY cap 1967. 6 England caps 1967-72 scoring 102 runs. (av 17.00), HS 59, and taking 21 wkts (av 21.71), BB 5-58. F-c career: 1,902 runs (av 13.78); 573 wkts (av 20.91). HS 73 MCC under-25 v Central Zone (Sahiwal) 1966-67. BB 8-41 v Glos (Oval) 1967.

A fine opening bowler with a very late away-swing. He has excellent control and, though not truly fast, has a good bouncer. Powerfully built, he can be relied upon to bowl for long spells. Takes the dropping of catches (and he suffered cruelly in last season's Old Trafford Test against Australia) rather more philosophically than most of his breed. A useful tail-end bat who hits straight.

†ASIF IQBAL RAZVI, b Hyderabad, India 6 Jun 43. RHB, RM. KENT cap 1968. 20 Pakistan caps 1964-71, scoring 1,032 runs (av 33.29) with 2 hundreds, HS 146, and taking 44 wkts (av 24.31), BB 5-48. F-c career: 10,487 runs (av 35.30), 14 hundreds; 223 wkts (av 30.13). HS 175 Pakistan v New Zealand (Dunedin) 1972-73. BB 6-45 Pakistan Eaglets v Cambridge U. (Cambridge) 1963.

An exciting strokemaker, capable of changing the course of any game by the virtuosity of his batting. He is a graceful and exciting batsman who is very quick on his feet. He is at his most effective when attacking. A useful seam and swing bowler, but not often used in this capacity owing to a suspect back. A brilliant all-purpose fieldsman.

BAILEY, Raymond Reginald, b Bedford, Beds 16 May 44. RHB, RFM. NORTHAMPTONSHIRE – uncapped. F-c career: 253 runs (av 9.37) 108 wkts (av 26.90). HS 25 v Middx (Lord's) 1971. BB 5-25 v Hants (Northampton) 1964.

Fast medium opening bowler who excelled in the John Player League but was something of a disappointment in Championship matches, for which he was unable to command a regular place.

BAIRSTOW, David Leslie, b Bradford 1 Sep 51. RHB, WK. YORKSHIRE – uncapped. F-c career: 1,083 runs (av 14.83); 166 dismissals (149 ct, 17 st). HS 67* v Notts (Leeds) 1971.

Most competent wicket-keeper who promises to become even better. Also promising batsman.

BAKER, Richard Kenneth, b Gidea Park 28 Apr 52. RHB, WK. ESSEX – uncapped. F-c career (1 match): 14 runs; 2 dismissals. HS 14* v Kent (Maidstone) 1972.

A promising wicket-keeper, now at Cambridge University, who deputised for the injured Taylor in one match last season.

A full-blooded pull from Asif Iqbal, Kent's dashing Pakistani strokemaker. His willingness to attack all bowling makes him ideal for the one-day game

BALDERSTONE, John **Christopher,** b Huddersfield, Yorks 16 Nov 40. RHB, SLA. LEICESTERSHIRE – uncapped. Played for Yorks 1961–69. F-c career: 1,944 runs (av 21.13); 57 wkts (av 20.94). HS 82 Yorks v Indians (Sheffield) 1967. BB 6–84 v Derbys (Leicester) 1971.

An experienced all-rounder who could walk into most county teams. His soccer career leaves him with less than half a season's cricket.

BARCLAY, John Robert Troutbeck, b Bonn, West Germany 22 Jan 54. RHB, OB. SUSSEX – uncapped. F-c career: 43 runs (av. 4.77); 1 wkt. HS 25 v Essex (Hove) 1972. BB 1–24.

An outstanding schoolboy all-rounder who captained Eton 1970–72 and led the first touring team of England Young Cricketers to the West Indies last year.

BARLOW, Graham Derek, b Folkestone, Kent 26 Mar 50. LHB. MIDDLESEX – uncapped. F-c career: 194 runs (av 19.40). HS 38 v Glam (Lord's) 1970.

Brilliant schoolboy batsman whose opportunities are limited by studies at Loughborough Colleges.

†**BEDI, Bishen** Singh, b Amritsar, India 25 Sep 46. RHB, SLA. NORTHAMPTONSHIRE cap 1972. 27 India caps 1966–71, scoring 253 runs (av 8.43), HS 22, and taking 96 wkts (av 28.94), BB 7–98. F-c career: 1,404 runs (av 10.55); 594 wkts (av 21.64), 1 hat-trick. HS 61 Delhi v Jammu & Kashmir (Srinagar) 1970–71. BB 7–19 N. Zone v S. Zone (Madras) 1969–70.

Slow left-arm bowler in the classic mould. He has superb control and the skill to deceive opponents in the air, as well as off the pitch. This is one of the reasons he has been so successful in Tests on India's perfect pitches, where the ball seldom deviates to any extent. A joy to watch and a true weaver of spells.

†BIRKENSHAW, Jack, b Rothwell, Yorks 13 Nov 40. LHB, OB. LEICESTERSHIRE cap 1965. Played for Yorks 1958–60. England debut in India 1972–73. F-c career: 8,242 runs (av 22.15), 3 hundreds; 714 wkts (av 26.27), 2 hat-tricks. HS 131 v Surrey (Guildford) 1969. BB 8–94 v Somerset (Taunton) 1972.

A fine all-rounder who is inclined to be underrated. He is not helped by living in the shadow of his captain who is similar – and even better. Spins his off-breaks considerably and has a deceptive, dipping flight. Relatively more dangerous on a dry, than a wet, turner. Steady, stubborn batsman, always difficult to remove and a good fighter, who is especially sound against spin bowling.

BLACK, Christopher James Robert ('Sam'), b Johannesburg, South Africa 15 Dec 47. RHB, RM MIDDLESEX – uncapped. F-c career: 246 runs (av 15.37); 9 wkts (av 50.66). HS 71 v Hants (Lord's) 1971. BB 3–51 v Cambridge U. (Cambridge) 1971.

Talented and aggressive all-rounder who has done well in limited-overs matches. Has had few opportunities at f-c level.

BLENKIRON, William, b Newfield, Co Durham 21 Jul 42. RHB, RFM. WARWICKSHIRE cap 1969. F-c career: 1,266 (av 13.91); 268 wkts (av 28.16). HS 62 v Worcs (Dudley) 1969. BB 5–37 v Leics (Leicester) 1968.

Honest, strongly-built seamer with a big heart.

BOLUS, John Brian, b Whitkirk, Yorks 31 Jan 34. RHB, occ LM. DERBYSHIRE cap 1973. Appointed captain 1973. Played for Yorks 1956–62 and for Notts 1963–72 (captain 1972). The third player after R. Berry and R. Swetman to be capped by three f-c counties and the first to captain different counties in successive seasons. 7 England caps 1963–64, scoring 496 runs (av 41.33), HS 88. F-c career: 22,319 runs (av 34.38), 35 hundreds; 24 wkts (av 36.91). HS 202* Notts v Glam (Nottingham) 1963. BB 4–40 Yorks v Pakistanis (Bradford) 1962.

Knowledgeable and thoroughly dependable bat, strong off his legs. Though usually seen in a grafting role, he has been known to cut and carve gayly – not merely for the odd innings but for long periods. At his peak he was an opening bat, but now can be relied on to bring stability to the middle batting.

BOOTH, Brian Joseph, b Blackburn, Lancs 3 Dec 35. RHB, occ LB. LEICESTERSHIRE cap 1964. Played for Lancs 1956–63. F-c career: 15,275 runs (av 27.97), 18 hundreds; 143 wkts (av 32.39). HS 183* Lancs v Oxford U. (Manchester) 1961. BB 7–143 Lancs v Worcs (Southport) 1959.

An experienced batsman who sensibly keeps within his limitations. Very right-handed and open, he is inclined to play across the line more than most. An occasional purveyor of leg-breaks.

BORE, Michael Kenneth, b Hull 2 Jun 47. RHB, LM/SLA. YORKSHIRE – uncapped. F-c career: 194 runs (av 7.18); 90 wkts (av 28.31). HS 21* v Northants (Northampton) 1970. BB 6–63 v Glos (Sheffield) 1971.

Came into the Yorkshire team in 1969 as a left-arm seamer of military medium pace but has since been converted into a spinner operating just below Underwood's pace.

BORRINGTON, Anthony John, b Derby 8 Dec 48. RHB, occ LB. DERBYSHIRE – uncapped. F-c career: 408 runs (av 21.47). HS 70 v Essex (Ilford) 1971 – on debut.

Studies at Loughborough Colleges have so far curtailed opportunities for this highly promising opening batsman.

†**BOYCE, Keith** David, b St Peter, Barbados 11 Oct 43. RHB, RFM. ESSEX cap 1967. 1 West Indies cap 1970–71. F-c career: 5,787 runs (av 21.51), 3 hundreds; 534 wkts (av 25.02). HS 147* v Hants (Ilford) 1969. BB 9–61 v Cambridge U. (Brentwood) 1966 – on Essex debut.

A natural entertainer, worth watching whether batting, bowling or in the field because there is such a grace about his movements. Would score more runs if he were prepared to restrain his natural aggression a little, but does hit the ball exceptionally hard. Even when mistimed, it will often carry the boundary. A lively fast bowler who has become even more effective since learning to deliver from closer to the stumps. A world-class fielder; it is doubtful if there is a finer performer in every position at the present time. Possesses a deadly throw of high velocity.

BOYCOTT, Geoffrey, b Fitzwilliam 21 Oct 40. RHB, occ RM. YORKSHIRE cap 1963. Captain since 1971. 53 England caps 1964–72, scoring 3,880 runs (av 48.50) with 11 hundreds, HS 246*, and taking 7 wkts (av 49.42), BB 3–47. F-c career: 22,416 runs (av 54.01), 68 hundreds; 21 wkts (av 44.95). Only English batsman to average 100 in a home season: 100.12 in 1971. HS 260* v Essex (Colchester) 1970 BB 3–47 England v South Africa (Cape Town) 1964–65.

A great opening bat with a superb technique who is especially adept at hitting boundaries off the back foot through the covers. Currently England's finest batsman, he passionately loves batting and is perhaps the finest acquirer of runs in the world. Has made himself into a good cover fielder through application.

BRAIN, Brian Maurice, b Worcester 13 Sep 40. RHB, RFM. WORCESTERSHIRE cap 1966. F-c career: 497 runs (av 6.80); 288 wkts (av 26.06). HS 38 v Glos (Cheltenham) 1964. BB 6–38 v Notts (Nottingham) 1969.

Tall, lean, fast-medium bowler who retired from f-c cricket in 1971 but who is still available for one-day matches.

BREAKWELL, Dennis, b Brierley Hill, Staffs 2 Jul 48. LHB, SLA. SOMERSET – uncapped. Played for Northants 1969–72. F-c career: 1,015 runs (av 15.85); 141 wkts (av 26.03). HS 97 Northants v Derbys (Chesterfield) 1970. BB 8–39 Northants v Kent (Dover) 1970.

One of the most promising of the young left-arm spinners. Decided to move because of the arrival of Bedi. His batting also shows promise.

BREARLEY, John **Michael,** b Harrow 28 Apr 42. RHB, occ WK. MIDDLESEX cap 1964. Captain since 1971. F-c career: 10,793 runs (av 33.41), 13 hundreds; 227 dismissals (215 ct, 12 st); 1 wkt. HS 312* MCC under-25 v N. Zone (Peshawar) 1966–67. BB 1–21.

A fine captain and a good batsman who has yet to produce for Middlesex the big innings his

Mike Brearley of Middlesex

ability promises. Although he scores plenty of runs, the centuries elude him – which makes one wonder whether there is something slightly wrong with his basic technique.

BRIERS, Nigel Edwin, b Leicester 15 Jan 55. RHB. LEICESTERSHIRE – uncapped. F-c career (2 matches): 26 runs (av 13.00). HS 12* v Cambridge U. (Cambridge) 1971.

Leicestershire's youngest f-c cricketer, he was 16 years and 104 days on debut and is still attending Lutterworth Grammar School. Exceptionally promising colt.

†BROWN, Anthony Stephen, b Bristol 24 Jun 36. RHB,RM. GLOUCESTERSHIRE cap 1957. Captain since 1969. F-c career: 10,549 runs (av 17.87), 3 hundreds: 1,045 wkts (av 25.69); 419 ct. HS 116 v Somerset (Bristol)1971. BB 8–80 v Essex (Leyton) 1963. Held 7 catches in an innings v Notts (Nottingham) 1966 to set world record.

Far better all-rounder than is generally appreciated with over 10,000 runs and 1,000 wickets to his credit. A natural free-scoring bat, and a seamer who has the advantage of being more difficult to play than he looks. He has led Gloucester with great keenness and considerable success.

†BROWN, David John, b Walsall, Staffs 30 Jan 42. RHB,RFM. WARWICKSHIRE cap 1964. 28 England caps 1965–70, scoring 390 runs (av 12.18), HS 44*, and taking 82 wkts (av 29.63) BB 5–42. F-c career: 2,951 runs (av 13.00); 776 wkts (av 24.51). HS 79 v Derbys (Birmingham) 1972. BB 8–64 v Sussex (Birmingham) 1964.

Big hearted fast bowler who never gives up. This important attribute accounted for the fact that he did rather better in Test matches than his ability warranted. His height and action enable him to extract bounce and he has refused to be dismayed by the setbacks he has experienced through injury. Stubborn tail-ender who plays straight.

BURGESS, Graham Iefvion, b Glastonbury 5 May 43. RHB,RM. SOMERSET cap 1968. F-c career: 4,240 runs (av 17.96); 237 wkts (av 29.15). HS 73 v Yorks (Taunton) 1971. BB 6–51 v Glos (Bath) 1971.

Useful county all-rounder. Hard hitting bat who has not quite lived up to his early promise, but on the other hand his medium-paced seam bowling has improved considerably.

BUSS, Antony, b Brightling 1 Sep 39. RHB, RFM. SUSSEX cap 1963. F-c career: 4,177 runs (av 13.26); 927 wkts (av 24.84), 2 hat-tricks. HS 83 v Northants (Hove) 1969. BB 8–23 v Notts (Hove) 1966.

Wiry opening bowler who, though not quick, does move the ball about and has a leg-cutter that really bites.

†BUSS Michael Alan, b Brightling 24 Jan 44. Brother of A. Buss. LHB,SLA/LM. SUSSEX cap 1967. F-c career: 8,279 runs (av 25.01), 8 hundreds; 326 wkts (av 29.31). HS 159 v Glam (Swansea) 1967. BB 7–58 v Hants (Bournemouth) 1970.

Attractive left-handed opening bat who likes going for his shots and drives sweetly. His nagging swing bowling is difficult to get away.

BUTCHER, Alan Raymond, b Croydon 7 Jan 54. LHB,LM. SURREY – uncapped. F-c career: 28 runs (av 9.33); 11 wkts (av 25.54). HS 20 and BB 6–48 v Hants (Guildford) 1972.

A most talented left-handed all-rounder for whom Surrey followers predict great things. He came into the senior team immediately on leaving Heath Clark Grammar School last July and this will be his first full season.

BUXTON, Ian Ray, b Cromford 17 Apr 38. RHB,RM. DERBYSHIRE cap 1962. Captain 1970–72. F-c career: 11,063 runs (av 23.89), 5 hundreds; 454 wkts (av 25.97), 1 hat-trick, HS 118* v Lancs (Derby) 1964. BB 7–33 v Oxford U. (Derby) 1969.

Competent county all-rounder. Attractive middle-order bat with a high backlift and a liking for the drive; natural medium-paced in-dipper with a good leg-cutter.

CARTWRIGHT, Harold, b Halfway 12 May 51. RHB. DERBYSHIRE – uncapped.

A promising batsman and superb cover fielder whose opportunities have so far been restricted to 14 limited-overs matches spread across two seasons.

CARTWRIGHT, Thomas William, b Coventry, Warwicks 22 Jul 35. RHB,RM. SOMERSET cap 1970. Played for Warwicks 1952–69. 5 England caps 1964–65, scoring 26 runs (av 5.20) and taking 15 wkts (av 36.26), BB 6–94. F-c career: 13,075 runs (av 21.86), 7 hundreds; 1,396 wkts (av 19.26), 1 hat-trick; 307 ct. HS 210 Warwicks v Middx (Nuneaton) 1962. BB 8–39 Warwicks v Somerset (Weston-s-Mare) 1962.

Outstanding medium-paced seam bowler with exceptional control. Originally an inswinger, he now moves the ball either way and gives absolutely nothing away. His action is very high, and he can be deadly on green or crumbling pitches. An effective, rather than attractive, middle-order bat with a distinct partiality for the sweep.

†CASS, George Rodney, b Overton, Yorks 23 Apr 40. LHB,WK. WORCESTERSHIRE cap 1970. Played for Essex 1964–67. F-c career: 2,811 runs (av 19.65), 1 hundred; 136 dismissals (116 ct, 20 st). HS 104* Essex v Warwicks (Birmingham) 1967.

Determined wicket-keeper batsman who has refused to be discouraged despite several setbacks through injury.

CLAPP, Robert John, b Weston-super-Mare 12 Dec 48. RHB,RM. SOMERSET – uncapped. F-c career (1 match): 3 wkts (av 39.33). BB 2–48 v Kent (Glastonbury) 1972.

Reserve seam bowler who is a master at Trent College.

CLIFFORD, Christopher Craven, b Hovingham 5 Jul 42. RHB,OB. YORKSHIRE – uncapped. F-c career: 39 runs (av 4.87); 26 wkts (av 25.61). HS 12* v Lancs (Manchester) 1972. BB 5–70 v Surrey (Oval) 1972.

Schoolmaster who first appeared for Yorkshire 2nd XI in 1963 and who in 1972 returned from South Africa in time to replace the unfortunate Cope in the 1st team. Immediately proved himself worthy of the honour.

†CLOSE, Dennis Brian, b Rawdon, Yorks 24 Feb 31. LHB,RM/OB. SOMERSET cap 1971. Captain since 1972. Played for Yorks 1949–70 (captain 1963–70). Did the 'double' and was awarded York cap in his first season (1949). 19 England caps 1949–67 (7 as captain), scoring 721 runs (av 24.03), HS 70, and taking 18 wkts (av 29.55), BB 4–35. Recalled to lead England in Prudential Trophy one-day internationals v Australia 1972. F-c career: 29,125 runs (av 32.98), 46 hundreds; 1,087 wkts (av 25.65); 692 ct, 1 st. HS 198 Yorks v Surrey (Oval) 1960. BB 8–41 Yorks v Kent (Leeds) 1959.

One of the most naturally talented players to come into cricket since World War II, yet he failed to establish himself as a permanent member of the England side. A fine left-hand bat strong in attack and defence, an off-spin bowler and seamer, and a brilliant fielder anywhere, he eventually proved himself a fine skipper with a deep knowledge of the game. Displays great physical courage fielding in suicidal positions and standing up to the really fast bowlers. Now primarily a batsman, he retains the eye and reaction to pick up good length deliveries and deposit them over the boundary. He has had two most successful seasons with Somerset.

COOK, Geoffrey, b Middlesbrough, Yorks 9 Oct 51. RHB. NORTHAMPTONSHIRE – uncapped. F-c career: 1,517 runs (av 25.71), 1 hundred. HS 122* v Sussex (Hove) 1971.

Highly promising young batsman who is one of the few under-25s currently commanding a place in a county XI. If he continues to improve, he might well attain highest honours.

COOKE, Robert Michael Oliver, b Adlington, Lancs 3 Sep 43. LHB, occ LB. ESSEX – uncapped. F-c career (1 match): 46 runs (av 23.00). HS 43 Minor Counties v Australians (Longton) 1972.

A newcomer to the Essex camp, this hard-hitting, left-handed, bespectacled batsman has played many remarkable innings for Lancashire 2nd XI and Cheshire. Could be an exciting prospect.

COOPER, Howard Pennett, b Bradford 17 Apr 49. LHB, RM. YORKSHIRE – uncapped. F-c career: 104 runs (av 10.40); 33 wkts (av 22.87). HS 47 v Surrey (Scarborough) 1972. BB 4–37 v Hants (Southampton) 1972.

Talented seam bowler who has quickly adapted to both forms of cricket. His batting could develop sufficiently to lift him into the 'all-rounder' category.

COOPER, Richard Claude, b Malmesbury, Wiltshire 9 Dec 45. RHB. SOMERSET – uncapped. F-c career (1 match): 4 runs.

Heavyweight batsman who strikes the ball with the power one would expect from a discus and shot-put specialist. Availability limited to one-day matches.

COPE, Geoffrey Alan, b Leeds 23 Feb 47. RHB, OB. YORKSHIRE cap 1970. F-c career: 689 runs (av 9.84); 247 wkts (av 23.36), 1 hat-trick. HS 66 v Northants (Northampton) 1970. BB 7–36 v Essex (Colchester) 1970.

Hopes that he would prove to be Illingworth's successor in the Yorkshire XI were dampened when he was forced to change his action owing to doubts about its legitimacy. Until he satisfies the authorities, a question mark surrounds his cricketing future.

†COTTAM, Robert Michael Henry, b Cleethorpes, Lincs 16 Oct 44. RHB, RFM. NORTH-AMPTONSHIRE cap 1972. Played for Hants 1963–71. 2 England caps 1969, scoring 8 runs and taking 9 wkts (av 20.00), BB 4–50. F-c career: 771 runs (av 6.02); 784 wkts (av 20.92). HS 35 Hants v Somerset (Portsmouth) 1969. BB 9–25 Hants v Lancs (Manchester) 1965.

Tall, fast-medium bowler who uses his body to full effect in a rather slinging delivery action. He thumps the ball in and can be distinctly unpleasant on a helpful pitch. Bowls a nasty break-back, and his cutters can be extremely effective in certain conditions. His departure from Hampshire has already benefited Northants, and his selection for the MCC tour of India and Pakistan, after a great first season, was fully deserved.

COWDREY, Michael Colin, b Bangalore, India 24 Dec 32. RHB, occ LB. KENT cap 1951. Captain 1957–71. 113 England caps 1954–71 (27 as captain), scoring 7,700 runs (av 44.76) with 22 hundreds, HS 182, and holding 121 ct (Test record). F-c career: 39,306 runs (av 43.43), 98 hundreds; 57 wkts (53.45), 574 ct. HS

307 MCC v South Australia (Adelaide) 1962–63. BB 4–22 v Surrey (Blackheath) 1951.

One of the greatest batsmen England has produced since World War II. Has opened for his country with success, but is happiest a shade lower in the order. A superb timer of the ball, he can reach the boundary by stroking rather than hitting it. The only surprise is that he has not made even more runs. His technique is excellent and yet, for a world-class bat, he does from time to time look ordinary. Captained both Kent and England with distinction on many occasions. An outstanding slip fieldsman with an enormous number of catches to his credit. Played in over 100 Test matches and is a true credit to the game he has adorned for so long.

CROSS, Graham Frederick, b Leicester 15 Nov 43. RHB, RM. LEICESTERSHIRE – uncapped. F-c career: 1,741 runs (av 17.58); 87 wkts (av 28.57). HS 78 v Hants (Portsmouth) 1964. BB 4–28 v Lancs (Manchester) 1970.

Footballing cricketer; hard-hitting middle-order batsman with a good eye, a useful seamer, and a fine fieldsman. His opportunities to play are restricted because of the overlap of the seasons.

CUMBES, James, b East Didsbury, Lancs 4 May 44. RHB, RFM. WORCESTERSHIRE – uncapped. Played for Lancs 1963–67 and 1971, and for Surrey 1968–69. F-c career: 105 runs (av 8.07); 133 wkts (av 22.93). HS 25* Surrey v West Indians (Oval) 1969. BB 6–35 Surrey v Oxford U. (Oxford) 1968.

Tall, athletic soccer goalkeeper who bowls at lively fast-medium and can extract bounce from the deadest pitches. Enthusiastic outfielder. Availability restricted by soccer commitments.

DALTON, Andrew John, b Horsforth 14 Mar 47. RHB. YORKSHIRE – uncapped. F-c career: 710 runs (av 24.48), 3 hundreds. HS 128 v Middx (Leeds) 1972.

Attractive strokemaker who, having missed virtually all of last season through injury, returned in time to score a fine hundred against Middlesex.

DAVEY, Jack, b Tavistock, Devon, 4 Sep 44. LHB, LFM. GLOUCESTERSHIRE cap 1971. F-c career: 259 runs (av 5.18); 225 wkts (av. 28.54). HS 17 (twice) BB 6–95 v Notts (Gloucester) 1967.

Promising left-arm fast-medium bowler who made a great advance last summer. He moves the new ball sharply.

DAVIES, Thomas **Clive,** b Pont-rhyd-y-fen 7 Nov 51. RHB, SLA. GLAMORGAN – uncapped. F-c career: 9 runs (av 4.50); 18 wkts (av 34.72). HS 5. BB 3–22 v Leics (Cardiff) 1971.

An economical slow left-arm spinner whose opportunities are limited by Walker's presence in the team.

DAVIS, Roger Clive, b Cardiff 15 Jan 46. RHB, OB. GLAMORGAN cap 1969. F-c career: 4,376 runs (av 19.71), 3 hundreds; 166 wkts (29.50). HS 134 v Worcs (Cardiff) 1971. BB 6–82 v Glos (Cheltenham) 1970.

Valuable member of Glamorgan side in all departments: has the batting technique and temperament ideally suited to opening; can bowl his off-breaks economically; was a brilliant short-leg catcher until his near-fatal injury in 1971.

†DAVISON, Brian Fettes, b Bulawayo, Rhodesia 21 Dec 46. RHB, RM. LEICESTERSHIRE cap 1971. F-c career: 3,682 runs (av 29.45), 3 hundreds; 62 wkts (av 30.74). HS 137* Rhodesia v Griqualand West (Kimberley) 1970–71. BB 5–52 Rhodesia v Griqualand West (Bulawayo) 1967–68.

Mike Denness became only the second Scot to captain a first-class county – Ian Peebles was the first – when he took over Kent in 1972

Especially aggressive, match-winning batsman who hits the ball uncommonly hard but who, because he takes so many chances, is liable to have bad patches, as occurred in 1972. Useful change seam bowler, and a superbly athletic fieldsman who regularly stops the unstoppable and catches the uncatchable. A dynamic cricketer in every sense.

DENMAN, John, b Crawley 13 Jun 47. RHB, RM. SUSSEX – uncapped. F-c career: 555 runs (av 14.23); 63 wkts (av 43.22). HS 42 v Cambridge U. (Horsham) 1971. BB 5–45 v Cambridge U. (Cambridge) 1972.

Sturdily-built seamer whose methods are well-suited to one-day cricket.

†DENNESS, Michael Henry, b Bellshill, Lanarks 1 Dec 40. RHB. KENT cap 1964. Captain since 1972. 2 England caps 1969–70, scoring 94 runs (av 31.33), HS 55*. F-c career: 15,065 runs (av 31.84), 16 hundreds; 1 wkt; 280 ct. HS 174 v Derbys (Folkestone) 1965. BB 1–36.

Graceful, elegant batsman with an upright stance and wide range of handsome strokes. Probably at his best as an opener, but can fill the 3 or 4 spot most capably. Has captained Kent with skill and enthusiasm and is an inspiration to any team in the field. He was selected as the vice-captain of the MCC in India and Pakistan, despite limited experience of Test cricket.

DENNING, Peter William, b Chewton Mendip 16 Dec 49. LHB. SOMERSET – uncapped. F-c career: 1,073 runs (av 17.30). HS 69 v Essex (Taunton) 1969.

With the experience of his first full season behind him, this 'home-grown' lefthander should produce the consistent scores Somerset are expecting. Alert and enthusiastic outfielder.

†D'OLIVEIRA, Basil Lewis, b Cape Town, South Africa 4 Oct 31. RHB,RM/OB. WORCESTERSHIRE cap 1965. 48 England caps 1966–72, scoring 2,792 runs (av 40.46), with 6 hundreds (HS 158), and taking 56 wkts (av 38.16), BB 4–43. F-c career: 12,833 runs (av 39.85), 33 hundreds; 371 wkts (av 27.29). HS 174* v Indians (Worcester) 1967. BB 6–29 v Hants (Portsmouth) 1968.

Learnt his cricket in South Africa and has given great service to both England and Worcestershire. A natural competitor who has the happy knack of producing his finest performances in times of crisis, he is a most effective bat. And despite his short backlift, he still manages to hit the ball extremely hard. Outstanding puller and cutter. His defence is sound, although he is inclined to be somewhat suspect at the beginning of an innings. A good medium-pace swing bowler (a fourth rather than a third seamer at Test level) who regularly breaks up awkward stands.

DUDLESTON, Barry, b Bebington, Cheshire 16 Jul 45. RHB,SLA. LEICESTERSHIRE cap 1969. F-c career: 5,978 runs (av 30.19), 11 hundreds; 17 wkts (av 32.47). HS 171* v Kent (Canterbury) 1969. BB 4–6 v Surrey (Leicester) 1972.

Correct, reliable, and unspectacular batsman who is at his best opening the innings.

DUDLEY-JONES, Robert David Louis, b Bridgend 26 May 52. RHB,RM GLAMORGAN – uncapped. F-c career: 6 runs; 9 wkts (av 25.11). HS 4. BB 4–31 v Hants (Portsmouth) 1972 – on debut.

A seam bowler from Millfield School who took seven wickets on his Championship debut. Opportunities restricted by teaching studies.

†DYE, John Cooper James, b Gillingham, Kent 24 Jul 42. RHB,LFM. NORTHAMPTONSHIRE cap 1972. Played for Kent 1962–71. F-c career: 383 runs (av 5.47); 453 wkts (av 23.80). HS 29* v Worcs (Northampton) 1972. BB 7–118 Kent v Notts (Nottingham) 1971.

Big, strong left-arm opening bowler who enjoyed a truly remarkable first season with Northants, Kent having discarded him at the end of 1971. Always a great trier, he is prepared to pound away in all conditions, and his reward last season was 79 wickets at 18.06 apiece, topping his new county's bowling averages.

EALHAM, Alan George Ernest, b Ashford 30 Aug 44. RHB, occ OB. KENT cap 1970. F-c career: 4,354 runs (av 27.38), 3 hundreds; 2 wkts. HS 105 v Somerset (Glastonbury) 1972. BB 1–1.

Fine fieldsman and distinctly promising middle-order batsman who has had comparatively few opportunities to establish himself in the senior team.

EAST, Raymond Eric, b Manningtree 20 June 47. RHB,SLA. ESSEX cap 1967. F-c career: 2,245 runs (av 15.48); 406 wkts (av 25.39). HS 89* v Worcs (Leyton) 1972. BB 8–63 v Warwicks (Leyton) 1968.

Probably spins the ball as much, if not more, than any other left-armer in the country. He has good control while his height makes him an extremely nasty proposition on a helpful pitch. Has yet to reach his full potential. At times he suggests that he has the basic ability to develop into a genuine all-rounder and is capable of producing an off-drive of classical proportions. A splendid fieldsman, who seldom drops a catch, and a natural, often very funny, comedian.

EDMEADES, Brian Ernest Arthur, b Matlock, Derbys 17 Sep 41. RHB,RM. ESSEX cap 1965. F-c career: 9,170 runs (av 25.33), 12 hundreds;

322 wkts (av 25.25). HS 163 v Leics (Leyton) 1972. BB 7–37 v Glam (Leyton) 1966.

Technically a most correct player who has developed into an effective acquirer of runs. He is at his best opening the innings, when he can afford to play himself in against the pace bowling before encountering the spinners. Originally a bowler of big inswingers, he has become a useful reserve seamer. A brilliant outfielder with a splendid pair of hands and a fine throw.

EDMONDS, Phillippe Henri, b Lusaka, Northern Rhodesia 8 Mar 51. RHB, SLA. MIDDLESEX – uncapped. Cambridge U. captain 1973. F-c career: 416 runs (av. 13.41); 79 wkts (av 28.59). HS 56* Cambridge U. v Glam (Pontypridd) 1971. BB 7–56 Cambridge U. v Oxford U. (Lord's) 1971.

Promising left-arm slow bowler who, if he is prepared to spend sufficient time on his difficult profession, might develop into a really good one. A somewhat limited batsman, he could nonetheless develop into an all-rounder of Championship standard. A superb close catcher.

†EDRICH, John Hugh, b Blofield, Norfolk 21 Jun 37. LHB. SURREY cap 1959. Appointed captain 1973. 61 England caps 1963–72, scoring 3,979 runs (av 41.02), with 10 hundreds (HS 310*). F-c career: 31,664 runs (av 46.29), 83 hundreds; 244 ct. HS 310* England v New Zealand (Leeds) 1965.

Tough little fighter who has established himself as one of the most dependable opening batsmen in the world. Not a pretty player to watch, but a great acquirer of runs who can attack as well as graft. Exceptionally strong in the forearms, he is able to punch the ball powerfully through the covers and off his legs. One of the secrets of his success has undoubtedly been the way he gets right behind the line. He has just been made captain of Surrey and he can be expected to respond to the challenge of the Surrey captaincy with the same skill and dedication that has always characterised his batting. Although he has recently had a lean spell in Test cricket, he has continued to score heavily for his county and there is no reason to suppose that he could not play again for England.

EDWARDS, Michael John, b Balham 1 Mar 40. RHB, occ OB. SURREY cap 1966. F-c career: 10,216 runs (av 27.24), 11 hundreds; 2 wkts (av 89.50); 257 ct. HS 137 v MCC (Oval) 1969. BB 2–53 Cambridge U. v Pakistanis (Cambridge) 1962.

Experienced a lean summer in 1972, but he has the ability to come again and has even been spoken of as a possible England opener. A superb catcher close to the wicket.

ELLIS, Geoffrey Phillip, b Llandudno, Caernarvons 24 May 50. RHB. GLAMORGAN – uncapped. F-c career: 601 runs (av 24.04). HS 55 v Glos (Swansea) 1970.

A promising opening bat, good close fielder, and former Welsh Schools captain.

ELMS, Richard Burtenshaw, b Sutton, Surrey 5 Apr 49. RHB, LFM. KENT – uncapped. F-c career: 79 runs (av 15.80); 19 wkts (av 36.31). HS 28* v Essex (Chelmsford) 1971. BB 4–84 v Warwicks (Birmingham) 1971.

Lively fast-medium bowler who has yet to reach his peak and might become quicker.

†ENGINEER, Farokh Maneksha, b Bombay, India 25 Feb 38. RHB, WK. LANCASHIRE cap 1968. 35 Test caps 1961–71 (33 for India, 2 for Rest of the World), scoring 1,782 runs (av 28.28) with 1 hundred (109), and making 72 dismissals (58 ct, 14 st). F-c career; 9,684 runs (av 29.16), 9 hundreds; 582 dismissals (480 ct, 102 st); 1 wkt. HS 192 Rest of the World XI v Combined XI (Hobart) 1971–72. BB 1–40.

His wicket-keeping has improved enormously since he joined Lancashire and he is now rated as one of the most talented exponents of this vital art. In contrast, his gay batting has not produced the number of runs it really warrants, although he has played several memorable innings for his county. A dashing and attractive bat capable of upsetting class bowling and a natural favourite with crowds everywhere.

†FEATHERSTONE, Norman George, b Que Que, Rhodesia 20 Aug 49. RHB, OB. MIDDLESEX cap 1971. F-c career: 4,035 runs (av 28.41), 1 hundred; 30 wkts (av 30.23). HS 120* v Glos (Gloucester) 1971. BB 3–32 v Notts (Worksop) 1971.

Graceful and exhilarating strokemaker who experienced a rather lean time in 1972. He appears to have the class and ability to develop into a really outstanding performer.

†FLETCHER, Keith William Robert, b Worcester, Worcs 20 May 44. RHB, occ LB. ESSEX cap 1963. 19 England caps 1968–72, scoring 833 runs (av 27.76), HS 89, and taking 1 wkt. F-c career: 17,748 runs (av 36.44), 27 hundreds; 19 wkts (av 51.26); 315 ct. HS 228* v Sussex (Hastings) 1968. BB 4–50 MCC under-25 v North Zone (Peshawar) 1966–67.

One of the most exciting and talented batsmen in the country. He is equally at home on either his front or his back foot and possesses an extensive repertoire of strokes. Occasionally, and inexplicably, allows himself to be tied down by ordinary bowling and has, as yet, failed to show his true potential at international level. Capable of taking an attack apart and not afraid to loft the ball deliberately. Brilliant all-purpose fieldsman and an occasional leg-spinner of uncertain length and direction who can turn the ball considerably.

FLICK, Barry John, b Coventry 5 Mar 52. RHB, WK. WARWICKSHIRE – uncapped. F-c career: 8 runs (av 4.00); 4 dismissals (1 ct, 3 st). HS 6* v Cambridge U. (Cambridge) 1972.

Reserve wicket-keeper who has played in only four friendly f-c matches during three seasons on the staff.

FOAT, James Clive, b Salford Priors, Warwicks 21 Nov 52. RHB. GLOUCESTERSHIRE – uncapped. F-c career: 87 runs (av 8.70). HS 20 v Hants (Basingstoke) 1972.

An outstanding schoolboy batsman (Millfield) who was unable to produce any form at all in six Championship appearances last season.

†FRANCIS, Bruce Collin, b Sydney, Australia 18 Feb 48. RHB. ESSEX cap 1971. 3 Australia caps 1972, scoring 52 runs (av 10.40), HS 27. F-c career: 3,884 runs (av 32.63), 9 hundreds; 1 wkt. HS 210 Australians v Oxford & Cambridge Us. (Oxford) 1972. BB 1–10.

This cheerful Australian has shown with Essex that he is a good county opener. He likes to attack, showing a marked preference for the on side, but he was unable to establish himself as a regular member of Ian Chappell's Test team.

†FREDERICKS, Roy Clifton, b Blairmont, Berbice, B.G. 11 Nov 42. LHB, SLC. GLAMORGAN cap 1971. 19 West Indies caps 1968–72, scoring 1,254 runs (av 34.83) with 1 hundred (163). F-c career: 7,744 runs (av 43.50), 17 hundreds; 32 wkts (av 30.18). HS 228* v Northants (Swansea) 1972. BB 4–36 Guyana v Trinidad (Port-of-Spain) 1971–72.

Chirpy little West Indian opener who likes to play strokes but is still a shade suspect against the ball that moves. He is inclined to get himself out when well set. At the moment a good lefthander and the next few seasons will show if he is going to become an outstanding one.

FROST, Graham, b Old Basford 15 Jan 47. RHB, RM. NOTTINGHAMSHIRE – uncapped. F-c career: 2,995 runs (av 23.21), 2 hundreds; 9 wkts (av 49.66). HS 107 v Surrey (Nottingham) 1970. BB 3–33 v West Indians (Nottingham) 1969.

Correct batsman who has yet to make the runs he originally promised. He hits well with a straight bat off the back foot but appears vulnerable to pace.

†**GIBBS, Lancelot** Richard, b Georgetown, B.G. 29 Sep 34. RHB, OB. WARWICKSHIRE cap 1968. 57 Test caps 1958–72 (53 for West Indies, 4 for Rest of the World), scoring 372 runs (av 6.88), HS 25, and taking 215 wkts (av 29.74), including one hat-trick, BB 8–38. F-c career: 1,525 runs (av 8.81); 863 wkts (av 26.62), 1 hat-trick. HS 43 West Indians v Combined XI (Hobart) 1960–61. BB 8–37 v Glam (Birmingham) 1970.

Lance Gibbs, off-spinner supreme

Superb off-spinner who has proved himself one of the greatest slow bowlers to come out of the West Indies. A high action, combined with the ability to make the ball dip late in flight, enables him to achieve more bounce than most of his kind. He is relatively more dangerous on hard pitches and has been happier operating over the wicket than round. With his accuracy he can be used as a stock bowler on perfect Test wickets, but he likes to experiment, and really gives the ball a tweak. Originally met with only limited success with Warwickshire, but in the last two seasons he has turned in some great performances, despite the lack of adequate spin support.

GIBBS, Peter John Keith, b Buglawton, Cheshire 17 Aug 44. RHB occ OB. DERBYSHIRE cap 1968. F-c career: 8,885 runs (av 29.13), 11 hundreds; 4 wkts (av 80.25). HS 138* v Somerset (Chesterfield) 1969. BB 2–54 v Northants (Derby) 1968.

Careful opener with a good defence. Happiest in a sheet-anchor role.

†**GIFFORD, Norman,** b Ulverston, Lancs 30 Mar 40. LHB, SLA. WORCESTERSHIRE cap 1961. Captain since 1971. 9 England caps 1964–72, scoring 94 runs (av 11.75), HS 17, and taking 20 wkts (av 25.80), BB 4–43. F-c career 3,892 runs (av 12.88); 1,106 wkts (av 19.83), 1 hat-trick. HS 89 v Oxford U. (Oxford) 1963. BB 8–28 v Yorks (Sheffield) 1968.

Fine left-arm spinner who is a natural match-winner in the right circumstances. He tends to bowl from wide of the stumps and has a rather flat trajectory, with the result that he is not easy to hit, or to cut. He never gives anything away and spins the ball rather more than most. A determined tailender, he has often held up the opposition with his essentially practical approach. A shrewd, thoughtful captain.

GILLIAT, Richard Michael Charles, b Ware, Herts 20 May 44. LHB, occ LB. HAMPSHIRE cap 1969. Captain since 1971. F-c career: 6,712 runs (av 27.73), 9 hundreds; 1 wkt. HS 223* v Warwicks (Southampton) 1969. BB 1–8.

Has captained Hampshire with considerable charm. Initially a solid middle-order lefthander, he met with considerable success when he first adopted a more swashbuckling approach. Sadly, the large scores began to dry up and at present he is faced by that difficult problem of whether to graft or to try to hit his way out of trouble.

†GOMES, Lawrence Angelo (**'Larry'**), b Arima, Trinidad 13 Jul 53. LHB, SLA. MIDDLESEX – uncapped. Qualified to play for County in 1973. F-c career (1 match): 14 runs (av 7.00). HS 14 Trinidad v New Zealanders (Pointe-à-Pierre) 1971–72.

Young West Indian who is likely to make a big impression this summer. He has the strokes and the class to make the runs come attractively.

GOODWIN, Keith, b Oldham 21 Jun 38. RHB, WK. LANCASHIRE cap 1965. F-c career: 612 runs (av 5.71); 253 dismissals (227 ct, 26 st). HS 23 v Glam (Swansea) 1965.

Lancashire's regular wicket-keeper until Engineer joined the staff in 1968, since when his senior team appearances have been few and far between. He has made a valuable contribution as captain of the 2nd XI and has developed his love of coaching. Spent the winter of 1971–72 in India, instructing leading coaches.

GRAHAM, John Norman, b Hexham, Northumberland 8 May 43. RHB, RM. KENT cap 1967. F-c career: 309 runs (av 3.76); 462 wkts (20.77) HS 23 v Cambridge U. (Cambridge) 1967. BB 8–20 v Essex (Brentwood) 1969.

Very tall (6 ft 7½ in), fast-medium bowler. His height enables him to extract considerable lift from some pitches and, though by no means quick, he can be a distinctly unpleasant proposition on certain wickets.

GRAVENEY, David Anthony, b Bristol 2 Jan 53. Son of J.K. Graveney, former Glos captain. RHB, SLA. GLOUCESTERSHIRE – uncapped. F-c career: 29 runs (av 5.80); 14 wkts (av 25.85). HS 11. BB 5–63 v Derbys (Cheltenham) 1972.

A tall, slow left-arm bowler from Millfield School who showed a marked ability to bowl a line and length in his five Championship appearances last season.

GRAVES, Peter John, b Hove 19 May 46. LHB, occ SLA. SUSSEX cap 1969. F-c career: 5,636 runs (av 23.88), 2 hundreds; 15 wkts (av 51.20). HS 117* v Kent (Tunbridge Wells) 1970. BB 3–69 Orange Free State v Australians (Bloemfontein) 1969–70.

For several years this naturally aggressive lefthander has looked the part but has failed to score the runs. Last summer he batted higher in the order and responded well to the added responsibility. A first-class fieldsman.

†GREENIDGE, Cuthbert Gordon, b St. Peter, Barbados 1 May 51. RHB, occ RM. HAMPSHIRE cap 1972. F-c career: 2,745 runs (av 30.50), 3 hundreds; 8 wkts (av 28.75). HS 142 v Sussex (Hove) 1972. BB 5–49 v Surrey (Southampton) 1971.

Compact, opening bat with pleasing strokes who is steadily improving and did extremely well last summer. He could well develop into a genuine Test cricketer and will certainly score many runs for Hampshire in the years ahead.

†GREENIDGE, Geoffrey Alan, b Bridgetown, Barbados 26 May 48. RHB, occ LB. SUSSEX cap 1970. 2 West Indies caps 1972, scoring 144 runs (av 48.00), HS 50. F-c career: 5,381 runs (av 28.62), 11 hundreds; 13 wkts (av 58.46).

HS 205 and BB 7–124 Barbados v Jamaica (Bridgetown) 1966–67.

Highly promising opener from the West Indies who is steadily improving and could well establish himself as a batsman of Test calibre this summer.

†GREIG, Anthony William, b Queenstown, South Africa 6 Oct 46. RHB, RM. 6 ft 7 in tall. SUSSEX cap 1967. Appointed captain 1973. 8 England caps 1970–72, scoring 384 runs (av 29.53), HS 62, and taking 21 wkts (av 32.66), BB 4–59. F-c career: 8,591 runs (av 27.71), 9 hundreds; 489 wkts (av 27.36), 1 hat-trick. HS 156 v Lancs (Hove) 1967. BB 8–25 v Glos (Hove) 1967.

Established himself as an all-rounder of international class with two fine series against Australia, for the Rest of the World and for England. With his great reach it is only to be expected that he should be an extremely fine driver off the front foot. His fast-medium seam bowling has improved enormously now that he has acquired the necessary control, and he should serve England well as a third seamer. An excellent fieldsman, desperately keen, and a hard competitor, he should prove a successful captain and will undoubtedly upset some opponents on the way.

GRIFFITH, Kevin, b Warrington, Lancs 17 Jan 50. RHB, OB. WORCESTERSHIRE – uncapped. F-c career: 795 runs (av 15.00); 50 wkts (av 35.06). HS 59 v Yorks (Sheffield) 1971. BB 7–41 v Oxford U. (Oxford) 1969.

A promising all-rounder (middle-order bat and off-spinner) who has yet to make his mark at County Championship level.

GRIFFITH, Mike Grenville, b Beaconsfield, Bucks 25 Nov 43. Son of S.C. Griffith (Sussex and England). RHB, WK. SUSSEX cap 1967. Captain 1968–72. F-c career: 7,906 runs (av 25.17), 4 hundreds; 248 dismissals (229 ct, 19 st); 1 wkt. HS 158 v Cambridge U. (Hove) 1969. BB 1–4 Cambridge U. v Sussex (Cambridge) 1965.

Very quick on his feet and a splendid runner between the wickets. If his technique is somewhat unconventional, he has nonetheless frequently rescued his county after those above him have failed. Indeed, it might have paid dividends had he batted higher up the order.

HADLEY, Robert John, b Neath 22 Oct 51. RHB, LFM. GLAMORGAN – uncapped. F-c career: 29 runs (av 2.90); 35 wkts (av 26.97). HS 9. BB 5–31 Cambridge U. v Sussex (Cambridge) 1972.

An interesting left-arm, fast-medium, over-the-wicket bowler with a good, high action. Took 5–32 in the first of his only two appearances for the county. Now in his third year at Cambridge University.

†HAMPSHIRE, John Harry, b Thurnscoe 10 Feb 41. RHB, occ LB. YORKSHIRE cap 1963. 7 England caps 1969–72, scoring 389 runs (av 29.92), with 1 hundred – 107 on debut. F-c career: 13,983 runs (av 30.66), 20 hundreds; 26 wkts (av 54.50); 251 ct. HS 183* v Sussex (Hove) 1971. BB 7–52 v Glam (Cardiff) 1963.

Has the time, the strokes, and the ability, but there has been a strange unevenness about his performances that is difficult to explain. Here is a player clearly capable of demoralising a Test attack, yet his overall figures in county cricket simply do not match up to his basic potential. He might have become a useful change leg-spinner but has suffered from lack of opportunities.

Above: England and Surrey opening bowler Geoff Arnold. Throughout his career he has been bedevilled by injury, with the result that his Test appearances have been limited

Far left: Bishen Bedi, having spun England's batting into confusion during the 1972–73 Test series in India, will return to Northamptonshire for 1973 with a great psychological advantage

Left: Kent captain Mike Denness is one of those who will be hoping to take his revenge on Bedi

Above: Clive Lloyd is bowled by the promising young Sussex seamer Paul Phillipson, who finished this John Player League match at Hove with 4 for 26

Left above: England captain Ray Illingworth batting against Australia. An astute tactician, Illingworth enjoyed a notable season in 1972, leading Leicestershire to victory in the Benson and Hedges Cup and ensuring the Ashes remained in England

Left: David Lloyd, Lancashire's new captain for 1973

HARDIE, Brian Ross, b Stirlingshire 14 Jan 50. RHB. Joined ESSEX 1973 – uncapped. Played for Scotland 1970–72. F-c career (4 matches): 158 runs (av 26.33). HS 49 Scotland v Ireland (Greenock) 1972.

Young Stenhousemuir batsman who came to notice with two centuries for Scotland against MCC at Aberdeen in 1971. His father and brother have also played for Scotland.

HARE, William Henry ('Dusty'), b Newark 29 Nov 52. RHB occ WK. NOTTINGHAMSHIRE – uncapped. F-c career (1 match): 34 runs. HS 28* v Oxford U. (Oxford) 1971.

An all-round sportsman – he has played stand-off for the East Midlands rugby team – who has yet to be given a chance in the senior team.

HARRIS, Michael John, b St Just-in-Roseland, Cornwall 25 May 44. RHB,LB. NOTTINGHAMSHIRE cap 1970. Played for Middx 1964–68. F-c career: 9,747 runs (av 36.36), 21 hundreds; 66 wkts (av 44.13). HS 177 v Kent (Nottingham) 1971. BB 4–16 v Warwicks (Nottingham) 1969.

Solidly-built opener with a fine technique who has looked a better player since joining Notts. Far stronger off the back foot than most, he is the type of batsman who would thrive overseas. Can bowl leg-breaks to greater effect than is sometimes appreciated.

HARRISON, Stuart Charles, b Cwmbran, Monmouths 21 Sep 51. RHB,RM. GLAMORGAN – uncapped. F-c career: 28 runs (av 7.00); 5 wkts (av 38.00). HS 15 v Derbys (Derby) 1971. BB 3–55 v Somerset (Cardiff) 1971.

A competent seam bowler whose progress has been interrupted by teaching studies.

HARROP, Douglas John, b Cosby 16 Apr 47. LHB,WK. LEICESTERSHIRE – uncapped. F-c career (1 match): 11 runs (av 11.00); 3 dismissals (3 ct). HS 11* v Oxford U. (Oxford) 1972.

Reserve wicket-keeper who joined the county staff and made his f-c debut last season.

HASSAN, Basharat, (*not 'S.B.'*) b Nairobi, Kenya 24 Mar 44. RHB, occ WK. NOTTINGHAMSHIRE cap 1970. F-c career: 4,968 runs (av 27.91), 5 hundreds. HS 125* v Pakistanis (Nottingham) 1971.

Must have the ugliest stance in first-class cricket, but he is an unconventional, cross-bat-minded striker capable of changing the whole course of a match with his far-from-text-book methods. A tremendous enthusiast, he is a useful stop-gap wicket-keeper who can be relied upon to hold remarkable catches.

†HAYES, Frank Charles, b Preston 6 Dec. 46. RHB. LANCASHIRE cap 1972. F-c career: 1,595 runs (av 31.27). HS 99 v Hants (Southampton) 1970.

Attractive player who has yet to translate his obvious ability into runs at f-c level. Might blossom into one of the best middle-order batsmen in the country.

HAYWOOD, Paul Raymond, b Leicester 30 Mar 47. RHB,LB/RM. LEICESTERSHIRE – uncapped. F-c career: 1,322 runs (av 21.67), 1 hundred; 9 wkts (av 32.00). HS 100* v Middx (Lord's) 1972. BB 4–60 v Surrey (Leicester) 1972.

Enjoyed a refreshingly successful first full season and looks a fine batting prospect.

HEADLEY, Ronald George Alphonso, b Kingston, Jamaica 29 Jun 39. Son of G.A. Headley (Jamaica and West Indies). LHB occ LB. WORCESTERSHIRE cap 1961. F-c career: 19,381 (av 30.71), 27 hundreds; 12 wkts (av 48.16); 333 ct. HS 187 v Northants (Worcester) 1971. BB 4–40 v Glam (Worcester) 1963.

Essentially a forward player with a full flowing

Worcestershire opener Ron Headley, a beautifully balanced player with a repertoire of handsome, full-flowing strokes

drive, in sharp contrast to his father. A lovely, natural mover and an exceptional close-to-the-wicket catcher.

HEMMINGS, Edward Ernest, b Leamington Spa 20 Feb 49. RHB, RM. WARWICKSHIRE – uncapped. F-c career: 1,397 runs (av 22.53); 85 wkts (av 37.84). HS 80 v Worcs (Worcester) 1971. BB 6–90 v Hants (Basingstoke) 1968.

Straight-forward all-rounder whose progress has been restricted by lack of opportunities.

HEMSLEY, Edward John Orton, b Norton, Staffs 1 Sep 43. RHB, RM. WORCESTERSHIRE cap 1969. F-c career: 3,351 runs (av 29.13), 1 hundred; 41 wkts (av 30.17). HS 138* v Oxford U. (Oxford) 1969. BB 3–5 v Warwicks (Worcester) 1971.

Cricketer-footballer who would do even better at the former if the two seasons did not overlap to such an extent. It would be no exaggeration to say that in 1972 he looked as good as and promised rather more than most uncapped middle-order batsmen in the country.

HENDERSON, Andrew Arthur, b Chadwell Heath, Essex 14 Jul 41. RHB, RM. SUSSEX – uncapped. F-c career (1 match): 11 runs (av 5.50); 5 wkts (av 26.40). HS 9 and BB 3–65 v Glos (Gloucester) 1972.

Tall seam bowler who appeared in one Championship match.

HENDRICK, Michael (*not 'M.J.'*), b Darley Dale 22 Oct 48. RHB, RFM. DERBYSHIRE cap 1972. F-c career: 169 runs (av 6.25); 91 wkts (av 26.90). HS 18 v Glos (Cheltenham) 1972. BB 8–50 v Northants (Chesterfield) 1972.

Over the years Derbyshire have a remarkable record for finding good, hostile opening bowlers and Michael Hendrick looks as if he will more than uphold the tradition. Hostile and accurate, he is patently a far-above-average prospect.

†HERMAN, Robert Stephen, b Southampton 30 Nov 46. RHB, RFM. HAMPSHIRE cap 1972. Played for Middx 1965–71. F-c career: 574 runs (av 8.31); 277 wkts (av 27.10) HS 56 v Worcs (Portsmouth) 1972. BB 8–42 v Warwicks (Portsmouth) 1972.

Celebrated signing on for Hampshire with the best season of his career. Until 1972 he had been regarded as just another opening seamer, but suddenly he discovered a new penetration that produced a rich haul of wickets. Easily the most improved young cricketer of the year.

HIGGS, Kenneth, b Sandyford, Staffs 14 Jan 37. LHB, RFM. LEICESTERSHIRE cap 1972. Played for Lancs 1958–69. 15 England caps 1965–68, scoring 185 runs (av 11.56), HS 63, and taking 71 wkts (av 20.74), BB 6–91. F-c career: 3,044 runs (av 10.94); 1,215 wkts (av 23.26), 2 hat-tricks. HS 63 England v West Indies (Oval) 1966. BB 7–19 Lancs v Leics (Manchester) 1965.

Powerfully-built stock seam bowler who formerly did extremely well both for Lancashire and England. From a short run-up, he hits the deck sufficiently hard to jar a batsman's right hand much more than many bowlers who are much quicker through the air. Tempted out of early retirement by Leicester, he played an important part in their success last summer. A left-handed tailender, he has used his ability to push forward with a straight bat to considerable effect on a number of occasions.

HILL, Alan, b Buxworth 29 June 50. RHB. DERBYSHIRE – uncapped. F-c career: 120 runs (av 20.00). HS 82 v Lancs (Blackpool) 1972.

Playing in Derbyshire's last three matches of 1972, this opening batsman revealed a sound technique with a good range of off-side strokes. He is now studying physical education.

HILL, Leonard Winston, b Caerleon, Monmouths 14 Apr 42. RHB, occ WK. GLAMORGAN – uncapped. F-c career: 1,202 runs (av 21.46); 24 dismissals (23 ct, 1 st). HS 80 v Oxford U. (Oxford) 1970.

A soccer professional who is available in mid-season only. Useful bat and outstanding cover fielder who can also keep wicket.

†HOBBS, Robin Nicholas Stuart, b Chippenham, Wilts 8 May 42. RHB, LB. ESSEX cap 1964. 7 England caps 1967–71 taking 12 wkts (av 40.08), BB 3–25, and scoring 34 runs (av 6.80), HS 15*. F-c career: 3,825 runs (av 11.87), 1 hundred; 896 wkts (av 25.49); 233 ct. HS 100 v Glam (Ilford) 1968. BB 8–63 v Glam (Swansea) 1966.

Almost an anachronism in first class cricket; an English-born leg-spinner who has commanded a regular place in a county side for many years, made several MCC tours, and been capped by his country. He is very accurate for this style of bowler and, although not a big spinner, varies his flight and pace skilfully. As a batsman he is an unconventional striker of the ball, with an excellent eye, a remarkable ability to cut seemingly uncuttable deliveries, and some highly individual and unusual strokes of his own design. He is such a fine cover that, when on tour and not in the team, he is an automatic choice for 12th man.

HODGSON, Alan, b Moorside Consett, Co Durham 27 Oct 51. LHB, RFM. NORTHAMPTONSHIRE – uncapped. F-c career: 52 runs (av 4.72); 27 wkts (av 29.88). HS 18 and BB 4–54 v Hants (Northampton) 1971.

Tall (6 ft 4½ in), well-built fast medium bowler whose career prospects with Northants have not been improved by the registration of Cottam and Dye.

†**HOLDER, Vanburn** Alonza, b Bridgetown, Barbados 8 Oct 45. RHB, RFM. WORCESTERSHIRE cap 1970. 10 West Indies caps 1969–72, scoring 218 runs (av 16.76), HS 42, and taking 27 wkts (av 30.07), BB 4–41. F-c career: 1,209 runs (av 11.29); 437 wkts (av 23.31). HS 52 v Glos (Dudley) 1970. BB 7–44 Barbados v Jamaica (Bridgetown) 1971–72.

Tall, West Indian fast bowler who can keep going for long periods and did remarkably well last summer without receiving much support. Though not truly fast, he can be distinctly hostile, achieving plenty of lift from his good, high action. Improved control has made him a much more effective and threatening bowler than when he was first picked for his country.

HOOPER, John Michael Mackenzie, b Milford 23 Apr 47. RHB, occ RM. SURREY – uncapped. F-c career: 406 runs (av 15.61); 1 wkt (av 10.00). HS 41* v Oxford U. (Guildford) 1970. BB 1–10.

An attractive strokemaker who abandoned his cricket career for the Stock Exchange in 1971 but who is still available for some one-day matches.

HOPKINS, John Anthony, b Maesteg 16 Jun 53. RHB, WK. GLAMORGAN – uncapped. F-c career: 332 runs (av 15.80); 8 dismissals (7 ct, 1 st). HS 88 v Glos (Colwyn Bay) 1971.

A mature, compact batsman and promising reserve wicket-keeper.

†**HOWARTH, Geoffrey** Philip, b Auckland, New Zealand 29 Mar 51. RHB, OB. SURREY – uncapped. F-c career: 138 runs (av 17.25); 3 wkts (av 31.66). HS 55 v Kent (Oval) 1972. BB 2–14 v Cambridge U. (Cambridge) 1971.

Brother of the New Zealand Test bowler, Hedley Howarth. A useful middle-order batsman, Geoff has the potential to develop into more than just a useful county player. A fine fielder – he substituted for England in the fifth Test last summer – he is also a distinctly handy change off-spinner.

†**HUGHES, David** Paul, b Newton-le-Willows 13 May 47. RHB, SLA. LANCASHIRE cap 1970. F-c career: 1,698 runs (av 15.57); 298 wkts (av 29.03). HS 78* v Northants (Southport) 1971. BB 7–24 v Oxford U. (Oxford) 1970.

Young left-arm orthodox bowler with excellent line and length. He is invariably tidy, but still does not spin the ball viciously enough to reap the benefits of a bad track. Produces useful scores with the bat from time to time.

HUTTON, Richard Anthony, b Pudsey 6 Sep 42. Son of Sir Leonard Hutton (Yorks and England). RHB, RFM. YORKSHIRE cap 1964. 5 England caps 1971, scoring 219 runs (av 36.50), HS 81, and taking 9 wkts (av 28.55), BB 3–72. F-c career: 7,106 runs (av 22.06), 4 hundreds; 592 wkts (av 23.35), 1 hat-trick. HS 189 v Pakistanis (Bradford) 1971. BB 8–50 Cambridge U. v Derbys (Burton upon Trent) 1963.

Fine aggressive county all-rounder; penetrating bowler, competent No. 5 or 6, and safe slip. Since he came down from Cambridge his bowling has improved rather more than his batting, though he drives well and can be relied on to pull out that little extra in a crisis, as he has shown for both England and Yorkshire. His career as a stockbroker will limit his availability to Sunday games and occasional appearances this season.

ILLINGWORTH, Raymond, b Pudsey, Yorks 8 Jun 32. RHB, OB. LEICESTERSHIRE cap 1969. Captain since 1969. Played for Yorks 1951–68. 60 England caps 1958–72 (30 as captain), scoring 2,104 runs (av 26.97), with 2 hundreds, HS 113, and taking 127 wkts (av 30.06), BB 6–29. F-c career: 20,268 runs (av 28.15), 20 hundreds; 1,797 wkts (av 19.57); 367 ct. HS 162 Yorks v Indians (Sheffield) 1959. BB 9–42 Yorks v Worcs (Worcester) 1957.

Very shrewd captain with exceptional tactical knowledge of the game; only really likes to gamble on certainties. An ideal all-rounder, he is capable of winning and saving matches with both ball and bat. His accurate off-spin is invariably tidy and can be devastating in the right conditions, his batting is defensively very sound, though in recent years he has displayed rather more shots than he seemed to possess in his Yorkshire days. He is especially good against seamers and off-spinners.

Illingworth's record since he took over the England captaincy has been outstanding. He may have occasionally underbowled himself, but his batting has frequently been an inspiration – and a revelation. Most surprisingly, all this has happened after it was generally believed that his Test career, not all that distinguished till then, was over.

†**INTIKHAB ALAM KHAN,** b Hoshiarpur, India 28 Dec 41. RHB, LB. SURREY cap 1969. 34 Test caps 1959–71 (29 for Pakistan – 6 as captain – 5 for Rest of World), scoring 1,042 runs (av 22.17), HS 61, and taking 71 wkts (av 45.18), BB 6–113. F-c career: 7,651 runs (av 22.77), 5 hundreds; 843 wkts (av 26.77), 1 hat-trick. HS 182 Karachi Blues v PIA 'B' (Karachi) 1970–71. BB 8–54 Pakistanis v Tasmania (Hobart) 1972–73.

Cheerful captain and leg-break bowler. An accurate spinner with a teasing flight, he is usually happier on the fast pitches abroad than at The Oval. Unlike some, he does not wilt under pressure and will simply go on bowling, but there is a danger that, in taking on the role of stock bowler, he will forget that wrist spinners should primarily be attackers. He hits straight with remarkable power and ferocity and is the ideal person to have coming in at No. 8 when quick runs are the order of the day.

†**JACKMAN, Robin** David, b Simla, India 13 Aug 45. RHB, RFM. SURREY cap 1970. F-c career: 976 runs (av 11.34); 431 wkts (av 24.98), 2 hat-tricks. HS 50 Rhodesia v Eastern Province (Bulawayo) 1972–73. BB 8–30 Rhodesia v Natal (Durban) 1972–73.

Proven opening bowler, lively rather than fast, who achieves a disconcerting amount of movement and has plenty of stamina.

†**JAMESON, John** Alexander, b Bombay, India 30 Jun 41. RHB, RM/OB, occ WK. WARWICKSHIRE cap 1964. 2 England caps 1971, scoring 141 runs (av 35.25), HS 82. F-c career: 12,026 runs (av 30.60), 14 hundreds; 60 wkts (av 35.23), 1 hat-trick. HS 231 v Indians (Birmingham) 1971. BB 4–22 v Oxford U. (Oxford) 1971.

Tall, powerfully-built batsman who is at his best as an aggressive opening bat. He is a very good driver and is usually severe on medium-paced bowling. An occasional medium-pace bowler who has even done the hat-trick.

JESTY, Trevor Edward, b Gosport 2 Jun 48. RHB, RM. HAMPSHIRE cap 1971. F-c career: 2,514 runs (av 23.71); 140 wkts (av 32.07). HS 80 v Kent (Folkestone) 1972. BB 5–37 v Kent (Southampton) 1972.

A capable 'bits and pieces' cricketer: handy middle-order batsman; medium-pace seamer; splendid fieldsman.

JOHNSON, Colin, b Pocklington 5 Sep 47. RHB, occ OB. YORKSHIRE – uncapped. F-c career: 849 runs (av 18.45); 4 wkts (av 58.00).

HS 61* v New Zealanders (Bradford) 1969 – on debut. BB 2–22 v Oxford U. (Oxford) 1971.

Promising middle-order batsman and superb cover fielder.

JOHNSON, Graham, William, b Beckenham 8 Nov 46. RHB, OB. KENT cap 1970. F-c career: 3,044 runs (av 20.56), 3 hundreds; 95 wkts (av 33.51). HS 116 v Sussex (Tunbridge Wells) 1970. BB 6–35 v Surrey (Blackheath) 1970.

Attractive strokemaker, superb fielder, and useful off-spinner.

JOHNSON, Ivan Nicholas, b Nassau, Bahamas 27 Jun 53. LHB, SLA. WORCESTERSHIRE – uncapped. F-c career: 75 runs (av 15.00); 7 wkts (av 44.28). HS 27 and BB 3–32 v Essex (Worcester) 1972.

Brilliant schoolboy (Malvern) all-rounder and outstanding success of the 1972 England Young Cricketers' tour of the West Indies.

JOHNSON, Laurence Alan, b West Horsley, Surrey 12 Aug 36. RHB, WK. NORTHAMPTONSHIRE cap 1960. F-c career: 1,573 runs (av 10.55); 329 dismissals (264 ct, 65 st); 1 wkt. HS 50 v Worcs (Dudley) 1967. BB 1–60.

Fine wicket-keeper who would probably still be a regular member of the 1st XI if he were a shade more productive with the bat.

JONES, Alan, b Swansea 4 Nov 38. LHB, occ OB. GLAMORGAN cap 1962. 1 England cap 1970. F-c career: 20,689 runs (av 31.53), 29 hundreds; 2 wkts; 218 ct. HS 187* v Somerset (Glastonbury) 1963. BB 1–24.

Neat, competent opening bat who has given fine service to Glamorgan over the years.

†**JONES, Allan** Arthur, b Horley, Surrey 9 Dec 47. RHB, RFM. SOMERSET cap 1972. Played for Sussex 1966–69. F-c career: 309 runs (av 5.72); 179 wkts (av 30.13). HS 22* v Lancs (Weston-s-Mare) 1972. BB 9–51 v Sussex (Hove) 1972.

Promising opening bowler who has made considerable progress since moving to Somerset.

JONES, Alan **Keith** Colin, b Solihull 20 Apr 51. RHB. WARWICKSHIRE – uncapped. Elected Oxford U. captain 1973. F-c career: 942 runs (av 21.90), 1 hundred. HS 111 Oxford U. v. Notts (Oxford) 1971.

Opening batsman who played one match for his County in 1969. Will be available when the Varsity season ends in July and, with Warwickshire almost certain to lose several batsmen on Test duty, has a fair chance of gaining valuable Championship experience in a confident team.

JONES, Eifion Wyn, b Velindre 25 Jun 42. Brother of Alan Jones. RHB, WK. GLAMORGAN cap 1967. F-c career: 3,906 runs (av 18.77), 2 hundreds; 446 dismissals (403 ct, 43 st). HS 146* v Sussex (Hove) 1968.

A quiet but highly competent wicket-keeper who can also score runs.

JONES, Keith Vaughan, b Park Royal 28 Mar 42. RHB, RM. MIDDLESEX cap 1971. F-c career: 1,566 runs (av 18.42); 186 wkts (av 26.27). HS 57* v Surrey (Oval) 1972. BB 7–52 v Warwicks (Coventry) 1971.

Had a highly commendable season with bat and ball in 1972. A good honest opening bowler, he has the advantage of being a shade quicker and more penetrating than he initially appears. Competent lower-order batsman who is ideal for limited-overs cricket.

†**JOSHI** Uday**kumar** Changanlal, b Rajkot, India 23 Dec 46. RHB, OB. SUSSEX cap 1971. F-c career: 1,119 runs (av 13.16); 281 wkts. (av 28.86). Took wicket with first ball in F-c cricket. HS 64 Gujerat v Maharashtra (Bulsar)

1971–72. BB 6–38 v Somerset (Eastbourne) 1971.

Has not yet properly adapted his off-break bowling to English conditions with the result that he has yet to return the figures Sussex need from their one recognised spinner.

†**JULIEN, Bernard** Denis, b Carenage, Trinidad 13 Mar 50. RHB, LM. KENT cap 1972. F-c career: 1,435 runs (av 18.88); 167 wits (av 28.34), 1 hat-trick. HS 90 v Northants (Dover) 1972. BB 7–63 N. Trinidad v S. Trinidad (Port-of-Spain) 1968–69.

A typical West Indian product; lively fast-medium bowler who can also bowl chinamen and googlies, ebullient batsman who could develop into something more, and a fine fieldsman. Rather slightly built for an opening bowler, but he does move the ball. It would come as no surprise if he eventually became a dashing strokemaker and a change, rather than a front line, bowler.

†**KALLICHARRAN, Alvin** Isaac, b Port Mourant, Berbice, B.G. 21 Mar 49. LHB, occ LB. WARWICKSHIRE cap 1972. 2 West Indies caps 1972, scoring 219 runs (av 109.50) with 2 hundreds – in his first two innings, HS 101. F-c career: 2,902 runs (av 45.34), 6 hundreds; 7 wkts (av 71.14). HS 164 v Notts (Coventry) 1972. BB 2–22 v Lancs (Birmingham) 1972.

Sparkling strokemaker from the Caribbean who has already proved himself a fine acquisition, both in the runs he has scored and the manner in which they have been made. Can bowl a useful leg-break, but length and line unreliable.

†**KANHAI, Rohan** Babulal, b Port Mourant, Berbice, B.G. 26 Dec 35. RHB, occ LB, former WK. WARWICKSHIRE cap 1968. 71 Test caps 1957–71 (66 for West Indies, 5 for Rest of the World), scoring 5,773 runs (av 47.31), with 14 hundreds (HS 256). F-c career: 22,888 runs (av 49.75), 68 hundreds; 13 wkts (av 53.92); 230 ct, 7 st. HS 256 West Indies v India (Calcutta) 1958–59. BB 2–5 Rest of the World XI v Pakistan XI (Karachi) 1970–71.

One of the finest, most exciting batsmen to come from the West Indies. Strong wrists and perfect timing enable him to hit the ball harder and further than seems possible for a player of his slight build. His ability to see the ball so early enables him to play several unconventional strokes – he has been known to finish flat on his back after smiting a six over square-leg. The hopes of bowlers that age would have dimmed his powers went unrewarded as he enjoyed a truly wonderful Indian summer in 1972, the runs flowing in an endless, fascinating stream from a bat that seemed to have a magical ring. Brilliant slip. Appointed West Indies captain against Australia 1972–73.

KENNEDY, Andrew, b Blackburn 4 Nov 49. LHB. LANCASHIRE – uncapped. F-c career (2 matches): 43 runs (av 21.50). HS 25 v Jamaica (Manchester) 1970.

A consistent 2nd XI batsman whose senior team chances have been reduced to two friendly matches spread over three years.

†**KHAN, MAJID JAHANGIR,** b Jullundur, India 28 Sep 46. Son of Dr Jahangir Khan (C.U. and India). RHB, RM/OB. GLAMORGAN cap 1968. Appointed captain 1973. Cambridge U. captain 1971–72. 12 Pakistan caps 1964–71, scoring 391 runs (av 24.43), HS 80, and taking 12 wkts (av 43.25), BB 2–32. F-c career: 12,929 runs (av 44.12), 36 hundreds; 170 wkts (av 30.27), 1 hat trick; 200 ct. HS 241 (Lahore Greens v Bahawalpur (Lahore) 1965–66. BB 6–67 Lahore 'B' v Khairpur (Lahore) 1961–62 – on f-c debut.

Captained Cambridge University with exceptional skill. A genuine world-class batsman with all the strokes who, amazingly, should become an even finer performer. Can demolish an attack with the power and brilliance of his batting and, in form, must rate as one of the most difficult people to bowl against. Was the only batsman to score more than 2,000 runs in first-class cricket in 1972. Originally a useful medium-paced swing bowler he now bowls off-breaks and might develop into more than an occasional spinner.

†KITCHEN, Mervyn John, b Nailsea 1 Aug 40. LHB, occ RM. SOMERSET cap 1966. F-c career: 11,526 runs (av 26.43), 14 hundreds; 2 wkts (av 39.50). HS 189 v Pakistanis (Taunton) 1967. BB 1–4.

Powerful middle-order lefthander who is at his best in an attacking role.

KNEW, George Alan, b Leicester 5 Mar 54. RHB. LEICESTERSHIRE – uncapped. F-c career (1 match): 19 runs (av 9.50). HS 14 v Oxford U. (Oxford) 1972.

Promising young 2nd XI batsman.

†KNIGHT, Roger David Verdon, b Streatham, London 6 Sep 46. LHB, RM. GLOUCESTERSHIRE cap 1971. Played for Surrey 1968–70. F-c career: 5,531 runs (av 28.07), 4 hundreds; 106 wkts (av 35.53). HS 164* and BB 6–65 Cambridge U. v Essex (Cambridge) 1970.

A recent recruit from Surrey, whose loss is Gloucester's gain. He is already one of their main run-getters and comes into the 'England possible' category. At the moment his front foot driving is the most impressive feature of his batting. A useful change bowler, he tends to move the ball into a righthander, and his height and action enable him to obtain lift. A batsman who can bowl rather than an all-rounder.

†KNOTT, Alan Philip Eric, b Belvedere 9 Apr 46. RHB, WK. KENT cap 1965. 41 England caps 1967–72, scoring 1,884 runs (av 34.88), HS 116, with 2 hundreds and making 137 dismissals (124 ct, 13 st). F-c career: 8,093 runs (av 27.90), 8 hundreds; 677 dismissals (592 ct, 85 st); 1 wkt. HS 156 MCC v South Zone (Bangalore) 1972–73.

Follows in the tradition of those great Kent wicket-keepers of the past, Leslie Ames and Godfrey Evans. Unless injured he is likely to remain an automatic first choice for England for many years to come. Exceptionally agile and nimble, he has already established himself as one of the great wicket-keepers of all time. His remarkable powers of concentration enable him to be as brilliant in the closing session of a long, hot, frustrating day as at the start. In addition to his value as a wicket-keeper, he is also a highly proficient, and on occasions dashing, batsman who has many outstanding innings to his credit when runs were really wanted for both Kent and England. Knott is the equivalent of another top-class all-rounder, for he is certainly worth his place in any county side for his batting alone.

LANCHBURY, Robert John, b Evesham 11 Feb 50. RHB. WORCESTERSHIRE – uncapped. Played for Glos 1971. F-c career: 112 runs (av 12.44). HS 38 Glos v Worcs (Cheltenham) 1971.

Correct opening batsman who has yet to appear in a f-c match for his native county.

LARKINS, Wayne, b Roxton, Beds 22 Nov 53. RHB. NORTHAMPTONSHIRE – uncapped. F-c career: 36 runs (av 4.50). HS 20 v Glos (Northampton) 1972.

A fairly consistent scorer in 2nd XI matches who failed to find any form at all during six f-c appearances last season.

LATCHMAN, Harry Chand, b Kingston, Jamaica 26 Jul 43. RHB,LB. MIDDLESEX cap 1968. F-c career: 1,520 runs (av 11.96); 383 wkts (av 27.28). HS 96 v Worcs (Kidderminster) 1972. BB 7–91 v Pakistanis (Lord's) 1967.

Although his successes in 1972 were limited, he can bowl his well flighted leg-breaks most effectively. Gives the ball plenty of air and is at his best on fast pitches. A reasonable lower-order batsman who looks better against spin than pace.

LAYCOCK, David Alan, b Woolwich 2 Sep 47. RHB. KENT – uncapped. F-c career: 264 runs (av 18.85). HS 58 v Leics (Canterbury) 1969 – on debut.

Reserve opening batsman whose opportunities have been limited to nine f-c matches in four seasons.

LEADBEATER, Barrie, b Harehills 14 Aug. 43. RHB, occ RM. YORKSHIRE cap 1969. F-c career: 2,727 runs (av 24.34); 1 wkt (av 5.00). HS 89* v Cambridge U. (Cambridge) 1970. BB 1–1.

Defensively correct opening batsman who has yet to score the runs expected of someone occupying that position for Yorkshire. Nevertheless the potential is there and he should blossom into a class player in the next two seasons.

LEE, Peter, b Arthingworth, Northants 27 Aug 45. RHB,RFM. LANCASHIRE cap 1972. Played for Northants 1967–71. F-c career: 316 runs (av. 8.77); 138 wkts (av 31.87). HS 26 Northants v Glos (Northampton) 1969. BB 6–86 Northants v Lancs (Northampton) 1969.

Promising fast-medium bowler who should improve with more experience.

†LEVER, John Kenneth, b Ilford 24 Feb 49. RHB,LFM. ESSEX cap 1970. F-c career: 838 runs (av 11.02); 299 wkts (av 26.00). HS 91 v Glam (Cardiff) 1970. BB 7–90 v Somerset (Leyton) 1971.

A most promising opening bowler with a fine build, good run-up, and a splendid body action. He does move the ball and could develop into an outstanding performer. Recent innings have furthered the impression that he might move from a bowler who can bat a little into the all-rounder category. A top-class outfielder.

LEVER, Peter, b Todmorden, Yorks 17 Sep 40. RHB,RFM. LANCASHIRE cap 1965. 13 England caps 1970–72, scoring 335 runs (23.92), HS 88*, and taking 34 wkts (av 32.23), BB 7–83. F-c career: 3,097 runs (av 15.64); 560 wkts (av 26.42), 1 hat-trick. HS 88* England v India (Manchester) 1971. BB 7–70 v Glam (Manchester) 1972.

Peter Lever really digs one in!

Determined fast-medium bowler who came into his own after the retirement of Statham and Higgs. Bowled particularly well for MCC in Australia. Has an over-long run-up for his pace, and a somewhat unattractive action, but he does move the ball about and his control is good. He was originally considered an all-rounder, and so it is only natural he should be an above-average tailender.

†**LEWINGTON, Peter** John, b Finchampstead, Berks 30 Jan 50. RHB,OB. WARWICKSHIRE – uncapped. F-c career: 60 runs (av 6.66); 47 wkts (av 26.40). HS 19 v Surrey (Oval) 1971. BB 4–39 v Glos (Gloucester) 1970.

Tall off-spinner whose opportunities, with Lance Gibbs around, are strictly limited.

†**LEWIS, Anthony** Robert, b Swansea 6 Jul 38. RHB, occ LB. GLAMORGAN cap 1960. Captain 1967–72. Captained MCC on 1972–73 tour of India, Sri Lanka, and Pakistan without previous Test experience. F-c career: 19,300 runs (av 33.10), 29 hundreds; 6 wkts (av 70.83). HS 223 v Kent (Gravesend) 1966. BB 3–18 v Somerset (Neath) 1967.

Good leader and sound tactician. At Cambridge he looked as if he was going to be the best bat the University had produced since Ted Dexter, but for some reason has never quite fulfilled that early promise. Makes runs attractively, is impressive against spin, and an innings of much character in the first Test against India – his debut – did much to establish him at international level.

LEWIS, Roy Markham, b Bromley, Kent 29 Jun 48. RHB, occ RM. SURREY – uncapped. F-c career: 1,611 runs (av 32.87). HS 87 v Kent (Blackheath) 1969.

Tall, powerfully-built opening batsman with a sound technique and fine range of strokes. His opportunities were limited until last season when he established himself in the side with a run of good scores.

LEWIS, Richard Victor, b Winchester 6 Aug 47. RHB, occ LB. HAMPSHIRE – uncapped. F-c career: 2,067 runs (av 20.06), 1 hundred; 1 wkt. HS 114 v Oxford U. (Oxford) 1968. BB 1–59.

The early promise of this attractive strokemaker has yet to mature. Perhaps lacking in concentration necessary for big scores. A keen fielder.

LLEWELLYN, Michael John, b Clydach 27 Nov 53. LHB,OB. GLAMORGAN – uncapped. F-c career: 263 runs (av 17.53), 1 hundred; 21 wkts (av 24.14). HS 112* v Cambridge U. (Swansea) 1972. BB 4–35 v Oxford U. (Oxford) 1970 – on debut.

A very exciting prospect. At 18 years, 7 months, this aggressive left-handed bat became the youngest Glamorgan century-maker when he hammered the Cambridge bowling for four sixes and ten fours last season. Useful close fielder.

LLOYD, Barry John, b Neath 6 Sep 53. RHB, OB. GLAMORGAN – uncapped. F-c career: 0 runs; 1 wkt.

A 19 year-old off-spinner, now studying teaching, who made one first-class appearance last season.

†**LLOYD, Clive** Hubert, b Georgetown, B.G. 31 Aug 44. LHB,RM. LANCASHIRE cap 1969. 30 Test caps (25 for West Indies, 5 for Rest of the World) 1966–72, scoring 1,920 runs (av 37.64) with 5 hundreds, HS 129, and taking 11 wkts (av 41.09), BB 3–34. F-c career: 9,892 runs (av 44.55), 23 hundreds; 89 wkts (av 36.00). HS 217* v Warwicks (Manchester) 1971. BB 4–48 v Leics (Manchester) 1970.

Superb West Indian strokemaker who has the

ability to win matches with his aggressive batting; is especially valuable in limited-overs cricket. Liable to be diffident at the start of an innings, but once established he invariably takes the initiative away from the bowlers. He is a world-class performer and a natural entertainer, the type of batsman spectators love, because he hits the ball so hard and so often. Useful medium-pace change bowler. One of the most exciting and brilliant fieldsmen the game has produced. Saves many runs in the covers, not only because he stops shots that many would consider boundaries, but also because batsmen are understandably wary of running when he is around.

LLOYD, David, b Accrington 18 Mar 47. LHB, SLA. LANCASHIRE cap 1968. Appointed captain for 1973. F-c career: 7,204 runs (av 29.52), 11 hundreds; 112 wkts (av 28.46). HS 177 v Worcs (Worcester) 1972. BB 7–38 v Glos (Lydney) 1966.

Reliable left-handed bat with an excellent temperament. He plays straight and possesses an attractive cover drive. Orthodox slow left-arm bowler.

†**LONG, Arnold,** b Cheam 18 Dec 40. LHB, WK. SURREY cap 1962. F-c career: 4,412 runs (av 15.70); 706 dismissals (618 ct, 88 st). HS 92 v Leics (Leicester) 1970. Held 11 catches in match v Sussex (Hove) 1964 to set world f-c record.

Chirpy little wicket-keeper whose unspectacular but efficient handling of a vital job has not always received the praise it deserved. Useful lower-order batsman.

LUCKHURST, Brian William, b Sittingbourne 5 Feb 39. RHB, occ SLA. KENT cap 1963. 22 England caps 1970–72, scoring 1,585 runs (av 42.83) with 5 hundreds, HS 131, and taking 1 wkt. F-c career: 18,257 runs (av 39.77), 40 hundreds; 53 wkts (av 46.60); 315 ct. HS 203* v Cambridge U. (Cambridge) 1970. BB 4–32 v Somerset (Gravesend) 1962.

A dependable, sound, and effective opening bat who, for the past decade, has been among the most consistent run-getters. He has an effective, rather than an attractive, style. His defence is very solid and he invariably sells his wicket dearly. Like so many batsmen whose right hand has become the dominant partner, he is an expert cutter. Although not by nature a fast scorer, he has played a number of fine knocks for Kent in limited-overs cricket, where his ability to pace an innings has proved an enormous asset. One of the best all-purpose fieldsmen in the game.

LUMB, Richard Graham, b Doncaster 27 Feb 50. RHB. YORKSHIRE – uncapped. F-c career: 795 runs (av 27.41). HS 79 v Worcs (Sheffield) 1972.

Probably the most promising of the current batch of Yorkshire colts, this tall (6 ft 3 in) opening bat scored consistently last season and should now produce some really big scores.

†**McKENZIE, Graham** Douglas, b Cottesloe, Australia 24 Jun 41. RHB, RFM. LEICESTERSHIRE cap 1969. 63 Test caps 1961–71 (60 for Australia, 3 for Rest of the World), scoring 955 runs (av 12.08), HS 76, and taking 255 wkts (av 29.84), BB 8–71. F-c career: 4,968 runs (av 15.62); 1,009 wkts (av 27.62). HS 76 Australia v South Africa (Sydney) 1963–64. BB 8–71 Australia v West Indies (Melbourne) 1968–69.

World-class fast bowler who was unlucky not to have been chosen to yet again tour this country with the Australians last season. With a short run-up, and relying for his pace on a fine body action, he is very much a rhythm bowler, and, when not 'clicking', is liable to spray the ball about. Is less put off by the run-up limitation in Sunday cricket than most of his breed and therefore is more effective.

McVICKER, Norman Michael, b Radcliffe, Lancs 4 Nov 40. RHB, RFM. WARWICKSHIRE cap 1971. F-c career: 1,206 runs (av 15.86); 254 wkts (av 26.37). HS 65* v Lancs (Manchester) 1972. BB 7-29 v Northants (Birmingham) 1969.

Emerged from Minor Counties cricket at a comparatively late age for a seamer, but immediately made his mark for Warwickshire with his persistent bowling.

MALTBY, Norman, b Marske-by-the-Sea, Yorks 16 Jul 51. LHB, RM. NORTHAMPTONSHIRE – uncapped. F-c career: 79 runs (av 19.75); 2 wkts (av 27.50). HS 36 and BB 2-43 v Somerset (Wellingborough) 1972.

Medium-paced seam bowler and useful middle-order bat who gained valuable experience in three 1st team matches at the end of last season. Could be especially useful in one-day games.

MANSELL, Alan William, b Redhill, Surrey 19 May 51. RHB, WK. SUSSEX – uncapped. F-c career: 82 runs (av 16.40); 23 dismissals (19 ct, 4 st). HS 51 v Hants (Portsmouth) 1971.

Extremely talented young wicket-keeper, similar in build to Alan Knott, for whom Sussex predict a great future. Succeeds Jim Parks as 1st team wicket-keeper this season.

MARRIOTT, Dennis Alston, b Annotto Bay, Jamaica 29 Nov 39. RHB, LM. MIDDLESEX – uncapped. Played for Surrey 1965–67. F-c career: 98 runs (av 14.00); 46 wkts (av 29.23). HS 24* Surrey v Leics (Leicester) 1967. BB 4-45 Surrey v Leics (Guildford) 1967.

Formerly with Surrey; has after several successful seasons in club cricket, been signed by Middlesex. A left-arm medium-pace bowler who, rather surprisingly, prefers to bowl round the wicket, cutting the ball into the right-hander.

MATTHEWS, Robin Birkby, b Stockton-on-Tees, Co Durham 30 Jan 44. RHB, RM. LEICESTERSHIRE – uncapped. F-c career: 58 runs (av 11.60); 31 wkts (av 25.51). HS 16* and BB 7-51 v Sussex (Hove) 1972.

Tall (6 ft 4 in) seamer whose build and action allow him to extract lift from the 'flattest' pitches. Played for Oxfordshire 1964–69 and is a latecomer to the f-c game.

MILTON, Clement Arthur, b Bristol 10 Mar 28. RHB, RM. GLOUCESTERSHIRE cap 1949. Captain 1968. 6 England caps 1958–59, scoring 204 runs (av 25.50), with 1 hundred – 104* on debut. F-c career: 31,606 runs (av 34.13), 56 hundreds; 79 wkts (av 45.94); 740 ct. HS 170 v Sussex (Cheltenham) 1965. BB 5-64 v Glam (Gloucester) 1950.

Now at the end of a fine career in which he has scored thousands of runs in his neat, unobtrusive fashion. Uncharacteristically for a player brought up on Bristol pitches, he has a marked preference for the back foot and is particularly adept at keeping the scoreboard moving with well placed singles. Almost certainly the last of that rare breed, the double international, who has represented his country at both cricket and soccer. As one would expect from a former First Division footballer he was very agile in the field and became one of the great close fieldsmen.

MORLEY, Jeremy Dennis, b Newmarket, Suffolk 20 Oct 50. LHB. SUSSEX – uncapped. F-c career: 388 runs (av 24.25). HS 76 v Notts (Hove) 1972.

Left-handed opening batsman who played for Cambridgeshire 1969–70 and spent three years on the MCC staff. Has usually had to bat at No. 7 in the 1st team.

MORTIMORE, John Brian, b Bristol 14 May 33. RHB,OB. GLOUCESTERSHIRE cap 1954. Captain 1965–67. 9 England caps 1959–64, scoring 243 runs (av 24.30), HS 73*, and taking 13 wkts (av 56.38), BB 3–36. F-c career: 15,356 runs (av 18.61), 4 hundreds; 1,707 wkts (av 22.68); 335 ct. HS 149 v Notts (Nottingham) 1963. BB 8–59 v Oxford U (Oxford) 1959.

Continues in the long line of great Gloucester off-spinners. He is very much an all-purpose bowler who can be devastating on a bad pitch and is prepared to nag away on a good one. In both circumstances his accuracy is an enormous asset, because his immaculate length means that a batsman must take chances to score runs. Not as big a finger spinner as his former colleague David Allen, but he does enough to beat the bat and has an effective and well hidden away-drifter. A typical Gloucester-style batsman; upright, with a preference for the front foot and the ability to drive with the full follow-through from a high backlift.

†**MOSELEY, Hallam** Reynold, b Christchurch, Barbados 28 May 48. RHB,RFM. SOMERSET cap 1972. F-c career: 484 runs (av 17.92); 82 wkts (av 29.76). HS 67 v Leics (Taunton) 1972. BB 5–52 v Glam (Cardiff) 1971.

Springy opening bowler and a vigorous hitter of the ball.

MOTTRAM, Thomas James, b Liverpool, Lancs 7 Sep 45. RHB,RM. HAMPSHIRE – uncapped. F-c career: 4 runs; 20 wkts (av 20.25). HS 3. BB 5–45 v Worcs (Portsmouth) 1972.

This tall (6 ft 4 in) seamer took 20 wickets in his only four f-c matches last year. Good control of line and length – moves the ball late. His profession (architect) allows few opportunities for playing cricket.

†**MURRAY, Deryck** Lance, b Port-of-Spain, Trinidad 20 May 43. RHB,WK, occ LB. WARWICKSHIRE cap 1972. Played for Notts 1966–69. 13 Test caps 1963–70 (10 for West Indies, 3 for Rest of the World), scoring 369 runs (av 20.50), HS 95, and making 53 dismissals (50 ct, 3 st). F-c career: 7,246 runs (av 28.52), 7 hundreds; 407 dismissals (352 ct, 55 st); 4 wkts (av 51.00). HS 166* Notts v Surrey (Oval) 1966. BB 2–50 West Indians v President's XI (Nagpur) 1966–67.

First came to fame when he kept so well on the West Indies 1963 tour of England. One of the foremost wicket-keeper-batsmen in the game and a strong candidate to lead the West Indies in England this summer.

†**MURRAY, John** Thomas, b Kensington 1 Apr 35. RHB,WK, occ RM. MIDDLESEX cap 1956. 21 England caps 1961–67, scoring 506 runs (av 22.00) with 1 hundred (112), and making 55 dismissals (52 ct, 3 st). F-c career: 16,654 runs (av 23.29), 14 hundreds; 1,365 dismissals (1,138 ct, 227 st); 6 wkts (av 40.50). HS 142 MCC v North-Eastern Transvaal (Pretoria) 1964–65. BB 2–10 MCC v Bombay (Bombay) 1961–62.

Highly experienced wicket-keeper who has brought off brilliant catches standing back and is far better up at the stumps than he is given credit for. A dangerous attacking batsman, he relishes hooking and straight driving, and had it been not for his wicket-keeping he might well have developed into an outstanding batsman. Now he is an effective, slightly unreliable strokemaker.

†**MUSHTAQ MOHAMMAD**, b Junagadh, India 22 Nov 43. RHB,LB. NORTHAMPTONSHIRE cap 1967. 27 Test caps 1959–71 (25 for Pakistan, 2 for Rest of the World), scoring 1,387 runs (av 32.25), with 3 hundreds (HS 101),

Hard-hitting David Nicholls makes use of his powerful physique to deposit the ball over the boundary

and taking 15 wkts (av 44.66), BB 4–80. F-c career: 20,217 runs (av 42.74), 47 hundreds; 607 wkts (av 22.70); 219 ct. HS 303* Karachi Blues v Karachi U. (Karachi) 1967–68. BB 7–18 Karachi Whites v Khairpur (Karachi) 1963–64.

World-class all-rounder who enjoyed a superb summer for Northants in 1972. Excels in all three departments. He is a brilliant attacking batsman with a wide range of strokes, both conventional and unconventional, and a lovely cutter, despite a distinct partiality for the on-side. Fascinating leg-break and googly bowler who is essentially an attacker, always trying to remove the opposition rather than merely contain them. Consequently his willingness to experiment may make his wickets costly.

NANAN, Nirmal, b Preysal Village, Couva, Trinidad 19 Aug 51. RHB, LB. NOTTINGHAMSHIRE – uncapped. F-c career: 263 runs (av 20.23); 5 wkts (av 25.40). HS 72 and BB 3–12 v Oxford U. (Oxford) 1971.

Exciting all-round prospect who toured Britain with Wes Hall's Young West Indies team in 1970. Has still to adapt to English conditions.

NASH, Malcolm Andrew, b Abergavenny, Monmouths. 9 May 45. LHB, LM. GLAMORGAN cap 1969. F-c career: 2,809 runs (av 17.44); 370 wkts (av 24.15). HS 82 v Middx (Cardiff) 1972. BB 7–15 v Somerset (Swansea) 1968.

Effective swing bowler, especially dangerous with the new ball. Enthusiastic batsman with an invigorating approach that has proved both productive and entertaining.

NICHOLLS, David, b East Dereham, Norfolk 8 Dec 43. LHB, WK, occ LB. KENT cap 1969. F-c career: 4,903 runs (av 21.13), 2 hundreds; 187 dismissals (180 ct, 7 st); 2 wkts. HS 211 v Derbys (Folkestone) 1963. BB 1–0.

A chunky left-hand bat who hits the ball hard and is at his best opening, for he is particularly partial to seam bowling. Cuts well and is strong off the back foot. Useful reserve wicket-keeper.

NICHOLLS, Ronald Bernard, b Sharpness 4 Dec 33. RHB, occ OB, occ WK. GLOUCESTERSHIRE cap 1957. F-c career: 22,463 runs (av 26.33), 17 hundreds; 7 wkts (av 77.00); 278 ct, 1 st. HS 217 v Oxford U. (Oxford) 1962. BB 2–19 v Glam (Neath) 1964.

Most correct, stylish opening batsman in the Tom Graveney mould; a top-of-the-handle, upright player with a classical drive. He has been the backbone of the team's batting for a long time.

NICHOLSON, Anthony George, b Dewsbury 25 Jun 38. RHB, RFM. YORKSHIRE cap 1963.

F-c career: 1,298 runs (av 10.90); 757 wkts (av 19.53). HS 43 v Kent (Bradford) 1968. BB 9–62 v Sussex (Eastbourne) 1967.

One of the best opening bowlers in the country. Moves the ball away in the air and also bowls a sharp break-back. He is extremely accurate and gives little away. Pace closer to medium than fast.

NORMAN, Michael Eric John Charles, b Northampton, Northants 19 Jan 33. RHB, occ RM. LEICESTERSHIRE cap 1966. Played for Northants 1952–65. F-c career: 16,959 runs (av 29.85), 24 hundreds; 2 wkts (av 82.00). HS 221* v Cambridge U. (Cambridge) 1967. BB 2–0 Northants v Lancs (Northampton) 1961.

Experienced grafter who showed his ability in the few matches for which he was available.

†**O'KEEFFE, Kerry** James, b Sydney, Australia 25 Nov 49. RHB, LB. SOMERSET cap 1971. 2 Australia caps 1971, scoring 42 runs (av 14.00), HS 27, and taking 6 wkts (av 43.33), BB 3–48. F-c career: 1,784 runs (av 22.58); 232 wkts (av 29.30). HS 81* New South Wales v South Australia (Adelaide) 1970–71. BB 7–38 v Sussex (Taunton) 1971.

Leg-break bowler of the faster, flatter variety. He should thrive in English conditions but was disappointing with the ball last summer. Like most Australian bowlers, he bats well enough to come into the all-rounder category, at least in county cricket.

†**OLD, Christopher** Middleton, b Middlesbrough 22 Dec 48. LHB, RFM. YORKSHIRE cap 1969. 2 England caps 1970, scoring 42 runs (av 10.50), HS 37, and taking 2 wkts (av 92.00), BB 2–70. F-c career: 1,532 runs (av 15.79); 271 wkts (av 21.33). HS 92* v Somerset (Taunton) 1970. BB 7–20 v Glos (Middlesbrough) 1969.

Highly promising fast bowler who moves the ball away from the righthander. Could become an England regular in the next few seasons. No mean performer as a left-hand bat with a liking for the drive. Toured with MCC this past winter.

ORMROD, Joseph Alan, b Ramsbottom, Lancs 22 Dec 42. RHB, occ OB. WORCESTERSHIRE cap 1966. F-c career: 10,082 runs (av 26.95), 7 hundreds; 24 wkts (av 41.37); 209 ct. HS 157* v Leics (Worcester) 1972. BB 5–27 v Glos (Bristol) 1972.

Correct middle-order batsman whose straight-bat shots off the back foot are especially impressive.

†**O'SULLIVAN, David** Robert b Palmerston North, New Zealand 16 Nov 44. RHB, SLA. HAMPSHIRE – uncapped. Test debut for New Zealand 1972–73. F-c career: 131 runs (av 14.55); 37 wkts (av 27.27). HS 33 v Glam (Portsmouth) 1972. BB 5–116 v Indians (Bournemouth) 1971 – on debut.

Slow left-arm bowler who did not qualify to play for Hampshire until halfway through last season.

OWEN-THOMAS, Dudley Richard, b Mombasa, Kenya 20 Sep 48. RHB, OB. SURREY – uncapped. F-c career 3,198 runs (av 32.96), 7 hundreds; 20 wkts (av 39.60). HS 182* Cambridge U. v Middx (Cambridge) 1969. 3–20 Cambridge U. v Worcs (Halesowen) 1969.

Most promising young player who has the makings of a good performer at county level. Time alone will tell if he has that little extra to take him into the international category. Small, correct, and quick on his feet, he has produced pleasant little innings of 30 and 40 but insufficient big ones.

PAGE, Michael Harry, b Blackpool, Lancs 17 Jun 41. RHB, occ OB. DERBYSHIRE cap 1964. F-c career: 8,627 runs (av 27.65), 8 hundreds; 7 wkts (av 71.57); 202 ct. HS 162 v Leics (Leicester) 1969. BB 1-0.

Elegant with a graceful style; always looks as if he should score more runs than he does.

PARFITT, Peter Howard, b Billingford, Norfolk 8 Dec 36. LHB, OB. DERBYSHIRE – uncapped. Played for Middx 1956–72 – captain 1968–70. 37 England caps 1961–72, scoring 1,882 runs (av 40.91), with 7 hundreds (HS 131*), and taking 12 wkts (av 47.83), BB 2-5. F-c career: 26,811 runs (av 36.28), 58 hundreds; 277 wkts (av 30.32); 562 ct. HS 200* Middx v Notts (Nottingham) 1964. BB 6-45 Middx v Oxford U. (Oxford) 1969.

Highly experienced lefthander who may join Derbyshire after a long and very successful career with Middlesex. He is bound to do well for his new county for he is still batting impressively, as was shown last summer when he was recalled to the England side. Small and compact, he has always looked happier on his front foot than his back, which may explain why he never completely bridged the gap between the very good county batsman and the great player. Splendid all-purpose fieldsman in his youth and still a well above-average performer anywhere near the bat. Bowls off-breaks.

†**PARKER, John** Morton, b Dannevirke, New Zealand 21 Feb 51. RHB, occ LB. WORCESTERSHIRE – uncapped. Test debut for New Zealand 1972–73. F-c career: 960 runs (av 41.73), 1 hundred; 1 wkt (av 14.00). HS 195 Northern Districts v Canterbury (Whangarei) 1972–73. BB 1-14.

Promising New Zealand batsman with character and an obvious appetite for batting. Could well develop into a class player.

†**PARKS, James** Michael, b Haywards Heath, Sussex 21 Oct 31. RHB, WK, occ LB. SOMERSET – uncapped. Played for Sussex 1949–72 – captain 1967–68. 46 England caps 1954–68, scoring 1,962 runs (av 32.16), with 2 hundreds (HS 108*), making 114 dismissals (103 ct, 11 st), and taking 1 wkt. F-c career: 34,709 runs (av 35.09), 50 hundreds; 51 wkts (av 43.25); 1,145 dismissals (1,052 ct, 93 st.) HS 205* Sussex v Somerset (Hove) 1955. BB 3-23 Sussex v Cambridge U. (Horsham) 1955.

Long-serving wicket-keeper-batsman for Sussex and England. A graceful, free-flowing bat with a very open stance, he uses his feet to attack the spinners far better than most of his contemporaries and can hit over the top of fielders with precision. Originally an outstanding fieldsman, he turned himself into an adequate, and at times brilliant, county wicket-keeper. Misses few chances standing back, which has been all he has been required to do for Sussex for 90 per cent of the time.

PEARMAN, Hugh, b Birmingham, Warwicks 1 Jun 45. RHB, SLA. MIDDLESEX – uncapped. F-c career: 294 runs (av 18.37); 16 wkts (av 36.12). HS 61 v Glos (Cheltenham) 1972. BB 4-56 Cambridge U. v Oxford U. (Lord's) 1969.

A talented all-rounder: attractive strokemaker and slow bowler who plays for Hornsey CC.

PHILLIPSON, Christopher Paul, b Brindaban, India 10 Feb 52. RHB, RM. SUSSEX – uncapped. F-c career: 47 runs (av 4.27); 33 wkts (av 35.60). HS 10* v Middx (Lord's) 1971. BB 6-56 v Notts (Hove) 1972.

Tall seam bowler, remarkably like John Snow in appearance, who did well in the John Player League and could easily develop into a stock bowler in f-c matches.

Above: Sussex keeper Jim Parks ended his long association with the county early in 1973

Left: Kent's chunky David Nicholls shows his liking for the cut

Below: Chris Old, Yorkshire's young fast bowler who served England well in India and Pakistan

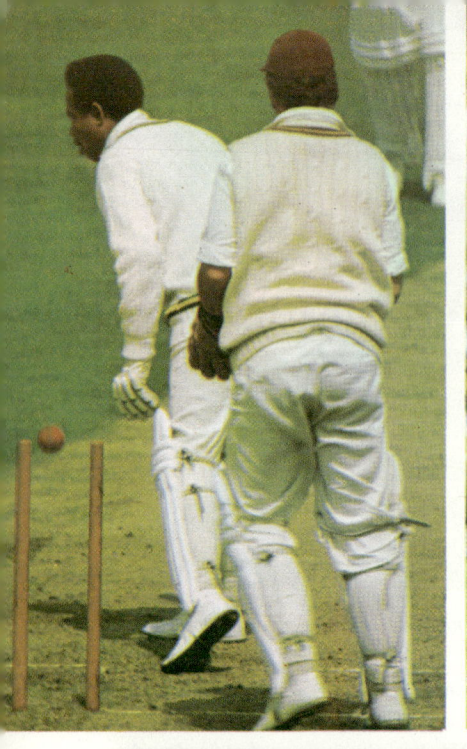

Above left: Gary Sobers is well and truly bowled by Bedi. Sobers, troubled by injury, did not enjoy the happiest of seasons in 1972. For 1973, however, he returns to Nottinghamshire much rested and again as captain. Both Notts and the West Indies, who tour Britain in 1973, hope the great all-rounder will be back to his old form

Above: Graham Roope will return to Surrey in 1973 as an England Test cricketer, having won his first cap in India – as an opening batsman!

Left: Barry Wood batting against Australia on his Test debut at The Oval. In his second innings he looked set for a century before falling lbw to Massie for 90

Diminutive he may be, but Harry Pilling is never reluctant to put bat to ball in a most attractive and productive style

Register of County Cricketers

PILLING, Harry (*not 'H.R.'*), b Ashton-under-Lyne 23 Feb 43. RHB, occ OB. LANCASHIRE cap 1965. Is the shortest (5 ft 3 in) current British f-c cricketer. F-c career: 10,472 runs (av 31.92), 17 hundreds; 1 wkt. HS 133* v Hants (Portsmouth) 1963. BB 1–42.

Diminutive middle-order batsman who, like so many little men, is an extremely effective cutter. Has the ability to improvise, which makes him more valuable in limited-overs cricket than many big hitters. At a distinct disadvantage on a 'lifting' pitch.

†POCOCK, Patrick Ian, b Bangor, Caernarvons 24 Sep 46. RHB, OB. SURREY cap 1967. 4 England caps 1968–69, scoring 48 runs (av 6.85), HS 13, and taking 12 wkts (av 42.75), BB 6–79. F-c career: 2,615 runs (av 11.94); 762 wkts (av 24.14), 2 hat-tricks. HS 75* v Notts (Oval) 1968. BB 7–57 v Essex (Romford) 1968. Took 7 wkts in 11 balls (incl. 4 in 4, 5 in 6, and 6 in 9) v Sussex (Eastbourne) 1972.

A fine off-break bowler with a deceptive dipping flight who is still improving. A thoughtful, attacking bowler, who gives the ball a considerable tweak, he is prepared to experiment rather more than the average English off-spinner. A rather awkward-looking tailender, he nonetheless makes some useful scores when he gets his head down.

PONT, Keith Rupert, b Wanstead 16 Jan 53. RHB, occ RM. ESSEX – uncapped. F-c career: 365 runs (av 26.07); 1 wkt. HS 75* v Worcs (Leyton) 1972. BB 1–15.

Young player whose performances have already suggested he could develop into a fine batsman. Also a useful change seamer.

PRICE, John Sidney Ernest, b Harrow 22 Jul 37. LHB, RF. MIDDLESEX cap 1963. 15 England caps 1964–72, scoring 66 runs (av

7.33), HS 32, and taking 40 wkts (av 35.02), BB 5–73. F-c career: 1,006 runs (av 8.17); 760 wkts (av 23.77). HS 53* D. H. Robins's XI v West Indians (Eastbourne) 1969. BB 8–48 v Derbys (Lord's) 1966.

Opening bowler of genuine pace with an unusual, rather ugly, round-the-corner run-up of considerable length. He may not be an aesthetically pleasing speed-merchant, but he is quick enough to inconvenience any batsman and to worry the faint-hearted. Has a powerful body action and can bring the odd ball back sharply from the off. Unavailable on a full-time basis this summer.

†**PRIDEAUX, Roger** Malcolm, b Chelsea, London 31 Jul 39. RHB, occ RM. SUSSEX cap 1971. Played for Kent 1960–61 and for Northants 1962-70 (captain 1967–70). 3 England caps 1968–69, scoring 102 runs (av 20.40), HS 64. F-c career: 23,828 runs (av 34.63), 40 hundreds; 2 wkts (av 38.00); 280 ct. HS 202* Northants v Oxford U. (Oxford) 1963. BB 2–13 v Cambridge U. (Cambridge) 1972.

Possesses one of the soundest defences in the game and is probably at his best as an opener, a job he has done well for both Northants and England. He can, however, bat anywhere and has brought much needed solidarity to Sussex.

PRIDGEON, Alan Paul, b Wall Heath, Staffs 22 Feb 54. RHB, RM. WORCESTERSHIRE – uncapped. F-c career: 9 runs (av 2.25); 7 wkts (av 81.14). HS 4*. BB 3–50 v Leics (Worcester) 1972.

Flame-haired seamer who has yet to make his mark at county level.

†**PROCTER, Michael** John, b Durban, South Africa 15 Sep 46. RHB, RF. GLOUCESTERSHIRE cap 1968. 12 Test caps 1967–70 (7 for South Africa, 5 for Rest of the World), scoring 518 runs (av 34.53). HS 62, and taking 56 wkts (av 17.41), BB 6–73. F-c career: 9,058 runs (av 36.08), 24 hundreds – including 6 in successive innings 1970–71; 616 wkts (av 17.75), 1 hat-trick. HS 254 Rhodesia v Western Province (Salisbury) 1970–71. BB 9–71 Rhodesia v Transvaal (Bulawayo) 1972–73.

The most potent individual force in county cricket, a Test-class opening fast bowler and forcing bat. He is genuinely quick and his unusual, very open-chested and whippy action enables him to achieve a big inswing. This ability to move the ball so much allows him to operate from round the wicket and still get lbw decisions. A fluent and powerful strokemaker, he can pierce a deep-set field with the force of his driving off both his front and his back foot. He is also more than prepared to hit the ball out of the ground. The pity is that his South African qualifications debar him from the international scene, for he is quite clearly one of the finest all-rounders in the history of the game – a match winner with either bat or ball.

PULLAN, David Anthony, b Farsley, Yorks 1 May 44. RHB, WK. NOTTINGHAMSHIRE cap 1971. F-c career: 473 runs (av 9.65); 189 dismissals (169 ct, 20 st). HS 34 v Warwicks (Nottingham) 1972.

An efficient wicket-keeper who is improving season by season. Regularly exceeds 50 f-c dismissals each year, possibly favoured by keeping wicket to a predominantly seam attack.

†**RADLEY, Clive** Thornton, b Hertford, Herts 13 May 44. RHB, occ LB. MIDDLESEX cap 1967. F-c career: 8,852 runs (av 33.15), 12 hundreds; 2 wkts (av 12.00). HS 139 v Sussex (Hove) 1967. BB 1–7.

Among the most consistent uncapped batsmen in the country. Somewhat squat in method, he is effective rather than attractive, but he does score runs and is certainly no slouch. His adaptability and redoubtable fighting qualities suggest he might make it at Test level. He has the added advantage of being a brilliant fieldsman.

RANDALL, Derek William, b Retford 24 Feb 51. RHB. NOTTINGHAMSHIRE – uncapped. F-c career: 550 runs (av 22.91). HS 78 v Essex (Newark) 1972 – on debut.

A most exciting stroke-maker who hit five sixes in his first f-c innings. Brilliant cover fielder, particularly in one-day games. One of several colts who should put Nottinghamshire cricket back on the map.

RATCLIFFE, Robert Malcolm, b Accrington 29 Nov 51. RHB,RM. LANCASHIRE – uncapped. F-c career (2 matches); 2 runs.

A Lancashire League all-rounder who joined the county staff in 1971 and made two unsuccessful Championship appearances last season.

RICE, John Michael, b Chandler's Ford 23 Oct 49. RHB,RM. HAMPSHIRE – uncapped. F-c career: 163 runs (av 9.58); 34 wkts (av 39.41). HS 26 v Worcs (Portsmouth) 1972. BB 4-64 v Sussex (Bournemouth) 1972.

Like so many tall, lean bowlers, Rice has been plagued by knee injuries. Extracts surprising lift and is quicker than his gentle approach suggests.

†RICHARDS, Barry Anderson, b Durban, South Africa 21 Jul 45. RHB,OB. HAMPSHIRE cap 1968. One appearance for Glos 1965. 9 Test caps 1970 (4 for South Africa, 5 for Rest of the World), scoring 765 runs (av 54.64) with 2 hundreds, HS 140, and taking 1 wkt. F-c career: 15,504 runs (av 55.97), 42 hundreds; 44 wkts (av 37.00). HS 356 South Australia v Western Australia (Perth) 1970–71. BB 7–63 v Rest of the World XI (Bournemouth) 1968.

An opening batsman who would grace a Test XI of any era, which underlines how unfortunate it is that his South African birth prevents him from participating in international cricket. It is doubtful whether there has ever been his superior in terms of pure technical perfection. He sees the ball early, has every shot in the book, the footwork and the timing. A truly great orthodox batsman who can also improvise. His only weakness is that, because he finds run scoring so much easier than practically anyone else, he has been known to become bored with the proceedings. He needs an additional incentive, or to be playing in the higher level of Test cricket, to maintain his true potential.

RICHARDS, Gwyn, b Maesteg 29 Nov 51. RHB. GLAMORGAN – uncapped. F-c career: 205 runs (av 14.64). HS 41 v Cambridge U. (Swansea) 1972.

A moderately successful 2nd XI batsman who has yet to be given an extended 1st team trial. Good close fielder.

ROBINSON, Arthur Leslie (**'Rocker'**), b Brompton 17 Aug 46. LHB,LFM. YORKSHIRE – uncapped. F-c career: 6 wkts (av 32.50). BB 2–22 v Sussex (Hove) 1971.

This tall, strongly-built fast-medium bowler has a splendid chance of establishing a 1st team place this season now that Hutton has retired and Nicholson's health is uncertain. Has yet to bat in a f-c match but plays for Leeds as an all-rounder.

ROBINSON, Peter James, b Worcester, Worcs 9 Feb 43. LHB,SLA. SOMERSET cap 1966. Played for Worcs 1963–64. F-c career: 4,626 runs (av 22.02), 3 hundreds; 292 wkts (av 27.35). HS 140 v Northants (Northampton) 1970. BB 7–10 v Notts (Nottingham) 1966.

Valuable utility player who was relegated to the 2nd XI for most of last season. Grafting opener who fields superbly and, on a pitch giving assistance, can win a match with his left-arm leg-breaks.

†**ROOPE, Graham** Richard James, b Fareham, Hants 12 Jul. 46. RHB, RM. SURREY cap 1969. England debut in India 1972–73. F-c career: 6,724 runs (av 33.78), 8 hundreds; 127 wkts (av 34.62); 218 ct, 1 st. HS 171 v Yorks (Oval) 1971. BB 5–14 v West Indians (Oval) 1969.

A batsman who can bowl, rather than a real all-rounder. One of the few young middle-order English batsmen to catch the eye. A correct, interesting strokemaker, he might establish himself in the England XI following last winter's MCC tour, especially as he has the considerable advantage of being a superb fielder. With the ball he is, at the moment, just another typically English seamer.

ROSE, Brian Charles, b Dartford, Kent 4 Jun 50. LHB, occ LM. SOMERSET – uncapped. F-c career: 682 runs (av 17.48), 1 hundred; 1 wkt. HS 125 v Kent (Glastonbury) 1972. BB 1–5.

Tall, elegant lefthander who, after an abortive couple of seasons on the staff, abandoned cricket for a teacher's training course. Last summer he returned to the Somerset team for three matches during his vacation and scored 252 runs, average 50.40, including a splendid hundred against Kent.

ROUSE, Stephen John ('**Mick**'), b Merthyr Tydfil, Glam 20 Jan 49. LHB, LM. WARWICKSHIRE – uncapped. F-c career: 260 runs (av 11.81); 69 wkts (av 31.07). HS 38* v Notts (Birmingham) 1971. BB 5–47 v Lancs (Manchester) 1972.

Tall, well-built, left-arm seamer.

RUMSEY, Frederick Edward, b Stepney, London 4 Dec 35. RHB, LFM. Played for Worcs 1960–62 and for Somerset 1963–68. Joined DERBYSHIRE 1969 as PRO – uncapped. 5 England caps 1964–65 scoring 30 runs (av 15.00) and taking 17 wkts (av 27.11), BB 4–25 F-c career: 1,015 runs (av 8.45); 580 wkts (av 20.29). HS 45 Somerset v Sussex (Weston-s-Mare) 1967. BB 8–26 Somerset v Hants (Bath) 1965.

Big strong left-arm fast bowler whose appearances are limited to John Player League matches.

†**SADIQ MOHAMMAD,** b Junagadh, India 3 May 45. LHB, LB. GLOUCESTERSHIRE – uncapped. 6 Pakistan caps 1969–71, scoring 327 runs (av 32.70), HS 91. F-c career: 4,317 runs (av 33.72), 7 hundreds; 88 wkts (av 25.14). HS 167 Karachi Blues v Rawalpindi Greens (Karachi) 1969–70. BB 5–29 PIA v Dacca (Dacca) 1964–65 and for Karachi Blues v Lahore Greens (Karachi) 1970–71.

Neat, diminutive opening bat who has yet to find his true form for his county. Also a reasonable county spinner.

SAINSBURY, Peter James, b Southampton 13 Jun 34. RHB, SLA. HAMPSHIRE cap 1955. F-c career: 17,469 runs (av 26.42), 5 hundreds; 1,107 wkts (av 24.92); 570 ct. HS 163 v Oxford U. (Oxford) 1962. BB 8–76 v Glos (Portsmouth) 1971.

Has given Hampshire outstanding service in all departments – as a stubborn bat, as a slow left-armer, as a brilliant short leg, and as a fine club man. He is the ideal person to come to the crease after a collapse and always sells his wicket dearly. He has a lovely action but has never captured as many victims as expected, largely because he has never been able to cash in on the odd 'sticky' to the extent expected of a spinner.

SAVILLE, Graham John, b Leytonstone 5 Feb 44. RHB, occ LB. ESSEX cap 1970. F-c career: 4,340 runs (av 24.11), 3 hundreds; 3 wkts (av 25.33). HS 126* v Glam (Swansea) 1972. BB 2–30 v Kent (Chelmsford) 1971.

A sound opening bat who possesses a limited range of strokes and has to graft for his runs. He watches the ball very carefully and is especially good at the cut and the nudge off the legs. A reliable, if unspectacular, slip.

SELVEY, Michael Walter William, b Chiswick 25 Apr 48. RHB,RFM. MIDDLESEX – uncapped. Played for Surrey 1968–71. F-c career: 131 runs (av 10.07); 78 wkts (av 29.56). HS 42 Cambridge U. v Pakistanis (Cambridge) 1971. BB 6–43 v Sussex (Lord's) 1972.

Fast-medium bowler who moves the ball both ways. Enjoyed a fairly successful first full season in 1972. His batting failed to produce a run during nine successive innings though, which suggests there is room for improvement.

†**SELWOOD, Timothy**, b Prestatyn, Flintshire 1 Sep 44. RHB. MIDDLESEX – uncapped. F-c career: 155 runs (av 11.92). HS 89 Central Districts v Pakistanis (Wanganui) 1972–73.

Consistently successful opening batsman for the 2nd XI who has been selected for only nine f-c matches in seven seasons.

SHACKLETON, Julian Howard, b Todmorden, Yorks 29 Jan 52. Son of Derek Shackleton (Hants and England). RHB,RM. GLOUCESTERSHIRE – uncapped. F-c career (1 match): 7 runs; 4 wkts (av 12.25). HS 5*. BB 4–38 v Surrey (Bristol) 1971.

Former Millfield schoolboy who, after a splendid debut in 1971, suffered from back trouble throughout last season. A tall, slim, seam bowler with a good, high action.

SHARP, George, b West Hartlepool, Co Durham 12 Mar 50. RHB,WK. NORTHAMPTONSHIRE – uncapped. F-c career: 687 runs (av 18.56); 80 dismissals (69 ct, 11 st). HS 76* v Sussex (Hove) 1972.

Competent wicket-keeper who is steadily improving.

SHARPE, Philip John, b Shipley 27 Dec 36. RHB, occ OB. YORKSHIRE cap 1960. 13 England caps 1963–70, scoring 792 runs (av 41.68), with 1 hundred (111). F-c career: 18,705 runs (av 31.01), 23 hundreds; 2 wkts (av 84.00); 532 ct. HS 203* v Cambridge U. (Cambridge) 1960. BB 1–1.

An attractive batsman, at his best on firm pitches because he tends to play from a basically half-cock position. As a result of this, Sharpe's defence is not the soundest, and he is infinitely more effective going for his shots. However, he will be best remembered for his fielding – as one of the greatest first slips of all time. His catching is so brilliant that he is one of the few players to hold his England place primarily for his fielding. Not only has he taken many more catches than most, but he has the knack of making the difficult ones look simple. Some he has caught from fierce cuts, with the wicketkeeper up at the stumps, have bordered upon the miraculous.

SHEPHERD, David Robert, b Bideford, Devon 27 Dec 40. RHB, occ RM. GLOUCESTERSHIRE cap 1969. F-c career: 6,400 runs (av 24.06); 9 hundreds; 1 wkt. HS 153 v Middx (Bristol) 1968. BB 1–1.

A batsman built on heavyweight lines who, while regularly producing several impressive innings each season, lacks consistency.

SHEPHERD, John Neil, b St Andrew, Barbados 9 Nov 43. RHB,RM. KENT cap

1967. 5 West Indies caps 1969–71, scoring 77 runs (av 9.62), HS 32, 19 wkts (av 25.21), BB 5–104. F-c career: 4,608 runs (av 23.15), 4 hundreds; 405 wkts (av 25.84). HS 170 v Northants (Folkestone) 1968. BB 8–40 West Indians v Glos (Bristol) 1969.

A fine, natural, all-round cricketer who bowls just above medium pace with a whippy action. Moves the ball a little bit off the seam either way, is accurate, and can keep going for extremely long spells. His batting has probably suffered from his representing a county with so much talent in this department. This has meant that his chances of playing a normal innings are limited and he frequently has to throw his wicket away in the pursuit of quick runs. A brilliant all-purpose fieldsman and just the type of player, and person, any captain would like to have in his side.

SHUTT, Albert, b Stockton-on-Tees, Co Durham 21 Sep 52. RHB, RM. WORCESTERSHIRE – uncapped. F-c career (2 matches): 2 wkts (av 90.50). BB 1–36.

Tall, well-built seamer from the north-east who joined the county last August.

SHUTTLEWORTH, Kenneth, b St Helens 13 Nov 44. RHB, RFM. LANCASHIRE cap 1968. 6 England caps 1970–71, scoring 47 runs (av 7.83), HS 21, and taking 12 wkts (av 42.66), BB 5–47. F-c career: 1,711 runs (av 16.29); 423 wkts (av 23.79). HS 71 v Glos (Cheltenham) 1967. BB 7–41 v Essex (Leyton) 1968.

On his day a destructive fast bowler with an action not dissimilar to Fred Trueman's. 1972 proved a disappointing season, but at his best he is an England possible. A tailender, with the ability to score runs and hit the ball exceptionally hard.

†**SIMMONS, Jack,** b Clayton-le-Moors 28 Mar 41. RHB, OB. LANCASHIRE cap 1971. F-c career: 1,232 runs (av 18.38), 1 hundred; 209 wkts (av 27.76). HS 112 v Sussex (Hove) 1970. BB 7–65 v Derbys (Blackpool) 1972.

Burly off-spinner with excellent control but a very flat trajectory and little flight. He has proved a great success in limited-overs cricket when he fires in full-length deliveries at the batsman. Competent batsman who can defend or attack according to the situation.

SKINNER, Lonsdale Ernest, b Plaisance, B.G. 7 Sep 50. RHB, WK. SURREY – uncapped. F-c career: 75 runs (av 18.75); 2 dismissals (2 ct). HS 30 v Glam (Oval) 1972.

Reserve wicket-keeper who is also a front-line batsman.

SMEDLEY, Michael John, b Maltby, Yorks 28 Oct 41. RHB. NOTTINGHAMSHIRE cap 1966. F-c career: 10,197 runs (av 31.76), 21 hundreds. HS 149 v Glam (Cardiff) 1970.

Good looking, upright, middle-order batsman who has tended to promise rather more than he has produced. Especially impressive off the back foot.

SMITH, Alan Christopher, b Birmingham 25 Oct 36. RHB, WK, RM. WARWICKSHIRE cap 1961. Captain since 1968. Test selector since 1969. 6 England caps 1962–63, scoring 118 runs (av 29.50), HS 69*, and making 20 dismissals (all ct). F-c career: 10,209 runs (av 20.83), 3 hundreds; 65 wkts (av 22.92), 1 hat-trick; 760 dismissals (699 ct, 61 st). HS 145 Oxford U. v Hants (Bournemouth) 1959. BB 5–32 Oxford U. v Free Foresters (Oxford) 1960.

One of the less graceful performers behind the stumps, but sufficiently effective to play for England. Useful acquirer of runs, or stubborn defender in the later order. With Deryck

Murray now Warwickshire's regular wicket-keeper, A.C. has turned in some surprisingly good performances with the ball as a medium-paced seamer with a whippy, hoppy, slightly improbable action.

†SMITH, Michael John, b Enfield 4 Jan 42. RHB,SLA. MIDDLESEX cap 1967. F-c career: 10,284 runs (av 29.38), 19 hundreds; 57 wkts (av 31.77). HS 181 v Lancs (Manchester) 1967. BB 4–13 v Glos (Lord's) 1961.

Did so well last summer as an opening bat that he must have come close to playing for England. He was in the party for the Headingley Test but not included in the twelve. Tall, he uses his height to hit the ball straight, and is also strong off his legs. Excellent fieldsman and occasional left-arm spinner.

SMITH, Michael John Knight, b Leicester, Leics 30 Jun 33. RHB, occ RM. WARWICKSHIRE cap 1957. Captain 1957–67. Played for Leics 1951–55. 50 England caps 1958–72 (25 as captain), scoring 2,278 runs (av 31.63), with 3 hundreds (HS 121), taking 1 wkt and holding 53 catches. F-c career: 36,722 runs (av 42.45), 66 hundreds; 5 wkts (av 60.40); 545 ct. HS 204 Cavaliers v Natal (Durban) 1960–61. BB 1–0.

One of the most popular captains to have led England. Also captained Warwickshire with distinction for many years. A splendid batsman with a wonderfully consistent record in first-class cricket, he retired from the game for a short period, but, on returning, was immediately among the most prolific scorers. Was recalled to the England side last summer in an effort to bring some much needed class to the middle order, but his Test record was a shade disappointing, probably because he has always looked a shade suspect against pace at the start of his innings. Once established, he was an expert at on-side placement and hence a master of off-spinners. Originally a brilliant short-leg especially effective in the bat-pad position, he still possesses a wonderfully safe pair of hands, as he showed against Ian Chappell's team.

SMITH, Neil, b Dewsbury, Yorks 1 Apr 49. RHB,WK. Played for Yorks 1970–72. Joined ESSEX 1973 – uncapped. F-c career: 111 runs (av 15.85); 18 dismissals (14 ct, 4 st). HS 24* Minor Counties v Australians (Longton) 1972.

This talented but undemonstrative wicketkeeper was overshadowed by Yorkshire's extrovert, Bairstow, and will now understudy Brian Taylor.

SNELLGROVE, Kenneth Leslie, b Shepton Mallet, Somerset 12 Nov 41. RHB. LANCASHIRE cap 1971. F-c career: 2,889 runs (av 24.90), 2 hundreds. HS 138 v Middx (Manchester) 1970.

Hard-hitting middle-order batsman with a wonderful eye. He is the ideal player to force the pace towards the end of an innings or to chase runs against the clock or, in one-day games, the overs.

SNOW, John Augustine, b Peopleton, Worcs 13 Oct 41. RHB,RF. SUSSEX cap 1964. 43 England caps 1965–72, scoring 725 runs (av 15.76), HS 73, and taking 179 wkts (av 27.02), BB 7–40. F-c career: 2,661 runs (av 12.15); 853 wkts (av 22.39). HS 73 England v India (Lord's) 1971. BB 7–29 v West Indians (Hove) 1966.

World-class fast bowler who thrives on the big occasion and has, relatively speaking, usually looked more hostile for England than Sussex. Like so many of his breed he is a controversial character with an obvious distaste for opposing batsmen. From a relatively short run-up and with a fine body action, he tends to make the odd ball run away off the pitch and has a distinctly menacing bouncer. Can be a fine outfield and is a far better batsman than the majority of tailenders.

†**SOBERS, Garfield** St Aubrun, b Bridgetown, Barbados 28 Jul 36. LHB, LFM/SLA/SLC. NOTTINGHAMSHIRE cap 1968. Captain 1968–71 and reappointed for 1973. 91 Test caps 1954–72 (86 for West Indies, 5 for Rest of the World), including 44 as captain (39 West Indies), scoring 8,214 runs (av 59.52), with 27 hundreds (HS 365* – world Test record), taking 236 wkts (av 33.30), BB 6–21, and holding 109 catches. F-c career: 25,752 runs (av 55.98), 79 hundreds; 967 wkts (av 27.63); 366 ct. HS 365* West Indies v Pakistan (Kingston) 1957–58. BB 9–49 West Indians v Kent (Canterbury) 1966.

The ultimate cricketer; the greatest and most complete all-rounder in cricket history, and an athlete with the grace and presence of a master. A glorious left-hand batsman who would grace any Test team of any era, he has also been good enough to command a place in international XIs as an opening bowler, wrist spinner, and orthodox slow left-armer. As if that is not enough, Gary Sobers has been a world-class fieldsman anywhere and, had he wished it, would have made a superb wicket-keeper. As a captain possessing an exceptional knowledge of the game he has been more adventurous than most. But he has suffered from playing too much cricket and last summer was often absent through injuries.

SOLANKY, John William, b Dar-es-Salaam, Tanganyika 30 Jun 46. RHB, RM/OB. GLAMORGAN – uncapped. F-c career: 326 runs (av 20.37); 15 wkts (av 24.06). HS 53 East Africa v MCC (Kampala) 1963–64 – on f-c debut. BB 5–37 v Notts (Cardiff) 1972.

A useful all-rounder who gained valuable experience with Devon before moving to Wales in 1971.

SPENCER, Charles Terry, b Leicester 18 Aug 31. RHB, RFM. LEICESTERSHIRE cap 1952. F-c career: 5,847 runs (av 10.76); 1,363 wkts (av 26.60); 380 ct. HS 90 v Essex (Leicester) 1964. BB 9–63 v Yorks (Huddersfield) 1954.

Tall, big-hearted fast-medium bowler who retired from the game, only to be persuaded to return and make a highly successful comeback. His fine, high action enables him to achieve bounce and good control. Safe fieldsman and a useful occasional hitter.

SPENCER, John, b Brighton 6 Oct 49. RHB, RM. SUSSEX – uncapped. F-c career: 508 runs (av 8.46); 189 wkts (av 25.55). HS 55 Cambridge U. v Glam (Swansea) 1972. BB 6–40 Cambridge U. v Pakistanis (Cambridge) 1971.

Has shown for both Cambridge University and Sussex that he is among the best young opening bowlers around. Will never be truly fast, but he does move the ball about and should develop.

SQUIRES, Peter John, b Ripon 4 Aug 51. RHB. YORKSHIRE – uncapped. F-c career: 210 runs (av 15.00). HS 64 v Surrey (Scarborough) 1972.

Bespectacled batsman who also plays rugby union for his county. Had his first experience of Championship cricket last season but made only one good score in 14 innings.

STEAD, Barry, b Leeds, Yorks 21 Jun 39. LHB, LFM. NOTTINGHAMSHIRE cap 1969. Played for Yorks 1959. F-c career: 1,123 runs (av 12.34); 429 wkts (av 26.83), 1 hat-trick. HS 58 v Glos (Bristol) 1972. BB 8–44 v Somerset (Nottingham) 1972.

Useful county opening bowler for many years. He has improved dramatically recently because he has discovered how to move the ball late in its flight. He enjoyed his best summer in 1972, when he was one of the most effective bowlers in the country, despite not having much support.

STEELE, David Stanley, b Stoke-on-Trent, Staffs 29 Sep 41. Brother of J.F. Steele (Leics). RHB, SLA. NORTHAMPTONSHIRE cap 1965. F-c career: 9,727 runs (av 29.74), 12 hundreds; 196 wkts (av 22.54); 267 ct. HS 140* v Worcs (Worcester) 1971. BB 8–29 v Lancs (Northampton) 1966.

Has gradually developed from a sound county batsman into a well-above-average player. He followed up a most successful season in 1971 with an even better one in 1972, including five centuries. Dogged and determined, he, together with Mushtaq, provided the backbone of Northamptonshire's batting. Fine fielder, and an occasional slow bowler whose chances these days are limited by the presence of two other spinners in the team.

STEELE, John Frederick, b Stafford, Staffs 23 Jul 46. Brother of D.S. Steele (Northants). RHB, SLA. LEICESTERSHIRE cap 1971. F-c career: 2,661 runs (av 28.01), 3 hundreds; 99 wkts (av 29.56). HS 195 v Derbys (Leicester) 1971. BB 5–15 v Northants (Leicester) 1971.

Dedication and enthusiasm have quickly made this talented all-rounder an integral part of the Leicestershire side and, in some books, a candidate for higher honours. Originally a grafting bat, he is now more eager to play his strokes. Bowls with a flat, containing trajectory. Excellent fielder and close catcher.

STEPHENSON, George **Robert,** b Derby, Derbys 19 Nov 42. RHB, WK. HAMPSHIRE cap 1969. Played for Derbys 1967–68. F-c career:

1,978 runs (av 15.95); 275 dismissals (237 ct, 38 st) HS 82 v Sussex (Bournemouth) 1970.

A neat, diminutive wicket-keeper who secured a large haul of dismissals last season. Useful batsman with an unusually upright stance.

STEWART, David Ernest Robertson, b Bombay, India 22 May 48. RHB. WORCESTERSHIRE – uncapped. F-c career: 508 runs (av 19.53). HS 51 Scotland v Warwicks (Birmingham) 1969.

A reserve middle-order batsman with one of the more unusual winter jobs among the cricketing fraternity: ski instructor in the Cairngorms.

STIMPSON, Peter John, b Aberfan, Glam 25 May 47. RHB. WORCESTERSHIRE – uncapped. F-c career: 1,327 runs (av 26.01), 1 hundred. HS 103 v Glam (Worcester) 1971.

Grafting opener who, with Turner and Headley in the side, frequently has to bat in the middle-order.

STOREY, Stewart James, b Worthing, Sussex 6 Jan 41. RHB, RM. SURREY cap 1964. F-c career: 8,888 runs (av 24.21), 9 hundreds; 457 wkts (av 25.99), 1 hat-trick; 285 ct. HS 164 v Derbys (Oval) 1971. BB 8–22 v Glam (Swansea) 1965.

Honest county all-rounder – hard-hitting batsman, accurate medium-paced seamer with a good leg-cutter, and a reliable slip.

STRETTON, Terry Kevin, b Cosby 23 May 53. RHB, RM. LEICESTERSHIRE – uncapped. F-c career (2 matches): 2 runs. HS 1.

Tall medium-paced seamer who joined the staff last year.

SULLIVAN, John, b Ashton-under-Lyne 5 Feb 45. RHB, RM. LANCASHIRE cap 1969. F-c career: 3,740 runs (av 20.54); 61 wkts (av

29.40). HS 81* v Hants (Bournemouth) 1972. BB 4–44 v Surrey (Oval) 1970.

A good middle-order county batsman who is still improving. Useful change bowler. His opportunities are limited in a very talented side.

SWETMAN, Roy, b Westminster, London 25 Oct 33. RHB,WK. GLOUCESTERSHIRE cap 1972. Played for Surrey 1954–61 and Notts 1966–67. The second cricketer after R. Berry to be capped by three f-c counties. 11 England caps 1959–60, scoring 254 runs (av 16.93), HS 65, and making 26 dismissals (24 ct, 2 st). F-c career: 6,174 runs (av 19.53), 2 hundreds; 555 dismissals (494 ct, 61 st); 1 wkt. HS 115 Notts v Essex (Nottingham) 1966. BB 1–10.

Diminutive, very experienced wicket-keeper who is normally a perky batsman, but who experienced a disastrous summer in 1972.

SWINDELL, Robert Stephen, b Derby 22 Jan 50. RHB,OB. DERBYSHIRE – uncapped. F-c career: 147 runs (av 18.37); 26 wkts (av 31.07). HS 38 v Somerset (Chesterfield) 1972. BB 5–69 v Notts (Ilkeston) 1972.

This tall off-spinner was brought into Derbyshire's team for ten matches last season and soon showed the control and variety necessary to fill the gap caused by Edwin Smith's retirement.

TAIT, Alar, b Washington, Co Durham 27 Dec 53. LHB. NORTHAMPTONSHIRE – uncapped. F-c career: 825 runs (av 18.75). HS 67 v Surrey (Northampton) 1972.

Although his overall figures may be disappointing, he remains one of the most exciting prospects in the country. A player who is well worth watching.

TAYLOR, Brian, b West Ham 19 Jun 32. LHB,WK. ESSEX cap 1956. Captain since 1967. Made 301 consecutive Championship appearances 1961–72. F-c career: 18,942 runs (av 21.89), 9 hundreds; 1,270 dismissals (1,064 ct, 206 st); 1 wkt. HS 135 v Middx (Lord's) 1959. BB 1–16.

Has led his team with success and enthusiasm since taking over the captaincy. He has given Essex fine service as a sound, unspectacular wicket-keeper who possibly was unfortunate to make his one MCC tour before he had reached his peak. A remarkably uninhibited batsman who, over the years, has really hammered such fine bowlers as Jackson, Shackleton, and Cartwright thanks to his ability to hit seamers on the up. His most devastating shot is a cross between a pull and a lefthander's 'hoick' that is capable of sending good-length bowling to all quarters of the legside boundary.

Essex keeper Brian Taylor watches Chris Old hit out

TAYLOR, Chilton Richard Vernon, b Birkenhead, Cheshire 3 Oct 51. RHB,WK. GLOUCESTERSHIRE – uncapped. F-c career: 141 runs (av 6.71); 44 dismissals (40 ct, 4 st). HS 25 Cambridge U. v Warwicks (Cambridge) 1972.

A keen student of the game, this enthusiastic young wicket-keeper, now in his final year at Cambridge, will join Gloucestershire on trial when the Varsity season ends in July. Played for Cheshire 1969–72, and toured the Far East with the Oxbridge team last season.

TAYLOR, Derek John Somerset, b Amersham, Bucks 12 Nov 42. Twin brother of M.N.S. Taylor (Notts and Hants). RHB,WK. SOMERSET cap 1971. Played for Surrey 1966–69. F-c career: 1,584 runs (av 18.20); 192 dismissals (168 ct, 24 st). HS 60* Griqualand West v Orange Free State (Kimberley) 1971–72.

A highly competent wicket-keeper who could become a useful front-line batsman if given the opportunity – as his performances in the Currie Cup have proved.

TAYLOR, Michael Norman Somerset, b Amersham, Bucks 12 Nov 42. Twin brother of D.J.S. Taylor (Somerset). RHB,RM. HAMPSHIRE – uncapped. Played for Notts 1964–72. F-c career: 4,385 runs (av 18.04), 1 hundred; 522 wkts (av 27.88) 1 hat-trick. HS 105 Notts v Lancs (Nottingham) 1967. BB 7–106 Notts v Glam (Nottingham) 1967.

Typical modern all-rounder – accurate medium-pace seamer; pleasant-looking, attacking bat; fine outfielder.

TAYLOR, Robert William, b Stoke, Staffs 17 Jul 41. RHB,WK. DERBYSHIRE cap 1962. 1 England cap 1970–71. F-c career: 5,714 runs (av 15.69); 841 dismissals (753 ct, 88 st). HS 74* v Glam (Derby) 1971.

Extremely efficient, undemonstrative wicket-keeper of Test calibre who maintains the highest standard day after day. A competent tailender with plenty of determination. But for the presence of Alan Knott he must have won more than his single cap.

TAYLOR, William, b Manchester, Lancs 24 Jan 47. RHB,RFM. NOTTINGHAMSHIRE – uncapped. F-c career: 74 runs (av 4.11); 95 wkts (av 27.22). HS 26* v Leics (Nottingham) 1972. BB 6–42 v Warwicks (Nottingham) 1972.

A Staffordshire League product, this enthusiastic fast-medium bowler showed marked improvement and established a regular place in the side last year. Still not at his peak.

TIDY, Warwick Nigel, b Birmingham 10 Feb 53. RHB,LB. WARWICKSHIRE – uncapped. F-c career: 70 runs (av 3.68); 81 wkts (av 33.55). HS 12* v Cambridge U. (Cambridge) 1972. BB 5–24 v Leics (Nuneaton) 1970.

A comparative rarity in modern first-class cricket – a young English-born leg-spinner. Although he has not yet established himself, he is, at 20, a most intriguing possibility.

TITMUS, Frederick John, b St Pancras 24 Nov 32, RHB,OB. MIDDLESEX cap 1953. Captain 1965–68. 49 England caps 1955–68, scoring 1,311 runs (av 23.00), HS 84*, and taking 146 wkts (av 31.30), BB 7–79. F-c career: 19,782 runs (av 23.94), 5 hundreds; 2,453 wkts (av 22.11), 1 hat-trick; 439 ct. HS 137* MCC v South Australia (Adelaide) 1962–63. BB 9–52 v Cambridge U. (Cambridge) 1962.

Excellent all-rounder who has given exceptional service to his county and country. Approaching the end of a long and distinguished career, he is still easily the best Middlesex slow bowler, accurate and thus more than able to hold his own in limited-overs cricket. With the ball he is a master craftsman with many variations, including a well disguised delivery that floats away towards the slips. His batting style is utilitarian rather than classical, but it has brought him runs the world over.

TODD, Paul Adrian, b Morton 12 Mar 53. RHB. NOTTINGHAMSHIRE – uncapped. F-c career (1 match): 66 runs. HS 66* v Warwicks (Nottingham) 1972 – on debut.

Another exhilarating strokeplayer who should help a revival of Nottinghamshire's fortunes. He looked certain to score a century in his first f-c innings when he had to retire hurt with a hairline fracture of the jaw.

TOLCHARD, Jeffrey Graham, b Torquay, Devon 17 Mar 44. Brother of R.W. Tolchard. RHB. LEICESTERSHIRE – uncapped. F-c career: 673 runs (av 18.18). HS 66 v Warwicks (Leicester) 1972.

Played for Devon 1963–69 and has found scoring runs at f-c level difficult. Two 50s in his last three innings of 1972 show that he may well have overcome this problem.

†TOLCHARD, Roger William, b Torquay, Devon 15 Jun 46. RHB, WK. LEICESTERSHIRE cap 1966. Vice-captain. F-c career: 5,313 runs (av. 26.30), 4 hundreds; 448 dismissals (395 ct, 53 st); 1 wkt. HS 126* v Cambridge U. (Cambridge) 1970. BB 1–4.

Lively, aggressive young wicket-keeper who thoroughly deserved his selection to tour India and Pakistan with MCC. A pugnacious batsman, he has played some fine innings, proving particularly successful chasing runs in limited-overs cricket.

TOPLEY, Peter Aland, b Canterbury 29 Aug 50. RHB, SLA. KENT – uncapped. F-c career 32 runs (av 8.00); 3 wkts (av 66.33). HS 15* v Warwicks (Dartford) 1972. BB 2–76 v Hants (Folkestone) 1972.

Reserve slow left-arm bowler who played in six f-c matches last year when Underwood was on Test duty.

†TURNER, David Roy, b Chippenham, Wiltshire 5 Feb 49. LHB, occ RM. HAMPSHIRE cap 1970. F-c career: 4,242 runs (av 26.18), 5 hundreds; 1 wkt. HS 181* v Surrey (Oval) 1969. BB 1–4.

This diminutive young lefthander has proved himself to be a good and attractive county performer. If he continues to display the form he showed in 1972, until his injury, he must stake a claim to international recognition. Like most small men, he is very quick on his feet and is also a brilliant outfielder with a devastating throw either over or underarm.

†TURNER, Glenn Maitland, b Dunedin, New Zealand 26 May 47. RHB, occ RM/OB. WORCESTERSHIRE cap 1968. 16 New Zealand caps 1969–72, scoring 1,382 runs (av 53.15), with 3 hundreds. (HS 259). F-c career: 12,064 runs (av 42.78), 29 hundreds; 5 wkts (av 37.60). HS 259 New Zealand v West Indies (Georgetown) 1971–72 and New Zealanders v Guyana (Georgetown) 1971–72. BB 3–18 v Pakistanis (Worcester) 1967.

This outstanding young opening batsman has always shown an excellent defensive technique, but since 1970, when he scored a record ten Championship centuries for Worcestershire, he has blossomed into a player of the highest class. His appetite for runs rivals that of Boycott. Last year was easily the best of his career. He produced a whole series of big innings for New Zealand in the Caribbean and for Worcestershire in both f-c and one-day matches. At the moment he must rate among the best and most prolific openers in the world. Also a fine slip.

David Turner, the Hampshire lefthander, plays a delicious cover slash off the front foot, sending the ball all the way along the ground to the ropes

Register of County Cricketers

TURNER, Stuart, b Chester, 18 Jul 43. RHB,RM. ESSEX cap 1970. F-c career: 2,017 runs (av 16.13), 2 hundreds; 211 wkts (av 25.44) 1 hat-trick. HS 121 v Somerset (Taunton) 1970. BB 5–39 v Somerset (Colchester) 1972.

Useful county all-rounder and a natural for limited-overs cricket. He is an accurate fast-medium bowler – a shade nippier than he looks – an attacking batsman, and a splendid fieldsman.

†UNDERWOOD, Derek Leslie, b Bromley 8 Jun 45. RHB,LM. KENT cap 1964. 30 England caps 1966–72, scoring 280 runs (av 12.72), HS 45*, and taking 127 wkts (av 20.66), BB 7–32. F-c career: 2,076 runs (av 8.75); 1,181 wkts (av 18.51). HS 80 v Lancs (Manchester) 1969. BB 9–28 v Sussex (Hastings) 1964.

On a pitch giving any assistance at all, he is probably the most devastating bowler in the world. His pace is close to medium, so that he gives batsmen few opportunities to use their feet. On perfect pitches he can be employed as a stock bowler because his accuracy always makes him difficult to score against. On the last tour to Australia he bowled more overs and took more wickets than anyone, apart from Snow, in the Tests, while in all the first-class matches he both headed the averages and was the leading wicket-taker. This proved that he can be effective abroad as well as at home. Although he has already established himself as a true international bowler, he is young enough to become even better. At present it is noticeable that he is less effective against lefthanders, and he could do with a well-disguised slower ball that turns as much as his normal delivery. He can bat stubbornly but would probably score more runs if he did not depend so exclusively on a peculiar shovel shot that is liable to despatch the ball, usually in the air, anywhere in the region between fine-leg and mid-on.

†**VENKATARAGHAVAN,** Srinivasaraghavan ('**Venkat**'), b Madras, India 21 Apr 46. RHB, OB. Joined DERBYSHIRE on special overseas registration 1973 – uncapped. 22 India caps (1965–71) scoring 421 runs (av 15.59), HS 51, and taking 82 wkts (av 27.76), BB 8–72. F-c career: 2,967 runs (av 18.89), 1 hundred; 580 wkts (av 21.90). HS 137 Tamil Nadu v Kerala (Calicut) 1970–71. BB 9–93 Indians v Hants (Bournemouth) 1971.

Fine, accurate off-spinner who, with his fairly flat flight, should find English conditions much to his taste. He is also a useful batsman, with plenty of determination and a beautiful cut, and should make runs in county cricket. A top-class fieldsman.

†**VIRGIN, Roy** Thomas, b Taunton, Somerset 26 Aug 39. RHB, occ LB. NORTHAMPTONSHIRE – uncapped. Played for Somerset 1957–72. F-c career: 16,153 runs (av 28.84), 24 hundreds; 4 wkts (av 80.25); 310 ct. HS 179* Somerset v Lancs (Manchester) 1971. BB 1–6.

For many seasons has been Somerset's opener and the county's main source of runs. But 1972 proved an unhappy season for him and he has now moved to Northamptonshire where he is likely to prove a big asset. A most accomplished batsman, he has, on several occasions, almost made the national XI.

WALKER, Peter Michael, b Bristol, Glos 17 Feb 36. RHB, LM/SLA. GLAMORGAN cap 1958. 3 England caps 1960, scoring 128 runs (av 32.00), HS 52. F-c career: 17,650 runs (av 26.03), 13 hundreds; 834 wickets (av 28.63); 697 ct. HS 152* and BB 7–58 v Middx (Lord's) 1962.

Tall, most articulate cricketer with a South African background. A slightly unusual all-rounder in that one thinks first of him as a superlative fielder and then as a good bat and reasonable change bowler. He was one of the original, and best, specialists in the bat-pad position, but has now retired to the slips. A practical, slightly ungainly batsman, he is, like many very tall men, suspect against pace at the start of an innings. He now usually bowls slow left-arm, but at his peak he was a medium-pace swinger.

WALLACE, Kenneth William, b Romford 27 Aug 36. RHB. ESSEX – uncapped. F-c career: 219 runs (av 13.68). HS 55 v Hants (Ilford) 1967.

Prolific run-getter in club cricket. Has made occasional appearances for the county, and is stronger against seam than spin.

WALLER, Christopher Edward, b Guildford 3 Oct 48. RHB, SLA. SURREY cap 1972. F-c career: 148 runs (av 8.70); 83 wkts (av 22.66). HS 47 v Pakistanis (Oval) 1971. BB 7–64 v Sussex (Oval) 1971.

A class left-arm spinner whose career prospects have been hindered by the registration of Intikhab. He will be hoping that the belated award of his county cap last November will guarantee a regular place in the 1st XI.

WARD, Alan, b Dronfield 10 Aug 47. RHB, RF. DERBYSHIRE cap 1969. 5 England caps 1969–71, scoring 51 runs (av 10.20), HS 21, and taking 14 wkts (av 31.85), BB 4–61. F-c career: 548 runs (av 9.13); 291 wkts (av 20.91). HS 44 v Notts (Ilkeston) 1969. BB 6–30 v Sussex (Buxton) 1970.

A genuinely fast bowler who would almost certainly hold a regular place in the England side had he not been plagued by a series of injuries in the last few seasons.

WARD, Brian, b Chelmsford 28 Feb 44: RHB, occ RM. ESSEX cap 1970. F-c career, 4,799 runs (av 23.64), 4 hundreds; 5 wkts (av

13.60). HS 164* v Notts (Nottingham) 1970. BB 2–5 v Northants (Northampton) 1969.

A correct opening or middle-order batsman, usually happier against seam than spin. He is a great trier – a little short of flair – who has also made himself into a very reliable outfielder.

WATSON, Ian Ronald, b Teddington, Middx 9 Jun 47. RHB. HAMPSHIRE – uncapped. F-c career (2 matches): 31 runs (av 15.50). HS 16 Northants v Oxford U. (Oxford) 1971.

A product of the MCC staff who joined Hampshire in 1972 after unsuccessful trials with Middlesex and Northants. Splendid fielder.

WATTS, Patrick James, b Henlow, Beds 16 Jun 40. LHB, RM. NORTHAMPTONSHIRE cap 1962. Captain since 1971. F-c career: 11,693 runs (av 28.24), 8 hundreds; 317 wkts (av 25.30); 224 ct. HS 145 v Hants (Bournemouth) 1962. BB 6–18 v Somerset (Taunton) 1965.

Dependable left-hand bat with a preference for the front foot. Plays straight, has a fluent off-drive, and is not easy to remove.

WHITE, David William (**'Butch'**), b Sutton Coldfield, Warwicks 14 Feb 35. LHB, RFM. Played for Hants 1957–71. GLAMORGAN – uncapped. 2 England caps 1961–62, taking 4 wkts (av 29.75), BB 3–65. F-c career: 3,080 runs (av 10.58); 1,143 wkts (av 23.54), 2 hat-tricks. HS 58* Hants v Essex (Portsmouth) 1963. BB 9–44 Hants v Leics (Portsmouth) 1966.

Big, strong, inswing bowler who for years was the battering ram of Hampshire's attack.

WHITE, Robert Arthur, b Fulham, London 6 Oct 36. LHB, OB. NOTTINGHAMSHIRE cap 1966. Played for Middx 1958–65. F-c career: 9,084 runs (av 24.09), 5 hundreds; 367 wkts (av 28.71). HS 116* v Surrey (Oval) 1967. BB 7–41 v Derbys (Ilkeston) 1971.

Competent middle-order lefthander who has proved a valuable asset to his adopted county. Originally an occasional bowler, he has been pressed into service as a slow bowler so often by Notts that he has improved considerably and now rates as an all-rounder.

WHITEHOUSE, John, b Nuneaton 8 Apr 49. RHB, occ OB. WARWICKSHIRE – uncapped. F-c career: 1,969 runs (av 31.75), 2 hundreds; 3 wkts (av 63.33). HS 173 v Oxford U. (Oxford) 1971 – on debut. BB 1–39.

Right-handed No. 1 with an open, somewhat ugly, stance and an inclination to play across the line. He had such an outstanding first season in 1971 that he was being tipped for England – distinctly prematurely as his less-rewarding second summer showed.

WILCOCK, Howard Gordon, b New Malden, Surrey 26 Feb 50. RHB, WK. WORCESTERSHIRE – uncapped. F-c career: 575 runs (av 14.02); 82 dismissals (73 ct, 9 st). HS 39 v Surrey (Oval) 1972.

Lively young wicket-keeper with the knack of holding highly improbable catches. Could also develop into a useful batsman.

WILKINSON, Keith William, b Fenton, Staffs 15 Jan 50. LHB, LM. WORCESTERSHIRE – uncapped. F-c career: 431 runs (av 20.52); 46 wkts (av 32.08). HS 49* v Lancs (Worcester) 1972. BB 5–60 v Sussex (Worcester) 1971.

Left-handed all-rounder – middle-order bat and seam bowler – who has proved more suited to three-day than one-day cricket.

WILKINSON, Philip Alan, b Hucknall 23 Aug 51. RHB, RM. NOTTINGHAMSHIRE – uncapped. F-c career: 24 runs (av 4.80); 4 wkts (av 81.75). HS 14 v Worcs (Nottingham) 1972. BB 3–50 v Hants (Nottingham) 1972.

A tall seam bowler who proved rather expensive during a six-match f-c trial last season.

WILKINSON, Stephen George, b Hounslow, Middx 12 Jan 49. RHB, occ SLA. SOMERSET – uncapped. F-c career: 299 runs (av 24.91). HS 69 v Surrey (Oval) 1972.

A tall product of the MCC staff who did not do as well as expected in his introductory nine f-c matches last year. Nevertheless, with that experience behind him he should find the confidence to play his strokes and score much quicker.

†**WILLEY, Peter**, b Sedgefield, Co Durham 6 Dec 49. RHB, RM. NORTHAMPTONSHIRE cap 1971. F-c career: 3,365 runs (av 21.70), 2 hundreds; 136 wkts (av 29.00). HS 158* v Oxford U. (Oxford) 1971. BB 5–14 v Middx (Lord's) 1970.

Useful middle-order batsman and dependable seam bowler whose batting showed a marked improvement last summer and whose final bowling figures did not do him full justice.

WILLIAMS, David Lawrence, b Tonna 20 Nov 46. LHB, RFM. GLAMORGAN cap 1971. F-c career: 227 runs (av 4.63); 231 wkts (av 25.78). HS 37* v Essex (Chelmsford) 1969. BB 7–60 v Lancs (Blackpool) 1970.

A steady, stock seam-bowler with a good outswinger.

†**WILLIS, Robert** George Dylan, b Sunderland, Co Durham, 30 May 49. RHB, RF. WARWICKSHIRE cap 1972. Played for Surrey 1969–71. 5 England caps 1971, scoring 47 runs (av 11.75), HS 15*, and taking 14 wkts (av 28.42), BB 3–58. F-c career: 349 runs (av 13.96); 149 wkts (av 27.94), 1 hat-trick. HS 34 D.H. Robins' XI v Combined 'B' Section XI (Pretoria) 1972–73. BB 8–44 v Derbys (Birmingham) 1972.

Tall, rather open-chested fast bowler who impressed when he went to Australia as a replacement. Disillusioned with Surrey on his return when he failed to maintain a regular place in their Championship-winning team he joined Warwickshire and spent part of last season qualifying. Can extract more life and lift from a docile pitch than most bowlers of his pace. Useful lower-order batsman and splendid fielder.

WILSON, Donald, b Settle 7 Aug 37. LHB, SLA. YORKSHIRE cap 1960. 8 England caps 1964–71, scoring 82 runs (av 9.11), HS 42, and taking 15 wkts (av 44.73), BB 2–17. F-c career: 6,149 runs (av 14.30), 1 hundred; 1,164 wkts (av 20.82), 3 hat-tricks; 248 ct. HS 112 MCC v S. Zone (Hyderabad) 1963–64. BB 8–36 MCC v Ceylon (Colombo) 1969–70.

Orthodox slow left-armer whose figures have been disappointing since Close left Yorkshire. Very experienced, he varies his flight cleverly and achieves a reasonable amount of movement off the wicket. A dangerous, uninhibited hitter and an athletic fielder.

†**WOOD, Barry**, b Ossett, Yorks 26 Dec 42. RHB, RM. LANCASHIRE cap 1968. 1 England cap 1972, scoring 116 runs (av 58.00), HS 90. F-c career: 6,979 runs (av 31.29), 12 hundreds; 133 wkts (av 29.39). HS 186 v Leics (Leicester) 1972. BB 7–52 v Middx (Manchester) 1968.

Conscientious opening bat who combines a solid defence with many good strokes, including the hook, but possibly shuffles too much before making each shot. Quick on his feet and between the wickets. Medium-pace change bowler and a truly outstanding and enthusiastic fieldsman. A natural competitor.

WOODFORD, John Douglas, b Little Horton 9 Sep 43. RHB, RM. YORKSHIRE – uncapped. F-c career: 1,204 runs (av 20.40), 1 hundred; 4

Barry Wood's Test debut was marked by his willingness to stand up to Australia's fast bowlers. Here he plays a powerfully controlled square cut

wkts (av 46.25). HS 101 v Warwicks (Middlesbrough) 1971. BB 2–20 v Worcs (Dudley) 1971.

A useful all-rounder and fine fielder whose teaching duties restrict his appearances almost entirely to one-day matches.

WOOLMER, Robert Andrew, b Kanpur, India 14 May 48. RHB, RFM. KENT cap 1970. F-c career: 1,524 runs (av 21.46); 131 wkts (av 22.71). HS 86 v Derbys (Derby) 1971. BB 7–47 v Sussex (Canterbury) 1969.

Very useful seam-bowling all-rounder who is ideally suited to limited-overs cricket. His pace is just above medium, and his accuracy, combined with an ability to move the ball a little either way, means that he is able to keep batsmen quiet as well as dismiss them. His batting is promising, with a pleasing style, and so there are hopes that he will develop into an England player. Only time will tell whether he has the ability to score the runs expected of an all-rounder at international level.

WORRELL, Lawrence Roosevelt (**'Larry'**) b St Thomas, Barbados 28 Aug 43. RHB, OB. HAMPSHIRE – uncapped. F-c career: 289 runs (av 11.56); 65 wkts (av 32.55). HS 50 v Kent (Canterbury) 1971. BB 5–67 v Leics (Southampton) 1971.

West Indian off-break bowler who can spin the ball considerably. Possibly bowls a shade too flat – a natural tendency over here.

YARDLEY, Thomas **James,** b Chaddesley Corbett 27 Oct 46. LHB, occ WK. WORCESTERSHIRE cap 1972. F-c career: 2,877 runs (av 24.38), 1 hundred. HS 104* v Indians (Worcester) 1971.

Solid lefthander who experienced a lean season last year after two highly successful ones.

Like many young middle-order batsmen he usually starts his innings at the biff-bang stage of a Championship bonus points chase or during the last overs of a one-day innings.

†**YOUNIS AHMED,** Mohammad, b Jullundur, India 20 Oct 47. LHB, occ SLA/LM. SURREY cap 1969. 2 Pakistan caps 1969, scoring 89 runs (av 22.25), HS 62. F-c career: 8,617 runs (av 34.88), 13 hundreds: 18 wkts (av 39.55). HS 147* PIA 'A' v Rawalpindi Blues (Lahore) 1969–70. BB 3–12 Rest of Pakistan v Pakistan XI (Sahiwal) 1969–70.

Dashing lefthander with numerous fine innings for his adopted county – yet he gives the impression that the best are still to come. He is gradually curing the impetuosity that has cost him his wicket too often in the past.

†**ZAHEER ABBAS,** Syed, b Sialkot, Pakistan 24 Jul 47. RHB, occ OB. GLOUCESTERSHIRE – uncapped. 4 Pakistan caps 1969–71, scoring 425 runs (av 70.83), with 1 hundred (274). F-c career: 4,951 runs (av 51.57), 15 hundreds; 7 wkts (av 32.42). HS 274 Pakistan v England (Birmingham) 1971. BB 4–54 Pakistan PWD v Karachi (Karachi) 1968–69. Scored 4 hundreds in successive innings in Pakistan 1970–71.

Delighted all with his elegant batting when he toured England with Pakistan. Clearly a young player of enormous potential who should provide both Pakistan and Gloucester with many runs in the years that lie ahead.

ADDENDA

CORDLE, Anthony Elton, b St Michael, Barbados 21 Sep 40. RHB, RFM. GLAMORGAN cap 1967. F-c career: 3,221 runs (av 14.84); 368 wkts (av 24.30). HS 81 v Cambridge U. (Swansea) 1972. BB 9–49 v Leics (Colwyn Bay) 1969.

Experienced county all-rounder whose style of batting is especially valuable in limited-overs games. Re-engaged by Glamorgan to cover shortage of bowlers.

LANGFORD, Brian Anthony, b Birmingham, Warwicks 17 Dec 35. RHB, OB. SOMERSET cap 1957. Captain 1969–71. F-c career: 7,483 runs (av 13.78); 1,363 wkts (av 24.86); 226 ct. HS 68* v Sussex (Hove) 1960 and v Glamorgan (Taunton) 1972. BB 9–26 v Lancs (Weston-s-Mare) 1958.

Off-spinner who left the Somerset staff last season after 20 years of sterling service. Will be available on a match-contract basis. Achieved the ultimate in economy by bowling eight overs in a John Player League match without conceding a run.

PATAUDI, Mansur Ali Khan ('Tiger'), (formerly the Nawab of Pataudi, jnr), b Bhopal, India 5 Jan 41. RHB, occ RM. SUSSEX cap 1963. Captain 1966. 39 India caps 1961–70 (36 as captain), scoring 2,552 runs (av 36.98), with 6 hundreds (HS 203*), and taking 1 wkt. F-c career: 14,249 runs (av 34.58), 30 hundreds; 8 wkts (av 91.25); 200 ct. HS 203* India v England (Delhi) 1963–64. BB 1–0.

A high-class strokemaker who should be a considerable asset to Sussex if he accepts their invitation to return for the 1973 season. He learnt his cricket in England and should easily re-adapt to our wickets.

Looking Ahead to 1973

Preview of 1973

Will the upward trend in first-class cricket in England continue? That is the big question for 1973. Thanks to heavy sponsorship the counties should again show a profit, but the coming Test matches cannot arouse the same amount of interest as the Australians provided in 1972. This is a great pity because a Test series sets the tone for all other forms of cricket.

This is no criticism of either New Zealand, who could prove to have their best side ever, or the West Indies. It is simply that three-Test, mini tours can never hope to provide as much excitement as a closely fought five-Test series, which spans the entire season. Rain has only to interfere with two Tests – and after the wonderfully fine weather that prevailed throughout the fight for the Ashes this is distinctly probable – and then the unsatisfactory situation arises of the entire rubber being decided on the result of one match. It happened the last time Pakistan and India came to this country and provided a false overall picture.

One of the reasons why the Australians drew crowds was that their team contained a number of exciting new faces. In contrast the West Indies are almost certain to include a number of cricketers who are currently members of county teams. Although all of these are fine players, they can hardly be expected to be as big an attraction, when playing against England, as a brilliant newcomer. They have been seen so often before. This is yet another handicap that stems from having introduced far too many overseas players into our domestic scene.

The West Indies do have a special appeal because of the calibre of their cricket, and because they have so many supporters in this country. What is required is for them to bring over a batsman as efficient and exciting as Everton Weekes, a fast bowler of the Wes Hall calibre, and a spinner as intriguing as Sonny Ramadhin; crowd-pleasers who have not been seen in England. Perhaps that really is asking too much.

Apart from Glenn Turner, and possibly one other member, the New Zealand party will be relatively fresh to this country and could, given the right conditions and breaks, be hard to beat. But they are more likely to be an efficient, effective combination than spectacular entertainers. However, there is every reason to suppose that they will emulate their predecessors by proving extremely popular wherever they play.

From the domestic angle 1973 should be a fascinating summer; one that will pose many questions. Who, for example, will captain England? In some quarters it is felt that Ray Illingworth should give way to a younger man and, provided Tony Lewis is as successful in India and Pakistan as he was, both as captain and player, in the opening Test, he must be a strong candidate. Mike Denness, if he is able to establish himself as a Test-class batsman, is another possibility. Should Tony Greig be able to make Sussex play to their real potential he could come into the reckoning, as he is a certainty for the team as an all-rounder.

The English attack should remain powerful, with plenty of capable seamers about. The spin section is not so strong, but there should be sufficient. The big problem concerns the batting, as at the moment, on form and figures, only Geoff Boycott could justifiably claim to be an automatic selection.

Looking for the most likely winner of the County Championship is far from easy. The difference in ability between the top 12 teams is so small that an outstanding season from two players, established or otherwise, could be enough to tip the scales. Much will clearly depend also on who are required by the tourists. If, for example, the West Indies picked Kanhai, Kallicharran, Murray, and Gibbs, Warwickshire's chance of retaining the title would be slim.

It would be fair to say that Kent, who are bound to be handicapped by representative calls, are, on paper, probably the best balanced team and are likely to finish there or thereabouts in most of the competitions. And Leicestershire are another side with serious hopes of carrying off at least one major honour. Those limited-overs experts, Lancashire, must start favourites in this particular field, even though the inspiration of Clive Lloyd is likely to be missing for part of the summer. Essex, who have at last engaged some new batsmen, must also stand a good chance. They have a varied attack, which is splendidly supported in the field, and, if the newcomers could supply the runs that have been missing, they could have a memorable season, with the John Player League as their most probable success. With that additional batting depth, however, they should finish among the leaders in the County Championship.

Gloucestershire are very unpredictable, but are clearly a force to be reckoned with. They have tended to rely too much on Procter, but once their two Pakistan Test batsmen have acclimatised themselves to English conditions, they should provide some of the solidarity that has been missing.

Northants have a fine attack for three-day matches and Virgin ought to be capable of lifting some of the burden from Mushtaq and Steele. Derbyshire do not look Championship material, but a fit Ward and the presence of two experienced players to strengthen their fragile batting line-up could mean a big improvement and take them clear of the bottom. The acquisition of Venkataraghavan should boost Derbyshire's chances no end, but the presence of the Indian off-spinner is bad luck for Swindell. A good outside bet might be Somerset, who have in Close one of the shrewdest of captains, while Yorkshire will be hoping to continue the improvement they showed last summer. Now they have come to terms with the requirements of limited-overs cricket the Yorkshiremen could capture one of the titles.

Two of the least satisfactory features of domestic cricket have been the slow over-rate and the shortage of outstanding young players, especially batsmen.

The first is being tackled by imposing substantial fines on counties that offend. The fines should cure this particular evil, but a simpler method might have been to make the fielding side continue during the intervals or after the close whenever they failed to maintain an agreed rate. The umpires would be allowed to deduct time for injuries, weather, and other such contingencies. The players would not be keen on overtime and this would effectively prevent the slowing down of the over-rate, sometimes deliberate, which does occur.

The second problem, this lack of brilliant youngsters, is not nearly so easy to cure. Reducing the number of imports from overseas will help, but this does not entirely explain why there appear to be so few brilliant teenage cricketers around.

One of the reasons is that fewer young men are prepared to take up what must always be a somewhat hazardous profession, especially as the financial remuneration has not kept up with the general rise in wages. Before World War II professional cricket not only provided a pleasant way of life but provided a standard of living far better than could be hoped for by the average working man. Now, although the money earned by a professional cricketer is much greater, its purchasing power has been much reduced.

Who are the young English-born players to look out for in 1973?

The seam division is in a reasonably healthy state, even if one ignores Old, Ward and Willis (who have all been capped), because there are some fine prospects among the lesser known. In Phillipson and Spencer, Sussex have two bowlers who could play a considerable part in their County's revival, and there may be something really special about the former. Hendrick of Derbyshire turned in some excellent performances last summer, while the strongly-built Essex left-armer, John Lever, cannot be all that far from representative cricket.

It normally takes time for slow bowlers to reach their peak, but Graveney of Gloucestershire might prove an exception. Breakwell will benefit from more opportunities with his new county, Somerset, and Tidy of Warwickshire must be close to establishing himself as a wrist spinner.

Three fine off-break bowlers retired at the end of last summer and three more, Illingworth, Titmus, and Mortimore, must be nearing the end of their careers. But their successors, apart from Pocock, in what for so long has been one of the strongest sections of English cricket, are not all that obvious.

The standard of wicket-keeping throughout the counties remains very high and Bairstow from Yorkshire continues to impress.

The main concern is among the batsmen. There are some young players about who are clearly going to be good, but are any of them likely to be great or really exciting? Searching through the counties it is hard to pick a Hutton, a Compton, a May, a Graveney, a Dexter, or a Cowdrey, all of whom had shown their ability before they were 20.

High among the most promising prospects come Cook and Tait of Northamptonshire. The former will probably make more runs, but the latter suggests greater natural panache. Turner from Hampshire has had the proper grounding, something that is now not always feasible with minute staffs and insufficient match play, and there were indications last summer that here is a player of genuine quality. Owen-Thomas is another possibility. He has enjoyed the considerable advantage of gaining experience on that ideal nursery at Fenners. It has always been a wonderful place to improve one's batting, and it is not sheer coincidence that so many of the best players in the country since the war have come from Cambridge and Oxford. In some respects it is even more beneficial today. The young cricketer at the university is blessed with being able to concentrate on the vital matter of making runs, without having to worry about extraneous problems like bonus points or the special demands of one-day cricket.

In Glamorgan, Wilf Wooller is confident that two or three of their home-grown products will be making the grade. But it is time that Yorkshire, where there is more talent than anywhere else, unearthed another top-class batsman.

England v New Zealand

(The W.J. Jordan Trophy)

RESULTS

Season	England	New Zealand (Captains)	Played	Won by E	Won by NZ	Drawn
1929–30	A.H.H. Gilligan	T.C. Lowry	4	1	0	3
1931	D.R. Jardine	T.C. Lowry	3	1	0	2
1932–33	D.R. Jardine[1]	M.L. Page	2	0	0	2
1937	R.W.V. Robins	M.L. Page	3	1	0	2
1946–47	W.R. Hammond	W.A. Hadlee	1	0	0	1
1949	F.G. Mann[2]	W.A. Hadlee	4	0	0	4
1950–51	F.R. Brown	W.A. Hadlee	2	1	0	1
1954–55	L. Hutton	G.O. Rabone	2	2	0	0
1958	P.B.H. May	J.R. Reid	5	4	0	1
1958–59	P.B.H. May	J.R. Reid	2	1	0	1
1962–63	E.R. Dexter	J.R. Reid	3	3	0	0
1965	M.J.K. Smith	J.R. Reid	3	3	0	0
1965–66	M.J.K. Smith	B.W. Sinclair[3]	3	0	0	3
1969	R. Illingworth	G.T. Dowling	3	2	0	1
1970–71	R. Illingworth	G.T. Dowling	2	1	0	1
		In England	21	11	0	10
		In New Zealand	21	9	0	12
		Totals	42	20	0	22

[1] R.E.S. Wyatt captained in second Test
[2] F.R. Brown captained in third and fourth Tests
[3] M.E. Chapple captained in first Test

RECORD INNINGS TOTAL

	Highest			Lowest		
England in England	546–4d	(Leeds)	1965	187	(Manchester)	1937
England in New Zealand	562–7d	(Auckland)	1962–63	181	(Christchurch)	1929–30
New Zealand in England	484	(Lord's)	1949	47	(Lord's)	1958
New Zealand in New Zealand	440	(Wellington)	1929–30	26	(Auckland)	1954–55

HIGHEST INDIVIDUAL INNINGS

England in England	310*	J.H. Edrich	Leeds	1965
England in New Zealand	336*	W.R. Hammond	Auckland	1932–33
New Zealand in England	206	M.P. Donnelly	Lord's	1949
New Zealand in New Zealand	136	C.S. Dempster	Wellington	1929–30

*Not out

BEST INNINGS AND BOWLING ANALYSIS

England in England	7–32	D.L. Underwood	Lord's	1969
England in New Zealand	7–75	F.S. Trueman	Christchurch	1962–63
New Zealand in England	6–67	J.A. Cowie	Manchester	1937
New Zealand in New Zealand	6–76	R.S. Cunis	Auckland	1970–71

MOST RUNS BY A BATSMAN IN ONE SERIES

England in England	469	av 78.16	L. Hutton	1949
England in New Zealand	563	av 563.00	W.R. Hammond	1932–33
New Zealand in England	462	av 77.00	M.P. Donnelly	1949
New Zealand in New Zealand	341	av 85.25	C.S. Dempster	1929–30

MOST WICKETS BY A BOWLER IN ONE SERIES

England in England	34	av 7.47	G.A.R. Lock	1958
England in New Zealand	17	av 9.34	K. Higgs	1965–66
	17	av 12.05	D.L. Underwood	1970–71
New Zealand in England	20	av 19.45	A.R. MacGibbon	1958
New Zealand in New Zealand	10	av 15.10	R.O. Collinge	1970–71
	10	av 18.90	R.S. Cunis	1970–71

RECORD WICKET PARTNERSHIPS—ENGLAND

1st	147	L. Hutton and R.T. Simpson	The Oval	1949
2nd	369	J.H. Edrich and K.F. Barrington	Leeds	1965
3rd	245	J. Hardstaff, jnr. and W.R. Hammond	Lord's	1937
4th	166	K.F. Barrington and M.C. Cowdrey	Auckland	1962–63
5th	242	W.R. Hammond and L.E.G. Ames	Christchurch	1932–33
6th	240	P.H. Parfitt and B.R. Knight	Auckland	1962–63
7th	149	A.P.E. Knott and P. Lever	Auckland	1970–71
8th	246	L.E.G. Ames and G.O. Allen	Lord's	1931
9th	163*	M.C. Cowdrey and A.C. Smith	Wellington	1962–63
10th	41	K.F. Barrington and F.E. Rumsey	Birmingham	1965

RECORD WICKET PARTNERSHIPS—NEW ZEALAND

1st	276	C.S. Dempster and J.E. Mills	Wellington	1929–30
2nd	131	B. Sutcliffe and J.R. Reid	Christchurch	1950–51
3rd	150	B.E. Congdon and B.F. Hastings	Nottingham	1969
4th	142	M.L. Page and R.C. Blunt	Lord's	1931
5th	141	M.G. Burgess and M.J.F. Shrimpton	Auckland	1970–71
6th	99	W.A. Hadlee and M.L. Page	Manchester	1937
7th	104	B. Sutcliffe and V. Pollard	Birmingham	1965
8th	104	D.A.R. Moloney and A.W. Roberts	Lord's	1937
9th	64	J.A. Cowie and T.B. Burtt	Christchurch	1946–47
10th	57	F.L.H. Mooney and J.A. Cowie	Leeds	1949

*Unbroken partnership

England v West Indies

(The Wisden Trophy)

RESULTS

Season	Captains England	West Indies	Played	Tests Won by E	Won by WI	Drawn
1928	A.P.F. Chapman	R.K. Nunes	3	3	0	0
1929–30	F.S.G. Calthorpe	E.L.G. Hoad[1]	4	1	1	2
1933	D.R. Jardine[2]	G.C. Grant	3	2	0	1
1934–35	R.E.S. Wyatt	G.C. Grant	4	1	2	1
1939	W.R. Hammond	R.S. Grant	3	1	0	2
1947–48	G.O. Allen[3]	J.D.C. Goddard[4]	4	0	2	2
1950	N.W.D. Yardley[5]	J.D.C. Goddard	4	1	3	0
1953–54	L. Hutton	J.B. Stollmeyer	5	2	2	1
1957	P.B.H. May	J.D.C. Goddard	5	3	0	2
1959–60	P.B.H. May[6]	F.C.M. Alexander	5	1	0	4
1963	E.R. Dexter	F.M.M. Worrell	5	1	3	1
1966	M.C. Cowdrey[7]	G.St.A. Sobers	5	1	3	1
1967–68	M.C. Cowdrey	G.St.A. Sobers	5	1	0	4
1969	R. Illingworth	G.St.A. Sobers	3	2	0	1
		In England	31	14	9	8
		In West Indies	27	6	7	14
		TOTALS	58	20	16	22

[1] M.I. Grell, M.P. Fernandes and R.K. Nunes captained in second, third and fourth Tests respectively
[2] R.E.S. Wyatt captained in third Test
[3] K. Cranston captained in first Test
[4] G.A. Headley and G.E. Gomez captained in first and second Tests respectively
[5] F.R. Brown captained in fourth Test
[6] M.C. Cowdrey captained in fourth and fifth Tests
[7] M.J.K. Smith and D.B. Close captained in first and fifth Tests respectively

RECORD INNINGS TOTALS	Highest			Lowest		
England in England	619–6d	(Nottingham)	1957	103	(The Oval)	1950
England in West Indies	849	(Kingston)	1929–30	103	(Kingston)	1934–35
West Indies in England	558	(Nottingham)	1950	86	(The Oval)	1957
West Indies in West Indies	681–8d	(Port-of-Spain)	1953–54	102	(Bridgetown)	1934–35

HIGHEST INDIVIDUAL INNINGS

England in England	285*	P.B.H. May	Birmingham	1957
England in West Indies	325	A. Sandham	Kingston	1929–30
West Indies in England	261	F.M.M. Worrell	Nottingham	1950
West Indies in West Indies	270*	G.A. Headley	Kingston	1934–35

*Not out

BEST INNINGS BOWLING ANALYSES

England in England	7–44	T.E. Bailey	Lord's	1957
	7–44	F.S. Trueman	Birmingham	1963
England in West Indies	7–34	T.E. Bailey	Kingston	1953–54
West Indies in England	8–104	A.L. Valentine	Manchester	1950
West Indies in West Indies	7–69	W.W. Hall	Kingston	1959–60

MOST RUNS BY A BATSMAN IN ONE SERIES

England in England	489	av 97.80	P.B.H. May	1957
England in West Indies	693	av 115.50	E.H. Hendren	1929–30
West Indies in England	722	av 103.14	G.St.A. Sobers	1966
West Indies in West Indies	709	av 101.28	G.St.A. Sobers	1959–60

MOST WICKETS BY A BOWLER IN ONE SERIES

England in England	34	av 17.47	F.S. Trueman	1963
England in West Indies	27	av 18.66	J.A. Snow	1967–68
West Indies in England	33	av 20.42	A.L. Valentine	1950
West Indies in West Indies	23	av 24.65	W.F. Ferguson	1947–48
	23	av 24.30	S. Ramadhin	1953–54

RECORD WICKET PARTNERSHIPS – ENGLAND

1st	212	C. Washbrook and R.T. Simpson	Nottingham	1950
2nd	266	P.E. Richardson and T.W. Graveney	Nottingham	1957
3rd	264	L. Hutton and W.R. Hammond	The Oval	1939
4th	411	P.B.H. May and M.C. Cowdrey	Birmingham	1957
5th	130*	C. Milburn and T.W. Graveney	Lord's	1966
6th	161	T.E. Bailey and T.G. Evans	Manchester	1950
7th	197	M.J.K. Smith and J.M. Parks	Port-of-Spain	1959–60
8th	217	T.W. Graveney and J.T. Murray	The Oval	1966
9th	109	G.A.R. Lock and P.I. Pocock	Georgetown	1967–68
10th	128	K. Higgs and J.A. Snow	The Oval	1966

RECORD WICKET PARTNERSHIPS – WEST INDIES

1st	173	G.M. Carew and A.G. Ganteaume	Port-of-Spain	1947–48
2nd	228	R.K. Nunes and G.A. Headley	Kingston	1929–30
3rd	338	E.de C. Weekes and F.M.M. Worrell	Port-of-Spain	1953–54
4th	399	G.St.A. Sobers and F.M.M. Worrell	Bridgetown	1959–60
5th	265	S.M. Nurse and G.St.A. Sobers	Leeds	1966
6th	274*	G. St.A. Sobers and D.A.J. Holford	Lord's	1966
7th	154	O.G. Smith and J.D.C. Goddard	Nottingham	1957
8th	99	C.A. McWatt and J.K. Holt	Georgetown	1953–54
9th	63*	G.St.A. Sobers and W.W. Hall	Port-of-Spain	1967–68
10th	55	F.M.M. Worrell and S. Ramadhin	Nottingham	1957

*Unbroken partnership

Fixtures 1973

New Zealand Tour
All matches 3 days unless otherwise stated

APRIL
Tuesday 24th EASTBOURNE – D.H. Robin's XI
Saturday 28th* WORCESTER – Worcestershire

MAY
Wednesday 2nd BOURNEMOUTH – Hampshire
Saturday 5th CANTERBURY – Kent
Wednesday 9th BRISTOL – Gloucestershire
Saturday 12th* TAUNTON – Somerset
Wednesday 16th CARDIFF – Glamorgan
Saturday 19th LORD'S – MCC
Wednesday 23rd DERBY – Derbyshire
Saturday 26th LEICESTER – Leicestershire
Wednesday 30th NORTHAMPTON – Northamptonshire

JUNE
Saturday 2nd MANCHESTER – Lancashire
Thursday 7th NOTTINGHAM – ENGLAND, 1st Test (5 days)
Wednesday 13th CAMBRIDGE – Combined Universities
Saturday 16th BIRMINGHAM – Warwickshire
Thursday 21st LORD'S – ENGLAND, 2nd Test (5 days)
Thursday 28th Venue undecided – Cricketers' Association (1 day)
Saturday 30th* THE OVAL – Surrey

JULY
Thursday 5th LEEDS – ENGLAND, 3rd Test (5 days)
Wednesday 11th DUNDEE – Scotland (2 days)
Saturday 14th WESTCLIFF-ON-SEA – Essex
Wednesday 18th SWANSEA – ENGLAND (1 day)
Friday 20th MANCHESTER – ENGLAND (1 day)

*Denotes Sunday play

West Indies Tour
All matches 3 days unless otherwise stated

JUNE
Wednesday 20th CHELMSFORD – Essex
Saturday 23rd SOUTHAMPTON – Hampshire

Wednesday 27th EASTBOURNE – D.H. Robin's XI
Saturday 30th NOTTINGHAM – Nottinghamshire

JULY
Wednesday 4th LORD'S – Middlesex
Saturday 7th SWANSEA – Glamorgan
Sunday 8th SWANSEA – Glamorgan (1 day)
Thursday 12th PORTSMOUTH – Combined Services (2 days)
Saturday 14th HOVE – Sussex
Wednesday 18th CANTERBURY – Kent
Saturday 21st MANCHESTER – England Under-25 XI
Thursday 26th THE OVAL – ENGLAND, 1st Test (5 days)

AUGUST
Wednesday 1st TORQUAY – Minor Counties
Saturday 4th CHELTENHAM – Gloucestershire
Thursday 9th BIRMINGHAM – ENGLAND, 2nd Test (5 days)
Thursday 16th Venue undecided – Cricketers' Association (1 day)
Saturday 18th SCARBOROUGH – Yorkshire
Thursday 23rd LORD'S – ENGLAND, 3rd Test (5 days)
Wednesday 29th CHESTERFIELD – Derbyshire

SEPTEMBER
Saturday 1st SCARBOROUGH – T.N. Pearce's XI
Sunday 2nd SCARBOROUGH – T.N. Pearce's XI (1 day)
Wednesday 5th LEEDS – ENGLAND (1 day)
Friday 7th THE OVAL – ENGLAND (1 day)

County Championship

MAY
Wednesday 2nd
LORD'S – Middlesex v Gloucestershire
TAUNTON – Somerset v Essex
HASTINGS – Sussex v Kent
BIRMINGHAM – Warwickshire v Yorkshire
Saturday 5th
LEICESTER – Leicestershire v Hampshire

347

Wednesday 9th
SOUTHAMPTON – Hampshire v Sussex
LORD'S – Middlesex v Somerset
NORTHAMPTON – Northamptonshire v Lancashire
THE OVAL – Surrey v Essex
WORCESTER – Worcestershire v Yorkshire

Saturday 12th
CHESTERFIELD – Derbyshire v Warwickshire

Wednesday 16th
CHELMSFORD – Essex v Derbyshire
MANCHESTER – Lancashire v Middlesex
LEICESTER – Leicestershire v Sussex
THE OVAL – Surrey v Gloucestershire
BIRMINGHAM – Warwickshire v Somerset
LEEDS – Yorkshire v Hampshire

Saturday 19th
NOTTINGHAM – Nottinghamshire v Middlesex

Wednesday 23rd
CARDIFF – Glamorgan v Yorkshire
BRISTOL – Gloucestershire v Hampshire
LORD'S – Middlesex v Essex
NORTHAMPTON – Northamptonshire v Somerset
BIRMINGHAM – Warwickshire v Leicestershire

Saturday 26th
SWANSEA – Glamorgan v Hampshire
MANCHESTER – Lancashire v Yorkshire
LORD'S – Middlesex v Sussex
NORTHAMPTON – Northamptonshire v Derbyshire
NOTTINGHAM – Nottinghamshire v Warwickshire
TAUNTON – Somerset v Gloucestershire
THE OVAL – Surrey v Kent
WORCESTER – Worcester v Essex

Wednesday 30th
NOTTINGHAM – Nottinghamshire v Lancashire

JUNE
Saturday 2nd
HOVE – Sussex v Gloucestershire

Wednesday 6th
DERBY – Derbyshire v Worcestershire
ILFORD – Essex v Glamorgan
LORD'S – Middlesex v Kent
THE OVAL – Surrey v Leicestershire
COVENTRY – Warwickshire v Hampshire
MIDDLESBROUGH – Yorkshire v Northamptonshire

Saturday 9th
ILFORD – Essex v Sussex
PORTSMOUTH – Hampshire v Surrey
MANCHESTER – Lancashire v Derbyshire

LEICESTER – Leicestershire v Nottinghamshire
LORD'S – Middlesex v Glamorgan
NORTHAMPTON – Northamptonshire v Kent
WORCESTER – Worcestershire v Warwickshire
SHEFFIELD – Yorkshire v Somerset

Saturday 16th
CHESTERFIELD – Derbyshire v Yorkshire
CARDIFF – Glamorgan v Surrey
GLOUCESTER – Gloucestershire v Essex
TUNBRIDGE WELLS – Kent v Nottinghamshire
LIVERPOOL – Lancashire v Leicestershire
NORTHAMPTON – Northamptonshire v Middlesex
BATH – Somerset v Worcestershire
HOVE – Sussex v Hampshire

Wednesday 20th
GLOUCESTER – Gloucestershire v Yorkshire
TUNBRIDGE WELLS – Kent v Hampshire
LEICESTER – Leicestershire v Glamorgan
NEWARK – Nottinghamshire v Northamptonshire
BATH – Somerset v Surrey
HOVE – Sussex v Lancashire

Saturday 23rd
BURTON UPON TRENT – Derbyshire v Middlesex
CHELMSFORD – Essex v Somerset
SWANSEA – Glamorgan v Lancashire
BRISTOL – Gloucestershire v Kent
NORTHAMPTON – Northamptonshire v Warwickshire
NOTTINGHAM – Nottinghamshire v Sussex
WORCESTER – Worcestershire v Surrey
LEEDS – Yorkshire v Leicestershire

Saturday 30th
MAIDSTONE – Kent v Somerset
LEICESTER – Leicestershire v Derbyshire
LORD'S – Middlesex v Worcestershire
BIRMINGHAM – Warwickshire v Essex

JULY
Wednesday 4th
CARDIFF – Glamorgan v Derbyshire
MAIDSTONE – Kent v Surrey
LEICESTER – Leicestershire v Somerset
KIDDERMINSTER – Worcestershire v Northamptonshire

Saturday 7th
DERBY – Derbyshire v Kent
MANCHESTER – Lancashire v Nottinghamshire
LEICESTER – Leicestershire v Middlesex
NORTHAMPTON – Northamptonshire v Essex
TAUNTON – Somerset v Hampshire
THE OVAL – Surrey v Warwickshire
HOVE – Sussex v Yorkshire
WORCESTER – Worcestershire v Gloucestershire

Saturday 14th
BUXTON – Derbyshire v Lancashire
BRISTOL – Gloucestershire v Northamptonshire
PORTSMOUTH – Hampshire v Glamorgan
DOVER – Kent v Middlesex
GLASTONBURY – Somerset v Nottinghamshire
THE OVAL – Surrey v Yorkshire
BIRMINGHAM – Warwickshire v Worcestershire

Wednesday 18th
WESTCLIFF-ON-SEA – Essex v Northamptonshire
BRISTOL – Gloucestershire v Leicestershire
BASINGSTOKE – Hampshire v Middlesex
HOVE – Sussex v Warwickshire
WORCESTER – Worcestershire v Glamorgan
BRADFORD – Yorkshire v Nottinghamshire (or July 21st if neither county in Benson and Hedges Cup final)

Saturday 21st
NEATH – Glamorgan v Somerset (or September 1st if either county in Benson and Hedges Cup final)
BRADFORD – Yorkshire v Nottinghamshire (or July 18th if either county in Benson and Hedges Cup final)

Wednesday 25th
CHESTERFIELD – Derbyshire v Surrey
CARDIFF – Glamorgan v Worcestershire
SOUTHPORT – Lancashire v Hampshire
NOTTINGHAM – Nottinghamshire v Gloucestershire
BIRMINGHAM – Warwickshire v Kent

Saturday 28th
CHELMSFORD – Essex v Leicestershire
SWANSEA – Glamorgan v Kent
MANCHESTER – Lancashire v Gloucestershire
NORTHAMPTON – Northamptonshire v Sussex
WORKSOP – Nottinghamshire v Surrey
WORCESTER – Worcestershire v Hampshire
SHEFFIELD – Yorkshire v Derbyshire

AUGUST
Wednesday 1st
BRADFORD – Yorkshire v Middlesex (or September 8th if either county in Gillette Cup quarter-finals)

Saturday 4th
ILKESTON – Derbyshire v Nottinghamshire
CARDIFF – Glamorgan v Warwickshire
PORTSMOUTH – Hampshire v Essex
CANTERBURY – Kent v Sussex
LEICESTER – Leicestershire v Worcestershire
LORD'S – Middlesex v Surrey
WESTON-SUPER-MARE – Somerset v Northamptonshire
SHEFFIELD – Yorkshire v Lancashire

Wednesday 8th
LEYTON – Essex v Lancashire
CHELTENHAM – Gloucestershire v Worcestershire
PORTSMOUTH – Hampshire v Derbyshire
CANTERBURY – Kent v Yorkshire
LEICESTER – Leicestershire v Northamptonshire
LORD'S – Middlesex v Warwickshire
WESTON-SUPER-MARE – Somerset v Glamorgan
HOVE – Sussex v Surrey

Saturday 11th
LEYTON – Essex v Kent
CHELTENHAM – Gloucestershire v Warwickshire
LORD'S – Middlesex v Yorkshire
WELLINGBOROUGH – Northamptonshire v Glamorgan
NOTTINGHAM – Nottinghamshire v Leicestershire
WESTON-SUPER-MARE – Somerset v Derbyshire
THE OVAL – Surrey v Lancashire
WORCESTER – Worcestershire v Sussex

Wednesday 15th
WORCESTER – Worcestershire v Nottinghamshire (or September 1st if either county in Gillette Cup semi-finals)

Saturday 18th
*SWANSEA – Glamorgan v Gloucestershire
SOUTHAMPTON – Hampshire v Northamptonshire
DARTFORD – Kent v Worcestershire
MANCHESTER – Lancashire v Somerset
LEICESTER – Leicestershire v Essex
THE OVAL – Surrey v Middlesex
EASTBOURNE – Sussex v Derbyshire
BIRMINGHAM – Warwickshire v Nottinghamshire

Wednesday 22nd
DERBY – Derbyshire v Gloucestershire
BLACKPOOL – Lancashire v Warwickshire
NORTHAMPTON – Northamptonshire v Leicestershire
NOTTINGHAM – Nottinghamshire v Glamorgan
TAUNTON – Somerset v Sussex
SCARBOROUGH – Yorkshire v Essex

Saturday 25th
DERBY – Derbyshire v Leicestershire
CHELMSFORD – Essex v Worcestershire
BRISTOL – Gloucestershire v Somerset
BOURNEMOUTH – Hampshire v Nottinghamshire
FOLKESTONE – Kent v Lancashire
HOVE – Sussex v Middlesex
BIRMINGHAM – Warwickshire v Northamptonshire
LEEDS – Yorkshire v Surrey

Wednesday 29th
CHELMSFORD – Essex v Nottinghamshire
BOURNEMOUTH – Hampshire v Gloucestershire
FOLKESTONE – Kent v Leicestershire
MANCHESTER – Lancashire v Worcestershire

John Player Cricket Yearbook 1973

GUILDFORD – Surrey v Northamptonshire
HOVE – Sussex v Glamorgan

SEPTEMBER
Saturday 1st
NEATH – Glamorgan v Somerset (if not played July 21st)
WORCESTER – Worcestershire v Nottinghamshire (if not played August 15th)

Saturday 8th
BRISTOL – Gloucestershire v Glamorgan
SOUTHAMPTON – Hampshire v Kent
NOTTINGHAM – Nottinghamshire v Derbyshire
THE OVAL – Surrey v Sussex
BIRMINGHAM – Warwickshire v Lancashire
BRADFORD – Yorkshire v Middlesex (if not played August 1st)
*Denotes Sunday play

Other First-Class Matches
APRIL
Saturday 21st
CAMBRIDGE – Cambridge U. v Warwickshire

Wednesday 25th
LORD'S – MCC v Warwickshire
CAMBRIDGE – Cambridge U. v Leicestershire

Saturday 28th
CAMBRIDGE – Cambridge U. v Yorkshire

MAY
Wednesday 2nd
CAMBRIDGE – Cambridge U. v Northamptonshire
OXFORD – Oxford U. v Surrey

Wednesday 9th
CAMBRIDGE – Cambridge U. v Glamorgan
OXFORD – Oxford U. v Warwickshire

Saturday 12th
CAMBRIDGE – Cambridge U. v Surrey

Wednesday 16th
CAMBRIDGE – Cambridge U. v Kent
OXFORD – Oxford U. v Worcestershire

Wednesday 23rd
OXFORD – Oxford U. v Sussex

Wednesday 30th
HOVE – ENGLAND v THE REST (Test Trial)

JUNE
Wednesday 6th
OXFORD – Oxford U. v Lancashire

Saturday 9th
OXFORD – Oxford U. v Gloucestershire

Wednesday 20th
OXFORD – Oxford U. v Derbyshire

JULY
Wednesday 4th
BIRMINGHAM – Warwickshire v Oxford U.
NOTTINGHAM – Nottinghamshire v Cambridge U.

Saturday 7th
LORD'S – Cambridge U. v Oxford U.

AUGUST
Saturday 11th
Venue undecided—Ireland v Scotland

John Player League
(All matches start at 2 p.m.)

APRIL
Sunday 29th
COLWYN BAY – Glamorgan v Yorkshire

MAY
Sunday 6th
DERBY – Derbyshire v Hampshire
MAIDSTONE – Kent v Middlesex
LEICESTER – Leicestershire v Glamorgan
NOTTINGHAM – Nottinghamshire v Yorkshire
THE OVAL – Surrey v Lancashire
HOVE – Sussex v Warwickshire
WORCESTER – Worcestershire v Northamptonshire

Sunday 13th
CHELMSFORD – Essex v Kent
CARDIFF – Glamorgan v Hampshire
MORETON-IN-MARSH – Gloucestershire v Surrey
MANCHESTER – Lancashire v Nottinghamshire
LORD'S – Middlesex v Sussex
NORTHAMPTON – Northamptonshire v Leicestershire
BIRMINGHAM – Warwickshire v Derbyshire
WORCESTER – Worcestershire v Yorkshire

Sunday 20th
CHELMSFORD – Essex v Derbyshire
BOURNEMOUTH – Hampshire v Kent
MANCHESTER – Lancashire v Middlesex
LEICESTER – Leicestershire v Warwickshire
TAUNTON – Somerset v Glamorgan
TOLWORTH – Surrey v Northamptonshire
HOVE – Sussex v Gloucestershire

Sunday 27th
EBBW VALE – Glamorgan v Essex
FOLKESTONE – Kent v Surrey
LEICESTER – Leicestershire v Sussex
NOTTINGHAM – Nottinghamshire v Middlesex
BRISTOL (Imperial) – Somerset v Gloucestershire
BIRMINGHAM – Warwickshire v Northamptonshire
DUDLEY – Worcestershire v Derbyshire
LEEDS – Yorkshire v Lancashire

JUNE
Sunday 3rd
BURTON UPON TRENT – Derbyshire v Leicestershire
HARLOW – Essex v Hampshire
BRISTOL – Gloucestershire v Glamorgan
LORD'S – Middlesex v Somerset
NORTHAMPTON – Northamptonshire v Yorkshire
HOVE – Sussex v Surrey
BIRMINGHAM – Warwickshire v Kent

Sunday 10th
ILFORD – Essex v Sussex
SOUTHAMPTON – Hampshire v Surrey
LEICESTER – Leicestershire v Kent
KETTERING – Northamptonshire v Glamorgan
NOTTINGHAM (John Player Ground) – Nottinghamshire v Gloucestershire
BRADFORD – Yorkshire v Somerset

Sunday 17th
CARDIFF – Glamorgan v Surrey
GLOUCESTER – Gloucestershire v Essex
PORTSMOUTH – Hampshire v Sussex
CANTERBURY – Kent v Nottinghamshire
MANCHESTER – Lancashire v Leicestershire
LORD'S – Middlesex v Northamptonshire
BATH – Somerset v Worcestershire
BIRMINGHAM – Warwickshire v Yorkshire

Sunday 24th
CHESTERFIELD – Derbyshire v Middlesex
CHELMSFORD – Essex v Somerset
SWANSEA – Glamorgan v Lancashire
BRISTOL – Gloucestershire v Kent
LUTON – Northamptonshire v Nottinghamshire
SUNBURY – Surrey v Warwickshire
WORCESTER – Worcestershire v Sussex
SHEFFIELD – Yorkshire v Leicestershire

JULY
Sunday 1st
BUXTON – Derbyshire v Glamorgan
CANTERBURY – Kent v Somerset
LEICESTER – Leicestershire v Essex
LORD'S – Middlesex v Worcestershire
NOTTINGHAM – Nottinghamshire v Warwickshire

Sunday 8th
CHESTERFIELD – Derbyshire v Kent
MANCHESTER – Lancashire v Northamptonshire
LEICESTER – Leicestershire v Gloucestershire
LORD'S – Middlesex v Warwickshire
BATH – Somerset v Hampshire
THE OVAL – Surrey v Essex
HASTINGS – Sussex v Yorkshire
DUDLEY – Worcestershire v Nottinghamshire

Sunday 15th
WESTCLIFF-ON-SEA – Essex v Middlesex
SOUTHAMPTON – Hampshire v Leicestershire
DOVER – Kent v Yorkshire
NORTHAMPTON – Northamptonshire v Derbyshire
GLASTONBURY – Somerset v Nottinghamshire
HOVE – Sussex v Glamorgan
BIRMINGHAM – Warwickshire v Lancashire
WORCESTER – Worcestershire v Gloucestershire

Sunday 22nd
LYDNEY – Gloucestershire v Middlesex
BASINGSTOKE – Hampshire v Warwickshire
BRACKLEY – Northamptonshire v Kent
NOTTINGHAM – Nottinghamshire v Essex
TORQUAY – Somerset v Leicestershire
BYFLEET – Surrey v Worcestershire
HOVE – Sussex v Lancashire
SCARBOROUGH – Yorkshire v Derbyshire

Sunday 29th
DERBY – Derbyshire v Surrey
SWANSEA – Glamorgan v Kent
MANCHESTER – Lancashire v Hampshire
LORD'S – Middlesex v Leicestershire
NORTHAMPTON – Northamptonshire v Essex
NOTTINGHAM – Nottinghamshire v Sussex
BIRMINGHAM – Warwickshire v Worcestershire
LEEDS – Yorkshire v Gloucestershire

AUGUST
Sunday 5th
CARDIFF – Glamorgan v Warwickshire
BOURNEMOUTH – Hampshire v Gloucestershire
TUNBRIDGE WELLS – Kent v Sussex
MANCHESTER – Lancashire v Derbyshire
LEICESTER – Leicestershire v Worcestershire
WESTON-SUPER-MARE – Somerset v Northamptonshire
THE OVAL – Surrey v Middlesex

Sunday 12th
LEYTON – Essex v Lancashire
CHELTENHAM – Gloucestershire v Warwickshire
LEICESTER – Leicestershire v Surrey
LORD'S – Middlesex v Yorkshire
WELLINGBOROUGH – Northamptonshire v Sussex
NOTTINGHAM – Nottinghamshire v Glamorgan
YEOVIL – Somerset v Derbyshire
WORCESTER – Worcestershire v Hampshire

Sunday 19th
CANTERBURY – Kent v Worcestershire
MANCHESTER – Lancashire v Somerset
LORD'S – Middlesex v Hampshire
NOTTINGHAM – Nottinghamshire v Leicestershire
EASTBOURNE – Sussex v Derbyshire
HULL – Yorkshire v Essex

351

Sunday 26th
CHELMSFORD – Essex v Worcestershire
BRISTOL – Gloucestershire v Northamptonshire
PORTSMOUTH – Hampshire v Nottinghamshire
MAIDSTONE – Kent v Lancashire
BIRMINGHAM – Warwickshire v Somerset
MIDDLESBROUGH – Yorkshire v Surrey

SEPTEMBER
Sunday 2nd
CHESTERFIELD – Derbyshire v Gloucestershire
SWANSEA – Glamorgan v Middlesex
MANCHESTER – Lancashire v Worcestershire
GUILDFORD – Surrey v Nottinghamshire
HOVE – Sussex v Somerset
BIRMINGHAM – Warwickshire v Essex
BRADFORD – Yorkshire v Hampshire

Sunday 9th
DERBY – Derbyshire v Nottinghamshire
TEWKESBURY – Gloucestershire v Lancashire
BOURNEMOUTH – Hampshire v Northamptonshire
THE OVAL – Surrey v Somerset
WORCESTER – Worcestershire v Glamorgan

Benson and Hedges Cup

APRIL
Saturday 28th
CHESTERFIELD – Derbyshire v Nottinghamshire
BRISTOL – Gloucestershire v Somerset
CANTERBURY – Kent v Middlesex
MANCHESTER – Lancashire v Minor Counties (N)
OXFORD – Oxford U. v Leicestershire
THE OVAL – Surrey v Sussex
COVENTRY – Warwickshire v Northamptonshire
AMERSHAM – Minor Counties (S) v Hampshire

MAY
Monday 7th
BRISTOL – Gloucestershire v Glamorgan
LORD'S – Middlesex v Surrey
NOTTINGHAM – Nottinghamshire v Lancashire
OXFORD – Oxford U. v Warwickshire
TAUNTON – Somerset v Minor Counties (S)
HOVE – Sussex v Essex
WORCESTER – Worcestershire v Northamptonshire
BRADFORD – Yorkshire v Derbyshire

Saturday 12th
SWANSEA – Glamorgan v Hampshire
CANTERBURY – Kent v Essex
MANCHESTER – Lancashire v Yorkshire
LEICESTER – Leicestershire v Worcestershire
LORD'S – Middlesex v Sussex
NORTHAMPTON – Northamptonshire v Oxford U.
NOTTINGHAM – Nottinghamshire v Minor Counties (N)
SWINDON – Minor Counties (S) v Gloucestershire

Saturday 19th
ILKESTON – Derbyshire v Lancashire
CHELMSFORD – Essex v Surrey
SOUTHAMPTON – Hampshire v Gloucestershire
LEICESTER – Leicestershire v Warwickshire
CHESTER-LE-STREET – Minor Counties (N) v Yorkshire
YEOVIL – Somerset v Glamorgan
HOVE – Sussex v Kent
WORCESTER – Worcestershire v Oxford U.

JUNE
Saturday 2nd
HARLOW – Essex v Middlesex
SWANSEA – Glamorgan v Minor Counties (S)
BOURNEMOUTH – Hampshire v Somerset
NORTHAMPTON – Northamptonshire v Leicestershire
CHEADLE – Minor Counties (N) v Derbyshire
THE OVAL – Surrey v Kent
BIRMINGHAM – Warwickshire v Worcestershire
HULL – Yorkshire v Nottinghamshire

Wednesday 13th – Quarter-Finals
Wednesday 27th – Semi-Finals
JULY
Saturday 21st—Final (LORD'S)

Gillette Cup

JUNE
Saturday 30th – First Round
LUTON – Bedfordshire v Lancashire
CARDIFF – Glamorgan v Gloucestershire
SOUTHAMPTON – Hampshire v Wiltshire
NORTHAMPTON – Northamptonshire v Sussex
STONE – Staffordshire v Dorset
HARROGATE – Yorkshire v Durham

JULY
Wednesday 11th – Second Round
BEDFORD/MANCHESTER – Bedfordshire/Lancashire v Staffordshire/Dorset
CHESTERFIELD – Derbyshire v Northamptonshire/Sussex
SWANSEA/BRISTOL – Glamorgan/Gloucestershire v Surrey
CANTERBURY – Kent v Hampshire/Wiltshire
LORD'S – Middlesex v Nottinghamshire
TAUNTON – Somerset v Leicestershire
BIRMINGHAM – Warwickshire v Worcestershire
SHEFFIELD/CHESTER-LE-STREET – Yorkshire/Durham v Essex

AUGUST
Wednesday 1st – Quarter-Finals
Wednesday 15th – Semi-Finals
SEPTEMBER
Saturday 1st – Final (LORD'S)